Three underlying principles guide the authors' approach to cultural anthropology:

An emphasis on learning how to ask important and interesting anthropological questions

Applying anthropology to understand and solve human problems

Respecting anthropological tradition, with a focus on contemporary perspectives

Every chapter, every feature of the book, has been written with these principles in mind

"The importance of coming up with good questions is a difficult but primary task for any researcher, student, or teacher. The emphasis on this approach is refreshing and helpful in terms of letting students know that there is still much to learn in the field of anthropology."

—Meghan Ference, *Brooklyn College, CUNY*

A Conversation with the Authors

Tell us about yourselves

We are curious people, especially about the fact that people in all societies do things that people in other societies—and even different communities in the U.S.—find strange and exotic. We have spent our careers studying these differences. We bring a variety of experiences and perspectives to our classrooms that come from our different ages, when we were trained, and the places and topics that we have studied.

Tell us about your experiences teaching the Introduction to Cultural Anthropology Course

We realize that the vast majority of our students will not become anthropologists. But we believe that all students can benefit from anthropological thinking in their lives. What we enjoy most about teaching is introducing students to the things that people do around the world that challenge students' (and our own) current way of thinking. We also like exploring the things we as Americans do that people from other cultures find perplexing, but which seem so normal and natural to us. We use these stories and facts from cultures around the globe in order to help our students make sense of the symbolic, social, and political–economic forces that shape everyday life, including our own. This kind of thinking will help our students become engaged members of the community, whatever their careers.

What inspired you to write the book?

Our classrooms are active and energetic places. Students are learning how to think anthropologically about many different kinds of issues and problems, both familiar and unfamiliar. We were searching for a textbook that could capture that energy, and at the same time be engaging, accessible, and comprehensive, both for students and for the instructors teaching them. It didn't exist, so we decided to write it.

What was your goal when you wrote this book?

Our goal was to create a textbook that guides students through an active process of developing their own abilities to pose good anthropological questions and to begin to approach problems and issues anthropologically. A commitment to an active, learner-centered pedagogy has informed us throughout the planning and writing of each chapter and every feature of this book.

How is your book different than other texts for Intro to Cultural Anthropology?

Most textbooks present anthropology as a settled body of knowledge. However, as older questions endure, new questions are emerging. We begin by emphasizing what anthropologists know and acknowledging areas of ongoing inquiry and debate, rather than beginning with traditional content and embedding unresolved questions deep within each chapter, as many other textbooks do. One of the unique features of our book is that at the end of each chapter we include a set of general questions that anthropologists have generally reached a consensus about, and another set of questions for which no settled answer has emerged. We elaborate on these general questions more explicitly in the Instructor's Manual so that faculty can have more ammunition in the classroom to demonstrate for students how anthropology is a living social science, not a set of dead ideas that were asked and answered a half-century ago.

Each chapter opens with a contemporary situation or fieldwork story

Introduces the overarching question or problem of the chapter

Ethnography

Studying Culture

YOU DON'T HAVE to travel far and wide to study culture, and anthropologists have long studied the social lives of people in their home countries and communities. One such study was conducted during the 1980s and 1990s in East Harlem, a neighborhood in New York City, by American anthropologist Phillippe Bourgois. East Harlem is largely cut off from mainstream America, if not from the very city in which it exists. Its residents, who are largely Puerto Rican, are isolated because of language and educational barriers, unemployment, poverty, and ethnic segregation. Bourgois, who had previously conducted research on Costa Rican banana plantations, lived in East Harlem to study how people experience this marginalization and how they make a living in an economy that does not seem to want them.

Bourgois soon discovered that the neighborhood was saturated with crack cocaine, which came to the market in the 1980s. Over the next four years he spent hundreds of nights on the street and in crack houses, building trust with dealers and addicts. He tape-recorded and carefully transcribed many of his conversations with them, recorded their life histories, and visited with their families. He attended parties, family reunions, Thanksgiving dinners, and New Year's Eve celebrations. He heard many stories about being excluded from mainstream jobs in midtown Manhattan, and thus falling back on crack as dealers

Life in Spanish Harlem. Ethnographic methods have been used to study the lives of many distinct societies and communities, including the lives of residents of East Harlem, New York City, such as those pictures here, who are watching a parade from their apartment. (Getty Images)

Helps students see how classic anthropological concerns relate to contemporary situations

Explains why anthropologists might ask such a question

"I think the authors have done a great job of choosing stories to open the chapters with. The stories are both engaging and relevant to the chapter material."

—Karen Kapusta-Pofahl, *Washburn University*

Anthropologist as Problem Solver

🌱 **Introduces individual, active anthropologists from around the globe**

🌱 **Followed by "Questions for Reflection," which promote active learning**

KNOWN FOR ITS high-quality cheeses and as the home of the iconic ice cream brand Ben and Jerry's, the New England state of Vermont has long enjoyed a reputation as an idyllic agrarian landscape full of milking cows. But dairy

farming is a difficult ye̶ returns due to fluctua̶ has shifted in the past̶ marily as small-scale f̶ a highly mechanized̶ number of large farm̶ longer want to work ̶ dustry has increasing̶ ment of low-wage ̶ undocumented labore̶ Chiapas, Veracruz, an̶

University of Vermo̶ who studies how the ̶ grants change as a resu̶ nographically what the̶ how their dietary patte̶ on dairy farms. She qui̶ farmworkers and imm̶ on a dairy farm in rural̶ perience. These farmw̶ of work because they̶ insignificant concern b̶ where federal immigra̶ Moreover, they have li̶ distances from the far̶

Mares conducted a̶ ment of farmworkers,̶ culture survey that ̶ food availability and̶ production resources.̶ most of us take for g̶ market to get nutriti̶ these farmworkers, a̶ the shopping for the̶ else who lives on or ̶ irregular, and miscon̶ English speakers is a c̶ due to inconsistent a̶ culturally familiar and̶

There are multiple i̶ ous one being that the very people producing an iconic food product themselves suffer from food insecurity and hunger. Another irony is that most of these people left their homes in rural Mexico in the first place because of food insecurity brought on by the kinds of globalizing factors now opening

🌱 Teresa Mares.

🌱 A Pastoral Vermont?

MEDICAL ANTHROPOLOGIST NANCY Scheper-Hughes has conducted research in a variety of contexts around the world: in the parched lands and shantytowns of northeast Brazil, in the squatter camps of South Africa, and in the AIDS sanatoria of Cuba. In each of these contexts she saw structural poverty and blatant examples of what she called "useless suffering." For years anthropologists have adopted a position of cultural relativism that she feels often puts us in a position of trying to be morally neutral when confronting issues of institutional or state violence against "vulnerable bodies and fragile lives." In her view, to be ethical, anthropologists need to focus critically on the institutions and embedded power relations that shape the health of poor, underserved, and disadvantaged people.

Recently, Scheper-Hughes has been studying the illegal sale of body parts (Scheper-Hughes 2004; Sheper-Hughes and Wacquant 2003). She has interviewed a Brazilian organ trafficker in his prison cell, people whose kidneys had been sold, and other people involved in this trafficking. In July 2009 Scheper-Hughes assisted authorities in arresting a Brooklyn man accused of selling black market kidneys. The *New York Daily News* heralded Scheper-Hughes as having an anthropological "'Dick Tracy' moment" when she turned over information to the FBI that allowed them to bring this suspected organ-trafficker to justice (*Daily News* 2009).

This led to exposing an extensive network that involved people in several countries. She told NPR's Brian Lehrer (National Public Radio 2009), "I had begun to unravel a huge network—a criminal network that really looks like, smells like, a kind of a mafia. The head office of the pyramid scheme originated in Israel; with brokers placed in Turkey; in New York City; in Philadelphia; in Durban; in Johannesburg; in Recife, Brazil; Moldova—all over the place." She went on to say, "And I used my ethnographic investigative skills to just go country-hopping and try to connect the dots. Eventually, it brought me to Isaac Rosenbaum being the head broker for Ilan Peri in Israel, who is the don, basically, of the operation, and who is a slippery guy."

Questions for Reflection

1. To what extent is understanding the perspective of people without a voice a contribution to addressing and resolving those issues?

2. Anthropology has become a much more "hands-on" discipline in the past two decades. But does such involvement in shaping policy get in the way of our being able to understand all perspectives holistically?

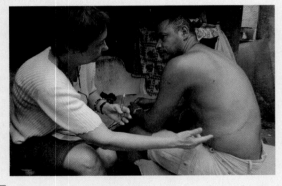

🌱 **Nancy Scheper-Hughes.** Here the anthropologist interviews a man who was trafficked from his home in Recife, Brazil, to Durban, South Africa, so his kidney could be illegally sold. For his kidney he received $6,000, a large sum of money in the slums of Brazil.

🌱 **Helps students learn how to think critically about the material in the chapter**

THINKING CRITICALLY ABOUT MEDICAL ANTHROPOLOGY

Medical anthropologists have traditionally been involved in public health efforts to vaccinate children, to provide clean drinking water, and more recently to assist with combatting HIV/AIDS. Why would such public health efforts be a natural role for anthropologists rather than involvement in clinical settings that involve physicians and their patients in modern urban settings?

Doing Fieldwork

CULTURAL ANTHROPOLOGIST ELLEN Lewin is a lesbian who had been in a long-term committed relationship with her partner. Some years into their relationship, the two decided to have a formal commitment ceremony. At the time, no state recognized any form of legal status for same-sex couples. In the mid-1990s Lewin noticed that across the country hundreds of other same-sex couples were holding commitment ceremonies, even though none of these relationships was recognized by any court. These were not legal ceremonies but a public recognition of their relationships.

She began a three-year study of these rituals to understand why these couples were performing ceremonies that had no legal implications whatsoever. Why were gay and lesbian couples, who had been marginalized by mainstream America for so long, adopting the rituals and ceremonies of those who had marginalized them?

Using participant-observation, Lewin observed these ceremonies and conducted open-ended interviews about the ceremonies of twenty-two male and thirty female couples. Her research challenged conventional anthropological methods, because Lewin was in a sense studying her own community. During interviews with couples planning their ceremonies, her informants sometimes relied on her as an "expert" on commitment ceremonies, because she had planned one herself. Throughout three years of research Lewin worked hard to be objective in her interviews, but she feels that having experienced her own commitment ceremony actually gave her insights that might have escaped other researchers.

Some ceremonies were religious services in churches or synagogues, while others were extremely secular. She also observed that some rites were structured to parallel or even mimic wedding ceremonies of the sort that straight couples might have. Yet others were organized almost defiantly in opposition to traditional American wedding ceremonies. Still other gay and lesbian couples objected to the whole idea of a commitment ceremony, arguing that holding such a ritual at all undermined the distinctiveness of being a lesbian or a gay man. She found that "no single lesbian or gay wedding is typical or exemplary." They take on many different forms and styles in ways that straight weddings do not. At the same time she concluded that each expresses many different sorts of symbolic messages simultaneously. All of the ceremonies she observed or studied were acts of accommodation to mainstream culture as much as they were simultaneously acts of resistance and rebellion.

Lewin (1998:44) contends that "same-sex weddings are cultural constructions grounded in a particular social, political, and historical context." A key part of this context at the time was the fact that gay marriage, civil unions, or even domestic partnerships were not recognized anywhere in the United States. These ceremonies drew on meanings from American weddings and common American notions about families, as well as meanings that come directly from the gay and lesbian counterculture. But these rites coopted these meanings, appropriating them for the participants' own personal and political agendas. The ceremonies derived meaning as much in opposition to images of gay promiscuity as they did by challenging straight ideas about family. Her analysis confirms what anthropologists working in exotic communities around the world have long observed: marriages and wedding ceremonies in particular are not just for the bridal couple; they offer powerful statements to the couple's social network.

Questions for Reflection

1. What benefits and disadvantages did Lewin have in being a lesbian anthropologist studying lesbian and gay commitment ceremonies?

2. What different problems might she have encountered if she had been a straight, married woman?

3. Since her commitment ceremony, a number of U.S. states have legalized same-sex marriage. How would this fact change Lewin's research if she conducted her study today?

A Lesbian Commitment Ceremony. Anthropologist Ellen Lewin studied commitment ceremonies for same-sex couples before same-sex marriage was legal in any state in the nation.

⭐ **Draws upon actual field projects to explore methods used by anthropologists to address questions and problems**

⭐ **Demonstrates how anthropologists collect data**

"This feature allows students to see anthropologists at work, with the particularities of different field and theoretical situations."

Thinking Like an Anthropologist

ANTHROPOLOGISTS BEGIN THEIR research by asking questions. In this box, we want you to learn how to ask questions as an anthropological researcher. Part One describes a situation and follows up with questions we would ask. Part Two asks you to do the same thing with a different situation.

PART ONE: OBSERVING THE USE OF SPACE IN THE AMERICAN SHOPPING MALL

We've all been to a shopping mall, but have you ever stopped to consider how people actually use malls? Anthropologist Paco Underhill (2005) has spent his career studying the American shopping mall and advising retail businesses on how to use space to sell products to the American consumer. From his observations it is clear that visiting a mall is a socially patterned experience, although visitors may not realize how their actions are being shaped by others.

Underhill begins his research on a mall, perhaps surprisingly, in the parking lot. There, he observes the possible entrances to the mall and the fact that, from the outside, the shopper can see little of what is inside. Landscaping is minimal, as is any other attraction that might keep the would-be shopper outside, and so they stream in to the building. The goal of the mall, Underhill infers, is to get people inside to begin spending money.

Once people enter, Underhill observes, they need time to slow down and adjust to the space of the mall, so shops are rarely placed at the entrance; instead, these spaces are rented to doctors, accounting firms, and other businesses whose customers require appointments. After leaving this "decompression area," visitors come to the excitement of the mall proper: shop after shop with brightly colored merchandise pouring out into the hallways to attract attention.

Unlike the halls of a hospital or office building, those at the mall are extra wide. Underhill seeks to understand what goes on in these spaces that requires room for two broad lanes of foot traffic, often separated by stalls, carts, and tables filled with merchandise. While most people pop in and out of the many shops, others stop to look at the shop windows and the merchandise that lies on tables or hangs along the way. Still others—particularly during cold or stormy weather—power-walk alone or in pairs, getting their exercise.

Underhill pays close attention to the people in these hallways and what they do, taking careful notes of his

▼ Inside an American Shopping Mall.

PART TWO: OBSERVING THE USE OF SPACE IN THE COLLEGE LIBRARY

Consider the library at your college or university. Most libraries have a variety of tables, desks, and study carrels. The stacks may be open, or students may need to show their ID cards to get inside. Audiovisual materials may be accessible to everyone in the student body, or professors may put some videos or DVDs on reserve. Modeling your work on Paco Underhill's, what kinds of questions would you pose to orient your observations of a college library?

Participant Observation: "Disciplined Hanging Out"

Participant observation is a key element of anthropological fieldwork. It is a systematic research strategy that is, in some respects, a matter of just hanging out. Many of you probably spend a lot of your free time hanging out with friends, without a specific plan or agenda, taking things as they come. For anthropologists, participant

● **Participant observation.** The standard research method used by sociocultural anthropologists that requires the researcher to live in the community he or she is studying to observe and participate in day-to-day activities.

> **"I really like the immediate appeal of the examples in the *Thinking Like an Anthropologist* boxes, which will attract students' attention and get them to see anthropology at work. These are tailor-made for in-class projects/discussions."**
>
> —Beau Bowers, *Winthrop University*

"Classic Contributions," featured in every chapter, consider the history of anthropological thought

Bronislaw Malinowski on the Ethnographic Method

THE POLISH-BORN ANTHROPOLOGIST Bronislaw Malinowski (1884–1942) was the leading figure in British social anthropology between the First and Second World Wars. Before Malinowski, nearly all anthropological fieldwork consisted of regional surveys, and researchers stayed for short periods in any one community, rarely learning the local language. Malinowski turned this all on its head. Between 1914 and 1917, he spent some eighteen months in Omarakana in the Trobriand Islands of Papua New Guinea, in the process realizing that the best way to understand native life was to live with native people, rather than with the white men—missionaries, traders, and colonial officers—who knew so little about native life. In this excerpt from Malinowski's (1922) best-known book, *Argonauts of the Western Pacific*, he outlines his basic approach to fieldwork, later celebrated as the "ethnographic method":

Conducting Participant Observation. Bronislaw Malinowski sits on a canoe chewing betel nuts with the white trader Billy Hancock and one of his Trobriand Islander informants, 1918.

Soon after I had established myself in Omarakana, I began to take part, in a way, in the village life, to look forward to the important or festive events, to take personal interest in the gossip and the developments of the small village occurrences; to wake up every morning to a day, presenting itself to me more or less as it does to the native. I would get out from under my mosquito net, to find around me the village life beginning to stir, or the people well advanced in their working day according to the hour and also to the season, for they get up and begin their labours early or late, as work presses. As I went on my morning walk through the village, I could see intimate details of family life, of toilet, cooking, taking of meals; I could see the arrangements for the day's work, people starting on their errands, or groups of men and women busy at some manufacturing tasks. Quarrels, jokes, family scenes, events usually trivial, sometimes dramatic but always significant, formed the atmosphere of my daily life, as well as of theirs.

It must be remembered that as the natives saw me constantly every day, they ceased to be interested or alarmed, or made self-conscious by my presence, and I ceased to be a disturbing element in the tribal life which I was to study, altering it by my very approach, as always happens with a new-comer to every savage community. . . .

Also, over and over again, I committed breaches of etiquette, which the natives, familiar enough with me, were not slow in pointing out. I had to learn how to behave, and to a certain extent, I acquired "the feeling" for native good and bad manners. With this, and with the capacity of enjoying their company and sharing some of the games and amusements, I began to feel that I was indeed in touch with the natives, and this is certainly the preliminary condition of being able to carry on successful field work. (Malinowski 1922:7–8)

Questions for Reflection

1. Up to the time that Malinowski came to stay with them, few of the islanders had had more than a quick glimpse of a white man. What was it about Malinowski's way of living that led the islanders to begin to take Malinowsk[...]

2. As newcomers to any community mi[...] breaching or violating the local etique[...] to his advantage?

3. How did Malinowski go from simply [...] islanders to beginning to look at even[...]

4. Do you think he understood the nati[...] why not?

Offers excerpts from original classic studies

Followed by "Questions for Reflection," which highlight themes of continuity and change in the discipline

"Reviewing the Chapter" boxes at the end of each chapter highlight key ideas

Chapter Section	What We Know	To Be Resolved
Do all people conceive of nature in the same way?	Different cultures have different ways of conceptualizing the boundaries between humans and the natural world. Metaphors often play a major role in these conceptualizations.	Anthropologists continue to debate the extent to which general conceptual models and metaphors, or the material forces of nature itself, shape human relations with the environment.
How is non-western knowledge of nature similar to and different from science?	Different societies have developed highly systematic and sophisticated knowledge systems for classifying the natural world, some of which resemble closely Western science. Unlike Western science, however, which views its methods and findings as universally applicable, these knowledge systems are often highly localized and customized to particular ecosystems and rooted in local moralities.	Anthropologists are still working to understand the specific ways in which traditional ecological knowledge shapes practices of ecological and agricultural management.
Do only industrialized western societies conserve nature?	While Western conservation practice is based on the separation of humans and nature, the stewardship traditions of non-Western societies often start from principles that view humans as important actors in nature. Western nature conservation practices have often disrupted and marginalized local cultures, many of which have had highly successful adaptations to their environments.	As some conservationists have realized new opportunities of co-managing natural resources with indigenous communities, anthropologists are divided over whether these approaches actually benefit indigenous communities.
How do social and cultural factors drive environmental destruction?	The ecological impact of a society depends on its ecological footprint, or the amount of natural resources people require to live their lifestyles. The negative impacts of environmentally harmful activities tend to fall disproportionately on lower-income people and minority groups.	Anthropologists are still identifying the conditions under which social groups can adopt new cultural ideas and practices that promote resilience and sustainability.

ENSURING STUDENT SUCCESS

Oxford University Press is proud to offer a complete and authoritative supplements package for both instructors and students. When you adopt *Cultural Anthropology: Asking Questions About Humanity*, you will have access to a truly exemplary set of ancillary materials to enhance teaching and support students' learning.

DASHBOARD

The Dashboard platform by Oxford University Press delivers high-quality content, tools, and assessments to track student progress in an intuitive, web-based learning environment. Full access to Dashboard can be packaged with new copies of the text for a discounted price or purchased separately through your college bookstore or at www.oup.com/us/welsch.

For each chapter, you will find learning objectives, chapter outlines, interactive exercises, a glossary of key terms, flashcards, additional links and recommended readings, self-grading review questions, and ethnographic film clips.

COMPANION WEBSITE

(www.oup.com/us/welsch)

A free and open-acces companion website provides a variety of learning and review tools for students, including outlines, interactive exercises, a glossary of key terms, flashcards, additional links, additional recommended readings, and self-grading review questions for each chapter.

INSTRUCTOR'S MANUAL

Developed by the authors, and designed to help instructors build and implement a course around *Cultural Anthropology: Asking Questions About Humanity*, the Instructor's Resource Manual includes chapter outlines, key terms and definitions, lecture outlines, PowerPoint-based slides, web links, in-class activities and project assignments, suggestions for class discussion, and additional readings.

ANCILLARY RESOURCE CENTER (ARC)

Accessed online through individual user accounts, the ARC provides instructors with access to up-to-date ancillaries at any time while guaranteeing the security of grade-significant resources. In addition, it allows OUP to keep instructors informed when new content becomes available.

The ARC for *Cultural Anthropology: Asking Questions About Humanity* includes:

- Digital copy of the Instructor's Manual
- Computerized Test Bank
- Ethnographic film clips
- Image bank

COMPUTERIZED TEST BANK

Using the test authoring and management tool Diploma, the computerized test bank that accompanies this text is designed for both novice and advanced users and features multiple-choice, true/false, fill-in-the-blank, and essay questions.

In addition, complete Course Management cartridges are available to qualified adopters. Contact your Oxford University Press sales representative for more information.

E-BOOK

Available through CourseSmart for $44.98.

CourseSmart®

Cultural Anthropology

Cultural Anthropology

ASKING QUESTIONS ABOUT HUMANITY

Robert L. Welsch
FRANKLIN PIERCE UNIVERSITY

Luis A. Vivanco
UNIVERSITY OF VERMONT

NEW YORK   OXFORD
OXFORD UNIVERSITY PRESS

Oxford University Press is a department of the University of Oxford.
It furthers the University's objective of excellence in research,
scholarship, and education by publishing worldwide.

Oxford   New York
Auckland   Cape Town   Dar es Salaam   Hong Kong   Karachi
Kuala Lumpur   Madrid   Melbourne   Mexico City   Nairobi
New Delhi   Shanghai   Taipei   Toronto

With offices in
Argentina   Austria   Brazil   Chile   Czech Republic   France   Greece
Guatemala   Hungary   Italy   Japan   Poland   Portugal   Singapore
South Korea   Switzerland   Thailand   Turkey   Ukraine   Vietnam

For titles covered by Section 112 of the US Higher Education
Opportunity Act, please visit www.oup.com/us/he for the
latest information about pricing and alternate formats.

Published by Oxford University Press
198 Madison Avenue, New York, NY 10016
www.oup.com

Library of Congress Cataloging-in-Publication Data
Welsch, Robert Louis, 1950–
    Cultural anthropology : asking questions about humanity / Robert L.
Welsch, Franklin Pierce University, Luis A. Vivanco, University of Vermont.
        pages cm.
    Includes bibliographical references and index.
    ISBN 978-0-19-992572-8
    1. Ethnology. I. Vivanco, Luis Antonio, 1969– II. Title.
    GN316.W47 2015
    305.8—dc23
                                                    2014033451

Printing number: 9 8 7 6 5 4 3 2 1

Printed in the United States of America
on acid-free paper

Robert L. Welsch:

To Sarah for her love and support, and to my students who have nudged me toward a broader and more complex view of the human condition and humanity's remarkable diversity.

Luis A. Vivanco:

To Peggy, Isabel, Felipe, and Camila for their love and support, and to my students who have taught me much about the importance of inspired teaching and learning.

Brief Contents

Contents

3 Beyond Nature and Nurture: The Individual, Biology, and Culture 55

6 Globalization and Culture: Understanding Global

7 Foodways: Finding, Making, and Eating Food 157

8 Environmental Anthropology: Relating to the Natural World 185

10 Politics: Cooperation, Conflict, and Power Relations 237

11 Race, Ethnicity, and Class: Understanding Identity and Social Inequality 265

15 Medical Anthropology: Health, Illness, and Culture 371

16 The Arts: Objects, Images, and Commodities 393

Letter from the Authors

Dear Reader,

Imagine how people would react to you if the next time you went to the university bookstore you tried to haggle at the cash register for your textbooks. Or if the next time you caught a cold you explained to your friends that you were sick because a jealous person had hired a witch to cast a spell on you. In both cases, a lot of people would think you are crazy. But in many societies throughout the world, a lot of ordinary people would consider you crazy for *not* haggling or for *not* explaining your misfortunes as the workings of a witch.

Issues such as these raise some interesting questions. How do people come to believe such things? How are such beliefs reflected in and bolstered by individual behavior and social institutions in a society? Why do *we* believe and act in the ways *we* do? Such questions are at the core of the study of culture. The idea of culture is one of anthropology's most important contributions to knowledge.

The goal of our textbook is to help students develop the ability to pose good anthropological questions and begin answering them, our inspiration coming from the expression "99% of a good answer is a good question." We present problems and questions that students will find provocative and contemporary, and then use theories, ethnographic case studies, and applied perspectives as ways of explaining how anthropologists have looked at these topics over time. Our approach emphasizes what is currently known within the study of cultural anthropology and issues that continue to challenge.

Central to the plan of this book are three underlying principles that guide our approach to cultural anthropology:

- An emphasis on learning how to ask important and interesting anthropological questions.
- Applying anthropology to understand and solve human problems.
- Respecting tradition, with a contemporary perspective.

Every chapter, every feature of the book has been written with these principles in mind. We have written a book about anthropology that draws on insights anthropologists have learned during the twentieth century. At the same time, with its cutting-edge content and pedagogy, this is a textbook that provides what students need for the twenty-first century.

For most students, an introductory course in cultural anthropology is the only educational exposure they will have to anthropological thinking. Most readers are unlikely to see anthropological thinking as relevant to their own lives unless we find a way to make it so. This book represents our endeavor to do just that.

Here's wishing you greater appreciation of cultural anthropology and a lifetime of cultural revelations to come.

Sincerely,

Robert L. Welsch

Luis A. Vivanco

About the Authors

Robert L. Welsch currently teaches cultural anthropology at Franklin Pierce University and previously taught for many years at Dartmouth College. He was affiliated with The Field Museum in Chicago for more than two decades. Trained in the 1970s, at a time when anthropologists still focused mainly on non-Western village-level societies, and when cultural materialist, Marxist, structuralist, and interpretive theories dominated the discipline, Welsch's research has focused on medical anthropology, religion, exchange, art, and museum studies in the classic anthropological settings of Papua New Guinea and Indonesia.

Luis A. Vivanco teaches cultural anthropology and global studies at the University of Vermont, where he has won several of the university's top teaching awards. He was trained in the 1990s when post-structuralist perspectives and "studying up" (studying powerful institutions and bureaucracies, often in Western contexts) was becoming commonplace. Vivanco has worked in Costa Rica, Mexico, Colombia, and the United States, studying the culture and politics of environmentalist social movements, the media, science, ecotourism, and urban mobility with bicycles. In addition to this book, he is author of two ethnographic monographs, co-editor of two others, as well as numerous articles and book chapters.

Preface

What is cultural anthropology, and how is it relevant in today's world? Answering these core questions is the underlying goal of this book.

Cultural anthropology is the study of the social lives of communities, their belief systems, languages, and social institutions, both past and present. It provides a framework to organize the complexity of human experience and comprehend global cultural processes and practices. The practice of cultural anthropology also provides knowledge that helps solve human problems today.

Thinking Like an Anthropologist

Unlike textbooks that emphasize the memorization of facts, *Cultural Anthropology: Asking Questions About Humanity* teaches students how to think anthropologically. This approach helps students view cultural issues as an anthropologist might. In this way, anthropological thinking is regarded as a tool for deciphering everyday experience.

Organized Around Key Questions

Inspired by the expression "99% of a good answer is a good question," each chapter opens with a contemporary story and introduces key questions that can be answered by cultural anthropology. Each main section of a chapter is built around these questions. Through these unique chapter-opening and follow-up questions, students will see how classic anthropological concerns relate to contemporary situations.

Solving Human Problems

At the heart of *Cultural Anthropology: Asking Questions About Humanity* is the belief that anthropology can make a difference in the world. We explain how anthropologists have looked at a wide range of human issues over time—mediating conflict, alleviating social problems, contributing to new social policies—exploring examples but also explaining challenges that still remain.

The Past Through a Contemporary Perspective

Cultural Anthropology: Asking Questions About Humanity represents our effort to close the gap between the realities of the discipline today and traditional views that are also taught at the introductory level. We believe that there is much to be gained, for ourselves and our students, by strengthening the dialogue between generations and subfields of anthropologists. We endeavor to bring classic anthropological examples, cases, and analyses to bear on contemporary questions.

Why We Wrote This Book

In view of how most academic work and life is organized and practiced today, our co-authorship is a somewhat unlikely collaboration. We come from different generations of anthropological training, teach at different kinds of institutions, do our research in opposite corners of the world, and work on different topics. Given the pressures and realities of regional and topical specialization within the discipline, we might not even run into each other at conferences, much less have reason to work together.

But as teachers concerned with sharing the excitement of anthropological findings and thinking with our undergraduate students, we share a lot in common. For one, we believe that there is strength in diversity, and we think our differing backgrounds are more representative of the breadth of the discipline and who actually teaches introductory courses in cultural anthropology. Because both of us feel that anthropological thinking is for everyone, we wrote this textbook to appeal to instructors who blend traditional and contemporary views of anthropology and teach students of many cultural backgrounds. We do this by treating the learning experience as a process of actively asking questions about real-world problems and applying theoretical insights to understand them, as nearly all anthropologists actually do.

Guiding You Through the Book

Cultural Anthropology is distinguished by three underlying principles:

- An emphasis on learning how to ask important and interesting anthropological questions.
- Applying anthropology to understand and solve human problems.
- Respecting tradition, with a contemporary perspective.

Each of these principles informs the scholarship, narrative, and features of the book.

Chapter Introductions

1. Each chapter opens with a real-life story introducing the theme of the chapter.

2. The chapter-opening narrative concludes with the core questions at the heart of the chapter.

3. The core questions posed at the beginning of the chapter are reflected in the titles of each major section in the chapter.

7 CHAPTER

Foodways
Finding, Making, and Eating Food

IN RECENT DECADES, India has experienced a rapid explosion in the number of people suffering from diabetes, currently at about 63 million (Kleinfield 2006; Chakrabarty 2012). Most of these people suffer from Type 2 diabetes, which is a chronic disease of high blood sugar that can lead to blindness, heart failure, and limb amputations. Type 2 diabetes is linked to obesity and diets based on fat-rich and sugar-dense processed foods. It is also related to the inactivity and sedentary nature of contemporary lifestyles. In India, it is a disease of the prosperous and overnourished, mainly afflicting the country's burgeoning population of urban middle-class professionals, such as computer programmers and merchants.

Simultaneously, about 300 million people in India are undernourished, and 42 percent of children under the age of five suffer from malnutrition (Yardley 2012). Many of these people live in rural areas, where for thousands of years small farmers have produced grains and vegetables for household consumption. But India's government has yielded to pressures from industry and encouraged a shift to industrial agriculture based on GMO crops (genetically modified organisms), fertilizers, and pesticides. Promising access to global markets and big profits, this industrial agriculture dictates a type of farming

IN THIS CHAPTER

Why Is There No Universal Human Diet?
- Human Dietary Adaptability and Constraints
- Cultural Influences on Human Evolution: Digesting Milk

Why Do People Eat Things That Others Consider Disgusting?
- Foodways and Culture
- Foodways Are Culturally Constructed
- Foodways Communicate Symbolic Meaning
- Foodways Mark Social Boundaries and Identities
- Foodways Are Dynamic

How Do Different Societies Get Food?
- Foraging
- Horticulture
- Pastoralism
- Intensive Agriculture
- Industrial Agriculture

Foodways
Finding, Making, and Eating Food

THINKING CRITICALLY ABOUT ENVIRONMENTAL ANTHROPOLOGY

The idea that traditional ecological knowledge provides an effective basis for managing natural resources is often resisted most strongly by Western agricultural scientists, who often dismiss these knowledge systems as not scientific and rigorous. How should environmental anthropologists respond to these kinds of claims?

4. The end of each section is capped with a thought-provoking question in Thinking Critically About Anthropology

THEMATIC BOXES

Four types of thematic boxes are used throughout to highlight key themes and principles of the book.

5. Classic Contributions considers the history of anthropological thought on a particular topic, presenting a classic passage from an important historical figure in the discipline. It is followed up with questions to promote anthropological problem solving.

6. Thinking Like an Anthropologist invites the student to exercise his or her own anthropological IQ. This is a two-part box. The first presents students with a concrete ethnographic situation and several proposed questions for further inquiry. The questions serve as a model for thinking anthropologically about the scenario. The second part introduces another scenario and prompts students to formulate questions of their own about this new but related subject matter.

Classic Contributions

Margaret Mead and the Sex/Gender Distinction

Margaret Mead.

SINCE THE BEGINNING of her career in the 1920s, anthropologist Margaret Mead (1901–1978) was interested in the differences between males and females, the cultural roles assigned to each, and how sexual differences shaped an individual's life experiences and personality. Mead was possibly the first social scientist to distinguish between biological sex and culturally distinct gender roles (Viswesaran 1997), which she did in her 1935 book *Sex and Temperament in Three Primitive Societies*. This book, which analyzes sex differences in three Papua New Guinea societies (the Arapesh, the Mundugumor, and the Tchambuli), ends with this influential theoretical reflection on the cultural influences on male and female difference.

The material suggests that we may say that many, if not all, of the personality traits which we have called masculine or feminine are as lightly linked to sex as are the clothing, manners, and the form of head-dress that a society at a given period assigns to either sex. When we consider the behavior of the typical Arapesh man or woman as contrasted with the typical Mundugumor man or woman, the evidence is overwhelmingly in favour of the strength of social conditioning. In no other way can we account for the almost complete uniformity with which Arapesh children develop into contented, passive, secure persons, while Mundugumor children develop as characteristically into violent, aggressive, insecure persons. Only to the impact of the whole of the integrated culture upon the growing child

can we lay the formation of the contrasting types. There is no other explanation of race, or diet, or selection that can be adduced to explain them. We are forced to conclude that human nature is almost unbelievably malleable, responding accurately and contrastingly to contrasting cultural conditions. The differences between individuals who are members of different cultures, like the differences between individuals within a culture, are almost entirely to be laid to differences in conditioning, especially in early childhood, and the form of this conditioning is culturally determined. Standardized personality differences between sexes are of this order, cultural creations to which each generation, male and female, is trained to conform. (Mead 1935/1963:280–281)

Questions for Reflection

1. Why would an anthropologist study three different societies in New Guinea to demonstrate that gender roles are culturally constructed rather than innately biological?

2. Some scholars have claimed that Mead's New Guinea examples are cultural stereotypes from within the three cultures she studied. If true, would these indigenous stereotypes undermine or support her claim that gender roles are cultural rather than biological?

Thinking Like an Anthropologist

Fieldwork in an American Mall

ANTHROPOLOGISTS BEGIN THEIR research by asking questions. In this box, we want you to learn how to ask questions as an anthropological researcher. Part One describes a situation and follows up with questions we would ask. Part Two asks you to do the same thing with a different situation.

PART ONE: OBSERVING THE USE OF SPACE IN THE AMERICAN SHOPPING MALL

We've all been to a shopping mall, but have you ever stopped to consider how people actually use malls? Anthropologist Paco Underhill (2005) has spent his career studying the American shopping mall and advising retail businesses on how to use space to sell products to the American consumer. From his observations it is clear that visiting a mall is a socially patterned experience, although visitors may not realize how their actions are being shaped by others.

Underhill begins his research on a mall, perhaps surprisingly, in the parking lot. There, he observes the possible entrances to the mall and the fact that, from the outside, the shopper can see little of what is inside. Landscaping is minimal, as is any other attraction that might keep the would-be shopper outside, and so they stream in to the

building. The goal of the mall, Underhill infers, is to get people inside to begin spending money.

Once people enter, Underhill observes, they need time to slow down and adjust to the space of the mall, so shops are rarely placed at the entrance; instead, these spaces are rented to doctors, accounting firms, and other businesses whose customers require appointments. After leaving this "decompression area," visitors come to the excitement of the mall proper: shop after shop with brightly colored merchandise pouring out into the hallways to attract attention.

Unlike the halls of a hospital or office building, those at the mall are extra wide. Underhill seeks to understand what goes on in these spaces that requires room for two broad lanes of foot traffic, often separated by stalls, carts, and tables filled with merchandise. While most people pop in and out of the many shops, others stop to look at the shop windows and the merchandise that lies on tables or hangs along the way. Still others—particularly during cold or stormy weather—power-walk alone or in pairs, getting their exercise.

Underhill pays close attention to the people in these hallways and what they do, taking careful notes of his

Inside an American Shopping Mall.

7. Doing Fieldwork draws upon an actual field project to explore the special methods used by anthropologists to address specific questions and problems.

8. Anthropologist as Problem Solver describes how a particular anthropologist has applied disciplinary insights and methods to help alleviate a social problem, mediate a conflict, or (re)define a policy debate related to the central problem of the chapter. These cases also provide insight into careers that take advantage of an anthropology background.

9. Visual program
A rich ensemble of relevant photographs, maps, and figures underscore the key points of each chapter.

Doing Fieldwork
Conducting Holistic Research with Stanley Ulijaszek

STANLEY ULIJASZEK IS a British anthropologist who has been conducting research for several decades in the swamplands of coastal Papua New Guinea, an island state in the Southwest Pacific. In recent years, he has turned his attention to an interesting question: in this difficult landscape that is unsuited to agriculture, how do people acquire a sufficient, safe, and nutritious food supply? To answer this question properly requires substantial knowledge of the human biology, prehistory, and culture of coastal New Guinea.

At the center of this story is the sago palm, a palm tree that grows abundantly in swamps. Its stem contains starch, a staple food for the people who cultivate it. People cook sago in long sticks resembling dense French bread, eating it with a bit of fish. Sago is not a great staple food, because it is 99.5 % starch, making it an excellent energy food, but it has few other nutrients. Worse, perhaps, is that sago is toxic when eaten uncooked or improperly prepared. Its toxicity threatens people with a specific genetic mutation that does not allow the red blood cells to carry the toxins out of the body, a mutation common among coastal New Guinea populations. Thus, because of this toxicity, eating sago presented a risk to these coastal people (Ulijaszek 2007).

It turns out, however, that this same genetic mutation confers some resistance to malaria, a mosquito-borne infectious disease common in the tropics. The key to protecting the people while releasing the nutritional energy of sago is to separate the starch from the pith at the center of the sago palm by washing and straining it, then cooking the starch, all of which reduces its toxicity to safe levels. Archaeological evidence indicates that people in this region figured out this process at least 6,000 years ago, which is when they began leaving behind their hunting-and-gathering way of life to take up agriculture. Ulijaszek concludes that they adapted sago for human consumption by detoxi-

Cultivating Nutrition from the Sago Palm. Transforming the pith of the sago palm into food is a complex process. First the pith must be chopped out of the trunk and pulverized using simple cutting and pounding tools (top), and then the starch must be leached from the dense mass of fiber using a frame made from the base of the leaf stalk in which the starch is pounded with water to release and strain the edible starch, leaving the inedible fiber behind in the frame. Later the raw flour is collected from a basin where it has settled (bottom).

Anthropologist as Problem Solver
Nancy Scheper-Hughes on an Engaged Anthropology of Health

MEDICAL ANTHROPOLOGIST NANCY Scheper-Hughes has conducted research in a variety of contexts around the world: in the parched lands and shantytowns of northeast Brazil, in the squatter camps of South Africa, and in the AIDS sanatoria of Cuba. In each of these contexts she saw structural poverty and blatant examples of what she called "useless suffering." For years anthropologists have adopted a position of cultural relativism that she feels often puts us in a position of trying to be morally neutral when confronting issues of institutional or state violence against "vulnerable bodies and fragile lives." In her view, to be ethical, anthropologists need to focus critically on the institutions and embedded power relations that shape the health of poor, underserved, and disadvantaged people.

Recently, Scheper-Hughes has been studying the illegal sale of body parts (Scheper-Hughes 2004; Scheper-Hughes and Wacquant 2003). She has interviewed a Brazilian organ trafficker in his prison cell, people whose kidneys had been sold, and other people involved in this trafficking. In July 2009 Scheper-Hughes assisted authorities in arresting a Brooklyn man accused of selling black market kidneys. The *New York Daily News* heralded Scheper-Hughes as having an anthropological "'Dick Tracy' moment" when she turned over information to the FBI that allowed them to bring this suspected organ-trafficker to justice (*Daily News* 2009).

This led to exposing an extensive network that involved people in several countries. She told NPR's Brian Lehrer (National Public Radio 2009), "I had begun to unravel a huge network—a criminal network that really looks like, smells like, a kind of a mafia. The head office of the pyramid scheme originated in Israel; with brokers placed in Turkey; in New York City; in Philadelphia; in Durban; in Johannesburg; in Recife, Brazil; Moldova—all over the place." She went on to say, "And I used my ethnographic investigative skills to just go country-hopping and try to connect the dots. Eventually, it brought me to Isaac Rosenbaum being the head broker for Ilan Peri in Israel, who is the don, basically, of the operation, and who is a slippery guy."

Questions for Reflection

1. To what extent is understanding the perspective of people without a voice a contribution to addressing and resolving those issues?

2. Anthropology has become a much more "hands-on" discipline in the past two decades. But does such involvement in shaping policy get in the way of our being able to understand all perspectives holistically?

...anthropologist interviews a man who was trafficked from ...South Africa, so his kidney could be illegally sold. For his ...of money in the slums of Brazil.

Figure 6.1 Bollywood in Africa. "Bollywood" movies—musicals produced in India, which has the largest film industry in the world—have become popular in countries like South Africa (pictured here) and Nigeria because of recent increases in the global distribution of media.

in very remote places can be in contact with people almost anywhere on the globe (Figure 6.2). Never before has this capability been possible.

But access to these innovations is extremely limited for some, while readily accessible for the wealthier and better educated. In sub-Saharan Africa (excluding South Africa), for example, only one in 5,000 people has computer access. As a result, some observers—to highlight real inequalities of access—prefer to talk about the globalization of communication in terms of wealth and poverty.

Figure 4.3 The Wave Theory of Language Change. Uvular, trilled, and flapped 'r' in European languages. Note that pronunciation patterns sweep across language boundaries from French to German and even to Scandinavian languages.

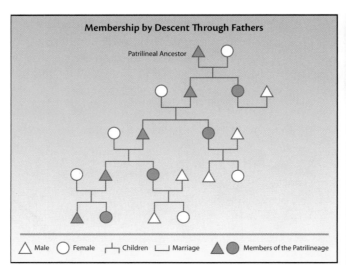

Membership by Descent Through Fathers

Patrilineal Ancestor

△ Male   ○ Female   ⌐_⌐ Children |_| Marriage   ▲ ● Members of the Patrilineage

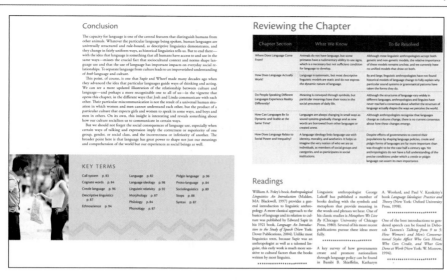

10. Each chapter closes with key terms, recommended readings, and a unique table recapping the main points of each section and unresolved matters that cultural anthropology is still exploring.

Ensuring Student Success

Oxford University Press offers students and instructors a comprehensive ancillary package for *Cultural Anthropology.*

For Students

Dashboard

The Dashboard platform by Oxford University Press delivers high-quality content, tools, and assessments to track student progress in an intuitive, Web-based learning environment. Full access to Dashboard can be packaged with new copies of the text for a discounted price or purchased separately through your college bookstore or at www.oup.com/us/welsch. For each chapter, you will find:

- **Learning Objectives**
- **Chapter Outlines** to help guide students through the chapter material
- **Interactive exercises** to engage students in fieldwork experience
- **Glossary of key terms** as a helpful reference for key concepts
- **Flashcards** to assist students in studying and reviewing key terms
- **Additional links** to websites providing supplemental information on the topics and ideas covered in the chapter
- **Additional recommended readings** that delve more deeply into the topics discussed in the chapter and that broaden student conceptions of what one can do with an anthropology degree
- **Self-grading review questions** to help students review the material and assess their own comprehension
- **Ethnographic film clips**

Companion Website

Cultural Anthropology: Asking Questions About Humanity is also accompanied by an extensive **companion website (www.oup.com/us/welsch)**, which includes materials to help students with every aspect of the course. For each chapter, you will find:

- **Chapter Outlines**
- **Flashcards**

- **Additional links**
- **Self-grading review questions**

For Instructors

Oxford University Press is proud to offer a complete and authoritative supplements package for both instructors and students. When you adopt *Cultural Anthropology: Asking Questions About Humanity,* you will have access to a truly exemplary set of ancillary materials to enhance teaching and support students' learning.

Ancillary Resource Center (ARC) at www.oup-arc.com is a convenient, instructor-focused single destination for resources to accompany *Cultural Anthropology: Asking Questions About Humanity.* Accessed online through individual user accounts, the ARC provides instructors with access to up-to-date ancillaries at any time while guaranteeing the security of grade-significant resources. In addition, it allows OUP to keep instructors informed when new content becomes available.

The ARC for *Cultural Anthropology: Asking Questions About Humanity* includes:

- Digital copy of **Instructor's Manual**, which includes:
  - Statement from the authors describing their pedagogical vision
  - Chapter outlines
  - Key controversies
  - Key terms and definitions and summaries
  - Lecture outlines
  - PowerPoint slides
  - Web links
  - In-class activities and project assignments, organized by class size (small to large)
  - Suggestions for class discussion
  - Additional readings
  - Supplements to each box figure
  - Image bank
  - Ethnographic film clips
- Computerized **Test Bank** including:
  - Multiple-choice questions
  - True/false questions
  - Fill-in-the-blank questions
  - Essay prompts

As an alternative to Dashboard, instructors may order a complete **Course Management cartridge**. Contact your Oxford University Press Sales Representative for more information.

Acknowledgments

The authors would like to thank the many individuals who have supported this project from its inception to the final stages of production. The impetus for this book lies with Kevin Witt, who had an inspired vision for a new kind of anthropology textbook and the foresight to identify and support the team to write it. In its early stages while this project was with McGraw-Hill, development editors Pam Gordon, Nanette Giles, Susan Messer, and Phil Herbst each played an important role in shaping the manuscript.

At Oxford University Press, Sherith Pankratz, our acquisitions editor, and Thom Holmes, our development editor, have managed this project and helped us further refine our vision with exceptional care and expertise. We would also like to thank editorial assistants Meredith Keffer and Katy Albis, development assistant Paul Longo, photo researcher Bethany Montagano, and permissions editor Cailen Swain. In production, we would like to thank art director Michele Laseau, production editor Keith Faivre, copy editor Debbie Ruel, and proofreader Linda Westerhoff. And last, but by no means least, we would like to acknowledge and thank our marketing team Tony Mathias, Frank Mortimer, Jolene Howard, and the other hardworking men and women who are marketing this book and getting it into the hands of the students for whom we wrote it. Although the sales and marketing team often go unsung and unacknowledged by many authors, we know their work is critical to the success of a project like this one.

It is important to acknowledge and thank Agustín Fuentes of the University of Notre Dame, co-author of our forthcoming general anthropology textbook, who has helped shape our thinking on numerous dimensions of cultural anthropology.

We are grateful to Franklin Pierce University, the University of Vermont, Dartmouth College, the Hood Museum of Art, The Field Museum, the U.S. National Museum of Natural History (a branch of the Smithsonian Institution), the American Museum of Natural History in New York, the University of Costa Rica, and the National University of Colombia, all of whom have provided support in diverse ways. In particular we appreciate the support and encouragement of Kim Mooney, Franklin Pierce University Provost; Kerry McKeever and Paul Kotila, Academic Dean at Franklin Pierce; and John Villemaire, Division Chair of the Social and Behavioral Sciences at Franklin Pierce. At the University of Vermont the Provost's Office and the Office of the Dean of the College of Arts and Sciences have provided important institutional support for this project.

Numerous librarians aided the development of this project at various stages, including Paul Campbell, Leslie Inglis, Melissa Stearns, and Jill Wixom at Frank S. DiPietro Library at Franklin Pierce University in Rindge, New Hampshire; Laurie Kutner at Bailey-Howe Library at the University of Vermont; Amy Witzel, Fran Oscadal, and John Cocklin, at Baker Library at Dartmouth College; and staff of Alden Library at Ohio University in Athens, Ohio.

We want to especially thank our colleagues Kirk M. and Karen Endicott, Robert G. Goodby, Debra S. Picchi, Douglas Challenger, John E. Terrell, Robert J. Gordon, and Richard Robbins, all of whom have offered support, encouragement, and insights throughout the various phases of writing this book. Many other colleagues have contributed to this project in direct and indirect ways, including shaping our thinking about various anthropological topics, sparking ideas and being a sounding board about matters of content and pedagogy, and reading and responding to draft chapters. These colleagues include: at Dartmouth College, Hoyt Alverson, Sienna R. Craig, Brian Didier, Nathaniel Dominy, Seth Dobson, Dale F. Eickelman, Kathy Hart, Sergei Kan,

Brian Kennedy, Kenneth Korey, Joel Levine, Deborah Nichols, and John Watanabe; and at the University of Vermont Ben Eastman, Scott Van Keuren, Cameron Wesson, Brian Gilley, Jennifer Dickinson, Teresa Mares, Amy Trubek, Scott Matter, Deborah Blom, and the late Jim Petersen.

Several students at Franklin Pierce, the University of Vermont, and Dartmouth College have helped with research during the various stages of writing and rewriting. These include: Adam Levine, Adam Slutsky, Nathan Hedges, Michael Surrett, Rebecca Nystrom, Scott Spolidoro, Kevin Mooiman, Matthew Dee, Kelsey Keegan, Kyle Brooks, Cory Atkinson, Taber Morrell, Saige Kemelis, Shannon Perry, Catherine Durickas, and Kristin Amato.

We want to thank our students at Franklin Pierce University and the University of Vermont who have test driven various earlier drafts of this book. Their feedback and insights have been invaluable. But in particular we want to thank Courtney Cummings, Kimberly Dupuis, John M. Gass, Kendra Lajoie, Holly Martz, Scott M. McDonald, Lindsay Mullen, and Nick Rodriguez, all of whom were students in AN400 at Franklin Pierce during the Fall Semester of 2012. Having used drafts of the text in their Introduction to Cultural Anthropology, they reviewed all of the chapters in the book in focus-group fashion and offered useful insights about examples and writing in each chapter.

Last but certainly not least, we would like to thank our families for all the critical emotional and logistical support they have provided over the years to ensure the success of this project. Luis's children Isabel, Felipe, and Camila have aided us in various ways, from prodding questions about the book and anthropology to, at times, comic relief when we needed it. Our wives, Sarah Welsch and Peggy O'Neill-Vivanco, deserve our deepest gratitude for all their wise counsel at many junctures in the development of this book, their behind-the-scenes support to enable us to research, write, and revise it, and their (long-suffering) patience until finally seeing it finished.

Manuscript Reviewers

We have greatly benefited from the perceptive comments and suggestions of the many talented scholars and instructors who reviewed the manuscript of *Cultural Anthropology*. Their insight and suggestions contributed immensely to the published work.

Augustine Agwuele
Texas State University

Data D. Barata
California State University, Sacramento

O. Hugo Benavides
Fordham University

Keri Brondo
University of Memphis

Leslie G. Cecil
Stephen F. Austin State University

Carolyn Coulter
Atlantic Cape Community College

Mathew Dalstrom
Ford University

Joanna Davidson
Boston University

Henri Gooren
Oakland University

Liza Grandia
Clark University

Ulrike M. Green
Orange Coast College

Shawn Dead Haley
Columbia College

Douglas Hume
Northern Kentucky University

Su Il Kim
Metropolitan State College of Denver/ Pikes Peak Community College

Diane E. King
University of Kentucky

Frances Kostarelos
Governors State University

J. Christopher Kovats-Bernat
Muhlenberg College

Kuinera de Kramer-Lynch
University of Delaware

Scott M. Lacy
Fairfield University

Louis Herns Marcelin
University of Miami

Linda Matthei
Texas A&M University, Commerce

Faidra Papavasiliou
Georgia State University

Mark Allen Peterson
Miami University

Harry Sanabria
University of Pittsburgh

Elizabeth A. Scharf
University of North Dakota

Rocky L. Sexton
Ball State University

Carolyn Smith-Morris
Southern Methodist University

Victor D. Thompson
University of Georgia

James E. Todd
Modesto Junior College/California
State University, Stanislaus

Susan R. Trencher
George Mason University

Neeraj Vedwan
Montclair State University

Jennifer R. Wies
Eastern Kentucky University

Cherra Wyllie
University of Hartford

Ancillary Authors

Our sincere thanks also to our ancillary authors, who created high-quality additional resources specifically for this text:

Jason Fancher
Mt. Hood Community College
(Instructor's Manual, PowerPoint
slides, web links)

Meghan Ference
Brooklyn College, CUNY (Test
Bank, interactive exercises, self-
quizzes, additional readings)

K. Patrick Fazioli
Medaille College
(Web links, interactive exercises,
additional readings)

Cultural Anthropology

Anthropology

Asking Questions About Humanity

HUMAN BEINGS ARE one of the world's most adaptable animals. Evolutionary history has endowed our species with certain common physical characteristics, instincts, and practices that have helped us to survive, even thrive, in every conceivable terrestrial environment. Yet no group of people is exactly like another, and as a species we exhibit tremendous variations across groups, variations in our adaptations to the environment, physical appearance, language, beliefs, and social organization.

Humans have always encountered groups of people who look different, speak peculiar languages, and behave in unexpected or unpredictable ways. Although sometimes hostility and wars break out between groups because of such differences, usually people have found ways to get along, often through trade and alliances. To be effective at establishing strong social and political bonds in spite of human differences has always required that people have a practical understanding of human variation.

Some of history's great travelers and explorers developed that practical understanding, among them the Venetian Marco Polo (1254–1324), the Norman cleric Gerald of Wales (1146–1223), the Franciscan missionary William of Rubruck (1220–1292), the North African Muslim Ibn Batuta (1304–1433), and the Chinese admiral Zheng He (1371–1433). These individuals were all deeply interested in other peoples, and their writings express sophisticated understandings

---

⚘ **Intercultural Interactions.** In 1867 Captain Samuel Wallis and his crew were the first Westerners to reach Tahiti. Their first interactions were peaceful and included an exchange of gifts between Wallis and Queen Oberea. The cultural differences between Tahitians and the English raised many important questions about human differences and similarities, for both parties—the kinds of dynamics that interest anthropologists today.

of how and why the groups they encountered looked, acted, worshiped, and spoke as they did (Larner 1999, Bartlett 1982, Khanmohamadi 2008, Fazioli 2014, Harvey 2007, Menzies 2002, Dreyer 2007). Similarly, there is a rich historical legacy of intellectual thought about human variation. The great Chinese philosopher Confucius (551–479 BCE) wrote in two of his *Analects* some principles for establishing relationships with *yi* [yee], meaning cultural and ethnic outsiders. A generation later, the Greek historian Herodotus (484–425 BCE), in his seven-volume *Histories*, described the diverse peoples and societies he encountered during his travels in Africa, Southwestern Asia, and India, offering a number of possible explanations for the variations he observed across groups.

While all of these individuals were curious about other peoples and at times quite rigorous in their ways of thinking about human variation, they were not anthropologists as we think of anthropology today. They were not researchers asking systematic questions about humanity, and anthropology as a discipline did not emerge from their writings. Still, their various studies show that getting along with peoples from different cultures has always been important, a point that is sometimes lost on us in the United States, where our international prominence and our preoccupation with American exceptionalism may lead us to think that we don't need to understand people and cultures from other countries. But if we Americans want to be most successful in dealing with people internationally in politics, trade, treaties, and global environmental or health policies, we need to understand in systematic ways the people from other countries and the cultures that guide and motivate them.

These points lead us to our first question, the question at the heart of this chapter: *What is anthropology, and how is it relevant in today's world?* Embedded in this broader question are the following problems, around which this chapter is organized:

How did anthropology begin?

What are the four subfields of anthropology, and what do they share in common?

How do anthropologists know what they know?

How is anthropology put to work in the world?

What ethical issues does anthropology raise?

Anthropology is the study of human beings, their biology, their prehistory and histories, and their changing languages, cultures, and social institutions. Anthropology provides a framework for asking questions about and grasping the complexity of human experience, both past and present. Anthropology is about where humans have been, but it also provides knowledge that helps solve human problems today.

How Did Anthropology Begin?

During the nineteenth century, **anthropology** emerged in Europe and North America as an academic discipline devoted to the systematic observation and analysis of human variation. It was made possible once intellectuals and scholars had developed rigorous ways of comparing different species and people with different cultures. The Enlightenment or Age of Reason, which began in the early 1700s with the rise of modern science, demonstrated that careful observation and analysis could lead to understanding the natural world. Sir Isaac Newton explained the principles of physics and gravity; geologists demonstrated that many species of animals, like the dinosaurs and (later) enormous elephant-like creatures such as wooly mammoths and mastodons, had once lived on Earth; and biologists began to describe different species of plants, insects, birds, and mammals, grouping them into families and larger level groupings. But while scholars acknowledged differences among peoples living on the different continents, they did not attempt to explain these variations until their own societies had begun to change as a result of industrialization. Previously, cultural differences were assumed to be a given; cultural variation in the 1800s was thought to be essentially as it always had been. But as intellectuals began to notice that their own societies were changing because of the rise of factories, they realized that other societies around the world had also been changing.

Three key concerns began to emerge by the 1850s that would shape professional anthropology. These were (1) the disruptions of industrialization in Europe and America, (2) the rise of evolutionary theories, and (3) the growing importance of Europe's far-flung colonies with large indigenous populations whose land, mineral wealth, and labor Europeans and Americans wanted to control.

- **Anthropology.** The study of human beings, their biology, their pre-prehistory and histories, and their changing languages, cultures, and social institutions.

The Disruptions of Industrialization

Industrialization refers to the economic process of shifting from an agricultural economy to a factory-based one. Industrialization disrupted American and European societies by bringing large numbers of rural people into towns and cities to work in factories. The rise of industrial towns and cities raised questions about how society was changing, including how a factory-based economy and the attendant growth of cities shaped society, government, residential patterns, and culture. These were the questions that motivated great social thinkers, in particular German political economists Karl Marx (1818–1883) and Max Weber (1864–1920) and the French anthropologist-sociologist Émile Durkheim (1858–1917), each of whom influenced the rise of anthropology as a social scientific discipline.

At the beginning of the nineteenth century most people in Western countries were rural and were usually engaged in farming. Industrial inventions like the cotton gin, the steam engine, and factory machinery made it possible to produce goods in large numbers and quickly that used to be made slowly by hand. In the factories, workers did repetitive tasks for long hours to mass-produce goods. Factory economies affected such basic aspects of life as who individuals would marry, what activities they would spend their days doing, and the role of religion in their lives.

In the midst of these social and economic upheavals, anthropology developed as a discipline that sought to understand and explain how people in rural and urban settings organize their communities and how they change. It also led these scholars to consider how industrialization affected peoples in European colonies in Africa, Asia, Latin America, and the Pacific Islands. Important new questions were posed: Why did these diverse societies organize their lives in the ways they did? Why had Native Americans and Africans not developed industrial societies as

- **Industrialization.** The economic process of shifting from an agricultural economy to a factory-based one.

European societies had? Why had the civilizations of China, India, and the Arab world developed social, political, and economic patterns distinct from those of Europeans? And why had these other civilizations not experienced industrialization as Europeans had? Asking about how European villages and cities were structured and how they perpetuated their cultures ultimately led to questions about how all sorts of non-Western societies worked as well.

The Theory of Evolution

- **Evolution.** The adaptive changes organisms make across generations.

A second key influence on the development of anthropology was the rise of evolutionary theory to explain biological variation between and within species. **Evolution** refers to the adaptive changes organisms make across generations. English naturalist Charles Darwin (1809–1882) developed a theory of how different species of plants and animals had evolved from earlier forms. He based his ideas on personal observations made during his travels with the British survey ship HMS *Beagle,* as well as his own backyard experiments raising pigeons, among other things. The key mechanism of his evolutionary theory was what he called "natural selection," a process through which certain inheritable traits are passed along to offspring because they are better suited to the environment. Thus in Darwin's view, in subtle ways nature was sorting out, or selecting, those forms best adapted for their environment.

Darwin had developed his theory of evolution in the late 1830s but delayed publishing his findings. He knew that his theory would be controversial, and he feared a backlash from the conservative religious community and from more established scientists. The idea of biological evolution was a remarkable notion for people used to thinking of species as fixed and stable. Religious scholars interpreted the book of Genesis in the Old Testament to suggest that God had created all of the natural species once at the time of creation and that no new species had been created since then. For Darwin, however, the question of the origin of species was not a religious one but

- **Empirical.** Verifiable through observation rather than through logic or theory.

an **empirical** one. It was a question that could be answered by observing whether species had changed and whether new species had emerged over time. From the findings of contemporary geologists, Darwin knew that many early species such as the dinosaurs had arisen and died out. For him, such changes were evidence that the natural environment had selected some species for survival and that extinction was the outcome for those not well suited to changing environments.

When Darwin published his groundbreaking work, *On the Origin of Species,* in 1859, he experienced the backlash he feared, and few scientists accepted Darwin's ideas immediately. Indeed, as late as the 1920s some biologists continued to be uncomfortable with the idea that species might change over time. But as the older generation left the scene, younger scientists recognized how easily this simple theory explained most kinds of biological variation both within and between species. Today, biologists and anthropologists no longer view biological evolution as controversial, and nearly all anthropologists and biologists accept evolution as the only way to explain the relationship among animal and plant species and the only way to explain why humans have the biological abilities and characteristics we can observe today.

Since Darwin's time, the broader scientific community has borrowed from his theory to produce a wave of new ideas involving evolution. Evolution seemed to provide a framework for studying both the biological and cultural development of humans and their societies. Among biological anthropologists, the inheritance of physiological traits allowed science to understand the history of human origins and our relationship to other primates. Among early cultural anthropologists, evolutionary models seemed ideal for explaining how different societies had come to be as they were when Europeans encountered them for the first time. The notion of evolution allowed early anthropologists to rank societies along an evolutionary scale, which they assumed showed which societies were more "advanced" because they had passed through more "primitive" forms of society with simpler technologies by adapting to their environments with more complex tools. Anthropologists today challenge such models of cultural evolution because this model does not fit the observed facts, but these early models motivated anthropologists to collect data from these so-called "primitive" societies before industrialization caused them to change or die out.

Colonial Origins of Cultural Anthropology

A third driving force behind anthropology was **colonialism,** the historical practice of more powerful countries claiming possession of less powerful ones. Although both China and Japan have had colonies, when we think about the development of anthropology, we usually think of colonialism as practiced by Europeans and Americans. We can think of American domination over Indian lands as a form of colonialism, particularly when government policies moved Native Americans from the southeastern states to what is now Oklahoma, largely because white settlers wanted their land. Overseas the colonial period flourished from the 1870s until the 1970s, and whites established mines, fisheries, plantations, and other enterprises using local peoples as inexpensive labor. Colonies enriched the mother countries, often impoverishing the indigenous inhabitants.

Colonial peoples everywhere had different cultures and customs, and their actions often seemed baffling to white administrators, a fact that these officials chalked up to their seemingly primitive or savage nature. To understand how to govern such radically different peoples Europeans and Americans began developing methods for studying those societies.

Most Europeans and Americans expected their colonial subjects to die out, leading to the urgent collection of information about tribal societies before it was too late. Well into the 1920s, anthropologists pursued an approach known as the **salvage paradigm**, which held that it was important to observe indigenous ways of life, interview elders, and assemble collections of objects made and used by indigenous peoples because this knowledge of traditional languages and customs would soon disappear (Figure 1.1). Of course, today we know that while some Indian tribes, especially along the East coast, largely died out, many other groups have survived and grown in population. But these Native American cultures have had to adjust and adapt to the changing American landscape and all the changes that Americans of different national origins have brought to the continent.

Anthropology as a Global Discipline

By the end of the nineteenth century, anthropology was already an international discipline, whose practitioners were mainly based in Western Europe and the United States. Although they had some shared concerns, anthropologists in particular countries developed specific national traditions, studying distinct problems and developing their own styles of thought. Throughout the twentieth century, anthropology began to emerge in

- **Colonialism.** The historical practice of more powerful countries claiming possession of less powerful ones.

- **Salvage paradigm.** The paradigm which held that it was important to observe indigenous ways of life, interview elders, and assemble collections of objects made and used by indigenous peoples.

Figure 1.1 The Salvage Paradigm. Efforts to document indigenous cultures "before they disappeared" motivated anthropologists and others to record the ways of traditional people, including well-known Western photographer William S. Prettyman, who took this picture of an Otoe family in Kansas in the 1880s.

many other non-European countries as well. Many students in colonial territories had gone to European and American universities where they learned anthropology and, in many cases, brought anthropology back home. In these countries, anthropology often focuses on practical problems of national development and on documenting the minority societies found within the country's borders. Today, anthropology is a truly global discipline with practitioners in dozens of countries asking many different kinds of questions about humanity.

• •

THINKING CRITICALLY ABOUT ANTHROPOLOGY

Can you think of something you do at your college or university that feels "natural" but is probably done somewhat differently at another college? Consider, for example, how your experiences in high school classes may have led you to expect something different from your college classes.

• •

What Are the Four Subfields of Anthropology and What Do They Share in Common?

Anthropology has traditionally been divided into four subfields: cultural anthropology, archaeology, biological anthropology, and linguistic anthropology (Figure 1.2).

Cultural anthropology focuses on the social lives of living communities. Until the 1970s, most cultural anthropologists conducted research in non-Western communities, spending a year or two observing social life. We call this kind of research anthropological fieldwork. These anthropologists learned the local language and studied broad aspects of the community, recording information about people's economic transactions, religious rituals, political organizations, and families, seeking to understand how these distinct domains influenced each other. In recent decades they have come to focus on more specific issues in the communities they study, such as how and why religious conflicts occur, how environmental changes affect agricultural production, and how economic interactions create social inequalities. Today, anthropologists are as likely to focus on modern institutions, occupational groups, ethnic minorities, and the role of computer technology or advertising in their own cultures as they are on cultures outside of their own.

Archaeology studies past cultures, by excavating sites where people lived, worked, farmed, or conducted some other activity. Some archaeologists study prehistory (life before written records), trying to understand how people lived before they had domesticated plants and animals. Or they may reconstruct the patterns of trade or warfare between ancient settlements. Two themes have been traditional concerns of prehistoric archaeology: (1) the transition from hunting and gathering to agriculture and (2) the rise of cities and states, when complex social, political, and economic institutions arose, along with occupational specializations, social class distinctions, and the emergence of early political forms that resemble states.

• **Cultural anthropology.** The study of the social lives of living communities.

• **Archaeology.** The study of past cultures, by excavating sites where people lived, worked, farmed, or conducted some other activity.

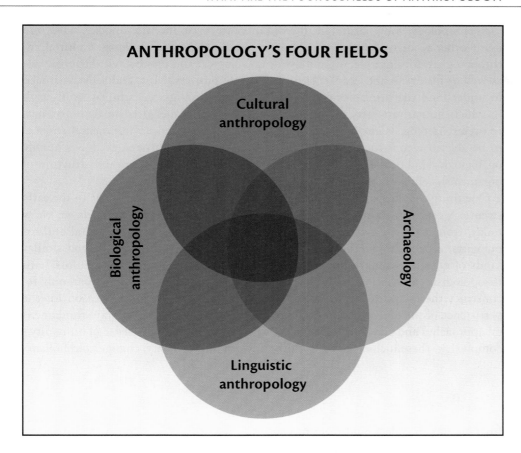

ANTHROPOLOGY'S FOUR FIELDS

Cultural anthropology

Biological anthropology

Archaeology

Linguistic anthropology

Figure 1.2 Anthropology's Four Fields.

Another branch of archaeology is historical archaeology, in which archaeologists excavate sites where written historical documentation about the sites also exists. The goal is to supplement what we know about a community or society from what is found in the ground with written records. Interestingly, historical archaeologists often find that few people actually lived as they described themselves in diaries and published accounts. For example, excavations on American cotton plantations have added a great deal to what we already know about the living conditions of slaves on plantations, information that does not generally appear in written records because the lives of slaves and poor white farmers were rarely documented in more than cursory ways.

Biological anthropology (also called physical anthropology) focuses on the biological aspects of the human species, past and present, along with those of our closest relatives, the nonhuman primates (apes, monkeys, and related species). A mainstay of biological anthropology has been the attempt to uncover human fossils and reconstruct the pathways of human evolution. By the 1950s and 1960s, biological anthropologists expanded into the study of human health and disease and began to look at the nonhuman primates (especially monkeys and apes) to reveal what is part of our basic primate biology and what comes with culture. Biological anthropology is currently a field of many specializations; researchers still explore human evolution, health and disease, and primate behavior, but they also work in areas such as human genetics, how social stress impacts the body, and human diet and nutrition.

Linguistic anthropology studies how people communicate with one another through language, and how language use shapes group membership and identity. Linguistic anthropologists also look at how language helps people organize their cultural beliefs and ideologies. These anthropologists have traditionally studied the categories that indigenous people use in their own languages, attempting to understand how they classify parts of their social and natural worlds differently from peoples in other societies.

- **Biological anthropology.** The study of the biological aspects of the human species, past and present, along with those of our closest relatives, the nonhuman primates.

- **Linguistic anthropology.** The study of how people communicate with one another through language and and how language use shapes group membership and identity.

Anthropology is by nature an interdisciplinary discipline. Its subfields cross into many other academic disciplines across the social and natural sciences. Cultural anthropologists, for example, often draw on sociological and psychological approaches, as well as historical and economic data for some projects. Most archaeologists need to understand the principles of geology, including stratigraphy (the layers of earth in which human artifacts might be found) and techniques used to date artifacts. Many archaeologists also need to understand ecological and environmental sciences to be able to reconstruct ancient landscapes. Biological anthropology draws heavily on biological subfields of morphology (which deals with the form and structure of organisms), cellular biology, and genetics.

One thing that keeps such diverse subfields together is a shared history. In the early twentieth century, anthropology became organized into the four subfields we know today, from a shared evolutionary perspective. Archaeologists and cultural anthropologists, especially in North America, generally see themselves as asking similar kinds of questions about human cultures. The major difference is that cultural anthropologists can observe cultures as they are lived, while archaeologists can only reconstruct these cultures from what they have left behind. Another reason for the persistence of the four-field approach is that anthropologists share certain fundamental approaches and concepts they agree are important for making sense of humanity's complexity. These include culture, cultural relativism, diversity, change, and holism.

Culture

Imagine how people would react to you if the next time you went to the university bookstore to buy your textbooks you tried to haggle at the cash register for them. Or if the next time you caught a cold you explained to your friends that your sickness was caused by someone's jealousy, and this jealous person had hired a witch to cast a spell on you. In both cases most people would think you are crazy. But in many societies throughout Africa, Asia, Latin America, the Pacific, and other regions, a lot of ordinary people would think you are crazy for *not* haggling or for not explaining your misfortunes as the workings of a witch.

Every human group has particular rules of behavior and a common set of explanations about how the world works. Within the community, these behaviors and explanations feel totally natural, which is to say, self-evident and necessary. People who behave differently are strange, wrong, maybe even evil. What feels natural to us may seem totally arbitrary to another group of people, because the rules and explanations vary from one group to another. In anthropology, the term **culture** refers to these taken-for-granted notions, rules, moralities, and behaviors within a social group that feel natural and the way things should be.

• **Culture.** The taken-for-granted notions, rules, moralities, and behaviors within a social group.

The idea of culture is one of anthropology's most important contributions to knowledge. It is also one of anthropology's oldest concepts, its first use commonly credited to British anthropologist Edward Burnett Tylor in the 1870s. In "Classic Contributions: E. B. Tylor and the Culture Concept," we examine his original definition of culture.

Anthropologists believe that people have culture in two senses: the general and the particular. Culture in the general sense refers to humans' possession of a generalized capacity, even necessity, to create, share, and pass on their understandings of things through culture. From this point of view, the development of culture is *the* defining feature of our species' evolutionary history, and thus of great relevance to the subfield of biological anthropology.

Culture in the particular sense refers to the fact that people live their lives within particular cultures, or ways of life. For example, although the "American way of life" is actually culturally diverse, with differences across regions, social classes, and ethnic groups, most Americans share very similar beliefs about such things as the value of a formal education, what kinds of clothes women and men should wear to the office,

Classic Contributions

E. B. Tylor and the Culture Concept

LIKE OTHER ANTHROPOLOGISTS of the latter half of the nineteenth century, Edward B. Tylor believed that the social and cultural differences of humanity could be explained as the product of evolutionary forces. Tylor's primary intellectual concern throughout his career was developing an evolutionary sequence that would explain how people evolved from a state of what he called "primitive savagery" to more "advanced" levels of civilization. In his book *Primitive Culture*, published in 1871, he advanced his argument that humans are subject to evolutionary forces in all aspects of their lives, including what he called "culture," offering the now classic definition presented here. Although contemporary uses of the term *culture* have changed since Tylor's definition—mainly because anthropologists today reject Tylor's evolutionary perspective—Tylor's definition is important because it provided a basis for the scientific study of culture that has been central to the discipline ever since.

❦ **E. B. Tylor.**

Culture or Civilization, taken in its wide ethnographic sense, is that complex whole which includes knowledge, belief, art, morals, law, custom, and any other capabilities and habits acquired by man as a member of society. The condition of culture among the various societies of mankind, in so far as it is capable of being investigated on general principles, is a subject apt for the study of laws of human thought and action.... [I]ts various grades may be regarded as stages of development or evolution, each the outcome of previous history, and about to do its proper part in shaping the history of the future. (Tylor 1871:1)

Questions for Reflection

1. How is this definition different from or similar to the notion of culture you had before taking an anthropology course?

2. Tylor believed that people acquire culture as members of a society. But how specifically might someone acquire his or her culture?

and what side of the road to drive on. Archaeologists, linguistic anthropologists, and cultural anthropologists tend to study people's lives in the context of a particular culture. In Chapter 2 we explore the concept of culture more deeply, but here it is important to know that when anthropologists use the term *culture* they are nearly always referring to ideas about the world and ways of interacting in society or in the environment in predictable and expected ways.

Cultural Relativism

All humans participate in culture. Anthropologists, of course, also carry with them basic assumptions about how the world works and what is right or wrong, which typically become apparent when one is studying a culture that makes completely different assumptions. One possible response to the gap in understanding that comes with being in another culture is **ethnocentrism**, assuming our way of doing things is

● **Ethnocentrism.** The assumption that one's own way of doing things is correct, while dismissing other people's practices or views as wrong or ignorant.

correct, while simply dismissing other people's assumptions as wrong or ignorant. Such a position would render the attempt to understand other cultures meaningless, and can lead to bigotry and intolerance. To avoid such misunderstandings, anthropologists have traditionally emphasized **cultural relativism**, the moral and intellectual principle that one should withhold judgment about seemingly strange or exotic beliefs and practices.

- **Cultural relativism.** The moral and intellectual principle that one should withhold judgment about seemingly strange or exotic beliefs and practices.

Human Diversity

- **Diversity.** The sheer variety of ways of being human around the world.

Another of anthropology's major contributions to knowledge has been to describe and explain human **diversity**, the sheer variety of ways of being human around the world. When anthropologists talk about diversity, they mean something different from the popular usage of the term in the United States, which typically refers to different kinds of art, cuisine, dress, or dance, as well as to differences among various racial and ethnic groups.

Early anthropologists of Tylor's day assumed that physical characteristics like skin tone, hair texture, stature (height), hair and eye color, and the shape of the nose, eyes, and lips were the defining characteristics of distinct races. Most of these early anthropologists assumed that race was closely associated with the sophistication of cultural development. Many believed that lighter skin tones were associated with more "advanced" peoples while darker skin tones were associated with more limited mental abilities. These ideas were based on the notion that the several different races represented different species of humans, each endowed with different mental and physical abilities and characteristics. In reality, the so-called races are not different species, because people from these groups can intermarry and produce healthy and intelligent children who are themselves able to reproduce. Tylor and other early anthropologists also assumed that people from the "lower races" were incapable of developing sophisticated cultures with rich and refined traditions as Europeans had. We now know that people from any society can learn the cultural patterns of any other society. We also know that there are variations among different individuals in their apparent abilities. Such differences are not associated with so-called racial differences but with individual ability and the families and communities in which they are raised. As we discuss in a later chapter, the idea of race continues to exercise a powerful influence in the world, but it has no relevant bearing on intelligence or cultural sophistication. Differences of skin color and hair textures are merely aspects of human diversity that exist in the world.

Defined anthropologically, diversity refers to multiplicity and variety, which is not the same as mere difference. Within multiplicity and variety, there is both difference *and* similarity. This idea of diversity-as-multiplicity can shed light not just on racial differences but on another important issue of our time, the cultural effects of globalization, which refers to the rapid movement of money, people, and goods across national boundaries. People now drink Coca-Cola, wear Levi's jeans, and watch CNN all over the world, leading many observers to believe that the diversity of human cultures is in decline because more and more people are participating in a global economy. Yet cultural differences do not just disappear. In fact, globalization creates many new opportunities for cultural diversity—differences *and* similarities—to thrive.

An example drawn from the southern Mexican state of Chiapas illustrates this point (Figure 1.3). In Chiapas, some indigenous people have adapted Coca-Cola for use in their religious and community ceremonies. For many generations Tztotzil Mayas [**tso**-tseel **my**-ahs] in the community of San Juan Chamula used alcoholic drinks, particularly fermented corn drinks and distilled sugar cane liquor, in their public and religious rites (Nash 2007) (Figure 1.4). To create these rites, traditional Mayan religious leaders blended Catholic and indigenous traditions, combining

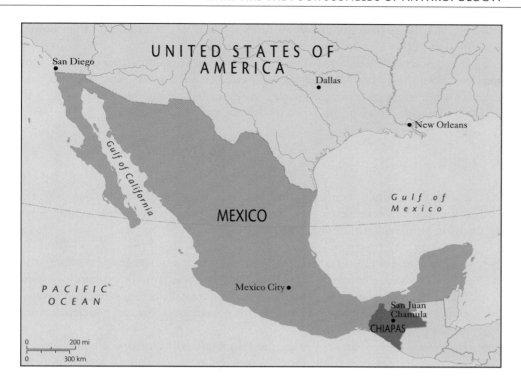

Figure 1.3　San Juan Chamula, Chiapas, Mexico.

Catholicism's celebration of saints' days with the Maya belief that consuming intoxicating spirits helps individuals access sacred powers. Alcoholism, however, became a severe problem, and beginning in the 1940s many Maya began converting to Protestant sects that ban alcohol, eroding the power of traditional religious leaders. In the 1980s these leaders began substituting Coca-Cola for alcoholic drinks in ceremonies. Some leaders gained great personal wealth as distributors of Coca-Cola, deepening socioeconomic class divisions in the community (Nash 2007). But community members incorporated Coke into their ritual lives easily, accepting the notion that the soft drink's bubbles have powers once associated with alcohol, for

Figure 1.4　San Juan Chamula, Chiapas, Mexico.

example, the ability to help individuals belch out bad spirits residing in their bodies (M. Thomas 2008).

Here is a powerful example of diversity-as-multiplicity: Globalization has brought changes to San Juan Chamula that resemble conditions in many other places around the globe, but Maya have imposed their own meanings on the soft drink, using it in ways that reinforce some of their own distinctive cultural traditions.

Change

As the previous example about globalization and Coca-Cola demonstrates, our world is dynamic and constantly changing. Anthropologists in each subfield are specialists in studying human change. For example:

- In *cultural anthropology*, researchers study topics as diverse as how and why religious change happens; what happens when a dominant economic system like socialism collapses or a new one like capitalism is incorporated into a traditional economy; and how and why political violence can erupt in societies experiencing rapid social change.
- In *archaeology*, researchers study the effects of environmental change on past societies; how changes in material culture reflect ongoing social, economic, and political changes; and the processes through which complex state societies were formed and disintegrated.
- In *biological anthropology*, researchers study the specific processes of human evolution, and how our bodies and genetic makeup change in relation to environmental changes, migration, diseases, and other dynamics.
- In *linguistic anthropology*, researchers study how new languages are formed when different languages come together; and how social changes, such as changes in gender relations, are reflected in and emerge from how people communicate with each other.

Some of these changes—particularly changes in cultural practices such as the consumption of Coca-Cola—can emerge over a few years or a generation or two. Others, like changes in human biology, can take many generations and are imperceptible to most living observers. Americans, for example, have gotten considerably taller than we were in colonial times 250 years ago, probably because of changes in diet, especially in the first few years of life. But this fact is largely unnoticed by modern Americans unless we tour fine colonial houses from the 1700s when we notice that the doors are not nearly as tall as the standard door of today.

Anthropology also mirrors the changing world in which it is practiced. As new topics, issues, and problems emerge, anthropologists study things they would not have studied several decades before. Today, for example, archaeologists may study garbage dumps and how high technologies are made in contemporary Silicon Valley computer factories to understand what people actually consume and throw away. Cultural and linguistic anthropologists explore how people create communities and identities and produce new forms of communication in cyberspace. Biological anthropologists specializing in primate behaviors design studies to aid wildlife conservation officials.

Moreover, the face of anthropology has changed dramatically in recent decades. Once a discipline dominated by white European and American men, anthropology is increasingly practiced by women and members of many ethnic and racial minority groups. In the United States today, in fact, women constitute the majority of professional anthropologists. Around the world, decolonization of former colonies has brought once excluded indigenous peoples and members of internal minority groups into universities where many studied anthropology, further expanding the kinds of backgrounds and perspectives represented in the global discipline.

Holism

In bringing together the study of human biology, prehistory, language, and social life under one disciplinary roof, anthropology offers powerful conceptual tools for understanding the entire context of human experience. The effort to synthesize these distinct approaches and findings into a single comprehensive explanation is called **holism**. It is American anthropology that has strived to be the most holistic. This was a legacy of German-born Franz Boas, later known as the "Founder of American Anthropology," through his work in the American Anthropological Association and at Columbia University in the early twentieth century. His student Alfred Kroeber once described four-field anthropology as a "sacred bundle" (Segal and Yanagisako 2005).

In the discipline's early years, it was possible for individuals like Boas, Kroeber and some of their students to work in all four subfields, because the body of anthropological knowledge was so small. But within several decades, the expansion of the discipline and increasing specialization within its branches forced anthropologists to concentrate on a single subfield and topics within subfields, a continuing trend today. In the face of specialization and calls to "unwrap the sacred bundle" (Segal and Yanagisako 2005)—that is, have the subfields go their separate ways—anthropology has struggled to retain its holistic focus.

And yet many anthropologists are deeply dedicated to holism, citing its ability to explain complex issues that no single subfield, much less any other social science, could explain as effectively (Parkin and Ulijaszek 2007). In "Doing Fieldwork: Conducting Holistic Research with Stanley Ulijaszek," we highlight how one anthropologist conducts research in a holistic fashion.

As Ulijaszek's research demonstrates, no single subfield by itself could address complex research problems. Working together, however, the subfields draw a compelling holistic picture of a complex situation. So how do anthropologists actually come to know such things? We turn to this issue in the next section.

• **Holism.** Efforts to synthesize distinct approaches and findings into a single comprehensive interpretation.

• •

THINKING CRITICALLY ABOUT ANTHROPOLOGY

Can you suggest ways that you may learn how people in your town or city view college students from your campus?

• •

How Do Anthropologists Know What They Know?

Anthropology employs a wide variety of methodologies, or systematic strategies for collecting and analyzing data. As we explore in this section, some of these methodologies are similar to those found in other natural and social sciences, including methods that involve the creation of statistics and even the use of mathematical

Doing Fieldwork

Conducting Holistic Research with Stanley Ulijaszek

STANLEY ULIJASZEK IS a British anthropologist who has been conducting research for several decades in the swamplands of coastal Papua New Guinea, an island state in the Southwest Pacific. In recent years, he has turned his attention to an interesting question: in this difficult landscape that is unsuited to agriculture, how do people acquire a sufficient, safe, and nutritious food supply? To answer this question properly requires substantial knowledge of the human biology, prehistory, and culture of coastal New Guinea.

At the center of this story is the sago palm, a palm tree that grows abundantly in swamps. Its stem contains starch, a staple food for the people who cultivate it. People cook sago in long sticks resembling dense French bread, eating it with a bit of fish. Sago is not a great staple food, because it is 99.5 % starch, making it an excellent energy food, but it has few other nutrients. Worse, perhaps, is that sago is toxic when eaten uncooked or improperly prepared. Its toxicity threatens people with a specific genetic mutation that does not allow the red blood cells to carry the toxins out of the body, a mutation common among coastal New Guinea populations. Thus, because of this toxicity, eating sago presented a risk to these coastal people (Ulijaszek 2007).

It turns out, however, that this same genetic mutation confers some resistance to malaria, a mosquito-borne infectious disease common in the tropics. The key to protecting the people while releasing the nutritional energy of sago is to separate the starch from the pith at the center of the sago palm by washing and straining it, then cooking the starch, all of which reduces its toxicity to safe levels. Archaeological evidence indicates that people in this region figured out this process at least 6,000 years ago, which is when they began leaving behind their hunting-and-gathering way of life to take up agriculture. Ulijaszek concludes that they adapted sago for human consumption by detoxifying it, which in turn allowed people's

Cultivating Nutrition from the Sago Palm. Transforming the pith of the sago palm into food is a complex process. First the pith must be chopped out of the trunk and pulverized using simple cutting and pounding tools (top), and then the starch must be leached from the dense mass of fiber using a frame made from the base of the leaf stalk in which the starch is pounded with water to release and strain the edible starch, leaving the inedible fiber behind in the frame. Later the sago flour is collected from a basin where it has settled (bottom).

genetic mutation to survive, thus providing some resistance to malaria in this difficult environment. People then continued to pass on the genetic trait of malarial resistance.

Ulijaszek's research addresses an interesting puzzle about how humans can successfully adapt to a challenging natural environment, and how those changes are intertwined with genetic factors like the resistance to malaria. To achieve this, he drew on the evidence of cultural and linguistic anthropology, gained by observing how people cultivate, process, consume, and talk about sago. He also drew on archaeological evidence of sago production that goes back thousands of years, not necessarily by conducting the excavations himself, but by relying heavily on the evidence

archaeologists working in that area had produced. He also drew on evidence about the genetic make-up of local populations drawn from blood samples and genetic analyses.

Questions for Reflection

1. How do you think Ulijaszek's findings would have differed if he relied only on the evidence of cultural anthropology? Archaeology? Biological anthropology?

2. Do you think Ulijaszek's approach would be applicable to a study of low-fat diets in the United States? How would you apply it?

models to explain things. Other methods aimed at describing cultures very different from our own are more closely allied with the humanities.

The Scientific Method in Anthropology

Anthropology often uses the **scientific method**, the most basic pattern of scientific research. The scientific method is quite simple. It starts with the observation of a fact, a verifiable truth. Next follows the construction of a hypothesis, which is a testable explanation for the facts. Then that hypothesis is tested with experiments, further observations, or measurements. If the data (the information the tests produce) show that the hypothesis is wrong, the scientist develops a new hypothesis and then tests it. If the new tests and the data they produce seem to support the hypothesis, the scientist writes up a description of what he or she did and found, and shares it with other scientists. Other scientists then attempt to reproduce those tests or devise new ones, with a goal of disproving the hypothesis (Figure 1.5).

Note that this way of doing things is a method, not pursuit of ultimate truths. The goal of the scientific method is to devise, test, and disprove hypotheses. Life's big questions—"Why are we here?" "Why is there evil in the world?" and so on—are *not* the goal of science. At best science can provide a reasonable degree of certainty only about more limited questions—"Do the planets revolve around the sun?" "Do mold-encrusted bagels cause people to get sick?" "How did our species develop the traits we now have?" and so on. Scientists regularly disagree among themselves, often passionately. Researchers with differing backgrounds and orientations ask different types of questions and look at data in different ways. Scientists tend to see such debates as beneficial to the practice of science because the more questions asked, the more observations made, and the more tests conducted, the more knowledge is produced.

Theories Guide Research

Theories, which are tested and repeatedly supported hypotheses, are key elements of the scientific method. A **theory** not only explains things, it also helps guide research by focusing the researcher's questions and making the findings meaningful. It is important to note that while many Americans assume that a theory is some wild hunch

- **Scientific method.** The standard methodology of science that begins from observable facts, generates hypotheses from these facts, and then tests these hypotheses.

- **Theory.** A tested and repeatedly supported hypothesis.

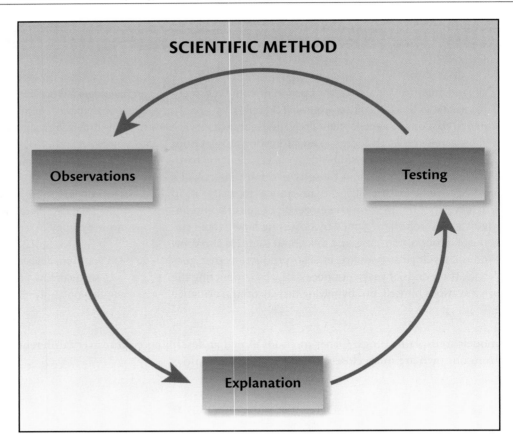

SCIENTIFIC METHOD

Observations

Testing

Explanation

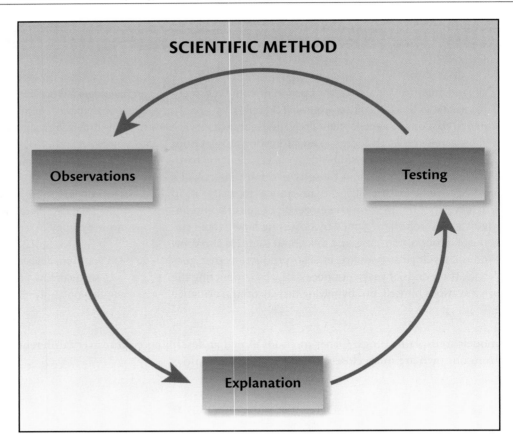

🌿 **Figure 1.5 The Scientific Method.** The process is circular, not linear.

or guess, when scientists in the natural and social sciences use the term *theory*, they mean a carefully constructed hypothesis that has been tested and retested. There is rarely any guessing involved.

Quantitative Data Collection

To build and test hypotheses and theories requires data. Anthropology's subfields employ a number of techniques for gathering and processing data. Some of these techniques use **quantitative methods**, which classify features of a phenomenon, count or measure them, and construct mathematical and statistical models to explain what is observed. Most quantitative research takes place in the subfields of biological anthropology and archaeology, although some cultural and linguistic anthropologists use quantitative techniques as well.

As an illustration of quantitative research, consider the work of Agustín Fuentes, a biological anthropologist at the University of Notre Dame. His research examines the nature of human–monkey interactions, and how, when, and why diseases, such as viruses, get passed between these species. Fuentes and his team (including many undergraduate anthropology students) observe monkeys and humans interacting in Bali, Singapore, and Gibraltar. In each location they record quantitative details about interactions: Who interacts, how many individuals interact, the length of interactions, whether interactions are aggressive or friendly, whether physical contact between species occurs, and whether food is involved in the contact. They interview humans at the locations, sometimes using surveys or administering questionnaires, and collect detailed physical information about the landscape inhabited by the people and monkeys. They also take blood or fecal samples from both the monkeys and the humans, analyzing them for pathogens and parasites. All these variables are considered independently and then compared statistically to see what patterns

• **Quantitative method.** A methodology that classifies features of a phenomenon, counting or measuring them, and constructing mathematical and statistical models to explain what is observed.

emerge. Fuentes has discovered that human–monkey interactions vary depending on the species of monkey, human cultural patterns, gender differences in humans, and sex differences in the monkeys.

Qualitative Data Collection

Anthropologists also employ **qualitative methods**, in which the aim is to produce an in-depth and detailed description of social behaviors and beliefs. Qualitative research usually involves interviews with people as well as observations of their activities. Research data comes in the form of words, images, or objects. In contrast with quantitative methods, qualitative research does not typically use research instruments like surveys or questionnaires. The research instrument is the researcher himself or herself, whose subjective perceptions and impressions in the subject matter also become the basis for knowledge. The **ethnographic method**, which involves prolonged and intensive observation of and participation in the life of a community, is a qualitative methodology and is a hallmark of cultural anthropology.

Luis Vivanco, one of this book's authors, is a cultural anthropologist who uses qualitative methods to ask how global environmentalism changes people's relationships with nature in Latin America. He has conducted more than twenty months of research in Monteverde, Costa Rica, a rural community bordering a tropical cloud forest, and renowned worldwide as a site of conservation and ecotourism. He interviewed local farmers, environmental activists, ecotourists, and scientists, usually on multiple occasions, sometimes with a tape recorder and notepad and other times in informal conversations at the local grocery store or in some other public setting (Figure 1.6). He observed these people interacting with others and participated in community events, including celebrations and public protests. Working as a volunteer in a nature preserve, he listened to how its managers and the ecotourists talk about tropical rain forests. He collected newspaper clippings and reports from local environmental groups and took pictures of people doing things. His fieldnotes, recordings, images, documents, and personal experiences with environmentalists and farmers have helped him understand environmentalism to be a complex arena of social conflict where people struggle not just over how to protect nature, but also how to deal with rapid social changes caused by globalization.

- **Qualitative method.** A research strategy producing an in-depth and detailed description of social activities and beliefs.

- **Ethnographic method.** A prolonged and intensive observation of and participation in the life of a community.

Figure 1.6   Monteverde Bus. In Vivanco's research on environmentalism in Costa Rica, his interest in the social dynamics of ecotourism led him to spend a lot of time among ecotourists, such as the ones shown here arriving in Monteverde by bus.

The Comparative Method

Unlike other scientists, anthropologists do not conduct experiments or make predictions. Instead, anthropologists use the **comparative method** (Kaplan and Manners 1972:42–43). The comparative method allows anthropologists to derive insights from careful comparisons of two or more cultures or societies. The actual "method" is nothing like a precise recipe for research, however, but a general approach, which holds that any particular detail of human behavior or particular social condition should not be seen in isolation, but should be considered against the backdrop of the full range of behaviors and conditions in their individual social settings.

The research of this book's other author, cultural anthropologist Robert Welsch, illustrates how anthropologists can use the comparative method. Welsch has conducted extended ethnographic research both in Papua New Guinea and in Indonesia. One of his research projects explicitly made use of comparative research strategies to understand the social and religious meanings of masks and carved objects in three societies along the Papuan Gulf of New Guinea. The carvings were collected a century ago and are now in museum collections. To conduct his comparative study, Welsch studied the museum collections, pored over published and unpublished accounts of the people who collected the masks, and interviewed older villagers about their traditional practices (Figure 1.7). He learned that although these three societies used the same kinds of objects, their differing decorative styles suggested differences in the social purposes for which each society used the objects. In one society, similarity in designs minimized differences between clans to create group cohesion in war. In another the designs supported social competition among clans within the village, while in the third the way men displayed these decorative boards gave a visual recognition of each man's social networks and where men in his clan had married. These three societies had similar types of carvings and masks, but these objects were used in three distinct ways for different social purposes.

When Anthropology Is Not a Science: Interpreting Other Cultures

Not all anthropologists characterize what they do as science. Prominent British anthropologist E. E. Evans-Pritchard (1902–1973) pronounced in 1961 that anthropology should

- **Comparative method.** A research method that derives insights from careful comparisons of aspects of two or more cultures or societies.

Figure 1.7   Boards Inside Longhouse at Naharo. Welsch visited many longhouses to discuss ritual carvings and their meaning as part of his comparative analysis of art and its social contexts in traditional societies of the Papuan Gulf. This image shows boards he was discussing with elders and their families in Naharo village.

be grouped with the humanities, especially history, rather than natural sciences (Evans-Pritchard 1961). Describing other people, he argued, requires an understanding of their inner lives and beliefs that no scientific methodology can grasp. His view was that the complexity of social behavior prevents any completely objective analysis of human culture.

These days most cultural anthropologists agree with this position. They disregard the scientific ideal of the researcher's detachment from their subject of study: the belief that researchers are not supposed to talk about what they feel and experience, or how emotions and experiences influence what they learn and know as anthropologists (Fabian 2001). The work of American anthropologist Renato Rosaldo (b. 1941), who studied head-hunting in a Filipino society called the Ilongot [Ill-**lahn**-goht], illustrates this point of view. When Rosaldo (1989) asked the Ilongots to explain why they take heads, they explained that when a loved one dies, their grief turns to rage, and the only way to vent that rage and get on with life is to take the head of a traditional enemy. Rosaldo initially dismissed this explanation, assuming there had to be a "deeper" purpose for head-hunting, such as creating group cohesion or allowing young men to prove their worthiness for marriage by showing they could kill an enemy.

That is, until his wife Shelly, also an anthropologist, died in an accident during fieldwork in the Philippines. His own devastating loss generated a similar combination of grief and rage. While he was adjusting to Shelly's death, Rosaldo could grasp emotionally what the Ilongot were getting at. Dealing with the death opened his eyes to the force of emotions in social life, something he and most other anthropologists had never really considered. Rosaldo (1989) realized that his training as an anthropologist, which emphasized scientific detachment, accounted for his initial dismissing of Ilongot notions of head-hunting. He concluded that his other interpretations of head-hunting were not wrong, they just gave him an incomplete picture of why Ilongot did it. He also concluded that ethnographic knowledge is an open-ended process so that as the ethnographer's own life experiences and knowledge change, so do his or her insights into other cultures.

Ethnographers know other cultures from particular points of view. Although they strive to see things from many perspectives—the perspectives of the many people they interview and observe—anthropologists' insights are always partial, indeed, only some of many possible interpretations of culture. But anthropologists do not just try to understand the world of culture and other human concerns, they also intervene in it in practical ways, which is an issue we explore next.

THINKING CRITICALLY ABOUT ANTHROPOLOGY

How might you use a comparative perspective even if you only visit just one country while on vacation? Consider the other cultural contexts you have experienced and how these might provide a comparative framework for experiencing a novel society and culture.

How Is Anthropology Put to Work in the World?

Anthropological research is relevant and useful for addressing many social problems. At some point in their careers, most anthropologists get involved in work with practical, real-world concerns, applying their research skills and knowledge to the creation or implementation of policies, management of social programs, conduct of legal proceedings, or even the design of consumer products.

Applied and Practicing Anthropology: "The Fifth Subfield"?

- **Applied anthropology.** Anthropological research commissioned to serve an organization's needs.

- **Practicing anthropology.** Anthropological work involving research as well as involvement in the design, implementation, and management of some organization, process, or product.

Practical applications are such an important component of anthropology that some anthropologists consider them the "fifth subfield." These practical applications include those of **applied anthropology**, anthropological research commissioned to serve an organization's needs, and those of **practicing anthropology**, the broadest category of anthropological work, in which the anthropologist not only performs research but also gets involved in the design, implementation, and management of some organization, process, or product. One reason some consider these two enterprises a fifth subfield is that the numbers of anthropologists doing these things has swelled in recent decades as university budget cuts have diminished job opportunities in academia.

Not all anthropologists, however, agree with the "fifth subfield" idea because it implies that putting anthropological knowledge to work is a different enterprise from the other subfields. Moreover, the fifth subfield notion sets up a false dichotomy between academic (or theoretical) and practical (or applied) work, which have often been intertwined throughout the history of the discipline (Field and Fox 2007).

Putting Anthropology to Work

Putting anthropological skills and knowledge to work is a challenging enterprise, not least because of tensions it creates with some anthropologists who feel that "we should never forget that a commitment to improving the world is no substitute for understanding it" (Hastrup and Elass 1990:307). In spite of the challenges, however, anthropologists have effectively put their discipline to work addressing difficult social, health, and educational problems, as the following snapshots demonstrate.

Figure 1.8   Cultural Anthropologist Mary Amuyunzu-Nyamongo.

Figure 1.9   Archaeologist Davina Two Bears.

Mary Amuyunzu-Nyamongo: Bringing Cultural Knowledge to Health Programs in Kenya

Like many other anthropologists, Kenyan anthropologist Mary Amuyunzu-Nyamongo works on pressing social and health problems confronting her country. She is currently director and co-founder of the African Institute for Health and Development, an organization that provides research and training on the social dimensions of debilitating illnesses in Kenya, including HIV/AIDS. Amuyunzu-Nyamongo was among the first students of anthropology at the University of Nairobi. She went on to postgraduate studies in medical anthropology at Cambridge University. Some of the problems Amuyunzu-Nyamongo has studied include the lack of detailed knowledge of local communities necessary to make health programs work. Amuyunzu-Nyamongo collected the local knowledge from insights about people's health beliefs and practices through qualitative research. For example, during a campaign to control mosquito-borne illness in a coastal village, government officials wanted to conduct blood screenings to identify levels of infection. They told school children to tell their parents to get screened, which failed. Amuyunzu-Nyamongo knew that in this culture, male heads of households control decision-making . She organized a meeting where the issue of screenings was introduced to them. Once these men became involved, the screenings became successful (Amuyunzu-Nyamongo 2006).

Davina Two Bears and Applied Archaeology on the Navajo Reservation

Because archaeologists often encounter burials when they excavate prehistoric Indian sites, American Indian communities have often found themselves at odds with archaeologists over the question of what to do with the human remains uncovered. Some Indians object to any excavation at all. But the work of Navajo archaeologist Davina Two Bears (2006) runs counter to the expectations many people may have about the inherent tensions between Indians and archaeologists. For several years now, she has worked with the Navajo Nation Archaeology Department, which emerged in 1988 from the Navajo Nation Cultural Resource Management Program. As both an archaeologist and a cultural resource management professional for the Navajo tribe, she advises on potential damage to archaeological sites that might be caused by road construction or building projects. Two Bears uses her professional archaeological training to prevent damage to ancient sites, which many Navajo people view as deserving great respect. Two Bears identifies and records the locations and characteristics of sites. When proposed projects would damage archaeological sites, Two Bears and her colleagues try to identify alternative locations. She feels that although she has been professionally trained, her work is more an extension of what Navajos have always done in protecting their ancestors and their ancestors' special sites.

James McKenna: The Naturalness of Cosleeping

In much of the Western world, it is considered "healthy" for an infant to sleep in a crib, alone, for long stretches during the night. When a baby wakes frequently or wants to sleep alongside the parents, many see the child as too dependent and not doing well. In our society we also have many deaths from sudden infant death syndrome (SIDS) where infants die in the night for unknown reasons. After decades examining how humans and their infants share social and physiological space, biological anthropologist James McKenna (1996) and his colleagues developed an explanation for how and why many SIDS deaths occur in the United States. They collected biological and evolutionary evidence to demonstrate that the advice of the medical establishment and many popular parenting books is plain wrong.

Through their intensive studies of sleeping mothers and infants around the planet, McKenna and his colleagues discovered the complex relationship associated with mothers and infants sleeping together. He found that the frequent stirring of young infants, nursing, and the carbon dioxide and oxygen mix created by bodies close together are important aspects of the healthy development of human babies. The physical closeness to the parent not only fosters the healthy development of the child's body, but it also facilitates feelings of well-being in both mother and child. It appears that cosleeping assists the infant's development and dramatically reduces the risks of SIDS. With these studies he is challenging the assumption that "a healthy baby sleeps alone."

Figure 1.10   Biological Anthropologist James McKenna.

Akira Yamamoto: Supporting Indian Language Revitalization in Arizona

A number of linguistic anthropologists now work on the revitalization of endangered languages, including professor emeritus Akira Yamamoto at the University of Kansas, who has supported language revitalization efforts among the Hualapai [**wah**-lah-pie] Indians of Northwestern Arizona. Yamamoto helped convince school officials of the value of using Hualapai language in schools, and he co-designed and implemented a bilingual school curriculum (Watahomigie and Yamamoto 1992). Yamamoto emphasizes a collaborative approach with native speakers. Recognizing that no language will survive if it relies on an outside specialist to promote it, Yamamoto supports these people with his linguistic skills in their everyday use of their language.

Figure 1.11   Linguistic Anthropologist Akira Yamamoto.

These snapshots offer a small sample of the range of ways anthropologists put their discipline to work. As we discuss in the next section, anthropology—whether practical or academic in its orientation—raises important ethical issues.

THINKING CRITICALLY ABOUT ANTHROPOLOGY

Compare how an anthropologist and an engineer might each approach a problem involving where to situate a bridge or highway in a heavily populated area.

What Ethical Issues Does Anthropology Raise?

• **Ethics.** Moral questions about right and wrong and standards of appropriate behavior.

Issues of **ethics**—moral questions about right and wrong and standards of appropriate behavior—are at the heart of anthropology, in two senses. First, anthropologists learn about how and why people in other cultures think and act as they do by researching their moral standards. Anthropologists often find these things out in the process of adjusting themselves to that culture's rules of ethical behavior.

Second, doing anthropology itself involves ethical relationships between researchers and others, raising many important and complex issues about the ethical conduct of anthropological research and practice. Ethics in anthropology—the moral principles that guide anthropological conduct—are not just a list of dos and don'ts. Nor is ethics just cautionary tales of research gone awry. Ethics is organically connected to what it means to be a good anthropologist (Fluehr-Lobban 2003).

Ethical matters tend to reflect the issues and events of the day. For example, a contentious issue in Franz Boas's time—he harshly criticized fellow anthropologists working as spies for the U.S. government during and after World War I—is no longer a front-burner issue, mainly because anthropologists today routinely reject clandestine research. The reason anthropologists reject work as spies overseas is because doing so puts all anthropologists under suspicion. Ethical issues also change because new topics of study emerge. In recent years, for example, anthropologists have begun considering the ethics of research and of publishing documents in cyberspace, or the ethics of new scientific techniques such as control over human DNA. The discipline also faces challenges about its ethics from outsiders, particularly indigenous groups who have challenged archaeologists over how they handle artifacts. Two common ethical dilemmas that face all anthropologists have to do with the effects of their research on the people, objects, or animals they study and on those to whom they are responsible, which we introduce here.

Do No Harm. But Is That Enough?

The Nuremberg trials after World War II revealed that Nazi scientists had conducted harmful experiments on people in concentration camps. Scientists responded by establishing informal ethical codes for dealing with research subjects. But in 1974 abuse of medical research subjects in the United States led the Congress to pass a law

Figure 1.12 Scandal at Tuskegee. Between 1932 and 1972, the U.S. Public Health Service studied syphilis among white and black men. When scientists learned they could treat syphilis with penicillin, they gave it to the white men, but not the black men. This abuse precipitated reform in the use of humans as research subjects in the United States.

preventing unethical research with human subjects (Figure 1.12). This new law required all research institutes and universities where research was conducted to establish an Institutional Review Board (IRB) to monitor all human subjects–based research. Medical, scientific, and social science organizations, including anthropologists, published codes of ethics emphasizing avoiding harm for people and animals who are the subjects of research.

"Do no harm" continues to be a bedrock principle in anthropology's primary code of ethics, the American Anthropological Association's Principles of Professional Responsibility (see inside front cover). Anthropologists routinely explain to people involved in their research any risks their participation might carry, and obtain their "informed consent" to participate. Anthropological publications avoid sharing confidential information and commonly disguise their informants' identities, in case those individuals could be targeted for harm because of what they say.

Some anthropologists believe the principle of "do no harm" is not enough, however. They assert that anthropologists also have a moral imperative to go further by doing good, for example, by working for social justice and the alleviation of suffering in powerless and marginalized communities (Scheper-Hughes 1995; Fluehr-Lobban 2003).

To Whom Are Anthropologists Responsible?

The primary ethical responsibility of anthropologists is to the people, species, or artifacts they study. Whether it is a pottery shard, baboon, or person, anthropologists are expected to side with their subjects. It does not mean an archaeologist is expected to throw himself or herself in front of a bulldozer to prevent an archaeological site from being destroyed, or a cultural anthropologist to take up arms in defense of informants threatened by police or military. It means that anthropologists should take whatever action is possible when their subjects are threatened, short of doing something illegal. Such action might include helping prepare legal paperwork necessary to stop the bulldozer and conserve the artifacts.

What complicates this principle is that anthropologists are also responsible to other parties. For example, anthropologists also have a responsibility to the public, including the obligation to disseminate the findings of their research—even when something

Thinking Like an Anthropologist

Anthropological Responsibilities to Informants and People in Authority

ANTHROPOLOGISTS BEGIN THEIR research by asking questions. In this box, we want you to learn how to ask questions as an anthropological researcher. Part One describes a situation and follows up with questions we would ask. Part Two asks you to do the same thing with a different situation.

PART ONE: ANTHROPOLOGISTS AND THE WARS IN IRAQ AND AFGHANISTAN

The U.S. government has been an influential supporter of anthropological research and researchers. For example, many anthropologists in all the discipline's subfields work in U.S. governmental service. The types of jobs anthropologists do is as wide-ranging as the discipline's interests and strengths, among them genetics research at the National Institutes of Health; working on the protection and conservation of archaeological sites for the National Park Service; and facilitating community involvement in watershed conservation programs at the Environmental Protection Agency. The U.S. government also provides substantial financial support for university-based anthropologists not directly in its employment through research funding

agencies like the National Science Foundation and the Fulbright Scholars Program.

The responsibility anthropologists have to the government may be nothing more than conducting rigorous, accurate, and either publishable research or research useful for decision-makers, which is what most private foundations that sponsor anthropological research also expect. But sometimes the sponsor's desire to know something particular can conflict with the anthropologist's ethical obligation to protect informants.

An example of this conflict emerged in the context of the U.S. military's involvement in wars in Iraq and Afghanistan beginning in 2001. U.S. military leaders recognized that a basic lack of cultural and linguistic knowledge about local people among U.S. troops can negatively impact their abilities to identify enemy combatants and the social networks that support those combatants, as well as to build alliances with local people necessary to help U.S. troops complete their missions.

As a result, the Department of Defense established a unit called the "Human Terrain System" (HTS), composed of applied social science and humanities researchers. Some of these researchers have been cultural anthropologists. Their

Human Terrain Systems Member Conducting Interviews in Afghanistan.

work involves accompanying troops into villages to conduct interviews of local people, identify village leaders and power brokers, and advise military commanders and State Department officials about the possible social consequences of their decisions. These social scientists are not intended to be combatants themselves, although they are allowed to carry weapons for self-defense. As one member of the program said, "One anthropologist can be much more effective than a B-2 bomber—not winning a war, but creating a peace one Afghan at a time" (HTS 2010).

HTS researchers undergo training in research ethics and internal ethics reviews to help them better manage relations with the vulnerable populations with which they work. They sometimes even find themselves at odds with the military commanders they advise when they express military action could negatively affect those populations. The American Anthropological Association has nevertheless condemned this use of anthropology as an ethical violation because the primary responsibility and accountability of the anthropologists is to the military, not to their informants. Furthermore, critics argue that anthropologists are also responsible to the discipline's standards of integrity, truth, and openness. An individual anthropologist who does not follow these standards can affect the reputation of other anthropologists. One reason for rejecting military-oriented research, for example, is that the association of anthropology with military action hurts other anthropologists' abilities to gain people's trust, a key component of anthropological research.

What questions does this situation raise for anthropological researchers?

1. What are the possible consequences of such research for the individual researchers and the discipline at large?

2. Is the anthropologist obliged to tell everything he or she finds out through research, or can and should some information be held back?

3. Should loyalty to one's nation transcend loyalty to one's informants?

4. Would hiding the identity of the informants be enough to quell ethical concerns raised by the military's use of anthropology?

PART TWO: ANTHROPOLOGY STUDENTS AND ETHICAL RESPONSIBILITIES

As a student of anthropology, you may be confronted with ethical dilemmas about your responsibilities to your informants and people in authority. For example, it is possible that you will be asked to conduct basic research, such as studying a club or fraternity on campus, or a social setting or group in the community. It is not unlikely that during the course of your research, you may witness an illegal activity—such as alcohol use by a minor, drug dealing, or some other situation in which a law is broken. What questions would you ask about this situation as an anthropological researcher? (Sample questions can be found at the end of this chapter. There is no single set of correct questions, but some questions are more insightful than others.)

that is published can lower public opinion about a group of people. Anthropologists also have responsibilities to their sponsors who fund their research—a theme we explore in "Thinking Like an Anthropologist: Anthropological Responsibilities to Informants and People in Authority."

THINKING CRITICALLY ABOUT ANTHROPOLOGY

If you were studying a local Head Start program with few resources and observed problems with local funding for the facility, could you suggest some "Action Anthropology" projects that might help the organization?

Conclusion

Ever since the 1850s, anthropologists have been asking questions about and developing perspectives on human societies past and present. Their expertise is on culture, diversity, how and why social change happens, the dynamics of human biology, and the ways people communicate with each other. The four subfields of anthropology—cultural anthropology, archaeology, biological anthropology, and linguistic anthropology—sometimes come together to offer powerful conceptual tools for understanding the whole context of human experience, an approach called holism. Together with the range of methodological tools represented in the discipline—sophistication with theory, quantitative methods, qualitative methods, and the comparative method—anthropology offers a highly relevant discipline for today's world.

But because anthropology deals with people, their bodies, and cultural artifacts meaningful to people, nearly everything anthropologists study invokes ethical concerns. Throughout this book we consider the ethics and application of anthropology research as we consider the anthropological research in all four subfields. But let us begin our journey toward an understanding of anthropology with a fuller discussion of the concept of culture.

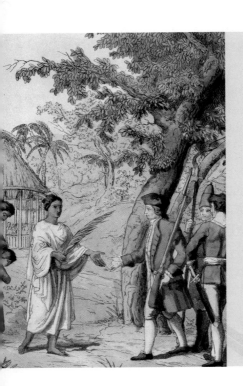

KEY TERMS

Anthropology   p. 5

Applied anthropology
 p. 22

Archaeology   p. 8

Biological anthropology   p. 9

Colonialism   p. 7

Comparative method   p. 20

Cultural anthropology   p. 8

Cultural relativism   p. 12

Culture   p. 10

Diversity   p. 12

Empirical   p. 6

Ethics   p. 24

Ethnocentrism   p. 11

Ethnographic method
 p. 19

Evolution   p. 6

Holism   p. 15

Industrialization   p. 5

Linguistic anthropology   p. 9

Practicing anthropology
 p. 22

Qualitative methods   p. 19

Quantitative methods   p. 18

Salvage paradigm   p. 7

Scientific method   p. 17

Theory   p. 17

Reviewing the Chapter

Chapter Section	What We Know	To Be Resolved
How did anthropology begin?	During the nineteenth century, the rise of industrialization, the influence of evolutionary theory, and colonial contact with less industrialized cultures led to the discipline of understanding how cultures operate and interact.	Anthropologists are still fascinated—and challenged—by the contrasts and changes in culture worldwide as a result of globalization.

What are the four subfields of anthropology, and what do they share in common?	Anthropologists in all subfields share certain fundamental approaches and concepts including culture, cultural relativism, diversity, change, and holism.	Some anthropologists continue to debate the idea that the subfields, with their distinct methods and specialized research interests, belong together in the same discipline.
How do anthropologists know what they know?	Anthropology has a strong relationship with the scientific method; all anthropologists use theories, collect data, and analyze that data.	While most cultural anthropologists reject the possibility of a completely objective analysis of human culture, other subfields of anthropology, such as archaeology and biological anthropology, are thoroughly committed to the scientific method.
How is anthropology put to work in the world?	All four of the subfields have both theoretical and applied aspects. Applied research uses the insights of anthropological theory to solve problems.	Most anthropologists see an anthropological approach as providing a better way of understanding people from different backgrounds than that of any other discipline, but anthropologists continue to disagree among themselves about how to apply that understanding to address human problems.
What ethical issues does anthropology raise?	Issues of ethics—moral questions about right and wrong and standards of appropriate behavior—are at the heart of anthropology.	Certain ethical issues have no easy resolution, such as the ideal that anthropologists should do no harm, or how to resolve sometimes conflicting responsibilities anthropologists have to different communities and publics.

Readings

There are numerous books that examine the historical emergence and intellectual history of anthropology. One of the best is the 2007 book *A New History of Anthropology,* edited by Henrika Kuklick (Malden, MA: Wiley-Blackwell).

●●●●●●●●●●●●●●●●●●●●●●●

The 2005 book *Anthropology Put to Work,* edited by Les Field and Richard G. Fox (Oxford: Berg Publishers), offers an introduction to both the opportunities and the disciplinary, social, and political complexities involved in applying anthropological expertise.

●●●●●●●●●●●●●●●●●●●●●●●

For a detailed exploration of the primary ethical concerns and dilemmas involved in anthropological research across the subfields, see Carolyn Fluehr-Lobban's 2003 book *Ethics and the Profession of Anthropology: Dialogue for Ethically Conscious Practice* (Walnut Creek, CA: AltaMira Press).

●●●●●●●●●●●●●●●●●●●●●●●

The 2007 book *Holistic Anthropology: Emergence and Convergence,* edited by David Parkin and Stanley Ulijaszek (New York: Berghahn Books), provides a contemporary perspective on the development of cross-subfield collaborations

dedicated to the notion of holism. For a critical perspective on that desire for holism, see the 2005 book *Unwapping the Sacred Bundle: Reflections on the Disciplining of Anthropology* (Durham: Duke University Press), edited by Daniel Segal and Sylvia Yanigasako.

●●●●●●●●●●●●●●●●●●●●●●●

Renato Rosaldo's 1989 book *Culture & Truth: The Remaking of Social Analysis* (Boston: Beacon Press) is a classic text that reflects critically on cultural anthropology's complicated relationship with the sciences and objectivity.

●●●●●●●●●●●●●●●●●●●●●●●

SUGGESTED ANSWERS TO "THINKING LIKE AN ANTHROPOLOGIST"

Use these examples as a guide to answering questions for other "Thinking Like an Anthropologist" boxes in the book.

1. Does withholding information about illegal activities compromise the integrity of the discipline?
2. Would you be obliged to tell your professor everything you've found out through research, or can and should some information be held back?
3. Should loyalty to one's peer group transcend loyalty to one's university, or the discipline of anthropology?
4. How could you protect the identity of your informants?

Culture

Giving Meaning to Human Lives

IN 2005, THE body that governs intercollegiate sports in the United States, the National Collegiate Athletic Association (NCAA), banned teams with American Indian names and mascots from competing in its postseason tournaments. Clarifying the ruling, an official stated, "Colleges and universities may adopt any mascot that they wish. . . . But as a national association, we believe that mascots, nicknames, or images deemed hostile or abusive in terms of race, ethnicity or national origin should not be visible at the championship events that we control" (NCAA 2005). The ruling affected a number of schools with competitive sports programs: Florida State ("Seminoles"), University of North Dakota ("Fighting Sioux"), and University of Illinois ("Fighting Illini"), among others.

The ruling concluded decades of pressure from American Indians, students, and others who have argued that these mascots stereotype and denigrate Indian traditions. As one Oneida woman expressed, "We experience it as no less than a mockery of our cultures. We see objects sacred to us—such as the drum, eagle feathers, face painting, and traditional dress—being used, not in sacred ceremony, or in any cultural setting, but in another culture's game" (Munson 1999:14). Moreover, most Indian activists point out that the same institutions and states that use Indian symbols are the very places where white people stole Indian lands, forcibly moving Indian people to much less desired areas on reservations. To Indians, the mascots seem to be just

Mascot Chief Illiniwek. Chief Illiniwek performs during a University of Illinois football game. In 2007, after a long controversy, the university retired the mascot.

31

another attack on the Indian cultures that non-Indians have tried to eliminate for several centuries.

Outraged students, alumni, and political commentators have countered that these mascots honor Indian traditions, pointing to the strength and bravery of Native Americans they hope to emulate in their teams. They also point out that the mascots are part of venerable traditions, part of the living cultures of their universities. Abandoning their mascots is like turning their backs on a part of their own cultural heritage.

This battle of words over college mascots has brewed for decades, participants on both sides sometimes making exaggerated claims about the other side's motivations or intentions. Yet each side in the controversy calls into play an issue of deep concern to them that divides the participants into two opposed groups, each with a radically different interpretation of the issue that often views the opposing point of view as irrational or wrong.

For this reason, this conflict provides a compelling illustration of the power of culture. The word *culture* is widely interpreted in society. To some it refers to aspects of popular culture such as art, music, fashion, theater, and other forms of self-expression and creativity. An even broader definition of culture encompasses the many elements of society often associated with ethnicity, from flags and banners to ethnic costumes, songs, and styles of cooking.

Culture is also at the heart of anthropology. But anthropologists interpret culture differently from these uses of the term and provide it with its most foundational and scientific definitions. Culture as anthropologists use the term is a concept that refers to the perspectives and actions that a group of people consider natural and self-evident. These perspectives and actions are rooted in shared meanings and the ways people act in social groups. Culture is, as we will see, a uniquely human capacity that helps us confront the common problems that face all humans, like communicating with each other, organizing ourselves to get things done, making life predictable and meaningful, and dealing with conflict and change. From an anthropological perspective, culture is a central component of what it means to be human.

The culture concept provides a powerful lens for making sense of the differences and similarities across and within societies, a point that leads to a key question: *How does the concept of culture help explain the differences and similarities in people's ways of life?* Embedded in this broader question are the following problems, around which this chapter is organized:

What is culture?

If culture is emergent and dynamic, why does it feel so stable?

How is culture expressed through social institutions?

Can anybody own culture?

In this chapter, we present an overview of how anthropologists approach culture and explain why it is so relevant to understanding human beliefs and actions. We also offer a definition of culture that informs and shapes the rest of this textbook. We start with the key elements that all anthropologists accept as central to any definition of culture.

What Is Culture?

Culture has been defined many ways by anthropologists, and there are nearly as many approaches to studying it as there are anthropologists. This lack of agreement does not frustrate or paralyze anthropologists. In fact, most anthropologists see this diversity of perspective as the sign of a vibrant discipline.

What is most striking about how different anthropologists define culture in somewhat different ways is that most of these definitions share a number of features in common. Culture is learned. It uses symbols. It is dynamic and is integrated with daily experience. It is also shared by groups of people, who by following its rules and guiding principles construct it anew for each new generation. We explore each of these elements of culture in turn.

Elements of Culture

English scholar Sir Edward B. Tylor (1832–1917) was a founding figure of cultural anthropology. He offered the first justification for using the word *culture* to understand differences and similarities among groups of people. He defined culture as "the complex whole which includes knowledge, belief, art, law, morals, custom, and any other capabilities acquired by man as a member of society" (1871:1). Two aspects of Tylor's definition, especially that culture is *acquired* (today we say *learned*) and that culture is a "complex whole," have been especially influential.

Since Tylor's time, anthropologists have developed many theories of culture, the most prominent of which are summarized in Table 2.1. We discuss many of these theories in later chapters, and explore in more detail how they have changed over time. One of the most important changes in cultural theory is that early anthropologists tended to see cultures in societies with simple technologies as more fixed and stable than anyone does today. We now know that every culture is quick to change as conditions around them change, giving rise to several modern evolutionary and ecological perspectives. Another key change is that since the 1960s cultural anthropologists have focused more intensively on the symbolic lives of people in all societies. These approaches have led to more emphasis in recent times on interpretive theories of culture. Nevertheless, across all these theories, there are seven basic elements that anthropologists agree are critical to any theory of culture.

Culture Is Learned

Although all human beings are born with the ability to learn culture, nobody is born as a fully formed cultural being. The process of learning a culture begins at birth, and that is partly why our beliefs and conduct seem so natural: we have been doing and thinking in certain ways since we were young. For example, the Ongee [ahn-**gay**], an indigenous group who live in the Andaman Islands in the Indian Ocean, learn from a very early age that ancestors cause periodic earthquakes and tidal waves, a fact that is as given to them as it would be strange to you, who were not raised with such beliefs.

TABLE 2.1		PROMINENT ANTHROPOLOGICAL THEORIES OF CULTURE	
Theory	Period	Major Figures	Definition
Social evolutionism	1870s–1910s	E. B. Tylor, Herbert Spencer, L. H. Morgan	All societies pass through stages, from primitive state to complex civilization. Cultural differences are the result of different evolutionary stages.
Historical particularism	1910s–1930s	Franz Boas, Alfred Kroeber, Edward Sapir	Individual societies develop particular cultural traits and undergo unique processes of change. Culture traits diffuse from one culture to another.
Functionalism	1920s–1960s	Bronislaw Malinowski	Cultural practices, beliefs, and institutions fulfill psychological and social needs.
Structural-functionalism	1920s–1960s	A. R. Radcliffe-Brown	Culture is systematic, its pieces working together in a balanced fashion to keep the whole society functioning smoothly.
Neo-evolutionism	1940s–1970s	Leslie White, Julian Steward	Cultures evolve from simple to complex by harnessing nature's energy through technology and the influence of particular culture-specific processes.
Cultural materialism	1960s–1970s	Marvin Harris	The material world, especially economic and ecological conditions, shape people's customs and beliefs.
Cognitive anthropology	1950s–1970s	Ward Goodenough, Roy D'Andrade	Culture operates through mental models and logical systems.
Structuralism	1960s–1970s	Claude Lévi-Strauss	People make sense of their worlds through binary oppositions like hot–cold, culture–nature, male–female, and raw–cooked. These binaries are expressed in social institutions and cultural practices like kinship, myth, and language.
Interpretive anthropology	1970s–present	Clifford Geertz, Victor Turner, Mary Douglas	Culture is a shared system of meaning. People make sense of their worlds through the use of symbols and symbolic activities like myth and ritual.
Post-structuralism	1980s–present	Renato Rosaldo, George Marcus	Not a single school of thought, but a set of theoretical positions that rejects the idea that there are underlying structures that explain culture. Embraces the idea that cultural processes are dynamic, and that the observer of cultural processes can never see culture completely objectively.

• **Enculturation.** The process of learning the social rules and cultural logic of a society.

Anthropologists call this process of learning the cultural rules and logic of a society **enculturation**.

Enculturation happens both explicitly and implicitly. Your student experience illustrates how both explicit and implicit enculturation processes have shaped you. Throughout your schooling, your teachers have explicitly taught you many things you need to know to be a productive member of society: to write, to analyze a text, to do mathematics, and so on (Figure 2.1). But you have also learned many other things that are more implicit, that is, not clearly expressed. The more implicitly learned lessons in your school years included obedience to authority and respect for social

Figure 2.1   Do You Get It? You were enculturated to read from left to right. But when speakers of Hebrew language are taught to read, such as those who might read this cartoon from a Hebrew language newspaper, they begin on the right and move left.

hierarchy. You learned these lessons from sitting in class. In the typical classroom, chairs face forward in rows so the teacher, who represents authority, can control your attention and movement. Bells and announcements over the loudspeakers also regulate your activities and the flow of your day. By the time you reach the university, these patterns are so ingrained that you take them for granted. But that does not mean enculturation has stopped. It will, in fact, continue throughout your life. You might notice that you are also involved in enculturation, explicit and implicit, as a student at your university, as you learn its specific traditions, which might include creating loyalty to certain mascots and other university symbols.

Culture Uses Symbols

Clifford Geertz (1926–2006) was one of the best known American anthropologists of recent time. He proposed that culture is a system of **symbols**—a symbol being something that conventionally stands for something else—through which people make sense out of the world. Symbols may be verbal or nonverbal. Symbols are things that people in a given culture associate with something else, often something intangible, such as motherhood, family, God, or country. To illustrate this point, Geertz posed an interesting question: How do we know the difference between a wink and a twitch (1973:6–7)?

As movements of the eye, winks and twitches are identical. But the difference between them is enormous, as anyone who has experienced the embarrassment of taking one for the other can attest. A twitch is an involuntary blink of the eye, and generally speaking has no symbolic significance. A wink, however, communicates a particular message to a particular someone, and it takes a lot of implicit knowledge, first, to decide if it is a wink or a twitch, and second, to understand what it communicates.

In an instant, we must consider a number of questions: Is there intent? What is the intent—conspiracy, flirtation, parody, ridicule, or something else? Would it be socially appropriate for this person to wink at me, and under what conditions? Underlying our considerations, which may barely rise to the surface of consciousness, is a shared system of meaning in which we (and the winker) participate that helps us communicate with and understand each other. Interestingly, what sounds like a complex computational process when broken down into these many decision points actually comes quite naturally to the human mind. This is because of the human capacity for learning with symbols and signs that otherwise have little meaning outside of a given culture.

Geertz's concept of culture, often called the **interpretive theory of culture**, is the idea that culture is embodied and transmitted through symbols. This fundamental concept helped anthropologists clarify the symbolic basis of culture, something virtually all anthropologists take for granted today. Because culture is based on symbols, culture is implicit in how people think and act, so they rarely, if ever, recognize culture for what it is; it is simply natural to them. In fact, people express culture in *everything* they do—playing games, speaking a language, building houses, growing food, making love, raising children, and so on (Figure 2.2). The meanings of these things—and the symbols that underlie those meanings—differ from group to group, and, as a result, people do things and organize themselves differently around the world. These differing meanings are what make the Balinese Balinese, Zapotecs Zapotecs, and Americans Americans.

Cultures Are Dynamic, Always Adapting and Changing

In a globalized world with high levels of migration across cultural borders, communication flowing in all directions, and social and

- **Symbol.** Something—an object, idea, image, figure, or character—that represents something else.

- **Interpretive theory of culture.** A theory that culture is embodied and transmitted through symbols.

Figure 2.2 It's Like Getting a Joke. When a popular comedian like Jerry Seinfeld tells a funny joke, most of us barely think about what makes it so funny. Like other examples of culture Geertz discussed, we just "get it."

ethnic mixing, it is often impossible to say with any certainty where one culture or social group ends and another begins. As a result, many anthropologists today talk less about culture as a totally coherent and static *system* of meaning and more about the *processes* through which social meanings are constructed and shared.

Attention to cultural processes yields another insight: culture is *dynamic*. Social groups are not uniform or homogeneous, because not everybody interprets the events of everyday life in the same way, nor do they blindly act out scripts already laid out for them to perform. Cultural processes are emergent, fluid, and marked by creativity, uncertainty, differing individual meaning, and social conflict. Relations of power and inequality often permeate these cultural processes. No social group in the United States is composed of people who are absolutely equal, despite American insistence that we all have equal opportunity. Some people seem to be natural leaders, perhaps because of their charm, intelligence, or wealth. People who are leaders of a group of people, like the most influential students in your dorm, can help others accept burdensome rules or help develop ways to evade them, whereas someone who is less a leader or trendsetter will have much less influence in shaping the culture of the same dorm. And university administrators and RAs on dorm floors know that their direct power over student behavior is limited to imposing or enforcing a few rules. But we all know that some RAs can influence their dorm residents better than others, even though everybody knows that colleges and universities have it in their power to expel students for violating basic rules. When conflicts emerge in such settings, those with much less "official" power may have more influence on the people involved. In the same way, understanding the changing culture of any group requires understanding who is powerful and how they come by this influence.

Culture Is Integrated with Daily Experience

As cultural beings, how we relate to the world seems natural to us, transparent, obvious, inevitable, and necessary. Our sense of passing time, for example, might contrast sharply with people in other cultures. In Western cultures, we think of time as an entity that moves from past to present to future. This concept—an element of culture—has a critical influence on our daily lives, because it helps us organize and regulate our activities every day. It also motivates us to make plans, since this concept of time leads us to believe that time must be used or it will be lost.

Our values and beliefs are shaped by many integrated elements of life experience that can be grouped under the term *culture*. Which foods we eat, the jobs we have, the clothes we wear, how we worship, the way we behave toward others on the street—these and other aspects must work well together to keep a culture fully functional. Understanding that culture comprises a dynamic and interrelated set of social, economic, and belief structures is a key to understanding how the whole of culture operates.

The integration of culture across these domains leads to expectations that are specific to a given social group. For example, white middle-class American parents think it is "natural" for their babies to sleep in single beds, often in their own rooms (Small 1998:116–18). They believe that sleeping with their babies creates emotional dependence. In our society, which prizes personal independence and self-reliance, such dependence seems damaging to the child. American couples often think of their own bed, the parents' bed, as a place of privacy and sexual intimacy where children do not belong. Other societies find these ideas strange and exotic. The Gusii of Kenya, for example, think it is "natural" to sleep with their babies, not to mention hold them constantly during waking hours, precisely because they *want* them to grow up to be dependent on others. For them, proper human behavior means constantly relying on other people.

Sleeping also demonstrates that activities you might think of as "natural"—that is, biologically based, as sleeping is, and therefore universally the same for all humans—are actually culturally patterned. Culture helps shape the basic things all humans must do for biological survival, like eating, sleeping, drinking, defecating, having sex, and so on. There is no better illustration of this fact than food preferences. As omnivores, humans can eat an enormous range of foods. But many Americans' stomachs churn at the thought of eating delicacies like rotten shark flesh (Iceland), buffalo penis stew (Thailand), or dogs (East Asia) (Figure 2.3).

No other animal so thoroughly dwells in artificial, or human-made, worlds of its own creation. Anthropologists stress that a **cross-cultural perspective** (analyzing a human social phenomenon by comparing that phenomenon in different cultures) is necessary to appreciate just how "artificial" are our beliefs and actions. A cross-cultural perspective demonstrates the incredible flexibility and plasticity of the human species—human belief and practices come in all shapes and forms.

Culture Shapes Everybody's Life

White middle-class North Americans tend to believe they have no culture, in the same way that most people feel they have no accent. But just as people from Dallas, Boston, or Oklahoma City may each feel they have no accent, they will likely feel their culture is not very distinctive either. They will likely feel that they possess the most mainstream aspects of American culture, even though each of the others, not to mention people from Los Angeles, Honolulu, or Seattle, will almost certainly feel that they have a fairly distinctive accent and an equally distinctive culture that varies from mainstream "American culture." These are understandable reactions to the transparency and naturalness of culture.

But the other side of the coin is the tendency to view minorities, immigrants, and others who differ from white middle-class norms as "people with culture," as compared to people who have what they understand as a fairly general American culture. In the United States, these ideas are tied to social and institutional power: the more "culture" in this sense of the term one appears to have, the less power one wields; the more power one has, the less one appears to have culture (Rosaldo 1989). This power of mainstream culture over ethnic cultures is about the relationships of power and inequality that we mentioned earlier. In fact, by differing from mainstream patterns a group's culture becomes more visible to everyone. It is in this sense that groups with the most obvious cultures tend to be the least powerful.

Culture Is Shared

The notion that culture is shared refers to the idea that people, through their participation in social groups, make sense of their worlds and order their lives. Until recently, most anthropologists thought about culture as being transmitted and participated in through face-to-face networks in real communities. But, as every student knows, today we can participate in social groups virtually through the Internet. Culture is not a product of individual psychology or biology, nor is it reducible to either individual psychology or biology. As a result, anthropologists generally accept that purely psychological and biological explanations of human experience are inadequate.

An individual's comprehension of anything is always based on what his or her group defines collectively as proper and improper. Anthropologists commonly refer to such definitions as **cultural constructions**, which refers to the fact that people collectively "build" meanings through common experience and negotiation. In the

Figure 2.3 Yummy . . . Or Not. A meal of insect larvae might make some Americans vomit or wretch, which shows how powerful cultural beliefs are: they actually provoke a biological response to something that is perfectly digestible, if not healthy and delicious.

- **Cross-cultural perspective.** Analyzing human social phenomenon by comparing that phenomenon in different cultures.

- **Cultural construction.** The meanings, concepts, and practices that people build out of their shared and collective experiences.

debate over college mascots, for example, both sides collectively "constructed" the significance of these images and symbols for both Indians and colleges through their debates, protests, and discussions. A "construction" derives from past collective experiences in a community, as well as lots of people talking about, thinking about, and acting in response to a common set of goals and problems.

Cultural Understanding Involves Overcoming Ethnocentrism

One of the key features of culture is that it makes us feel that the ways we do things are correct, that is, that we do things—or think things out—in the "right" way and everybody else thinks and does things wrongly. As we mentioned in the previous chapter, feeling that everyone else does things the wrong way and that our way of doing things is right is called *ethnocentrism*. You may think of this process as a community-wide form of egocentrism. But for anthropologists, who like all other humans have a culture, ethnocentrism presents a major problem. How can we as anthropologists overcome our own ethnocentric biases to view any other culture or group of people objectively? Going and living with a community provides access to understanding what other people do, say, think, and believe, but if we are constantly judging their society and how it does things by our own goals, morals, and understandings we cannot ever understand them in their own terms.

From the beginning of cultural anthropology in America, anthropologists have argued that the only way to understand other cultures is in terms of that other culture's own goals, ideas, assumptions, values, and beliefs. The concept of *relativism*, by which we interpret and make sense of another culture in terms of the other culture's perspective, using their own goals, values, and beliefs rather than our own to make sense of what people say and do, is a central means of overcoming ethnocentrism, and it is a major feature of the anthropological perspective on culture.

But understanding another culture in its own terms does not mean that anthropologists necessarily accept and defend all the things people do. Even though the job of an anthropologist is not to judge other cultures but learning to understand how and why other peoples do things as they do, anthropologists still carry basic values as individuals and as members of a particular society. A relativistic perspective is simply a useful tool that can help anthropologists overcome ethnocentrism and begin to see matters from the point of view of another culture.

A number of anthropologists, in fact, advocate a "critical relativism," or taking a stance on a practice or belief only after trying to understand it in its cultural and historical context. Critical relativism also holds that no group of people is homogeneous, so it is impossible to judge an entire culture based on the actions or beliefs of a few. For example, many North Americans practice male circumcision, which other societies consider abhorrent, including people in the German city of Cologne who banned circumcision in 2012 as a human rights abuse. There is even a small but growing social movement in the United States that condemns the practice along similar lines. But when people from other societies or members of this movement criticize this practice they are not condemning our entire culture. Similarly, anthropologists can take critical perspectives on particular cultural practices and beliefs without indicting an entire culture as if it were a homogeneous entity (Merry 2003).

Another motive for advocating critical relativism is that, in an extreme form, cultural relativism can be a difficult position to uphold. It can lead to **cultural determinism**, the idea that all human actions are the product of culture, which denies the influence of other factors like physical environment and human biology on human behavior. Some critics also argue that extreme relativism can justify atrocities like genocide, human rights abuses, and other horrific things humans do to one another. For some background on the origins of relativism in anthropology, see "Classic Contributions: Franz Boas and the Relativity of Culture."

• **Cultural determinism.** The idea that all human actions are the product of culture, which denies the influence of other factors like physical environment and human biology on human behavior.

Classic Contributions

Franz Boas and the Relativity of Culture

GERMAN-BORN FRANZ BOAS (1858–1942) was a pioneer anthropologist and the major figure responsible for establishing anthropology in America. Although he had a doctorate in physics, he became interested in studying non-Western cultures while conducting research on Baffin Island (Newfoundland) on the color of ice and sea water. He befriended many Inuit (so-called Eskimos), and learned that they thought about the world differently; for example, they did not distinguish between the colors green and blue. From these conversations he learned a valuable lesson that would be at the heart of his work for the rest of his life: to learn about another people's perspective, one has to try to overcome one's own cultural framework. This perspective has come to be known as cultural relativism.

Franz Boas (posing for a museum display about the Hidatsa at the American Museum of Natural History).

The data of ethnology prove that not only our knowledge, but also our emotions are the result of the form of our social life and the history of the people to whom we belong. If we desire to understand the development of human culture we must try to free ourselves of these shackles. This is possible only to those who are willing to adapt themselves to the strange ways of thinking and feeling of primitive people. If we attempt to interpret the actions of our remote ancestors by our rational and emotional attitudes we cannot reach truthful results, for their feeling and thinking were different from ours. We must lay aside many points of view that seem to us self-evident, because in early times they were not self-evident. It is impossible to determine a priori those parts of our mental life that are common to mankind as a whole and those due to the culture in which we live. A knowledge of the data of ethnology enables us to attain this insight. Therefore it enables us also to view our own civilization objectively. (Boas 1940:636, translated from the original German published in 1889 as Die Ziele der Ethnologie)

Questions for Reflection

1. Do you think it is really possible to, as Boas said, "free ourselves of these shackles" (our own self-evident points of view)? Why and how? If you do not think it is possible, why not?

2. Do you think we can even know what our self-evident points of view are? How?

Defining Culture in This Book

Although all anthropologists agree that these seven elements of culture are critical to any definition, in their research different anthropologists emphasize or interpret these elements differently, which contributes to the diversity of culture theories expressed in Table 2.1. So while we too accept the importance of these key elements to any definition, reflecting our backgrounds as interpretive anthropologists working in regions of rapid social change due to globalization, as authors of this book we define culture in the following way: *Culture consists of the collective processes that make the artificial seem natural.*

What we mean with this definition is that culture is not a static set of rules, or a totally coherent system of symbolic beliefs that people "have" or "carry" like a toolbox that gets passed down from generation to generation, which have been rather common views of culture among anthropologists. Culture, in fact, is more dynamic, emergent, and changing than these ideas allow, as cultures intermingle due to cross-border interconnections such as migration, global media, economic globalization, and other such dynamics of our contemporary world. So we emphasize culture as the processes through which people in social groups collectively construct or accept certain ways of thinking and acting such that they feel "natural," that is, obvious, appropriate, or even necessary. This definition emphasizes that those feelings of naturalness people experience about their beliefs and actions are in fact artificial, that is humanly constructed and variable across social groups, and they can change somewhat quickly. It also assumes that culture is emergent and even unstable, responding to innovation, creativity, and struggles over meaning. The power of this definition is that by presenting culture as a dynamic and emergent process based on social relationships, it leads anthropologists to study the ways cultures are created and re-created constantly in people's lives. Throughout this chapter and in subsequent chapters we illustrate how this approach to understanding culture works.

But this definition does raise an immediate question: if culture is a dynamic process, why doesn't it always feel that way to people? We deal with this question in the next section.

THINKING CRITICALLY ABOUT CULTURE

How can an understanding of the complexities of culture help us make sense of the day-to-day world in which we live? Give an example from your life to illustrate your answer.

If Culture Is Emergent and Dynamic, Why Does It Feel So Stable?

Imagine how chaotic life would be if you could not expect the same rules and processes for interacting with others from one week to the next. People need cultural stability. If we always had to stop and think about changes in the rules of social interaction, we could not function in our society. The very power of culture is that its processes feel totally natural and simultaneously predictable. Yet the previous section defined culture in a way that emphasizes its processes as dynamic and emergent. So how does something feel stable if it is so dynamic?

The concept of enculturation—the idea that people have been doing or believing things for much of their lives—only partly explains why culture feels so stable. There are a number of other features of culture—symbols, values, norms, and traditions—that help explain the sense of stability that people feel about it.

Symbols

One way of approaching the issue of cultural stability and change is by examining symbols. Leslie White, a prominent American anthropologist, once said, the symbol is "the origin and basis of human behavior" (1949). Human life, in all of its social and material dimensions, is symbolically constituted (Sahlins 1999:400). A symbol, as we have already said, is something that conventionally stands for something else. The relationship between the symbol and what it refers to is arbitrary, based on no particular rhyme or reason (Figure 2.4). Symbols can be more than just images or concepts, however; people also use their bodies as symbols. In Japan, for example, bowing is a form of greeting, but depending on how low one bows, it may also symbolize respect, apology, gratitude, sincerity, remorse, superiority, or humility.

A society will store its conventional meanings in symbols because their meanings tend to be stable. But symbols and their meanings can and do change, sometimes dramatically. For example, during the Spanish conquest of the Peruvian Andes during the sixteenth century, the Spaniards carried banners of their patron saint, Santiago Matamoros, to ensure victory over the Indians. The Indians quickly absorbed Santiago into their native religion. They identified Santiago as their own god of thunder and lightning, Illapa, who they believed changes forms. To the Indians, Santiago symbolized the power of their own mountain gods and encouraged resistance against the Spaniards (Silverblatt 1988).

Figure 2.4   Love, Affection . . . and Toilets. Symbols are arbitrary. In the United States and several other countries, the heart conventionally symbolizes love and affection. But the Swedish associate the heart symbol with defecation and toilets.

Values

Studying values also helps us to understand how change and stability are so closely related. **Values** are symbolic expressions of intrinsically desirable principles or qualities. They refer to that which is moral and true for a particular group of people. For example, "mom and apple pie" symbolize American core values (values that express the most basic qualities central to a culture), such as patriotism or loyalty to country. In the United States, "Mom" expresses the purity of selfless sacrifice for the greater good. "Apple pie," a common food since colonial times, expresses Americans' shared heritage. Of course, not everybody eats apple pie and not every mother is loyal to her family, much less sacrifices herself for the greater good. The point is not that these ideals reflect what actually happens in the real world. Rather, they orient thinking about one's obligations as a citizen, like putting aside differences with other Americans and being willing to sacrifice oneself for love of family and country.

Values are conservative in that they conserve prevailing ideas about social relations and morality. Yet, this does not mean that a community's values do not change. Nor does it mean that within a society or community people will not have opposing values. It is not even uncommon for people to hold conflicting values simultaneously.

- **Values.** Symbolic expressions of intrinsically desirable principles or qualities.

Norms

While values provide a general orientation for social relations, norms are more closely related to actual behavior. **Norms** are typical patterns of behavior, often viewed by participants as the rules of how things should be done. In our society, for example, it would be unimaginable to try to haggle over the price of toothpaste at the grocery store because everyone expects you to pay the listed price. But in many other societies, especially in the Arab world and in Indonesia, the norm is just the opposite: no matter how small the item, it is considered rude to *not* haggle. In such places, taking the first asking price disrespects the seller. For more expensive items, such as a digital camera, buyers and sellers may expect to haggle over the price for an hour. The norm is for the starting price to be three to five times the item's actual worth, and buyers may break off negotiations and leave the shop two or three times so the buyer can run after them, bringing them back into the shop with a lower price.

- **Norms.** Typical patterns of actual behavior as well as the rules about how things should be done.

Norms are stable because people learn them from an early age and because of the social pressure to conform. Norms also tend to be invisible (we're usually not conscious of them) until they are broken, as visitors to a different society or even city often find when they do things the "wrong" way. In Chicago, for example, pedestrians at a stoplight rarely pay much attention to a "Don't Walk" light; many people cross the street whenever they see a break in the traffic. But in Seattle, the social norm is different. People wait for the light to change to "Walk" before crossing the street, even in the rain and even when there is no traffic. When people from Seattle visit Chicago they are pushed and bumped by other pedestrians rushing to cross the street. When Chicagoans visit Seattle they tend to cross against the light while Seattleites wait patiently at the corner, scowling at the norm-breaking visitors. The scowl provides a **social sanction**, a reaction or measure intended to enforce norms and punish their violation. To avoid this public display of disapproval, Chicagoans in Seattle quickly learn to follow the norm. Long-established norms may eventually become **customs**, which have a codified and lawlike aspect.

- **Social sanction.** A reaction or measure intended to enforce norms and punish their violation.

- **Customs.** Long-established norms that have a codified and lawlike aspect.

- **Tradition.** Practices and customs that have become most ritualized and enduring.

Traditions

Tradition usually refers to the most enduring and ritualized aspects of a culture. People often feel their traditions are very old, which justifies actions that make no logical sense in contemporary times. With such justifications individuals and groups go to great lengths to protect their traditions. The controversy between Indians and NCAA schools over mascots with which we opened this chapter illustrates how powerful such traditions can be.

But anthropologists are careful not to assume that traditions are as old as people may say, because appearances can be deceiving (Hobsbawn and Ranger 1983). For example, Scottish people often celebrate their identity with bagpipes and kilts made from tartans, plaid textiles that comprise stripes of different widths and colors that identify the wearers' clans. But these traditions, while indeed venerable, are not actually ancient. As a matter of fact, these objects, and the sense of a distinctive tradition they symbolize, emerged only during the eighteenth and nineteenth centuries (Trevor-Roper 1983). An English iron industrialist designed the kilt as we know it for his workers in the late 1700s. As the kilt caught on in the Scottish highlands, textile manufacturers began producing distinctive plaids to expand sales and found willing buyers among clan chiefs. The chiefs wanted to distinguish themselves and their ancestry as unique, so they adopted particular designs. When England's King George IV made a state visit to Scotland in 1822, the organizers heavily promoted the use of kilts and tartans to enhance the pageantry of the visit. This occasion legitimized highlands culture and established the look as a national institution. The power of tartans comes not from their antiquity, but from their association with the clans that have long been central to Scottish highlander social life. Figure 2.5 shows another example drawn from Japanese culture of a similarly recent and flexible tradition.

Such examples demonstrate that what we take as timeless and authentic examples of tradition may be quite recent innovations. But knowing that a particular tradition may be a recent invention does not mean people are any less protective of it (just ask defenders of Indian mascots on college campuses; most mascots came about only during the early twentieth century).

Historically, anthropologists have emphasized that culture is "shared" among a group of people, implying a kind of uniformity and stability in culture. Clearly, people need a relatively stable and common base of information and knowledge in order to live together. But these different aspects of culture—symbols, values, norms, and traditions—are features that seem stable and common even though they may not

Figure 2.5 Another "Tradition" That Might Surprise You. Like the use of tartans in Scotland, Sumo wrestling in Japan feels ancient, although key features of it—such as the practice of awarding one person champion—are less than one hundred years old.

be shared by everybody in a society. There is another reason culture feels stable. It is that culture is expressed through social institutions, a theme we turn to next.

THINKING CRITICALLY ABOUT CULTURE

Most students think it is easy to identify the symbols, values, norms, and traditions that support other people's practices. But they find it more difficult to think about their own daily practices in the same terms. Use any of your own daily practices to illustrate how these four features of culture reinforce your own behavior.

How Is Culture Expressed Through Social Institutions?

The **social institutions** of any society are the organized sets of social relationships that link individuals to each other in a structured way in a particular society. These institutions include patterns of kinship and marriage (domestic arrangements, the organization of sex and reproduction, raising children, etc.), economic activities (farming, herding, manufacturing, and trade), religious institutions (rituals, religious organizations, etc.), and political forms for controlling power. Each culture has its norms, values, and traditions for how each of these activities should be organized, and in each case they can vary greatly from one society to another because each society has a different culture.

• **Social institutions.** Organized sets of social relationships that link individuals to each other in a structured way in a particular society.

Let us consider how mid-twentieth-century anthropologists approached culture's relationship to social institutions. Then we will consider how changes in these institutions can shape cultural patterns, which ultimately transform the social institutions themselves.

Culture and Social Institutions

From the 1920s to the 1960s, the dominant answer to this question about how culture was expressed in social institutions was that culture is like the glue that holds people together in ordered social relationships. Associated with British anthropologists Bronislaw Malinowski and A. R. Radcliffe-Brown, this theory, known as **functionalism**, holds that cultural practices and beliefs serve purposes for society, such as explaining how the world works, organizing people into roles so they can get things done, and so on. Functionalists emphasize that social institutions function together in an integrated and balanced fashion to keep the whole society functioning smoothly and to minimize social change.

As an illustration of functional analysis, think back to the case of the Ongee, the people who believe their ancestors make earthquakes and tidal waves. A functionalist would focus on how Ongee beliefs about their ancestors explain how the natural world works, and that these beliefs in turn help shape and are shaped by their migratory hunting-and-gathering existence. Working together with other structures of Ongee society, such as political organization, economics, kinship, and so on, these beliefs contribute to the maintenance of an ordered society.

For functionalists, cultures were closed, autonomous systems. But even at its height of popularity, critics insisted that functionalism's vision of culture was *too* stable. In fact, not all societies function smoothly, and functionalism's static view of culture could not explain history and social change. One of Britain's most prominent anthropologists, E. E. Evans-Pritchard, famously broke with functionalists in 1961 when he said that anthropology should not model itself on the natural sciences but on humanistic disciplines, especially history with its processual focus.

In spite of its shortcomings, functionalism has left important legacies, especially that of the **holistic perspective**, a perspective that aims to identify and understand the whole—that is, the systematic connections between individual cultural beliefs, practices, and social institutions—rather than the individual parts. This does not mean contemporary anthropologists still see a society as wholly integrated and balanced. Rather, the holistic perspective is a methodological tool that helps show the interrelationships among different domains of a society, domains that include environmental context, history, social and political organization, economics, values, and spiritual life. Thus, the life of a community becomes expressed through the social relationships among its members, organized as they are through their social institutions. To understand how changes in cultural values can lead to changes in social institutions, consider the relationship between diet, industrialization, and sexual deviance.

American Culture Expressed Through Breakfast Cereals and Sexuality

Let us begin by posing a simple question: Why do so many Americans prefer cereal for breakfast? Most of us today prefer cereal because it is part of a "healthy and nutritious diet" (the standard industry line) or because of its convenience. In any event,

- **Functionalism.** A perspective that assumes that cultural practices and beliefs serve social purposes in any society.

- **Holistic perspective.** A perspective that aims to identify and understand the whole—that is, the systematic connections between individual cultural beliefs and practices—rather than the individual parts.

eating cereal for breakfast has become a social norm for a majority of Americans. It builds on positive cultural values attributed to health and on the symbolism of "healthy food = a healthy body." But corn flakes began in the nineteenth century as a cure for sexual deviance, masturbation being the most worrisome.

Nineteenth-century religious leaders considered masturbation an abomination, and the emerging scientific disciplines of psychiatry and surgery claimed that masturbation caused shyness, hairy palms, jaundice, insanity, cancer, and murderous behaviors (Figure 2.6). From 1861 to 1932, the U.S. Patent Office issued some two dozen patents on antimasturbation devices to prevent boys from masturbating, among them a safety pin to close the foreskin of the penis, various kinds of male chastity belts, and an electric bell attached to the penis that would notify parents if their son got an erection during the night. As recently as 1918, a U.S. government brochure advised new parents to prevent their babies from masturbating by tying their hands and legs to the sides of their cribs. Circumcision became the most commonly performed surgery in the United States based on the view that it prevented masturbation.

John Harvey Kellogg (1852–1943), the inventor of corn flakes, was a physician from Battle Creek, Michigan. He was a nutritional enthusiast and a follower of the health food movement of vegetarian and dietary reformer Sylvester Graham (1797–1851), who had developed graham flour used in graham crackers. Kellogg became director of a Seventh-day Adventist sanitarium in Battle Creek, where he built on Graham's ideas, inventing corn flakes and various granolas as food for his patients (Figure 2.7). Both men were concerned with health and sexuality—they especially abhorred masturbation—which they attributed to animalistic passions that were enhanced by a rich, meaty, or spicy diet. Both believed that bland but healthy foods were the way to soothe these volatile and unhealthy sexual urges (Money 1985).

Of course, their solution to the perceived problems of sexual passion was based on the symbols of passion being fiery that could be quenched (symbolically) only with bland cereals. None of these efforts ever prevented masturbation, of course, and no one defends them for that purpose anymore. But these assumptions were enough to create corn flakes and graham crackers. The meanings we give to eating cereal and masturbation have changed as our lifestyles and diets have changed. In fact, an increasing number of medical professionals embrace masturbation as good for mental health.

During the nineteenth century, the American breakfast, like the rest of the diet, was a hearty meal of meat, eggs, fish, biscuits, gravy, jams, and butter. Although farmers worked off the calories in their fields, as America became more urban such rich meals became a sign of prosperity, just as the ideal body type was full-bodied for both men and women. But as American culture began to value healthy eating early in the twentieth century, industrial cereal makers, like C. W. Post and Kellogg's brother William, took advantage of this connection between cereals and good health to market their creations as nutritious foods. By the 1920s the American diet had shifted dramatically along with the ideal body type becoming much thinner. The result was an increased demand from consumers for convenient and tasty breakfast cereals, spawning a giant breakfast cereal industry associated with good taste and health rather than with preventing sexual deviance.

Figure 2.6   The Effects of Masturbation, Circa 1853. This image comes from a book called *The Silent Friend* about the "horrors of masturbation." At the time, common wisdom held that masturbation would lead to insanity.

Figure 2.7   Happiness Is Wellness in the Bowels. John Harvey Kellogg's Battle Creek Sanatarium, opened in 1876, served corn flakes, granolas, and yogurts to promote good bowel health. There was also an enema machine that could pump fifteen gallons of water through a person's bowel in seconds. It was a popular and fashionable vacation destination.

In answering our initial question, we see interrelationships between separate domains like beliefs (about sexual morality, good health), social institutions and power (expert knowledge, medical practices), and daily life (changes in labor organization and economic life, dietary preferences). This is the holistic perspective.

Second, it shows the integration of specific domains. For example, beliefs about sexual morality are intertwined with institutions of social authority, such as sanitariums and medical disciplines like psychiatry and surgery, and those institutions in turn regulate people's sexual relationships. Similarly, changes in people's economic relationships and work habits help shape and are shaped by their ideas about what is good to eat. At any historical moment, these domains feel stable because they are reflected in the other domains, even though some may be highly transitory and dynamic. The values, norms, and traditions in one domain are buttressed and supported by values, norms, and traditions in many other domains.

And herein lies the power of a cultural analysis: it shows how doing something that feels totally "natural" (pouring yourself a bowl of cereal in the morning) is really the product of intertwined "artificial" processes and meanings. In "Thinking Like an Anthropologist: Understanding Holism" we present a scenario to illustrate how simple innovations can lead to changes in social institutions.

Thinking Like an Anthropologist

Understanding Holism

ANTHROPOLOGISTS BEGIN THEIR research by asking questions. In this box, we want you to learn how to ask questions as an anthropological researcher. Part One describes a situation and follows up with questions we would ask. Part Two asks you to do the same thing with a different situation.

PART ONE: INTRODUCING CASH CROPS TO HIGHLAND NEW GUINEANS

When anthropologist Ben Finney (1973) studied coffee as a cash crop in the Eastern Highlands of Papua New Guinea, he observed that some younger men planted large fields in coffee and some had become coffee buyers. In the years since Finney's field research, many of these men became very successful coffee planters and buyers. Several acquired whole fleets of Isuzu and Toyota trucks, which they used to bring coffee beans to local warehouses and to coastal cities (Westermark 1998).

On the face of it, this program was dramatically successful in introducing a valuable cash crop to a region that had only known subsistence horticulture. But a holistic approach illustrates that coffee also brought important social consequences for Highland communities.

In the 1950s an Australian colonial ban on tribal warfare opened up large tracts of no-man's-land between formerly hostile groups. Colonial officers brought coffee seedlings for villagers to plant in this formerly useless land. Some highlanders planted coffee, others rejected the whole idea, saying "what good is coffee, you can't eat it and pigs can't eat it either," pigs being an especially important form of wealth in Highlanders' political and economic lives. Most of the village leaders and prominent elders continued planting sweet potatoes and tending pigs as they always had. The pigs ate surplus sweet potatoes and were used in feasts and ceremonial exchanges with friends and rivals in other villages. Men with extensive exchange networks became village leaders called "big men." Big men achieved prominence and influence over others from their own hard work, assisted by the hard work in the gardens of their wives and female relatives. Traditional subsistence farmers made fun of their coffee-planting neighbors.

But after seven years, the coffee trees began to bear fruit, and the officers showed the coffee planters how to pick, process, and sell the beans. The young coffee planters now had larger sums of cash than people had ever seen.

Coffee profits increased as more and more trees matured. Unexpectedly, younger men found themselves with money that they would have had to work for months or years on a coastal plantation to earn.

These young coffee growers used this money to achieve social status because they, unlike the old men, had access to all sorts of imported goods in the stores. In some cases, the prestige of these new big men was even greater than that of the older big men. Suddenly, everyone wanted to become a coffee planter, but after seven or eight years nearly all of the open land was already planted in coffee.

Elimination of tribal warfare and the introduction of coffee did not eliminate the big man political system or the cultural logic upon which it is based. But a holistic perspective shows that it did have important ramifications throughout the society.

What questions does this situation raise for anthropological researchers?

1. How did Highland's society change as a result of coffee?

2. What were the unexpected effects of introducing coffee on this small-scale egalitarian society?

3. Which effects were positive? For whom were they positive? Who experienced negative consequences from the introduction of coffee?

PART TWO: INTRODUCING SMARTPHONES TO AMERICAN COLLEGE STUDENTS

Consider the relatively recent rise in the use of smartphones by high school and college students. As little as ten or fifteen years ago, students were forced to use a land line if they wanted to talk to their friends, which usually meant that they were calling from home. Nowadays, growing numbers of students have their own smartphones, not just for making phone calls but for taking pictures, surfing the Internet, texting, and so on. Students use their smartphones in a variety of ways not possible on their parents' land lines. They have brought lifestyle changes for young people that might be considered unexpected effects when cell phones were initially introduced.

(continued)

Thinking Like an Anthropologist (continued)

Using a holistic approach, think about some of the changes that smartphone use and texting have introduced into the lives of high school and college students. What questions would you ask about this situation as an anthropological researcher? (Sample questions can be found at the end of this chapter.)

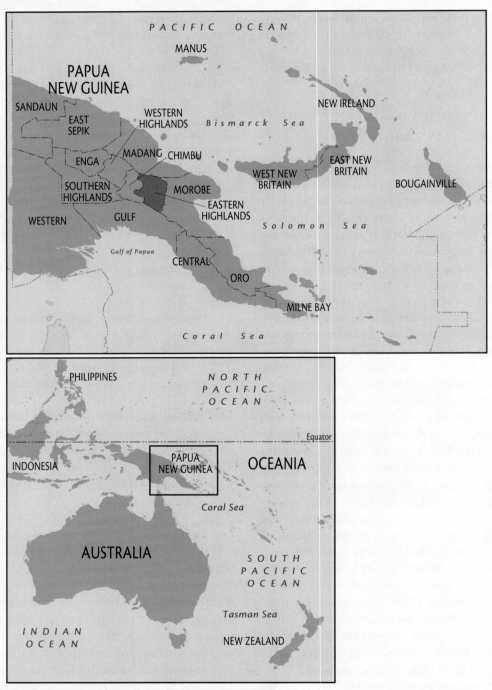

Eastern Highlands of Papua New Guinea.

Can Anybody Own Culture?

As we have defined culture, the question of owning culture may appear to make little sense. How can somebody own the collective processes that make the artificial seem natural? For the most part, owning culture is about power relations between people who control resources and (typically) minority communities who have been kept out-side the mainstream. At one level, nobody can own culture, but many will claim the exclusive right to the symbols that give it power and meaning.

The debate over sports teams' Indian mascots is only one example of a conflict over who has the right to use, control, even "own," symbols, objects, and cultural processes. This conflict is related to the phenomenon of **cultural appropriation**, the unilateral decision of one social group to take control over the symbols, practices, or objects of another. Cultural appropriation is as old as humanity itself. The fact that people adopt ideas, practices, and technologies from other societies demonstrates the fluidity of social boundaries and partly explains why societies and cultures are changing all the time.

Yet cultural appropriation also often involves relationships of domination and subor-dination between social groups. For American Indians, for example, the pressure to assimilate into dominant white Euro-American society has coincided with the domi-nant society's appropriation of Indian cultural symbols. That appropriation goes beyond the use of Indian images as sports mascots and includes, among others, kids "playing Indian," New Age religion's imitation of Indian spirituality and rituals, Hollywood's endless fascination with making movies about Indians, even the use of the Zia Pueblo sun symbol on the New Mexico state flag (Strong 1996; Brown 2003). While some Indians do not mind, others find these uses of Indian symbolism degrading and simplis-tic, because they ignore the realities of Indian communities and traditions, or because nobody asked permission to use the culturally meaningful objects and symbols.

Some of these conflicts have taken shape as dramatic protests, as in the 2002 case of Australian Aboriginal activists who removed the coat of arms at the Old Parliament House in Canberra. They declared that images of the kangaroo and emu (a large flightless Australian bird resembling an ostrich) on the national seal are the cultural property of Aboriginal people (Brown 2003). Other conflicts have happened in courts, such as the highly publicized law suit Zia Pueblo brought against the state of New Mexico in 1994, formally demanding reparations for the use of the Zia sun symbol in the state flag (Figure 2.8).

Anthropologists have not escaped indigenous scrutiny and criticism for claiming expertise about native cultures. Anthropologist Kay Warren (1998), for example, studied the rise of the Pan-Maya ethnic movement in Guatemala. When she gave an

● **Cultural appropriation.** The unilateral decision of one social group to take control over the symbols, practices, or objects of another.

Anthropologist as Problem Solver

Michael Ames and Collaborative Museum Exhibits

FOR SEVERAL DECADES indigenous activists in the United States and Canada have criticized museums for mishandling sacred indigenous artifacts and displaying objects without the permission of tribal leaders. Until the 1990s most museums paid little attention to these concerns. They rarely sought indigenous input into museum exhibits, and when they did, it was usually long after planning for an exhibit was complete.

In the United States, the passage of the Native Americans Graves Protection and Repatriation Act (NAGPRA) in 1990 changed the playing field substantially. The law provides a framework for the return of human remains, burial goods, and religious objects to tribes that can demonstrate a direct connection (Brown 2003). At first, museum professionals worried that their collections would be cleaned out by Indian claims. But for the most part museums and Indian tribes have made concerted efforts to find effective solutions to these problems. Anthropologists have played key roles as mediators and advocates—for both museums and Indians—in many of these situations.

One pioneer in creating a partnership between native communities and museums in Canada was Michael M. Ames (1933–2006), who was director of the Museum of Anthropology (MOA) at the University of British Columbia from 1974 until 1997. Ames made several changes in the relationships between museums and their publics, including museum visitors and native peoples. While he was director of the MOA, he put all of the museum's ethnographic collections on display in visible storage so that the ordinary visitor could see everything in the collection. This was a striking shift for a museum, but nothing compared to his efforts in the 1990s to establish a new relationship between the MOA and the local First Nations—as Indian communities are referred to in Canada. He pioneered collaborative exhibitions in the museum.

Two proposed exhibitions dealt with archaeological material excavated on the lands of First Nations communities. Early in the planning process, Ames contacted tribal leaders from the communities, who agreed to participate and wanted to participate fully in managing the exhibitions and interpreting the objects displayed. The tribal leaders insisted on meaningful consultation at every stage of the process, including selection of objects, the final design of the exhibition, interpretation of each object, installation, promotion, and exhibit maintenance.

🌱 **Michael Ames and Margaret Mead.**

Tribal leaders became so involved in developing these exhibits that some museum staff feared that MOA was giving up its scholarly role altogether. After extensive negotiations with tribal leaders facilitated by Ames, First Nations communities acknowledged that museum professionals were experts in research, interpretation, and exhibition design. But they asked that this expertise be used toward the Indians' educational goals (1999:46). For example, even though the objects displayed were prehistoric and archaeological, they had contemporary relevance for the native groups involved. Ames (1999:48) suggests that these archaeological pieces "have a powerful resonance for the living descendants and thus in a very real sense are contemporary as well as prehistoric" objects, especially since these prehistoric objects and sites are part of their historical record and thus part of their assertion of continuing sovereignty over their territories. These objects have current meaning in much the same way that documents and historic sites from the American Revolution have ongoing meaning for Americans.

Ames's efforts to have real participation by native groups in the museum's exhibitions have changed the museum's relationships with native communities throughout British Columbia. These communities feel that every object in the museum from their area is part of their own cultural patrimony. Museums may hold them, but they do so in trust for the native communities, who made, used, and continue to value these objects. Ames's work helped build bridges where previously there had been little more than suspicion toward anthropologists and museum professionals.

Questions for Reflection

1. From the perspective of museum curators, what might be lost if they make indigenous peoples partners in an exhibition?

2. What are the possible benefits to the museum of accepting indigenous input?

3. Even though museums may purchase cultural artifacts from members of indigenous communities, who really owns these objects?

Figure 2.8   The Cause of Indigenous Rights. Indigenous groups forced the United Nations to establish the Permanent Forum on Indigenous Issues in 2000. The Forum's goal is to address the human, cultural, and territorial rights of indigenous peoples around the world.

academic presentation on Maya political activism, Maya intellectuals and political leaders in attendance responded by challenging the right of foreign anthropologists even to study Maya culture. As Warren points out, indigenous movements like Pan-Mayanism reject the idea that anthropological knowledge is neutral or objective. They insist that doing anthropology raises important political and ethical questions: Who should benefit from anthropological research? Why do the people studied by anthropologists not get an opportunity to help define and evaluate research projects?

Responding to such questions, a number of anthropologists like Warren have modified how they do cultural research, including inviting the subjects of their research to be collaborators in all stages of the research, from the definition of the study all the way through to publication. In "Anthropologist as Problem Solver: Michael Ames and Collaborative Museum Exhibits" we explore how one anthropologist collaborated with indigenous people in the creation of museum exhibitions.

THINKING CRITICALLY ABOUT CULTURE

Discuss whether people from one culture could "own" a dance—like the samba from Brazil—that originated with people from another ethnic group. Could anyone own a style of pop music?

Conclusion

At the heart of all anthropological discussions of culture is the idea that culture helps people understand and respond to a constantly changing world. As we have defined it, culture consists of the collective processes that make the artificial seem natural. Based on symbols and expressed through values, norms, and traditions, culture offers a relatively stable and common base of information and knowledge so that people can live together in groups. A holistic perspective on culture illustrates how different domains of a society interrelate. But culture is also dynamic, responding to innovation, creativity, and struggles over meaning.

In spite of the many difficulties involved in studying culture, it is more important than ever to understand culture, what it is, and how cultural processes work. The big and urgent matters of our time have cultural causes and consequences. These matters range from the problems posed by development and change for indigenous groups and heated conflicts about social identity over mascots and traditions on college campuses, to others like terrorism, environmental degradation and sustainability, ethnic diversity and racial conflict, religious intolerance, globalization, and health care. As you read this book, you will learn how anthropologists use cultural perspectives to understand, explain, and even contribute to resolving problems related to these matters.

KEY TERMS

Cross-cultural perspective   p. 37

Cultural appropriation   p. 49

Cultural construction   p. 37

Cultural determinism   p. 38

Customs   p. 42

Enculturation   p. 34

Functionalism   p. 44

Holistic perspective   p. 44

Interpretive theory of culture   p. 35

Norms   p. 41

Social institutions   p. 43

Social sanction   p. 42

Symbol   p. 35

Tradition   p. 42

Values   p. 41

Reviewing the Chapter

Chapter Section	What We Know	To Be Resolved
What is culture?	Culture is a central component of what it means to be human. Culture involves the processes through which people comprehend, shape, and act in the world around them.	Although most definitions of culture emphasize common themes, anthropologists have never agreed on a single definition of culture.
If culture is emergent and dynamic, why does it feel so stable?	Cultural processes are emergent, fluid, and marked by creativity, uncertainty, differing individual meaning, and social conflict. Yet culture is also remarkably stable.	Anthropologists continue to debate which is more important—dynamism or stability—in explaining how culture works in people's lives.
How is culture expressed through social institutions?	A holistic perspective enables anthropologists to understand how different social institutions and domains of a society are interrelated.	Anthropologists continue to debate how and why social institutions in any society change.
Can anybody own culture?	The phenomenon of cultural appropriation illustrates the tensions between cultural change and stability, and raises important ethical and political questions about anthropological knowledge itself.	Anthropologists continue to debate over which research and collaborative strategies are most effective to respond to the ethical and political issues raised by the creation of anthropological knowledge about culture.

Readings

For an overview of different theories of culture in anthropology and how and why they differ across schools of thought within the discipline, see Adam Kuper's *Culture: The Anthropologists' Account* (Harvard University Press, 2000). In this book Kuper actually expresses deep skepticism about the centrality of the culture concept to anthropology, and illustrates why anthropologists continue to debate what culture means.

For an intellectual history of the development of the culture concept in anthropology and its place in the discipline during the early twentieth century, the essays in George Stocking's book *Race, Culture, and Evolution: Essays in the History of Anthropology* (University of Chicago Press, 1968) are classics and remain relevant today.

The book *Who Owns Culture?* by anthropologist Michael Brown (Harvard University Press, 2003) is a highly readable account of the vexing legal, ethical, and methodological issues involved in who owns native cultural symbols and heritage.

SUGGESTED ANSWERS TO "THINKING LIKE AN ANTHROPOLOGIST"

Use these examples as a guide to answering questions for other "Thinking Like an Anthropologist" boxes in the book.

1. How has cultural life on campus changed because of smartphones?
2. Are there unexpected effects of introducing smartphones into college life?
3. How has the proliferation of smartphones changed college students' patterns of communication with their parents and friends?
4. Are people more connected socially than they were before?
5. Are there ways that people are less connected socially?
6. Does smartphone use have any impact on the ways university classrooms operate?

Beyond Nature and Nurture

The Individual, Biology, and Culture

IN 2001, THE U.S. Equal Employment Opportunity Commission filed a court action against the Burlington Northern Santa Fe Railroad, alleging that the company had violated the Americans with Disabilities Act. The commission claimed that the company had secretly run genetic tests on the blood of 36 employees who suffered from carpal tunnel syndrome, a painful wrist condition usually brought on by repetitive motion. The blood was drawn during a comprehensive medical exam required of any worker claiming disability from carpal tunnel syndrome. The company's apparent goal was to identify workers who might be genetically predisposed to the development of carpal tunnel syndrome so they could deny those people worker's compensation benefits for the injuries. The company settled the case, paid a fine, and stopped the testing, denying any wrongdoing.

Medical experts questioned the legitimacy of the test being used and pointed out that the disease is associated much more closely with conditions in the workplace environment than with genetics (Hawkins 2001). It caused many commentators to worry openly about a future in which employers and insurance companies would provide coverage for only the "genetically fit." It also raised questions about how individuals might guard the privacy of data about their genetic constitution.

This case underscores a kind of blind faith that the general public has developed in relation to the genetic screening itself. We often believe that our biological hardwiring—the innate components of our

Working on the Railroad. Given that labor conditions in railways are dangerous and physically demanding, it is difficult if not impossible to reduce worker injuries to genetic predisposition.

makeup such as genes, hormones, neurons, and the like—defines human nature, that is, the fundamental dispositions of who people are as individuals, the maladies they suffer, and even their intelligence. News outlets confirm these beliefs nearly every day, with proclamations that scientists have discovered a new gene or hormone that explains disease, mental illness, gender characteristics, sexual preference, racial type, personality, or emotional states. The high profile of genetic studies naturally leads people to believe that "biology is destiny." But the reality is more complex than that.

In the era of the Human Genome Project—the multibillion dollar scientific research venture begun in 1990 to identify and map the human genetic makeup—"nature" (biology) appears to be winning out over "nurture" (environmental and cultural influences) as the key to understanding ourselves. But anthropologists, as well as many biologists and other scientists, are deeply skeptical of grandiose claims about biological destiny. These scholars recognize that this sort of "it's-all-in-your-genes-and-hormones" thinking is a cultural idiom our society uses to understand human nature, just as other societies use other idioms and metaphors to understand their own individual and collective selves. This is not to deny that biology plays a role in who we are as individuals, but our biology works together with our culture to make us who we are and to determine what we can accomplish and which diseases we will experience.

Nature and nurture (a common shorthand term that refers to biological and cultural or environmental influences) are not opposed and mutually exclusive, but rather intertwined and emergent, processes. That is, our genes work together with our culture and environment to shape our lives as individuals. A full appreciation of the human condition requires that we avoid thinking of ourselves as *either* cultural *or* biological (natural) beings, but through a new and emerging paradigm that emphasizes humans as **biocultural** beings in which biological, psychological, and cultural processes interact in complex ways.

At the heart of the debate over whether biology or culture controls our behavior as individuals is the question around which this chapter is organized: *How should we make sense of the biological and cultural factors that together shape human nature?*

Embedded in this broader question are the following problems, around which the chapter is organized:

- **Nature and nurture.** A kind of shorthand for biological (nature) and cultural or environmental (nurture) influences.

- **Biocultural.** The complex intersections of biological, psychological, and cultural processes.

What can the biology of brain development teach us about culture?

How do anthropologists understand other people's psychologies?

What role does evolution play in human lives?

Is biotechnology changing our bodies?

The claim that humans are biologically hardwired ignores crucial biocultural variations in how we experience our bodies as individuals. We can appreciate this point by exploring two major issues covered in this chapter: the dynamics of human cognition and psychology, and the role of evolution in human lives. Together these themes demonstrate the complex ways that culture interacts with human biological processes to create many possible human natures, not just one human nature.

What Can the Biology of Brain Development Teach Us About Culture?

The idea of human nature as something fixed in our biology has been central to Western European and American ideas about humanity for more than a century. This view, which is still deeply entrenched in American culture, holds that the physiological make-up of our brain governs, if not fully determines, how we will respond to various physiological and emotional stimuli and the lengths we will go to satisfy them. From this perspective, it is just "our nature," "who we are." The norms of our society and culture may temper these reactions to some extent, but it seems hard to fight human nature. Most people would assume that this biological hardwiring is in our brains and is what directs our thoughts and responses to the world.

But over the past several decades a revolution in the cognitive sciences—the study of the processes of thought (or cognition)—has taught us many lessons about human brain development, thinking, and evolution. One of the most powerful findings is that culture plays a key role in growth and development of neurons in the brain that allows for cognition. Neurons are the brain cells that transmit information through chemical and electrical signals. Cultural influence on neuron growth has striking implications for understanding the human mind. The human brain does not exist in some idealized natural state; it is continually influenced by cognition and bioculturally variable phenomena that depend on the cultures in which we grow up and live. Our mind is therefore the logical place to begin to mend the perceived gap between culture and biology (Hruschka, Lende, and Worthman 2005).

The Adaptable Human Brain

Understanding the adaptability of the human brain can begin by comparing it to the brains of non-human primates. Most non-human primates are born with their brains largely developed. At birth, the brain of a macaque (a type of monkey), for example, is 60% of its adult size. That of a chimpanzee, our nearest primate relative, at birth is 45%. After birth, the rate of neural development in both species slows considerably (Shore 1996) (Figure 3.1). But when humans are born, our brains are only 25% of their eventual weight, meaning that a full 75% of human brain development occurs after birth. During the first two years of life, human brain construction does not slow down, as among other primates, but continues at the same rate it did in the womb. As our neural pathways develop they allow for more complex thoughts and are tied to the development of cultural behavior. Our brains do not mature until puberty, although they are still

Figure 3.1   Infant Macaque and Chimpanzee.

developing significantly into our early twenties and beyond into old age, giving humans a degree of mental flexibility and dexterity unparalleled anywhere else in the animal kingdom.

The most crucial processes of human brain construction take place during the first five years after birth, a period that coincides with the most intensive processes of enculturation in an individual's life. Our brains develop and grow in the context of a particular culture and within a set of social relationships. As we learn language, how to behave in certain settings, how to hunt or plant crops, or how to read or play computer games, humans are enculturated to think and act in the conventional ways of their society. Our brains build neural pathways that reflect these lessons. It therefore makes sense to refer to the human brain as a "cultured" brain.

Far from being fixed at birth by genetic and neural factors, our brains are functionally pliable and adaptable organs that operate as generalized learning and problem-solving devices (Gibson 2005). The evolution of our species appears to have favored brains that are flexible, responsive to a much wider range of environments and novel situations than any other primate (Gibson 2005). Even before the emergence of anatomically modern humans (*Homo sapiens*), our ancestors demonstrated behavioral versatility and problem-solving abilities and were able to adapt to a wide variety of specific and changing natural environments. We know this because *Homo erectus* (an ancestral species of *Homo sapiens*) was able to expand its range from Eastern and Southern Africa to most of Europe and Asia nearly two million years ago.

- **Neural plasticity.** The moldability and flexibility of brain structure.

Evidence of what cognitive scientists call **neural plasticity**, or the moldability and flexibility of brain structure, is illustrated by the fact that people born without hands can develop the ability to feed themselves or use simple tools with their feet, and that blind people can develop acute hearing and heightened tactile senses. Our brains also help us acquire skills that are culturally defined and not part of our species' evolutionary heritage, such as reading, writing, and playing computer games.

Neural plasticity is also evident in the role that culture plays in shaping some basic aspects of perception. For example, people growing up in societies with little two-dimensional art must learn how to understand photographs after first seeing them (Shore 1996). Cultural differences in perception suggest that mental development varies with cultural practices (Figure 3.2).

The Mind and Culture

- **Mind.** Emergent qualities of consciousness and intellect that manifest themselves through thought, emotion, perception, will, and imagination.

The human **mind** is the emergent qualities of consciousness and intellect that manifest themselves through thought, emotion, perception, will, and imagination. More than just an information processor, the mind also constructs cognitive models—an identifiable set of patterns—to make sense of the world around us. Such models are a kind of operator's manual for the mind, providing a pattern for one's own behavior or for interpreting other people's actions. These models help us make meaning out of raw information by filling in the gaps in our direct knowledge. Anthropologists have long recognized the importance of these cognitive models, referring to them as **cultural models**, because they are external, or public, and shared by a social group (D'Andrade 1990:809). Anthropologists also recognize *personal* models, or an individual's idiosyncratic way of making sense of things.

- **Cultural model.** Implicit and typically non-conscious cognitive models shared by a group of people of what is real or natural.

To understand the difference between cultural and personal cognitive models, imagine, for example, that you are at a baseball game. You stand and take off your hat to sing the national anthem. If you are watching the game at home, you do neither (Shore 1996). These are cultural models, public and conventional in the sense that we all know how to act in these different situations. When invested with great social importance, cultural models can become social institutions. Forms of greeting, calendars,

Figure 3.2   A Rabbit, a Duck, or Both? When he presented this image to them in the 1950s, anthropologist Edward Carpenter was amazed to learn that Inuit (Eskimo) people do not see only one image at a time, but can identify both simultaneously.

games, chants, conventional body postures, rituals—to name just a few—are examples of social institutions that began as cultural models.

A personal model is quite different. Consider, for example, how you personally think about your city, which probably has little to do with your city's actual layout. While some of you might think of it in terms of business districts and residential neighborhoods, others might think of it in terms of important landmarks, and still others might think of places where they had significant experiences. More likely, your personal model of the city is a combination of these mental representations and is unique to you.

Uniting Mind and Matter: A Biocultural Perspective

Increasing biocultural evidence also suggests that cognition does not happen separately from our bodies. The human nervous system is a complex neurological network that reads and regulates chemical and biological conditions throughout the entire body, not just our thinking brains. Human biology sets certain broad outer limits that all humans share, but the actual character of cognitive processes differs from one individual to the next and across cultures because of the influence of external factors.

These external factors include social context and culture, with which the nervous system interacts through individual cognition. For example, the mental stresses people experience because of rapid social and political-economic change, or contradictions between cultural and personal models, have well-documented physical and bodily consequences, including raising blood pressure, affecting immunity to disease, and creating symptoms of fatigue or feelings of inadequacy (Dressler 2005). These mental stresses may accompany other biological impacts, including changes in diet, nutrition, and general health (Daltabuit and Leatherman 1998). The mind manifests itself through the whole person, throughout an individual's lifetime (Toren 1996). Taking this biocultural approach to the mind and cognition seriously requires us to rethink our basic assumptions about what an individual person is and how we might understand the psychology of people in other cultures.

THINKING CRITICALLY ABOUT BIOLOGY AND CULTURE

The notion that humans are simultaneously biological and cultural beings is what we mean when we say humans are biocultural. Think of an example of typical behavior from your ordinary life that suggests that neither a purely biological or a purely cultural perspective is enough to understand why we behave as we do.

How Do Anthropologists Understand Other People's Psychologies?

The biocultural perspective has only recently begun to take root in the field of cultural anthropology. But it also builds on a rich history of research regarding how cultural and social contexts shape the psychologies, emotions, and personalities of individuals. In this section, we consider a variety of theories suggested by anthropologists to explain culturally distinct notions of individual psychology. To begin, it is helpful to consider how anthropologists have thought about the individual person.

What Is an Individual Person?

This question might seem strange, partly because the answer seems so simple and straightforward. We tend to think individual persons are like onions: peel back the layers from the surface and underneath humans are all organisms of a certain anatomy, physiology, and cognition. Moving outward from that essential (biological) core, we see other layers, with social and cultural influences usually nearest the surface. But anthropologists have long resisted such a simple perspective, because it downplays how central culture is to shaping what a person is.

For much of the discipline's history cultural anthropologists have been keenly interested in the individual person, even though the discipline's primary interest lies in the collective and social aspects of human life. Important work on the individual has taken place in the subfield of **psychological anthropology**, which studies the psychological states and conditions of individuals (G. White and Lutz 1992:1). It closely parallels and often intersects with cognitive anthropology. It seeks to reconcile psychology's focus on the individual with anthropology's focus on culture and society (Toren 1996).

• **Psychological anthropology.** The subfield of anthropology that studies psychological states and conditions.

The Culture and Personality School

Psychological anthropology grew out of mid-twentieth century "culture and personality" studies by anthropologists. The **culture and personality school** focused on how patterns of child-rearing, social institutions, and cultural ideologies shaped individual experience, personality characteristics, and thought patterns (Hsu 1972). The assumption was that how children are bathed, fed, and attended to while infants and toddlers shapes their approach to the world. Most culture and personality studies tried to show that our individual (or collective) psychologies were primarily shaped by environment (nurture) rather than by our biology (nature).

An important culture and personality scholar was Ruth Benedict, a student of Franz Boas and a teacher and close friend of Margaret Mead, an American anthropologist who gained popular fame in the twentieth century for her writings on culture. Benedict's classic book *Patterns of Culture* (1934) is a major work in American anthropology and is popular in its own right, read by millions of undergraduates and selling nearly two million copies (and translated into two dozen languages). Benedict argued that particular cultures produce more or less consistent patterns of thought and action in individuals. For example, she argued that the Zuñi of the southwestern Pueblos are moderate in temperament and prefer not to stand out in a crowd, closely following their cultural norms. In contrast she observed that Kwakiutl culture, a Native American culture of the Northwest Coast, exhibits a patterned "will to superiority" that expresses itself in the aggressive and competitive personality characteristics of individual Kwakiutl. The box "Classic Contributions: Ruth Benedict, the Individual, and Culture" elaborates on Benedict's contributions to thinking about the relationship between the individual and culture.

Culture and personality studies represented an effort to reconcile the divide between the individual and culture, but they had several important weaknesses. For example, they assumed that a society has only one personality type and that childhood enculturation determines adult personality; we now know that neither is true. They also minimized how much our Western cultural constructions about individual persons can shape, and even get in the way of, our understanding of other cultures that have different concepts of individual persons.

The Individual: Persons and Selves

During the twentieth century, European and American anthropologists who were not part of the culture and personality school were also interested in the individual. Rather than dwelling on personality types and subjective personal experience, they focused on the individual as a social category and what it revealed about how a society works. French sociologists Emile Durkheim (1858–1917) and Marcel Mauss (1872–1950) focused on the **person**, the socially recognized individual, as a universal social category—that is, one found among all peoples—whose characteristics would vary depending on a society's customs and beliefs. For example, they observed that "modern" (European and American) societies value each unique individual, and define the person as a bounded and sacred being with an inner self and consciousness (Carrithers 1996). In contrast, they claimed that so-called pre-modern societies primarily value social solidarity, emphasizing the fulfillment of family roles as a basic condition of personhood. While the former was understood as an "egocentric" view of personhood, the latter emphasized a "sociocentric" view of the person.

In fact, anthropologists have observed great variation across cultures in terms of how they define full personhood. For example, in parts of Melanesia, individuals are

- **Culture and personality school.** A school of thought in early and mid-twentieth-century American anthropology that studied how patterns of child-rearing, social institutions, and cultural ideologies shaped individual experience, personality characteristics, and thought patterns.

- **Person.** The socially recognized individual.

Classic Contributions

Ruth Benedict, the Individual, and Culture

RUTH BENEDICT (1887–1948) was an American anthropologist of the mid-twentieth century who was a strong advocate for culture and personality studies. Like her mentor Franz Boas, under whom she studied at Columbia University, she argued for the power of culture over biology in explaining how and why individuals develop their personalities. This point was Benedict's argument in her book *Patterns of Culture*, which compared the personalities of people in three indigenous societies. Here she promoted the idea that different cultures encourage individuals to develop distinct personality types and other psychological characteristics. In this excerpt from *Patterns of Culture*, Benedict offers her perspective on the relationship between the individual and culture.

Ruth Benedict.

The vast proportion of all individuals who are born into any society always and whatever the idiosyncrasies of its institutions, assume, as we have seen, the behaviour dictated by [that] society. This fact is always interpreted by the carriers of that culture as being due to the fact that their particular institutions reflect an ultimate and universal sanity. The actual reason is quite different. Most people are shaped by the form of their culture because of the enormous malleability of their original endowment. They are plastic to the moulding force of the society into which they are born. It does not matter whether, with the Northwest Coast, it requires delusions of self-reference, or with our own civilization the amassing of possessions. In any case the great mass of individuals take quite readily the form that is presented to them. (Benedict 1934:254–255)

Questions for Reflection

1   Do you think our culture dictates your individual personality? Why and how, or why not?

2.   Can you think of institutions in our society that, as Benedict suggests, encourage some kinds of expressions while inhibiting others?

not born as persons, but gain full personhood only after they begin exchanging objects with others. In many Zapotec Indian villages in the southern Mexican state of Oaxaca, individuals do not gain full rights that any person enjoys, such as owning land, using resources, or even residing in a community until they marry, assume normal adult social roles, and fulfill communal duties in local fiestas and governance.

There is also great variation in the specific attributes different cultures recognize in personhood. The Dinka of South Sudan, for example, think of the conscience—an obligation to fulfill personal responsibilities—not as a property that lies deep inside the individual psyche (as we do), but as an external spirit named *Mathiang Gok* that seizes an individual and forces him or her to own up to his or her responsibilities (Lienhardt 1961).

Contemporary psychological anthropologists take the cultural variability of concepts of personhood for granted. But they have also added a new element, viewing persons as "cultural bases for formulating and exploring subjective experience," a theme that did not directly interest the Durkheimians (Kirkpatrick and White 1985:9). To differentiate this interest, psychological anthropologists use the term **self** to refer to an individual's conception of his or her fundamental qualities and consciousness.

Although not all anthropologists have seen the distinction between persons and selves as fully satisfactory, these revelations about cultural variation in concepts of person and selfhood do raise questions about the universality of our own American notions of individual psychology. It has led to an anthropology of different psychologies around the world, which we sometimes refer to as ethnopsychology.

- **Self.** An individual's conception of his or her fundamental qualities and consciousness.

Ethnopsychology

One of the key lessons of psychological anthropology has been that our own assumptions about what a person is as well as our own psychological terms and concepts might differ greatly from—and could even get in the way of understanding—indigenous psychological concepts. In researching these themes, the challenge is to translate foreign concepts so they are intelligible to us while preserving as much of their original meaning as we can. This problem is not simply one of linguistic translation, but of rendering whole modes of thought and feeling intelligible (G. White 1992). This is the domain of **ethnopsychology**, or how other societies make sense of persons, selves, and emotions. The ethnopsychological approach, which accepts the validity of indigenous psychological categories and understanding, is also at the heart of so-called cultural psychology, an emerging field that straddles the disciplines of anthropology and psychology (Shweder 2003).

- **Ethnopsychology.** The study of culturally specific ideas of personhood, self, emotion, and other psychological states.

Emotions—the affects and feelings we experience as humans—represent one of those areas in which the concepts we take for granted may not have an exact equivalent in another culture (Lindholm 2005). For example, anthropologist Michelle Rosaldo (1984), who was the spouse of Renato Rosaldo, whose work on emotions we mentioned in Chapter 1, studied the emotional lives of the Ilongot of the Phillipines, who have a history of headhunting. The motivation for headhunting, she describes, comes from *liget,* a concept that overlaps with but is distinct from our concept of "anger." Western understandings of anger assume that underlying anger causes hostility. But Rosaldo cautions that Ilongot do not recognize that anger, or *liget,* underlies hostility and violence, much less headhunting (Figure 3.3). According to Ilongot, "passion" and a "heavy heart," not anger, motivate headhunting. They also do not recognize anger as the cause of other social tensions and conflicts. So do they really understand anger as we do? Rosaldo (1984:144) concluded that they do not, writing "in important ways their feelings and the ways their feelings work must differ from our own." Such studies suggest that not only do different cultures lead people to understand themselves differently from us, but when they experience emotional disturbances and even mental illnesses they behave and react differently as well.

Culture and Mental Illness

Accepting the existence of cross-cultural differences in how people think about even the most basic psychological and emotional processes and conditions has an important consequence: We have to approach mental illness in a culturally relative way.

Psychological abnormality is always defined culturally because what is considered abnormal is based on socially accepted norms. Not all societies define the same

Figure 3.3   Displaying *Liget* in a Ritual Duel Among the Ilongot.

- **Culture-bound syndrome.** A mental illness unique to a culture.

conditions as psychologically abnormal, nor do they necessarily share the same mental illnesses. A well-known example of a so-called **culture-bound syndrome** (a mental illness unique to a culture) is *koro,* the condition unique to Chinese and Southeast Asian cultures in which an individual believes his external genitalia—or, in a female, nipples—are shrinking and even disappearing. What counts as a mental illness can also change in a society. Homosexuality is one such example. Although today few people view it as an illness, until 1974 American psychiatrists classified homosexuality as a mental disorder, and the U.S. Immigration and Naturalization Service used the classification of homosexuality as "abnormal" as a reason for excluding immigrants until 1990.

The ability to define any condition or behavior as a psychiatric disturbance reflects great social power, and can have serious consequences for the course of an individual's life and for his or her experience of self. As we see in "Anthropologist as Problem-Solver: Kim Hopper, Homelessness, and the Mentally Ill in New York City," anthropologists have paid close attention to the relationship between psychiatry and social power.

Because different societies define mental illnesses differently based on specific understandings of individual psychology, their treatments can differ too. For example, on the Indonesian island of Bali, persons are not conceived of as isolated or indivisible, as we conceive of them in the West. Spirits and deceased ancestors commonly reside in individuals. Madness (*buduh*) can be caused by inherited factors, congenital influences, an ancestral or divine curse, or the blessings of gods (Connor 1982). The task of the village-level healer, called the *balian,* is to identify the specific causes of madness, which are usually related to some kind of social disruption or family conflict. The *balian* then resolves the conflict or disharmony in the family or neighborhood (Connor 1982) (Figure 3.4). Western psychiatry's approach, which often involves isolating the individual through institutionalization or providing pharmaceuticals, would clearly be inappropriate, if not socially disruptive, in these circumstances.

Anthropologist as Problem Solver

Kim Hopper, Homelessness, and the Mentally Ill in New York City

HOMELESSNESS DID NOT become a recognized social problem in the United States until the late 1970s. Before then, of course, there were people who had nowhere to live, but homelessness was commonly understood as an extension of their poverty, the result of alcoholism, or lifestyle choices (Beriss 2005). Few researchers tried to understand how and why some people were homeless, or what Americans thought about people without homes. One exception was anthropologist Kim Hopper of the City University of New York.

Since the 1970s, Hopper has lived among, studied, and worked as an advocate for homeless people in New York City. He has spent most of his professional life outside academia, working in non-profit agencies, advocacy organizations, and government (Hopper 2002). He helped draft legislation and legal briefs, submitted affidavits, served as a court-appointed monitor, testified as an expert witness, and served as a board member of the National Coalition for the Homeless.

According to Hopper, anthropology's strength in this arena is its ability to focus attention on the cultural concepts that shape our thinking about homelessness, the social and policy conditions that prevent adequate solutions, and the social control that service institutions exert on homeless people.

One area where these concerns come together is in the connection between homelessness and mental health. In the 1970s, the closing of mental hospitals, asylums, and psychiatric clinics led to an explosion of homelessness in large cities, leading many people to believe that most homeless people are mentally ill. Social service institutions were built on the assumption that people become homeless because of psychiatric problems. Their model suggests that the best way to approach homeless people is to treat them as mental patients.

Hopper has been highly critical of this model. Not only is there little evidence to prove its assumptions, there is no way of knowing if a perceived disorder is a *cause* or a *consequence* of homelessness. In other words, are the homeless people's patterns of behavior 'symptoms' of mental illness or caused by, if not adaptations to, the homeless way of life (Hopper 1988:158)? According to Hopper, homelessness typically has its roots in larger developments, like housing crises, increases in unemployment, changes in household composition, and the reduction of government assistance programs. Defining all homeless people as deviant mental patients is an exercise in social control, and leads to coercive policies of hospitalization. These actions preempt questions

♟ **Kim Hopper.**

both about the quality of immediate assistance offered such people and about the long-term subsistence alternatives to the hospital (Hopper 1988).

From Hopper's point of view, the issue is not whether the problem of homelessness will be solved, because it will not. One reason, Hopper argues, is that industrialized societies produce "surplus people," which means that there are more people than positions in technology-driven industrial economies, so there will always be people on the margins of the economy and out of work. One key issue is to recognize that the opposite of homelessness is not a homeless shelter. Rather, it is a home, which is currently lacking in treatments of homeless people.

Hopper insists that ethnographic research offers useful on-the-ground insights into these matters, because policymakers, judges, and social service bureaucrats are unlikely to find these things out for themselves. But, he argues, fieldwork is not enough: anthropologists also need to familiarize themselves with clinical knowledge and the government's legal, regulatory, and procedural constraints to be able to evaluate proposed interventions.

Questions for Reflection

1. How and why do you think homeless people might develop traits of mental illness?

2. Why would social institutions want to define people as mentally ill if they are not?

3. What might you say to officials in your hometown to explain American cultural attitudes toward homelessness?

Figure 3.4   Balinese *Balians.* *Balians* are ritual specialists and healers who use a mix of traditional herbs, prayers, and other rituals.

Nevertheless, as documented in Ethan Watters's book *Crazy Like Us: The Globalization of the American Psyche* (Watters 2011), Western psychological terms, notions, and illnesses are globalizing rapidly in recent years. For example, mental illnesses such as depression, anorexia, and post-traumatic stress disorder seem to now exist in places that have never had them before, such as Hong Kong, Sri Lanka, and Tanzania. Watters suggests that much of this is taking place because of the increasingly global flows of Western media and psychiatric practices, as well as the expansion of pharmaceutical companies into new markets throughout the globe. Watters argues that such practices, which are usually based on an assumption of "hyper-individualism," destabilize indigenous notions and ways of treating mental illness in social context.

We can bring these insights about psychological processes and mental illness beliefs even further with a biocultural approach that combines cultural and biological insights. Rebecca Seligman has conducted research on Candomblé, a spirit-possession religion in Brazil (Figure 3.5). Seligman asked a simple question: Why do certain people become spirit mediums and others do not? Biomedicine explains mediumship as a psychological disturbance with a biological basis, but fails to explain how and why such a disturbance might express itself specifically through mediumship. The cultural approach argues that oppressed and marginalized individuals gravitate toward mediumship, but it fails to explain why not all dispossessed people become mediums (Seligman 2005).

Seligman found that there is no single pathway to mediumship, but the interaction of biological, psychological, and cultural factors plays a crucial role. Among these are a physiological ability to achieve dissociation (trance states); conditions of poverty and oppression that cause emotional distress, which is often experienced through bodily pain; and a cultural outlet and social role that rewards people who exhibit the qualities of mediumship. Seligman concludes that without this holistic perspective on a medium's experience, we cannot appreciate the complexity of how people become mediums.

Such biocultural approaches in psychological anthropology open up new possibilities of collaboration between the natural and social sciences. As we will see in the next section, other

Figure 3.5   Candomblé Mediumship. In Brazil, where some two million people practice Candomblé religion, temples where rituals are carried out are managed by women priests, known as a "mothers-of-saint," often with support from men priests ("fathers-of-saint").

natural and social scientific collaborations aimed at increasing understanding of the relationship between individuals, biology, and culture focus on understanding the role of evolution in shaping individual behavior and cognition.

● ●

THINKING CRITICALLY ABOUT BIOLOGY AND CULTURE

If individual psychology differs from one culture to another, what might this suggest about the academic and clinical disciplines of psychology in which most psychologists treat patients who are Americans? What might these psychologists consider when dealing with recent immigrants from Africa or Asia?

● ●

What Role Does Evolution Play in Human Lives?

The phenomenon of evolution—that life forms make adaptive changes over generations—is widely believed to play a central role in shaping our human nature as individuals, and it has also played a key role in anthropological study. This section explains the basics of evolution and then explores the relationship between evolution and culture.

Understanding Evolution Among Human Populations

When Charles Darwin first published his revolutionary book *On the Origin of Species* in 1859, he argued that the visible characteristics of an organism (what has come to be known as a **phenotype**) were shaped over time through an evolutionary mechanism he called **natural selection**. Behind natural selection was Darwin's observation that life exists under complex, changing conditions and that those individuals having inherited traits best suited to a particular environment will survive and reproduce. For example, if the wild seeds available on one particular island are generally very large, birds with larger beaks will be better fed because their beaks are better suited to get nutrients from the seeds than birds with smaller beaks. Consequently, the larger-beaked birds normally have more offspring that survive into adulthood because they will inherit larger beaks from their parents. Conversely, these larger-beaked birds will be at a disadvantage on other islands where smaller seeds are most plentiful. Darwin observed this very pattern among several species of finches on the Galápagos Islands in the 1830s. According to Darwin's theory, we would expect the environment (in this case the size of the seeds) to "select" or favor the most appropriate beaks for the given localities.

Natural selection shapes all species, including our own. Once *Homo sapiens* became anatomically modern about 100,000 years ago, our species and those of our closest cousins, especially the Neanderthals, were capable of symbolic thought. This enhanced cognition had several advantages, including the making of better and more

● **Phenotype.** The visible characteristics of an organism.

● **Natural selection.** The process through which the natural environment selects those individuals with the most suitable characteristics for that environment to have more successful offspring than other, less well adapted individuals.

sophisticated tools, organizing social groups for hunting and building, and for defense against animals or even hostile humans. Those groups with more sophisticated strategies for organizing themselves were more likely to survive and reproduce than neighboring groups with less developed cognition.

Natural selection is one of four evolutionary mechanisms that shape the typical physical characteristics of any population of animals or humans. The second evolutionary mechanism is that of **mutation**. Mutations are slight, unpredictable variations in genetic code that occur when two organisms reproduce. Mutations may be passed along to offspring and become widespread, or they may simply disappear from the population. Mutations may have no effect on an organism's ability to survive or they may result in genetic changes that could help or hinder an individual. Some mutations cause genetic disorders and susceptibility to illness. Others may benefit an organism by making it more resistant to certain diseases or infection. Mutations may also affect the phenotype, or observable traits of an individual, such as the shape of the nose or length of the fingers, among many traits.

The third and fourth evolutionary mechanisms neither add to the variation in a population nor cause particular phenotypes to disappear. What they do is move existing traits around within populations.

Gene flow is the movement of genes though interbreeding or intermarriage among humans from distinct populations. For example, when hundreds of thousands of African slaves were brought to North America, many slave owners of European heritage had children with Africans, which changed the distribution of genes within the North American population. One result was that the physical characteristics, or phenotype, of the slave population, including skin color, gradually blended with those of white North Americans. Gene flow caused the two widely separated populations—the Africans in North America and those living in Africa—to diverge in certain traits, which is why many African-Americans have lighter complexions than African peoples.

Genetic drift, the last of the four evolutionary mechanisms, is only important when population sizes are small and possibly isolated geographically. It consists of random sampling effects—not natural selection—that bring changes to the distribution of traits within a population. Today this mechanism is most noticeable in small islands in the Pacific or among small isolated communities in which the arrival of a small group of immigrants with a peculiar characteristic has a significant but random effect on the genetic variations found in the population. For example, if a single male immigrant to a small, isolated population brings a rare genetic trait to the islands' population, this trait may be distributed among descendants of this individual after several generations. After a few hundred years it could be present in nearly all of the island's population.

Gene flow and genetic drift work on human populations in opposite ways. Groups that move farther apart and have less interaction experience genetic drift as the two groups gradually start to differ from one another. At the same time, when groups interact and share genes, the mechanism of gene flow neutralizes any differences that might exist within two populations by distributing genes over a number of generations within the interacting populations.

Natural selection also affects gene distribution. We can see this most clearly in the distribution of skin tone across human populations. All *Homo sapiens* emerged from Central Africa, but as they moved out of Africa into Europe and Asia, natural selection favored melanin and darker skin tones in more tropical areas with more direct sunlight. Simultaneously, groups that moved toward the Arctic benefitted by pale skin and less melanin. There were adaptive advantages for individuals with less skin pigment in northern, colder climates and similar advantages for individuals with more pigmentation in more equatorial regions and more direct sun. The traditional distribution of skin tone before the age of discovery around 1500 shows that groups

- **Mutation.** Seemingly random changes in an organism's genetic code.

- **Gene flow.** The movement of genes though interbreeding or intermarriage in humans between distinct populations so the two populations become more similar or maintain shared traits.

- **Genetic drift.** Random sampling effects—not natural selection—that bring changes to the distribution of traits within a population.

near the equator tend to have darker skin color whether in Africa, Asia, New Guinea, or the Americas. Simultaneously, groups living in far northern regions in Europe, Asia, and the Americas have less pigment and lighter skin tone irrespective of where their ancestors may have come from. Such patterns demonstrate natural selection at work by showing that skin color is most strongly shaped by available sunlight more than by ancestry.

Racism and Early Evolutionary Models in Anthropology

During the late nineteenth century, when racism permeated both the public and the intellectual climate in Europe and North America, the theory of evolution appeared to offer an objective way of classifying the world's diverse peoples (see also Chapter 11). Many anthropologists of this period saw their discipline as a branch of natural history. Like zoologists and botanists, many saw their goal as finding a suitable way to classify human cultures, as well as their religions, their kinship systems, their political forms, and the material objects in their daily lives. Many assumed that these other domains (religion, kinship, politics, and material culture) would all map onto observable physical traits (skin color, hair texture, etc.) that these same researchers used to classify human biological groupings.

Not surprisingly, these nineteenth-century classifications made by white Europeans were racial scales putting blacks and other non-white groups on the bottom and whites on the top (Figure 3.6). Such models were used to justify colonial conquest of people of color around the world. To distance itself from these ideas, mainstream anthropology avoided evolutionary explanations of human behavior for a long time. In order to understand how anthropologists can contribute to our understanding of the role of evolution in human lives, we need to first understand why that history of avoidance was justified, and consider how biocultural perspectives can help us understand the role of evolution in human lives.

Franz Boas and Antievolutionism

Swimming against the current of racial thought during these early years of anthropology was Franz Boas, who harshly criticized attempts to equate evolution with racial theories (Armelagos and Goodman 1998). For example, he rejected the idea that there are groups of people belonging to stable and unchanging races, and he used biological data to prove that human populations in fact change. He also rejected the idea that there is an average phenotype within any of the groups that biologists and earlier anthropologists had identified as racial groups, arguing rather that there is greater variability within any one group than between groups. He strongly resisted the linkage between race and individual character.

For instance, Boas challenged racial science's use of the cephalic index, a ratio derived from the maximum length of a skull to its maximum width, which many researchers had used trying to "prove" that the so-called superior racial groups had bigger brains. Boas (1912) measured the brain cavities of European immigrants to America and their children, and discovered that the cavities of individuals born in America were larger than those of individuals born in Europe because of improvements in diet and health in their adopted country. Boas's insight was to use biological data to show how "nurture"—cultural factors and in this case the food people consume—can influence the shape of "nature," that is, physiology and anatomy.

Fɪɢ. 339. — Apollo Belvidere.[553]

Fɪɢ. 840.[556]

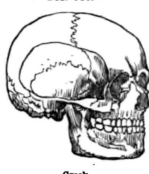

Greek.

Fɪɢ. 341. — Negro.[554]

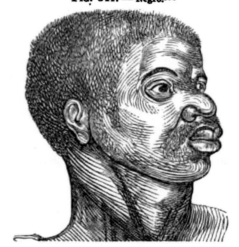

Fɪɢ. 342.[357]

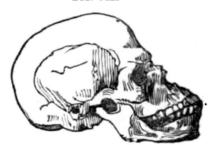

Creole Negro.

Fɪɢ. 843. — Young Chimpanzee.[555]

Fɪɢ. 844.[558]

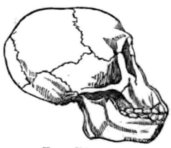

Young Chimpanzee.

Figure 3.6   Eighteenth-Century Racial Science. This image, from a book called *Types of Mankind* published in 1854, claims a close relationship between chimpanzees and Africans.

Ultimately, Boas's antiracial stand was not an argument that humans and their cultures were not shaped by their physical and social environments, but rather an attack on the process of classifying different peoples and cultures along some hierarchical scale based on skin color and hair texture. Boas's model came to be understood as antievolutionary. Nevertheless, antievolutionism was one of the most influential forces in anthropology and at least partly explains why most social and cultural anthropologists have emphasized culture's independence from biology.

Moving Beyond Purely Biological Notions of Evolution

Even though under Boas's influence the focus on culture *over* biology became dominant in twentieth-century anthropology, evolutionary thought never completely disappeared from cultural anthropology. One reason is that it has offered one way to address the question of why and how cultures change. For example, between the 1930s and 1950s, cultural anthropologists such as Julian Steward and Leslie White applied evolutionary theory to explain how and why cultures change, or the tendency of cultural systems to increase in complexity.

In more recent years several schools of evolutionary thought have emerged with relevance to anthropology, including sociobiology and evolutionary psychology. Both of these have similar goals, so we will consider only one of them—evolutionary psychology—here.

Evolutionary Psychology

Evolutionary psychologists seek to explain contemporary human behavior, cognition, and perception as the outcome of evolutionary processes. For example, they commonly argue that through natural selection human males evolved to be naturally aggressive and sexually promiscuous. Meanwhile females evolved to be innately passive, preferring a single mate with ample resources. These arguments are an example of **biological determinism**—the belief that human behaviors and beliefs are primarily, if not solely, the result of biological characteristics and processes. These seemingly common-sense explanations appear to explain why men cannot seem to be loyal to their girlfriends and wives, or why women are attracted to wealthy and powerful men. They have played well in the media hungry for eye-catching stories.

Similar behaviors among primates with whom we share common ancestry are often presented to "prove" that these conditions are "natural." But these claims rest on poor logic and flawed science, including the very use of contemporary primates as evidence for the naturalness of these behaviors. These other primates have also been evolving for a very long time, and adapting to circumstances sometimes quite different from the evolutionary conditions that have shaped humans, so we cannot assume that the behaviors we see in them today have any relationship with our common ancestry. In fact, ecological and social variability among primates is so great that it is impossible to identify any meaningful patterns except in the most general sense.

For example, in 40% of primate species, females actually dominate over males (MacKinnon and Fuentes 2005) (Figure 3.7). In addition, while all primates have the *capacity* for aggressive behavior, the *incidence* of aggression is not evenly distributed. Researchers studying primates have found that the reproductive success of individuals depends less on aggression than on the ability to get along with others in the social group. Paternity tests on

• **Biological determinism.** The belief that human behaviors and beliefs are primarily, if not solely, the result of biological characteristics and processes.

Figure 3.7 Female Dominance. Female dominance is characteristic of these ring-tailed lemurs from Madagascar.

primate species that are not seasonal breeders (i.e., who are capable of breeding at any time of the year, like humans) show that dominant and aggressive males do not necessarily have the most reproductive success (MacKinnon and Fuentes 2005).

No animal or human carries genes for dominance, aggression, or passivity. The capacity for dominance, aggression, and passivity are complex social and psychological conditions and states that involve biological processes, such as the production of certain hormones. But they are not fixed properties or traits carried on genes. Even if they were carried on genes, genes operate in such complex ways that there would be no way to ensure that this particular gene would express itself in behavior. It is much more accurate to think of the causes of aggression as coming from social and cultural processes—such as disagreements over land, women, and resources—not some adaptation humans made in a distant evolutionary past (MacKinnon and Fuentes 2005).

Evolution Still Matters

None of this is to say that humans are not continuing to evolve as a species with biocultural consequences for individuals. For example, improvements in travel technology and social changes promoting mobility have created high rates of global migration. In these processes, the intermixing of human populations is leading to gene flow, an evolutionary process in which genetic material moves between populations and creates changes in how people look, the distribution of susceptibility to disease, and other biological changes.

But it is difficult to accept that culture and cultural change follow the same principles of biological evolution, if only because genes do not transmit culture. People transmit culture, from individual to individual. We are not constrained to following the cultural patterns of our parents but can model our own ways of doing things on patterns we see among our neighbors. The interactions of individuals with each other, culture, economics, politics, and social processes, not to mention nature itself, are much too complex to reduce to biological arguments. Besides, as we explore in our final section, who is to say that we as individuals are subject to evolutionary pressures anyway, living in an era in which scientists can manipulate genes?

THINKING CRITICALLY ABOUT BIOLOGY AND CULTURE

In this section we have argued that people in America today, whose ancestors originated in Europe, Africa, Asia, and North America, have all experienced gene flow within North America and genetic drift away from their ancestral groups. We have also suggested that the environment has shaped these populations as well during the 100 to 400 years these communities have been in North America. What do these evolutionary mechanisms imply about how fixed and stable the social categories we call "race" are in America?

Is Biotechnology Changing Our Bodies?

Not so long ago, the idea that a person could clone himself or herself, that parents could choose the color of their child's eyes, or that scientists could transplant genetic material from another species into our own genes seemed like exotic possibilities.

But we hear constantly of the revolution in genetic research that has begun to accomplish such things through biotechnology, which refers to genetic engineering or any other technological modification of biological systems to make useful products. These facts have led some scholars to ponder if humans are no longer adapting to nature but transforming nature to fit their needs and desires (Singer 1996).

Humans play an active role in biological evolution. For thousands of years, humans have been manipulating the genetic makeup of other organisms to fit their needs and desires, through the selective breeding of plants and animals and the modification of natural environments. What is different in the age of biotechnology and genetically modified organisms is that genetic manipulation can occur at the level of specific gene sequences. For example, scientists perform "gene therapy" by taking out mutated gene sequences linked to disease and inserting new ones. Nobody really knows whether such techniques will be widely available and effective, or what the long-term genetic and ecological consequences of such practices will be. But it must also be said that to date there have been very few viable examples of medically useful gene therapies. Why? Because genes function in complex ways that scientists are still struggling to understand. In the first section here, we explain why, and in the second section we explain why that doesn't seem to stop the use of genes to explain all kinds of things going on with humans.

How Genes Work: The Basics

DNA consists of pairs of long molecules in the form of a spiral called a double helix (Figure 3.8). Each strand of DNA contains billions of nucleotide bases that contain the genetic blueprint for all living organisms. These DNA strands are found in the nucleus of every living cell. There are four nucleotide bases—adenine (A), cytosine (C), guanine (G), and thymine (T)—and each has a specific affinity, or chemical attraction, to one of the other bases. The rungs of the ladder of DNA are always composed of an A-T or C-G pair. When the nucleus of a cell divides to create two cells, the filaments of DNA separate, and each nucleotide base attracts its mate reproducing exactly the other filament of DNA for the new nucleus (Lewontin 1991).

A gene is a long sequence of nucleotides, found along a strand of DNA. The gene's primary purpose is to allow the cell to form specific proteins. These proteins are used for communicating with other cells and triggering other bodily processes. Other parts of the genes turn the production of proteins on and off in response to external conditions. Genes are necessary to produce proteins, but so are other things, including the nuclear and cellular machinery that actually makes proteins. So if you want to understand why one person with a gene linked to breast cancer gets the disease and another without the gene does not, you cannot study the offending gene alone. You also have to understand how that particular gene interacts with its environment—environments that range from the internal biological environment (at the nuclear, cellular, and somatic levels), to the external (familial, social, and ecological) (Taussig 2005). These interactions include everything from whether the machinery to produce proteins is in good shape to whether there are certain triggers present such as an individual's dietary patterns or the presence of a toxin in his or her environment. Scientists are just beginning to explore gene–environment interactions.

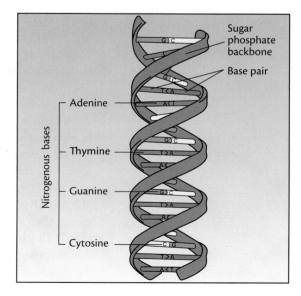

Figure 3.8   DNA Molecule.

The bottom line is that genes never work in isolation, and they do not cause anything by themselves. Herein lies a central flaw of using genetic explanations for almost anything having to do with people: genes are just one agent in the very complex processes that make us human, cause our maladies, make us intelligent, and so on (Lewontin 1991).

Expecting the revolution in genetics to solve human problems by decoding our individual gene sequences is unreasonable, not because geneticists will not identify most of our genes, but because what triggers genes to act is largely not coded in our DNA. If we think back to the situation we opened this chapter with regarding genetic testing for a propensity to get carpal tunnel syndrome, it is clear that the repetitive work of data entry at a keyboard (or some similar repetitive task in the workplace) was the likely precipitating cause. But even if some people had a propensity to get carpel tunnel syndrome, it is unlikely that these genes would be triggered without the environmental stimulus of repetitive tasks.

The hype about genetic testing comes from the fact that corporations and governments have invested billions of dollars in this research. What better justification can there be for the massive expenditures than unlocking the "secrets of life" itself? Clearly what has been unlocked, though, is life's enormous complexity (Keller 2000). We have to conclude that biotechnology is not changing our human nature, if only because human nature has never been a simple expression of our genes but the complex interplay of genetic, biological, and cultural factors.

The Dilemmas of Geneticization

- **Geneticization.** The use of genetics to explain health and social problems over other possible causes.

But if biotechnology is not changing who we are, it has impacted people's lives, particularly through the **geneticization** of many conditions, which is the use of genetics to explain health and social problems over other possible causes (Lippman 2001). A focus on geneticization sheds light on important ethical, philosophical, and legal dilemmas raised by genetics, especially surrounding the sensitive issue of who organizes, interprets, and controls genetic information (Taussig 2005). For example, the effort to identify a genetic predisposition for carpal tunnel syndrome among railroad workers, with the plan of using that information to deny them worker's compensation claims, is a clear example of geneticization and the concerns it raises about who controls genetic information. It also shows how geneticization can divert attention from the social causes of disease.

Another example of geneticization concerns how biotechnologies are changing women's experiences of pregnancy, a theme that anthropologist Rayna Rapp has studied at several clinics in New York City. Amniocentesis is a prenatal screening test for diagnosing genetic anomalies in a fetus, such as Down syndrome, a disorder arising from a defect in the DNA of certain chromosomes (Rapp 1999). Down syndrome causes intellectual impairment and certain abnormal physical features. Such anomalies become apparent in the chromosomes very early on as a fetus develops. If anomalies are detected early enough, usually in the first trimester, a woman can choose to terminate her pregnancy. Rapp's research shows that the impacts of these tests on women's lives are complex. For example, because the law protects the rights of disabled individuals after the second trimester of pregnancy, women face a conflict between their own reproductive rights and the disability rights of the fetus. These are clearly controversial social issues that surround geneticization. In "Thinking Like an Anthropologist: The Controversies Over I.Q. Testing and Mother-Infant Bonding," we consider some genetic controversies surrounding intelligence testing to help you develop your own critical perspective on geneticization.

Thinking Like an Anthropologist

Controversies Over I.Q. Testing and Mother-Infant Bonding

ANTHROPOLOGISTS BEGIN THEIR research by asking questions. In this box, we want you to learn how to ask questions as an anthropological researcher. Part One describes a situation and follows up with questions we would ask. Part Two asks you to do the same thing with a different situation.

PART ONE: I.Q. TESTING

At one point or another, most of us have taken an I.Q. ("Intelligence Quotient") test, the goal of which is to test our individual mental abilities. Proponents assert that I.Q. tests are accurate predictors of academic achievement, job performance, and social pathology. I.Q. testing has an aura of scientific objectivity and certainty about something we all know is complicated. Numerous social institutions, from schools to corporations, rely on it to identify appropriate applicants and placement (such as "tracking" in schools). The U.S. government also accepts the validity of I.Q. tests. The courts, including the Supreme Court, consider it in cases involving mentally retarded criminals; the Social Security Administration uses it when deciding certain disability claims; and the Department of Defense requires a minimum I.Q. to serve in the military. I.Q. testing is based on psychometrics, techniques for measuring knowledge, aptitudes, abilities, and personality traits. The Scholastic Aptitude Test (SAT) is another psychometric test.

I.Q. tests operate on several assumptions: (1) intelligence is a single entity that can be reduced to a number; (2) differences in intelligence are the result of fixed genetic differences between individuals; and (3) socioeconomic success, status, and power are the result of inherited intelligence. Poor people, minorities, and socially marginalized groups all tend to score low on these tests, a fact that supporters of I.Q. tests assume demonstrates that these groups have inherited intelligence that is lower than people who score higher on these tests. The inevitable conclusion is that social and racial inequality are a "natural" result of low intelligence (Gould 1981).

Many anthropologists, psychologists, and geneticists have challenged the validity of these assumptions, if not the whole enterprise of I.Q. testing. Critics point out that I.Q. tests are culturally loaded documents, that is, they ask questions that require specific cultural or social knowledge, such as that related to school performance. Because the tests mimic the content and circumstances of schoolwork, they tend to predict how well a student will do in school. This is not testing "intelligence" per se, but school performance (Lewontin, Rose, and Kamin 1984).

Critics argue that I.Q. tests cannot predict socioeconomic success, since many people with high I.Q. scores earn less than some others with lower scores. The real question is, how much more likely is it for a high-I.Q. child to end up in the top 10% of income, *all other things being equal*? When family income and school background are the same, a high-I.Q. child has only twice, not fifty times, the likelihood of ending up in the top 10% of income as a child in the lowest income group. But the more important result is that a child in the top 10% of family income has a twenty-five-times greater chance of being in the top income bracket than a child whose family is among the poorest 10% (Lewontin, Rose, and Kamin 1984:93–4). Socioeconomic class background is clearly a more important predictor of socioeconomic success than is I.Q.

The mystery of intelligence extends to its presumed heritability, which proponents of I.Q. have not been able to establish with any certainty. There is no single gene for intelligence, and intelligence does *not* seem to be part of an individual's genotype (fixed genetic inheritance). Rather, intelligence is a complex interplay between genetic makeup, environment, and behavior. Thus, intelligence is subject to cultural influences and changes throughout an individual's life.

What questions does this situation raise for anthropological researchers?

1. What and whose interests are served by geneticizing intelligence?
2. How and why do scientific experts and social institutions uphold the validity of I.Q.?
3. What are the impacts of I.Q. testing on the social prospects of people from different social classes, racial groups, and ethnicities?

PART TWO: MOTHER-INFANT BONDING

Many Americans feel it is important for mothers and their infants to be physically close for up to a year after birth in order for "bonding" to take place. Because pediatricians and child psychologists support these views, they have an aura of scientific certitude. Some pediatricians and nurses even blame social and physical problems in children on a mother's lack of bonding (Eyer 1993). Anthropological research on patterns of childrearing in other societies

(continued)

Thinking Like an Anthropologist (continued)

suggests that different societies have a wide variety of ways of treating infants in their first year that don't involve close physical contact between mother and child, and don't lead to social and physical problems in the child. What questions would you ask about the idea of mother-infant bonding as an anthropological researcher?

Prepared under the auspices of the National Research Council

NATIONAL INTELLIGENCE TESTS

By M. E. HAGGERTY, L. M. TERMAN, E. L. THORNDIKE G. M. WHIPPLE, and R. M. YERKES

THESE tests are the direct result of the application of the army testing methods to school needs. They were devised in order to supply group tests for the examination of school children that would embody the greater benefits derived from the Binet and similar tests.

The effectiveness of the army intelligence tests in problems of classification and diagnosis is a measure of the success that may be expected to attend the use of the National Intelligence Tests, which have been greatly improved in the light of army experiences.

The tests have been selected from a large group of tests after a try-out and a careful analysis by a statistical staff. The two scales prepared consist of five tests each (with practice exercises), and either may be administered in thirty minutes. They are simple in application, reliable, and immediately useful for classifying children in Grades 3 to 8 with respect to intellectual ability. Scoring is unusually simple.

Either scale may be used separately to advantage. The reliability of results is increased, however, by reexamination with the other scale after an interval of at least a day.

Scale A consists of an arithmetical reasoning, a sentence completion, a logical selection, a synonym-antonym, and a symbol-digit test. Scale B includes a completion, an information, a vocabulary, an analogies, and a comparison test.

Scale A: *Form* 1. 12 pages. Price per package of 25 Examination Booklets, 2 Scoring Keys, and 1 Class Record $1.45 net.
Scale A: *Form* 2. Same description. Same price.
Scale B: *Form* 1. 12 pages. Price per package of 25 Examination Booklets, Scoring Key, and Class Record $1.45 net.
Scale B: *Form* 2. Same description. Same price.
Manual of Directions. Paper. 32 pages. Price 25 cents net.
Specimen Set. One copy of each Scale and Scoring Keys and Manual of Directions. Price 50 cents postpaid.

Experimental work financed by the General Education Board by appropriation of $25,000

WORLD BOOK COMPANY
YONKERS-ON-HUDSON, NEW YORK
2126 PRAIRIE AVENUE, CHICAGO

❧ **Advertisement for Mass Mental Testing.**

●●

THINKING CRITICALLY ABOUT BIOLOGY AND CULTURE

What kinds of issues are raised beyond the purely biological when a doctor diagnoses a specific genetic problem in a child or adult? Give an example to illustrate your analysis.

●●

Conclusion

The idea that human nature is biologically fixed is a powerful dogma, confirmed at virtually every turn, from medical and psychiatric fields to media headlines. But biological determinism often obscures more than it reveals, mainly because it denies the central role of culture in shaping who we are as individuals. It also minimizes the important contribution culture makes to brain development, cognitive processes, the psychological experience of self, and processes of biological evolution. Biological determinism also diverts attention away from the social causes of illness, for example, the carpal tunnel syndrome of a railroad laborer whose worker's compensation claim is denied on genetic grounds, even though it was his work conditions that caused his condition.

But the alternative, cultural determinism, is not acceptable either, because it denies the biological factors that contribute to who we are and how we experience our selves. Our neural pathways may be "cultured" in important ways, and genes may not operate in isolation, but in both cases it is impossible to deny that there are biological factors at work that play a key role in shaping our possibilities as individual humans.

The biocultural approach, which emphasizes the complex interplay of culture, biology, and cognition, is breathing new life into classic anthropological questions, some of which we have examined here: What is the relationship between the individual and culture? What is the role of evolution in human lives? Even more exciting is its promise for reconciling the traditional divide between nature and nurture.

So what is "human nature?" This is perhaps the most beguiling and consequential question at the heart of anthropology. There is hardly consensus about how to characterize such a broad and abstract condition. Nevertheless, biocultural perspectives and evidence keep leading us toward the conclusion that there is no single human nature, but many human natures.

KEY TERMS

Reviewing the Chapter

Chapter Section	What We Know	To Be Resolved
What Can the Biology of Brain Development Teach Us About Culture?	Biocultural perspectives and evidence are breathing new life into classic anthropological interests in cognition, individuals and their psychologies, and evolutionary processes, suggesting that "human nature" is not a singular condition. We have also learned that human brains are not genetically and neurally fixed but functionally plastic organs that operate as generalized learning and problem-solving devices in the context of culture.	Many anthropologists find it difficult to even talk about something as broad and abstract as "human nature," maybe even rejecting the possibility that we can describe such a thing with any certainty.
How Do Anthropologists Understand Other People's Psychologies?	Ideas about personhood, self, experience, emotions, and mental illness are culturally variable and shaped by cultural and social context.	Anthropologists continue to debate how the cultural variability around psychology, emotions, and mental states relates to biological and other psychological processes.
What Role Does Evolution Play In Human Lives?	Human populations are subject to diverse evolutionary processes, although how those processes actually relate to individual behaviors and characteristics—as well as culture—are more complicated than biological determinist explanations allow.	The long-standing skepticism in cultural anthropology toward using theories of evolution to explain human behavior has made it difficult to advance discussions about the effects of evolution on human behavior and cognition in the discipline.

Is Biotechnology Changing Our Bodies?	Biogenetic engineering in plants and animals has produced a significant new mechanism for changing and altering genetic code and thus has a powerful role to play in the evolution of these species. Nevertheless, even though it is clear that human characteristics are not reducible to our genes, social interests and institutions still use genetic explanations to explain many cultural phenomena.	Neither anthropologists nor other scientists can predict with certainty how genetics may shape our species' biology.

Readings

Stephen Jay Gould's classic book *The Mismeasure of Man* (New York: W. W. Norton, 1981) remains one of the most authoritative histories of racist science. An excellent complement to that book is Richard Lewontin's *Biology as Ideology: The Doctrine of DNA* (New York: Harper Perennial, 1991).

• •

For an excellent and readable overview of recent developments in the anthropology of cognition and the opportunities of closing the gap between cultural anthropology and the brain sciences, see Bradd Shore's book *Culture in Mind: Cognition, Culture, and the Problem of Meaning* (New York: Oxford University Press, 1996).

• •

As the biocultural synthesis has gained steam in anthropology, several books have emerged that treat it in detail, including Alan H. Goodman and Thomas L. Leatherman's edited volume *Building a New Biocultural Synthesis: Political-Economic Perspectives on Human Biology* (Ann Arbor: University of Michigan Press, 1998) and Susan McKinnon and Sydel Silverman's edited book, *Complexities: Beyond Nature and Nurture* (Chicago: University of Chicago Press, 2005).

• •

To explore ethnopsychology and cultural psychology, see Richard's Shweder's *Why Do Men Barbeque? Recipes for Cultural Psychology* (Cambridge: Harvard University Press, 2003).

An anthropological analysis of fetal testing and its relationship with geneticization is Rayna Rapp's book *Testing Women, Testing the Fetus: The Social Impact of Amniocentesis in America* (New York: Routledge, 1999).

• •

Linguistic Anthropology

Relating Language and Culture

IN HER WELL-KNOWN book *You Just Don't Understand: Women and Men in Conversation*, linguist Deborah Tannen (1990) describes the tensions that arise between young couples because of the different ways they use language. Consider the case of Josh, a college student who has been dating his girlfriend, Linda, for more than a year. One day, he received a text from his close high school friend, who was coming through town. Josh invited him to spend the weekend and to go see the Red Sox play the Yankees. That evening, when Josh was over at Linda's he told her he was going to have a houseguest and wouldn't be able to see the film he had told her they would see on the day of the Sox–Yankees game. Linda became upset. Linda would never make such plans without talking about it with Josh first. In fact, she liked being able to say to her friends, "I'll have to check with Josh," because it showed how close they were. Josh's failure to check with her suggested to Linda a lack of intimacy in their relationship.

Josh was equally upset by Linda's reaction, although for different reasons. When Linda asked him why he did not consult her first, he replied, "I can't say to my friend, 'I have to ask my girlfriend for permission!'" For Josh, checking with Linda would make him feel subordinate to her, or worse, like a child. He felt Linda was trying to limit his freedom as an adult and as a man.

Josh and Linda speak the same language, yet they were clearly talking past one another. In their case, the same words "I'll have to check with Josh (or Linda)" meant very different things to each person. What

---

🌱 **Talking Past Each Other?**   Men and women in the United States are socialized to communicate in different ways, which can produce tensions when one party doesn't recognize or appreciate differences in the other's approach to using language.

explains the miscommunication? While the expression "Women are from Venus and men are from Mars" overstates the situation, in American culture, men and women do live in somewhat different worlds. We have different expectations of each other, expectations that help shape how we use language. If Linda were more direct, people would consider her harsh, aggressive, and unladylike. Josh's directness, however, would typically be a sign of his strength, independence, and maturity, the supposed ideal for a man in American culture. Taking this a step further, we can see how American patterns of gender inequality are built into how we use language. In some settings—the workplace, say—Linda's concern for preserving good social relationships could appear as a sign of weakness, dependence, and uncertainty, limiting her ability to climb the corporate ladder.

This perspective on language leads us to ask a question at the heart of anthropology's interest in language: *How do the ways people talk reflect and create their cultural similarities, differences, and social positions?* Embedded within this larger question are the following problems, around which this chapter is organized:

Where does language come from?

How does language actually work?

Do people speaking different languages experience reality differently?

How can languages be so dynamic and stable at the same time?

How does language relate to social power and inequality?

Language is one of the most rule-bound and structured aspects of human culture. Yet, ironically, language is also one of the least conscious aspects of culture. Moreover, while language is structured, it is also one of the most dynamic aspects of human life, because it can change so rapidly. Different languages have words for different sets of concepts, just as different words can be used for similar concepts. Furthermore, within a society social hierarchies and gender differences are both marked and reinforced by linguistic expressions. Before we get into these kinds of subtleties, it is important to find out where language comes from.

Where Does Language Come From?

● **Language.** A system of communication consisting of sounds, words, and grammar.

A **language** is a system of communication consisting of sounds, words, and grammar. This simple definition emphasizes three features: (a) language consists of sounds organized into words according to some sort of grammar, (b) language is used to communicate, and (c) language is systematic. But where does it come from? We can begin to answer this question in two ways: one is evolutionary—having to do with our biological heritage—and the other is historical, related to how languages have developed over time.

Evolutionary Perspectives on Language

The simple fact that we are able to make sounds and put them into meaningful sequences suggests two different biological abilities that both link us to and separate us from non-human animals. First is the ability to make linguistic sounds using the mouth and larynx. Second is the ability to reproduce these sounds in an infinite variety of ways to produce an equally diverse range of thoughts. To what extent do we share these capabilities with other animals?

There are clearly examples in which an animal appears to talk. Animal behaviorist Irene Pepperberg worked for several decades to train her famous African Grey Parrot Alex (1976–2007) to make similar simple sentences using symbolic concepts of shape, color, and number. Alex's ability to use language was quite rudimentary compared to human speech. He was one of the few non-primates to have an obituary published in the *New York Times* (Carey 2007). But do animals really talk?

Call Systems and Gestures

Most animals cannot talk because they do not have a larynx, which enables humans to make the meaningful sounds we call language. Yet most animals use sounds, gestures, and movements of the body intended to communicate. Anthropological linguists refer to these sounds and movements as **call systems,** which are patterned forms of communication that express meaning. But why is this communication not language? There are four major reasons:

● **Call systems.** Patterned sounds or utterances that express meaning.

1. *Animal call systems are limited in what and how much they can communicate.* Calls are restricted largely to emotions or bits of information about what is currently present in the environment, while language has few limitations in the content of what kind of information it can transmit.
2. *Call systems are stimuli-dependent, which means an animal can only communicate in response to a real-world stimulus.* Animal calls are responses to visible triggers in the external world and nothing more. In contrast, humans can talk about things that are not visible, including things and events in the past or future.
3. *Among animals each call is distinct, and these calls are never combined to produce a call with a different meaning, while the sounds in any language can be combined in limitless ways to produce new meaningful utterances.*
4. *Animal call systems tend to be nearly the same within a species with only minor differences between call systems used in widely separated regions.* In contrast, different members of our species speak between 5,000 and 6,000 different languages, each with its own complex patterns.

Humans are evolutionarily distinct from other animals in that we developed not just the biological capacity to speak through a larynx but the brain capacity to combine sounds to create infinite symbolic meanings. Both abilities form the basis of human language.

Teaching Apes to Use Sign Language

Nevertheless, it is clear that some apes have the ability to communicate, beyond the limits of a call system, as researchers who have attempted to teach American Sign Language (ASL) to apes demonstrate. A well-known example is a chimp named Washo, who grew up in captivity but heard no spoken language from her human caregivers, R. Allen Gardner and Beatrice Gardner. The Gardners instead used ASL whenever they were with her, and Washo learned just over 100 signs that had English equivalents. Even more striking, she was able to combine as many as five signs to form

Figure 4.1   Koko with Penny Patterson.

complete, if simple, sentences (Gardner, Gardner, and Van Cantfort 1989). Similarly, Penny Patterson (2003) worked with a female gorilla named Koko, who has learned to use more than 400 signs, and can also combine them in short sentences (Figure 4.1).

Chimpanzees and gorillas clearly have the cognitive ability to associate signs with concepts and then to combine them in original ways, comparable in some respects to the linguistic ability of a toddler. Such capabilities are not surprising among our nearest relatives in the animal kingdom, since the human capacity for language had to begin somewhere and we would expect other advanced primates to have some limited abilities.

Several anthropologists have nevertheless challenged whether apes like Washo and Koko actually demonstrate any innate linguistic ability (Wallman 1992). These critics argue that the two apes are extremely clever and have learned to respond to the very subtle cues of their trainers, in much the way circus animals learn remarkable tricks and know when to perform them. But as linguistic anthropologist Jane Hill (1978) has noted, most of these critics have never worked with primates. Whatever the case, such studies of ape sign language do suggest that our capacity for language may have begun to emerge with our ancestral apes. Most likely, from this rudimentary ability to associate meaning with signs and gestures, full-blown language evolved as human cognitive abilities became more complex.

Historical Linguistics: Studying Language Origins and Change

While primatologists take the evolutionary approach to the origins of language, historical linguistics focuses on how and where the languages people speak today emerged. This approach uses historical analysis of long-term language change. The approach began in the eighteenth century as **philology**, which is the comparative study of ancient texts and documents. Philologists like the German Jakob Grimm (1822), best known for his collections of fairy tales, observed that there were regular, patterned differences from one European language to another. To explain these patterns he hypothesized that English, German, Latin, Greek, Slavic, and Sanskrit all came from a common ancestor. As speakers of languages became isolated from one another—perhaps because of migration and geographic isolation—the consonants in the original language shifted one way in Sanskrit, another way in Greek and Slavic languages, in a different direction in Germanic and English, and yet another way in Latin and the Romance languages, all of which came to be known as Grimm's Law (Figure 4.2). The supposed common ancestor language, which became extinct after these divergences took place, is called a **proto-language**.

Genetic Models of Language Change

Contemporary historical linguists call Grimm's approach "genetic," since it explores how modern languages derived from an ancestral language. To identify languages that have a common ancestry, historical linguists identify **cognate words**, which are words in two or more languages that may sound somewhat different today but would have changed systematically from the same word (Table 4.1). As speakers became isolated from one another for geographic, political, or cultural reasons, consonants, vowels, and pronunciation diverged until they were speaking two or more new, mutually unintelligible languages. For example, German, Dutch, and English are descended from

- **Philology.** Comparative study of ancient texts and documents.

- **Proto-language.** A hypothetical common ancestral language of two or more living languages.

- **Cognate words.** Words in two languages that show the same systematic sound shifts as other words in the two languages, usually interpreted by linguists as evidence for a common linguistic ancestry.

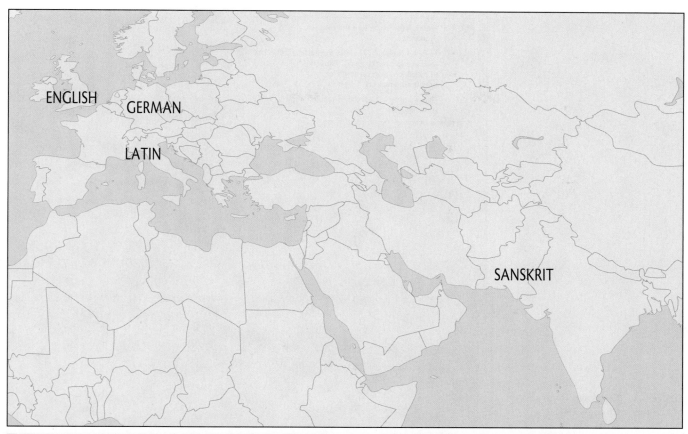

INDO-EUROPEAN INITIAL CONSONANT	ENGLISH	GERMAN	LATIN	SANSKRIT
*p	foot	Fuß	pes	pet
*p	father	Vater	pater	pita
*d	two	zwei	duo	dva
*d	tooth	zahn	dens	dan
*k	hundred	hundert	centum	satam
*k	heart	Herz	cor	
*k	hound	Hund	canis	sua

the same proto-Germanic language, but speakers of these three languages cannot usually understand each other unless they have studied the other language.

Non-Genetic Models of Linguistic Change: Languages in Contact

Languages also change by being in contact with another language, which is a "non-genetic" model of change. Such change generally takes place where people routinely speak more than one language. In the speech of multilingual persons, the use of

Figure 4.2 Grimm's Law. Early Indo-European forms using 'k' in Greek, Latin, and Irish shifted to "h" in the Germanic languages of English, German, Danish, and Norwegian. Many other examples include "head" and "heart."

TABLE 4.1			EXAMPLES OF COGNATE WORDS IN INDO-EUROPEAN LANGUAGES					
English	Dutch	German	Norwegian	Italian	Spanish	French	Greek	Sanskrit
three	drei	drei	tre	tre	tres	trois	tri	treis
mother	moeder	mutter	mor	madre	madre	mère	meter	matar
brother	broeder	bruder	bror	fra	hermano	frère	phrater	bhrator

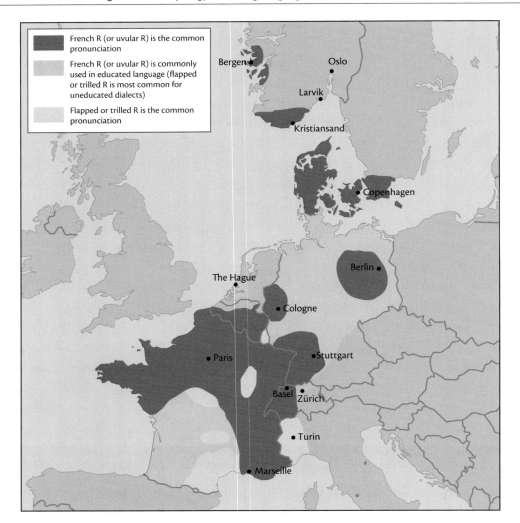

Figure 4.3   The Wave Theory of Language Change. Uvular, trilled, and flapped 'r' in European languages. Note that pronunciation patterns sweep across language boundaries from French to German and even to Scandinavian languages.

one of the languages is subtly influenced by the other language's sounds, syntax, grammar, and vocabulary. Evidence of this process can be seen in the use of the flapped and trilled 'r' in Europe. In southern parts of Western Europe, the trilled 'r' is typical, but this pronunciation seems to have given way in the north of France to a flapped 'r' as is common in German and Dutch. In this process, distinctive pronunciations move across language boundaries from community to community like a wave (Figure 4.3).

THINKING CRITICALLY ABOUT LANGUAGE

Many of us are familiar with how our pets respond to things we say in regular and predictable ways so that it often seems like they understand what we are saying. Although dogs and cats cannot make the normal sounds in English, we might sometimes think they understand simple English. Using some of the primate language studies as a guide, how would you respond to a friend who claims that his or her dog understands English? What do examples like this tell us about language generally?

Now that we have some understanding about the emergence of language, we can consider how language actually works.

How Does Language Actually Work?

Over the past century, linguists and linguistic anthropologists have studied the majority of the world's languages and found that each is highly structured. Moreover, most people, even those who speak unwritten languages, are largely unaware of the structure of their language until someone makes a mistake. Even then, they do not always know what is wrong, they just know the sentence sounded wrong.

To explain such reactions, the French linguist Ferdinand de Saussure (1916, 1986) suggested a distinction between the structure, or formal rules, of a language (*langue*) and how people actually speak it (*parole*). Distinguishing *langue* ('language') and *parole* ('speech') allows linguists to separate the rules and expected usage of language from what people actually say. The distinction is useful because it helps us realize that the rules we use to produce the sounds, word formation, and grammar as native speakers of a language can differ from how we actually speak, which is as much a social and cultural phenomenon as it is a function of language's structure. Here we explore how language is formally structured, which is the field of descriptive linguistics, and then sociolinguistics, the field that studies the social contexts of language use.

Descriptive Linguistics

The study of *langue,* or the formal structure of language, is called **descriptive linguistics**, which refers to the systematic analysis and description of a language's sound system and grammar. Linguists distinguish three types of structure in language: (a) **phonology,** the structure of speech sounds; (b) **morphology,** how words are formed into meaningful units; and (c) **syntax,** how words are strung together to form sentences and more complex utterances, such as paragraphs. (High school grammar classes mostly focus on morphology and syntax). All languages have predictable phonological, morphological, and syntactic structures.

- **Descriptive linguistics.** The systematic analysis and description of a language's sound system and grammar.

- **Phonology.** The systematic pattern of sounds in a language, also known as the language's sound system.

- **Morphology.** The structure of words and word formation in a language.

- **Syntax.** Pattern of word order used to form sentences and longer utterances in a language.

Phonology: Sounds of Language

The sounds of language are organized by marking systematic contrasts between pairs or groups of sounds. The majority of both these sounds and the contrasts appear in many of the world's languages, and yet each language has its own unique pattern of sounds. When linguists listen to natural language, such as when people talk unselfconsciously in ordinary conversations, they identify minimal pairs, which are pairs of words that differ only in a single sound contrast.

Sound Contrasts: Pan, Ban, and Man

Consider, for example, the initial sounds in the English words "pan," "ban," and "man." Three sounds, [p], [b], and [m], distinguish these three words, while the other sounds in these words are the same. The consonants p, b, and m are formed at the front of the mouth at the lips. The differences among three consonants parallel differences among the initial sounds in the words, "tab," "dab," and "nab," or the final sounds in the words "pig," "pick," and "ping."

- **Stops.** Sounds that are formed by closing off and reopening the oral cavity so that it stops the flow of air through the mouth, such as the consonants p, b, t, d, k, and g.

These nine contrasts distinguish three series of what linguists call **stops**, sounds that are made by an occlusion, or stopping, of the airstream though the oral cavity or mouth. But in addition, [b], [d], [g] differ from [p], [t], [k] in that the first group are voiced, formed by the vibration of the vocal cords (glottis), at the Adam's apple. The triplet of nasal consonants, [m], [n], [ng], are also voiced consonants that stop the airflow through the mouth, but allow the air to pass through the nasal cavity.

Mind you, these are examples from English. Other languages have different sounds. One of the most distinct from our language's point of view is the click (!) sound of Southern African peoples like the !Kung (Bushmen). Most speakers of English, !Kung, or for that matter any language, are not fully aware of how they form the different sounds they use when speaking, yet linguists recognize that sound systems are surprisingly systematic.

Dialects and Accents

Another interesting way to think about phonology is to consider dialects, which are regional or social varieties of a single language. Differences in vocabulary, grammar, and pronunciation, as well as regional accents such as those found in Brooklyn or Alabama in American English, are examples of a fairly minor dialect variation. Sometimes the variation occurs between generations or among people of different social classes. Part of the difference between these forms of speech is intonation, the pattern of rising and falling pitch, but usually careful analysis of the sounds shows that they also have systematic differences in their respective sound systems.

Up to the 1970s linguists assumed that American language was becoming increasingly homogeneous. It seemed that, owing to schools or to national broadcasts on television and radio where the accent is standardized, regional dialects would disappear. In fact, variation in sound systems seems to be greater now than ever before. The sociolinguist William Labov (1990; Labov, Ash, and Boberg 2006) observed in the 1980s that language change in the sound system of American English was concentrated in the cities. He also noted that sound change was most pronounced between generations in the same communities. Such findings suggest a much stronger role for peer groups in the transmission of linguistic forms than linguists had previously noticed.

Morphology: Grammatical Categories

The elements of grammar—tense, word order, which genders are marked, and so on—are also structured. Just like cultural patterns, grammatical patterns learned during childhood feel extremely natural to native speakers in any language, even though the same forms and structures would seem quite unnatural to speakers of most other languages. A couple of examples will illustrate how varied even the most basic grammatical categories can be.

Tenses

Americans tend to assume that there are only three natural tenses: past, present, and future. But not all languages use this same set of tenses, and some languages do not even require that tense be unambiguously marked in any particular sentence.

For example, the Ningerum language of Papua New Guinea uses five tenses: present, future, today-past, yesterday-past, and a-long-time-ago-past. Events that happened earlier in the day receive a different tense marking from those that happened yesterday or the day before. Similarly, events that happened several weeks, months, or years ago take a different tense marking altogether.

In contrast, Indonesian has no regular tense marking in its verbs but uses adverbs or other time references to emphasize when something has happened or will happen.

Pronouns

American English has fewer pronouns than many other languages. We distinguish between singular and plural, and among three persons (first person, second person, and third person). English also has two cases used when the pronoun is either the subject or the object. If we consider only person and number, we should have six basic pronouns, plus two extra pronouns for gender marking in the third person singular (he, she, and it).

This set of pronouns does not even begin to exhaust the possible pronoun distinctions that could be used. In French, for example, the second person singular pronoun ("you") takes two forms, *tu* and *vous* (an informal and a formal form). The Awin language of Papua New Guinea has singular, dual, and plural forms of its pronouns, meaning "you" (one person), "you two," and "you" (more than two).

Such basic examples as pronouns and tenses illustrate some of the wide range of possibilities that are possible in natural languages. Each configuration suggests certain distinctions that represent meaning encoded in the language's grammar. But such patterns do not alone create meaning.

Sociolinguistics

Sociolinguistics is the study of how sociocultural context and norms shape language use and the effects of language use on society. Sociolinguists accept whatever form of language a community uses—which de Saussure referred to as *parole*—as the form of language they should study.

When one examines the actual speech (*parole*) used in any community, one often finds that different people may use the same grammar and sound system (*langue*), but the actual sentences they make (*parole*) often carry different assumptions and connotations. This is because meaning emerges from conversation and social interaction, not just the formal underlying rules of language. We can see how sociocultural context shapes meaning by looking at signs, symbols, and metaphors.

- **Sociolinguistics.** The study of how sociocultural context and norms shape language use and the effects of language use on society.

Signs

Signs are words or objects that stand for something else, usually as a kind of shorthand. They are the most basic way to convey meaning. A simple example is the ordinary traffic sign that tells motorists to stop or not to park along a certain stretch of roadway. The colors, shapes, and designs used in these signs are largely arbitrary; when highway signs were invented early in the twentieth century, engineers could have selected any shape or color for the stop sign. The choice was not totally arbitrary, however, because Americans feel red is more dramatic than yellow or blue, and it may well have been associated with fire departments before the automobile (Figures 4.4 and 4.5).

Symbols

Symbols, which we introduced in Chapter 2, are basically elaborations on signs. When a sign becomes a symbol it usually takes on a much wider range of meanings than it may have had as a sign. For example, most colleges and universities in America have mascots and colors associated with their football teams. A mascot, such as a wildcat or panther, is a sign of the team, but mascots also readily become a symbol for the whole school, so that the wildcat represents all of the distinctive features of the institution and its people. But note that symbols work because signs

Figure 4.4 One of the Most Common Signs in American Life. Even without words on it, we all know the meaning of this sign.

Figure 4.5   The Productive Use of Signs Around the World. This sign in front of a business in Papua New Guinea bans the sale of betel nut. When chewing betel nut, a common practice in that island nation, one needs to spit out bright red spittle frequently.

themselves are productive, capable of being combined in innovative and meaningful ways.

Anthropologist Sherry Ortner (1971) distinguished three kinds of key symbols, or culturally powerful symbols. These are summarizing symbols, elaborating symbols, and key scenarios.

Summarizing symbols sum up a variety of meanings and experiences and link them to a single sign. An example would be the American flag, which many Americans see as summarizing everything good about America, especially such things as "democracy, free enterprise, hard work, competition, progress, and freedom" (Figure 4.6).

Elaborating symbols explain and clarify complex relationships through a single symbol or set of symbols. Elaborating symbols work in exactly the opposite way from summarizing symbols, because they help us sort out complex feelings and relationships. For example, the cow is an elaborating symbol among the Nuer and Dinka peoples of southern Sudan. For these herding groups, cows are used for bride wealth, and people spend an extraordinary amount of time thinking about their cows, their coloration, their body parts, and the like. A cow resembles the body of society with its varied and interlinked parts. By talking about cows, the Nuer and Dinka can talk about social relations within the community (Figure 4.7).

The key scenario differs from the other two kinds of symbols because it implies how people should act. A common American key scenario is the Horatio Alger myth. In Horatio Alger's many novels, this scenario often involves a young boy from a poor family, who works hard to become rich and powerful. It does not matter that most of us will not become these things, but the scenario does have meaning for how we feel about and evaluate hard work and persistence.

Metaphors

Metaphors are implicit comparisons of words or things that emphasize the similarities between them, allowing people to make sense of complex social relations around them. For example, in our culture we metaphorize ideas as food, as in "this textbook gives you *food* for thought, and some things to *chew* over, although you probably can't *stomach* everything we tell you here." Another example is how we metaphorize love as a disease, as in "he got over her, but she's got it bad for him, and it broke her heart" (Sheridan 2006:54).

Through signs, symbols, and metaphors language thus reinforces cultural values that are already present in the community. Simultaneously cultural norms and values reinforce the symbols that give language its power to convey meaning. Such relationships between language and culture raise a very interesting and old question: Do speakers of different languages see the world differently, just as people from different cultures might? We turn to this issue in the next section.

Figure 4.6   Making Use of a Summarizing Symbol. The Marine Corps War Memorial in Arlington, Virginia, pictured here is based on the famous photograph "Raising the Flag on Iwo Jima" by Joe Rosenthal. The image of Marines raising the flag has become a symbol of the American struggle for freedom.

Figure 4.7   An Elaborating Symbol to Make Sense of Social Relations. Nuer cattle have various kinds of markings and colors, and the Nuer use them to make sense of social differences in their community.

●●●

THINKING CRITICALLY ABOUT LANGUAGE

How might paying attention to the metaphors and symbols we use in our daily language allow us to frame important issues in more or less appealing ways? An example from national public life is the use of the term "downsizing" rather than "firing" staff. Consider an undesirable change at your college or university and think of different ways the administration might have made the change seem more appealing by talking about it differently.

●●●

Do People Speaking Different Languages Experience Reality Differently?

Most Americans generally assume that the world is what it is, and our experience of it is shaped by whatever is actually happening around us. But as we saw in Chapter 2, our culture predisposes us to presume some features of the world, while other people's culture leads them to assume something different. For many decades anthropologists and linguists have been debating a similar point in relation to language: Does the language we speak shape the way that we perceive the physical world? According to the Sapir-Whorf hypothesis, which we examine next, it does.

The Sapir-Whorf Hypothesis

In the 1920s, the linguistic anthropologist Edward Sapir (1929) urged cultural anthropologists to pay close attention to language during field research. Recognizing that most non-European languages organized tense, number, adjectives, color terms, and vocabulary in different ways from English, French, or German, he argued that a language inclines its speakers to think about the world in certain ways because of its specific grammatical categories. We explore this hypothesis further in "Classic Contributions: Edward Sapir on How Language Shapes Culture." It is anthropology's first expression of **linguistic relativity**, which is the idea that people speaking different languages perceive or interpret the world differently because of differences in their languages.

Sapir's student Benjamin Lee Whorf (1956) expanded on Sapir's work. Whorf had studied the language of the Hopi Indians and found that his knowledge of the grammars of European languages was little help in understanding Hopi grammar. He concluded that people who speak different languages actually do—are not just "inclined to," as his teacher Sapir would have said—perceive and experience the world differently. By the 1950s, linguistic anthropologists saw the ideas of Sapir and Whorf as related and began referring to them as the "Sapir-Whorf hypothesis." Let us illustrate the hypothesis with one of Whorf's best examples, the lack of tenses in Hopi.

Hopi Notions of Time

Whorf studied Hopi language and concluded that it lacked tenses like those we have in English. Hopi uses a distinction not expressed grammatically in European

● **Linguistic relativity.** The idea that people speaking different languages perceive or interpret the world differently because of differences in their languages.

Classic Contributions

Edward Sapir on How Language Shapes Culture

▼ **Edward Sapir.**

THE LINGUISTIC ANTHROPOLOGIST Edward Sapir (1884–1939) was the only professionally trained linguist among the students of Franz Boas, a founder of American anthropology. Sapir believed that language "provided the ethnographer with a terminological key to native concepts, and it suggested to its speakers the configurations of readily expressible ideas" (Darnell and Irvine 2006). In this excerpt we see Sapir's strongest statement about how language shapes the cultural expectations of the individual speaker:

It is an illusion to think that we can understand the significant outlines of a culture through sheer observation and without the guide of the linguistic symbolism which makes these outlines significant and intelligible to society....

Language is a guide to "social reality." Though language is not ordinarily thought of as of essential interest to the students of social science, it powerfully conditions all our thinking about social problems and processes. Human beings do not live in the objective world alone, nor alone in the world of social activity as ordinarily understood, but are very much at the mercy of the particular language which has become the medium of expression for their society. It is quite an illusion to imagine that one adjusts to reality essentially without the use of language and that language is merely an incidental means of solving specific problems of communication or reflection. The fact of the matter is that the "real world" is to a large extent unconsciously built up on the language habits of the group. No two languages are ever sufficiently similar to be considered as representing the same social reality. The worlds in which different societies live are distinct worlds, not merely the same world with different labels attached.... We see and hear and otherwise experience very largely as we do because the language habits of our community predispose certain choices of interpretation.... From this standpoint we may think of language as the symbolic guide to culture. (Sapir 1929:209–210)

Questions for Reflection

1. Can you think of an example, either from your native language or another language you know, in which language predisposes you to think in certain ways?

2. How does thinking of language as a "symbolic guide to culture" impact how you think about culture?

languages, which he called "assertion categories." These include (1) statements that report some fact (e.g., "he is running" or "he ran"), (2) declaration of an expectation, whether current or past (e.g., "he is going to eat" or "he was going to run away"), and (3) statements of some general truth (e.g., "rain comes from the clouds" or "he drinks only iced tea"). These three assertion categories do not overlap and are mutually exclusive. When translating these Hopi concepts into English, most people will use our tenses (past, present, and future), partly because we have to express tense in English to make a sentence, and partly because this is the only convenient way to express these different types of assertions in English.

Figure 4.8   A Hopi Ceremony of Regeneration. Tendencies in language are reflected in and reinforced by social action, such as this ritual which emphasizes regeneration and the recycling nature of the world. Non-Hopi people are now prohibited from seeing most Hopi rituals and religious dances today; this historic image of one of these celebrations of renewal is from a century ago, when outsiders were permitted to see them.

Whorf argued that the structure of the Hopi language suggested different ideas to Hopi than their translations would to English-speakers. He also linked these grammatical categories to Hopi "preparing" activities that surrounded certain rituals and ceremonies, arguing that "To the Hopi, for whom time is not a motion but a 'getting later' of everything that has ever been done, unvarying repetition is not wasted but accumulated" (1956). Americans, in contrast, might see repetitive actions before a celebration as a sapping of effort or as inefficiency (Figure 4.8).

Since Whorf's death in 1941, several linguists have challenged his interpretation of Hopi grammar. Malotki (1983), for example, argues that Hopi does, in fact, have tenses that resemble English tenses. Malotki's claims have not gone unchallenged, but if true, such a finding would call Whorf's example into question, although not necessarily his theory of the relationship between language and culture. Moreover, in the time between Whorf's and Malotki's research, Hopi have become more knowledgeable and conversant in English, suggesting that if Hopi now has tenses, these may be evidence of language change since the 1930s.

Ethnoscience and Color Terms

In the 1960s anthropologists began to explore how different peoples classified the world around them, focusing on how people conceptually group species of plants and animals or other domains, such as planets or colors. The study of how people classify things in the world became known as **ethnoscience** (see also Chapter 8). These studies began with a very different set of assumptions about the relationship between language and culture from those accepted by Sapir and Whorf. These scholars assumed that the natural world was a given, and that all human beings perceived it in the same way. Differences in classification were simply different ways of mapping categories onto empirical reality.

For example, anthropologists Brent Berlin and Paul Kay (1969) analyzed the color terms of more than 100 languages and found that basic color terms are consistent

• **Ethnoscience.** The study of how people classify things in the world, usually by considering some range or set of meanings.

across languages. For example, if a language has only two basic color terms, they are terms for dark (black) and light (white). But if a language has three terms, they were black, white, and red. The third term is never green, blue, purple, or orange. An example of a language with three basic color terms is Lamnso, spoken in the Central African country of Cameroon (see Figure 4.9). If a fourth color is present, then the terms are black, white, red, and blue/green. Some anthropologists suspect that these patterns are universal and may have to do with the way our optic nerve responds to light of different wavelengths (Figure 4.9).

This universal pattern does not disprove the Sapir-Whorf hypothesis or linguistic relativity more generally. But when informants with limited numbers of basic color terms were given paint chips displaying a wide range of colors, they could distinguish the different colors from other chips, but they classified them into groups that corresponded to their basic color categories. People speaking different languages did not appear to see colors any differently, they just classified them differently. For example, as Franz Boas discovered early in his career, Inuit of Newfoundland would not make a distinction between blue and green as he and other Europeans did because they did not separate the colors into distinct categories. But the Sapir-Whorf hypothesis would not necessarily have predicted that people see color differently anyway.

Is The Sapir-Whorf Hypothesis Correct?

By the late 1960s ethnoscience had largely dismissed the Sapir-Whorf hypothesis as having no significance for understanding human cognition. The most powerful argument against the idea that our language shapes our thought is that we have no way of knowing for sure what cognitive processes are involved when we distinguish different sets of pronouns, or have no English-style tenses. All we have is the language, which is where we started in the first place, plus our own researcher's intuition (Pinker 1994).

Today most anthropologists accept what has come to be called the weak or non-deterministic version of the linguistic relativity argument, which suggests (much as Sapir wrote) that the language habits of a community lead people to think about the world in certain ways and not others. Such a reading of the Sapir-Whorf hypothesis supports the idea that some ways of thinking are guided by the language we use while others are not.

There are implications here for language change. Over the long term such suggested ways of thinking would lead to a preference in each language for some kinds of linguistic change over others. If we take a rather static view of language, this issue might

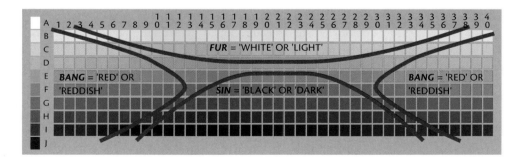

🌿 **Figure 4.9 The Munsell Color Chart.** The Cameroon language of Lamnso has three basic color terms that center on the colors called *sin*, *fur*, and *bang*, which we would gloss as 'black' (or 'dark'), 'white' (or 'light'), and 'red' (or 'reddish'), respectively. But as we can see from the plot of these three color terms on a standard Munsell color chart, our American sense of black, white, and red are not at all typical of the range of colors included in each of these Lamnso terms.

lead us to believe that languages are very stable, slow to change; and yet throughout this chapter we have suggested that language is dynamic. Let us now consider how language can constantly be changing, yet seem so stable.

● ●

THINKING CRITICALLY ABOUT LANGUAGE

How might the coarse slang used in daily conversations by college students be interpreted differently by parents or grandparents?

● ●

How Can Languages Be So Dynamic and Stable at the Same Time?

A striking paradox in linguistics is that, like culture, language constantly changes, yet most people experience their own language as stable and unchanging. We tend to notice the changes only when we hear other people in our communities using different words, pronunciations, or grammatical forms from our own. Usually national policies come into play to enforce or support the use and stabilization of certain linguistic forms over others, leading to language change within a strong framework of stability.

Linguistic Change, Stability, and National Policy

The increase of commerce, communication, and migration around the world over the past few centuries has produced new environments for language change. Colonial powers such as Great Britain, France, and Spain learned about new plants, peoples, and ways of living in their far-flung colonies. In the Americas, these powers also introduced slave labor from Africa, resulting in the blending of diverse African cultures, which were also blending with Native American cultures. These societies developed dynamic new languages, such as creole and pidgin languages, and implemented national language policies, in some cases to stabilize rapid linguistic change.

Creole and Pidgin Languages

- **Creole language.** A language of mixed origin that has developed from a complex blending of two parent languages that exists as a mother tongue for some part of the population.

- **Pidgin language.** A mixed language with a simplified grammar, typically borrowing its vocabulary from one language but its grammar from another.

In the Americas, local colonized societies developed hybrid languages that linguists call **creole languages,** languages of mixed origin that developed from a complex blending of two parent languages. A prominent example is the language commonly spoken in Haiti that combines several African languages with Spanish, Taíno (the language of Caribbean native peoples), English, and French.

In Asia and the Pacific, these hybrid forms have generally been called **pidgin languages**, which refers to a mixed language with a simplified grammar that people rarely use as a mother tongue (which is the case of Haitian creole), but to conduct business and trade. In the independent Melanesian countries of Vanuatu, the Solomon Islands, and Papua New Guinea, for example, local forms of Pidgin that combine various local languages and English have become national languages along with the colonial languages of English or French. In all three countries, ability to speak Pidgin has positive social status.

National Language Policies

Different countries have tried to control language change through the creation of national language policies. Short of making one particular regional dialect the national language, however, countries have found it nearly impossible to dictate what language or what form of the national language the public will speak. Three examples—taken from the Netherlands, France, and Quebec (Canada)—demonstrate different approaches to controlling processes of language change.

In the Netherlands during the twentieth century, Dutch linguists recognized that pronunciation and vocabulary had changed so much that spelling no longer reflected how people pronounced words. Dutch linguists recommended that spelling be changed to keep up with changing language use, and twice in the twentieth century the ruling monarchs, Queen Wilhelmina and Queen Juliana, issued royal decrees changing the official spelling of Dutch words to parallel actual use. The Dutch approach is quite tolerant of changing language.

In contrast, the French spent much of the twentieth century trying to preserve traditional French words that were being replaced by English loans, such as "le hamburger." The French parliament has passed several laws restricting English words from formal French documents, and prominent leaders have spoken out against the use of foreign words in proper French. But such laws have had little effect on the everyday speech of French people—especially the young, who readily borrow from English when discussing music, the arts, film, and anything trendy (Figure 4.10).

French Canadians in the Province of Quebec have been considerably more successful in preserving Quebecois (the form of French spoken in Quebec) against the pressure of English-speaking Canadians, who have historically considered English to be the superior language. Although government officials throughout Canada must be bilingual in English and French, the Province of Quebec conducts all government business primarily in French. To stem the tide of Anglicization (the creeping influence of English), the provincial parliament passed laws that require signs in public places to be in French. If English is also used, the English words cannot be longer than their French translations (Figure 4.11). In this case, language use coupled with nationalist control of the provincial parliament has encouraged the use of French throughout the population of Quebec.

Language Stability Parallels Cultural Stability

As the situations of language use in France and Quebec demonstrate, the potential loss of a native language can be a critical issue for a group of people. In such cases, people view the use of a particular language not just as a means of communication but as integral to their cultural identities and worldviews. As a result, the preservation of language and culture are often seen to go hand in hand.

The connection between cultural stability and the ongoing use of language is an especially critical one for many indigenous peoples around the world, who are striving to protect their languages and distinctive ways of life in face of rapid social change. In many cases, the cultural disruptions created by rapid social changes such as colonization and globalization have undermined the use of native languages. As a result, many indigenous groups around the world are facing what scholars call "language death," referring to the dying out of many minority languages. Some linguists argue that nearly half of the world's 5,000 or 6,000 languages are in jeopardy of dying out within a century (Hale 1992).

Figure 4.10 Mock Language and Exoticization. The American firm that produces LeSports Sac uses mock French words to exoticize its products.

Figure 4.11 Defending Quebecois from Anglicization. In Quebec, many store signs in English are smaller than French ones.

In many cases government actions have systematically set the stage for native language death by discouraging younger members of the community from using their indigenous language in favor of the national language. For example, in the United States the Bureau of Indian Affairs sent many American Indians to schools where until the 1970s they were prohibited from using their native languages and were taught that their languages were inferior and stupid. The effect has been that many Indians stopped using their native tongues and most indigenous North American languages are spoken by only small numbers of old people.

Many scholars believe that these dramatic losses will have considerable impact on the world's linguistic diversity, even as new languages are created all the time. And because of the close relationship between language and culture, the world's cultural diversity will suffer as well. As our discussion of the Sapir-Whorf hypothesis suggests, language is the primary medium through which people experience the richness of their culture, and loss of language suggests a genuine loss of a culture's fullness.

As we have seen in this section, issues of language stability and change are closely tied to questions of domination, control, and resistance, a theme we explore in more detail in our final section.

THINKING CRITICALLY ABOUT LANGUAGE

What is it about our language that makes it feel so personal and so much a part of us? How is it that our language actually changes so seamlessly as we hear and adopt new words and expressions?

How Does Language Relate to Social Power and Inequality?

Anthropological linguists established long ago that language use influences the cultural context and social relationships of its speakers. But in recent years, they have become especially attuned to issues of power and inequality in language use, specifically how language can become an instrument of control and domination. We explore these issues here by introducing the concept of language ideology.

Language Ideology

- **Language ideology.** Widespread assumptions that people make about the relative sophistication and status of particular dialects and languages.

The concept of **language ideology** refers to the ideologies people have about the superiority of one dialect or language and the inferiority of others. A language ideology links language use with identity, morality, and aesthetics. It shapes our image of who we are as individuals, as members of social groups, and as participants in social institutions (Woolard 1998). Like all ideologies, language ideologies are deeply felt beliefs that are considered truths. In turn, these truths are reflected in social relationships, as one group's unquestioned beliefs about the superiority of its language justifies the power of one group or class of people over others (Spitulnik 1998:154). In the accompanying "Thinking Like an Anthropologist" box, we explore how the use of mock Spanish by Anglo-Americans in the United States reflects and reinforces the impression of social inferiority of Latinos.

Gendered Language Styles

In our daily interactions, men and women often experience miscommunication as Josh and Linda did in the vignette at the beginning of this chapter. Typically, each speaker feels that she or he has expressed things correctly and that the other speaker is at fault. When a man feels that his way of speaking is better, and the woman's is wrong, a language ideology about gendered use of language has come into play.

Despite what your high school English teachers may have told you, there is no "proper" way to speak English or any other language. From the anthropological perspective of language ideology, there are only more and less privileged versions of language use. This is to say, language use either legitimates an individual or group as "normal" or even "upstanding" or defines that individual or group as socially inferior. Consider, for example, the findings of a classic study in sociolinguistics that explores how gendered expectations of how women speak English in our culture can reflect and reinforce the idea that women are inferior to men. In her research, Robin Lakoff described how "talking like a lady" involved the expectation that a woman's speech patterns should include such things as tag questions ("It's three o'clock, *isn't it*?"); intensifiers ("It's a *very* lovely hat!"); hedge ("I'm *pretty* sure"); or hesitation and the repetition of expressions, all of which can communicate uncertainty and were largely absent in expectations about men's speech (Lakoff 1975). Lakoff argued that the social effects of speaking in this way can marginalize women's voices in contexts like a courtroom or a workplace, where speaking in a way that implies uncertainty—even if the speaker is not intentionally expressing uncertainty—can undermine a woman's testimony (as in a court of law) or trustworthiness (as in a workplace). Such situations, she suggested, are used to justify elevating men to positions of authority over women.

Lakoff herself recognized that some men may communicate in female-preferential ways, and not all women use the patterns just described, since language ideologies are not hard and fast for every speaker. Indeed, more recent research of email communications between men and women (Thomson, Murachver, and Green 2001) suggests that men and women can actually be quite flexible in their use of gendered language styles, changing these depending on who they are talking to. As a result, men may use female-preferential language when interacting with a woman, and vice versa, further suggesting that language ideologies do not always exercise total control over how people speak.

Language and Social Status

As we saw with gendered language, language ideologies are closely tied to the creation of social difference. They are also closely tied to the creation and maintenance of social status. Let us see how this works in a particular society by considering language and social status among the Javanese, for whom language use reflects and reinforces a highly stratified and unequal society.

The people of the Indonesian island of Java are among the most status conscious people on earth. In any social setting one person has a higher social position, while the other is lower. Politeness—and through it, social position—is expressed in Javanese in nearly every sentence. Nearly every word takes on a different form in each of

Thinking Like an Anthropologist

Exploring Relationships of Power and Status in Local American Dialects

ANTHROPOLOGISTS BEGIN THEIR research by asking questions. In this box, we want you to learn how to ask questions as an anthropological researcher. Part One describes a situation and follows up with questions we would ask. Part Two asks you to do the same thing with a different situation.

PART ONE: MOCK SPANISH IN THE AMERICAN SOUTHWEST

Anthropological linguist Jane Hill (1993, 1998), who lives and teaches in Arizona, noticed that White Anglo residents of southwestern states, who were monolingual speakers of English, incorporated a large number of Spanish words and phrases in their everyday speech. Hill notes that these borrowings are not just random uses of Spanish or Spanish-like words in English, but they are often used in jokes or in contexts intended to be humorous. Usually such utterances are grammatically incorrect both in English and in Spanish. Nor would these sentences be acceptable in Spanglish dialects. Hill describes these utterances as "Mock Spanish."

Speakers and hearers can only get jokes in Mock Spanish if they already assume that Mexicans or Mexican Americans have traits that are viewed as negative in mainstream Anglo culture. Although Hill found that working-class whites used and understood some Mock Spanish jokes, she feels that the most productive use of Mock

Spanish was found among middle- and upper-income, college educated whites. The domain of Mock Spanish is instead to be found in the university seminar, in the board room, or the country club party. For Hill, Mock Spanish serves as a covert form of racism in which the jokes or utterances implicitly disparage Latinos, simultaneously identifying the speaker and hearers as members of different social classes. To many listeners these jokes may not seem overtly racist, and in any event, they can be dismissed as merely evidence that the speaker had lived around Spanish-speaking people, or that it was just a joke.

Examples of Mock Spanish include such phrases as "no problemo," "cojones" used as a euphemism for the vulgar English "balls," the use of "mucho" to mean "much," "numero uno" and its Mock Spanish variants like "numero ten-o," as well as more seeming benign words "amigo," and "Comprende?" Hill suggests that it is the seemingly innocuous nature of these Mock Spanish forms that creates a powerful racist distinction between the superior Anglo-speaker and the inferior Mexican American.

What questions does this raise for anthropological researchers?

1. How does language use serve to create or at least reinforce social distinctions?

2. What is it about Spanglish that makes its speakers seem neither mainstream American nor mainstream Mexican, Cuban, Salvadoran, etc.?

Examples of Mock Spanish. "Hasta la vista" is a common expression used in a mocking way (left). On the right is another type of Mock Spanish, in this case by Hispanicizing an English word ("cheap") that doesn't exist in Spanish. In these examples Mock Spanish marks Hispanic Americans, their culture, and their language as inferior.

3. What is it about the use of Mock Spanish that allows White Anglos who are monolingual in English to feel superior to their Spanish-speaking neighbors?

PART TWO: LANGUAGE USE ON YOUR CAMPUS

On your campus, students and faculty most likely use colloquial forms of English, most likely words and phrases that you and your friends use that your parents and surrounding community members would likely not understand. What kinds of questions could you pose about how this colloquial dialect draws boundaries between different groups of people, or enhances and builds on distinctions between social groups, social classes, ethnicities, and the like?

three different registers (varieties or levels of speech used by people of a certain social status or social class): *Ngoko* (informal speech), *Madya* (intermediary register), and *Karya* (polite speech). Throughout Java, every sentence marks the speaker's social status in relation to his or her listener, both by choice of vocabulary and by the pronoun used to refer to the listener. Most verbs and many nouns have at least three different forms representing the lower, intermediate, and polite registers. Younger people use the more polite words with their elders, and peasants or other low status people use the more polite forms to nobles. But elders and nobles usually respond with informal word forms. In Java, the vocabulary used in any conversation differs for speaker and hearer.

As the linguist Robbins Burling (1971) noted, poorer and low-status people may only know the lowest and crudest register of Javanese, while higher status people are conversant with a much wider range of registers. Using these registers, with their different choices of words, helps Javanese sort out a wide variety of social positions beneath theirs (see Table 4.2).

Note that Javanese registers differ from the distinctive vocabulary of occupational or youth dialects in America, which tend to be unfamiliar to speakers of mainstream English. In these American dialects, distinctive words indicate common membership in a group, occupation, or cultural movement. For example, in the hip-hop youth subculture, speakers use a shared vocabulary—words like "crib" ('place of residence') and "fly" ('cool')—to build solidarity within the group in opposition to mainstream American culture. By contrast, the Javanese words used by each speaker and hearer will be different and mark their relative social positions in society.

TABLE 4.2	THE THREE BASIC REGISTERS OF JAVANESE THAT MARK SOCIAL STATUS						
	Are	you	going	to eat	rice	and	cassava	now?
3 (high)	menap	sampéjan	bade	neḍa	sekul	kalijan	kaspé	samenika
2 (middle)	napa	sampéjan	adjeng	neḍa	sekul	lan	kaspé	saniki
1 (low)	apa	kowe	arep	mangan	sega	lan	kaspé	saiki

Note: All three registers are Javanese, but the vocabulary changes depending on a person's social class. Elites use the highest register with higher ranking people. They use the second register with one another, and the lowest register with servants. Servants use the highest register with high-status people but the lowest register within their families. The point is that the vocabulary and pronunciation mark one's social status with respect to the person they are speaking to. Unlike English, there is no neutral register; a speaker must mark social position.
Source: Robbins Burling (1970:82–87).

Doing Fieldwork

Untangling Language Ideologies in Contemporary Egypt

IN RECENT YEARS the Middle East has taken on an important role in American business and diplomacy, but few American businessmen or diplomats have a firm grasp of Arabic, the most important language in this region. Each of the dozen or so Arab countries has its own vernacular, or locally distinct, form of Arabic that is the mother tongue of its citizens. These forms of Arabic vary widely from Morocco to the Persian Gulf, and most people from other Arab countries have difficulty understanding the vernaculars of other Arab countries.

Each of these Arab states has chosen Classical Arabic—the language of the Quran—as its official language. Most Arabs feel that Classical Arabic is more sophisticated and appropriate for official business than any of the local versions of Arabic. But nobody has spoken Classical Arabic as his or her mother tongue for a thousand years. What people learn to speak from childhood is a vernacular Arabic.

For the anthropologist concerned with language ideologies, this situation raises questions about how language use is linked to political power in a region that is so important in international affairs and the world's economy. To address some of these concerns and to offer policy-makers and others insight into the relationship between language and patterns of dominance and politics in Arab countries, linguistic anthropologist Niloofar Haeri (1997, 2003) has studied the use of language in Cairo, Egypt, the largest and most cosmopolitan Arab city. During 19 months of fieldwork she interviewed dozens of native speakers from a diverse set of social classes. These informants ranged from those with no schooling to physicians, diplomats, professionals, and bureaucrats.

She found that nearly all of the educated Cairo elite had studied at private schools where the medium of instruction was a foreign language such as English, French, or Italian. Nearly all of these people had studied Classical Arabic only a few hours a week, and nearly all felt they had very weak skills in the official language. Most had good command of colloquial Egyptian Arabic, which gave them credibility in the national arena. But nearly all of these professionals had succeeded because of their command of a foreign language, which has much higher caché than the vernacular.

Haeri observed a very different pattern among the middle class, who took midlevel jobs as clerks and secretaries in government or business. These middle-class people had good command over Classical Arabic, which they had studied in national schools. Unlike the elites, the middle class used Classical Arabic as their road to success in work; often it was their ability to write the official language that landed them their jobs. Ironically, Haeri found that nearly all of the high-ranking bureaucrats and professionals succeeded because they relied heavily on their secretaries and aides for drafting any formal written documents, which were necessarily written in Classical Arabic.

Thus, contrary to the pattern in Europe and America, where command of the official language helps elites remain elite, in Egypt it is command of a foreign language that serves this role. One implication of Haeri's research is that if one wishes to succeed in an Arab country, knowledge of Classical Arabic may not be sufficient. In such cases, however, familiarity with the county's vernacular form of Arabic may be helpful, since this is the language of the financial and political elite.

Questions for Reflection

1. Why would Classical Arabic, a language nobody speaks, seem a better choice as an official language than one of the vernacular forms of Arabic?

2. What significance should we give to the fact that all Arab countries have chosen Classical Arabic as their official language? How does this choice of a common official language help create or reinforce a pan-Arab identity?

3. Why do Egyptian elites not bother to learn Classical Arabic? What does this say about the relative importance of the official language in Egypt as compared with other languages?

Secretaries Working in an Office in Cairo.

Language and the Legacy of Colonialism

In places like sub-Sarahan Africa, nineteenth-century European colonial powers introduced their own language as the official language, because they viewed indigenous languages as socially inferior to their European languages. When these countries acquired independence, many of these languages became one of several national languages. As a way of building a national identity, many newly independent nations have had to make decisions about which language or languages among its many vernaculars to select as its official language. In Zambia, for example, which gained independence from Great Britain in 1964, the government recognized seven of the most important of its 73 local languages, plus English, as national languages, since nearly everyone in Zambia knows one or another of these languages. In theory each is equal to the others, but in practice they are not, as listening to Zambian radio broadcasts reveals (Spitulnik 1998).

Although all eight Zambian languages were given air time, English dominated the airwaves, both in the number of hours per week and in having a more sophisticated and cosmopolitan content. Certain of the more widely spoken indigenous local languages also got more air time than minority languages. Over the past decades, broadcasters have presented to their ethnically diverse listening public what they feel are appropriate topics in each of the different languages, such as themes related to subsistence farming for certain language groups considered less sophisticated, and themes related to business and politics for others deemed linguistically superior. These broadcasting decisions have shaped how the public evaluates each indigenous language, presenting some as more sophisticated than others, but all as less sophisticated than English. In this case, broadcasts not only become models of language hierarchy in Zambia, but they also reinforce these views of different languages and the ethnicities associated with them.

The broader point about language ideologies that comes across in each of our examples is that language can be used to exclude or marginalize some people in workplaces and social programs. In "Doing Fieldwork: Untangling Language Ideologies in Contemporary Egypt," we consider the practical implications for anthropologists concerned about the implications this situation has for democracy and social justice.

THINKING CRITICALLY ABOUT LANGUAGE

Students often feel they will never be able to participate in the professional lives of their advisors because their advisors and other professors seem to speak a language that many students do not understand. Of course, they are speaking English, but they use many complex words that few students know. How does language in this situation become a tool of control and power over students?

Conclusion

The capacity for language is one of the central features that distinguish humans from other animals. Whatever the particular language being spoken, human languages are universally structured and rule-bound, as descriptive linguistics demonstrates, and they change in fairly uniform ways, as historical linguistics tells us. But to end there—with the idea that language is something that all humans have access to and use in the same ways—misses the crucial fact that sociocultural context and norms shape language use and that the use of language has important impacts on everyday social relationships. To separate language from culture leads to an impoverished understanding of *both* language and culture.

This point, of course, is one that Sapir and Whorf made many decades ago when they advanced the idea that particular languages guide ways of thinking and acting. We can see a more updated illustration of the relationship between culture and language—and perhaps a more recognizable one to all of us—in the vignette that opens this chapter, in the different ways that Josh and Linda communicate with each other. Their particular miscommunication is not the result of a universal human situation in which women and men cannot understand each other, but the product of a particular culture that expects girls and women to speak in some ways, and boys and men in others. On its own, this insight is interesting and reveals something about how our culture socializes us to communicate in certain ways.

But we should not forget the social consequences of language use, especially when certain ways of talking and expression imply the correctness or superiority of one group, gender, or social class, and the incorrectness or inferiority of another. The broader point here is that language has great power to shape not just our meanings and comprehension of the world but our experiences as social beings as well.

KEY TERMS

Reviewing the Chapter

Chapter Section	What We Know	To Be Resolved
Where Does Language Come From?	Animals do not have language, but some primates have a rudimentary ability to use signs, which is a necessary but not sufficient condition for language to develop.	Although most linguistic anthropologists accept both genetic and non-genetic models, the relative importance of these models remains unclear, and we currently have no unified models that draw on both.
How Does Language Actually Work?	Language is systematic, but most descriptive linguistic models are static and do not express the dynamic nature of language.	By and large, linguistic anthropologists have not found historical models of language change to fully explain why particular sound systems or grammatical patterns have taken the forms they do.
Do People Speaking Different Languages Experience Reality Differently?	Meaning is conveyed through symbols, but particular meanings have their roots in the social processes of daily life.	Although the structures of language vary widely in different languages, anthropologists and linguists have never reached a consensus about whether the structure of language actually shapes the ways we perceive the world.
How Can Languages Be So Dynamic and Stable at the Same Time?	Languages are always changing in small ways as sound systems gradually change and as new words are borrowed from other languages or created anew.	Although anthropologists recognize that languages change as cultures change, there is no current consensus about how these changes emerge.
How Does Language Relate to Social Power and Inequality?	A language ideology links language use with identity, morality, and aesthetics. It helps us imagine the very notion of who we are as individuals, as members of social groups and categories, and as participants in social institutions.	Despite efforts of governments to control their populations by shaping language policies, creole and pidgin forms of languages are far more important than was thought to be the case half a century ago. Yet anthropologists do not have a full understanding of the precise conditions under which a creole or pidgin language can assert its own importance.

Readings

William A. Foley's book *Anthropological Linguistics: An Introduction* (Malden, MA: Blackwell, 1997) provides a general introduction to linguistic anthropology. A more classical approach to the basics of language and its relation to culture was published by Edward Sapir in his 1921 book, *Language: An Introduction to the Study of Speech* (New York: Dover Publications, 2004). Unlike most linguistics texts, because Sapir was an anthropologist as well as a talented linguist, this early work is much more sensitive to cultural factors than the books written by most linguists.

• • • • • • • • • • • • • • • • • • • •

Linguistic anthropologist George Lakoff has published a number of books dealing with the symbols and metaphors that provide meaning in the words and phrases we hear. One of his classic studies is *Metaphors We Live By* (Chicago: University of Chicago Press, 1980). Several of his more recent publications pursue these ideas more fully.

• • • • • • • • • • • • • • • • • • • •

A key survey of how governments create and promote nationalism through language policy can be found in Bambi B. Shieffelin, Katharyn

A. Woolard, and Paul V. Kroskrity's book *Language Ideologies: Practice and Theory* (New York: Oxford University Press, 1998).

• • • • • • • • • • • • • • • • • • • •

One of the best introductions to gendered speech can be found in Deborah Tannen's *Talking from 9 to 5: How Women's and Men's Conversational Styles Affect Who Gets Hired, Who Gets Credit, and What Gets Done at Work* (New York: W. Morrow, 1994).

• • • • • • • • • • • • • • • • • • • •

Ethnography

Studying Culture

YOU DON'T HAVE to travel far and wide to study culture, and anthropologists have long studied the social lives of people in their home countries and communities. One such study was conducted during the 1980s and 1990s in East Harlem, a neighborhood in New York City, by American anthropologist Phillippe Bourgois. East Harlem is largely cut off from mainstream America, if not from the very city in which it exists. Its residents, who are largely Puerto Rican, are isolated because of language and educational barriers, unemployment, poverty, and ethnic segregation. Bourgois, who had previously conducted research on Costa Rican banana plantations, lived in East Harlem to study how people experience this marginalization and how they make a living in an economy that does not seem to want them.

Bourgois soon discovered that the neighborhood was saturated with crack cocaine, which came to the market in the 1980s. Over the next four years he spent hundreds of nights on the street and in crack houses, building trust with dealers and addicts. He tape-recorded and carefully transcribed many of his conversations with them, recorded their life histories, and visited with their families. He attended parties, family reunions, Thanksgiving dinners, and New Year's Eve celebrations. He heard many stories about being excluded from mainstream jobs in midtown Manhattan, and thus falling back on crack as dealers

Life in Spanish Harlem. Ethnographic methods have been used to study the lives of many distinct societies and communities, including the lives of residents of East Harlem, New York City, such as those pictured here, who are playing dominoes on the sidewalk.

or users. He documented the many self-destructive behaviors that so often accompany addictions. At times, the research was dangerous for Bourgois.

Bourgois found that census records and other official documents gave an inaccurate picture about wealth and poverty in East Harlem, because they did not account for the thriving underground drug economy. Studies by other social scientists were no more helpful, because they typically confirmed the stereotype that poor people in the inner city deserve their poverty, in large part because of their drug-related illegal activities. But during his conversations and interviews, Bourgois was stunned to learn that people who run crack houses work much like any business owner pursuing the American dream. As he wrote, "They are aggressively pursuing careers as private entrepreneurs, they take risks, work hard, and pray for good luck. They are the ultimate rugged individualists braving an unpredictable frontier where fortune, fame and destruction are all just around the corner" (Bourgois 1995:326).

Such insights came to Bourgois only because as an anthropological fieldworker, he participated in the lives of the crack dealers over a long period. Never a crack user himself, Bourgois got to know dealers and users personally in ways that almost no one who sets American policy about poverty and drug use does. And he came away with an appreciation of the community's all-too-American aspirations, even when mainstream opportunities and employment had been denied to them.

For those of you accustomed to stereotypes of anthropologists working in far-flung corners of the world with non-Western people, Bourgois's research might seem surprising. In fact, until the 1970s, the typical path of the anthropologist was to seek an out-of-the-way place where cultural differences appear most pronounced. Today, cultural anthropologists are as likely to be doing fieldwork among advertising executives, factory workers, transnational migrants—or, in this case, urban drug dealers and users—as we are to live in villages in remote settings. Bourgois's five years of research involved a longer stay in "the field" than most anthropologists spend. But the distinctive methods he used were essentially the same as those of any cultural anthropologist fifty years ago who was studying people's lives in small villages in Africa, Latin America, or Oceania. At the heart of all of these research projects is a central goal, to learn about people who often live in different cultural circumstances from our own. It leads us to ask: *How do anthropologists learn about other ways of life?* Embedded within this question are several more specific questions around which this chapter is organized:

What is so distinctive about anthropological fieldwork?

Aside from participant observation and interviews, do anthropologists use other methods?

What special ethical dilemmas do ethnographers face?

Ethnographic research methods have been around for the better part of a century because they have proven to be an effective tool for helping anthropologists gather the kind of information they require to understand social complexities and the inner lives and beliefs of people. We begin by examining what traditional ethnographic research is all about.

What Is So Distinctive About Anthropological Fieldwork?

In popular culture, an aura of mystery has long surrounded the question of what cultural anthropologists do. In part, this is because anthropology is generally less well known than other social scientific fields such as economics, psychology, or political science. But even anthropologists can sometimes find it difficult to define precisely how they collect and produce data. Graduate students preparing to do their research still hear, with an awkward humor, advice such as the American anthropologist Cora Dubois (1903–1991) heard before she went off to study the Wintu Indians of Northern California to "carry a stick as the dogs are vicious," or to "take plenty of pencils and paper" for taking notes (Goldschmidt 2000). Anthropologists are well advised to take the right equipment along to do fieldwork in a foreign culture. But to focus on equipment only suggests that the persons giving the advice do not know enough about the culture to offer anything more significant. Cultural anthropologists do research by building personal relationships over a long period, and it is difficult to tell a student how to do that with people who are culturally different. Thus, although cultural anthropology shares some methods with other social sciences, it also has distinctive and effective methodological tools.

In general, social scientists gather data or information about human beings and the social, economic, political, and psychological worlds they inhabit. They use methods that are either quantitative (e.g., statistical) or qualitative (e.g., descriptive and interpretive). Although most anthropologists use quantitative data, cultural anthropology is the most qualitative of the social sciences. Aside from this fact, two additional features distinguish anthropology from these other disciplines. One is that anthropologists are more holistic, traditionally studying all aspects of social life simultaneously, rather than limiting ourselves to a single dimension of people's lives, such as economic, political, psychological, or religious dimensions. The second is that researchers have found that long-term immersion and participation in a community (at least a year or more) as well as an open mind yield insights we would never achieve had we started with preconceived ideas about the relationships among social, economic, political, and religious institutions.

Fieldwork

We call this long-term immersion in a community **fieldwork**. It is *the* defining methodology of the discipline, to the point that an observer once said, "What blood was to the martyrs of the early Church, fieldwork is to anthropologists" (Haviland, Gordon, and Vivanco 2006). During fieldwork, anthropologists become involved in people's daily lives, observe and ask questions about what they are doing, and record those observations. Being involved in people's lives for a long period of time is critical to the method, generating insights we would not have if we simply visited the community

- **Fieldwork.** Long-term immersion in a community, normally involving firsthand research in a specific study community or research setting where people's behavior can be observed and the researcher can have conversations or interviews with members of the community.

Thinking Like an Anthropologist

Fieldwork in an American Mall

ANTHROPOLOGISTS BEGIN THEIR research by asking questions. In this box, we want you to learn how to ask questions as an anthropological researcher. Part One describes a situation and follows up with questions we would ask. Part Two asks you to do the same thing with a different situation.

PART ONE: OBSERVING THE USE OF SPACE IN THE AMERICAN SHOPPING MALL

We've all been to a shopping mall, but have you ever stopped to consider how people actually use malls? Anthropologist Paco Underhill (2005) has spent his career studying the American shopping mall and advising retail businesses on how to use space to sell products to the American consumer. From his observations it is clear that visiting a mall is a socially patterned experience, although visitors may not realize how their actions are being shaped by others.

Underhill begins his research on a mall, perhaps surprisingly, in the parking lot. There, he observes the possible entrances to the mall and the fact that, from the outside, the shopper can see little of what is inside. Landscaping is minimal, as is any other attraction that might keep the would-be shopper outside, and so they stream in to the building. The goal of the mall, Underhill infers, is to get people inside to begin spending money.

Once people enter, Underhill observes, they need time to slow down and adjust to the space of the mall, so shops are rarely placed at the entrance; instead, these spaces are rented to doctors, accounting firms, and other businesses whose customers require appointments. After leaving this "decompression area," visitors come to the excitement of the mall proper: shop after shop with brightly colored merchandise pouring out into the hallways to attract attention.

Unlike the halls of a hospital or office building, those at the mall are extra wide. Underhill seeks to understand what goes on in these spaces that requires room for two broad lanes of foot traffic, often separated by stalls, carts, and tables filled with merchandise. While most people pop in and out of the many shops, others stop to look at the shop windows and the merchandise that lies on tables or hangs along the way. Still others—particularly during cold or stormy weather—power-walk alone or in pairs, getting their exercise.

Underhill pays close attention to the people in these hallways and what they do, taking careful notes of his

▼ **Inside an American Shopping Mall.**

observations. He pays close attention to the ages and sexes of people there, if they walk by themselves or with others, who those others might be (children? middle aged?), and if these patterns change by day of the week and time of day. Entering the food court, Underhill observes the types of restaurants, the ways people interact with those restaurants, the kinds of shops near them, and how long people linger before returning to shopping. Underhill then turns his attention to the restrooms, observing where they are located, which is often hidden away in distant corners and corridors, intended not to affect the shopping experience negatively.

As Underhill wanders in and out of the large anchor stores, he makes other observations. Merchandise is piled up in the entryways, some on sale, some seasonal. He observes what grabs people's attention, getting them to slow down and pause. He observes how and where stores place different kinds of products, which influences how people move through the store, and what they are likely to see (and possibly purchase even though they did not come to buy that particular thing).

Underhill's research shows that by looking at the architecture and observing closely the flow of shoppers through it we can sense what kinds of behavior the store managers had hoped to encourage, what they might have hoped to discourage, and how people actually make use of these semi-public spaces.

The experience of walking through the mall with Paco Underhill raises important questions for anthropological researchers, such as:

1. What might an anthropologist learn about the use of space from watching and observing what people do as opposed to interviewing them?
2. How can an anthropologist check the inferences he or she might make about the goals of store managers?

PART TWO: OBSERVING THE USE OF SPACE IN THE COLLEGE LIBRARY

Consider the library at your college or university. Most libraries have a variety of tables, desks, and study carrels. The stacks may be open, or students may need to show their ID cards to get inside. Audiovisual materials may be accessible to everyone in the student body, or professors may put some videos or DVDs on reserve. Modeling your work on Paco Underhill's, what kinds of questions would you pose to orient your observations of a college library?

a few hours a day, to administer a survey or questionnaire, or conduct a brief interview. As virtually every anthropologist will tell you, people may say one thing but then go and do something completely different. Sticking around helps us put what people say in context.

Fieldwork also helps us achieve one of our discipline's central goals, which Clifford Geertz (1973) once described as deciphering "the informal logic of everyday life," which is to say, trying to gain access to the implicit assumptions people make and the tacit rules they live by. Most Americans, for example, assume that drug dealers have a different set of values from their own, but Bourgois's long-term involvement with them suggests otherwise, even if their style of talking and their way of interacting with one another differ from those other Americans. By participating directly in community activities, we can observe what is important to the community, what they discuss among themselves, and how these matters intertwine with social institutions. This approach can yield rich insights about people's behaviors, actions, and ideas that people themselves might not notice or understand, as we explore in "Thinking Like an Anthropologist: Fieldwork in an American Mall."

Participant Observation: "Disciplined Hanging Out"

Participant observation is a key element of anthropological fieldwork. It is a systematic research strategy that is, in some respects, a matter of just hanging out. Many of you probably spend a lot of your free time hanging out with friends, without a specific plan or agenda, taking things as they come. For anthropologists, participant

• **Participant observation.** The standard research method used by sociocultural anthropologists that requires the researcher to live in the community he or she is studying to observe and participate in day-to-day activities.

Figure 5.1   Fieldwork and Traditional Dress. Anthropologist Margaret Mead wearing clothing typical of young Samoan women during her fieldwork in 1925–1926. This was not what she ordinarily wore, but something that she did to help build rapport.

- **Informant.** Any person an anthropologist gets data from in the study community, especially people interviewed or who provide information about what he or she has observed or heard.

- **Intersubjectivity.** The realization that knowledge about other people emerges out of relationships and perceptions individuals have with each other.

Figure 5.2   Cultural Anthropologist Robert L. Welsch. Wearing appropriate clothing, whether traditional or contemporary, helps build rapport with the community by allowing the anthropologist to demonstrate that he or she respects traditional customs and culture. One of the authors wears traditional Mandarese clothing including a silk sarong, batik shirt, and cap to attend a wedding reception near Majene on the island of Sulawesi in Indonesia.

observation is similarly unstructured. But one of the things that distinguishes anthropologists from college students is that anthropologists record much of what transpires while we are hanging out. We are also in a very different social position than we are normally accustomed to, and we must work hard to build rapport and friendships in a community where we have no friends (Figure 5.1). Establishing rapport requires a lot of discipline, as well as acceptance of local customs and practices, however peculiar, unfamiliar, or uncomfortable.

Participant observation makes the anthropologist a professional stranger. Participant observation has been compared to living on the edge of a razor (Delaney 1988); it is neither pure observation nor pure participation. As observers, anthropologists cannot remove themselves from the action (Figure 5.2). Yet giving into participation too easily prevents one from noticing subtleties of behavior and learning to intuit their significance. Too much participation is sometimes referred to as "going native," because the researcher stops being an engaged observer and starts to become a member of the community, dressing like them and even assuming some of their mannerisms.

Some years ago, anthropologist Johannes Fabian (1971) suggested that any notion that an anthropologist in the field is collecting "objective" data misses the point of the discipline. The data anthropologists bring home in their field notebooks were not out there to be gathered like blackberries; they were created by the relationships between an anthropologist and his or her **informants**, the people from whom he or she gathers information. The anthropologist observes things in the field setting, observes them a second or third time, and later inquires about them, gradually pulling together an enriched sense of what has been observed. Both the anthropologist and his or her informants have been actively creating this synthesis that becomes field data. For Fabian such observations and understanding are neither objective nor subjective, but the product of **intersubjectivity**, which means that knowledge about other people emerges out of relationships individuals have with each other.

Interviews: Asking and Listening

Participant observation gives us many insights about how social life in another society is organized, but it is up to us as anthropologists to find systematic evidence for our

perceptions. So another key goal of fieldwork is to flesh out our insights and gain new perspectives from **interviews**, or systematic conversations with informants, to collect data.

There are many kinds of interview, ranging from highly structured, formal ones that follow a set script, to unstructured, casual conversations. Anthropologists use structured interviews to elicit specific kinds of information, such as terms for biological species, details about the proceedings of a village court case, or the meaning of symbols and behavior in rituals (Figure 5.3). Anthropologists might also conduct systematic surveys, such as a village census or a survey of attitudes about an event, using carefully structured interviews so that all informants are asked the same questions and their responses are thus comparable. In an **open-ended interview**, or unstructured interview, informants discuss a topic and in the process make connections with other issues. Open-ended questions usually encourage informants to discuss things the anthropologist wants to hear about, or that informants find especially meaningful. Table 5.1 outlines the various contexts for asking and listening that are possible.

Knowing What to Ask

How do anthropologists know what questions to ask? From the 1870s until the 1950s, many British and American anthropologists relied on a volume published by the British Association for the Advancement of Science (1874) entitled *Notes and Queries in Anthropology* as a guide for what questions field researchers should use (Figure 5.4). This little book was updated and reissued every decade or so. *Notes and Queries* was initially created to help colonial-era travelers, missionaries, and administrators gather data to send back to Europe for **armchair anthropologists**, people who never went to the field but relied on others for their ethnographic data (Urry 1972).

With the professionalization of anthropology in the early 1900s, however, such guides became less relevant since anthropologists themselves were collecting data. Today, anthropologists no longer have a prescribed set of good questions to ask. Usually we go with certain questions we want answered—drawn from theories and background literature, from an advisor or other colleague, or from simple curiosity. These questions change during fieldwork as we experience and confront new cultural

- **Interview.** Any systematic conversation with an informant to collect field research data, ranging from a highly structured set of questions to the most open-ended ones.

- **Open-ended interview.** Any conversation with an informant in which the researcher allows the informant to take the conversation to related topics that the informant rather than the researcher feels are important.

- **Armchair anthropologist.** An anthropologist who relies on the reports and accounts of others rather than original field research.

Figure 5.3 Interviews in the Field. Interviews take place in all kinds of settings, from the most formal and sterile, such as in an office, to settings like this one, in which coauthor Luis Vivanco (left, holding plants) interviews an environmental activist in rural Costa Rica who is showing him an agricultural demonstration project.

TABLE 5.1	CHARACTERISTICS AND NATURE OF DIFFERENT KINDS OF INTERVIEWS		
Kinds of Interviews	Nature of Interview	Clear Focus for Interview	Kind of Fieldnotes
Interview schedule	Questions are read from a printed script exactly as written to all subjects of the interview. Often used for survey data collection. Researcher has decided ahead of time what is important to ask.	Yes	Interview schedule form
Formal interview Structured interview	Interviewer has a clear goal for the interview and writes down the informant's answers or tape-records the interview. Often used for survey data collection. Researcher has decided ahead of time what is important to ask.	Yes	Transcript of answers or of questions and answers.
Informal interview Open-ended interview	Interviewer has a focus for the interview but may not have a clear goal of what information he or she wants from the interview. While the researcher may begin with certain questions, he or she develops new questions as the interview proceeds. The interviewer may have a notebook present, but most of the time is spent in conversation rather than writing notes.	Sometimes	Preliminary notes that outline the discussion. Later writes up a full description of context and content of discussion.
Conversation Casual conversation	Most people would not recognize this as an interview, notebooks are not present, and it would appear that the anthropologist and informants are simply having an ordinary conversation. The anthropologist might ask certain questions, but the flow is much more conversational. Afterward the anthropologist takes a few jot notes so he or she can remember the topics discussed or goes somewhere private to write up more detailed raw notes that can be fleshed out later.	No	Headnotes and jot notes. Later writes up a full description of context and content of discussion. Notes often include topics to follow up on in future interviews or conversations.
Hanging out	At the heart of anthropology is participant observation, and participating by just hanging out with members of the community in sex- and age-appropriate ways is the best way to participate. Hanging out may involve helping with fishing, cooking, planting, or weeding in rural or traditional societies, or playing in some pickup sport like basketball or soccer. It could involve hanging out in a local coffee shop, diner, or bar, or in a work environment such as an office, water cooler, lunch room, or cafeteria. Anthropologists may occasionally make jot notes, but most of the time they record details in their notes later, when people are not around.	No	Headnotes and jot notes. Later writes up a full description of context and content of discussion. Notes often include topics to follow up on in future interviews or conversations.

realities. A solid education prepares us to ask insightful questions. As the expression goes, "99% of a good answer is a good question." For example, anthropologists find that questions posed to elicit a "yes" or "no" answer are almost always unproductive. Our goal is, quite simply, to get people talking, not to get them to provide simple, short answers. The more they talk, the more people tell us about the cultural logic they use in their daily lives that they may not even be conscious of.

Taking Fieldnotes

- **Fieldnotes.** Any information that the anthropologist writes down or transcribes during fieldwork.

Much of the time in the field is spent scribbling **fieldnotes**, information that the anthropologist writes down or transcribes. Unlike historians, who go into archives and search

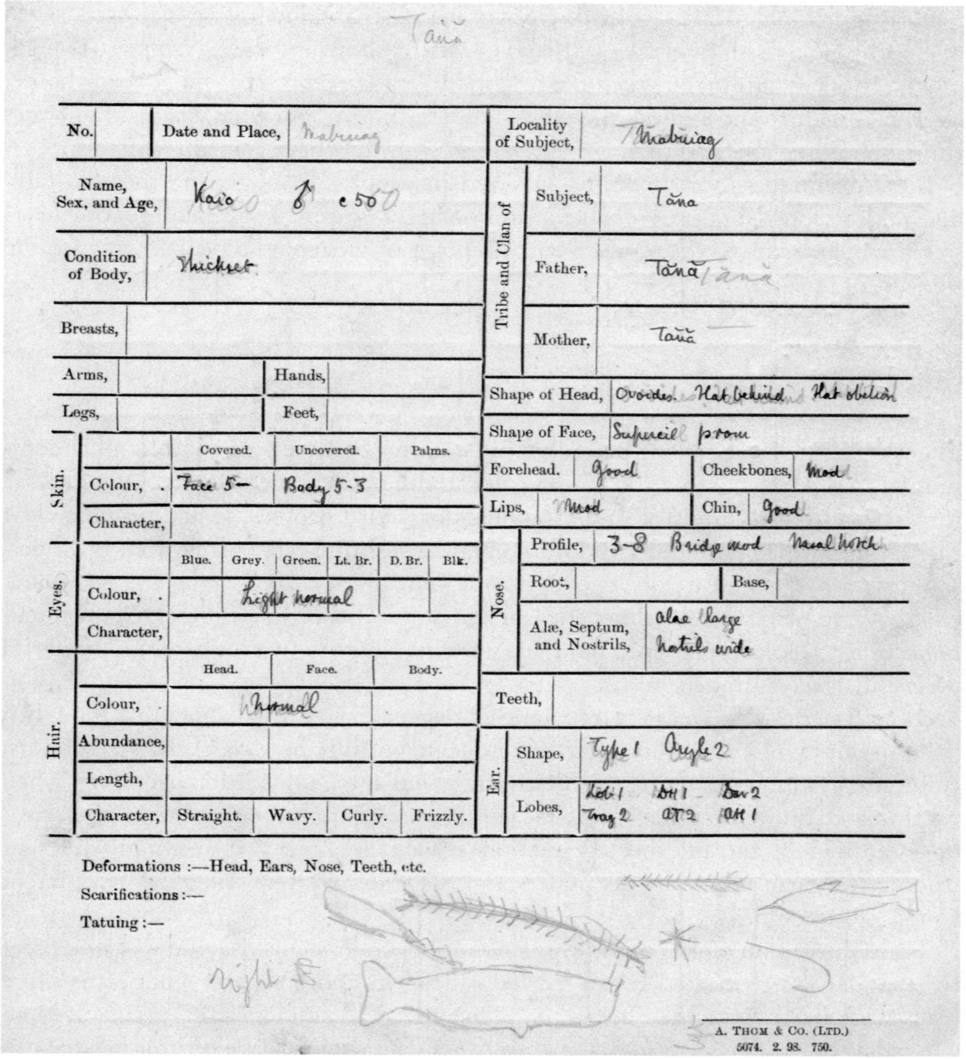

Tana

No.	Date and Place, Mabuiag	Locality of Subject,	Mabuiag

Name, Sex, and Age, Kaio ♂ c 50

Condition of Body, Thickset

Breasts,

Arms, Hands,

Legs, Feet,

Tribe and Clan of — Subject, Tana; Father, Tana; Mother, Tana

Shape of Head, Ovoides. Flat behind Flat obelion

Shape of Face, Superciliary prom

Forehead. Good — Cheekbones, Mod

Lips, Mod — Chin, Good

Skin. — Covered. Uncovered. Palms. — Colour, Face 5— Body 5-3 — Character,

Nose. — Profile, 3-8 Bridge mod Nasal notch — Root, Base, — Alæ, Septum, and Nostrils, alae large nostrils wide

Eyes. — Blue. Grey. Green. Lt. Br. D. Br. Blk. — Colour, Light normal — Character,

Hair. — Head. Face. Body. — Colour, Normal — Abundance, — Length, — Character, Straight. Wavy. Curly. Frizzly.

Teeth,

Ear. — Shape, Type 1 Angle 2 — Lobes,

Deformations :—Head, Ears, Nose, Teeth, etc.

Scarifications :—

Tatuing :—

A. Thom & Co. (Ltd.) 5074. 2. 98. 750.

Figure 5.4 A Guide for Ethnographic Research. Shown here is an anthropological Record card used in the 1898 Cambridge Expedition to the Torres Straits. Anthropological guides such as this asked for anthropometric measurements, general assessments about how a particular community did things, or what they believed. Of course, today we recognize that people in every society have a variety of opinions and ideas about almost everything.

out documents written by others, we primarily make our own (Lederman 1990). Some of this happens in the ebb and flow of everyday life, as we jot down notes in conversation with others, or when a festival, ritual, or some other activity is taking place. Usually these scribbles are only shorthand notes made in small, unobtrusive notebooks. Unlike your professors, most people in the world are not comfortable when somebody opens a notebook and starts writing notes. But with time and plenty of explanation about what we plan to do with the information, people become accustomed to it. Anthropologists have an ethical commitment to share our reasons for doing research with our informants openly, and explaining our goals often helps build rapport with informants.

In fact, many anthropologists only bring out a notebook when they are conducting structured interviews and surveys. We also write down many details after the fact, or after we have had a chance to reflect more deeply on something. It is simply too difficult to capture everything taking place or being said in the moment. Every day—early in the morning, during the evening, or whenever we tear ourselves away from the flow of everyday life—we write up the details about what we did during the day, who we spoke with, what struck us as odd or puzzling, and the context in which we heard about certain details. A lot of us keep diaries where we express personal frustrations and keep what anthropologist Simon Ottenberg referred to as **headnotes**, which are the mental notes we make while in the field (Sanjek 1990:93–95), all of which can prove to be useful later.

- **Headnotes.** The mental notes an anthropologist makes while in the field, which may or may not end up in formal fieldnotes or journals.

Writing fieldnotes takes great discipline. It is also absolutely essential because, as one anthropologist has written, "if it's not written down, it didn't happen" (Sanjek 1990). Think about it. You are in the field for at least a year. Once you get back home, settle in, organize and analyze all your fieldnotes, think about what you want to write, think about it again, and then write it, *several years* may have passed.

These techniques—of becoming involved in people's lives, getting them to talk, and taking notes about it—enable anthropologists to pursue a major goal of fieldwork, which is to see the world from the point of view of the people who are the subjects of research.

Seeing the World From "The Native's Point of View"

The decision to live for a long period of time—a year or more—in an unfamiliar community in order to observe and record cultural differences emerged after 1914 and led to profoundly new kinds of understandings of native peoples. It had become clear that living in the community did not guarantee cultural relativism—that is, understanding a native culture on its own terms—nor did it promise that the researcher could overcome his or her ethnocentrism and cultural bias. But it increased the likelihood that the anthropologist could get some sense of the world in terms that local people themselves understood.

Of course, nobody ever gets into another person's mind or has the same thoughts. Even in our own community, we rarely understand fully how classmates, neighbors, colleagues, roommates, or teammates think about some topic. Moreover, even when we think we understand how someone thinks, a similar but new situation often produces a different and unexpected reaction. If we talk about two seemingly different reactions, we can nearly always understand that the two were triggered by different conditions or contexts.

As an illustration of this point, think about how politicians respond to scandals. If the scandal is perpetrated by an elected official in another party politicians often react with harsh criticism, but when someone in their own party is involved in a scandal they rarely seem to make a fuss. It is tempting to write off this behavior as paradoxical or hypocritical, but a more accurate view is that their moral outrage is situational, conditioned by the context of who is involved, how well they know them, and perhaps how much impact the incident might have on a party's outcome in the next election.

Now, put yourself in an anthropologist's shoes. As outsiders we might initially think that our informants can be similarly paradoxical. But after some time and effort to see things in terms of local context, things people say and do begin to make sense and we generally feel we are beginning to see the world from an emic (or insider's) perspective. Anthropologist Bronislaw Malinowski referred to this perspective as "the native's point of view" and asserted that it lay at the heart of the ethnographic method he claimed to have invented when he famously pitched his tent on the beach near the houses of Trobriand Islanders (Figure 5.5), as we discuss in "Classic Contributions: Bronislaw Malinowski on the Ethnographic Method."

Avoiding Cultural "Tunnel Vision"

Most people assume that their own way of doing things is inherently better than everyone else's. No matter how much we think we understand the world better than

Figure 5.5   "The Native's Point of View." The ethnographer's tent on the beach of Nu'agasi, Trobriand Islands.

anyone else, we can never understand others' reactions until we see the world from their point of view. We face a similar problem when we first interact with people from another culture. Their reactions to nearly everything seem foreign and strange, and our own cultural "tunnel vision"—unquestioned tacit meanings and perspectives drawn from our own culture that prevent us from seeing and thinking in terms of another culture's tacit meanings and perspectives—can lead to ethnocentrism. But as we get to know them and see more of their culture, their reactions seem less puzzling and unexpected, even reasonable. We do not usually start thinking the way they do, and we will often continue to feel that their way of doing things is peculiar or even wrong, but we will gradually come to accept their reactions as making sense in terms of the local culture. Until we can make sense of the local cultural logic, we will inevitably use tunnel vision to understand another culture, complete with all its ethnocentric biases.

Of course, people in other societies are ethnocentric as well. They feel that their way of doing things, their moral, ethical, and legal codes, and their ways of thinking about the world are correct, while everyone else's are flawed. In other words, they have their own tunnel vision. When anthropologists attempt to see the world "from the native's point of view" we are not claiming that the other culture's way of thinking is necessarily better than our own. But by understanding the native's point of view we are attempting to unravel the cultural logic within which unthinkable actions in our own society become commonplace in another culture.

For example, when Philippe Bourgois (1995) studied the lives of crack dealers in East Harlem, he recognized that addiction had taken a toll on the lives of many of his informants. He did not use crack himself, and he does not believe that using crack is a good thing. Nevertheless, to understand the lives of his informants, he had to suspend his tunnel vision—that is, the perspectives and judgments that so many Americans make about those who sell and use crack cocaine. He was not condoning the harm crack dealers did to their bodies, their lives, and their families. But as an anthropologist he was trying to understand their lives, and the only way to do that was to suspend his own view of crack dealers to get at the cultural logic of their beliefs and actions. Participant observation was key to getting at that logic, but it was not the only method that he used. In the next section, we explore some of the other methods anthropologists use.

Classic Contributions

Bronislaw Malinowski on the Ethnographic Method

THE POLISH-BORN ANTHROPOLOGIST Bronislaw Malinowski (1884–1942) was the leading figure in British social anthropology between the First and Second World Wars. Before Malinowski, nearly all anthropological fieldwork consisted of regional surveys, and researchers stayed for short periods in any one community, rarely learning the local language. Malinowski turned this all on its head. Between 1914 and 1917, he spent some eighteen months in Omarakana in the Trobriand Islands of Papua New Guinea, in the process realizing that the best way to understand native life was to live with native people, rather than with the white men—missionaries, traders, and colonial officers—who knew so little about native life. In this excerpt from Malinowski's (1922) best-known book, *Argonauts of the Western Pacific*, he outlines his basic approach to fieldwork, later celebrated as the "ethnographic method":

Conducting Participant Observation. Bronislaw Malinowski sits on a canoe chewing betel nuts with the white trader Billy Hancock and one of his Trobriand Islander informants, 1918.

Soon after I had established myself in Omarakana, I began to take part, in a way, in the village life, to look forward to the important or festive events, to take personal interest in the gossip and the developments of the small village occurrences; to wake up every morning to a day, presenting itself to me more or less as it does to the native. I would get out from under my mosquito net, to find around me the village life beginning to stir, or the people well advanced in their working day according to the hour and also to the season, for they get up and begin their labours early or late, as work presses. As I went on my morning walk through the village, I could see intimate details of family life, of toilet, cooking, taking of meals; I could see the arrangements for the day's work, people starting on their errands, or groups of men and women busy at some manufacturing tasks. Quarrels, jokes, family scenes, events usually trivial, sometimes dramatic but always significant, formed the atmosphere of my daily life, as well as of theirs.

It must be remembered that as the natives saw me constantly every day, they ceased to be interested or alarmed, or made self-conscious by my presence, and I ceased to be a disturbing element in the tribal life which I was to study, altering it by my very approach, as always happens with a new-comer to every savage community. . . .

Also, over and over again, I committed breaches of etiquette, which the natives, familiar enough with me, were not slow in pointing out. I had to learn how to behave, and to a certain extent, I acquired "the feeling" for native good and bad manners. With this, and with the capacity of enjoying their company and sharing some of the games and amusements, I began to feel that I was indeed in touch with the natives, and this is certainly the preliminary condition of being able to carry on successful field work. (Malinowski 1922:7–8)

Questions for Reflection

1. Up to the time that Malinowski came to stay with them, few of the islanders had had more than a quick glimpse of a white man. What was it about Malinowski's way of living that led the islanders to begin to take Malinowski for granted and to pay little attention to him?

2. As newcomers to any community might do, Malinowski made many mistakes breaching or violating the local etiquette. How do you think he turned this situation to his advantage?

3. How did Malinowski go from simply pitching his tent next to the houses of the islanders to beginning to look at events from the "native's point of view"?

4. Do you think he understood the native's view completely, on every topic? Why or why not?

THINKING CRITICALLY ABOUT ETHNOGRAPHY

Just hanging out, interviewing, and taking fieldnotes are not enough to shake an anthropologist out of his or her own cultural tunnel vision. Why not? What are some other ways you can think of for an anthropologist to avoid cultural tunnel vision?

Aside from Participant Observation and Interviews, Do Anthropologists Use Other Methods?

Although participant observation and unstructured, open-ended interviews are the core research methods for cultural anthropologists, some projects require additional strategies to understand social complexity and the native's point of view. Some of the most important other methods include some we review here: the comparative method; the genealogical method; life history; ethnohistory; rapid appraisals; action research; anthropology at a distance; and analyzing secondary materials.

Comparative Method

Since the beginning of the discipline, anthropologists have used the **comparative method**, which involves systematic comparison of data from several societies. The first American anthropologist, Lewis Henry Morgan, for example, sent letters to people all over the world requesting lists of kinship terms in local languages. From these scattered reports he conducted a comparative study of kinship terminologies around the world, which he published as *Systems of Consanguinity and Affinity of the Human Family* (1871). Early anthropologists also used comparative data to establish models of how they believed the cultures of modern Europe had evolved from so-called primitive societies.

Comparative method is still relevant in anthropology. For example, anthropologists studying globalization use a version of the comparative method called multi-sited ethnography, which involves conducting participant observation research in many different social settings. Another kind of comparative research strategy is exhibited by the **Human Relations Area Files** (HRAF), which collects and finely indexes ethnographic accounts of several hundred societies from all parts of the world. Each paragraph has been subject-indexed for a wide variety of topics such as type of kinship system, trading practices, etc. This facilitates the ability of researchers to conduct statistical analyses about whether particular traits appear to be randomly associated or whether they are regularly found together in human cultures (Figure 5.6).

Genealogical Method

The **genealogical method** is an old method, developed by English anthropologist William H. R. Rivers in 1898 during the Cambridge Anthropological Expedition to the

- **Comparative method.** Any anthropological research that involves systematic comparison of several societies.

- **Human Relations Area Files (HRAF).** A comparative anthropological database that allows easy reference to coded information about several hundred cultural traits for more than 150 societies. The HRAF allows statistical analysis of the relationship between the presence of one trait and the occurrence of other traits.

- **Genealogical method.** A systematic methodology for recording kinship relations and how kin terms are used in different societies.

🌱 **Figure 5.6   Opening Page of HRAF's Website.**

Torres Straits, the islands between Australia and New Guinea (Figure 5.7). Rivers was studying visual perception among the Torres Straits Islanders and observed that they had an unusually high incidence of mild color blindness. To understand whether color blindness was genetically passed only in certain families or was a more generalized trait, Rivers needed to discern the relationships between the islanders.

The task was at first confusing, because Torres Straits islanders' kinship terminology used terms that Rivers interpreted as "mother," "brother," and "grandfather" for a much wider variety of people than just the relatives Euro-Americans refer to with these terms. Rivers developed a simple but systematic way of classifying all kin according to their relationship to his informants. This was essentially a system of notation—for example, using MBD to refer to the mother's brother's daughter—so that he could classify how terms were used. This methodology was widely used during the past century and became a key tool for understanding all sorts of relationships in non-industrial societies, where political, economic, and social institutions are based on kin relationships. It is increasingly used in hospitals today to understand genetic propensity for certain diseases, such as breast and ovarian cancers.

Life Histories

Understanding the **life histories** of informants has been an important tool for anthropologists in understanding past social institutions and how they have changed. During the 1920s, American anthropologists developed life histories as part of their fieldwork on Indian reservations, because the questions they were studying had to do with the American Indian societies before they had been profoundly transformed by contact with white American society. Anthropologists quickly recognized that by interviewing elders about their lives, they could get an understanding of how life was before contact.

Life histories reveal important aspects of social life, such as whether or not the society being studied has changed dramatically. As people develop, become adults, mature, and grow old,

🌱 **Figure 5.7   Members of the Cambridge Anthropological Expedition to the Torres Straits.** A. C. Haddon (standing left), W. H. R. Rivers (behind and to left), C. G. Seligman (top right), linguist Sidney Ray (to his left), and Charles Wilkin (standing front right). Each studied different aspects of Torres Straits life, but their conversations provided a holistic view of the culture.

people take on different roles in society and in its social institutions. By recording the life histories of a number of individuals, the anthropologist can build an image of how a person's age influences his or her role in the community and how typical social roles unfold over a lifetime.

Ethnohistory

Ethnohistory combines historical and ethnographic approaches to understand social and cultural change. The approach has been most important in studying non-literate communities, where few written historical documents exist, and those documents that do exist can be enhanced with archaeological data and ethnographic data such as life histories.

Ethnohistorians are also interested in how societies understand and recount the past. The concepts of history and how to tell it may differ from one society to another. Western history is linear, reflecting a view of time as marching through past and present straight toward the future. But Mayan societies, for example, view time as cyclical, which is to say repeating itself during regular periodic cycles, so their notion of history is different from that in the Western world. And as societies have changed over the past century, museum collections have become another source of data about historic conditions.

Rapid Appraisals

While typical anthropological studies involve an extended stay of a year or two in the field community, some field projects—including many applied anthropological studies—do not have time for twelve months of fieldwork and require answers to focused research questions within a month or two. In such cases, what is an anthropologist to do?

The only solution is to use a focused research strategy known as a **rapid appraisal**, sometimes jocularly referred to as parachute ethnography, because the researcher drops in for a few weeks to collect data. Such focused fieldwork requires a general knowledge of both the region and the topic under investigation. This kind of research requires that the anthropologist have considerable field experience to begin with, so she or he knows to focus on the features that distinguish the community under study from other similar ones (Figure 5.8).

- **Life history.** Any survey of an informant's life, including such topics as residence, occupation, marriage, family, and difficulties, usually collected to reveal patterns that cannot be observed today.

- **Ethnohistory.** The study of cultural change in societies and periods for which the community had no written histories or historical documents, usually relying heavily on oral history for data. Ethnohistory may also refer to a view of history from the native's point of view, which often differs from an outsider's view.

- **Rapid appraisal.** Short-term, focused ethnographic research typically lasting no more than a few weeks about narrow research questions or problems.

Figure 5.8 Short-Term Ethnography. Some projects have no time for long-term field research. Applied anthropologist Anthony Oliver-Smith investigates the impact of an earthquake in Peru.

Action Research

One criticism of all social scientific research—not just ethnography—is that research often benefits the researcher more than the subjects of research. Even if the researcher publishes a study at the end, it may advance his or her career more than it improves the conditions of the people being studied. This problem is especially acute for disenfranchised communities, where the gap between a community's needs and a researcher's own personal interests may be greatest. Policy makers have even used reports about a marginalized or underserved community to justify their limited efforts to help the community.

In the 1950s, prominent American anthropologist Sol Tax began advocating **action anthropology**, or research committed to making social change. He encouraged anthropologists to offer voluntary help to disenfranchised communities in airing their grievances and solving their collective problems. Tax believed in the importance of inserting one's political values into anthropological research and of treating research subjects as equal partners (Bennett 1996). Today, some anthropologists use a variant of action research methods by promoting the involvement of community members in formulating the research questions, collecting data, and analyzing the data. Often called **participatory action research**, it is based on the idea that poor people can and should do much of their own investigation, analysis, and planning (Chambers 1997). This approach not only aims to place the researcher and subjects on a more even plane; it also encourages researchers to share their methods so people can act to improve their own social, economic, and political conditions.

- **Action anthropology.** Research in which the goal of a researcher's involvement in a community is to help make social change.

- **Participatory action research.** A research method in which the research questions, data collection, and data analysis are defined through collaboration between the researcher and the subjects of research. A major goal is for the research subjects to develop the capacity to investigate and take action on their primary political, economic, or social problems.

Anthropology at a Distance

While "parachute anthropologists" may not have much time in a field setting, at other times anthropologists have no way of getting into the field at all. In times of war or political repression, for example, an anthropologist may be unable to conduct fieldwork, so the researcher conducts interviews with people who are from the community but who live elsewhere. Such studies can be thought of as anthropology at a distance.

One famous example is Ruth Benedict's research on Japanese society and culture during the Second World War, *Chrysanthemum and the Sword* (1946). Because the United States was at war with Japan, Benedict could not visit Japan, so she interviewed Japanese living in the United States and read widely in the published literature about that country and its customs. The result was a solid account of Japanese culture as it was in the 1890s when most of her Japanese informants had left Japan for California.

Analyzing Secondary Materials

Anthropologists also use both published and unpublished materials to learn about other people's lives. For example, we can learn a great deal from media clippings, government reports, scientific studies, institutional memos and correspondence, newsletters, and so on.

- **Secondary materials.** Any data that come from secondary sources such as a census, regional survey, historical report, other researchers, and the like that are not compiled by the field researcher.

These materials, called **secondary materials** because they are not primary, that is, original, sources (such as fieldnotes) from someone with direct personal knowledge of the people, provide yet another level of context for what we observe and learn in interviews. Like historians, though, anthropologists must read documents critically, paying attention to issues like who wrote them, what their author's motivations (thus biases) might have been, and any other factors that may have influenced the writing and distribution of the document.

Many anthropologists make provisions to donate their fieldnotes to an archive, such as the National Anthropological Archives at the Smithsonian Institution, and these notes can become a form of secondary materials (Figure 5.9). Margaret Mead,

Figure 5.9   The National Anthropological Archives. Besides fieldnotes written by anthropologists, the National Anthropological Archives hold many things collected by anthropologists in the past. Here, anthropologist Jake Homiak and Achu Kantule from the San Blas Kuna community of Panama (left) examine a map of the Kuna sacred landscape drawn around 1925 by Mr. Kantule's grandfather. It was collected by anthropologist John Peabody, who was a field ethnologist for the Smithsonian's Bureau of American Ethnology during the early 1900s.

for example, deposited most of her fieldnotes at the Library of Congress where many younger anthropologists have pored over her notes from Samoa, New Guinea, Bali, the Omaha, and other field sites (Figure 5.10). Some, however, feel that their fieldnotes could harm their informants and thus lodge those notes at an archive with the provision that they may not be consulted for twenty or fifty years. Still others say that once everything useful from their notes has been published, the notes should be destroyed to prevent harm to their informants or misunderstandings. But when fieldnotes exist, they nearly always contain data that can help us understand the culture of the people studied as well as the perspective of the earlier anthropologist.

For the most part anthropologists developed their methods in village settings in out-of-the-way places. These methods especially made sense when applied in non-Western

Figure 5.10   Preservation of Ethnographic Data. Anthropologists Margaret Mead and her husband Gregory Bateson typing up their fieldnotes in their mosquito room on the Sepik River of Papua New Guinea. Most of Mead's field notes are at the Library of Congress.

communities because they were effective at helping anthropologists gain critical insights into cultures radically different from their own. But as anthropologists have increasingly focused their research on communities in their own countries, they have been confronted by social groups whose cultures do not always differ so much from our own. Next we consider how anthropologists can study their own societies.

Special Issues Facing Anthropologists Studying Their Own Societies

An important reason anthropologists can understand other cultures is that when we go overseas or work with a community different from our own, the differences between our culture and theirs are immediately obvious. The effect of being a proverbial "fish out of water," struggling to make sense of seemingly senseless actions, heightens our sensitivities to the other society's culture. These sensitivities allow us to ask questions and eventually understand what seems obvious to members of the other community. What happens if we try to do this work within our own society?

When we understand the language and already have well-formed views about people's behavior and attitudes, being a "professional stranger" becomes more difficult. We are more likely to think we know what is going on and miss the local particularities that make people's actions sensible. A common technique to overcome these limitations is to study social conflicts, because when people are complaining or making allegations against others, their informal logic emerges quite clearly. For example, when anthropologist Laura Nader wanted to understand how American culture deals with relatively minor injustices—such as when a product breaks and consumers have a difficult time getting it fixed—she studied hundreds of consumer complaint letters received by her brother, the nationally prominent consumer rights activist Ralph Nader. In these letters, Laura Nader found people asserting their basic values about fairness and accountability.

It is important to remember as well that anthropology has always been an international discipline, conducted by people from many different countries outside of Europe and North America. In non-industrialized countries where poor and/or indigenous populations are common, the goals of anthropology have often been closely aligned with national development needs, such as researching the health conditions of rural and poor people to improve government programs. Some anthropologists have also taken an activist stance such as fighting for minority rights, a theme we explore in the "Anthropologist as Problem Solver: Alcida Rita Ramos and Indigenous Rights in Brazil."

It is important to recognize that indigenous people also practice anthropology themselves. As one Maya ethnolinguist has observed, indigenous peoples often conduct anthropological research as a way of speaking not just *about* their own societies, but *for* their societies: "Our dominators, by means of anthropological discourse, have reserved for themselves the almost exclusive right to speak for us. Only very recently have we begun to have access to this field of knowledge and to express our own world" (Alonzo Camal 1997:320). For example, the Pan-Maya ethnic movement in Guatemala, which is led by linguists (like the one just mentioned) who have studied anthropological theory and methods, aims to assert a research agenda and methods derived from and relevant to Maya social interactions and worldviews. This anthropology is often in direct tension with that of other national and foreign anthropologists, because one of its central goals is to support the political claims and self-determination of a particular indigenous group (Warren 1998).

Although issues like indigenous rights are highly political, for anthropologists what often underlies their involvement is the feeling of an ethical commitment to a certain group or issue. In our last section, we explore in more detail the ethical issues facing ethnographers.

Anthropologist as Problem Solver

Alcida Rita Ramos and Indigenous Rights in Brazil

BRAZILIAN ANTHROPOLOGIST ALCIDA Rita Ramos (1990, 2000) has been championing the rights of indigenous Brazilian Indians for many years. She argues that anthropology in Brazil has a different feel from anthropology as practiced by Americans or Europeans. When American or European anthropologists study Amazonian tribes, they often overlook the harshness of the Indians' contact with mainstream Brazilian society, spending many more pages

The Yanomami of Brazil. Yanomami Indians have suffered a great deal from the steady intrusion of more than 50,000 Brazilian peasants onto their traditional territory. Yanomami villagers (top); land encroachment by Brazilian peasants (bottom).

(continued)

Anthropologist as Problem Solver (continued)

on the traditional cultural practices than on the cultural contact that destroys so many indigenous communities today. As a result, she argues, American anthropologists tend to romanticize Indian culture. Brazilian anthropologists, in contrast, are deeply invested in writing about the intercultural strife that faces Amazonian tribes and are equally engaged in activist efforts to protect those tribes.

In recent decades, anthropologists like Ramos have needed to get permission from the Brazilian government to conduct research among indigenous peoples in the Amazon. The 1970s, when Ramos began research there, was a period when the authoritarian Brazilian regime had lightened its restrictions on domestic and foreign anthropologists, allowing them to go into indigenous areas. The government even allowed anthropologists to help them create development programs for these areas. Many Brazilian and foreign researchers helped, suggesting formation of a Yanomami Park that would shield the indigenous people from the onslaught of Brazilian developers who wanted to cut down rain forest and replace it with agriculture.

By the 1980s the government had decided to support industrial interests and clamped down on anthropological research in the Amazon. Then, in 1987, gold was discovered in the Yanomami region, an area that straddles the Brazil-Venezuela border. Some fifty thousand poor Brazilian prospectors and miners flocked to the area, disrupting the Yanomami economy, diet, and way of life. Prohibited from visiting the Yanomami, anthropologists could not see the effects of malnutrition caused by economic disruption. When images of the local tragedy were broadcast on TV, the situation became a national scandal, and the Brazilian government allowed anthropologists to assist.

Ramos was among those who insisted on getting involved. She gave numerous interviews to reporters, criticizing the government for inaction, pleading that the Brazilian peasants be removed from Yanomami territory. In this way, the Yanomami became a symbol of exotic peoples in danger of extinction at the hands of the Brazilian government. Ramos helped raise awareness in the international community, which also exerted pressure on the Brazilian government. Ramos also offered herself as an expert witness in legislative inquiries and court cases. While she has not been able to reverse the depredation of Yanomami lands and resources, she has been one of the loudest voices advocating the interests of this indigenous group on the national political stage. This approach to anthropological research and scholarship is highly valued at her university, and she believes her work as an activist anthropologist is no less important than her academic contributions.

Questions for Reflection

1. How might an activist anthropologist justify his or her approach to more theoretically minded anthropologists?

2. Given that she lacked government support for her views and had no direct power to control the situation among the Yanomami, what kinds of tools and strategies do you think Ramos might have used to influence conditions among the Yanomami?

3. If a researcher practices activist anthropology, should she or he abandon a teaching position at the university? Or are the two roles compatible? How?

THINKING CRITICALLY ABOUT ETHNOGRAPHY

Because the methods associated with action anthropology involve explicitly political commitments, some critics view them as less "objective" than some of the other methods described in this chapter. How would you respond to such a claim?

What Special Ethical Dilemmas Do Ethnographers Face?

When Philippe Bourgois decided to conduct research among crack dealers and users in East Harlem, he knowingly entered a situation in which he would witness illegal activities that could put him and his informants at great risk. One central ethical dilemma he confronted was ensuring that he did not betray the people who trusted him. His commitment to protecting their interests was tested every day, since the dealers and users he interviewed would be subject to arrest, prosecution, and prison if he uncovered their identities to authorities (Figure 5.11).

Unlike Bourgois, most anthropologists do not set out to study illegal activities, in part because of the risks both to themselves and to their informants. But all anthropologists, nevertheless, face certain common ethical dilemmas, no matter where they conduct their research, including the commitment to do no harm; considerations about to whom anthropologists are responsible; and who should control anthropology's findings. Here we explore how such issues play out in the specific context of ethnographic research.

Figure 5.11   Philippe Bourgois in East Harlem. His research with crack dealers required great sensitivity to the interests of his informants, most of whom were engaged from time to time in illegal activities. But his presence in a predominately Puerto Rican community led police to stop him frequently on the street because they assumed that the only reason a young white man would be in East Harlem was if he wanted to buy drugs.

Protecting Informant Identity

Social research can impact its subjects in powerful ways. For example, when living in a community, anthropologists often learn about matters that their informants would prefer to keep secret from other members of their community. Disclosure of these secrets may lead to social isolation of an informant, contention in the community, or even criminal investigation, as Bourgois knew all too well in East Harlem.

Any kind of objectionable behavior or medical conditions can cause difficulties or harm to informants and members of their family or community. For example, many communities around the world stigmatize HIV/AIDS, alcohol use, and certain sexual practices. In some settings, such as in countries with repressive governments, simply talking with a foreign researcher may harm an informant by casting doubt on his or her loyalty or patriotism.

In order to do no harm, anthropologists need to conceal the identities of everyone they have interviewed and, sometimes, conceal content. Typically we use pseudonyms for informants in published accounts, but we might also change details to further disguise an informant's identity. In her monograph on Samoa, for example, Margaret Mead (1928) changed details about characteristics of the adolescent girls she interviewed so nobody, even within the small community she studied, could identify them. She was especially concerned about informants who had admitted to having had premarital sex, which Mead knew some old Samoans would disapprove of.

The Limits of Anthropology's First Amendment Protections

In some respects anthropological fieldwork resembles the work of journalists in that we interview people to learn what is happening in a community. But anthropologists differ from journalists in several important ways. First, anthropologists tend to stay in a community gathering field data for a long time, and most anthropological data come directly from participant observation and interviews with informants.

In contrast, journalists often get their information secondhand and rarely stay on assignment for more than a few days or weeks.

Second, unlike reporters, in the United States anthropologists have no constitutional protections, such as the First Amendment, that allow them to conceal their informants or the sources of their data, as reporters have traditionally had. This means that while anthropologists are obligated to protect their informants, their fieldnotes, tape recordings, and photographs are nevertheless subject to a subpoena from a court should the police or some similar legal authority show cause that one should be issued.

Who Should Have Access to Fieldnotes?

Generally anthropologists have worked hard to protect their fieldnotes from scrutiny, because they inevitably contain information that was given in confidence. When anthropologists publish excerpts, they do so in short passages that give the flavor of the field experience or of an interview. The purpose is not to reveal an informant's secrets. Most of us feel that our fieldnotes are too personal and private for public dissemination, and if they are published on the Internet, they have nearly always been heavily edited.

In some communities, informants insist they should have access to and control of anthropological fieldnotes, since they helped create the data and should benefit from it (Brown 2003). This situation can create a dilemma for the anthropologist. On the one hand, many anthropologists share the sentiment that their research should benefit the community. On the other hand, they know that many communities are divided into factions and so raw data turned over to the community can benefit some and harm others. In situations where an anthropologist agrees to share fieldnotes, he or she negotiates with community members what will be shared.

Anthropology, Spying, and War

Anthropologists ask prying questions and seem to stick their noses into many aspects of people's lives, which has led many anthropologists to be accused of spying. Anthropological research does bear some similarities to the work of spies, since spying is often a kind of participant observation. When anthropologists conduct participant observation, however, we are ethically obligated to let our informants know from the outset that we are researchers. As researchers, our primary responsibility is to our informants, not government agencies or the military.

Yet many anthropologists have used their anthropological skills in service to their countries. For example, during World War II a number of anthropologists assisted with the war effort. Ruth Benedict studied Japanese culture from interviews with Japanese people living in the United States. Sir Edmond Leach assisted the British government in Burma, and E. E. Evans-Pritchard used his knowledge of the Sudan to mobilize the war effort against Germany there (Geertz 1988). Recently David Price (2002) has explored American anthropologist Gregory Bateson's wartime work with the OSS—the predecessor to the CIA. Bateson willingly used his anthropological insights about how to influence tribal peoples in order to ensure they sided with the Allies. In later years Bateson came to view his wartime service with regret because he had inadvertently assisted in the ill treatment, manipulation, and disempowerment of native peoples.

More recently, controversy has swirled around the use of anthropological researchers in the U.S. wars in Iraq and Afghanistan. After the events of 9/11, some anthropologists like Murray Wax and Felix Moos (2004) asserted that every American anthropologist has a moral obligation to help fight terrorism. A handful of anthropologists agreed and joined a new U.S. military program called the Human Terrain System, which places a non-combatant social scientist with combat units to aid officers in gathering information and working with local communities in Iraq and Afghanistan. This program was based on the reasonable assumption that the U.S. military had little knowledge or experience in these foreign cultures, and that military success required the insights provided by cross-cultural research (McFate 2005). But the American Anthropological Association—with the strong support of the vast majority of its members—condemned this program and its use of anthropology, recognizing the dilemma that Bateson's experience suggests, that anthropologists may end up helping the state act against minority groups by providing cultural insights that can harm or disadvantage them. The deeper obligation of anthropology, some have asserted, is to reveal to the public the oversimplified images of the enemy offered by politicians and the media (Price 2002). Others have worried that the military use of anthropology in one place can undermine the trust local communities elsewhere have about anthropological researchers, compromising the trust and rapport all anthropologists strive to create with their informants.

CRITICAL THINKING ABOUT ETHNOGRAPHY

In addition to disguising the identity of specific informants, anthropologists often disguise the identity of a village or community to protect it from scrutiny by outsiders. But individuals and sometimes whole communities decline that anonymity, and even strenuously object to efforts to be anonymous. How do you think an anthropologist should act in such a situation?

Conclusion

Anthropologists have used the ethnographic methods of participant observation and open-ended interviews for about a century and have developed systematic ways to get holistic data that are accessible to few other social scientists. Such methods were tested and developed as research strategies in remote, non-Western communities. But for the past thirty years anthropologists have shown that the same methods are effective for studying modern American culture, even the culture of urban drug dealers.

Participant observation provides rich insights because it emphasizes a holistic perspective, direct experience, long-term participation in people's lives, and responsiveness to unexpected events. And, as Bourgois has shown, the insights that come from living in a community and participating in its daily life often yield unexpected and startling findings. For example, many other social scientists have studied the problem of drug use in urban minority neighborhoods. Few, however, have recognized, as Bourgois did, that although most crack dealers in East Harlem lacked the benefits that many college students take for granted, they still pursue the American dream as active and energetic entrepreneurs.

Anthropologists use other methods besides participant observation and interviews, including the comparative method, the genealogical method, collecting life histories, ethnohistory, and rapid appraisal. Each of these research strategies is effective in tackling different research questions where participant observation may not be possible. And, as always, sociocultural anthropologists have an ethical responsibility to protect their informants from coming to any harm as a consequence of our research.

KEY TERMS

Action anthropology   p. 122

Armchair anthropologist
    p. 113

Comparative method   p. 119

Ethnohistory   p. 121

Fieldnotes   p. 114

Fieldwork   p. 109

Genealogical method   p. 119

Headnotes   p. 115

Human Relations
    Area Files (HRAF)
    p. 119

Informant   p. 112

Intersubjectivity   p. 112

Interview   p. 113

Life history   p. 121

Open-ended interview
    p. 113

Participant observation
    p. 111

Participatory action
    research   p. 122

Rapid appraisal   p. 121

Secondary materials
    p. 122

Reviewing the Chapter

Chapter Section	What We Know	To Be Resolved
What is so distinctive about anthropological fieldwork?	Anthropology's most important advances emerged once anthropologists abandoned their armchairs and took up fieldwork, living in the communities of the peoples they were studying. Participant observation is the anthropologist's key research method. It provides rich and nuanced insights about the cultural logic of social life and cultural practices because it offers the researcher a chance to see what people do, not just what they say.	Although nearly all anthropologists accept participant observation as a reliable research tool, scholars in other disciplines, particularly economics, political science, and psychology, do not accept participant observation as reliable because it seems to them subjective.
Aside from participant observation and interviews, do anthropologists use other methods?	The anthropologist in the field is not there simply collecting "objective" data. The data anthropologists bring home in their field notebooks were not out there to be gathered like blackberries; they were created by the interaction between an anthropologist and her or his informants.	No anthropologist is ever fully able to see the world from the native's point of view, and anthropologists disagree about how successful we are in this respect.

| What special ethical dilemmas do ethnographers face? | In the past few decades, anthropologists have increasingly attempted to establish new relationships with their study communities, helping these communities with locally defined goals or standing up for the rights of individuals in these communities.

Anthropologists' primary ethical obligation is to protect the interests of informants. | While anthropologists increasingly take on dual roles as academic and applied anthropologists, many disagree about whether we can do both simultaneously.

Efforts to protect our informants are now well established, but questions still persist as to who owns ethnographic data. |

Readings

There are many useful introductions to ethnographic methods, but Michael Agar's *The Professional Stranger: An Informal Introduction to Ethnography* (2nd edition, 1996, Academic Press) is a classic resource for the beginning student. There are also numerous historical analyses of the development of ethnographic methods, and among them George Stocking's edited volume *Observers Observed: Essays on Ethnographic Fieldwork* (1983, University of Wisconsin Press) is one of the most important.

• • • • • • • • • • • • • • • • • • • •

For a rich resource for exploring the intellectual and theoretical issues involved in the practice of writing and analyzing fieldnotes, see Roger Sanjek's *Fieldnotes: The Makings of Anthropology* (1990, Cornell University Press). A more practical guide to writing and analyzing fieldnotes is *Writing Ethnographic Fieldnotes,* by Robert Emerson, Rachel Fretz, and Linda Shaw (1995, University of Chicago Press).

• • • • • • • • • • • • • • • • • • • •

For a justification of anthropological involvement in the U.S. wars in Iraq and Afghanistan, see Montgomery McFate's 2005 article "The Military Utility of Understanding Adversary Culture" (*Joint Force Quarterly* 38:42–48). The author is one of the architects and largest proponents of the Human Terrain System program. Critical reactions against that program and the broader involvement of anthropologists in war are many, including David Price's 2011 book *Weaponizing Anthropology: Social Science in Service of the Militarized State* (AK/CounterPunch Books) and Roberto Gonzalez's *American Counterinsurgency: Human Science and the Human Terrain* (2009, Prickly Paradigm Press).

• • • • • • • • • • • • • • • • • • • •

Globalization and Culture

Understanding Global

Interconnections

IN THE EARLY 1980s, Walpiri (Wal-*peer*-ee) Aborigines living as hunter-gatherers in the remote Central Desert of Australia began watching movies and television in their temporary camps near cattle stations. By 1985, one observer wrote, "the glow of the cathode ray tube had replaced the glow of the campfire in many remote Aboriginal settlements . . . Of all the introduced Western technologies, only rifles and four-wheel-drive Toyotas had achieved such acceptance" (Michaels 1994:91). During the past century of contact with Europeans, the Walpiri had maintained their distinctive culture and language. Many observers began to worry, however, that the introduction of mass media would finally destroy their traditions.

But that was not what happened. The Walpiri turned this alien technology toward more familiar ends, by incorporating the genre of film and filmmaking into their own traditions of storytelling, and by imposing their own meanings on the videos they watch. In Walpiri settlements, viewing a video is a social event where people participate and collaborate in ways that are similar to how they view their traditional sand paintings or tell stories. If a movie like *Rambo*—that continues to circulate on DVD—fails to say who the main character's grandmother is, or who is taking care of his sister-in-law—meaningful kinship information for this hunting-gathering people—they debate the matter and fill in the missing content (Michaels 1994:92). Walpiri people view films in socially appropriate kin groups, on video players

Representing the Walpiri Landscape. Walpiri people of northern Australia have taken to watching—and producing—their own television programs. Their cinematic productions reflect particular social dynamics and cultural perspectives. (Image courtesy of PAW Media/Warlpiri Media Association)

133

that are collectively owned and shared according to traditional patterns. These practices help to reinforce rather than diminish their culture.

Walpiri also began making films to tell their traditional stories. Their films are disappointing to or misunderstood by Western audiences because of the slow and subtle way they unfold, taking their meaning from the Walpiris' own cultural style and aesthetic criteria. The camera pans slowly across a landscape, and the long, still shots seem empty of meaning to Westerners. But Walpiri examine these films closely for the important stories they are supposed to reveal, with the camera tracking locations where ancestors, spirits, or historical characters are believed to have traveled (Michaels 1994:93). Walpiri also pay close attention to what happens behind the scenes, because to them the authenticity of a film depends on whether the family that "owns" the story gave its permission to retell it and supervised its production. In short, the Walpiri use this global technology to express their own local traditions and worldviews, borrowing from the outside world what they want to maintain or even revitalize of their own.

The Walpiri fascination with television and film is not unique. Around the world, people living in even the most remote places now have television sets connected to video players or satellite dishes, on which they watch CNN International and movies from dozens of other countries. They also participate in a globalized world in other ways, by drinking Coca-Cola, wearing Western clothing, or migrating to and from distant lands. These international borrowings are happening everywhere, but does this mean that the world is losing its rich cultural diversity? Examples such as the Walpiri lead us to the question at the core of anthropologists' interest in globalization: *Are all the world's different cultures becoming the same because of globalization?* Embedded in this larger question are a number of problems, around which this chapter is organized:

Is the world really getting smaller?

Are there winners and losers in globalization?

Doesn't everyone want to be developed?

If the world is not becoming homogenized, what is it becoming?

What strategies can anthropologists use to study global

interconnections?

We aim to deepen your understanding of culture as a dynamic process by showing its importance for understanding contemporary global processes. For anthropologists, the cross-border connections we refer to as globalization are not simply a matter of cultural homogenization. It is a process that illustrates how people create and change their cultures because of their connections with others. Not everybody participates equally in these diverse kinds of global connections, which means we also have to consider power relationships and social inequality.

Is the World Really Getting Smaller?

Asian hip-hop in London. American retirement fund investments in a South Korean steel conglomerate. Indian "Bollywood" movies in Nigeria. Mexican migrants cooking Thai food in a North Carolina restaurant. Each of these situations confirms our sense that the world is getting smaller and cultural mixing is on the rise. This sense extends to anthropologists, who recognize that the people whose lives we study are often profoundly affected by global interconnections, migratory flows, and cultural mixing. During the past several decades, understanding how those processes of global interconnection affect culture has become an important issue for all anthropologists. For a discipline that has long tried to understand the differences and similarities between human groups and cultures, the idea that the world is getting smaller might suggest that the differences, in particular, are melting away. But is the world really getting smaller? To answer this question, we first need to understand what globalization is. Unfortunately, defining globalization is, as one scholar has observed, like eating soup with a fork (Nederveen Pieterse 2004). Why?

Defining Globalization

Defining globalization is a challenge for two reasons. First, different academic disciplines define globalization differently because they study different things. Economists focus on investment and the activity of markets, political scientists on international policies and interactions of nation-states, and sociologists on non-governmental organizations (NGOs) and other international social institutions. But there is a second problem. Is globalization a general *process* or a trend of growing worldwide interconnectedness? Is it a *system* of investment and trade? Or is it the *explicit goal* of particular governments or international trade bodies that promote free trade? Or is it, as some say, "globaloney," something that does not actually exist at all (Veseth 2005)?

Anthropologists define **globalization** as the contemporary widening scale of cross-cultural interactions owing to the rapid movement of money, people, goods, images, and ideas within nations and across national boundaries (Kearney 1995; Inda and Rosaldo 2002). But we also recognize that social, economic, and political interconnection and mixing are nothing new for humanity. Archaeological and historic records show that humans have always moved around, establishing contacts with members of other groups, and that sharing or exchanging things, individuals, and ideas are deeply rooted in human evolutionary history.

Early American anthropologists also recognized these facts. Franz Boas and his students Alfred Kroeber and Ralph Linton developed a theory of culture that emphasized the interconnectedness of societies. The Boasians thought of themselves as **diffusionists**, emphasizing that cultural characteristics result from either internal historical dynamism or a spread (diffusion) of cultural attributes from one society to another (Figure 6.1). Later, beginning in the 1950s, Marxist anthropologists like Eric Wolf argued against the isolation of societies, suggesting that non-Western societies could not be understood without reference to their place within a global capitalist system, which reaches across international boundaries with abandon. And yet, until the 1980s, such themes of interconnectedness rarely interested most cultural anthropologists.

Mainstream anthropology was locally focused, based on research in face-to-face village settings. But as encounters among societies have seemed to increase, anthropologists have realized that paying attention only to local settings gives an incomplete understanding of people's lives. It also gives an incomplete understanding of the causes of cultural differences. As we will see, differences often emerge not in spite of, but *because of,* interconnections.

- **Globalization.** The widening scale of cross-cultural interactions caused by the rapid movement of money, people, goods, images, and ideas within nations and across national boundaries.

- **Diffusionists.** Early twentieth-century Boasian anthropologists who held that cultural characteristics result from either internal historical dynamism or a spread (diffusion) of cultural attributes from other societies.

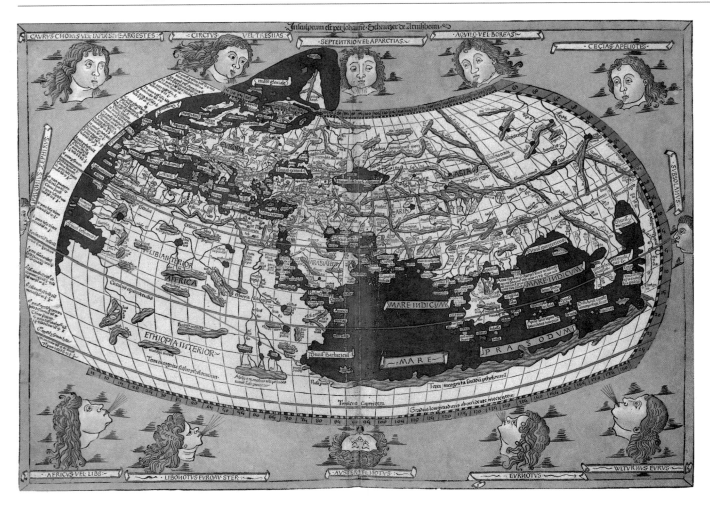

⚘ Figure 6.1   A Global Ecumene. The Greeks referred to an ecumene as the inhabited earth, as this map shows. Much later, anthropologist Alfred Kroeber (1876–1960) used the term to describe a region of persistent cultural interaction. The term became current again in the 1980s and 1990s as anthropologists adopted it to describe interactions across the whole globe.

- **Transnational.** Relationships that extend beyond nation-state boundaries without assuming they cover the whole world.

The World We Live In

How do anthropologists characterize the world in which we live today? Several factors stand out, including the scale of human interconnections and a growing awareness of these interconnections (Nederveen Pieterse 2004). But even if we acknowledge the intense interconnections, anthropologists know that these changes hardly mean everybody is participating equally in the same globalizing processes. Further, the word "globalization," unfortunately, tends to make us think of the entire globe, exaggerating the scale and expanse of financial and social interconnections, which, while great, are typically more limited and often more subtle than the word implies. Indeed some anthropologists prefer the term **transnational** to describe the circulation of goods and people instead of the word "global" because *transnational* imagines relationships that extend beyond nations without assuming they cover the whole world (Basch, Schiller, and Blanc 1993). Nevertheless, it is useful to think of globalization as indicating persistent interactions across widening scales of social activity in areas such as communication, migration, and finances.

Communication

At the heart of globalization are rapid increases in the scale and amount of communication. With cell phones, the Internet, and email possible in most parts of the world it is clear that the scale of contact has made a quantum leap forward over the past generation. Such rapid and much more frequent communication means that people

Figure 6.2 Bollywood in Africa. "Bollywood" movies—musicals produced in India, which has the largest film industry in the world—have become popular in countries like South Africa (pictured here) and Nigeria because of recent increases in the global distribution of media.

in very remote places can be in contact with people almost anywhere on the globe (Figure 6.2). Never before has this capability been possible.

But access to these innovations is extremely limited for some, while readily accessible for the wealthier and better educated. In sub-Saharan Africa (excluding South Africa), for example, only one in 5,000 people has computer access. As a result, some observers—to highlight real inequalities of access—prefer to talk about the globalization of communication in terms of wealth and poverty.

Migration

Another key feature of the changing scale of globalization is the mobility of people. Whether **migrants** (who leave their homes to work for a time in other regions or countries), or **immigrants** (who leave their countries with no expectation of ever returning), or **refugees** (who migrate because of political oppression or war, usually with legal permission to stay), or **exiles** (who are expelled by the authorities of their home countries) (Shorris 1992), people are on the move. These movements of people bring larger numbers of people in contact with one another, offering many possibilities for inter-cultural contact (Figure 6.3).

Finance

In the modern era, financial globalization involving the reduction or elimination of tariffs to promote trade across borders began in the 1870s. Although the two World Wars disrupted those processes, the past sixty years have seen their re-emergence. In recent decades, finance and the rapid movement of money across national boundaries have allowed corporations to move factories from one country to another. A generation ago, U.S. factories moved their operations to Mexico and China, but now many of these same factories have been shuttered and relocated to Honduras or Vietnam because of rising hourly labor costs in Mexico and China.

Under these conditions of globalized capital, many transnational corporations have accumulated vast amounts of capital assets. A number of these corporations now exceed entire governments in terms of their economic size and power. For example, if Wal-Mart, the world's largest retailer, were its own economy, it would rank 24th in the world, just ahead of Norway (D. S. White 2010). Because powerful corporate interests often influence the policies of governments, some see in this situation a movement of power away from nation-states (Korten 1995). But this economic growth and trade are also highly

- **Migrants.** People who leave their homes to work for a time in other regions or countries.

- **Immigrants.** People who enter a foreign country with no expectation of ever returning to their home country.

- **Refugees.** People who migrate because of political oppression or war, usually with legal permission to stay in a different country.

- **Exiles.** People who are expelled by the authorities of their home countries.

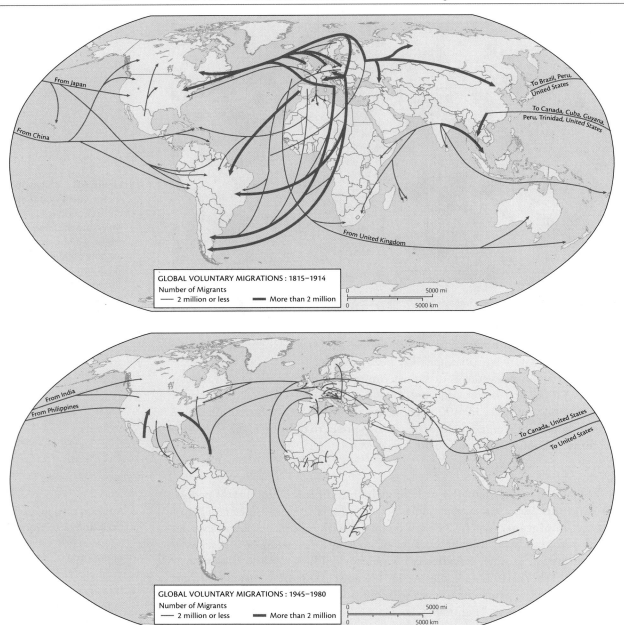

Figure 6.3 Global Voluntary Migrations. These two maps show dramatic differences in the directions of migratory flows. In Map A, during the European colonial era, Europeans were motivated to migrate out of Europe because of opportunities in the colonies. In Map B, after the Second World War, decolonization saw a reversal in the flow, as non-Europeans and non-U.S. Americans began moving into Europe and the United States in search of new opportunities for themselves.

uneven. "Thinking Like an Anthropologist: Understanding Global Integration Through Commodities" explores the complexities of contemporary economic globalization.

Such analyses raise a key question: who benefits from and who pays the costs of global interconnections? We turn to this important question in the next section.

THINKING CRITICALLY ABOUT GLOBALIZATION

Beyond communications, migration, and finance, what are some other culturally significant forces that make the world feel smaller?

Thinking Like an Anthropologist
Understanding Global Integration Through Commodities

ANTHROPOLOGISTS BEGIN THEIR research by asking questions. In this box, we want you to learn how to ask questions as an anthropological researcher. Part One describes a situation and follows up with questions we would ask. Part Two asks you to do the same thing with a different situation.

PART ONE: THE T-SHIRT ON YOUR BACK

Concepts like the "global economy," "economic integration," even "globalization" are pretty abstract. Here, by considering the common t-shirt as a concrete example of economic globalization, we can show how your life is touched by seemingly remote and abstract economic, social, and political forces.

The things people want and need depend increasingly on the interactions of numerous institutions, individuals, states, and corporations, many of which are anonymous to consumers. To understand these diffuse interconnections, it is helpful to start with some concrete object that circulates through and between these actors. All objects, such as the humble t-shirt, have biographies, that is, particular life stories and trajectories. You can learn a lot about a social system—especially global integration—by following the trajectory of an object such as a t-shirt: who produced it, how it has changed hands, who has used it, and the uses to which it has been put (Kopytoff 1986).

Let us begin in the most obvious place, the tag on your shirt. Chances are pretty good it says "Made in . . ." followed by an exotic port of call: Bangladesh, Malawi, Malaysia, the Philippines, Mexico, or maybe China, which since 1993, has been the world's largest producer and exporter of clothing, about 30% of the world's share. Each year, Americans buy about one billion garments from China, four for every U.S. citizen (Rivoli 2005:70).

To tell the full story of your t-shirt, though, we have to get the whole picture, which includes understanding the commodity chain, or the linked elements—labor, capital, raw materials, etc.—that contribute to the manufacture of a commodity. Quite likely, your t-shirt originated in a cotton field around Lubbock, Texas. The United States has dominated cotton production markets for two hundred years, thanks largely to our ability to be highly productive while controlling labor costs. Before the Civil War, slavery kept these costs down; now tractors and government subsidies do. Raw cotton is then shipped off, quite likely to China, to be made into thread and cloth, and then, if it does not stay in China to be manufactured into a t-shirt, off to somewhere else to be cut and sewn. The manufacturer then sells the t-shirts to a distributor, probably a U.S.-based business, and maybe after changing hands once again for silk-screening, it goes to the retailer who sells it to you.

But let's keep going. After you wear it for a while, you might toss it in the trash, where it finds its way into a landfill. Or you might donate it to a used clothing charity bin like those in the parking lots of grocery stores. The charities themselves rarely handle your clothing, but in turn sell it to companies like Ragtex or the Savers Company that sort, bundle, and ship used clothing in 1,000-pound bales to sub-Saharan Africa (the largest market for used U.S. clothing), Eastern Europe, East Asia, or Latin America. A whole new series of wholesalers and small traders take over from there (Veseth 2005).

In these markets, people rarely think of these clothes as cast-offs or rags, as we do. For example, in Zambia, in southern Africa, where anthropologist Karen Tranberg Hansen (2000) has researched the local trade in used clothing, people call this clothing *salaula*, which means opportunity, choice, and new chances. At the same time, the arrival of so many inexpensive t-shirts and other clothing to places like Zambia undermines the local clothing industry, which cannot compete with the low cost of these used items.

What questions does this situation raise for anthropological researchers?

Chinese Garment Factory. T-shirts are made in this garment factory.

(continued)

Thinking Like an Anthropologist (continued)

1. Is the supply chain that created your t-shirt really "global"?
2. Why are t-shirt production facilities no longer in the United States, and why are these facilities in the places they are?
3. Who are the different actors who participate in the processes of manufacturing and using your t-shirt, both before and after you own it?
4. What are the consequences for local people of this global trade in t-shirts?

PART TWO: CHILEAN TABLE GRAPES

In industrialized economies like the United States and Europe, food is also quite likely to come from far away. This is especially true of fruits and vegetables, which can be harvested in the Southern Hemisphere during the American winter when domestic fruits and vegetables are not available in the United States. Chile is a major exporter of fruits to the United States and Europe, because its summer harvests coincide with the winter off-season in the Northern Hemisphere. If you wanted to understand global economic integration through table grapes such as those produced in Chile, what questions would you ask as an anthropological researcher?

Are There Winners and Losers in Global Integration?

In public debates, the most common way of framing globalization is in terms of winners and losers. Globalization's promoters focus on winners, arguing that greater economic integration brings unprecedented prosperity to millions. They cite evidence that the more open a country is to foreign trade, the more rapidly its economy grows (Norberg 2006). Critics focus on losers, invoking images of sweatshops and poverty. They offer evidence that the gap between rich countries and poor countries has actually widened, and we are witness to a "globalization of poverty" (Chossudovsky 1997). In the face of such arguments, it is useful to remember that both sides are often discussing fairly narrow economic policy questions such as free trade, labor conditions, outsourcing of jobs, and so on. These are important issues, but they tend to ignore the cultural nuances of global interconnections, which include inequality, confrontation, domination, accommodation, and resistance.

World Systems Theory

- **World systems theory.** The theory that capitalism has expanded on the basis of unequal exchange throughout the world, creating a global market and global division of labor, dividing the world between a dominant "core" and a dependent "periphery."

For several decades, **world systems theory** has provided the social sciences with an important theoretical lens for understanding global inequality. Developed by economic historians André Gunder Frank and Immanuel Wallerstein, world systems theory rejects the idea that global interconnections are anything new, identifying the late fifteenth century as the beginning of a new capitalist world order that connected different parts of the world in new ways. During this historical period, according to world systems theory, European powers created a global capitalist market based on unequal exchange between a "core" (the home countries) and a "periphery" (the rest of the world). The core (the winners) develops its economy by exploiting the periphery (the losers), whose role is to provide labor and raw materials for the core's consumption. The result is the periphery's long-term poverty, underdevelopment, and dependency on the core. Anthropologists have made a particular contribution to world system

Classic Contributions

Eric Wolf, Culture, and the World System

ERIC WOLF (1923–1999) studied issues of power, inequality, and politics in Latin America. He insisted that the discipline needed to discover history, "a history that could account for the ways in which the social system of the modern world came into being" (1984:ix). He was interested in the origin and workings of peasant and tribal societies, but always in relation to the powerful governmental and business interests that so often kept peasants poor. In this selection, Wolf presents why anthropologists should view most societies over the past five hundred years as societies linked to other societies, often with tragic consequences for some of the people involved.

 Eric Wolf.

While some anthropologists thus narrow their focus to the ever more intensive study of the single case, others hope to turn anthropology into a science by embarking on the statistical cross-cultural comparisons . . . drawn from large samples of ethnographically known cases. . . .

What, however, if we take cognizance of processes that transcend separable cases, moving through and beyond them and transforming them as they proceed? Such processes were, for example, the North American fur trade and the trade in native American and African slaves. What of the localized Algonkin-speaking patrilineages, for example, which in the course of the fur trade moved into large nonkin villages and became known as the ethnographic Ojibwa? What of the Chipewayans, some of whose bands gave up hunting to become fur trappers, or "carriers," while others continued to hunt for game as "caribou eaters," with people continuously changing from caribou eating to carrying and back? . . . What moreover, of Africa, where the slave trade created an unlimited demand for slaves, and where quite unrelated populations met that demand by severing people from their kin groups through warfare, kidnapping, pawning, or judicial procedures, in order to have slaves to sell to the Europeans? In all such cases, to attempt to specify separate cultural wholes and distinct boundaries would create a false sample. These cases exemplify spatially and temporally shifting relationships, prompted in all instances by the effects of European expansion. If we consider, furthermore, that this expansion has for nearly 500 years affected case after case, then the search for a world sample of distinct cases is illusory. (Wolf 1984:17–18)

Questions for Reflection

1. What happened about five hundred years ago that changed the relations between societies from what they had been?

2. Why does Wolf feel that most societies have been in touch with Europeans and others outside of their society for the past five hundred years?

3. How would you explain to your younger brother or sister why Wolf feels anthropologists should not view societies as bounded and unconnected to other societies?

studies by posing a question other social scientists had not: How has this world system affected the native peoples and cultural systems of the periphery?

In his influential book *Europe and the People Without History*, anthropologist Eric Wolf took on this question. Wolf argued that long-distance trade and cultural interaction were around long before the development of capitalism, but that the expansion of European colonialism and capitalism drew non-European people into a global market, in which, as producers of commodities, they were to serve the cause of capital accumulation as a subordinate working class (Wolf 1984:352–3). These processes disrupted, even destroyed, many societies (Bodley 1999).

But Wolf rejected the customary divisions we make between "West" and "non-West." He insisted that people in the periphery also have helped shape the world system because they have not responded passively to capitalist expansion. In fact, they have often resisted it. These are the common people usually ignored by the victorious elites when they wrote their histories. Wolf argued that we need to pay close attention to the peripheral people's active role in world history. As we explore in "Classic Contributions: Eric Wolf, Culture, and the World System," Wolf's argument not only challenged popular stereotypes of indigenous people as isolated and passive, but he also challenged anthropology's bias toward the local, that is, the traditional ethnographic focus on villages and other small groups.

Because world systems theory focused on the rise of capitalism as a global system, this perspective did not readily lend itself to ethnographic research of smaller communities and non-global economics. But the theory helped anthropologists better explain the historical emergence and contemporary persistence of uneven development patterns around the world and has been of critical interest to scholars of **postcolonialism**, the field that studies the cultural legacies of colonialism and imperialism. It has also helped anthropologists understand the linkages between local social relations (families, kin networks, communities) and other levels of political-economic activity, like the regional, national, and transnational.

- **Postcolonialism.** The field that studies the cultural legacies of colonialism and imperialism.

Resistance at the Periphery

As Wolf observed, expansion of the capitalist world system did meet resistance from the peripheral peoples affected. Anthropologists have devoted considerable attention to this resistance, finding examples that range from open rebellion and mass mobilizations to more subtle forms of protest and opposition.

Many forms of resistance may not be obvious to us. For example, in one factory in Malaysia, spirit possession episodes have erupted, disrupting work and production goals (Ong 1988). According to the factory women of Malaysia, the facility violated two basic moral boundaries: Close physical proximity of the sexes, and male managers' constant monitoring of female workers. Young female workers, who as Muslims are expected to be shy and deferential, believe these two factors force them to violate cultural taboos that define social and bodily boundaries between men and women. They also believe that the construction of modern factories displaces and angers local spirits, who then haunt the toilets. For the women, these three transgressions combine to provoke spirit possession, in which the women become violent and loud, disrupting work in the factory. Spirit possession episodes help the women regain a sense of control over both their bodies and social relations in the factory (Ong 1988:34). Such resistance interests anthropologists because it shows how people interpret and challenge global processes through local cultural idioms and beliefs.

Globalization *and* Localization

- **Localization.** The creation and assertion of highly particular, often place-based, identities and communities.

Perhaps greater global integration also creates opportunities for local cultures to express themselves more vividly. This is a phenomenon that some anthropologists call **localization**, and it's the flip side, or side effect, of globalization. Localization is the creation and assertion of highly particular, often place-based, identities and communities (Friedman 1994). This is evidenced by the recent rise of autonomy movements among Hawaiian separatists and the Zapatistas in Mexico, movements that seek self-determination; nationalist and ethnic movements like the Basques in Europe; and other movements engaged in reinforcing local control, such as community-supported agriculture and local currencies (Friedman 1994). Each of these movements seeks to recuperate and protect local identities and places in the face of greater economic and cultural integration within a nation or a transnational network.

Other evidence of localization lies in people's patterns of consumption, which is a common way people express their local identities and ways of being. In our own society, people choose certain clothing and shoe brands because they believe it says something about them as individuals: their social status, lifestyles, and outlook on the world, in particular. People in other countries do this too, but because of local culture and history, patterns of consumption can communicate very different things.

For example, among the Bakongo in the People's Republic of Congo, a former French colony in Central Africa, poor Bakongo youths in urban shanty towns of the capital city, Brazzaville, compete with each other to acquire famous French and Italian designer clothes (Figure 6.4). Calling themselves *sapeurs* (loosely translated as "dandies"), the most ambitious and resourceful go to Europe where they acquire fancy clothes by whatever means they can. By becoming hyper-consumers, *sapeurs* are not merely imitating prosperous Europeans. Europeans may believe that "clothes make the man," but Congolese believe that clothes reflect the degree of "life force" possessed by the wearer (Friedman 1994:106). The *sapeur*'s goal is not to live a European lifestyle; his goal is to accumulate prestige by linking himself to external forces of wealth, health, and political power. In highly ranked Congolese society, the poor Bakongo urbanite ranks lowest. By connecting to upscale European fashion trends, the *sapeur* represents an assault on the higher orders of Congolese society who normally dismiss him as a barbarian.

Whether they are Walpiri Aborigines watching video, Malay factory women, or Congolese *sapeurs,* people continue to define their identities locally. What is different today from previous generations, perhaps, is that people increasingly express their local identities through their interaction with transnational processes, such as communications or consumerism, and with institutions, such as transnational businesses.

Figure 6.4   Bakongo *Sapeur*. The *Sapeur*'s engagement in both transnational fashion worlds and local processes of social stratification destabilizes any strong local-global dichotomy.

In today's world people participate in global processes *and* local communities simultaneously. But they rarely participate in global processes on equal footing, because of their subordinate place in the world system or in their own countries. Nevertheless, many anthropologists feel that to identify them in stark terms as *either* winners *or* losers of global integration greatly simplifies the complexity of their simultaneous involvement in globalization and localization processes.

As these examples show, people can be accommodating to outside influences, even while maintaining culturally specific meanings and social relations, whether because of defiance or because they actively transform the alien into something more familiar (Piot 1999). In these circumstances, cultural differences exist not in spite of, but because of, interconnection. But it still seems difficult to deny that so many millions of people are striving to become developed and pursue lifestyles similar to middle-class Americans.

THINKING CRITICALLY ABOUT GLOBALIZATION

Who should define who is a winner or loser in the processes of global integration? What kinds of criteria (financial, social, political, etc.) do you think are most appropriate for defining such a thing?

Doesn't Everyone Want to Be Developed?

Long before the current globalization craze, discussions about global integration were often framed as the problem of bringing "civilization" (Western, that is) and later, economic development, to non-European societies. But the question we pose here—Doesn't everyone want to be developed?—has no easy answer. Ideas differ about what development is and how to achieve it, so first we must ask: What is development?

What Is Development?

In 1949, U.S. President Harry Truman gave his inaugural address in which he defined the role of the United States in the post–World War II world, when the West confronted the communist nations. He said, "We must embark on a new program for making the benefits of our scientific advances and industrial progress available for the improvement and growth of the underdeveloped areas" (Truman 1949). He defined two-thirds of the world as "underdeveloped" and one-third as "developed." Truman believed that if poor people around the world participated in the "American dream" of a middle-class lifestyle, they would not turn toward communism (Esteva 1992).

The Cold War is over, but development is still with us. It is a worldwide enterprise that was never solely American. Many European nations give aid to their former colonies. The stated goals of this aid range from expanding capitalist markets through trade and new building to alleviating poverty, improving health, and conserving natural resources. Key actors include the United Nations, the government aid agencies of most industrialized countries, lending agencies like the World Bank, and non-governmental organizations (NGOs) like CARE International.

Contemporary international development still aims to bring people into the "modern" world and correct what it identifies as undesirable and undignified conditions like poverty and lack of modern conveniences. And, just as in the colonial era, "advanced" capitalist countries still provide the economic and social models for development.

But there is ambiguity to the concept of development. Is it a means to a particular end? Or is it the end itself? Who defines the shape and course of development? More importantly for our purposes, development has an ambiguous relationship with cultural diversity. Is its goal to foster the unfolding potential and purposeful improvement of people—from their own local cultural perspective? Or is it a program of forced change that is eliminating cultural diversity to create a world ordered on the universal principles of capitalist societies? Is it an effort to remake the world's diverse people to be just like us?

There are two distinct anthropological approaches to development: **development anthropology** and the **anthropology of development** (Gow 1993). While development anthropologists involve themselves in the theoretical and practical aspects of shaping and implementing development projects, anthropologists of development tend to study the cultural conditions for proper development, or, alternatively, the negative impacts of development projects. Often the two overlap, but at times they are in direct conflict.

Development Anthropology

Development anthropology is a branch of applied anthropology. It is a response to a simple fact: many development projects have failed because planners have not taken local culture into consideration. Planners often blame project failures on local peoples' supposed ignorance or stubbornness (Mamdani 1972). But it is often planners themselves who are ignorant of local issues or set in their ways. Projects are more likely to meet their goals when they are fine-tuned to local needs, capacities, perspectives, and interests.

A classic example recognized by many anthropologists is the work of Gerald Murray on deforestation in Haiti. In the 1970s and 1980s, the U.S. Agency for International Development (USAID) invested millions of dollars in Haitian reforestation projects that consistently failed (Murray 1987). Poor farmers resisted reforestation because it encroached on valuable croplands. Worse yet, aid money directed to farmers kept disappearing in the corrupt Haitian bureaucracy. Murray saw that planners misunderstood the attitudes and needs of local farmers, not to mention the most effective ways to get the resources to them. He suggested a different approach. Planners had conceived of this project as an environmental one. He convinced the United States Agency for International Development (USAID) instead to introduce it to farmers as planting a new cash crop, and to avoid involving the Haitian bureaucracy. Farmers would plant trees along the borders of their lands, allowing crops to continue to grow (Figure 6.5). After several years, they could harvest mature trees to sell as lumber. It was a very successful project: within four years, 75,000 farmers had planted 20 million trees, and many discovered the additional benefits of having trees on their land.

Development anthropologists often think of themselves as advocates for the people living at the grassroots—the poor, small farmers, women, and other marginalized people—who could be most affected, negatively or positively, by development but who lack the political influence to design and implement projects (Chambers 1997). As a result of pressure from anthropologists and other social activists, governments and major development organizations like the World Bank began to commission social impact studies to understand the potential impacts of their projects, and to try to alleviate the negative effects on local populations. Today, many anthropologists work in development agencies, both internationally (such as in USAID) and domestically (in community development organizations). One indication of how successful

- **Development anthropology.** The application of anthropological knowledge and research methods to the practical aspects of shaping and implementing development projects.

- **Anthropology of development.** The field of study within anthropology concerned with understanding the cultural conditions for proper development, or, alternatively, the negative impacts of development projects.

Figure 6.5   Haitian Farmers Planting Saplings for Reforestation.

anthropologists' contributions to development have been is that the current director of the World Bank, Dr. Jim Yong Kim, is an anthropologist.

And yet there are limits to what anthropologists can do. Policy makers and development institutions may not pay attention to their advice. Or the anthropologist may not have enough time to fully study a situation before having to make recommendations (Gow 1993).

Anthropology of Development

A number of anthropologists have supported the work of development anthropology by analyzing the social conditions that might help projects succeed. Other anthropologists have examined the development enterprise itself, and challenged its unpredictable and often harmful impacts on local cultures. These critics argue that no matter how well intentioned the developers, the outcome of most development projects is to give greater control over local people to outsiders, or the worsening of existing inequalities as elites shape development projects to serve their own political and economic interests (Escobar 1995). They also charge that the notion of development itself is ethnocentric and paternalistic (Escobar 1991).

Anthropologist James Ferguson applied some of these perspectives in his study of the Thaba-Tseka Rural Development Project. This project was a World Bank and U.N. Food and Agriculture Organization (FAO) project that took place between 1975 and 1984 in the southern African country of Lesotho (J. Ferguson 1994). Its goal was to alleviate poverty and increase economic output in rural villages by building roads, providing fuel and construction materials, and improving water supply and sanitation. But the project failed to meet its goals.

Ferguson argued that intentional plans like this one never turn out the way their planners expect, because project planners begin with a distinctive way of reasoning and knowing that nearly always generates the same kinds of actions. In this particular case, the planners believed that Lesotho's problems fit a general model: its residents are poor because they are subsistence farmers living in remote and isolated mountains, but they could develop further if they had technical improvements, especially roads, water, and sanitation.

But, according to Ferguson, this perspective has little understanding of on-the-ground realities. He noted that people in rural Lesotho have been marketing crops and livestock since the 1840s, so they have already been involved in a modern capitalist economy for a long time. They are also not isolated, since they send many migrants to and from South Africa for wage labor. In fact, most of the income for rural families comes from family members who have migrated to South Africa.

Ferguson's point is that people in rural Lesotho are not poor because they live in a remote area and lack capitalism; they are poor because their labor is exploited in South Africa. But by viewing poverty as a lack of technical improvements in the rural countryside, the project failed to address the socioeconomic inequalities and subordination that are the underlying causes of poverty in rural Lesotho. All of this misunderstanding led to one major unexpected consequence: the arrival of government development bureaucrats to put the development project's technologies in place undermined the power of traditional village chiefs. Ferguson concluded that development exists not to alleviate poverty, but to reinforce and expand bureaucratic state power at the expense of local communities.

Not all anthropologists, especially those working in development, are comfortable with such critiques. Some anthropologists counter that we cannot sit on development's sidelines, that we have a moral obligation to apply our knowledge to protect the interests of the communities we study. Others insist that critics ignore the struggles within development institutions that indicate that there is not simply one discourse of development but a variety of perspectives among developers (Little and Painter 1995). Still others insist that development is less paternalistic and more accountable to local communities than it has ever been (Chambers 1997).

These debates remain unresolved, but now that we have some background, we can begin to answer the bigger question: do people really want to be developed? The answer often depends on how much control over development processes people will have.

Change on Their Own Terms

In indigenous and poor communities around the world, it is not uncommon to hear variations on the following phrase, originally attributed to Lila Watson, an Australian Aboriginal woman: "If you have come here to help me, you are wasting your time. But if you have come here because your liberation is bound up with mine, then let us work together." According to this perspective, outside help is not automatically virtuous, and it can undermine self-determination. Some scholars view this basic desire—to negotiate change on one's own terms—as a fundamental challenge to development's real or perceived paternalism and negative effects on local culture (Rahnema and Bawtree 1997). As confirmation of that fact, they point to the explosion of grassroots social movements throughout the Third World that challenge capitalist development schemes and seek alternatives such as social justice and environmental sustainability (Escobar, Alvarez, and Dagnino 1998).

Understandably, in the face of forced change, people want to conserve the traditions and relationships that give their lives meaning. This point is one of the keys to understanding culture in the context of global change. Culture helps people make sense of and respond to constant changes in the world, and is itself dynamic. But culture also has stable and conservative elements, and different societies have different levels of tolerance for change, both of which mean that cultural change is not a uniform process for every society. This situation of uneven change partly explains why we see the persistence of cultural diversity around the world in spite of predictions that it would disappear.

● ●

THINKING CRITICALLY ABOUT GLOBALIZATION

Are anthropologists ethically obligated to help communities develop if members of the community want it?

● ●

If The World Is Not Becoming Homogenized, What Is It Becoming?

Like the previous question about whether everyone wants development, this one has no simple answer. Anthropologists are divided on this question. The interaction of culture with political, economic, and social processes is complex, and in many ways the world's material culture and associated technologies are becoming homogeneous. Anthropologists who study these processes pursue one or another form of cultural convergence theory. Other anthropologists however, see conflict and a clash of cultures. And still others see hunter-gatherers like the Walpiri using aspects of modern technology in their own ways and on their own terms. These scholars use an approach called hybridization theory. In this section we examine the strengths and relevance of each theory.

Cultural Convergence Theories

In the 1960s the famous media scholar Marshall McLuhan suggested that the world was becoming a "global village" in which cultural diversity was in decline. Many social scientists agree. The British philosopher and social anthropologist Ernest Gellner, for example, believed the spread of industrial society created a common worldwide culture, based on similar conditions of work within the same industry. Making t-shirts in a factory is going to be similar whether situated in Honduras, Tanzania, or Vietnam. Gellner wrote that "the same technology canalizes people into the same type of activity and the same kinds of hierarchy, and that the same kind of leisure styles were also engendered by existing techniques and by the needs of productive life" (1983:116–17). Gellner's view was that local distinctions and traditions will gradually fade as Western ideas replace those in non-Western communities.

Another version of convergence theory envisions a worldwide convergence of consumer preferences and corporate practices, invoking the image of "McDonaldization." Advocates of this version assert that the principles of the fast food restaurant— efficiency (quick service at a low cost), calculability (quantity over quality), predictability, tight control over production, and using technology over human labor—characterize American society and, increasingly, the rest of the world (Ritzer 1996).

Still another variation on this theme imagines "Coca-Colonization," alternatively called Westernization or Americanization. This model proposes that the powerful and culturally influential nations of the West (especially the United States) impose their products and beliefs on the less powerful nations of the world, creating what is known as **cultural imperialism**, or the promotion of one culture over others, through formal policy or less formal means, like the spread of technology and material culture.

The appeal of these theories is that they address the underlying causes of why the world feels smaller, as well as how rich societies systematically exploit poor societies by drawing them into a common political-economic system. They also appear to explain the appearance of a common **world culture**, based on norms and knowledge shared across national boundaries (Lechner and Boli 2005; Figure 6.6).

But many anthropologists disagree with the basic assumptions convergence theorists make about culture, and in fact most proponents of convergence are not anthropologists. As we discussed earlier in this chapter, the fact that people might consume the same goods, wear the same clothes, or eat the same foods does not necessarily mean that they begin to think and behave the same ways. A major limitation of convergence theories is that they underestimate variability and plasticity as key features of human culture and evolutionary history (J. Nash 1981).

- **Cultural imperialism.** The promotion of one culture over others, through formal policy or less formal means, like the spread of technology and material culture.

- **World culture.** Norms and values that extend across national boundaries.

Figure 6.6   World Culture and the Olympic Games. The Olympic Games is a quintessential global event: currently 203 countries participate in the Olympic Games, even more than are members of the United Nations. Drawing on certain core values—competitiveness, internationalism, amateurism, etc.—they foster an awareness of living in a single world culture.

Clash of Civilizations

One alternative to convergence theories is the "clash of civilizations" theory. Advanced by political scientist Samuel Huntington, it offers a direct challenge to convergence theorists by explaining why cultural differences have not disappeared. It argues that consciousness of culture is becoming greater around the world, and that states and people band together because of cultural similarities, not because of ideological similarities, as in the past (Huntington 1996). As a result, the world is divided into civilizations in perpetual cultural tension with each other. For example, Huntington pits Western civilization against Islamic and Confucian (Chinese) civilizations, arguing that their divergent values and worldviews generate geopolitical conflicts.

American neoconservatives used this theory during the early 2000s to justify the "War on Terror" as a clash between what they saw as an enlightened and democratic West versus a closed and autocratic Islam. Although a handful of anthropologists accept Huntington's premises (Wax and Moos 2004), most have dismissed this theory and its mosaic vision of the world as crude, ethnocentric, and inaccurate. Not only does it assume that cultural difference automatically generates conflict—which is not supported by historical facts—but it also denies overwhelming evidence of cultural mixing and fluidity.

Hybridization

An alternative theory that many anthropologists prefer is **hybridization**, which refers to open-ended and ongoing cultural intermingling and fusion. The word is actually drawn from nineteenth-century racial thinking, which idealized "racial" purity and abhorred racial mixing as hybridism (Nederveen Pieterse 2004). The difference is that anthropologists have reimagined the word so it is no longer perceived as a negative process, but descriptive of a key feature of human existence. While the convergence and clash of civilization theories imagine a world based on or moving toward cultural purities, hybridization emphasizes a world based on promiscuous mixing, border crossing, and persistent cultural diversity (García Canclini 1995; Piot 1999) (Figure 6.7).

Hybridization has several aliases, including syncretism and creolization. Anthropologists have usually applied the word *syncretism* to the fusion of religious systems; *creolization* is used to mean the intermingling of languages. Still another metaphor is the notion of "friction," which anthropologist Anna Tsing (2005) employs: just as rubbing two sticks together creates light and heat, the coming together of diverse and conflicting social interactions creates movement, action, and effects. Tsing's broader assertion is that globalizing processes produce important effects around the world but that these effects are rarely predictable given the particularities of how people situated in their local cultures relate to those effects. Debates continue over the relative usefulness of each of these terms. But anthropologists recognize that each revolves around a common theme: the synthesis of distinct elements to create new and unexpected possibilities.

Hybridization theory does have critics. Some argue that cultural mixing is merely a superficial phenomenon, the real underlying condition being convergence. Others charge that all the talk about boundary-crossing and mixture ignores the fact that boundaries—national, social, ethnic, and so on—have not disappeared (Friedman 1999). At the heart of this

• **Hybridization.** Persistent cultural mixing that has no predetermined direction or end-point.

Figure 6.7   Kabuki Meets Shakespeare. As an illustration of hybridization, consider how in recent years a quintessential Japanese theater form, Kabuki, has been used to stage the plays of William Shakespeare, such as this performance of *Twelfth Night*.

criticism is the charge that hybridization theory ignores real political and economic power and inequalities. Others assert that these three approaches do not have to be mutually exclusive, but that convergence is happening in some places, cultural conflict in others, and hybridization everywhere, all at the same time.

Although these debates can be contentious, for a discipline historically accustomed to studying culture from a local vantage point (the stereotype of the anthropologist in a village), there is widespread consensus that taking on big questions like these opens up exciting new possibilities for research.

THINKING CRITICALLY ABOUT GLOBALIZATION

Can you identify any examples of cultural hybridization in your community? How does the example you came up with connect to transnational dynamics and processes?

What Strategies Can Anthropologists Use to Study Global Interconnections?

Nowadays nearly every anthropologist accepts that it is impossible to make sense of local cultural realities without some understanding of the broader political, economic, and social conditions that also shape people's lives (Kearney 1995). The problem is that anthropologists have typically conducted their studies in a single field site (a village, community, tribe, or district), while the transnational or transregional connections may be very far away. So how can anthropologists simultaneously study a local phenomenon in a community and the national or international factors and forces shaping that community?

Defining an Object of Study

Some anthropologists, such as Eric Wolf, have defined their object of study as the world system itself. They focus on the role of culture in that system. Others who take a global system more or less for granted have focused on specific components within that system, especially objects, money, and ideas that "flow" and "circulate" around it (Appadurai 1996), or the "cosmopolitan" people (journalists, city people, world travelers) who move within and through it (Hannerz 1992). Some go a step further, observing that in a transient world, the migrant offers the most productive object of study (Kearney 1995; García Canclini 1995).

But some reject the notion of a unified global system altogether, and propose investigation of what Tsing (2000:348) describes as "interactions involving collaboration, misunderstanding, opposition, and dialogue" between transnational and local actors. A key component of this approach is learning how people find meaning in their places within broader political, economic, and cultural systems. For example, in September 2012, riots erupted throughout many Muslim countries after a crude video produced in the United States was posted on Youtube that portrayed the Muslim prophet

Doing Fieldwork

Studying Chernobyl's Aftermath With Adriana Petryna

IN APRIL 1986, the worst nuclear disaster of the twentieth century occurred in the Soviet Union, when Unit Four of the Chernobyl nuclear reactor exploded. Its radioactive cloud spread over Belarus, Ukraine, Russia, and Western Europe, exposing millions of people to dangerous levels of radiation. Three years later the Soviet Union and its socialist economy collapsed, leaving the newly independent country of Ukraine, where the ruined reactor lies, to deal with the reactor's technical maintenance, extensive radioactive contamination, and a major health crisis. Some 3.5 million Ukrainians (one of every 20 people) are suffering from the effects of radiation poisoning.

University of Pennsylvania anthropologist Adriana Petryna was one of the first to examine the political, scientific, and social aftermath of the disaster systematically (Petryna 2002). She was particularly interested in how technical, scientific, and political actors understood and responded to the disaster as well as its impacts on the everyday lives of the people.

How did Petryna go about studying a topic as complex as the way science, politics, and people intersected in their everyday lives in the aftermath of a nuclear disaster? The radiation did not simply involve Ukrainians; Petryna writes that "It became apparent that in order to do a fair analysis of the lived experience of Chernobyl, I had to do multisited work" (2002:17). First, between 1992 and 1997, she lived and worked for several brief and long periods of time in Kiev, the capital of Ukraine. There, she conducted participant observation among resettled families, radiation-exposed workers, and mothers of exposed children. Next, she interviewed government officials and civil servants in charge of dealing with Chernobyl's aftermath, as well non-governmental disability rights organizations. During some of this time she also did participant-observation research in the state-supported Radiation Research Center, where she studied the everyday activities and interactions of medical personnel and patients.

In between her stints in Kiev, the research also took her to other countries. She went to Russia to study the scientific knowledge and technical experience nuclear and radiation experts gained from the disaster. She conducted interviews and participant observation in the United States at the International Atomic Energy Agency in New York and in government laboratories such as the Lawrence Berkeley Laboratory, in California, where she learned techniques for measuring the biological impact of radiation at the cellular and genetic levels, which helped her better understand the scientific dimensions of these matters.

Multi-sited research like Petryna's requires following certain common themes and processes across widely dispersed research settings. Its goal is not to study the world system in its totality, but identify the connections that link these dispersed settings. The settings can be geographically dispersed, both within and across nation-states. But they can also be socially dispersed, as in the social distance that exists between a state-run research clinic and a neighborhood where resettled families live.

Her transient method provided rich perspectives on the complex changes in people's lives that came following the breakdown of state socialism following the collapse of the Soviet Union and the sudden rise of global capitalism and new laws. On the one hand, citizens gained new democratic opportunities, including the right to information and the ability to pressure their government to provide benefits for their suffering. On the other hand, to deal with the

Chernobyl Nuclear Power Plant Accident, Ukraine.

(continued)

Doing Fieldwork (continued)

suffering, the Ukrainian state's welfare system had to expand instead of contract, defying any predictions that the end of state socialism would automatically lead to a capitalist, free-market economy.

These complex changes have expressed themselves through what Petryna calls "biological citizenship." In the normal sense of citizenship, citizens bear certain natural and legal rights as their birthright. But in Ukraine, themes like biological damage, scientific knowledge, and suffering have become the grounds upon which many people claim citizenship.

Questions for Reflection

1. What would Petryna have gained if she had stayed in one place to do her research? What would she have lost?

2. What do you think are some of the practical problems facing an anthropologist who wants to conduct multi-sited research?

3. Do you think that multi-sited research raises any particular ethical issues?

Mohammed in a highly negative light. These riots ended in many injuries and even deaths. While American officials scrambled to communicate their agreement that the video was reprehensible, such arguments had little effect on Muslim publics who invoked a longer history of frustration with what they perceive to be a pattern of Western disrespect of Islam throughout the twentieth century.

Each of these approaches raises questions about the adequacy of anthropology's most distinctive methodological tool, ethnographic research. Understood as intensive participation and observation in the everyday life of a single place over a long period of time, ethnographic research has yielded incredibly rich insights into how people live and make sense of their lives. Yet ethnographers also assume that to learn about a community one should stay in one place. But what if the community or the issues one wants to study extend beyond that place?

Multi-Sited Ethnography

- **Multi-sited ethnography.** An ethnographic research strategy of following connections, associations, and putative relationships from place to place.

One technique is to use **multi-sited ethnography**, which is a strategy of following connections, associations, and putative relationships from place to place (Marcus 1995). Its goal is not a holistic representation of the world system as a totality. Rather, it seeks to track cultural themes as they express themselves in distinct places and settings that are typically connected in some concrete way. Its goal is to describe relationships and connections between these different places. In this sense, multi-sited ethnography offers a comparative method. Comparisons emerge from juxtaposing phenomena that were once thought "worlds apart" (Marcus 1995:102). "Doing Fieldwork: Studying Chernobyl's Aftermath With Adriana Petryna" considers how one anthropologist has taken advantage of the opportunities multi-sited ethnography presents for studying culture in transnational contexts.

Multi-sited fieldwork has been productive for studying transnational phenomena like environmentalism and other social movements, the media, certain religious societies whose membership extends across the borders of many countries, and the spread of science and technology. As the object of anthropological research has expanded to include topics like these, more and more anthropologists are doing multi-sited research. Multi-sited research is not appropriate for every research topic, but it is now becoming a common anthropological research strategy.

Conclusion

No anthropologist can claim to have easy answers to the dilemmas, dislocations, and problems raised by globalization. But anthropological research can provide critical perspectives on how and why people relate to large-scale social, economic, and political changes in the ways they do.

As we have established in this chapter, culture helps people make sense of and respond to constant changes in the world, which is itself dynamic. But cultural change is not a uniform process. There are many reasons for this. Different societies have differing levels of tolerance toward change, and some are more protective of their cultural traditions than others. In addition, as the story about Walpiri watching television demonstrates, people can be open to outside influences even while maintaining culturally specific meanings and social relations. They do this by actively transforming the alien into something more familiar. Even more important, perhaps, is that not all people participate in global processes on equal terms. Their position within broader political-economic processes helps shape their consciousness and experience of global cultural integration.

For these reasons alone, it is possible to see why cultural diversity continues to exist in the world. But there is another key reason. It is because cultures are created in connection with other cultures, not in isolation, as many anthropologists had previously thought. This is not to say that there are not certain elements that make the world feel smaller, including empirical changes in communications, migration, and finances. But does this mean we live in a global village as Marshall McLuhan once claimed? Only if we think of a village as a place in which diversity, and not uniformity, is the defining feature of that village.

KEY TERMS

Reviewing the Chapter

Chapter Section	What We Know	To Be Resolved
Is the World Really Getting Smaller?	It is impossible to make sense of local cultural realities without some understanding of the broader political, economic, and social conditions that also shape people's lives.	Anthropologists do not have easy answers for the cultural, economic, and political dilemmas raised by globalization.
Are There Winners and Losers in Global Integration?	Not everybody participates equally in the diverse kinds of interconnections that make up globalization, and taking globalization seriously means taking power relationships and social inequality seriously.	While some anthropologists emphasize the destructive and dominating effects of global capitalism's spread for many non-Western societies, others have argued that the expressions of resistance and creative localization are meaningful and important responses.
Doesn't Everyone Want to Be Developed?	Development raises complex and politically charged issues about socioeconomic and cultural change for anthropologists and the indigenous and poor communities that are the target of development initiatives.	Anthropologists are deeply divided over the positive and negative impacts of development, and they continue to debate the merits and drawbacks of anthropological involvement in development and other projects that promote globalization.
If the World Is Not Becoming Homogenized, What Is It Becoming?	Globalization is a complicated matter that illustrates how people create and change their cultures not in isolation but through connections with others.	Although many anthropologists accept that globalization is a process primarily of hybridization, others argue that it is a process of cultural convergence.
What Strategies Can Anthropologists Use to Study Global Interconnections?	Multi-sited ethnography is one approach for tracking cultural themes as they express themselves in distinct places and settings, and it seeks to identify concrete connections between those places and settings.	Anthropologists continue to debate whether or not multi-sited research is as effective for understanding culture as traditional community-based ethnographic methods.

Readings

Although anthropologists have been interested in cultural transmission from one society to another for more than a century, very few of these studies are studies of globalization as anthropologists now understand the concept. *The Anthropology of Globalization: A Reader,* edited by Jonathan Xavier Inda and Renato Rosaldo (Malden, MA: Blackwell, 2007) offers a rich overview of the history, topics, and debates in the anthropological study of globalization, including essays on themes such as migration, the creation of transnational identities, and the movement of goods and capitalist economic structures across political, economic, and cultural boundaries.

• •

Although he is not an anthropologist, Pico Iyer's book *The Global Soul: Jet Lag, Shopping Malls, and the Search for Home* (New York: Vintage, 2001) captures rich description of many of the cultural dilemmas and situations that draw anthropological attention about global processes. Anthropologist Michael Jackson's book *At Home in the World* (Durham, NC: Duke University Press, 1995) is a rich ethnographic and philosophical counterpart to Iyer's book, juxtaposing the author's own global travels and sense of uprootedness with how Australian

Walpiri construct a concept of home as hunter-gatherers who move across large geographic distances.

● ● ● ● ● ● ● ● ● ● ● ● ● ● ● ● ● ● ● ●

Many anthropologists have written noteworthy ethnographic monographs exploring the intersections of culture and globalization. Among the more thought-provoking are Anna Tsing's book *Friction: An Ethnography of Global Interconnection* (Princeton, NJ: Princeton University Press, 2005), which asserts the many global institutions and interactions that shape the problems facing Indonesian rain forests and indigenous peoples; Charles Piot's *Remotely Global: Village Modernity in West Africa* (Chicago: University of Chicago Press, 1999), which explores how village life among the Kabre of Togo is shaped by a complex mixture of local traditions and colonial and postcolonial histories; and Adriana Petryna's *Life Exposed: Biological Citizens After Chernobyl* (Princeton, NJ: Princeton University Press, 2002), which is described in the "Doing Fieldwork" box.

● ●

Foodways

Finding, Making, and Eating Food

IN RECENT DECADES, India has experienced a rapid explosion in the number of people suffering from diabetes, currently at about 63 million (Kleinfield 2006; Chakrabarty 2012). Most of these people suffer from Type 2 diabetes, which is a chronic disease of high blood sugar that can lead to blindness, heart failure, and limb amputations. Type 2 diabetes is linked to obesity and diets based on fat-rich and sugar-dense processed foods. It is also related to the inactivity and sedentary nature of contemporary lifestyles. In India, it is a disease of the prosperous and overnourished, mainly afflicting the country's burgeoning population of urban middle-class professionals, such as computer programmers and merchants.

Simultaneously, about 300 million people in India are undernourished, and 42 percent of children under the age of five suffer from malnutrition (Yardley 2012). Many of these people live in rural areas, where for thousands of years small farmers have produced grains and vegetables for household consumption. But India's government has yielded to pressures from industry and encouraged a shift to industrial agriculture based on GMO crops (genetically modified organisms), fertilizers, and pesticides. Promising access to global markets and big profits, this industrial agriculture dictates a type of farming that transforms local rural lands into expansive farms for export cash crops, such as cotton and soy, not food for local consumption.

Farmer Suicides in Rural India. Caught in a trap of indebtedness to keep up with the increasing industrialization of agriculture in rural India, tens of thousands of farmers have committed suicide in recent years.

This shift has been difficult for many of India's small farmers. Having to purchase expensive seeds, fertilizers, and pesticides to accommodate the new methods, many farmers have gone deeply into debt. Even when global prices go up, many farmers can barely make ends meet because their interest payments are so high. And when global prices drop, farmers become vulnerable to debt collectors and the social stigma of defaulting on their loans. The ecological costs are also high. Cash crops attract new insect pests, and so farmers have applied more pesticide. Overuse of pesticide has poisoned waterways, destroyed soils, and killed off natural predators that traditionally control pests. Even worse, many pests have become pesticide resistant. During the past two decades, the combined factors of increasingly dismal harvests, indebtedness, and the shame of defaulting on loans have come crashing down on the most vulnerable Indian farmers, leading tens of thousands—as many as 17,500 a year between 2002 and 2006—to commit suicide by drinking the very pesticide that contributed to their woes (D. Sharma 2004; Patel 2007).

These contrasting facts—desperate small farmers who don't have enough to eat and prosperous urbanites suffering from diabetes—offer a glimpse into one country's rapidly changing **foodways**, or the structured beliefs and behaviors surrounding the production, distribution, and consumption of food. What and how India's farmers produce, and what and how Indians eat, are clearly linked to that country's involvement with global markets. Similar changes in both food habits and production systems are happening all over the globe. These changes raise a variety of interconnected issues and challenges involving too much or too little access to food, both of which are related closely to diet-related diseases, as well as the environmental and social consequences of the shift to industrial agriculture.

Yet, in spite of such rapidly changing foodways in a global economy, there is still tremendous cultural variation in how people relate to food. This variation exists not just in how and why people obtain or raise certain foods, but how and why they consume them.

Central to anthropology's interest in food is the question around which this chapter is organized: *Why do we eat the things we eat?* Embedded in this larger question are the following problems, around which this chapter is organized:

• **Foodways.** Structured beliefs and behaviors surrounding the production, distribution, and consumption of food.

Why is there no universal human diet?

Why do people eat things that others consider disgusting?

How do different societies get food?

How are contemporary foodways changing?

Food is a fundamental aspect of culture: we organize our productive and social lives around it; reach out to friends, families, and enemies with it; find both pleasure and disgust in it; define social status and identity through it; get sick and die from it. Anthropologists bring a holistic perspective to the study of food and foodways, meaning that we focus on the complex interactions between human nutritional needs, ecology, cultural beliefs, industry, and political-economic processes. We begin by exploring the diversity of things people eat.

Why Is There No Universal Human Diet?

As a species, humans are omnivores, which means we eat both plants and animals. Our actual everyday diets usually come from a limited range of foods, determined by what is available, by dietary restrictions, and by what we have learned to prefer as individuals and as members of a particular social community. But, in theory at least, humans can eat a tremendous variety of things, and the fact that humans can and do eat almost anything tells us something important about the relationship between our species' biology and evolution, which is that the human diet evolved to be extremely fluid and adaptable.

Human Dietary Adaptability and Constraints

Six million years ago our non-human primate ancestors were largely tree-dwelling frugivores (fruit-eaters), following an evolutionary past that helped make them biologically suited to a plant- and fruit-rich diet. A pivotal evolutionary shift came some 1.8 to 2 million years ago as certain primates began to consume meat more regularly and in larger quantities. Eventually (sometime around 400,000 years ago), this dietary shift was supported by the ability to use fire for cooking, which breaks down tendons and toxins in meat. Meat eating provided high-quality proteins that drove the evolution of the human brain, making it even more complex. The human digestive system also evolved, becoming highly flexible and complex. The remarkable adaptation our species has made to so many different environments from the arctic tundra to tropical rainforests, savannas, and deserts, was likely possible because humans have no prescribed primary diet.

Humans do have certain biologically constrained nutritional needs and will get sick and die if we do not meet them. Some of these requirements include having sufficient calories, water, certain vitamins, lysine, and iron, to name but a few. But in different societies people get differing amounts of these vital nutrients. The differences can be staggering because of factors such as whether a diet is based principally on meat or plant foods, whether a group is cut off from nutritious foods for economic or political reasons, or because a particular food is not available or exists in limited quantities in the natural environment. For example, people living in the Tibetan plateau historically have suffered high rates of goiter, an enlargement of the thyroid gland, because their environment and diet lack a natural source of iodine, essential to keeping the thyroid in good health. In other cases, however, a population has developed biological adaptations to the lack of certain nutrients in their environments. One example is the Inuit, who live in icy northern latitudes. For obvious climatic reasons, the traditional Inuit diet is very low in plant carbohydrates, which is a basic source of energy for most human populations. To get their daily calories, the Inuit eat mostly animal fat and protein. They have a metabolic adaptation that allows them to efficiently transform the amino acids in animal protein into glucose, a key energy source for the body (Lieberman 1987).

Figure 7.1   Dinner in Costa Rica and Ethiopia. The core-legume-fringe pattern is generally not consciously apparent to eaters. But the pattern is more or less the same around the world: a dominant carbohydrate core, a smaller amount of protein, and fringe foods to provide flavor.

• **Lactase persistence.** Continuation of lactase production beyond early childhood that allows a person to digest milk and dairy products.

In spite of the sheer diversity of things humans *can* eat, the food we *actually* put on our plates does seem to follow somewhat reliable patterns. Anthropologist Sidney Mintz (1992) observes that, except in a handful of unusual cases of people who eat only plants *or* only animals, the typical human meal forms a common core-legume-fringe pattern: a core, consisting of a complex carbohydrate (the starchy seeds of grasses or tubers) that provides the caloric basis of a meal, a legume like beans or a small piece of meat that provides a small amount of protein, and a fringe, that provides flavor (relishes) (Figure 7.1). This meal serves both biological needs, providing us with key nutrients, and cultural needs, such as providing taste and flavor. When it comes to human diets, culture and biology interact in complex ways.

Cultural Influences on Human Evolution: Digesting Milk

The evolution of dietary flexibility in our species is not just a fact of biology but is complexly intertwined with cultural dynamics as well. One example concerns something many North Americans take for granted: the ability to digest milk. This ability is not normal for human adults around the world. In fact, it is unusual.

All mammalian babies produce an enzyme called lactase that allows them to digest lactose, a simple sugar found in their mothers' milk. For the majority of the world's human population, lactase production ceases before adulthood, and drinking fresh milk or eating dairy products can create symptoms of lactose intolerance, such as bloating, diarrhea, and cramps (Wiley 2004, 2011).

Only a few populations have developed the ability to digest lactose in adulthood, notably Northern Europeans (from whom many North Americans trace their ancestry), South Asians, and herders in the Middle East, Arabian Peninsula, and sub-Saharan Africa. People in these societies have a condition called **lactase persistence**, which refers to the ability to continue producing lactase in adulthood. People who do not have this trait are lactase impersistent, meaning unable to produce lactase in adulthood. Anthropologists use this terminology instead of the more popular "lactose intolerance" largely because of the negative connotations carried in the word "intolerance" to describe a condition that is actually the more typical condition around the world.

Lactase persistence is a genetically regulated trait, but it is made possible by a particular cultural environment (Wiley 2004). Domestication of animals, especially in the Middle East by 12,000 years ago, set the stage for lactase persistence, because fresh milk was constantly available to those adults with the genetic mutation that allowed them to take advantage of the nourishment milk provides. Other cultural factors today, such as the central role of milk production in the domestic economy, together with a belief system that views the consumption of fresh milk and dairy products as a healthy practice, also support lactase persistence (Wiley 2004).

In the United States, we see these cultural factors in the high profile of the dairy industry, in their "Got Milk?" ad campaign, and the advice we give to young children to drink their milk so they grow up to have strong bodies. Few Americans know about biological variations in the ability to digest milk, and both the federal government and the dairy industry appear to sanction this lack of awareness, routinely telling us that cow's milk is indispensable to healthy bones and brain development. This message remains strong even though as much as 25% of the American population is lactase impersistent.

Around the world there is no evidence that *not* drinking milk or not eating dairy products has created developmental or bone density problems among lactase impersistent populations, who get their calcium, fat, and proteins from other sources (Wiley 2004) (Figure 7.2). But we still assume that the ability to digest milk and other dairy

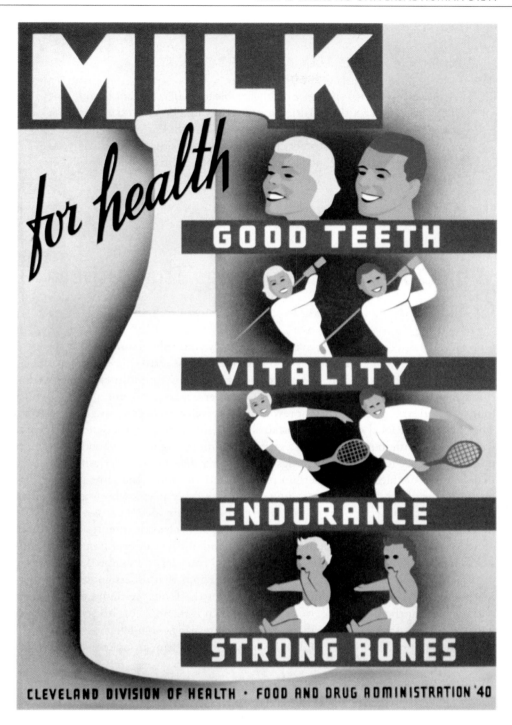

Figure 7.2   Drink Milk for Health? Participants in the anti-milk movement argue that milk consumption contributes to health problems like heart disease and obesity. They also point out that the majority of the world's population does not suffer from bone density problems because they get their calcium from other sources.

products is the norm, as demonstrated by the creation of new drugs that help lactase-impersistent people avoid the symptoms of lactose intolerance.

The milk example shows how flexible human bodies are in responding to their natural and cultural environments, depending on what is available and appropriate to consume. There is no universal human diet because our dietary physiology is open-ended, leaving our needs to be defined and fulfilled partly by the specific natural environments in which we find ourselves, and even more so by the particular societies in which we live. The cultural shaping of dietary particulars is so extreme that one group of people will eat things that another group considers disgusting, which is a theme we explore in the next section.

● ●● ● ●

THINKING CRITICALLY ABOUT FOODWAYS

Although the human species is highly flexible and able to adapt to different environments to get the nutrition it needs, it would be a mistake to assume that all human diets are optimal for human health. Can you think of examples of human dietary practices that do not maximize health? Why do people maintain them if such practices can make them get sick or even die?

● ●

Why Do People Eat Things That Others Consider Disgusting?

One exciting aspect of traveling to another country is the opportunity to eat the local cuisine. Yet for many of us food is also one of the most terrifying aspects of travel. Our health may be a concern. Who likes being laid up with intestinal problems due to bugs our bodies aren't immune to? But another concern is being presented with foods we find strange or downright revolting, as travelers to Iceland might experience when offered the local delicacy of rotten shark flesh; visitors to Thailand might find when offered buffalo penis stew; or a visitor to Zambia might find when eating caterpillars and other insects. These things are not only delectable to certain people but may be a reasonable source of certain proteins and vitamins. The same sense of disgust, of course, can be experienced by people from other places who find the things North Americans eat to be revolting. For example, many people around the world find one of our major staples—cheese—to be gross (it is, after all, intentionally spoiled secretions from an animal's glands), and others find our love of beef hamburgers and steaks horrifying (such as Hindus from India who consider cows sacred).

That one group of people finds some things delicious that others consider disgusting goes to the heart of how much culture shapes the foods we desire to eat, when and how we eat them, and why we eat them, which is the topic of this section. As we will see in this section, ideas about what is disgusting—or delicious—to eat are closely tied to processes of cultural construction, symbolism, group identity, and cultural change.

Foodways and Culture

When we talk about the relationship between food and culture, anthropologists take a holistic perspective on foodways, which refers to those structured beliefs and behaviors surrounding the production, distribution, and consumption of food (Anderson 2005). The foodways perspective distinguishes between food as a tangible object that provides nutrition, and food as a conduit, channeling social relationships and symbolic meanings that are formed while food is produced, prepared, shared, and eaten. Although the actual use of the term "foodways" is relatively new in anthropology, the holistic approach it emphasizes is in fact not at all new to anthropology. In "Classic Contributions: Audrey Richards and the Study of Foodways," we explore how one British social anthropologist pioneered the holistic analysis of foodways.

Classic Contributions

Audrey Richards and the Study of Foodways

THE BRITISH SOCIAL anthropologist Audrey Richards (1899–1984) is best known as a founder of the field of nutritional anthropology, which studies the relationship between human nutritional needs, ecological conditions, and what people actually eat (Anderson 2005). Because of Richards's influence, nutritional anthropologists today approach eating holistically, exploring how biology, health concerns, ecology, political-economic processes, and most of all culture shape people's relationships with food. In this selection, drawn from her classic 1939 book *Land, Labor, and Diet in Northern Rhodesia: An Economic Study of the Bemba Tribe*, Richards justifies a holistic perspective on what we now call foodways.

The study of . . . magico-religious attitudes to different foods must be an essential part of any nutritional survey as well as a record of the people's digestive theories and their beliefs as to the correct feeding of infants and the sick.

But if social values and nutritional dogmas shape a people's food habits, it is their economic institutions that enable them to produce their supplies. Here again the anthropological approach to diet problems is seen to be a very important one. Agricultural and pastoral activities are governed by cultural rules, some based on empirical knowledge and some on magico-religious beliefs. These vary from tribe to tribe, even in areas where environmental conditions are

very similar. Food is everywhere produced by co-operative action and it is on the success of their social organization that different people's diets depend. Man works to produce sufficient or surplus victuals under the urge of a number of economic incentives and these are culturally defined in each tribe. Distribution is a question of the utmost importance among peoples living for the most part on perishable foods, and it is their different legal systems and principles of social grouping that enable them to share their supplies between the different members or classes of the community. All these social and economic factors directly affect the production and consumption of food in a native area. (Richards 1939:8–9)

Questions for Reflection

1. What do you think Richards meant when she referred to the "magico-religious attitudes to different foods"? Why do you think these are important to understanding a society's foodways?

2. Richards said that the production and distribution of food are also culturally defined. Can you think of an example from our own society that illustrates her point? (Consider cheeseburgers and ice cream. How are their production and distribution culturally defined?)

Foodways Are Culturally Constructed

Foodways are culturally constructed in that they are always surrounded by cultural beliefs and governed by systematic rules and etiquette. These rules regulate what and how people hunt and gather; what plants they raise and how they harvest them; how and with whom they share and prepare food; and how and with whom they consume it. These rules, all culturally constructed, differ from one society to the next.

For example, those of us who get our food from supermarkets tend to think of food as material, impersonal, and dissociated from the producer and its natural environment. In contrast, the Hua, who live in the Eastern Highlands of Papua New Guinea, believe that food possesses mystical dynamism, vitality, and danger (Meigs 1997). For the Hua, the act of eating unites them with the individual who produced or shared food with them and invigorates them with the vital essences of the organisms they are consuming. Because food is so spiritually powerful, humans are susceptible to its influences. The Hua have devised many rules governing who can handle, share, and eat certain foods. Some of these rules, for example rules that disallow women or men from eating certain foods, strengthen the social distinction between male and female. Other rules, such as those that require certain foods to be shared, build stronger bonds among members of the same clan, village, and gender.

Foodways Communicate Symbolic Meaning

In every society, food is a rich source of meaning, and people use it to communicate specific messages. Particular foods and meals can draw people together, especially when they share and consume foods that symbolize concepts like home, family, or conviviality. When you are traveling and become homesick, the yearning for certain "comfort foods" is not just a desire for a familiar taste. It is also satisfying because it ties you symbolically to home and family.

But food can just as easily communicate division and unequal power relations, as with so-called Sumptuary Laws that limit consumption of certain items along class lines. For example, in Renaissance England the Parliament passed a law that allowed "gentlemen" to eat two courses of meat and fish during a meal, but restricted their servants to only one course of meat during the day, leaving them to eat only foods consisting of milk, butter, and cheese the rest of the day (Figure 7.3).

The use of food as a form of symbolic communication is so pervasive that some anthropologists, such as Mary Douglas and Claude Lévi-Strauss, have suggested that food operates with logic similar to that of language. English anthropologist Douglas, for example, observed that an English formal dinner takes on a certain precise order, just like a sentence: appetizers, soup, fish, and so on to dessert (Anderson 2005:110; Douglas 1966). Douglas also wrote about food taboos, which are prohibitions on eating certain foods. She argued that these are especially important modes of symbolic communication. For example, in her analysis of Jewish dietary laws (the "Abominations of Leviticus") that prohibit the consumption of pork, Douglas concluded that abiding by these taboos was a means through which ancient Israelites symbolically communicated their religious piety (Douglas 1966). And French anthropologist Claude Lévi-Strauss famously observed that food is good to think, not just eat. The anthropological theory of **structuralism**, which he established, argues that the human mind creates meaning and understanding by making patterned oppositions and contrasts. For example, Lévi-Strauss observed that all cultures make a distinction between food that is raw and food that is cooked, which on a symbolic level means that all cultures draw a distinction between nature and culture (Lévi-Strauss 1969b). The act of cooking marks the transition from nature to culture, easing the opposition between them and creating the meanings that people give to food.

Foodways Mark Social Boundaries and Identities

Food preferences, etiquette, and taboos also mark social boundaries and identities. As anthropologist Carole Counihan (1999:8) has observed, "One's place in a social

• **Structuralism.** An anthropological theory that people make sense of their worlds through binary oppositions like hot-cold, culture-nature, male-female, and raw-cooked. These binary oppositions are expressed in social institutions and cultural practices.

Á faut espérer q'eu jeu la finira ben tôt.

Un Païsant portant un Prélat, et un Noble.

Allusion aux impots dont le poids retombait en entier sur le peuple : M.M. les Ecclesiastiques et les Nobles non seulement ne payoient rien, mais encore obtenoient des graces, des pensions qui épuisoient l'Etat, et le Malheureux cultivateur pouvoit apeine fournir à sa subsistance.

Figure 7.3 Sumptuary Laws, Circa 1500s England. These laws reflected and strengthened everyone's awareness of the advantaged position of aristocrats at a time when the European preference for meat eating allowed it to symbolize aristocracy.

system is revealed by what, how much, and with whom one eats." Eating practices might mark gender differences, as when men and women eat different foods. They might mark ethnic or regional differences, as particular groups identify themselves closely with certain foods. Or they could mark profession or class status, as certain individuals consume certain foods identified with their social station (Lentz 1999). These social markers are closely related to differing notions of **taste** that may exist between or within groups. *Taste* can refer to both the physical sensation on the tongue (as in "this crab cake tastes good") and social distinction and prestige (as in "her consumption of fine wine shows she has good taste") (MacBeth 1997).

● **Taste.** A concept that refers to the sense that gives humans the ability to detect flavors, as well as the social distinction associated with certain foodstuffs.

Every society has a notion of the "perfect meal," which typically reflects people's culturally acquired tastes and is closely identified with their social identity as a group. For example, German anthropologist Gerd Spittler (1999) found that among the Kel Ewey Tuareg [kell **eh**-way **twar**-egg] nomads who live in the Sahara desert region in northern Mali, West Africa, the perfect meal is simple and always the same for everybody regardless of their relative wealth. Breakfast is a drink made of cheese, dates, and the grain millet, stirred in water. Lunch and dinner are millet, prepared in the style of polenta and sprinkled with soured camel or goat's milk, which might taste something like oatmeal or grits with yogurt. Spittler theorizes that Tuareg prefer these types of meals because it identifies them as a people that provides a stable diet for all its members in a precariously dry environment. These Tuareg view variety in the diet—something that many of us take for granted—as a characteristic of people who must be so desperately poor and hungry they are forced to eat anything they can find.

Changes in taste and food preferences are often linked to broader changes in social differentiation, such as an increasing social stratification within a population. Middle and upper class urban dwellers in Ghana, for example, tend to prefer drinking factory-produced bottled beer over sorghum beer, which is common in the villages. By drinking bottled beer, the members of the middle and upper classes distance themselves symbolically from poor and illiterate village dwellers and identify themselves with the prestige of modern institutions (Lentz 1999).

One of the most significant ways food shapes social differentiation is in the ways it mediates relationships between sexes. In many societies, producing, sharing, and eating food is a highly gendered experience (Counihan 1999). In "Thinking Like an Anthropologist: Food Preferences and Gender," we explore how gender differentiation helps organize women's and men's distinct preferences for food.

Foodways Are Dynamic

Because foodways are so bound up with people's identities, it is easy to assume that people always hold onto them tightly. In some cases, foodways are remarkably persistent. For example, the diet in the southern Spanish region of Andalucía is about the same as it was during Roman times: crusty bread, olive oil, eggs, pork, wine, cabbage, herbs, onions, and garlic (Anderson 2005:163).

But foodways change for many reasons. Environmental changes, like overhunting or overfishing, change what is available. Or people begin to identify certain foods with good health, such as the reputation beef held among North Americans during the mid-twentieth century, but which in recent decades has given way to new ideas about the healthiness of a diet based on vegetables or items like soy products, whole grains, or gluten-free foods. Or formerly expensive foods, like white bread and processed sugar, become inexpensive because of new industrial processing techniques. And changes in family dynamics force changes in eating habits, such as in North America where women's increasing involvement in the workforce (leaving nobody home to cook) has helped fuel the rapid rise of convenience foods such as fast food, frozen dinners, and family restaurants (Anderson 2005:165–68).

People construct their own foodways, but never independent of broader social dynamics or economic contexts. This is especially true of societies involved in geographically dispersed trading networks. For example, around Aitape on the North Coast of Papua New Guinea, sago (starch from the sago palm) and smoked fish are the staple foods for everyone, whether they live on the mainland or on small offshore islands. But only mainland villagers had access to sago palms, which grow in abundance in swampy areas. The islanders enjoyed an abundance of fish, but have no sago or other

Thinking Like an Anthropologist

Food Preferences and Gender

ANTHROPOLOGISTS BEGIN THEIR research by asking questions. In this box, we want you to learn how to ask questions as an anthropological researcher. Part One describes a situation and follows up with questions we would ask. Part Two asks you to do the same thing with a different situation.

PART ONE: FOOD PREFERENCES AMONG THE YAO OF THAILAND

In all societies maleness and femaleness are associated with certain foods, bolstered by social rules and etiquette that govern what men and women can eat and not eat (Counihan 1999). As a result, people learn to prefer the foods that are appropriately identified with their gender. Consider, for example, the case of the Yao people, who are farmers living in the forested mountains of northern Thailand. Yao men prefer raw meat and blood, spiced with chili pepper and fragrant leaves of mint, basil, and dill (Hubert 1997). When men get together as friends to socialize, they drink alcohol and snack on grilled bits of meat and offal. The men view their food preferences as a sign of their virility. In contrast, women are expected to show a slight repulsion toward raw meat and blood. Yao believe that if women prepare or consume these foods they will experience illness and conflict with their husbands. Their preference is for soft, boiled, tender, and bland foods, like rice-based meals and stews. They also prefer fruits, which in Yao culture symbolize femininity.

These food preferences are difficult to comprehend without a broader understanding of Yao cosmology and concepts of space and gender (Hubert 1997). Yao connect particular foods to particular spaces in the cosmic order, and in turn connect these foods and spaces with each sex. Their notion of the cosmos is like a set of concentric circles. The smallest circle, in the center, is the civilized space of the home. The next ring out is the swiddens—the fields they cultivate—which they consider to be semi-wild. The third ring represents the forest, which is a wild and dangerous space. Finally, the outer ring, which encompasses all the others, is the otherworld, a space beyond the pale of the living which is inhabited by ancestors and other spirits.

Women, as well as their foods—which are the staple foods everyone, male and female, eat on a daily basis—are associated with the inner circle, the civilized space of the home and

🌱 **Are These American Foods Gendered?**

kitchen where foods are cooked in cauldrons and woks. Men's foods—especially raw and grilled meats—are associated with the "wilder" outer rings of swidden and forest. Raw meats are prepared only on special occasions, such as a wedding banquet or sacrifice to the ancestors. The only occasion on which raw foods are permitted in the home is when a family offers a sacrifice to their ancestors at the home altar.

(continued)

Thinking Like an Anthropologist (continued)

In Yao cosmology, the more foods are cooked or the closer to home they are produced the more they are considered civilized. Raw and bloody foods are stronger and more dangerous. This arrangement reflects and reinforces ideas about the qualities of maleness and femaleness. Women should be mild, polite, and civilized, working primarily in or near the home in the swiddens. In the space of the home, men are expected to be polite as well. But they also go into the wild and dangerous space of the forests to hunt animals and collect useful plants, and as a result, they are permitted, even expected, to be virile and at times less civilized.

What questions does this situation raise for anthropological researchers?

1.   What are Yao qualities of maleness and femaleness?
2.   What are the qualities of female foods and what are the qualities of male foods?
3.   How do people learn to prefer one food over another?

4.   Are there cultural rules around who can prepare certain foods and how they prepare them?
5.   How do ideas about gender-appropriate foods relate to other notions of gender-appropriate behavior?

PART TWO: FOOD PREFERENCES IN NORTH AMERICA

In North America, we identify certain meals and foods with men, such as steaks, french fries, potato chips, hamburgers, donuts, beer, black coffee, and fried foods. But Americans also increasingly label them "unhealthy" and assume that most men have unhealthy diets. Alternatively, we identify "light" and "healthy" foods with women, such as fresh fruits and vegetables, and especially salads. We also associate flavored coffees, herbal teas, and cosmopolitan martinis with women. While there are exceptions to these patterns, most of us take these distinctions for granted.

What questions would you ask about this situation as an anthropological researcher?

vegetables. Islanders exchange smoked fish and other goods for foods like sago, yams, and bananas grown on the mainland. Even though the communities that comprise this trading system are scattered across a large geographical area, they are nevertheless intimately connected and reliant on each other.

Figure 7.4   Tortillas Sí, Pan No! In 2007, 75,000 people took to the streets in Mexico City to protest an increase in tortilla prices. Chanting "Tortillas Sí, Pan No!" ("Tortillas Yes, Bread No!"), protesters criticized policies that allowed American corn to flood the Mexican market, undermining Mexican farmers and raising the cost of tortillas.

Foodways are also dynamic because they are subject to the influence of large-scale political-economic processes such as cross-border trade and globalization policies (Watson and Caldwell 2005). In Mexico, where maize tortillas are a staple food, Mexican agricultural policies that favored the importation of more inexpensive American corn have resulted in the displacement of small farmers who traditionally produced many maize varieties. Many of these farmers have in turn migrated to cities in Mexico or to the United States, and because they don't grow them anymore, the many maize varieties in rural Mexico now are threatened with extinction (Wise 2007). As the United States has expanded corn-based ethanol production to offset oil imports, the demand for U.S. corn is increasing, and the cost to Mexico to import corn has risen sharply. Poor residents of Mexico City feel the burden of the new higher prices they have been forced to pay for their daily tortillas, and have organized massive protests (Figure 7.4). This situation has revealed certain vulnerabilities in how they get their staple food, which is a key dilemma for any society, as we explore in the next section.

THINKING CRITICALLY ABOUT FOODWAYS

To better understand the complex cultural dynamics of food, what is your idea of an ideal meal? Ask yourself: beyond its flavor, why is this food so good in your opinion? What does it communicate to you and others? Are there any special expectations about who should prepare it and how? Under what conditions do you eat it, especially when and with whom? Why do you think some people, like you, really like this meal, while others do not?

How Do Different Societies Get Food?

Whether a society's foodways are successful or not depends on a combination of environmental, economic, and historical conditions that shape how the community gets its food. Anthropologists call the social relationships and practices necessary for procuring, producing, and distributing food **modes of subsistence.** There are four major modes:

1. Foraging, or the search for edible things.
2. Horticulture, or small-scale subsistence agriculture.
3. Pastoralism, which means the raising of animal herds.
4. Intensive agriculture, or large-scale, often commercial, agriculture.

For the past several thousand years, intensive agriculture has furnished most people with most of their food supplies. But foraging, horticulture, and pastoralism are still important dimensions in many of the world's diets. Not only do these three modes persist in the contemporary world, but they also demonstrate the range and flexibility of human approaches to procuring and producing food. Societies are rarely committed to a single mode of subsistence, but often combine two or more modes. We explore each mode in turn.

• **Modes of subsistence.** The social relationships and practices necessary for procuring, producing, and distributing food.

Foraging

- **Foraging.** Obtaining food by searching for it, as opposed to growing or raising it.

Foraging refers to searching for edible plant and animal foods without domesticating them. Hunter-gatherers, who obtain their subsistence through a combination of collecting foods and hunting prey, are called foragers. Because of their limited storage and transportation technologies, most foragers live mobile lives, traveling to where the food happens to be rather than moving the food to themselves (Bates 1998).

A common stereotype about hunting and gathering is that it is a brutal struggle for existence. This stereotype is inaccurate, because in reality foragers tend to work less to procure their subsistence than people who pursue horticulture or pastoralism. For example, Richard Lee found that !Kung San (also known as Ju/'hoansi) hunter-gatherers of the Kalahari Desert in Southern Africa spent less than 20 hours per week getting food (Lee 1969) (Figure 7.5). Although some hunter-gatherer groups work more hours per week, none of them routinely work the equivalent of a 40-hour week as people in agricultural and industrial societies do. Anthropologist Marshall Sahlins (1972) used Lee's data to suggest that hunter-gatherer societies are the "original affluent society" because they had more leisure time than people in most other societies. Sahlins did not define affluence in terms of material possessions, as many of us might think of it, but in terms of how much free time hunter-gatherers have compared to everyone else in the world. In addition, Sahlins's idea of affluence reflects hunter-gatherers' view that their natural environments are not harsh (as we might view them), but as always providing for their needs, even in times of objective scarcity such as drought (Bird-David 1992).

It is all too easy to view foraging communities as a peculiar survival of our Paleolithic past since humans lived this way for 99% of our history. But contemporary foragers tend to inhabit extreme environments where horticulture or pastoralism are not feasible, such as the desert, the arctic tundra, or certain rainforests. There is plenty of ethnographic evidence that most contemporary foragers often integrate some gardening or herding into their hunting-gathering strategies. Many have also had trading relations with food producing communities, especially to obtain carbohydrates (Spielmann and Eder 1994). For example, the foraging Okiek (oh-**kee**-eck) of Kenya obtain more than half their calories from domesticated garden vegetables grown by neighboring settlers, which they trade for goods collected in forests, such as honey

Figure 7.5   !Kung San Hunter-Gatherers in Nambia.

and fruits. The trade networks in which foragers participate can even have a global reach. For example, during the nineteenth century, San hunter-gatherers in southern Africa hunted elephants and gathered the tusks to feed the booming global trade in ivory to produce piano keys (Gordon 2005).

One of the main questions surrounding foragers is why they persist in a world of food producers (Spielmann and Eder 1994). Why do they not turn to agriculture? Remember first that the foraging life is not as brutal a struggle for existence as stereotypes about it suggest. Foragers tend to give up their mode of subsistence only because they are forced to give it up. One explanation is that increased population density within foraging groups, which brings greater competition for plants and game, causes foragers to settle in one place and grow a reliable food source. Another explanation is the over-exploitation of a resource base by neighboring non-foraging people or foreign corporations. For example, the deforestation that accompanies the work of Japanese lumber companies has put major pressure on foraging communities in Southeast Asian rainforests, forcing them to settle because they can no longer live nomadically.

Foragers are typically ethnic minorities, and often they are treated in discriminatory ways by neighboring agricultural and herding peoples who view them as social inferiors. Sometimes maintaining a foraging existence is a form of resistance and a way of avoiding subordination to stronger groups (Dentan, Endicott, Gomes, and Hooker 1997; Gordon 2005). For example, some San foragers have fought to keep foraging which they view as means to maintain their social independence. They have also become politically active in recent years, seeking to gain rights over territory that they see as the key to their survival.

Horticulture

Horticulture is the cultivation of gardens or small fields to meet the basic needs of a household. It is sometimes referred to as subsistence agriculture, which refers to cultivation for purposes of household provisioning or small-scale trade, but not investment (Bates 1998). Horticulturists tend to be sedentary, living in one place. Horticulture emerged some twelve thousand years ago with domestication, which gave humans selective control over animal and plant reproduction. Domestication increases the amount of predictable or reliable food energy that humans can get out of a piece of land (Bates 1998:70) (Figure 7.6).

The primary goal of horticulture is to feed a single household, resulting in certain characteristics. First, farmers cultivate only small plots and employ relatively simple technologies (using hand tools like knives, axes, and digging sticks, for example) that have low impacts on the landscape. Horticulture relies heavily on human labor and energy (Bates 1998). Horticulturists have relatively small yields and are vulnerable to crop failures and soil depletion, and so they tend to rely on several plots of land scattered over a large area. Many horticulturalists also rely partly on hunting and products traded from other groups, particularly foragers who provide wild game, fruit, and nuts to round out their diets.

The most common form of horticulture is **swidden** (slash and burn) **agriculture**. In some geographic areas, such as the tropics, swidden agriculture is the most effective mode of agriculture because burning releases nutrients into the soil. Tropical soils are nutrient-poor because most nutrients reside in the vegetation, and heavy rainfall washes nutrients out of the soil. By clearing a patch of forest and burning the vegetation, the resulting ash fertilizes the soil for a single crop. A farmer can use this plot for several years (between three and seven or so, depending on local climate and soil conditions), usually planting ten to twenty different crops that mature or ripen at different times. These garden plots often imitate the ecological diversity and structure of

- **Horticulture.** The cultivation of gardens or small fields to meet the basic needs of a household.

- **Swidden agriculture.** A farming method in tropical regions in which the farmer slashes and burns small area of forest to release plant nutrients into the soil. As soil fertility declines, the farmer allows the plot to regenerate to forest.

Figure 7.6   Horticulture in Papua New Guinea. (a) Mixed garden in fence in lowland Ningerum area; (b) Freshly planted sweet potato mounds in Highland New Guinea; (c) A married couple in their mature sweet potato garden.

the rainforest itself, with some plants living in the understory shade, others in the twilit middle level, and others in the sunny top. By the time the crops are all harvested the soil is depleted, and the farmer will move to another plot to repeat the process. Old plots lie fallow so nitrogen-fixing bacteria in the soils can regenerate the soil and trees and shrubs. If there are no other pressures on them, such as population growth or new settlers coming to a rainforest area, a farmer might not return to work one of these fallow plots for several decades, rotating between several plots of land over a long period of time. Slash-and-burn agriculture tends to work best when population densities are low, because the land requires long fallow periods.

The shift from foraging to horticulture was not a matter of people "discovering" that seeds grew into plants, shrubs, and trees. Early foraging peoples knew more about these natural processes than most of us do today, because they lived within these complex natural environments. According to Danish economist Ester Boserup (1965), full-time horticulture takes more work than foraging, and foragers would never have shifted to planting crops unless forced to because a group's population was growing. Boserup theorized that with growing numbers of mouths to feed foragers would have started planting some crops, gradually becoming more settled and less nomadic. Although anthropologists still debate details of this theory, it has helped explain the role of population growth and technology in the transition from foraging to horticulture.

Pastoralism

Pastoralist societies live by **animal husbandry**, which is the breeding, care, and use of domesticated herding animals such as cattle, camels, goats, horses, llamas, reindeer, and yaks (Bates 1998). Rather than raising animals for butchering as food, pastoralists mainly consume their milk and blood and exploit their hair, wool, fur, and the ability of animals to pull or carry heavy loads. This approach allows them to

- **Pastoralist societies.** Groups of people who live by animal husbandry, which is the breeding, care, and use of domesticated herding animals such as cattle, camels, goats, horses, llamas, reindeer, and yaks.

- **Animal husbandry.** The breeding, care, and use of domesticated herding animals such as cattle, camels, goats, horses, llamas, reindeer, and yaks.

get more out of the animal in the long run. Pastoralists typically occupy the landscapes beyond the reaches of productive agricultural lands, especially arid scrublands where irrigation cannot reach (Figure 7.7).

While some pastoralists are sedentary, others live as nomads, moving themselves and their herds in search of grazing lands. One form of nomadic pastoralism is **transhumance**, or regular seasonal movement from one ecological niche to another. For example, during the dry season, the Maasai of Kenya move their cattle to areas where there are permanent water holes, and during the rainy season, to grazing lands that are normally dry (Igoe 2004). A different form of nomadic pastoralism is **horizontal migration**, which refers to movement across a large area in search of whatever grazing lands may be available. The Bedouins of the Arabian Peninsula, for example, move their herds across many thousands of square miles, making use of whatever scant vegetation might be available in this arid environment, periodically congregating at permanent water holes for short periods (Bates 1998).

Figure 7.7   Pastoralist in Afghanistan.

Because a livestock herd can do quick, even irreparable, damage to vegetation in arid landscapes, this mode of subsistence requires the constant movement of herds through a landscape (Igoe 2004). This movement does not depend on the whims of the animals or the individual herder, but is typically coordinated between herd-owning households. At the heart of this system is common ownership of land and social institutions that ensure that herders do not sacrifice the fragile environment for short-term individual gains. These social institutions include livestock exchanges to redistribute and limit herd size, punishments for individuals who diverge from planned movement patterns, and the defense of rangeland boundaries to ensure that neighboring pastoral groups cannot invade with their own livestock (McCabe 1990). When these institutions work successfully, pastoralism is an effective mode of subsistence, providing people with a stable source of nutritious foods (milk, blood, and meat) without irreversibly destroying the fragile landscape.

In recent decades certain pressures have forced some nomadic pastoralists to settle and abandon their mode of subsistence semi-permanently. Causes include drought, famine, livestock diseases, loss of common property, and the political turmoil of civil wars, such as in the Sahelian countries of Sudan and Somalia (Fratkin 2003). Also, a number of governments and development aid agencies view pastoralism as primitive or a sign of their country's underdevelopment and have tried to encourage or even force pastoralists to settle by digging wells and building villages for them, or dividing up common lands and privatizing them to exploit the resources "more rationally." But most of these schemes have had disastrous social, economic, and ecological consequences for pastoralist communities because they disrupt the mobility and collective control of resources that are so critical to effective pastoralism (Stiles 1993).

- **Transhumance.** Regular seasonal movement of herding communities from one ecological niche to another.

- **Horizontal migration.** Movement of a herding community across a large area in search of whatever grazing lands may be available.

Intensive Agriculture

While the goals of horticulture and pastoralism are to feed families, the goal of intensive agriculture is to increase yields to feed a larger community. There are a number of approaches to **intensification**, which refers to processes that increase yields (Bates 1998). These include:

- *Preparing the soil,* with regular weeding, mulching, mounding, and fertilizers.
- *Technology,* often simple, such as a harness or yoke that allows a farmer to use horses or oxen to plow a field; complex, such as a system of canals, dams, and

- **Intensification.** Processes that increase agricultural yields.

water pumps that provide irrigation to an arid landscape; or very complex, like a combine harvester, a machine that harvests, threshes, and cleans grain plants like wheat, barley, and corn.

- *Using a larger labor force,* such as in Asian rice farming, which sustains the nutritional and energy needs of large populations, and provides many people with employment (although the yield does not always increase enough to feed the additional workers) (Geertz 1963).
- *Water management,* ranging from the practice of adding pebbles to fields to retain soil moisture (as ancient Pueblo dwellers of North America did), to large-scale and sophisticated irrigation systems implemented by modern states.
- *Modifying plants and soils,* through selective breeding of plants to produce better yields, reduce the time needed to mature, or create a more edible product, as farmers have done for major grains like maize, rice, and wheat (Bates 1998).

Intensification carries certain trade-offs. On the one hand, it solves an important human problem, which is how to provide food for a large number of people, including those who do not work directly in food production. It also provides a relatively steady supply of food, though famines can still happen. For thousands of years, intensive systems around the world have provided large communities with a stable source of nutrition and energy and, many archaeologists insist, have made possible the rise of cities and states with their complex social organization.

On the other hand, intensification can create new problems, especially environmental ones. By rearranging ecosystems to achieve greater control over natural processes, intensive agriculture is vulnerable to declining environmental conditions. For example, clearing a hillside to plant crops, build terraces, or install water works may increase productivity in the short run, but these can lead to the erosion of topsoils, lowering of water tables, concentration of salts in soils, the silting up of waterworks, and so on. Farmers may not notice declining environmental conditions immediately, because these are often long-term effects. Eventually, however, farmers may have to work harder just to maintain the same level of productivity. Such is the case in California's Imperial Valley, where decades of irrigation to aid the production of vegetables for sale throughout the United States market have created salt concentration in the soil, worsening overall soil quality (Bates 1998).

Industrial Agriculture

The most intensive form of agriculture is **industrial agriculture**, which applies industrial principles to farming. Key principles include specialization to produce a single crop, and the obtaining of land, labor, seeds, and water as commodities on the open market (Figure 7.8). This form of agriculture is characteristic of highly industrialized and post-industrial economies in which only 1% to 5% percent of the population engages in farming. Many claim it is the only way to feed a burgeoning world population, although there is enormous global inequality in terms of how its benefits are distributed.

Through the use of machines, industrial agriculture harnesses sources of energy such as steam power and petroleum, vastly increasing the scale of productivity. Technology-based farming has also redefined our notion of what agricultural work is. On some farms, such as those that produce grains like corn and wheat, farming now means tending to huge machines that provide nearly all the actual farm labor (Bates 1998). As a result of mechanization, a small rural labor force (less than 2% of the total U.S. population) produces so much food that one of industrial agriculture's greatest economic problems is *over*production.

- **Industrial agriculture.** The application of industrial principles to farming.

🌱 **Figure 7.8   Factory Farms in the Twenty-First Century.** In the United States, most of the farms that produce meat, eggs, and dairy products are organized on industrial principles. These farms create economies of scale to reduce costs and maximize profits.

A key feature of industrial agriculture is the application of scientific research to increase crop yields. After World War II, scientists introduced "super crops" based on new genetic strains and synthetic chemical fertilizers, which were found to triple and quadruple crop yields (Bates 1998). The dramatic impacts of these new technologies became known as the **Green Revolution**. Today, biotechnology is a common feature of industrial agriculture, providing farmers not only with "improved" high-yield hybrid seeds and fertilizers, but with crops that are pest or pesticide-resistant or crops that ripen on a particular time frame. These high-tech developments are expensive to purchase, so it is either large landowners or increasingly giant agricultural corporations who benefit most from industrial agriculture. Another major effect of industrial agriculture is that it increases social and economic stratification in rural areas, which includes the creation of a peasant class. Because of industrial agriculture, foodways around the world are changing quickly, as we discuss in the next section.

- **Green Revolution.** The transformation of agriculture in the Third World that began in the 1940s, through agricultural research, technology transfer, and infrastructure development.

THINKING CRITICALLY ABOUT FOODWAYS

Even though most of us probably get our food from a supermarket, can you identify examples of other modes of subsistence in our own society? How and why do these multiple modes of subsistence persist? Can you identify situations in which people combine modes of subsistence?

How Are Contemporary Foodways Changing?

Industrial agriculture and dynamics like globalization are fueling major changes in foodways around the world, with important health and environmental consequences for many people. At the beginning of this chapter, for example, we contrasted how the growth of the Indian middle class was changing people's diets with dramatic negative impact on middle class health as millions of Indians are now diabetic, a disease associated with obesity. The diets rich in sugar and fat now available to Indians are similar in many ways to the typical American middle class diet since the 1970s. Note that Americans too are experiencing more diabetes as a consequence of more sugar and fat in the ordinary diet. These patterns in both India and the United States also correspond to much higher average consumption of fast foods, processed foods, and larger typical portion sizes.

But the situations in India and the United States differ in the plight of the poor. In India, the poor are mostly farmers, and in the United States the poor mostly live in urban areas. The diets of the American inner city poor, whether white, black, or Latino/a, are filled with inexpensive starches, fats, and sugars, while the diet of Indian farmers resembles more traditional Indian farm diets, predominantly vegetarian meals with an emphasis on rice or other cereal grains. The biggest shift for these farmers is that as industrial agricultural development has spread across India, most affected farmers have lost control of their production and now work as laborers or tenant farmers of large agribusinesses, most of whose production is for export to industrialized countries. There is little rice, grain, or vegetables available for the food needs of the local population. Thus, the diets of even the non-farmers in these rural

Anthropologist as Problem Solver

Migrant Farmworker Food Security in Vermont With Teresa Mares

KNOWN FOR ITS high-quality cheeses and as the home of the iconic ice cream brand Ben and Jerry's, the New England state of Vermont has long enjoyed a reputation as an idyllic agrarian landscape full of milking cows. But dairy

🌱 **Teresa Mares.**

🌱 **A Pastoral Vermont?**

farming is a difficult year-round job with unreliable financial returns due to fluctuations in the price of milk. The activity has shifted in the past sixty years from being managed primarily as small-scale family-run operations to what is now a highly mechanized industry consolidated into a small number of large farms. Not able to rely on locals, who no longer want to work on these farms, the Vermont dairy industry has increasingly staked its survival on the employment of low-wage migrant farmworkers, most of them undocumented laborers from southern Mexican states like Chiapas, Veracruz, and Oaxaca.

University of Vermont food anthropologist Teresa Mares, who studies how the diets and foodways of Latino/a immigrants change as a result of migration, set out to research ethnographically what the lives of these farmworkers are like and how their dietary patterns have changed now that they work on dairy farms. She quickly found out through interviews with farmworkers and immigrants' rights advocates that working on a dairy farm in rural Vermont is a stressful and isolating experience. These farmworkers rarely get away from their places of work because they are afraid of being deported, a not-insignificant concern being so close to the Canadian border where federal immigration enforcement agents are common. Moreover, they have limited transportation to travel the long distances from the farms to the nearest towns.

Mares conducted a Community Food Security Assessment of farmworkers, which is a U.S. Department of Agriculture survey that measures household access to food, food availability and affordability, and community food production resources. The results showed that something most of us take for granted—the ability to go to a supermarket to get nutritious food—is almost impossible for these farmworkers, and they have to rely on others to do the shopping for them, usually their employer or someone else who lives on or near the farm. These trips are often irregular, and miscommunication between Spanish and English speakers is a common problem, resulting in hunger due to inconsistent access to food, much less food that is culturally familiar and affordable.

There are multiple ironies to this situation, the most obvious one being that the very people producing an iconic food product themselves suffer from food insecurity and hunger. Another irony is that most of these people left their homes in rural Mexico in the first place because of food insecurity brought on by the kinds of globalizing factors now opening jobs for them in Vermont's dairy industry. Among these factors is the 1994 North American Free Trade Agreement, which displaced southern Mexican farmers who could not compete with cheaper American imports of Midwestern corn and milk from various dairy states, including Vermont.

Recognizing an opportunity to address an acute problem and to create new opportunities for collaborative research with colleagues in other fields like agriculture and health, Mares worked with her university's extension office and community volunteers to create a program that would make seeds, tools, and technical guidance available to farmworkers so that they could plant their own vegetable and herb gardens on the dairy farms. Mares met regularly with farmworkers participating in the program, interviewing them at length about issues such as their knowledge about gardening techniques, what kinds of foods they liked to eat, cooking patterns, and household spending patterns. She also worked alongside them in gardens and kitchens—hoeing soils, transplanting seedlings, making meals, etc.—which are useful vantage points from which to observe their actual food practices.

This research has produced rich ethnographic insights into how farmworkers cope with food insecurity and struggle to maintain food practices that are meaningful to them, as well as the successes the program has made in improving farmworker food security. It has also been useful to the people who run the program, who have used Mares's data to assess the effectiveness of the program and to improve its delivery as they begin to address other issues of food insecurity in rural Vermont.

Questions for Reflection

1. Go to the USDA's Community Food Security Assessment Toolkit website (http://www.ers.usda.gov/publications/efan-electronic-publications-from-the-food-assistance-nutrition-research-program/efan02013.aspx#.Uijrn7wzoTk) and review the kinds of data it seeks to collect. How do the data this toolkit elicits differ from the data one might gather from participant observation? In what ways do the two complement each other?

2. What kinds of ethical dilemmas accompany research with a community like undocumented farmworkers?

districts are becoming more and more meager with higher levels of malnutrition than before (Patel 2007). Cash crops, tenant farming, and wage labor have undermined local **food security**, which refers to access to sufficient nutritious food to sustain an active and healthy life. As we will see in "Anthropologist as Problem Solver: Migrant Farmworker Food Security in Vermont With Teresa Mares," concerns over what happens to rural people's food security when their foodways industrialize have become an important area of anthropological research and application.

The rise of industrial farming across the world continues to have important consequences for rural populations. The World Bank has encouraged some countries, such as Costa Rica, Honduras, and Colombia, to produce non-traditional agricultural exports. These are highly specialized commodities like houseplants, flowers, and melons. The goal is to generate foreign revenue by exporting items that other countries do not have, so that the countries can then pay back their World Bank loans and then make investments in domestic public improvements. Similar trends exist in the United States, where government policies favor industrial agriculture over small-scale or subsistence-oriented production (McDonald 1993). For example, in the so-called "Corn Belt" (the dozen or so Midwestern states that dominate corn production), the family farm has been in decline for decades. In the place of family farms, a handful of heavily government-subsidized agribusiness conglomerates produce enormous quantities of grain for export and for industrial processing into food. Industrially produced corn is currently a key ingredient in virtually everything Americans eat. Often found in the form of high fructose corn syrup, it has replaced cane sugar to become the leading sweetener in our food today. Industrial corn is also the major source of feed for the beef, dairy, pork, and poultry industries.

- **Food security.** Access to sufficient nutritious food to sustain an active and healthy life.

Growing Environmental Impacts of Industrial Agriculture

Industrial agriculture requires specific environmental conditions in order to be successful. These include heavy inputs of synthetic chemical fertilizers, pesticides, and large amounts of water. While fertilizer, pesticides, and water are necessary for successful plant growth, the large quantities of each used by industrial agriculture also threatens the environment by polluting rivers and lakes with phosphate from fertilizers, by poisoning ground water with dangerous pesticide residues, and by depleting water supplies. Over the long run, this technology actually destroys soil quality, and as soil quality declines, industrial farms become even more dependent on synthetic soil additives. Pests become resistant to pesticides, so farmers have to apply newer, more potent poisons to manage them, creating a situation called the "pesticide treadmill" that, as we saw in the beginning of this chapter, has motivated tragic suicides among Indian farmers.

Agricultural industrialization also depends largely on non-renewable fossil fuels for powering the combines and other machinery, and for transporting the products to markets. In the United States, the average food item travels 1,500 miles from farm to table, often spending time in two or three warehouses. As a result, about one-fifth of all energy consumption in the United States goes toward sustaining our industrialized foodways, which an increasing number of scientists believe is an unsustainable situation (Mark 2006).

Industrial Foods, Sedentary Lives, and the Nutrition Transition

Even as they can provide a reliable source of food, industrialized foodways have important consequences on people's health. One dimension of this problem is the role industrial foods have played in the dramatic global rise of people who are overnourished, as reflected in growing global rates of **obesity**, which is the creation of excess body fat to the point of impairing bodily health and function, and of **overweight**, or having abnormally high fat accumulation. There are now more people in the world who are suffering the effects of overnourishment—estimated at one billion overweight and 475 million obese people—than people classified as undernourished, estimated at 875 million (Food and Agriculture Organization of the United Nations [FAO]2012; International Obesity Task Force 2013). Thirty-three countries now have obesity rates exceeding 10% of their populations (Ulijaszek and Lofink 2006). Because obesity and being overweight can cause chronic diseases—diabetes and heart disease among them—health officials and researchers consider them to be among the most serious public health crises facing the world.

Obesity is not a genetically determined condition but a complex metabolic syndrome, or combination of medical conditions, that is related to non-genetic factors like maternal health and diet during pregnancy and environmental conditions. For example, smoking or insufficient nutrition during pregnancy appears to be linked to a higher likelihood of developing obesity later in life. New research also links obesity to the presence of certain environmental toxins that have disruptive effects on endocrine production. Individuals may be genetically predisposed to gain weight more easily than others, but it is also clear that obesity tends to develop in a person who eats a lot of food while expending little energy (Ulijaszek and Lofink 2006).

Social factors influence how much food people eat and contribute directly to the production of obesity and overweight. These factors include the presence of other

- **Obesity.** The creation of excess body fat to the point of impairing bodily health and function.

- **Overweight.** Having abnormally high fat accumulation.

individuals at a meal, television viewing, portion size, cultural attitudes toward body fat, and learned preferences (Ulijaszek and Lofink 2006). Consider how powerful just one of these factors—television viewing—can be: in the United States during the 1990s, a child watched on average 10,000 television advertisements for food per year, with 95% of those foods being sugared cereal, sweets, fast food, and soft drinks, all of which are fattening (Brownell 2002). Or consider portion sizes, which food corporations have increased to enhance profitability. Twenty years ago, for example, the average bagel was 3 inches in diameter and 140 calories. Today it is 6 inches and 350 calories!

Scholars have also traced the current worldwide rise of obesity and overweight to a global **nutrition transition**, the combination of changes in diet toward energy-dense foods (high in calories, fat, and sugar) and declines in physical activity. These changes in diet are related to an abundant, secure, and inexpensive food supply, which is the very definition of success for industrial agriculture. But this success is double-edged, because it is a food supply of relatively low nutritional quality, offering processed grains, fats, and refined sugars instead of fruits, vegetables, whole grains, and lean meats—the foods on which we thrive as a species. The other major change is the movement worldwide since the mid-nineteenth century of massive numbers of people away from rural areas, where they tend to lead physically active lives, to cities and suburbs, where they lead more sedentary lives and have more transportation options. For example, in 1900 only about 10% of the world population lived in cities. Today it is 50%, and rates of urbanization continue to be high around the world.

Both of these factors also explain why the problem of obesity is a problem not just in wealthy countries like the United States but also in poor countries. As we saw earlier, the importation of inexpensive foods from industrialized countries into poorer ones changes local diets. Because small-scale farms, which produce locally grown and nutrient-rich food, can rarely compete with the low-cost foods of transnational agribusinesses, many small-scale farms shut down their operations. With fewer farms to support rural livelihoods, people then migrate to urban areas where they occupy more sedentary and less physically active lives.

The Return of Local and Organic Foods?

Widespread concern over access to healthy foods is currently driving an explosion of interest in **sustainable agriculture** (farming based on integrating goals of environmental health, economic productivity, and economic equity), organic foods, and local food production, especially among consumers in Europe and the United States, who live in the heart of industrialized agriculture. During the past decade, farmers' markets have reappeared in many American cities and suburbs to support local production. Community-supported agriculture, in which neighbors buy shares in a local farm and receive its produce, has also proven to be a viable business model for a growing number of small farmers.

Researchers are also challenging the assumption that industrial agriculture consistently produces more, if not also better, food than traditional systems of farming do. A recent study of small farms in fifty-two countries found that when farmers adopted certain techniques of **agroecology** (integrating the principles of ecology into agricultural production) their average yields rose 93%, increases that were superior to industrial methods of production (Pretty 2002). These agroecological techniques emphasize organic production and, instead of turning to synthetic fertilizers and pesticides sold by international conglomerates, involve the integration of natural processes such as nutrient cycling, nitrogen fixation, soil regeneration, and natural enemies of pests into food production. These farming practices also incorporated the knowledge

- **Nutrition transition.** The combination of changes in diet toward energy-dense foods (high in calories, fat, and sugar) and declines in physical activity.

- **Sustainable agriculture.** Farming based on integrating goals of environmental health, economic productivity, and economic equity

- **Agroecology.** Integrating the principles of ecology into agricultural production.

and skills of the local farmers because of their superior understanding of local ecological conditions (Pretty 2002).

There are also important cultural dimensions to these efforts at localizing food, according to anthropologist Amy Trubek, who has studied local food movements in France and the United States. Trubek (2008) explains that the new interest in local foods taking the United States and a number of other countries by storm has its origins in the French ideal of *gout de terroir* ("taste of place"), which refers to the connection between locally based farming and cooking practices and the quality of a food's flavor. Being able to identify the origins of a food and know particular details of the landscape on which it was produced and the practices of the farmer who produced it, Trubek argues, is an important new way of expressing social discernment around food and drink. It also aligns closely with support for local and traditional methods of food production, such as organic and small-scale production. Trubek suggests that what is happening is an interesting process of globalization in its own right, as the ideal of eating "the taste of place" spreads around the globe through public culture like food television channels and other media.

The Biocultural Logic of Local Foodways

Although foodways are dynamic, people have a pretty stable concept of an appropriate diet that reflects their understanding of proper foods, good taste, and nutritional requirements. It is relatively stable because our biological requirements of adequate energy and nutrition and the cultural requirements of meaning and satisfaction are themselves fairly stable. Underlying these facts is a simple biocultural logic: if a diet works, if it provides sustenance and meaning, then people are unlikely to drop everything when something new comes along. People integrate new foods and cuisines into their existing dietary practices all the time, but since this biocultural logic of local foodways is also integrated into the production, preparation, and sharing of food, dramatic change is unlikely.

The biocultural logic of foodways is also related to the reason people do not automatically adopt industrial methods to increase productivity. The cultural logic underlying industrial agriculture is to create never-ending productivity and accumulation of profit. But many people around the world do not share this cultural logic. Their goal is to meet their basic subsistence needs, based on a cultural logic of sufficiency and adequacy. As long as population densities remain low, foraging, horticulture, pastoralism, and some forms of small-scale agriculture require a much smaller investment of work and financial investment while providing adequate nutrition and energy.

THINKING CRITICALLY ABOUT FOODWAYS

There is perhaps no more consequential issue for the future of human environmental and bodily health than the changing dynamics of foodways in the contemporary world. What role do you think anthropologists of food should play in the issues of changing foodways? What specific kinds of knowledge or interventions do you think are most appropriate for anthropologists?

Conclusion

Returning to where we opened this chapter, with a complex situation playing out in Indian foodways, we have to recognize that at the heart of that situation is a critical point: what and how people eat, the foods they find or grow, and how they share and prepare them are patterned and interlocking issues (Pottier 1999:25–26). The fact that each of these elements is subject to biological, ecological, political, economic, technological, historical, and social pressures means that changes in foodways are always complicated. In India, alarming numbers of people are developing diabetes from overnourishment and sedentary lifestyles while others living in rural areas are confronting poverty, starvation, and ecological ruin. Each of these processes is related to certain aspects of Indian society and history, but each is also a consequence of that country's involvement in broader global changes that affect the production, distribution, and consumption of food. Because these global dynamics also affect many other countries, India is not alone in confronting rapidly changing foodways.

But even as foodways are dynamic, we also know that there are certain relatively stable characteristics of human foodways, as can be seen with modes of subsistence. The simplest mode of subsistence is foraging, in which hunter-gatherers collect wild fruits, nuts, tubers, and greens and hunt for animals. As populations grew and the land could no longer provide sufficient food for communities, people began producing their own crops with simple horticulture, small fields for family-based subsistence. Some of these producers specialized into pastoralists, who tended herds, and intensive agriculturalists. Intensive agriculture was the first mode of subsistence able to feed people not engaged in food production, allowing for the rise of cities and states. With increasing mechanization, industrial agriculture has developed, with its potential for large yields per acre but fewer farmers and important consequences for the environment, food security, and people's health.

The panorama of human relationships with food is broader than any species, based on the highly fluid and adaptable aspects of our human dietary biology. But this does not explain why we eat the things we eat. The answer to that question has to do with the fundamental role of culture and political-economic processes in shaping how people meet their basic nutritional and energy needs.

KEY TERMS

Reviewing the Chapter

Chapter Section	What We Know	To Be Resolved
Why Is There No Universal Human Diet?	There is no universal human diet because our dietary physiology is open-ended, leaving our needs to be defined and fulfilled partly by the specific natural environments in which we find ourselves, and even more so by the particular societies in which we live.	Anthropologists are still trying to understand the complex interactions between human biological evolution, histories of food production, and the development of food preferences.
Why Do People Eat Things that Others Consider Disgusting?	Cultural processes strongly shape which foods we eat, when and how we eat them, and why we eat them.	Anthropologists continue to work through how cultural attitudes and social practices surrounding food relate to social categories and dynamics such as class, race, ethnicity, and gender.
How Do Different Societies Get Food?	Humans have developed four general modes of subsistence—foraging, horticulture, pastoralism, and intensive agriculture—each of which carries certain social and environmental trade-offs and opportunities.	Although they are under great pressure in a world increasingly dominated by industrial and other forms of intensive agriculture, foragers, horticulturists, and pastoralists still persist. Anthropologists are working to understand how and why they persist, as well as the pressures on these modes of subsistence.
How Are Contemporary Foodways Changing?	Industrial agriculture's rapid expansion around the globe is related closely to unequal political-economic relationships, creates new environmental and health risks, can diminish food security, and has important biocultural consequences.	Anthropologists of food are relatively new to public health policy discussions about critical issues like food security and obesity, and have just begun to define the anthropological dimensions of these issues.

Readings

There are many books produced mostly by ecological anthropologists on the diverse modes of subsistence described in the third section of this chapter. A useful introduction to that diversity is Daniel Bates's textbook *Human Adaptive Strategies: Ecology, Culture, and Politics* (Boston: Allyn and Bacon, 2005), which does a good job not only describing the social and ecological details of each individual mode of subsistence but also in explaining how they are affected by contemporary global political-economic dynamics.

• • • • • • • • • • • • • • • • • • • •

An excellent overview of the relationship between food and culture can be found in Eugene Anderson's *Everyone Eats: Understanding Food and Culture* (New York: New York University Press, 2005). It pairs well with Raj Patel's book, *Stuffed and Starved: The Hidden Battle for the World Food System* (Brooklyn: Melville House Press, 2008), which offers a culturally informed perspective on the globalization of industrialized foodways.

• • • • • • • • • • • • • • • • • • • •

Andrea Wiley's 2011 book *Re-Imagining Milk* (Routledge) offers a fascinating biocultural analysis of milk, explaining how and why cow's milk has become such a powerful marker of cultural identity for some people even as most people in the world cannot consume it without great discomfort.

● ● ● ● ● ● ● ● ● ● ● ● ● ● ● ● ● ● ● ●

Carole Counihan and Penny Van Esterik's 1997 edited volume *Food and Culture: A Reader* (New York: Routledge, 1997) is a classic compilation of essays by many of the top figures in the anthropology of food.

● ● ● ● ● ● ● ● ● ● ● ● ● ● ● ● ● ● ● ●

Amy Trubek's book *The Taste of Place: A Cultural Journey Into Terroir* (Berkeley: University of California Press, 2008) offers close ethnographic description of local food movements around Europe and the United States, with a particular focus on how these movements develop ways for people to talk about the relationship between the taste of a food and where it comes from.

● ● ● ● ● ● ● ● ● ● ● ● ● ● ● ● ● ● ● ●

Environmental Anthropology

Relating to the Natural World

ONCE EVERY TEN YEARS, people from all over the world attend the World Parks Congress, a conference on formally protected wilderness areas and national parks. During September 2003, several thousand park administrators, policy-makers, scientists, and a handful of global celebrities from over sixty countries convened in Durban, South Africa. Also in attendance were some 150 leaders of indigenous peoples from around the world. These leaders' clothing of colorful beadwork and headdresses with bright feathers provided a sharp contrast to the dark suits and blazers of the other attendees. Even more dramatic than their clothing, however, was their message of protest: conservationists had to stop abusing indigenous people who traditionally owned and used lands now in conservation areas.

Throughout the Congress's panels, workshops, and plenary sessions, indigenous leaders argued that the dominant model for administering protected areas, which is based on the idea that nature must be kept uninhabited by people, has been a disaster for their communities. They insisted that parks force evictions of indigenous peoples, disrupting their customary livelihoods and indigenous systems of environmental management. Parks deny traditional land rights, and sometimes lead to repression. In some cases, park administrators have allowed mining and fossil fuel exploration on the very lands formerly inhabited

❦ **Indigenous Rights and the Challenge to Conservation.** In recent years tensions between indigenous peoples and conservation have intensified over the perception that conservationists do not respect indigenous peoples' rights to land or the validity of their relationships with the environment. Indigenous people, such as the Indians from Brazil pictured above, have become increasingly assertive about protecting those rights in national and international conferences.

by indigenous groups. Jannie Lasimbang of the Asia Indigenous Peoples Pact asserted: "Protected areas have been made into big business and the danger is that this business is both unsustainable and may further marginalize us, indigenous peoples. . . . Funds would be better spent protecting our rights and involving us directly [in park management]" (Colchester 2003).

The organizers of the conference saw the situation quite differently. The Congress's theme was "Benefits Beyond Boundaries," implying that protected areas are good for communities. Organizers argued that parks contribute to economic development and help alleviate poverty. Their approach emphasized the ideals of **sustainable development**, defined as "development that meets the needs of the present without compromising the ability of future generations to meet their own needs" (WCED 1987). For advocates of protected areas, sustainable development means that nature protection must address local people's abilities to make a living, involve them in conserving natural resources, and create suitable alternatives to economic activities that deplete natural resources (Wapner 1996:83). Because indigenous people living in rural areas are often poor and marginalized within their countries, Congress organizers wanted to showcase how nature protection will lead to the sustainable development of indigenous and other rural communities.

On the surface, it would seem that indigenous people should be strong allies of those who seek sustainable development. Some of the world's most pristine landscapes have had indigenous people living on them for a long time. The late geographer Bernard Nietschmann called this "The Rule of Indigenous Environments: Where there are indigenous peoples with a homeland there are still biologically rich environments" (1992:3). Since the 1970s, environmentalists and indigenous groups have often come together to fight the destruction of some of those landscapes.

But as the Congress protests demonstrate, their interests often clash because they have different relationships to nature and histories of using it, and nature protection agendas often conflict with the agendas of communities who live on those landscapes. These issues lead us to the question at the center of **environmental anthropology**, the field that studies how different societies understand, interact with, and make changes to the natural world: *Why do some societies apparently have sustainable relations with the natural world while others seem to be more destructive?* Embedded in this broader question are the following problems, around which this chapter is organized:

- **Sustainable development.** Development that meets the needs of the present without compromising the ability of future generations to meet their own needs (WCED 1987).

- **Environmental anthropology.** The field that studies how different societies understand, interact with, and make changes to the natural world.

Do all people conceive of nature in the same way?

How is non-Western knowledge of nature similar to and different from science?

Do only industrialized Western societies conserve nature?

How do social and cultural factors drive environmental destruction?

Because different groups of people view the natural world differently, they also have different environmental management practices. Studying the environmental beliefs, knowledge, and practices of different societies has long been a major concern at the heart of cultural anthropology. The subfield of environmental anthropology traditionally studied these issues in the settings of small-scale, non-Western societies where beliefs, knowledge, and practices differ markedly from Western views and practices. But in recent years, as global concern with environmental degradation and the loss of biodiversity has mushroomed, environmental anthropologists have also been paying close attention to the effects of global economic changes on human–nature relations, the impacts of pollution and nature conservation initiatives on certain groups, and what sustainable development means for different people. We begin by exploring how a people's environmental values and behaviors emerge from particular ways of thinking about the natural world.

Do All People Conceive of Nature in the Same Way?

What nature means to people and how they see themselves in relation to it vary greatly around the world. Consider, for example, the relationships between indigenous settlement and natural ecosystems in southern Mexico and Central America (Figure 8.1). Some of these areas, such as the Yucatán Peninsula, the Petén region of Guatemala, and the Miskito Coast of Nicaragua, have been inhabited for many centuries. These lowlands provided Indians of the region productive environments in which to live. After the arrival of the Spanish in the 1500s they were safe areas for indigenous people because the Spanish conquerors found the tropical heat and diseases undesirable (Lovgren 2003). Why did the indigenous people not simply cut the forest down for fields, as European settlers did in other parts of the New World? One reason was their low population density and subsistence economies based on swidden agriculture in which fields go back to forest to fallow after harvesting. But economic practices alone do not explain good stewardship; for that we need to understand the indigenous views of their environment. As Ken Rapp of the Center for the Support of Native Lands recently observed, "It's part of their belief system. They don't see a division between nature and man" (Lovgren 2003).

The Human–Nature Divide?

A good example of Rapp's statement about beliefs and good stewardship of the environment is the Itzaj, a Maya group that has lived in the Petén tropical lowlands of Guatemala since pre–Spanish contact times (Figure 8.2). According to Itzaj beliefs, humans and nature do not occupy separate realms; there is both real and spiritual reciprocity and communication between plants, animals, and humans. For example, forest spirits called *arux* ("masters of the wind") continually monitor people, and they play tricks on those who cut down too many trees or kill too many animals (Atran 2001:169). Those who show respect by not wantonly destroying plants and animals receive help from the *arux*, who will lead people to animals they are hunting or to

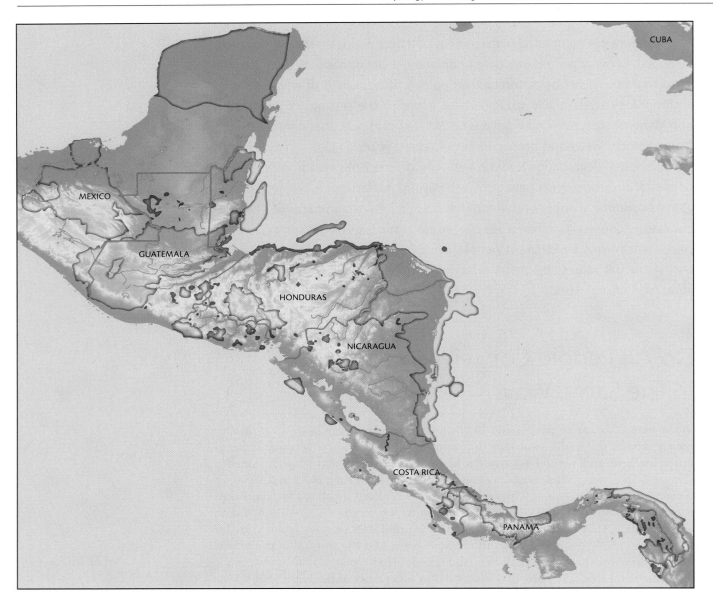

Figure 8.1   Linkages Between Biological and Cultural Diversity. This map, which is a simplified version of a map produced by the Center for the Support of Native Lands and originally published in *National Geographic* magazine, superimposes the distribution of cultural diversity and the distribution of biological diversity in Central America and Southern Mexico. The areas outlined in red mark zones where indigenous populations live and where intact biodiverse ecosystems can be found.

useful trees (Atran 2001:169). It is not accidental that Itzaj agricultural practices respect and preserve the forest.

These ideas are quite alien to most of us in North America, but Western thinking does not inherently divide humans from nature either. The medieval Italian friar St. Francis of Assisi, for example, put all creatures more or less on the same plane as humans. Nevertheless, Western thought does tend to emphasize detachment, if not opposition, between humans and nature. This detachment can be seen in the metaphor of "natural resources," in which we see nature as an object for humans to possess, control, exploit, and manage. The ancient Greek philosopher Aristotle's notion of the Great Chain of Being, which proposed that all living beings exist in hierarchical order with humans at the top (who are therefore closest to God), provides the basis for this metaphor. Western science later refined the idea of human dominion over "lower" beings. The English philosopher Sir Francis Bacon, the sixteenth-century originator of the scientific method, said that the "purpose of science was to restore to man the dominion that had been lost by the fall [from Eden]" (K. Thomas 1983:27). This view, that nature should be harnessed to make the world a better place for humans, is the basis of seeing nature as a resource (Igoe 2004:78).

Some Western philosophical traditions have emphasized an even more stark separation between humans and nature, viewing nature as an independent force outside of humans that shapes the very characteristics of their societies. This position extends back at least to the early Greeks. In his work *Historiae,* the renowned historian Herodotus (484–425 BCE) argued that biophysical factors shaped human events and societies. For example, he described the Scythians as fearsome warriors whose aggressiveness resulted from their struggle to survive in their barren desert environment. This idea is an early version of **environmental determinism**, the view that nature and environmental conditions shape the characteristics and lifeways of a group of people. Some cultural anthropologists have promoted a version of environmental determinism, such as the American anthropologist Marvin Harris (1979), who argued in the 1970s that customs develop as a direct way of regulating limited resources, acquiring protein for sustenance, controlling populations, and adapting to local ecological conditions.

Figure 8.2   The Petén Region of Lowlands Guatemala.

Harris's position that nature plays a shaping role in human cultural life became broadly accepted within **ecological anthropology**, the specific vein within environmental anthropology, prominent between the 1960s and 1980s, that studied directly the relationship between humans and natural ecosystems. But many other environmental anthropologists believe that Harris's extreme position leaves humans and nature divided, virtually in opposition, and that in fact, there is less of a stark division between people and nature and more of a give-and-take in which people's lives are affected by nature but people also shape nature to fit their own interests. Indeed, contemporary ecological science supports this second position, recognizing that humans have dramatic and subtle effects on their environments, acting as "keystone species," that is, predators that regulate animal populations and the functioning of **ecosystems**, which are natural systems based on the interaction of non-living factors and organisms (Stoffle, Toupal, and Zedeño 2003).

The Cultural Landscape

For anthropologists, however, one of the problems with purely ecological analyses of human–nature relations is that they do not account for the abstract ideas people have about landscapes and other ideas that influence people's behavior within it. One way to think of these abstract ideas is through the concept of a **cultural landscape**, which holds that people have images, knowledge, and concepts of the physical landscape that affect how they will actually interact with it (Stoffle, Toupal, and Zedeño 2003:99). For example, the Itzaj consider nature to be an extension of their social world, full of spirits that influence their everyday lives. As a result they are less likely to wantonly destroy the landscape in which they live because it would destroy their very selves. Clearly, different social groups can hold distinct, even conflicting, ideas and images of the same landscape, because it is just as easy to imagine another view (that many North Americans might hold) of that same landscape as a place with useful resources—tropical hardwoods, for example—to exploit.

Key to understanding the cultural landscape is the idea that people use metaphors to think about their natural environments, and these metaphors are connected to social behavior, thought, and organization (Bird-David 1993:112). For example, in many hunting and gathering societies, people use metaphors of personal relatedness—sexuality, marriage, or family ties—to describe human–nature relations. An illustration of this notion is from the Cree who live throughout northern Canada, who

- **Environmental determinism.** A theory that attempts to explain cultural characteristics of a group of people as a consequence of specific ecological conditions or limitations.

- **Ecological anthropology.** The specific vein with environmental anthropology that studies directly the relationship between humans and natural ecosystems.

- **Ecosystem.** Natural systems based on the interaction of non-living factors and living species.

- **Cultural landscape.** The culturally specific images, knowledge, and concepts of the physical landscape that help shape human relations with that landscape.

describe hunting through sexual metaphors. The hunter "courts" the prey, whether moose, bear, or caribou, using magic and songs to "seduce" it. Hunters describe the kill as sexual intercourse, and its result (the corpse) is believed to be the joint product of hunter and prey. The male hunters, and the women who prepare the corpse to be eaten, are expected to show great respect to the prey (especially by using all parts of the corpse), because they see killing animals as ensuring the reproduction of both humans and animals. In this metaphoric way the Cree think of animals as married to humans.

Another example of a metaphor that describes human–nature relations is that of "Mother Nature." During the past several decades it has become popular in North America and Europe to represent nature as a living force with feminine qualities of procreation and nurturing. The origin of this metaphor is popularly attributed to American Indian societies, although its Western use traces back at least to the ancient Greek goddess of the earth, Gaia. Mother Nature is an example of an "adult–child caring" metaphor. This kind of metaphor exists in a number of other societies, including the Nayaka of South India (Bird-David 1993:120). The Nayaka, for example, believe they are the offspring of ancestral forest spirits who regularly visit their hamlets to provide them with food. These spirits come to ensure that people are following the ways of their ancestors, while the people use the opportunity to demand to be cared for and fed (Bird-David 1993:120).

Metaphors are always complex, and different people may not understand them in the same ways. Nevertheless, metaphors offer insights into a community's cultural landscapes that symbolize the society's feelings and values about its environment. Anthropologists recognize that these metaphors also provide the intellectual and moral foundations upon which people construct more systematic environmental knowledge.

THINKING CRITICALLY ABOUT ENVIRONMENTAL ANTHROPOLOGY

People's images and metaphors of human–nature relatedness reflect and communicate what they know about how to work a landscape, and these are important guides to action. Besides "natural resources" and "Mother Nature" discussed previously, can you think of other metaphors of human–nature relatedness in our society? How do you think those metaphors relate to people's actual interactions with nature?

How Is Non-Western Knowledge of Nature Similar to and Different From Science?

Environmental anthropologists try to describe the traditional knowledge that different societies have of their natural environments, recognizing that all knowledge systems about nature, including science, are culturally based. This goal dates back to the beginnings of anthropology as a discipline. For example, during his years among the

Trobriand Islanders (1915–1918), Bronislaw Malinowski was keenly interested in people's knowledge of gardening, canoe building, and navigation. From observing these activities, he concluded that "primitive humanity was aware of the scientific laws of natural process" as well as magical processes, and went on to add that all people operate within the domains of magic, science, and religion (1948:196).

American anthropologist Paul Radin reached a similar conclusion from his fieldwork with Native Americans and wrote about it in his 1927 work *Primitive Man as Philosopher,* observing that "it is manifestly unfair to contend that primitive people are deficient either in the power of abstract thought or in the power of arranging these thoughts in a systematic order, or, finally, of subjecting them and their whole environment to an objective critique" (1927:354). In their time, these were highly controversial claims. Malinowski was implying that modern knowledge operated partly on non-scientific principles of magic and religion (which the West looked down upon as features of "less civilized" societies), and both were claiming that non-Western people could be scientific too.

Do native knowledge systems have scientific validity? Malinowski reasoned that if knowledge is born of experience and reason, and if science is an activity characterized by rationality, then indigenous knowledge is part of humankind's scientific knowledge (Nader 1996:7). Since his time, anthropologists have demonstrated that scientific attitudes and methods of validation—close observation, experimentation, and analysis—are not unique to the West (1996:8). It is also the case that modern sciences have borrowed extensively from non-European societies. Key concepts and methods in mathematics, for example, are derived from India and the Arab world; some agricultural products and techniques from the pre-Columbian Americas; and technologies such as the magnetic needle and gunpowder from China (Harding 1994:347). So other societies have what we think of as scientific attitudes and practices. One key difference that distinguishes many non-Western knowledge systems from Western sciences, however, is that they are not necessarily viewed as distinct realms of knowledge, being integrated into people's spiritual beliefs, social practices, and individual identities, while in the West people tend to think of science as separate from all these things, as its own special domain of knowledge.

Ethnoscience

Early interest within environmental anthropology concerned with knowledge in non-Western societies was called **ethnoscience** (see also Chapter 4). During the 1960s, when ethnoscience was at its peak influence, ethnoscientists aimed to describe and understand the conceptual models and rules with which a society operates, following Malinowski's call for anthropologists to see the world from the "native's point of view" (Sturtevant 1964:100). They began by comparing the systems of classification used by the different peoples they studied.

Classification systems are reference systems that group things or ideas with similar features. Examples include plant and animal taxonomies, kinship terminologies, color schemes, and medical diagnoses. Classification systems create a common intellectual framework that people use to work with the natural world, heal the sick, and communicate with each other.

The Linnaean classification system is what the scientific discipline of biology uses to classify all living organisms into species. Closely related species belong to the same genus, and related genuses are grouped into orders, and so on. Brent Berlin, who studied **ethnobiology** (indigenous ways of naming and codifying living things) of the Tzeltal Maya, has argued that the Tzeltal and most societies for whom we have data divide living things into groups based on shared morphological characteristics as the

- **Ethnoscience.** The study of how people classify things in the world, usually by considering some range or set of meanings.

- **Ethnobiology.** The subfield of ethnoscience that studies how people in non-Western societies name and codify living things.

Linnaen system does (Berlin 1973). Based on these findings, Berlin concluded that all human classification systems were basically reflective of an underlying cognitive structure of the human brain that organizes information in systematic ways—in other words, that all human minds more or less think alike.

But numerous challenges to Berlin's conclusions exist, based largely on the observation that some societies use non-morphological characteristics to classify plants and animals. For example, the Kalam people of the Papua New Guinea highlands do not consider the cassowary, a large flightless bird, as a bird. They also distinguish it from bats, which they put in the same category as birds. The Kalam classification system gives the cassowary a special taxonomic rank that places them close to humans (Bulmer 1967). Kalam mythology identifies the cassowary as sisters and cousins to Kalam men, and the Kalam place special restrictions on hunting them. The special taxonomic status of these creatures not only results from their unexpected physical characteristics (a bird that cannot fly) but also reflects certain social categories and relationships.

Another challenge comes from the existence of societies in which classification is a highly dynamic and unstable affair. For example, the Wola, who also live in the highlands of Papua New Guinea, have a classificatory system that leaves much room for disagreement. In itself, such disagreement is not especially surprising: people often disagree with one another when they classify natural phenomena, because different people have different knowledge (Sillitoe 2002:1162). But the extent of disagreement in Wola is such that it can undermine the entire classification system. People regularly disagree over the identification of particular animals, devise their own names and categories based on personal experiences, and even dispute the structure of taxonomy itself. Confronting this system, environmental anthropologist Paul Sillitoe argues that the Wola have a taxonomy less in the Greek sense of a *taxis* (arrangement) of natural phenomena for intellectual purposes, than an arrangement in the political sense of being a way of talking through and settling differences (Sillitoe 2002:1169). The main purpose of their taxonomy is not to provide certainty, Sillitoe believes, but to keep people talking to each other, working out the issues and disputes that arise in everyday life. This situation is especially important for a society like the Wola, which has a non-hierarchical political order and has no political authority to settle disputes.

Traditional Ecological Knowledge

- **Traditional ecological knowledge.** Indigenous ecological knowledge and its relationship with resource management strategies.

In environmental anthropology, ethnoscience's interests these days continue under the more general label **traditional ecological knowledge**, which studies indigenous ecological knowledge and its relationship with resource management strategies. One of the more important findings of this field is that many ecological relations recognized by indigenous peoples are not known to Western science. One reason for this lack of knowledge is that this knowledge may involve species that are endemic, which means they exist only in one place. Indigenous knowledge also sometimes makes connections that Western science does not make. For example, many indigenous groups in the Americas make a distinction between domesticated and wild chili peppers. Groups such as the Tohono O'odham [Toe-**hoh**-no Oh-**oh**-dom] people of the Sonora Desert in the American Southwest use a term akin to "bird peppers" for the wild ones, and when asked will name certain birds that consume those chilies and disperse their seeds. Ethnobiologist Gary Paul Nabhan designed an experiment to test this knowledge, and confirmed its accuracy (Nabhan 2001). He suggests that indigenous knowledge can serve to guide scientific research on plant–animal interactions.

Another reason local ecological knowledge is not well known to Western science is that knowledge often resides in local languages, songs, or specialized ritual knowledge. Healers and shamans are important repositories of local plant knowledge and lore, and they may even keep their knowledge secret from other people in their own society. In recent years, ethnobotanists working with pharmaceutical companies have been trying to gain access to the knowledge of traditional healers to identify plants that might be useful for developing new commercial drugs.

One famous example of traditional medicinal knowledge that led to a commercially viable drug is the Rosy Periwinkle plant from Madagascar. Healers there have traditionally used it to treat diabetes, and scientists discovered that it also contains chemicals that are highly effective in treating certain cancers, including Hodgkin's Disease. Eli Lilly, a U.S. pharmaceutical company, patented one of these chemicals and markets it as a pharmaceutical drug. Although traditional healers in Madagascar did not necessarily know about its ability to treat cancer, many critics point out that these healers—from whom Western scientists first learned of the plant's healing properties—never received any compensation. As a result, many indigenous healers around the world are increasingly becoming even more protective of their knowledge in fear that transnational corporations can reap profits from their collective wisdom without their permission.

Because traditional ecological knowledge is customized to particular environments, it can also provide a highly effective basis for managing resources. For example, in the Southern Mexican state of Oaxaca, Zapotec farmers have been growing maize on the same landscape for hundreds of years. Farmers have a highly systematic understanding of how soil qualities, weather patterns, lunar phases, plant–plant interactions, and plant–insect interactions affect the growing of maize (Gonzalez 2001). Western scientists have discovered that Zapotec practices of intercropping (planting multiple crops together), building soil mounds for planting maize, letting the land lie fallow, and planting and harvesting by the phases of the moon all contribute to creating a highly productive and sustainable agricultural system (Gonzalez 2001).

Some elements of Zapotec science do not correspond to Western science and beliefs about effective resource management, however. For example, the system of measurements that farmers use to cultivate fields, create tools, and measure the volume of their production is not standardized. The Zapotec base measurements on the human body, such as the length of the arm, and they are therefore highly variable. While such a system might seem confusing, it has distinct advantages: it is portable (no need to carry a measuring stick or tape measure), and tools are made to fit the user (Gonzalez 2001). Also, ecological knowledge is not separate from other forms of knowledge, such as ideas about morally acceptable behavior. Zapotecs believe that cultivations, especially maize, have a soul that rewards people who share with others. As a result, they believe that the success of a harvest is directly related to the farmer's positive social relations with other members of the community.

When environmental anthropologists seek to understand how traditional ecological knowledge works to guide human action in particular communities, they have to take into account that the insider's point of view about what is going on in nature—for instance, the Zapotec belief that maize has a soul and if cultivated and shared properly will grow well—is often different from the views of outsiders, such as scientists who would explain that soil and climate conditions are what make maize grow. As we explore in "Classic Contributions: Roy Rappaport's Insider and Outsider Models," one prominent anthropologist argued that both views have relevance to the environmental anthropologist.

The Zapotec case demonstrates that traditional ecological knowledge has allowed communities to thrive for a long time on a landscape without destroying it.

Classic Contributions

Roy Rappaport's Insider and Outsider Models

THE AMERICAN ANTHROPOLOGIST Roy Rappaport (1926–1997) was a major figure in the field of ecological anthropology, whose specific focus is on the relationship between humans and natural ecosystems. He was a pioneer in the use of systems theory for understanding human populations. In his landmark 1968 study *Pigs for the Ancestors: Ritual in the Ecology of a New Guinea People* (1984), Rappaport distinguished between the insider's mental models of human–nature relations called "cognized models" and "operational models," the ecological dimensions of human–nature relations identified by the observer. He argues that the goal of the anthropologist is to figure out how cognized models guide behavior, and how that behavior helps people adapt to specific environmental conditions:

> [T]wo models of the environment are significant in ecological studies, and I have termed these "operational" and "cognized." The operational model is that which the anthropologist constructs through observation and measurement of empirical entities, events, and material relationships. He takes this model to represent, for analytic purposes, the physical world of the group he is studying. . . .
>
> The cognized model is the model of the environment conceived by the people who act in it. The two models are overlapping, but not identical. While many components of the physical world will be represented in both, the operational model is likely to include material elements, such as disease germs and nitrogen-fixing bacteria, that affect actors but of which they may not be aware. Conversely, the cognized model may include elements that cannot be shown by empirical means to exist, such as spirits and other supernatural beings. . . . the important question concerning the cognized model, since it serves as a guide to action, is not the extent to which it conforms to "reality" (i.e., is identical with or isomorphic with the operational model), but the extent to which it elicits behavior that is appropriate to the material situation of the actors, and it is against this functional and adaptive criterion that we may assess it. (Rappaport 1984:237–238; emphasis in the original)

Questions for Reflection

1. What are some reasons Rappaport might advocate a balanced approach between "cognized" and "operational" models of human–nature interactions?

2. Can you identify some elements of the insider's view or "cognized model" of our own society?

Unlike Western sciences, which claim to have universal tools for understanding nature, the Zapotec knowledge of nature is rooted in local cultural traditions and beliefs. It is also not viewed as a separate domain of specialized knowledge but is integrated into people's daily lives, spiritual practices, and so on. The fact that such groups have not destroyed their environments, as many other societies have, has led some researchers to speculate that conservationist principles such as respect for local ecology and nature protection are embedded in traditional ecological knowledge. But do non-Western people actively conserve nature?

THINKING CRITICALLY ABOUT ENVIRONMENTAL ANTHROPOLOGY

The idea that traditional ecological knowledge provides an effective basis for managing natural resources is often resisted most strongly by Western agricultural scientists, who often dismiss these knowledge systems as not scientific and rigorous. How should environmental anthropologists respond to these kinds of claims?

Do Only Industrialized Western Societies Conserve Nature?

The World Parks Congress, described at the beginning of this chapter, is one aspect of a remarkable global phenomenon that began with the founding of the first national park at Yellowstone in 1872. Formal nature protection as we know it—national parks, wilderness areas, etc.—originated in the West, although it is spreading rapidly around the globe. Environmental anthropologists have studied these processes closely, because they often generate social conflict in communities with different cultural perspectives on and histories within the natural world.

In exploring whether or not non-Western societies have had similar intentions to conserve, it is necessary to overcome a powerful stereotype that a lot of Americans and Europeans hold about native peoples, that they are "natural environmentalists" always in tune with the natural world. In fact, environmental anthropologists have documented many examples of destructive indigenous relationships with nature. Examples include the Itzaj's neighbors in Guatemala's Petén region, the Maya Q'eqchi, whose cattle ranching economy is destroying the rainforests of that region. Scholars also point to the "aboriginal overkill" that led to human-caused extinctions toward the end of the Pleistocene Era (Ice Age) (Krech 1999). Stereotypes of Indians as "natural environmentalists" are romantic, and they often obscure the real conditions under which a group of people relate to nature (Figure 8.3). The key to answering this section's question is to consider first how indigenous societies have created landscapes that either deliberately or unintentionally have the effect of protecting natural ecosystems and wildlife and, second, the ways in which Western societies approach the same objective.

Artifactual Landscapes

Upon close examination, many landscapes that appear "natural" to Westerners—sometimes the very landscapes that Westerners want to conserve without people on them—are actually the result of indigenous involvement and manipulation. In other words, they are **artifactual landscapes**, or products of human shaping.

• **Artifactual landscapes.** The idea that landscapes are the product of human shaping.

Figure 8.3 **Stereotypes of Green Indians.** In 1971 the "Keep America Beautiful" campaign developed by the U.S. government aired an anti-pollution television ad featuring an American Indian (actually an Italian-American actor with the stage name of Iron Eyes Cody) who sheds a tear because of pollution. There is usually a large gap between such romantic stereotypes and the real conditions in which indigenous groups relate to the environment.

A good illustration of an artifactual landscape is the North American continent during the early period of European settlement. When British settlers arrived on the East Coast, they found a continent abundant with woodlands and wild game and apparently inhabited by few people, and it confirmed for them a sense that America was an unpeopled wilderness. Most Europeans did not realize that this landscape had been created by indigenous resource management systems, which included regular burning of underbrush to keep shrubs and grasses down as well as seasonal migration (Cronon 1983). The intention of these Indian groups was to create environments that were easy to move around and hunt in, though to European eyes they looked like purely natural environments.

Environmental anthropologists have documented numerous examples of the creation of artifactual landscapes through human manipulation and management that actively and self-consciously support the conservation of specific plants and animals. For example, the Tohono O'odham of the Sonora Desert, mentioned earlier, protect rare plants from overharvesting near sacred sites, transplant individual cacti and tubers to more protected sites, and promote the fruiting of certain rare food plants by pruning them (Nabhan 1997:162). The O'odham believe that humans are active participants in the desert ecosystem and that certain animals, plants, and habitats will "degenerate" unless humans care for them (Nabhan 1997:163).

Another important example of an artifactual landscape is the East African savannas of northern Tanzania and southern Kenya. The Maasai, who live there as pastoralists, have extensively modified their environment to support their cattle. They burn scrub brush to encourage the growth of nutritious pasture grass, an act that helps support wildlife biodiversity because these are the same nutritious pastures that the savanna's world-famous wildlife populations of zebras, wildebeest, and other large animals also eat (Igoe 2004). But today, some of these fragile scrublands are in crisis because Maasai pastoralists are undermining them with overgrazing. To understand why they now overgraze, we must look at the clash between Western and Maasai notions of managing and conserving nature.

The Culture of Modern Nature Conservation

To prevent overgrazing and conserve resources for themselves and wildlife populations, Maasai traditionally practiced a form of pastoralism called transhumant pastoralism in which they range over large territories of commonly held property on regular paths and cycles. During drought years, when pastures are most susceptible to overgrazing, the Maasai would traditionally bring cattle to swamp areas and permanent waterholes. But during the twentieth century national parks and nature reserves were typically formed around these permanent wet areas (since a lot of wild animals congregate there too), preventing Maasai access to them. Park administrators and scientists did not understand the delicate balance between people and wildlife that was sustained by the constant movement of people, their herds, and the wild animals. The result is that the Maasai were forced to overgraze areas outside the park during drought periods, not to mention great resentment among the Maasai that has generated conflicts with park officials (Igoe 2004).

These park officials practice what anthropologist Dan Brockington (2002) calls "Fortress Conservation," an approach to conservation that assumes that people are threatening to nature, and that for nature to be pristine the people who live there must be evicted. This approach to conservation is precisely what indigenous leaders were protesting at the World Parks Congress. One question for the anthropologist is: where does this culturally powerful idea that people and conservation of nature are incompatible originate? The philosophical divide in Western thought between nature and people is one influence. In addition, at least three historical trends came together to create the culture of modern conservation: enclosure in England, westward expansion in the United States, and European colonial expansion.

The English Enclosure Movement

For centuries, England's countryside was characterized by fields and pastures held in common by small farmers. Between the eighteenth and mid-nineteenth centuries, the English Parliament privatized these lands in what is known as the *enclosure movement*. The Napoleonic Wars had driven up the prices of grain and meat, and wealthy landowners saw opportunities to create large commercial farms to take advantage of these markets. Parliament turned over formerly common lands to private ownership, evicting farmers and sending them to work on the new farms or in urban factories. Rural people who tried to continue their lifestyles were branded criminals and sent off to the penal colony of Australia. The resulting depopulation of the English countryside accompanied a shift in how people thought about the landscape. Because the countryside was no longer populated by poor and working people, the wealthy began to idealize it as a place of scenic beauty and leisure (Igoe 2004:81). The connection between landscape appreciation and "civilized tastes" was born.

Westward Expansion in the United States.

During the nineteenth century, the idea of formally preserving wilderness took root in the Western United States. With the Louisiana Purchase in 1803, Americans had accepted the doctrine of Manifest Destiny, which presumed that the destiny of the United States was to colonize and civilize the entire North American continent. Always self-conscious about our national identity vis-à-vis Europeans, Americans believed that the spectacular and vast resources and natural beauty of the North American continent could compete with the monuments and civilized arts of Europe. Soon after the turmoil of the Civil War ended Americans set about showing our own "civilization" by establishing formally protected areas. The Indians who relied on these wilderness areas for their subsistence were branded as uncivilized and unappreciative of nature, and were forcibly removed. When the Congress created Yellowstone National Park in 1872, for example, it entailed the removal of six different Indian groups from park lands (Guha 2000).

European Colonial Expansion

European colonial regimes commonly instituted controls on native people's use of natural resources. The main reason was to eliminate native competition against the European businesses exploiting raw materials in the colonies (Grove 1995). British colonial officials took landscape control a step further in East Africa, where they created "Royal Game Reserves" in which English aristocrats and colonial officers could hunt. They forcibly removed people from these areas and criminalized local people (like the Maasai) who continued hunting as "poachers." The Society for the Preservation of the Wild Fauna of the Empire, founded in 1903 and a forerunner of organizations such as the World Wildlife Fund, played a central role in establishing these policies. This was the era of the big game hunter, and many animal populations—most notably wild elephant and rhinoceros—crashed as a result of overhunting by European elites (Figure 8.4). Many of these parks were later upgraded to national parks where hunting is no longer permitted.

By preventing native peoples in the colonies from engaging in their traditional businesses or gaining access to their commonly held properties, colonial administrators simultaneously eliminated most of the economic opportunities that would have been available had Europeans not come and taken over their territories. Native peoples became dependent on the colonial administration, encouraging the view among

Figure 8.4   Big-Game Hunters and Conservation. American President Teddy Roosevelt was an avid hunter who went on numerous hunting expeditions in East African Royal Game Reserves. He believed modern life degenerated manhood, and he advocated "getting back to nature" (which for him was hunting) as a way to correct this problem.

Europeans that natives were naturally lazy. To Europeans it seemed that native peoples were unable to look after their own interests, although, as the Malaysian sociologist Syed Hussein Alatas (1977) suggests, most of these native peoples had been quite industrious and able to manage complex businesses with extensive international trade relations until Europeans seized their lands, or banned international shipping, to ensure a government monopoly. Once the native inhabitants of a colony were impoverished from losing control over the best lands and resources, colonizers took on a paternalistic attitude toward native peoples. This view came to be known as the "White man's burden," the so-called duty of white men to look after the interests of their dark-skinned colonial subjects. In fact, however, had local people retained access to the lands and resources they had always made use of, they would not have been anyone's burden.

Is Collaborative Conservation Possible?

Environmental anthropologists recognize that the displacement of local people for the purposes of conserving nature is a powerful cultural idea born of complex historical dynamics. But many also recognize that this approach has been tied closely to colonial power over local natural resources and has tended to ignore subtle histories of how artifactual landscapes are produced through active human involvement in a landscape, in ways that can actually support wildlife biodiversity, such as the Maasai case.

Some conservationists have begun to agree, and during the past several decades there have been a number of experiments in "co-management" between international conservation groups and indigenous people. In places like Nepal, Alaska, Canada, Panama, Brazil, and Australia, indigenous people have been allowed to continue living in protected areas and have some say in park management. Environmental anthropologists have in turn begun studying these situations. They have found that a collaborative approach creates new kinds of opportunities for dialogue, power-sharing, and relationship-building between conservationists and indigenous communities (Natcher, Hickey, and Hickey 2005). But they can also create new dilemmas for indigenous communities. For example, national and international conservation groups still exercise considerable control, especially over funding, and government scientists often disrespect indigenous knowledge about wildlife and landscape dynamics even though they are supposed to be "co-managing" the resources with the indigenous community (Igoe 2004:158; Nadasdy 2005).

Some critics also assert that the drive to protect nature by creating preserves, even when it is done with the collaboration of indigenous groups, is merely treating a symptom of a deeper problem. Should we not really get to the root of that problem, which is the social practices and ideologies that lead to the destruction of nature itself in the first place? Who is really to blame for environmental destruction around the world? Anthropologists have a sophisticated understanding of what factors and who contribute to environmental destruction, an issue we turn to in the next section.

THINKING CRITICALLY ABOUT ENVIRONMENTAL ANTHROPOLOGY

Americans often assume that people interested in conserving nature tend to be middle-class people who give money to environmental groups because they have met their other basic requirements, such as getting access to food, shelter, clothing, and other necessities. In other words, protecting nature is a luxury and poor people cannot do it because they need to feed themselves. Based on what we have discussed in this section, why is this view skewed?

How Do Social and Cultural Factors Drive Environmental Destruction?

What are the root causes of environmental destruction? Greed and self-interest tend to rank high on the list. The same could be said for poor land management techniques, overpopulation, and old-fashioned ignorance. Trying to identify a root cause is tempting because it suggests a relatively clear course of action. Were it only as simple as that.

Environmental anthropologists have found that nature's destruction results from a complex interplay of social, cultural, natural, and political-economic factors that always come back to two important questions: How do people consume natural resources in their lifestyles, and who pays the cost of that consumption? The concept of ecological footprint and theories of political ecology will help us explore this issue in a later section. But before we review these, let us show how the search for root causes distracts us from understanding the complex interrelationships that produce environmental destruction. Let us first consider population growth, which is one of the most popular explanations as a root cause for environmental destruction.

Population and Environment

Eighteenth-century theologian Thomas Malthus argued that human population grows exponentially (as opposed to arithmetically), quickly overwhelming a limited resource base and leading to famine. Some modern environmentalists, such as Paul Erlich who in 1968 wrote a book with the alarming title *The Population Bomb,* have argued that the same is happening on a global scale in the world today. The numbers are stark: in the seventy-two years from 1927 to 1999, there was a three-fold increase in world population, from approximately two billion to six billion people. Barely over a decade later, that population has grown to more than seven billion. At these rates of growth, he and others have concluded that complete environmental collapse is likely. The problem seems self-evident: a small planet cannot indefinitely support a quickly expanding global population, and ecological ruin awaits us if we do not deal with it. However, social scientists have yet to identify any confirmed case of environmental and social collapse because of overpopulation or mass consumption (Tainter 2006).

• **Carrying capacity.** The population an area can support.

Second, humans have tended to adapt to the land's **carrying capacity**, which is the population an area can support, by intensifying agriculture (a dynamic we described in Chapter 7, "Foodways"). Sustainable social systems also often respond by adopting new cultural practices to cope with rapid ecological deterioration. In other words, they are resilient, able to absorb change by changing social practices. For example, in the floodplain of the Brazilian Amazon, attempts to make commercial fisheries more sustainable have focused on how communities can themselves regulate fisheries (de Castro and McGrath 2003). To ensure that overfishing does not take place, communities sign formal fishing accords that regulate who has access to fisheries and the amounts they are allowed to keep. These accords have had some success controlling commercial fishing, and they show that one of the keys to sustainability is to create innovative social institutions that help people collectively deal with changing environmental circumstances, in this case declining fisheries.

In addition, anthropologists have also shown that the environmental disruptions that lead to famines result from a complex interplay of natural conditions with existing patterns of social inequality. For example, during the 1985 Ethiopian famine, Western aid and relief agencies like the World Food Program the U.S. Agency for International Development argued that Ethiopia's population was too large, resulting in the overconsumption of natural resources, environmental collapse, and famine. Their solution was to implement programs of food relief and land reclamation projects to improve agricultural yield.

But these programs failed, because the experts who conceived them misunderstood the complex causes of the famine. The experts based their models on exaggerated data about land degradation and ignored other data, particularly the disastrous effects of the country's civil war and socialist government, which disrupted food distribution channels. Legal barriers that led to insecure access to land also discouraged farmers from investing in traditional soil conservation measures (Hoben 1995). This famine was not a consequence of overpopulation but the result of these other interrelated factors. No one of these factors by itself would have produced the famine.

Doing Fieldwork

James Fairhead and Melissa Leach on Misreading the African Landscape

IN THE WEST African country of Guinea, in the prefecture of Kissidougou [kee-see-**doo**-goo], the landscape is a mosaic of forests and savanna lands. From the nineteenth century to the present, French colonial administrators, environmentalists, and development officials have interpreted this landscape as a story of once-extensive forest fragmented by rapid population growth and native

James Fairhead and Melissa Leach.

mismanagement. As the forest has disappeared, the explanation goes, the savannas have been on the increase.

British anthropologists James Fairhead and Melissa Leach (1996) had heard stories that suggested the opposite was happening—that savannas are retreating and forests are on the increase. So, during the 1990s, they set out to test this counterintuitive claim. Their findings confirmed that forests are in fact increasing and that the real landscape history is a story of savannas being replaced by human-cultivated forests. Even more remarkable, perhaps, is their finding that these processes have intensified *as human populations have grown*. In some cases, forests had grown so successfully that local people no longer had access to useful savanna products, like straw grass for hut roofs. People grow forests for various reasons: forests create protective fortresses around villages, provide hunting grounds by attracting birds and animals, prevent grassland fires from reaching villages, and improve grassland soils for cultivation. The anthropologists' research indicates that elite misreadings of environmental history are not inconsequential. They underestimate how much people modify landscapes in ways that can even *enhance* biodiversity. Development personnel thus risk imposing poorly designed solutions on rural peoples (such as population control programs, instead of, say, technical support for reforestation).

How did Fairhead and Leach learn these things? First, they went to villages with distinct combinations of forest and savanna, and listened to local people's own stories of landscape transformation. They recorded oral histories of savanna–forest transformation, and found that landscape could be converted from savanna to dense forest rapidly, sometimes within a single lifetime. They asked people to show them the process of converting savannas to forest, which starts with the cultivation of useful plants like kola nuts (used to create cooking oil) to break up the dense grassland soils, and follows these with fast-growing tree species. Fairhead and Leach also learned by directly participating in people's agricultural activities, working side by side with them in fields and forests, so that they could understand land management techniques first-hand.

To complement these insider perspectives, Fairhead and Leach studied different kinds of official documents from government archives. They consulted colonial records that

(continued)

Doing Fieldwork (continued)

referred to the forests being used as protective fortresses. They looked at censuses to track population growth. They also consulted aerial photographs and satellite images going back several decades. These images helped them track the establishment of settlements and the resulting growth of forests. By measuring the growth of forest in these images, they could test the claims made by local people, finding support for what people told them.

In isolation, none of these methods would necessarily be sufficient to demonstrate this story: aerial photos can be ambiguous, censuses inaccurate, and oral histories exaggerated. But when combined and carefully executed, they can challenge basic assumptions about environmental degradation.

Questions for Reflection

1. Suppose you wanted to understand the landscape history of your hometown or city. Where and how would you gather information on this issue?

2. If you wanted to do oral histories of the landscape, with whom would you speak?

3. What kinds of documents do you think might help you understand the landscape history of your hometown or city?

The point is that it is impossible to isolate overpopulation as *the* cause of environmental collapse. To do so is a misreading of environmental degradation. In "Doing Fieldwork: James Fairhead and Melissa Leach on Misreading the African Landscape," we examine how one pair of environmental anthropologists has challenged these misreadings using careful ethnographic and historical research methods.

Ecological Footprint

● **Ecological footprint.** A quantitative tool that measures what people consume and the waste they produce. It also calculates the area of biologically productive land and water needed to support those people.

Another problem with overpopulation as a sole explanation for environmental degradation is that it does not address the fact that different societies, as well as people within those societies, consume differing amounts of resources. The concept of an **ecological footprint** addresses this issue by measuring what people consume and the waste they produce. It then calculates the amount of biologically productive land and water area needed to support them. Researchers estimate that 1.8 hectares (4.5 acres) are available for each person on earth, although the actual worldwide per capita footprint is 2.3 hectares (5.75 acres) (Wackernagel et al. 1997). In isolation these numbers do not tell us much, except perhaps that humanity as a whole is using more than the earth's projected ecological capacity. But when we compare the consumption rates of different countries, an important pattern emerges. People in industrialized countries consume much more than people in non-industrialized countries. For example, the average American needs 8.4 hectares (21 acres) to support his or her lifestyle, while the average (South Asian) Indian requires 0.8 hectares (2 acres) (Wackernagel et al. 1997) (Figure 8.5). Of course, these are just averages; some consume more and others less, usually related to their relative wealth or poverty.

The distinction between the average Indian and the average North American is the latter's involvement in consumer capitalism. Consumer capitalism promotes the cultural ideal that people will never fully satisfy their needs, so they will continually buy more and more things in their pursuit of happiness. This cultural ideal has enormous ecological consequences. We see these consequences in the production of goods (the extraction of non-renewable raw materials to make consumer products); the distribution of goods (the reliance on fossil fuels to transport goods to market); and the

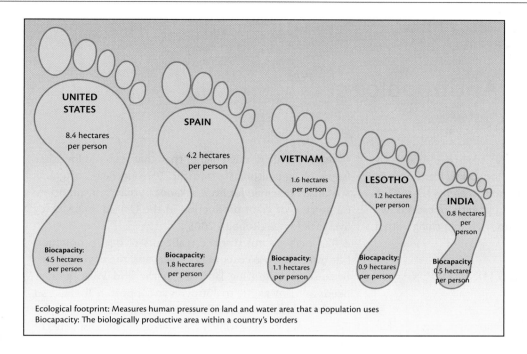

Ecological footprint: Measures human pressure on land and water area that a population uses
Biocapacity: The biologically productive area within a country's borders

Figure 8.5   The Ecological Footprints of Five Countries.

consumption of goods (the landfills that get filled with non-organic trash). As a result, while Americans make up only 5% of the world's population, they consume 25% of its resources.

Most Americans do not understand the ecological destructiveness of consumer lifestyles, although signs of it are everywhere: urban sprawl, polluted air and waterways, acid rain, unhealthy forests, global warming, and environmental health problems linked to contamination. In "Thinking Like an Anthropologist: Identifying Hidden Costs," we explore how the simple act of eating a hamburger relates to environmental degradation.

Political Ecology

The kinds of analyses that focus on the linkages between political-economic power, social inequality, and ecological destruction are typical of **political ecology**. Many environmental anthropologists align themselves closely with political ecology, which rejects singular-factor explanations, like overpopulation, ignorance, or poor land use, as explanations for environmental degradation. It asks questions like: What are the ecological and social consequences of an industrial economy? Who pays the real costs of capitalist development patterns that promote the exploitation, not the replenishment, of natural resources? How do pollution and other problems of environmental degradation reflect and reinforce patterns of social inequality? Political ecology emphasizes the idea that capitalism undermines itself over the long term because it exploits the labor and natural resources upon which it relies to produce commodities (O'Connor 1988).

Social and Economic Inequality:
The Case of Small Honduran Farmers

Political ecologists also ask how and why people in desperate poverty overexploit the few natural resources available to them (Peet and Watts 2004). Often, the answer has to do with their marginal position within unequal social and economic systems. Consider, for example, the small farmers in southern Honduras studied by anthropologist

- **Political ecology.** The field of study that focuses on the linkages between political-economic power, social inequality, and ecological destruction.

Thinking Like an Anthropologist

Identifying Hidden Costs

ANTHROPOLOGISTS BEGIN THEIR research by asking questions. In this box, we want you to learn how to ask questions as an anthropological researcher. Part One describes a situation and follows up with questions we would ask. Part Two asks you to do the same thing with a different situation.

PART ONE: IDENTIFYING THE HIDDEN COSTS OF A HAMBURGER

In his book *Fast Food Nation*, Eric Schlosser points out that the typical American eats three hamburgers and four orders of French fries every week (2001:6). This meal epitomizes American tastes, but its desirability is also due to its low cost to the consumer—this meal comes in at around $4 or $5, including a soda, at most fast-food restaurants. Why is the price so low? Traditional economists would answer that it is the fast food industry's technological efficiency and economy of scale that keep costs down. But these facts alone do not explain the low cost, because neither the consumer nor the industry actually pays the real costs for each of the ingredients that go into the meal. Revealing the hidden costs shows who and what bears the actual costs of fast food.

Each ingredient deserves analysis, but in the interest of space, let us consider only the beef that goes into the hamburger. Beef is a notoriously inefficient source of energy and protein. It takes about 2,700 pounds of grain or a couple of acres of pasture to produce a typical 1,050 pound steer (Robbins 2005). The amount of land and water it takes to

raise beef cattle is much higher than that required for other forms of agriculture. In fact, our "waving fields of grain" are largely destined for livestock, not human, consumption: 80 percent of grain production in the United States is for livestock forage (Robbins 2005).

Ranchers do not pay the real costs of beef production but transfer those costs to taxpayers and the environment. Because most grazing land lies in the arid West, a steer needs as many as 200 to 300 acres to support it. To make so much land available to ranchers, Congress passed the Taylor Grazing Act in 1934, which transferred millions of acres of public land to ranchers if they took responsibility for improving them (Robbins 2005:224). These "improvements" are generally minor and self-interested (such as barbed-wire fences), so taxpayers assume the greater costs of predator control, drought relief, disease control, and the costly reservoir and irrigation projects required to support cattle in arid lands. One estimate calculates that the government subsidizes public land grazing as much as $500 million per year. If the government charged ranchers fees that reflected the real costs of supporting cattle in the arid West, it would annually charge ranchers $175 per steer (Wuerthner 2003).

But most beef cattle are fed grains and cereals. Grains quickly fatten the steer and have become inexpensive to buy because of chemical fertilizers, herbicides, and pesticides, which keep production costs down and enhance the productivity of grain farmers. To keep grain costs low, the government offers reduced tax rates on agricultural lands and pays farmers direct subsidies to protect them from market variations. And approximately half the water we as a nation consume is used to grow the grain needed to feed cattle (Robbins 2005:217). The amount of water used to produce ten pounds of steak equals the household water consumption of a family for an entire year (Robbins 2005)! It is taxpayers, not grain farmers, who assume the costs of building and maintaining expensive water reclamation and irrigation projects.

Water reclamation projects also have enormous ecological impacts, including flooding to create dams, silting of waterways, diversion of waterways, and effects on fish populations. Use of so many chemical fertilizers, pesticides, and herbicides also carries high ecological costs, damaging soil and groundwater throughout grain producing areas. Finally, beef has to travel over subsidized highways with subsidized gasoline from where it is produced to where it is eaten.

❦ **A Hamburger With All the Trimmings.**

These costs are not borne exclusively by the people of the United States alone, because Americans produce about 9 percent of beef in the world but consume about 28 percent of the world's beef production (Robbins 2005:226). Clearly, our analysis of beef's hidden costs would also have to take into account the ecological and social costs of raising beef in other countries.

What questions does the hidden cost of a burger raise for anthropological researchers?

1. What are the different steps involved in the production, distribution, and consumption of beef, and who is involved in this chain of relationships?
2. Who and what assumes the actual costs of production at each of these steps?
3. Why do some actors in this chain pay the costs more than others?
4. Why are the ecological costs of producing beef not paid by agricultural producers?
5. Does anyone pay those ecological costs?

PART TWO: FILLING YOUR TANK

The analysis of hidden costs on people and environments can be applied to virtually any part of a consumer lifestyle, even the most mundane. Consider developing some questions about the hidden costs of filling an automobile gas tank, before and after the BP oil spill in the Gulf of Mexico of 2010. What questions would you pose as an anthropological researcher in order to explore the hidden environmental and social costs of pumping gasoline?

Susan Stonich (Stonich 1995). Since the 1950s, large commercial cotton plantations and cattle ranches have encroached on small farmers, pushing them into less productive land on mountain slopes. As commercial farms have gotten larger, the size of small farms has declined, causing many farmers to give up and migrate to the cities. Those who remain on the farm have shifted from subsistence agriculture to growing cash crops for export. The intense pressure to produce high yields has led them to deforest hillsides and abandon soil conservation measures that take more work because they are on steep land, both of which undermine the long-term fertility of their lands. Eventually farmers find themselves in a spiral of declining environmental quality on their farms.

The dynamics of the decline of small Honduran farmers are connected to political-economic forces operating simultaneously at local, regional, and international levels. Political ecologists explain the environmental degradation as the result of the Honduran government's laws encouraging concentration of land in few hands. To explain why the government creates policies favoring commercial agriculture's expansion, they look to the lending policies of countries like the United States and agencies like the World Bank, both of which have pressured the Honduran government to promote the growth of melons and shrimp for export to pay international debts instead of encouraging food for local consumption (Stonich 1995).

Social and Economic Inequality: Why Poor Neighborhoods Get the Toxic Waste Dumps

Political ecologists have also observed that environmentally harmful activities fall disproportionately on lower-income people and minority groups, especially African Americans, American Indians, and Latinos in the United States. These groups are less able to challenge the powerful economic and political interests behind environmentally harmful activities such as toxic waste dumps and polluting industries (Bullard 1994). This issue came to public attention in September 1982, when 400 protesters

Figure 8.6   The Birth of Environmental Justice. Although the Warren County, North Carolina, protest did not prevent the opening of a highly toxic PCB landfill site, it inspired others around the country to recognize and challenge situations of environmental discrimination.

● **Environmental justice.** A social movement addressing the linkages between racial discrimination and injustice, social equity, and environmental quality.

in Warren County, North Carolina, were arrested at the proposed site of a toxic waste landfill (Figure 8.6). At the time, Warren County was 84% African American and one of the poorest counties in the state. The leaders of the protest, some of them important civil rights leaders, argued that these facts, not the ecological suitability of the site to store toxic waste, motivated the decision to build the waste dump in their county (Sandweiss 1998). This protest marked the start of an **environmental justice** movement, a social movement that addresses the linkages between racial discrimination and injustice, social equity, and environmental quality.

Environmental justice is now a global movement, and unlike environmentalism oriented toward creating nature preserves that tend to focus on scenic landscapes and biodiversity, environmental justice tends to be organized around the defense of a people's livelihood and social justice concerns (Guha 2000:105). A good international example of this kind of activism is Kenya's Green Belt Movement, which has involved poor rural women in planting trees. Since its founding in 1977, these Kenyan women have planted 30 million trees, and today there are over 600 community networks that care for 6,000 tree nurseries (Green Belt Movement 2005). The goal is to address the sources of social problems directly, specifically poor land use and bad governance, by promoting environmental projects that enhance community self-determination. As one journalist has observed, the Green Belt Movement has "arguably done more to stall the expansion of deserts and destruction of soils in Africa than its big brother international body down the road, the United Nations Environmental Program with its grand but largely unsuccessful anti-desertification programs" (quoted in Guha 2000:102). In 2004, Wangari Maathai, the founder of the Green Belt Movement, received the Nobel Peace Prize, suggesting that environmental justice activism is gaining recognition among important global institutions.

THINKING CRITICALLY ABOUT ENVIRONMENTAL ANTHROPOLOGY

Environmental anthropologists reject population growth as a singular cause of environmental degradation around the world. But there are certain conditions in which population growth can play a role in environmental degradation, along with other factors described by political ecologists. What kinds of conditions do you think those would be?

Conclusion

Anthropologists agree that we must pay close attention to the social practices and structures that shape the way communities relate to their natural environments. When we do, we can see that non-industrialized people often have a deep understanding of their environments, and they routinely understand the behaviors of animals and plants as well as, if not better than, scientists from other regions. In such communities, the cultural landscape envisions nature differently than do people in the West, using metaphors that often express people's reciprocal ties to the land.

If we want to understand why indigenous leaders showed up in Durban, South Africa, at the World Parks Congress in protest—as related in the story that opens this chapter—it was at least partially because Westerners, with their cultural landscape of human–nature separation, have not appreciated these facts. Instead they have designed conservation programs that tend to expel indigenous peoples from landscapes they may have lived on sustainably for many years, even living in ways that support the biodiversity of other species, as is the case of the Maasai. Congress attendees apparently agreed, at least to some extent. In the consensus document published at the end of the congress, "The Durban Accord," the participants accepted the necessity of a new paradigm for protected areas. Although a decade later that new paradigm is still not yet worked out, this accord was widely viewed as a major victory for indigenous rights, because it recognizes that indigenous people conserve resources through their traditional practices, acknowledges that they have often suffered injustice because of protected areas, and urges commitment to involve indigenous peoples in managing protected areas (Colchester 2003:21).

Environmental anthropologists also agree that careful use of natural resources is the basis of a sustainable society. As a result, it is important to look critically at the current causes of the world's ecological crisis, which many prominent scholars and leaders claim is caused by recent, unchecked population growth. However, the causes of today's global ecological crisis—as was the case in past ecological crises—cannot be reduced to any singular cause. We have to consider factors like elite mismanagement of resources, government policy choices, inflexible responses to change, and consumption patterns that extract key resources and create waste. We also have to consider who pays the cost of these patterns and realize that questions of unequal access to resources and social patterns of injustice are often at the heart of the world's key ecological crises.

KEY TERMS

Artifactual landscapes
p. 195

Carrying capacity   p. 200

Cultural landscape   p. 189

Ecological anthropology
p. 189

Ecological footprint   p. 202

Ecosystem   p. 189

Environmental anthropology
p. 186

Environmental determinism
p. 189

Environmental justice
p. 206

Ethnobiology   p. 191

Ethnoscience   p. 191

Political ecology   p. 203

Sustainable development
p. 186

Traditional ecological
knowledge   p. 192

Reviewing the Chapter

Chapter Section	What We Know	To Be Resolved
Do all people conceive of nature in the same way?	Different cultures have different ways of conceptualizing the boundaries between humans and the natural world. Metaphors often play a major role in these conceptualizations.	Anthropologists continue to debate the extent to which general conceptual models and metaphors, or the material forces of nature itself, shape human relations with the environment.
How is non-western knowledge of nature similar to and different from science?	Different societies have developed highly systematic and sophisticated knowledge systems for classifying the natural world, some of which resemble closely Western science. Unlike Western science, however, which views its methods and findings as universally applicable, these knowledge systems are often highly localized and customized to particular ecosystems and rooted in local moralities.	Anthropologists are still working to understand the specific ways in which traditional ecological knowledge shapes practices of ecological and agricultural management.
Do only industrialized western societies conserve nature?	While Western conservation practice is based on the separation of humans and nature, the stewardship traditions of non-Western societies often start from principles that view humans as important actors in nature. Western nature conservation practices have often disrupted and marginalized local cultures, many of which have had highly successful adaptations to their environments.	As some conservationists have realized new opportunities of co-managing natural resources with indigenous communities, anthropologists are divided over whether these approaches actually benefit indigenous communities.
How do social and cultural factors drive environmental destruction?	The ecological impact of a society depends on its ecological footprint, or the amount of natural resources people require to live their lifestyles. The negative impacts of environmentally harmful activities tend to fall disproportionately on lower-income people and minority groups.	Anthropologists are still identifying the conditions under which social groups can adopt new cultural ideas and practices that promote resilience and sustainability.

Readings

For a century, anthropologists have taken a systematic interest in how humans vary in the ways they interact with the environment. There are several good general overviews of the subfield of Environmental Anthropology, among them Patricia Townsend's *Environmental Anthropology: From Pigs to Policies* (2nd edition, Long Grove, IL: Waveland Press, 2008) and Nora Haenn and Richard Wilk's edited reader *The Environment in Anthropology: A Reader in Ecology, Culture, and Sustainable Living* (New York: New York University Press, 2005). For a now-classic overview of political ecology, see Richard Peet and Michael Watts, eds., *Liberation Ecologies: Environment, Development, Social Movements* (2nd edition, New York: Routledge, 2004).

• •

Two books that explore the complex dimensions of indigenous ways of knowing and interacting with natural environment include Roberto

Gonzalez's ethnographic study of farming in Southern Mexico, *Zapotec Science: Farming and Food in the Northern Sierra of Oaxaca* (Austin: University of Texas Press, 2001) and ethnobotanist Gary Paul Nabhan's book, which is more poetic and story-driven, *Cultures of Habitat: On Nature, Culture, and Story* (Washington, DC: Counterpoint, 1997).

● ●

To explore the differences between insider and outsider understandings of landscapes and how they can lead to sharp conflicts over the conservation of natural resources, read James Fairhead and Melissa Leach's 1996 book *Misreading the African Landscape: Society and Ecology in a Forest-Savanna Mosaic* (Cambridge: Cambridge University Press, 1996) and James Igoe's book *Conservation and Globalization: A Study of National Parks and*

Indigenous Communities from East Africa to South Dakota (Belmont, CA: Wadsworth, 2004).

● ●

Shepard Krech's book *The Ecological Indian: Myth and History* (New York: W. W. Norton, 1999) offers an important and historically rooted challenge to romantic stereotypes of naturally "green" indigenous communities.

● ●

Economics

Working, Sharing, and Buying

WHEN THE SOVIET Union collapsed in 1989, so did the institutions and structures that gave meaning and material sustenance to the lives of millions of Russians. Inflation soared, and massive unemployment replaced the full state-employment that previously fed and clothed most Russians. Most people faced great scarcity, while a handful grew astonishingly wealthy.

With its vast natural resources, politicians and economists predicted Russia's quick transition to free-market capitalism and Western-style democracy. But it is now clear, several decades later, that the transition from state socialism has been complicated, uneven, and not easily destined to end in Western-style capitalism (Humphrey 2002). So how have people survived in their day-to-day lives?

In some respects, people have gotten along as they did under socialism. One strategy is what Russians call *blat* [blahtt], which refers to the give and take of favors among personal contacts to obtain hard-to-find goods and services, including food, well-made clothing, help fixing one's car, or assistance at the ministry of trade getting an import permit (Ledeneva 1998). *Blat* is based on long-term trusting relationships among family, friends, and neighbors. It differs from bribery, which Russians sometimes use when they have no personal connections. *Blat* was common during the Soviet era (1917–1989) when shortages and restrictions on consumption were frequent. In post-Soviet Russia, people do use money to buy things, but *blat* has

Pains of Privatization. The fall of the Soviet Union in 1989 disrupted people's economic lives, causing widespread difficulties and pain. But people also responded in culturally meaningful ways and mobilized economic practices long used during the Soviet period to get what they needed and wanted.

persisted because it is still useful for influencing decision-making and gaining access to all kinds of goods (Ledeneva 1998).

Barter, the direct swapping of goods, is another pervasive survivor of the Soviet period in Russia. It is especially useful when money is scarce or unreliable because of high inflation. Institutions and businesses, not just individuals, rely on barter to get what they need and want. For example, a collective farm might give meat to the electricity substation in exchange for its power, give milk to the local school for the farm children's education, and so forth (Humphrey 2002:xxvi).

But the decline of state socialism also created new economic realities and opportunities. For example, many small-scale traders bring goods like blue jeans and household electronics from other countries—a practice that was illegal during the Soviet era. Illicit protection rackets for small business owners have also flourished, permeating nearly all aspects of society in Russia. The Western media have dubbed these rackets "mafias" because of their reputations for brutality. The Russians, however, call them *krysha* [**kree**-shah], which translates as "roof" (Humphrey 2002). *Krysha* demand payments in exchange for providing protection (a "roof") to businesses and individuals from exploitation by criminals or corrupt politicians, as well as other "services" like coupons for rationed goods (Humphrey 2002).

Together, these relationships and practices have helped many people find their way through a complex new world of novel goods, lower wages, and puzzling new regulations to avert the most severe impoverishment. But protection rackets and economic uncertainty have also created widespread anxiety, disillusionment, and mistrust among Russians.

Many Western economists view survivors of socialism like *blat* and barter, and the emergence of new actors like protection rackets, as irrational—even corrupt—because they prevent the growth of markets and democracy in post-socialist economies. This Western capitalistic view, however, has several problems. First, markets have existed in these countries for a long time, even during the Soviet period; and second, people in these countries know that to get things done, they have to work within existing social hierarchies and relationships. The fact is, the economy that has taken shape in post-socialist Russia does not exist independently of local social relationships, cultures, and moralities. In fact, *all* economies are shaped by these factors.

At the heart of anthropology's interest in economics is the following question: *How do people get what they want and need to live?* Embedded in this larger question are the following problems, around which this chapter is organized:

Is money really the measure of all things?

How does culture shape the value and meaning of money itself?

Why is gift exchange such an important part of many societies?

Why does having some things make you cool?

Are there distinct cultures of capitalism?

Anthropologists who study economies and economic activities are interested in not only how people satisfy their needs, but why they want certain things in the first place. Although we have long debated the exact nature of the relationship between economy and culture, the two clearly interpenetrate each other, and one cannot be fully understood without the other. We begin exploring this relationship by considering the nature of value.

Is Money Really the Measure of All Things?

Many North Americans and Europeans are accustomed, if not also deeply committed, to the idea that money is the measure of all things. We hear all the time that everything has a price and that the price of an object reflects its real value.

But consider these questions. What would be the price in dollars of the original Declaration of Independence of the United States? A favorite blanket you have had since childhood? The Wailing Wall, Jerusalem's most sacred Jewish site? An antique gold wedding band that mothers have passed to their daughters for seven generations?

Somebody could try to set dollar values, or even try to buy or sell them, as when experts on the *Antiques Roadshow* give market values for heirlooms (Figure 9.1). But some objects and relationships carry such sacred or special qualities that they can never really be reduced to a monetary equivalent, even in our own society (Werner and Bell 2004). The awkwardness you might feel thinking about people doing so—as well as the controversies that erupt when someone tries to sell something over the Internet such as human body parts, virginity, Holocaust memorabilia, and so on—suggests that some deep set of processes defines what is an acceptable economic transaction, what is not, and how we establish monetary values for things. Those processes are cultural. Culture—those collective processes that make the artificial seem natural—not only shapes what is acceptable to transact, but how and why the transaction will take place, and how the objects or services being exchanged are valued.

Figure 9.1   How Much Is Grandmother's Antique Battle-Axe Worth? In the U.S. television show *Antiques Roadshow*, an expert evaluates the market value of household antiques. The popularity of the show, not to mention the motivation people have to go on it with their antiques, is ultimately less about the money than it is about other factors. What do you think those factors are?

Culture, Economics, and Value

- **Value.** The relative worth of an object or service that makes it desirable.

- **Economic anthropology.** The subdiscipline concerned with how people make, share, and buy things and services.

If money is not the measure of all things, where exactly within the processes of culture does **value**—the relative worth of an object or service—come from? **Economic anthropology**, the subdiscipline concerned with how people make, share, and buy things and services, has considered this question for a century. Economic anthropologists study the decisions people make about earning a living, what they do when they work, the social institutions that affect these activities, and how these three matters relate to the creation of value (Wilk and Cliggett 2007; M. E. Smith 2000).

Although both anthropologists and economists study the origins of value and how economies work, they generally have different goals. Economists typically try to understand and predict economic patterns, often with a practical goal of helping people (usually those with wealth) hold onto and increase their wealth. They may describe the economic lives of less-wealthy sectors of society, as one pair of economists recently did in an article entitled "The Economic Lives of the Poor" (Banerjee and Duflo 2006). But such studies tend to describe these communities in terms of economic statistics, and they assume that economic transactions in one country are like transactions in any other.

Anthropologists, on the other hand, do not assume transactions are the same everywhere, recognizing that culture shapes the character of any transaction. Furthermore, we tend to study how people lead their day-to-day economic lives by means of direct, long-term interaction with them. As a result, we tend to focus more than economists do on understanding the world's diversity of **economic systems**, the structured patterns and relationships through which people exchange goods and services, and making sense of how the world's diverse economic systems reflect and shape particular ways of life.

- **Economic system.** The structured patterns and relationships through which people exchange goods and services.

There are four major theoretical approaches to how economies create value used in anthropology: three of these are traditional approaches within the social sciences—neoclassical economics, substantivism, and Marxism—and a fourth approach, cultural economics, is one developed by anthropologists. Each approach reveals particular dimensions of an economic system, suggesting that no single theory can comprehensively represent the complexity of what an economy is and how it works. These approaches are summarized in outline form in Table 9.1 and discussed in more detail in the text that follows.

The Neoclassical Perspective

Scottish moral philosopher Adam Smith wrote about the creation of value in his influential book *The Wealth of Nations* (1776/1976). Smith observed that in "primitive" societies individuals did a lot of different kinds of work—growing and preparing food, making their own clothing, building their own homes, and so forth—but in the "civilized" societies of eighteenth-century Europe, such jobs were done increasingly by "the joint labor of a great multitude of workmen" (A. Smith 1776). This change was due to the **division of labor**, the cooperative organization of work into specialized tasks and roles (A. Smith 1776). Citing the example of sewing pins, Smith marveled at how dividing the process of making a sewing pin into distinct actions performed by different specialized laborers—one laborer to draw out the wire, a second to cut it, a third to straighten it, and so on—produced exponential growth in the number of pins that could be made in a day.

- **Division of labor.** The cooperative organization of work into specialized tasks and roles.

This change was revolutionary. Before the division of labor, Smith noted that a pin would take a lot of time and effort for an individual to make, and so the value of the pin lay in the amount of labor it took to make one. But with the division of labor

TABLE 9.1 THEORIES OF CULTURE, ECONOMY, AND VALUE			
Theoretical Approach	What Is the Economy?	How Does the Economic System Work?	How Is Value Created?
Neoclassical	The economy is a division of labor and the exchange of goods and services in a market.	Workers cooperate in the division of labor to produce goods. The market brings together buyers and sellers to exchange those goods.	Value and wealth are created by competition between buyers and sellers.
Substantivism	The economy is the substance of the actual transactions people engage in to get what they need and want.	Economic processes are embedded in and shaped by non-market social institutions, such as the state, religious beliefs, and kinship relations.	Value is relative, created by particular cultures and social institutions.
Marxism	Capitalism, which is a type of economic system, is a system in which private ownership of the means of production and a division of labor produce wealth for a few, and inequality for the masses.	People participate in capitalism by selling their labor. That labor is appropriated by those holding the means of production.	Labor, and especially the exploitation of others' labor, is a major source of value.
Cultural Economics	The economy is a category of culture, not a special arena governed by universal economic rationality.	Economic acts are guided by local beliefs and cultural models, which are closely tied to a community's values.	Value is created by the symbolic associations people make between an activity, good, or service and a community's moral norms.

reducing that time and effort, the value of the pin was now established by its **exchange** (the transfer of objects and services between social actors) in a **market**, a social institution in which people come together to buy and sell goods and services.

For Smith and the economists who follow him, market exchange reflects a natural human propensity to (as Smith famously said) "truck, barter, and exchange." It also acts like an "invisible hand" and was the most successful mechanism for determining value and making wealth possible. Within the market, individuals pursue their own self-interest, using their capacity for reason and calculation to maximize their individual satisfaction. The world has finite resources ("limited means"), but everybody has unlimited desires ("unlimited ends"), and the result is competition among individuals. Every person's struggle to get the most value theoretically keeps prices, costs of production, profits, and interest rates low while generating great wealth (Wilk and Cliggett 2007). This theory is the foundation of **neoclassical economics**, which studies how people make decisions to allocate resources like time, labor, and money in order to maximize their personal satisfaction (Figure 9.2).

Among anthropologists, this influential theory has provoked a long debate over the nature of the economy. It is, we will see, basically an unresolved debate, but exploring the positions illustrates how anthropologists interested in the relationship between culture, economics, and value have applied—and criticized—neoclassical thought.

The Substantivist–Formalist Debate

In 1944, the Hungarian-American economic historian Karl Polanyi published his book *The Great Transformation* to explain how modern **capitalism**—the economic system based on private ownership of the means of production, in which prices are set and goods distributed through a market—emerged in Europe (Polanyi 1944/1975). In contrast to Smith, who saw the market as emerging naturally from the human propensity to truck, barter, and exchange, Polanyi insisted that rather than being an expression of an assumed human nature, the rise of the market was a social process that went hand in hand with the creation of the modern state.

- **Exchange.** The transfer of objects and services between social actors.

- **Market.** A social institution in which people come together to exchange goods and services.

- **Neoclassical economics.** Economic theories and approaches that studies how people make decisions to allocate resources like time, labor, and money in order to maximize their personal benefit.

- **Capitalism.** An economic system based on private ownership of the means of production, in which prices are set and goods distributed through a market.

Figure 9.2   An Invisible Hand? Neoclassical economists emphasize that the pursuit of self-interest in markets works like an "invisible hand." In reality modern markets rarely, if ever, operate so freely, since governments impose regulations and enforce actions to keep markets operating smoothly, and in some cases, fairly.

- **Formal economics.** The branch of economics that studies the underlying logic of economic thought and action.

- **Substantive economics.** A branch of economics, inspired by the work of Karl Polanyi, that studies the daily transactions people engage in to get what they need or desire.

- **Redistribution.** The collection of goods in a community and then the further dispersal of those goods among members.

In developing that argument, Polanyi proposed that studying economies involves making a distinction between "formal" and "substantive" economics. By **formal economics**, he meant the underlying ("formal") logic that shapes people's actions when they participate in an economy, as we see in the apparently self-interested and rational decision-makers of neoclassical economic theory. By **substantive economics**, he referred to the daily transactions people actually engage in to get what they need or desire, or the "substance" of the economy. These transactions are embedded in and inseparable from other social institutions, such as politics, religion, and kinship. Anthropologists found this distinction useful for describing issues they were studying in other societies.

The Substantivist Position

Polanyi's own approach to economics was substantivist. Its primary goal was to describe how the production and **redistribution** of goods (collection of goods in a community and then re-division of those goods among members) were embedded in and shaped by non-market social institutions, such as the state, religious beliefs, and kinship relations. Substantivism was *relativistic*, holding that societies have unique social institutions and processes that influence economics like other aspects of culture. From this perspective, the value of goods in an economic system is culturally relative, rooted in particular cultures and social institutions. Second, it was *evolutionary*, recognizing that economies change over time. Third, its *main unit of analysis was a whole society and its institutions*, not individual behaviors and actions. Finally, it was *descriptive*, encouraging researchers to describe social institutions and their underlying principles, something anthropologists already did in a holistic and relativistic way (Wilk and Cliggett 2007).

Substantivists felt that the concept of an "economy" did not do justice to the way making a livelihood is inseparably interwoven with customs and social relations in other societies. They argued that research should focus on a broad field of social relations and institutions that provided people with what they needed to live instead of any predetermined or limited notion of an economy centered on a market. A major proponent of substantivism in anthropology was University of Chicago anthropologist Marshall Sahlins, as we examine in "Classic Contributions: Marshall Sahlins on Exchange in Traditional Economies."

The Formalist Reaction

By the 1960s, some anthropologists began to criticize substantivism's lack of attention to individual action and behavior, shifting their focus to formal economics. Formalists advocated scientific investigation into individual economic behavior and rationality, noting that markets based on supply and demand have long existed in many different kinds of societies.

To formalists, individuals in all societies are as rational as neoclassical economics says they are. People everywhere confront limited means and unlimited ends (wants), and therefore they make rational decisions that are appropriate to the satisfaction they desire (M. E. Smith 2000). Being anthropologists, the formalists understood that "satisfaction" could be culturally defined and variable but, they asserted, the decision-making processes people used to achieve satisfaction were basically the same everywhere. Formalists criticized the common argument that the poor and people of non-Western cultures were irrational and unable to efficiently handle resources, which some economists and policy-makers used to justify withholding financial aid from such people (Wilk and Cliggett 2007).

Classic Contributions

Marshall Sahlins on Exchange in Traditional Economies

Marshall Sahlins.

SINCE THE 1950s, cultural anthropologist Marshall Sahlins (b. 1930) has been interested in differences and similarities between the economies of small-scale non-Western societies and those of Europe. The following excerpt comes from Sahlins's statement about the nature of the economy in societies with non-industrial technologies, illustrating substantivist economic theory's emphasis on the social nature of economic transactions. To distinguish it from the modern capitalist economy, Sahlins calls this sort of economic system one of "primitive exchange." Although anthropologists no longer use terminology like "primitive," two important elements of Sahlins's explanation are that (1) nearly every transaction involves a social relationship and (2) production is organized by families in what he refers to as the "domestic mode of production."

What are [in] the received wisdom "noneconomic" or "exogenous" conditions are in the primitive reality the very organization of economy. A material transaction is usually a momentary episode in a continuous social relation. The social relation exerts governance: the flow of goods is constrained by, is part of, a status etiquette. . . .

Yet the connection between material flow and social flow is reciprocal. A specific social relation may constrain a given movement of goods, but a specific transaction suggests a particular social relation. If friends make gifts, gifts make friends. A great proportion of primitive exchange, much more than our own traffic, has as its decisive function this latter, instrumental one: the material flow underwrites or initiates social relations.

Even on its strictly practical side, exchange in primitive communities has not the same role as the economic flow in modern industrial communities. The place of transaction in the total economy is different: under primitive conditions it is more detached from production, less firmly hinged to production in an organic way. Typically it is less involved than modern exchange in the acquisition of means of production, more involved with the redistribution of finished goods. The bias is that of an economy in which food holds a commanding position, and day-to-day output does not depend on a massive technological complex nor a complex division of labor. It is the bias of a domestic mode of production: of household producing units, division of labor by sex and age. (Sahlins 1965:139–140)

Questions for Reflection

1. How do you think Sahlins was being a substantivist?

2. Why do you think transactions in a "primitive" society are more oriented toward redistribution and less toward the production of goods?

By the late 1970s, the debate between substantivists and formalists had fizzled out with no clear winner. The main reason is that the two sides were essentially arguing past each other: one side was talking about societies and their institutions, while the other was talking about individuals, their rationality, and their individual transactions. Both had a point and both had a role to play in the study of economic behavior. Non-Western people were rational in an economic sense, but used culturally constructed notions of value particular to their own society and its institutions.

The Marxist Perspective

The substantivist-formalist debate also fizzled because a number of anthropologists had begun to adopt Marxism, the political and economic theories associated with German political economist Karl Marx (1818–1883). In his analysis of British capitalism, Marx characterized the English system as pitting the conflicting interests of a wealthy class (who owned factories), against a poorer working class (laborers in the factories). A man's or woman's labor in a factory was only worth what the factory owner was willing to pay for it, which might not be enough for the worker to live on (Marx 1867). At the heart of this system, Marx argued, was a division of labor that produced inequality and conflict.

From the Marxist point of view, the substantivists and formalists had wasted their time debating the nature of exchange and redistribution, while the neoclassicists misunderstood economic activity as individual choice and decision-making. Marxism emphasizes that societies are divided into unequal classes, with a few individuals at the top accumulating wealth and power by appropriating the labor and property of the many below. The real problem, according to Marxists, is explaining why and how an economy and society based on inequality reproduces itself, in other words, how the production and trade of goods enforces and maintains the social inequality.

- **Surplus value.** The difference between what people produce and what they need to survive.

Marxists use the concept of **surplus value**, which is the difference between what people produce and what they need to survive, to address this problem. In a capitalist society, workers create greater output than they get paid, generating surplus value. For example, a worker in a widget factory might make $35 of widgets in an hour from $5 of materials, but only gets paid $10 per hour. What happens to the $20 of surplus value? The owner of the factory, who controls the **means of production**—the machines and infrastructure required to produce the widget—appropriates it, the Marxists argue, thus exploiting the worker's productivity. This surplus value is the basis of private wealth, but it also creates permanent conflict between the worker and owner classes. The institution of private property and the state, through its social and economic policies, support this inequality.

- **Means of production.** The machines and infrastructure required to produce goods.

Marxist analysis introduced issues of power, domination, and the unequal distribution of wealth into anthropology's discussions of culture and economy, which substantivists and formalists largely ignored. World Systems theory, for example, has applied Marxist analysis to study how indigenous societies have been drawn into the global capitalist system, usually serving the role of providing labor and raw materials for capitalistic countries with the result of falling into poverty and dependency on those countries (see Chapter 6, "Globalization and Culture").

Not all attempts to apply Marxist analysis to non-Western societies have been entirely satisfying, because non-capitalist economies work so differently. In particular, such studies do not always adequately address the culturally specific symbolic and moral dimensions of economic interaction, to which we turn next.

The Cultural Economics Perspective

- **Cultural economics.** An anthropological approach to economics that focuses on how symbols and morals help shape a community's economy.

The idea that symbols and morals help shape a community's economy lies at the heart of **cultural economics**. Cultural economics views the economy as a category of culture, not a special arena governed by universal utilitarian or practical reason (Sahlins 1972, 1976). As you might guess, the roots of this approach lie in substantivism. This view asserts that universalist theories of economy, such as neoclassical economics, Marxist analysis, and substantivism, prevent us from understanding local economic beliefs and behaviors (Gudeman 1986). The cultural economist's goal is to understand, from the "native's point of view," the local beliefs and cultural models that guide and shape economic activities.

To the cultural economist, a close relationship exists between the words "value" (desirability) and "values" (moral norms). Both refer to the symbolic expression of intrinsically desirable principles or qualities. This relationship also implies that moral norms and economic activity influence each other (Sayer 2000).

Anthropologists working in this vein have been especially interested in **prestige economies**, economies in which people seek high social rank, prestige, and power instead of money and material wealth. In indigenous Maya communities of Guatemala and southern Mexico, for example, men have traditionally participated in the Cofradía [ko-fra-**dee**-ah] system, a hierarchical system dating from colonial times that combines civic leadership and Catholic religious authority (M. Nash 1958) (Figure 9.3). As they enter higher offices with greater responsibilities and power, these men also have the obligation to spend more of their personal money and other wealth on community fiestas and infrastructure. Some will go broke or deep into debt doing so. Underlying this system is a moral philosophy (rather than individual self-interest) emphasizing that the path to status and rank requires an individual to share generously with others whatever material wealth he has.

Of course, people are not culturally programmed actors who automatically or continuously act out traditional roles scripted for them by their cultures, and cultures change (Wilk and Cliggett 2007). In recent years, for example, Cofradía systems have been eroding, as many Maya have converted to Protestantism and rejected the system's association with the Catholic Church. Others migrated to cities or other countries because of economic and political pressures. Similar kinds of changes are happening all over the world to traditional economic systems.

Recent studies in cultural economics have tended to focus on the dynamism of local economies, recognizing that one society may encompass several local economic models simultaneously, perhaps at different levels or among different institutions (Robben 1989; Gudeman 2001). Such a perspective can help us better understand how people in post-Soviet Russia got along, since it is a place where people held distinct and even competing ideas about appropriate ways to get what they need to survive, as we presented at the beginning of the chapter.

Returning to this section's broader focus on how value is created, it should be clear that none of these theoretical approaches—neoclassical economics, formalism, substantivism,

• **Prestige economies.** Economies in which people seek high social rank, prestige, and power instead of money and material wealth.

Figure 9.3 Members of a Cofradía in Guatemala. Cofradías, which are Catholic civil-religious associations, are a classic example of a prestige economy since members gain social prestige and authority even as they may go deeply into financial debt to participate.

Marxism, or cultural economics—accepts that money is the measure of all things. While the specifics of these theories differ—some might even say they are irreconcilable—each nevertheless accepts, at least partially, that cultural processes and social relationships play a central role in establishing value, and that culture and economics are intertwined in complex ways.

THINKING CRITICALLY ABOUT ECONOMICS

Cultural economics argues that a single society can have multiple local cultural models of appropriate economic action and behavior circulating in it. For example, in the United States, even as dominant cultural models of economic behavior resemble Adam Smith's rational economic actors, some religious communities have certain expectations about appropriate economic behavior, such as saving a certain amount of money, donating a certain percentage to the church, and so on, which make explicit connections between economic behavior and morality. Can you think of other cultural models of economic behavior in the United States?

How Does Culture Shape the Value and Meaning of Money Itself?

- **Money.** An object or substance that serves as a payment for a good or service.

If value and its meanings are created through the processes of culture, then it stands to reason that the value and meanings of **money** itself—an object or substance that serves as a payment for a good or service—are also created through culture. Money, which is a type of **currency** (an object used as a medium of exchange), provides a standard measure of value that allows people to compare and trade goods and services. Although we are most familiar with paper bills and metal coins, anything durable and scarce can serve as money. Cowrie (a type of mollusk) shells, rings made of precious metals, brass rods, and even enormous stone disks have been used as money. Money interests anthropologists not simply because it is a medium of economic exchange, but also because it has important cultural dimensions.

- **Currency.** An object used as a medium of exchange.

The Types and Cultural Dimensions of Money

Several cultural dimensions of money are of interest to anthropologists, especially the diverse types of money people use and the powerful moral meanings people project onto money and its uses. Together, these dimensions reveal important diversity and subtleties surrounding how people use money and establish its value.

Across the world, money is many things to many people, and not everybody wants it for the same reasons. In market-based economies like that in the United States, people want money because it can be used to buy nearly any good or service. Anthropologists call this **general purpose money** because it is money that is used to buy almost anything. Portability and mobility are important features of general purpose money, as we see in our dollar bills, coins, credit cards, checks, college "smart"

- **General purpose money.** Money that is used to buy nearly any good or service.

identity cards, and electronic transfers. General purpose money has some limits—for instance, most of us will not take a check from just anyone, and you cannot pay for a $50 pair of shoes with a pocketful of pennies—but most Americans are preoccupied with getting money because in order to get almost anything, including the goods necessary for basic subsistence, they need it.

Another type of money is **limited purpose money**, which refers to objects that can be exchanged only for certain things. For example, the pastoral Tiv people of Nigeria traditionally could purchase cattle and pay bride price (things of value a groom gives to his bride's father) only with brass rods. In Tiv society, people traditionally did not use money for basic subsistence, but primarily to gain access to goods that give social respectability and prestige, such as a marriage partner, cattle, and other livestock (Bohannon and Bohannon 1968).

In the Tiv case, powerful moral rules regulated the ways in which money was used. Paul Bohannan, who studied Tiv uses of money, argued that the Tiv traditionally had three separate **spheres of exchange**, or bounded orders of value in which certain goods can be exchanged only for others: ordinary subsistence goods, prestige goods, and rights in people, especially women and slaves (Bohannon and Bohannon 1968). They could not exchange goods across those spheres; to do so would have been immoral. So an individual could not trade, say, a basket of food for a prestige item like a brass rod or cow, but could have an "exchange marriage" in which a man gained a bride by exchanging a sister or a daughter. The British colonial period in Nigeria (1900–1960) undermined this traditional system, because the British introduced general purpose money. Young Tiv men working as laborers and paid in British currency began using it to pay for prestige goods like cattle and bride price. The acquisition of cash value for prestige goods, Bohannon observed, was not just an economic problem: it was a moral problem since it messed with Tiv notions about what money could be used for.

Even general purpose money, such as the use of dollars and cents, has cultural and moral dimensions beyond its function as a medium of exchange (Parry and Bloch 1989). We all know, for example, that you cannot simply walk into your university's accounting office, pay a large sum of money, and receive a diploma. Our ideas about getting an education involve a moral obligation to work hard and apply oneself before the diploma is awarded. If you tried to buy a diploma outright, your money would have no value for this purpose, and one could even imagine that seeking to buy a diploma could feel "dirty," contaminating the purity and goodness we associate with the process of education.

An anthropological explanation for this situation lies in the concept of **transactional orders**, or realms of transactions a community uses, each with its own set of symbolic meanings and moral assumptions (Parry and Bloch 1989). The transactions involved in getting an education, which are steeped in long-term obligations and expectations, are morally distinct from other short-term transactions that have no special moral obligations, such as buying a magazine at your university bookstore.

As money circulates through these transactional orders, it can gain different meanings. Langkawi [lahng-**kah**-wee], a Malaysian fishing community (Carsten 1989), illustrates this interesting relationship between culture and money. The people of Langkawi view money as a potentially threatening and subversive force because it circulates in the amoral domain of the marketplace, making it incompatible with the moral bonds of kinship and mutual obligation in the community. Yet men are quite willing to engage in commercial exchanges involving money, such as selling their fish to merchants. Once they earn the money, they turn it over to women, who are not involved directly with the marketplace. The women "de-contaminate" the money by using it to sustain the household and community. By insulating the women from

- **Limited purpose money.** Objects that can be exchanged only for certain things.

- **Spheres of exchange.** Bounded orders of value in which certain goods can be exchanged only for others.

- **Transactional orders.** Realms of transactions a community uses, each with its own set of symbolic meanings and moral assumptions.

these amoral transactions and letting them use money to benefit the family, people in Langkawi shift the money from one transactional order of short-term competitive relationships to another based on long-term family obligations and community relationships steeped in morality.

Although most of us take for granted the existence of money, its use is not universal and people have developed other ways to get what they need and want. Anthropologists have found that non-monetary exchanges are a central economic aspect of all societies, a theme we turn to in the next section.

● ●

THINKING CRITICALLY ABOUT ECONOMICS

Do you feel a need to protect certain relationships from money? What relationships? What is the meaning of money for you in these situations?

● ●

Why Is Gift Exchange Such an Important Part of All Societies?

Corporations make donations to political parties, adversaries trade insults, kin groups swap women in marriage, hunters placate the spirit of their prey with offerings, parents prepare meals for their children—all of these are acts of exchange, which anthropologists understand as the transfer of things and gifts between social actors (Carrier 1996a:218). Exchange is a universal feature of human existence and relates to all aspects of life, and as such it is a central topic of anthropological inquiry. In many societies, the exchange of gifts is the central defining feature of its economy.

Gift Exchange and Economy: Two Classic Approaches

● **Reciprocity.** The give-and-take that builds and confirms relationships.

It may sound strange to think of a gift exchange in economic terms. We tend to think of gifts as personal expressions of **reciprocity**, the give-and-take that builds and confirms relationships. For Americans the problem here is that we distinguish the economy from gift giving, while in the non-industrial societies anthropologists have traditionally studied, exchanging gifts is at the heart of the local economy.

So how are gifts related to economy? Two classic approaches to this question date back to the 1920s, one associated with Polish-born British anthropologist Bronislaw Malinowski and the other with French anthropologist Marcel Mauss. Each based his analysis on the theory of functionalism—that gift exchange fulfills certain needs—although the two men's views differed in a crucial way: Malinowski stressed the individualistic aspects of gift exchange, whereas Mauss emphasized the importance of gift exchange for maintaining social cohesion.

Malinowski and the Kula

The exchange of gifts is a central feature of life in Melanesian societies of the Southwest Pacific, a fact Malinowski discovered while he was in the Trobriand Islands. He wrote that for Trobrianders, "to possess is to give. . . . A man who owns a thing is expected to share it, to distribute it, to be its trustee and dispenser" (1922:97).

He found no better illustration of this phenomenon than the *Kula* [**koo**-la], an extensive inter-island system of exchange in which high-ranking men gave ornamental shell armbands (*mwali*) and necklaces (*soulava*) to lifelong exchange partners on other islands. In the highly structured *Kula,* armbands traveled in one direction and necklaces in the opposite direction (Figure 9.4). For Trobriand Islanders these shell valuables were about the most valuable things one could possess, even though men typically owned them for only a few months before they gave them to other partners (anthropologists call this **delayed reciprocity**—which means a long lag time between giving and receiving). These shell valuables had no real function, as they were rarely worn, and had no other use. Their value came when they were given away because that is when they brought renown to the man who gave them away. Malinowski saw islanders spend months preparing their canoes for the voyages that were focused so intently on getting objects with no real use.

He did observe that when men sailed to visit their partners on another island, in addition to the armbands and necklaces, they always brought along many utilitarian goods, such as vegetables, fish, or pots to exchange on the side for things they could not get on their own island. Malinowski theorized that these ritualized *Kula* exchanges functioned to enhance the status of individual men and distribute goods people could not otherwise get on their home islands.

Kula is such an important dimension of Trobriand society that colonialism did not undermine it. In fact, it has expanded in recent decades, involving more islands and lower-ranking individuals. Now, as before, the significance of *Kula* lies in the prestige an individual gains from giving away armbands and necklaces, not in accumulating these objects. The reason it has persisted and adapted to change is that it is so central to how Trobriand men establish their individual identities.

Although Malinowski did not discuss it, Trobriand women also participated in extensive exchange systems; "Thinking Like an Anthropologist: The Role of Exchange in Managing Social Relationships" explores the significance of women's exchange in the Trobriand Islands.

• **Delayed reciprocity.** A form of reciprocity that features a long lag time between giving and receiving.

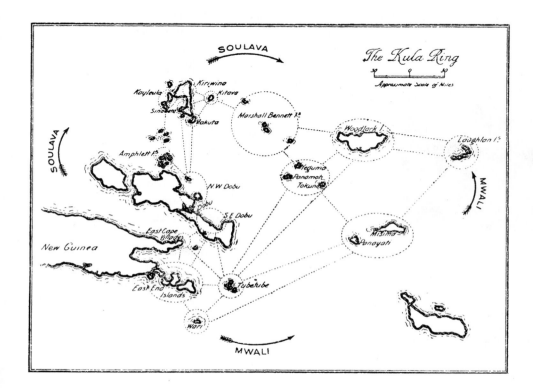

🌱 **Figure 9.4   The Kula Cycle with Mwali (Armbands) and Soulava (Necklaces).**

Thinking Like an Anthropologist

The Role of Exchange in Managing Social Relationships

ANTHROPOLOGISTS BEGIN THEIR research by asking questions. In this box, we want you to learn how to ask questions as an anthropological researcher. Part One describes a situation and follows up with questions we would ask. Part Two asks you to do the same thing with a different situation.

PART ONE: MORTUARY EXCHANGE IN THE TROBRIAND ISLANDS

During his field research in the Trobriand Islands, Malinowski paid considerable attention to the inter-island *Kula* exchange. Since then, other scholars have updated Malinowski's picture of the *Kula* and other Melanesian exchange systems. Most notable of these scholars was the American anthropologist Annette Weiner (1933–1997), who conducted fieldwork in the Trobriand Islands during the 1970s and 1980s.

Weiner noted that women rarely participated directly in *Kula*. But she also observed that women participate in their own elaborate exchange system based on delayed reciprocity. This exchange system, called *Sagali*, involves the exchange of grass skirts and bundles made of dried banana leaves and is used almost exclusively in women's exchanges (Weiner 1976, 1988).

In Plain Sight. Malinowski uncritically accepted certain European preconceptions about women's non-economic status, ignoring almost completely Sagali exchanges, even though they were going on all around him. Yet we know that he observed them, because he took photographs like this one of women exchanging banana leaf bundles and skirts that they had themselves made.

Sagali is a mortuary exchange ritual. When someone dies, Trobrianders go through months of mourning during which they shut themselves off from most normal activities. When they eventually emerge from this self-imposed seclusion, their closest relatives give gifts of decorative women's skirts and banana leaf bundles to all the in-laws and other relatives who have helped them out during their months of seclusion. Although the fancy skirts can be worn in traditional dances, the banana leaf bundles have no use whatsoever outside the *Sagali*. Women make them all the time, usually while sitting outside their homes with other women and discussing village news and gossip. Only women give or receive banana leaf bundles or skirts, and men play no role in the exchange except perhaps to help move the huge baskets of bundles from a house to the village plaza for their wives or sisters.

Weiner nevertheless found important similarities between *Sagali* and *Kula*. For example, they both involve delayed reciprocity. That is, just as a man would not receive any *Kula* valuables between visits to his trading partners on other islands, a woman who gave away all her bundles would not receive any back until the next *Sagali*. The significance of both kinds of exchange system lay in the prestige that came from giving away the objects involved—bundles and skirts, or armshells and necklaces—not in accumulating them. If a person hoarded Kula valuables or skirts and leaf bundles when called on to exchange them, he or she would be subject to ridicule as a stingy and selfish person.

What questions does this situation raise for anthropological researchers?

1. How can a woman guarantee that Sagali exchanges will eventually be repaid at some later exchange?
2. In a Sagali ritual, the recipients of bundles and skirts see tangible affirmation of their contributions to the family of the deceased. But what does the deceased's family get out of giving away hundreds of bundles and skirts?
3. How do these transactions build social bonds between the family of a dead person and the people who have supported them during the months of mourning?
4. How does giving and receiving bundles enhance an individual's social status?

PART TWO: EXCHANGE RELATIONS SURROUNDING AMERICAN FUNERALS AND MARRIAGES

Not all American transactions are about acquiring desired goods and services; some exchanges involve delayed reciprocity much as they do in the Trobriand Islands. Two socially based American transactions are best viewed as ritualized exchanges: giving wedding gifts and giving support to family and friends after a death. If you wanted to understand the ritualized aspects of American wedding gifts or mortuary transactions, what questions would you ask as an anthropological researcher?

Mauss and the Spirit of the Gift

Marcel Mauss (1872–1950), nephew and colleague of the French sociologist Emile Durkheim, was the founder of modern French anthropology. In 1924, he published his most influential work, *The Gift* (Mauss 1954), which compares gift exchange and its functions in a wide range of non-Western societies.

Unlike Malinowski, who viewed gift exchange primarily in terms of how it contributed to an individual's status and identity, Mauss viewed gift exchange in terms of how it builds group solidarity. Gift exchange, Mauss insisted, is based on obligation, which has three dimensions: (1) *the obligation to give,* which establishes the giver as generous and worthy of respect; (2) *the obligation to receive,* which shows respect to the giver; and (3) *the obligation to return the gift in appropriate ways,* which demonstrates honor. It thus creates and maintains bonds of solidarity between people who, Mauss believed, would otherwise pursue their own personal interests.

For Mauss, gift-giving is steeped in morality and spirituality. The objects people give even take on the identity of the giver. Among the Maori of New Zealand, for example, the gift has a spirit called *hau* that demands the return of the gift to its owner. (If this sounds strange, consider that we sometimes believe that objects take on their owner's life force, which is why many collectors buy personal effects of famous persons, or why it might feel creepy—or empowering, depending on your perspective—to wear a deceased friend's clothing.) (Figure 9.5)

Later anthropologists have built on Mauss's insights into how gift exchange lies at the heart of human society. One of the most influential of these was Marshall Sahlins (1972), who argued that gift exchanges help manage group boundaries. Sahlins identified three types of reciprocity involved in gift exchange—generalized reciprocity, balanced reciprocity, and negative reciprocity—each of which defines the social relationship between a giver and a receiver.

Generalized reciprocity refers to giving something without the expectation of return, at least not in the near term. It is uninhibited and generous giving, such as that which takes place between parents and children, married couples, or close-knit kin groups.

Balanced reciprocity occurs when a person gives something, expecting the receiver to return an equivalent gift or favor at some point in the future. The Kula, Sagali, and American birthday presents among good friends are examples.

Finally, **negative reciprocity**, which economists call barter, is the attempt to get something for nothing, to haggle one's way into a favorable personal outcome. It exists between the most distant relations, such as between strangers or adversaries.

Figure 9.5   Marilyn Monroe's Dress. In 1999 this dress sold at auction for $1.5 million. The dress by itself is beautiful, but it is the fact that Marilyn Monroe wore it that makes it so valuable to some collectors.

- **Generalized reciprocity.** A form of reciprocity in which gifts are given freely without the expectation of return.

- **Balanced reciprocity.** A form of reciprocity in which the giver expects a fair return at some later time.

- **Negative reciprocity.** A form of reciprocity in which the giver attempts to get something for nothing, to haggle one's way into a favorable personal outcome.

Sahlins's typology is useful because it suggests that social relationships shape the kinds of reciprocity people practice. But recent studies of gift-giving have focused less on the objective types of reciprocity and more on how people interpret gift exchange. For example, anthropologist Marilyn Strathern (1990) argues that certain Melanesian cultures believe that people acquire their individual identities through gift exchange. These Melanesians do not conceive of people as independent units who *enter into* gift exchange; instead, they see themselves as *made* into people by gift exchange itself. Strathern's broader point is that culturally different concepts of personhood and relationship lead to different understandings of and motivations for gift exchange.

Our current understandings of the gift clearly owe a great deal to the pioneering work of Malinowski and Mauss, especially the realization that many societies have met people's material and social necessities, not with money, but with highly organized and principled gift exchanges.

Gift Exchange in Market-Based Economies

Although our cultural models dismiss its economic significance, gift exchange is tremendously important in American and European societies for a lot of the same reasons it is in other societies: it establishes social status, reaffirms relationship, and gives people access to the goods and sometimes influence that they want and need. As in any society, important implicit rules guide our gift exchange.

Some of our gifts are blatantly self-interested, of the "If-You-Rub-My-Back-I'll-Rub-Yours" variety, including bribes, political donations, and the like. Yet such gifts are morally hazardous. That such gifts are given does not surprise us. But we also expect participants to go to great lengths to hide their transactions or, in the case of large political donations, obscure them behind elaborate rules and accounting procedures meant to build confidence that the politician accepting them does not give special favors.

Even the gifts we give for holidays and birthdays follow implicit rules. Gifts between siblings or good friends have to be repaid in equal value every bit as much as the Kula valuables do. Ideally, gifts should also be personal and embody the relationship between giver and receiver. Yet such gift exchanges among friends are delicate matters. Most Americans feel these gifts should not be cash, for example, in the form of a $20 bill, because it places a concrete value on the relationship. Somewhat less impersonal are **commodities** (mass-produced and impersonal goods with no meaning or history apart from themselves) bought at a mall. As commodities they are equivalent to the money spent to buy them. Somewhat between the two are gift cards, that have the double disadvantage of being the same as money and as impersonal as any commodity in the store. One solution described by anthropologist James Carrier (1995) is to turn impersonal commodities into personal gifts, by wrapping objects as personal presents, or if they are too difficult to wrap, putting bows on them. This simple action symbolically distances the goods from an anonymous retail environment, suggesting that the giver made a greater effort than simply going to a store (Figure 9.6).

Three points stand out here: (1) gift exchanges are deeply embedded in the social relations of every society, including our own; (2) by personalization we can transform impersonal commodities into personal gifts; and (3) we, like everyone else in the world, invest tremendous symbolic meaning in the things we give, receive, and consume. This third point has significant subtleties, which we explore in more detail in the next section.

- **Commodities.** Mass-produced and impersonal goods with no meaning or history apart from themselves.

Figure 9.6 Marketing Celebrities to Sell Goods. Retailers try to help us overcome the impersonality of commodities by creating marketing campaigns that personalize their products. One strategy is to associate a product with widely recognized celebrities, such as the Argentine soccer star Lionel Messi pictured here. Celebrities can generate positive feelings about a product even if they don't actually say anything about its quality.

THINKING CRITICALLY ABOUT ECONOMICS

The way anthropologists think about it, "reciprocity," "exchange," and "sharing" each have different meanings. In what ways do you think these are different from each other?

Why Does Having Some Things Make You Cool?

In U.S. society, people work hard and spend a great deal of time and money to buy things that make them appear "cool," that is, impressive, trendy, a bit better than other people. "Cool" people understand what is "in" and what is not. Marketing and advertising executives work hard to identify and create an image of coolness in ads and commercials—in the clothing we wear, the music we listen to, the foods we eat, the cars we drive, the smartphones we use, and so on—all to get us to buy more things. But coolness is more than just a tool for selling goods and services. It is also an important way people in a mass society identify who is and is not a member of their "in-crowd"—their social class, rank, lifestyle, ethnic identity, or other particular grouping (Bourdieu 1984).

But neither a Ferrari nor an Abercrombie & Fitch shirt, beloved by many college students, is naturally "cool." Whatever symbolic distinctions or qualities these goods have are culturally constructed. Their meaning results from social and cultural processes that create demand for these objects, such as the fact that everyone is talking about them or important and respected people own them. Less-trendsetting members of a society need and want them because higher status people who set trends have

- **Consumption.** The act of using and assigning meaning to a good, service, or relationship.

- **Appropriation.** The process of taking possession of an object, idea, or relationship.

- **Consumers.** People who rely on goods and services not produced by their own labor.

Figure 9.7   Prestige Goods. Although both of these bags are considered prestige goods in their specific cultures, a vast conceptual distance exists between how and why people consume them. String bags represent an individual's wealth in social relationships, while Gucci bags represent an individual's material wealth.

them, and those who do not set the trends can only satisfy their desires through the act of consumption.

Anthropologists define **consumption** as the act of using and assigning meaning to a good, service, or relationship (see also Chapter 16, "The Arts"). Through consumption people make cultural meaning, build social relationships, and create identities (Douglas and Isherwood 1978; Appadurai 1986). Every culture distinguishes between what is appropriate and what is inappropriate to consume, providing social avenues to consuming culturally accepted goods and limiting consumption of things considered inappropriate. For example, the noble families of the Mandar people of Sulawesi in Indonesia wear certain patterns of hand-woven silk sarongs at weddings and other formal occasions, but have placed restrictions on commoners from wearing these same designs. This restriction has raised the status of nobles, while simultaneously lowering that of commoners.

Consumption begins with an act of **appropriation**, which is a process of taking possession of the object (Carrier 1996b; Miller 1995). Consider, for example, the consumption of a smartphone. The initial act of appropriation takes place as you shop for it. Shopping entails narrowing your choices on the basis of price, size, look, brand, special features, and your sense of how you want to be seen by others until you identify the one you want to buy. After paying for it, you continue the appropriation process by personalizing it—by using it in certain ways, such as programming its memory with your special apps, putting a case with special designs on it, or otherwise customizing it to reflect what you want out of a phone. These customizations, as well as how and when you use your smartphone, in turn reflect and define who you are as a person. An informed techie who loves the latest gadgets, a social butterfly who is always networked, a creative and artistic type, or a serious businessperson. Depending on the brand you purchased or how you customize it, your consumption of this particular smartphone distinguishes your social position in society, as a member of the middle class, or some other grouping based on age, ethnicity, and so on.

In societies where people still make many of the things they consume, people may be just as concerned with wanting cool things—things that identify the owner as worthy of respect—as many Americans are. Of course, other cultures' ideas of what "cool" is may differ greatly from ours. For instance, when people around Aitape on the North Coast of Papua New Guinea exchange food and other subsistence goods with their friends in neighboring villages, they also often give their partners hand-made netted string bags with unique designs common to their home villages. String bags are a tangible manifestation of the trader's generosity and commitment to the social and economic relationship between the two exchange partners (Figure 9.7). People are especially proud of the bags that come from very distant villages, because they indicate an extensive network of friends.

Young Aitape villagers, whose definition of "cool" means wearing Bob Marley t-shirts and listening to world music CDs also circulate these objects through local exchange networks. So on Monday we might see one person wearing the Marley t-shirt, and by Friday this individual's cousin might be wearing it. The next week we might see it on somebody else, and pretty soon it has been given to someone in another community altogether.

The best way to think about consumption is as a key avenue through which people continuously recreate and modify both their cultures and their social relationships. Changes in consumption patterns are often visible manifestations of broader cultural changes (Miller 1995). For example, let us return to post-Soviet Russia. The shift toward a market economy made it possible for Russians to consume things they could not during the Soviet era. Consumerism itself was not new in Russia; during the Soviet era people were also **consumers**, that is, people who live through objects and images not of their own making (Humphrey 2002:40). But people's consciousness of consumption changed. During the Soviet era, when the state produced and allocated all industrial and agricultural goods, people were encouraged to identify these goods as "their own," because the state presented itself ideologically as an expression of the people.

Now that the state no longer controls consumer goods, and foreign goods pour in, Russians have a bewildering array of choices about how and what to consume. During the Soviet era, consuming foreign goods was viewed positively by many as an act of rebellion and defiance against the state. Today, however, many Russians distrust foreign goods—or even refuse to consume them—because they associate them with the domestic importers and sellers of these goods who are often shady and corrupt businessmen created by the decline of the state (Humphrey 2002:55). As Russians negotiate who they are through what and how they consume, we can see that the influx of Western consumer goods is not as culturally homogenizing as many of us assume. Instead, the influx is becoming the grounds of creating new cultural meanings and social relationships.

Consumption is a key feature of capitalism, but if consumption varies around the globe, does the capitalist system also vary?

THINKING CRITICALLY ABOUT ECONOMICS

If it is true that changing consumption patterns are visible manifestations of broader cultural changes, what can the massive acquisition of cellular and smartphones by millions of people during the past decade tell us about changes in how people communicate?

Are There Distinct Cultures of Capitalism?

For the better part of the twentieth century, capitalism and socialism existed as opposed forms of economic organization, an opposition that dominated global politics during the Cold War. After the collapse of the Soviet Union and Eastern Bloc regimes in 1989 and Communist China's increasing shift toward free markets, many economists and political leaders, especially in the United States, asserted that "capitalism won." But under the influence of local cultures, capitalism can take more varied forms than we might assume.

As defined previously, capitalism is an economic system based on private ownership of the means of production, in which prices are set and goods distributed through a market. Beyond this generally accepted definition, theoretical approaches to capitalism vary depending on the researcher's philosophical and political persuasions (Blim 2000). For example, followers of influential sociologist Max Weber study the distinct types of capitalism that have existed in different times and places; formalists study capitalism through the actions of individuals and institutions; and Marxists study the changing nature of industrial production, the conditions of workers, and the connection between small-scale economic activities and broader global economic trends.

In spite of theoretical orientation, however, anthropologists view capitalism as a cultural phenomenon. In fact, its deepest assumptions are cultural: capitalism assumes certain values and ideals to be natural, in the sense that this is the way things really are. It seems inevitable that well-being can be achieved through consuming material things. Anthropologist Richard Robbins (2005:2) suggests that capitalist systems are culturally organized into four distinct social roles. *Capitalists* invest money in real estate, buildings, machinery, and so on to make profit. *Laborers* work for the capitalists; their sole means of support comes from the sale of their labor. The primary role of *consumers* is to purchase and consume quantities of goods and services. Finally, the *state* institutes and enforces policies that structure the relationship between these three other actors, attempting to ensure that capitalists invest, workers work, and consumers consume. These social categories and the cultural ideals associated with them are the basic and universal elements of capitalism.

But anthropologists also recognize that the cultural contexts and meanings of capitalist activities take diverse forms. Let us compare two examples—one drawn from Wall Street, the other from Malaysia—to illustrate how capitalist activities and meanings can vary across cultures.

Culture and Social Relations on Wall Street

Investment banks on Wall Street, site of the New York Stock Exchange and America's financial capital, are popularly seen as a bastion of individual entrepreneurialism and cold rationalism in pursuit of profits (Figure 9.8). If Adam Smith were alive he'd probably see Wall Street as the epitome of capitalism. But anthropologists have found that social relationships and cultural processes shape transactions on Wall Street in far more complex ways than our image of Wall Street may suggest.

What interests anthropologists is how, in the context of such social relationships, people construct meanings, and how those meanings shape social action and individual conduct. For example, anthropologist Karen Ho (2009) studied investment banks and the international banking industry on Wall Street using participant observation and open-ended interviews just as an anthropologist working in a foreign village would. She reports that bankers and traders think of Wall Street as an entity that mediates vast and anonymous flows of capital throughout the world. One informant told her, "What Wall Street has been doing over the past 15 years is to make the whole world look like one big pool of capital and the whole world look like one big pool of people who need capital. Wall Street basically brings it all together." This banker stressed the seamlessness and anonymity of the global marketplace.

But Ho had conducted participant observation within these global networks as an investment banker herself. She found that these investment banks had transformed the goals of American capitalism since the 1980s, by shifting companies away from traditional corporate goals: producing a quality product in a sustainable way that would provide income for corporate investors, jobs for employees, and useful product for consumers. Instead, investment firms came to stress increasing "shareholder value" as a corporation's mission, a view that justified hundreds of mergers and acquisitions throughout the 1990s and 2000s. The consequence of most mergers and acquisitions was buying up less profitable firms, liquidating and breaking them up, selling off their assets at a profit, and firing all the employees. The acquiring hedge fund or investment bank added short-term shareholder profits, but no new production and many newly unemployed. The investment banks themselves benefited dramatically from commissions

🌱 **Figure 9.8   The New York Stock Exchange on Wall Street, the Heart of U.S. Capitalism.**

that they received for each step of the process, increasing their own shareholder value and bonuses for individual bankers.

But even the bankers themselves, she discovered, could be laid off at a moment's notice as the banks confronted regular economic crises because of poor investments. She concluded that the structure of the investment bank workplace, a crisis-prone setting in which workers are seen as expendable to protect the profits of the bank itself, has become a powerful cultural model that Wall Street bankers project onto the rest of the economy. Because they control access to money for many corporations, this Wall Street vision of how an economy should work is being imposed on many other businesses.

Throughout her time on Wall Street, Ho also found that strong personal relationships are essential to successful transactions, precisely because the market is so vast and because it is so difficult to decipher with assurance the risks and strengths of any particular global segment. As a result, bankers who tell their clients they have "global reach" and coverage "everywhere in the world"—which is a central part of the image they promote to convince investors to do business with them—are not being entirely honest. In reality, Ho found, most firms had minimal coverage in most parts of the world, often maintaining empty or barely staffed offices where they only occasionally did business. Their relationships with local banking firms and clients tend to lie nearly dormant, only being reactivated when new investment opportunities arise. Ho's point is that without the rich personal relationships and knowledge of local conditions and markets, these banks have almost no reach whatsoever, demonstrating that modern financial markets are every bit as dependent on social relationships and local knowledge as any daily transaction anthropologists might study in a rural village setting.

Entrepreneurial Capitalism Among Malays

The southeast Asian nation of Malaysia provides an example of a very different culture of capitalism. During the past several decades, Malaysia has aggressively pursued economic growth through industrialization and the creation of investment opportunities. Malaysia is an Islamic country whose majority are Muslim ethnic Malays. During British colonial times (early 1800s to the mid-1900s) the nation's Chinese minority dominated the economy and remained considerably better off than most of the Malay majority. Since the late 1960s the Malaysian government's goal for economic growth has been to reduce economic inequality between the country's ethnic Chinese and ethnic Malays by giving Malays preferential treatment and greater control over economic resources through set-aside provisions, government subsidies, special investment programs, and preferential opportunities for university education.

Anthropologist Patricia Sloane (1999) studied the impact of these laws on the culture of Malay entrepeneurs in urban Kuala Lumpur, Malaysia's capital. Few Malay capitalists in her study were extremely wealthy, but were part of the growing Malaysian middle class. These Malay capitalists' aspirations are not "global" but self-consciously local. The ideology of business was embedded in local values and committed to promoting the economic interests and growth of the Malay ethnic group.

These processes have created a new class of Malay entrepreneurs who think of themselves as the cornerstone of a new, modernized Malaysia. They accept that capitalism is a self-interested enterprise, but they also feel bound by traditional Malay values, insisting on investment and development that serve traditional obligations to family, community, and other Malays. Their idea of capitalism is one in which wealth, social balance, and even salvation are the rewards for those who abide by the moral dictates of social responsibility and obligation. At the heart of these values lie Islamic

Anthropologist as Problem Solver

Ashraf Ghani and the Reconstruction of the Afghan Economy

Ashraf Ghani.

SINCE THE 1970s, the people of Afghanistan have suffered through a Soviet invasion and occupation, a civil war, and the repressive government of the Taliban (a fundamentalist Islamic religious and political group). After the events of 9/11 in 2001, U.S. and NATO troops invaded Afghanistan to overthrow the Taliban who were supporting the 9/11 terrorists. All these events disrupted the country's agricultural economy and Afghanistan has become a chief supplier of opium for the production of heroin.

After the fall of the Taliban in 2001, Afghan anthropologist Ashraf Ghani, who received his Ph.D. from Columbia University, decided to return to his native country to help with its reconstruction. As a scholar, Ghani had studied social transformation, the role of religion in people's lives, and how states succeed or fail—topics that he taught about in U.S. and Afghan universities for several decades. In the 1990s, he worked at the World Bank on projects related to state reform, and later at the United Nations working on the Afghan peace agreement after the U.S. invasion. He was a well-known international expert on state-building and reform (Ghani and Lockhart 2009).

Within several months of his return, Ghani became Afghanistan's finance minister, a position he held between June 2002 and December 2004. As finance minister, Ghani implemented a number of major reforms, including issuing a new currency, creating a national budget, computerizing the operations of the treasury, and sharing treasury reports with the public to provide transparency and accountability in the use of public funds.

As a Marxist anthropologist, Ghani has been a staunch critic of capitalism, insisting that the majority of people in the world experience capitalism mainly through industries that come to extract their countries' resources and wealth, leaving the people with few benefits. But as finance minister, he understood that people in his country could benefit from participation in the global capitalist economy if given the opportunity to do it more or less on their own terms and in partnership with foreign investors. Toward this end, he raised $27.5 billion dollars of international assistance, with the goal of creating new capitalist development programs outside the opium economy.

In spite of his openness to the global economy, Ghani has insisted that elected village-level councils determine the priorities and ways of implementing development plans. Like many other anthropologists, he opposed the idea of having central government and aid officials create and implement development programs, because they have little knowledge of local priorities and social norms. Ghani's approach drew directly and explicitly on Afghan traditions of *Ashar* (community members working together voluntarily to improve community infrastructure), *Jirga* (councils composed of respected members of the community), and Islamic values of unity, equity, and justice (National Solidarity Programme 2014).

As finance minister, Ghani managed all the typical issues—currency, budgets, and treasury functions—but he drew explicitly on his anthropological training when he pressed his government to appreciate the importance of local culture in shaping how economies work. This approach has been tangibly successful from an economic point of view, since Afghan economic growth in recent years has been as high as 30% annually. From a social and political point of view it was also successful. He has become a popular political figure in Afghanistan, becoming president after the 2014 election.

Question for Reflection

1. What conditions might undermine Ghani's plan to have local communities determine the priorities and ways of implementing development plans?

2. Why might an agent of the World Bank or the U.S. State Department approach rebuilding the Afghan economy differently from Ghani?

economic principles—such as the prohibition on charging interest, prohibitions on exploitive or risky activities, and the obligation to share wealth after meeting one's family needs (Sloane 1999:73).

One effect of these ideals is that few enterprises are economically successful, so business failures are common. But Malays do not view these facts with embarrassment, because for many individuals the primary business goal is not to generate huge profits but to extend and deepen their social networks and to cultivate contacts with powerful people. Entrepreneurship is thus not simply about economic action and profit accumulation; it allows people to show how they are both fully engaged in the modern world of global capitalism and respectful of traditional Islamic and Malay obligations and values.

The challenge for Malays, in other words, has been how to pursue a capitalist economy that both improves their material quality of life and conforms to their local cultural values and social practices. This challenge is not unique to Malaysia. In "Anthropologist as Problem Solver: Ashraf Ghani and the Reconstruction of the Afghan Economy," we consider how one anthropologist has sought to create capitalist development that aligns with cultural priorities and social norms in Afghanistan.

THINKING CRITICALLY ABOUT ECONOMICS

If capitalism can vary across cultures, do you think models of capitalist behavior and thought can also differ within a society? Can you think of any examples drawn from what you know about the different kinds of industries and businesses you would find in the American capitalist economic system? How can you explain the variability of capitalism within a single society?

Conclusion

Most North Americans take for granted that the best way to get the things we need and want is to get a job and begin getting a paycheck. But this is definitely not how people do it everywhere in the world. Whether they are Russians gaining access to goods and services through the informal exchange of favors, Trobriand Islanders trading for goods on other islands, or Malaysian entrepreneurs building social ties with other entrepreneurs and powerful individuals, people differ in their cultural strategies and ideas about appropriate ways to conduct their economic lives. And, when we step back and look at our own economic lives in a consumer capitalist society, we can see that we too have developed distinctive strategies for exchanging goods and money, such as when we symbolically transform commodities into personalized gifts or possessions.

Economic ideas and behaviors never exist independently of culture, morality, and social relationships. Culture shapes what is acceptable to transact, how and why a transaction occurs, and how the goods and services being exchanged are valued. This point is especially important for understanding the complexities of contemporary global economic changes. In an economically interconnected world, the creation of new markets and economic relationships has an impact on whether and how people in a particular place will be able to acquire certain goods and services. But these processes never occur in a cultural and social vacuum, which is why economic processes continue to play out in distinct ways in communities around the world.

KEY TERMS

Reviewing the Chapter

Chapter Section	What We Know	To Be Resolved
Is Money Really the Measure of All Things?	Economies never exist independently of already existing social relationships and culture. Culture shapes what is acceptable to transact, how and why that transaction will take place, and how the goods or services being exchanged are valued.	Still unresolved is the issue of how to define the category "economic." Is it a particular logic and decision-making process? Or is it the substance of the economy, meaning the daily transactions of goods and services?
How Does Culture Shape the Value and Meaning of Money Itself?	People's relationships and attitudes toward money depend on factors such as whether their society uses general purpose money and/or limited purpose money; spheres of exchange; and cultural distinctions between transactional orders.	Anthropologists are still working through the diverse cultural meanings of money, especially the ways money circulates and shifts meanings through distinct transactional orders.
Why Is Gift Exchange Such an Important Part of All Societies?	The exchange of things is a universal feature of human existence. Many societies have met people's material and social necessities through highly organized and principled gift exchanges, but rich subtleties and cross-cultural variations exist in how, when, what, and why people engage in gift exchange.	Although anthropologists accept the central importance of gift exchange in all societies, they continue to embrace distinct theoretical models concerning reciprocity and gift exchange, and debates persist over whether these models adequately capture the complexity of other cultures' approaches to reciprocity.

Why Does Having Some Things Make You Cool?	The symbolic distinctions and qualities that make objects cool and worthy of respect are always culturally constructed.	People's relationships with objects are more complicated than economic perspectives on consumption suggest. Anthropologists are still documenting and seeking to understand those complexities.
Are There Distinct Cultures of Capitalism?	Capitalism is as much an economic system as it is a cultural phenomenon, whose actual practices and cultural models vary across and within cultures.	The idea that capitalism is not a monolithic economic structure but a variable culturally diverse set of practices is not universally accepted in anthropology, especially by Marxist anthropologists.

Readings

Since Bronislaw Malinowski's classic monograph on the Kula exchange among the Trobriand Islanders (*Argonauts of the Western Pacific,* London: G. Routledge and Sons, 1922), a considerable amount of anthropological research has focused on gift-giving systems around the world. Marcel Mauss's classic 1924 essay *The Gift: The Form and Reason for Exchange in Archaic Societies* (New York: W. W. Norton, 1990) is a necessary starting point. Marylin Strathern's *The Gender of the Gift: Problems with Women and Problems with Society in Melanesia* (Berkeley: University of California Press, 1988) offers an excellent overview of gift-giving in Melanesia—where gift-giving plays an especially prominent role in the social lives of many societies—and how anthropologists should think of those issues.

● ●

For a useful overview of the field of economic anthropology and its primary theoretical debates and orientations, see Richard R. Wilk and Lisa C. Cliggett's book *Economies and Cultures: Foundations of Economic Anthropology* (Boulder, CO: Westview Press, 2007).

● ●

When the Soviet Union fell, anthropologists working in Russia and Eastern Europe found themselves in an interesting position trying to document and analyze the dramatic social transformations that were playing out in front of them. Two excellent books on this transformation are Caroline Humphrey's *The Unmaking of Soviet Life: Everyday Economies After Socialism* (Ithaca, NY: Cornell University Press, 2002) and Katherine Verdery's book *What Was Socialism? What*

Comes Next? (Princeton, NJ: Princeton University Press, 1996).

● ●

The 2008 financial crisis in the United States, which spread to many other countries, revealed for many people the powerful role Wall Street plays in shaping the economic prospects of people who have nothing to do with investment banking. Karen Ho's *Liquidated: An Ethnography of Wall Street* (Durham, NC: Duke University Press, 2009) provides a rich and in-depth ethnographic description of how investment banking culture operates.

● ●

Politics

Cooperation, Conflict,

and Power Relations

IF YOU FOLLOW the news much, you'll know that reporting about politics is a major focus of any newspaper or news website. Stories about what the President recently said, conflicts between political parties in Congress, election results here or in another part of the world, or scandals involving local political figures tend to dominate the headlines. But even as these kinds of stories are the lifeblood of important public discourse in any country, they offer a fairly narrow view of what politics actually is. Why do we not find stories about the following in news reporting about politics?

- In Papua New Guinea, a young woman commits suicide out of protest for being abused by a man, intending to motivate her male relatives to seek justice and reparations.
- In a village in the Venezuelan Amazon, a Yanomamo headman scrapes the ground with a machete to shame others to join him in cleaning the village before a feast.
- In 1930s Italy, government officials concerned with the problem of declining fertility and reproductive rates among the Italian people introduce a census, social insurance programs, housing projects, and social work to support an increase in the size, growth rate, and "vitality" of the population.
- In Cameroon, high-ranking government officials use sorcery to undermine their rivals and impress villagers with their immunity from occult forces.

🌱 **Revenge Suicide as Politics.** This painting (detail) represents a suicide performed as a revenge against wrongdoing in Papua New Guinea, by native artist Apa Hugo. See page 247 for a discussion of the complete image.

• In Hawai'i, a community leader guides adversaries in a dispute and their immediate family members through a healing process in which everyone is expected to share their feelings and grievances openly.

Of course, one reason we do not find such reporting about politics in U.S. news is that these are minor events with no bearing on the lives of most of us. But in the 24–7 news world we live in, it is easy to come to the conclusion that politics is simply what politicians or political parties said and did in the latest news cycle. Anthropologists take a wider view on **politics**, understanding it to be those relationships and processes of cooperation, conflict, and power that are fundamental aspects of human life. There is considerable variety in how people think about politics and their reasons for engaging in political acts. It might be to enrich themselves materially or spiritually; to help their families, friends, or a social group to which they belong; to pursue personal power; to resolve a conflict; or to seek dignity or independence from oppression. It might be to produce relative order in a chaotic situation or to produce chaos in a relatively ordered situation.

The preceding brief list also suggests that people exert power in diverse ways. Some of these are formal and fairly stable, through institutions and procedures—government offices, armies, codified laws, rituals, or legal proceedings—that are easily identifiable elements of most societies. Others are less formal and more fleeting, such as the creation of temporary alliances, or acts of protest, manipulation, accusation, sorcery, and shame. Political acts may draw attention to the exercise of power, or they may be disguised, hiding the true source of power. Actual techniques range from coercion and oppression to persuasion and influence, but they may also include truth-seeking, the collection and sharing of information, and the desire to know intimate details about people's lives.

This approach to politics moves beyond the idea that modern states, which function through elections, bureaucracies, political parties, etc., should be the sole focus of anthropological interest. Even though states are the dominant political form in our contemporary world, the actual practices of modern states are not the same everywhere. More important is the diversity in how people around the world manage power relations at all levels of social life, from the interpersonal to the national and transnational. We can hardly begin to understand this diversity if we focus exclusively on the formal institutions of modern states, because that approach misses the fact that cooperation, conflict, and power are rooted in and emerge from people's everyday social interactions, belief systems, and cultural practices.

At the heart of anthropology's approach to politics is a key question: *How is power acquired and transmitted in a society?* Embedded in this broader question are the following problems, around which this chapter is organized:

• **Politics.** Those relationships and processes of cooperation, conflict, and power that are fundamental aspects of human life.

Does every society have a government?

What is political power?

Why do some societies seem more violent than others?

How do people avoid cycles of aggression, brutality, and war?

For anthropologists, power is not simply in the hands of state institutions and political offices. Politics is also about how people manage their everyday social relationships through force, influence, persuasion, and control over resources. But before we understand how these processes work in different societies, we need to address the opportunities and pitfalls of thinking about politics solely in terms of how formal political systems work.

Does Every Society Have a Government?

This question might seem strange because the answer seems so obvious. Our society has **government** (a separate legal and constitutional domain that is the source of law, order, and legitimate force) from the federal level down to the most local. We may assume other societies must have something similar. Otherwise, wouldn't they be in the throes of anarchy?

Not necessarily. Consider the !Kung San (also known as Ju/'hoansi), a hunter-gatherer society in the Kalahari Desert of southern Africa. !Kung have historically lived in egalitarian bands of fifteen to twenty people, and are an **acephalous society**, that is, they have no governmental head or hierarchical structure. Until they were brought under the control of the Namibian and South African governments, !Kung did not even have a notion of a distinct political sphere, and important band decisions were made by group consensus. Life was organized around sharing food, and those who did not share were taunted and shamed mercilessly, or even pushed out of the band (Figure 10.1). When a hunter killed a large animal, he shared it with everyone

- **Government.** A separate legal and constitutional domain that is the source of law, order, and legitimate force.

- **Acephalous society.** A society without a governing head, generally with no hierarchical leadership.

Figure 10.1 The Power of Sharing. In many hunter-gatherer societies, such as the !Kung San pictured here, individuals are obligated to share their goods, especially food. This obligation represents a powerful force for ensuring social stability.

- **Laws.** Sets of rules established by some formal authority.

in the band, belittling his own accomplishment lest he be considered arrogant. The emphasis on sharing and egalitarianism kept people more or less in line without the need for government or **laws**, which are a set of rules established by some formal authority. Leadership is informal, usually one of the senior men guiding the band, but without any power over others. In some hunter-gatherer groups, as anthropologists Kirk and Karen Endicott (2008) observed among the Batek people of Malaysia, even relations between men and women are egalitarian, and women can become leaders of a band.

The fact that the !Kung and other foraging societies do not have a formal political system like ours suggests that governments are not a universal feature of human existence. So why do we tend to think of politics primarily in terms of how formal governments work? Part of the reason is historical, the other part philosophical.

The Idea of "Politics" and the Problem of Order

Our modern notion of politics emerged during the Enlightenment (1650–1800), a period that saw the rise of science and modern philosophy emphasizing the use of reason. This was a period of social upheaval in Western Europe in which the rise of industrial capitalism and revolutionary democracies challenged the existing social and political order. Two of the major figures concerned with the problem of disorder caused by these changes were the English philosophers Thomas Hobbes (1588–1679) and John Locke (1632–1704). Hobbes believed that humans are naturally selfish, competitive, and warlike, leading to violence and a chaotic free-for-all as people use whatever means they have at their disposal to pursue their own personal interests, a condition avoided only by the absolute rule of a monarch (Hobbes 1909). Locke disagreed, arguing that chaos was avoidable by creating a more limited government based on a "social contract" in which certain basic individual rights are recognized (Locke 2003). This is our modern idea—and justification—for democratic government, and it is what modern politicians refer to when they talk about the "rule of law."

Europeans learned that societies exist around the world that do not have government, written laws, or "social contracts," but they largely dismissed them as primitive, uncivilized, and savage societies. Indeed, one of the central animating ideals of European colonialism in Africa, Asia, Latin America, and the Pacific was that bringing these people social order created by European forms of government and law would lift them out of their supposed savagery.

Structural-Functionalist Models of Political Stability

- **Structural-functionalism.** An anthropological theory that the different structures or institutions of a society (religion, politics, kinship, etc.) functioned to maintain social order and equilibrium.

During the early twentieth century, the global expansion of British colonialism coincided with and helped fuel the rise of British anthropology. Colonial authorities often turned to anthropologists to help them make sense of the foreign societies now under British control that did not have forms of government recognizable to the British. This situation presented British anthropologists with important opportunities to study the maintenance of order in societies without formal governments and political leaders. It also allowed these anthropologists to help formalize patterns of indirect rule in which local chiefs were incorporated into the new colonial administration. The theory they used to explain how these societies had maintained order was **structural-functionalism**, which held that the different structures of a society (such as religion, politics, kinship, etc.) functioned in an integrated way to maintain social order and equilibrium. In Africa, structural-functionalists identified numerous ways societies maintained order

Classic Contributions

E. E. Evans-Pritchard on Segmentary Lineages

E. E. EVANS-PRITCHARD (1902–1973) was a British social anthropologist and a proponent of structural-functionalism. Among the Nuer, Evans-Pritchard could find no central government, central chiefs, or powerful individuals, and he noted that the contentious Nuer were frequently feuding over stolen cattle, their principal form of wealth.

Evans-Pritchard called this situation "ordered anarchy," alluding directly to Hobbes's notion of anarchy. The Nuer are quite independent, tending their herds of cattle in small lineages of several dozen men descended from a single ancestor. These lineages see themselves as having arisen when larger lineage groups broke into smaller groups or segments. Yet, whenever a smaller lineage group faces an external threat, such as aggression from a distantly related lineage, it works together with other closely related lineages to confront the threat. The political unity of Nuer was thus flexible and non-centralized, allowing them to create larger groups according to need and dismantle them quickly. Evans-Pritchard described this political system as segmentary lineages. In this classic quotation he explains the logic of political organization.

▼ **E. E. Evans-Pritchard.**

A man is a member of a political group of any kind in virtue of his non-membership of other groups of the same kind. He sees them as groups and their members see him as a member of a group, and his relations with them are controlled by the structural distance between the groups concerned. But a man does not see himself as a member of that same group in so far as he is a member of a segment of it which stands outside of and is opposed to other segments of it. This is a fundamental principle of Nuer political structure. Thus a man is a member of his tribe in its relation to other tribes, but he is not a member of his tribe in relation to his segment of it to other segments of the same kind. Likewise a man is a member of his tribal segment in its relation to other segments, but he is not a member of it in the relation of his village to other villages of the same segment. A characteristic of any political group is hence its invariable tendency towards fission and the opposition of its segments, and another characteristic is its tendency toward fusion with other groups of its own order in opposition to political segments larger than itself. (Evans-Pritchard 1940:136–137)

Questions for Reflection

The Nuer live in a region that recently split from Sudan and created itself as the world's newest country, South Sudan (established in 2011). By 2013 the new country was experiencing internal strife, and Nuer have been embroiled in a bloody conflict with other prominent ethnic groups, such as the Dinka, over who should lead the country.

1. How would you expect the lineage dynamics described by Evans-Pritchard to be playing out in the current conflict?

2. What do you think the leadership structure is like on the Nuer side in this conflict?

without formal political institutions, among them (1) kinship systems, (2) associations, and (3) religious beliefs and practices (Radcliffe-Brown 1952).

A classic example of the political function of the kinship system is the Nuer, who are pastoralists in southern Sudan. In "Classic Contributions: E. E. Evans-Pritchard on Segmentary Lineages," this prominent British anthropologist explains how the Nuer maintain social order without political leaders or formal governmental structures.

In addition to kinship, various kinds of informal associations, which are groupings of individuals around non-political matters, can function as a political system. Secret societies, for example, might exercise control over territory, rituals, and the enforcement of certain customs. Many pastoralist societies, like the Maasai of Kenya and Tanzania, divide men from different families into **age-grades**, which are groupings of age-mates, who are initiated into adulthood together, and where senior grades have some authority over juniors (Kurtz 2001) (Figure 10.2).

Religious rituals can also function politically, integrating a community by bringing people together around common beliefs and activities. Rituals can also serve political ends, by legitimating community authority, ensuring group cohesion, organizing against enemies, and resolving disputes. Beliefs in witchcraft or sorcery, which provoke fear in many societies, can also promote order. Throughout Africa, for example, people who do not behave according to community norms are identified and punished as witches. They might be banished from a village, harassed, or abused physically (Marwick 1952). Without formal courts, structural-functionalists insisted, such practices operated as a rudimentary criminal justice system (Gledhill 2000).

Neo-Evolutionary Models of Political Organization: Bands, Tribes, Chiefdoms, and States

In the 1940s and 1950s as political anthropology was taking shape in the United States, American anthropologists, influenced by the neo-evolutionary theories of Leslie White and Julian Steward (see Chapter 3), sought to classify the world's diversity of political systems and explain how complex political systems, especially states, had evolved from simpler forms of social and political organization.

- **Age-grades.** Groupings of age-mates, who are initiated into adulthood together.

- **Band.** A small, nomadic, and self-sufficient group of anywhere from 25 to 150 individuals with face-to-face social relationships, usually egalitarian.

- **Tribe.** A type of pastoralist or horticulturist society with populations usually numbering in the hundreds or thousands in which leadership is more stable than that of a band, but usually egalitarian, with social relations based on reciprocal exchange.

- **Chiefdom.** A political system with a hereditary leader who holds central authority, typically supported by a class of high-ranking elites, informal laws, and a simple judicial system, often numbering in the tens of thousands with the beginnings of intensive agriculture and some specialization.

Figure 10.2 The (Changing) Life of the Maasai Warrior. The traditional duties of these young Maasai in Kenya whose age-grade is warrior is to protect cattle herds from raiders and large cats, and to raid the herds of others. As wildlife conservation and tourism have increasingly disrupted Maasai lives and cattle economy, the duties of warriors are in transition.

Anthropologists Marshall Sahlins and Elman Service (1960) suggested a typology of societies with different forms of political and economic organization. By considering who controls food and other resources in any given society, they defined four types of society: **bands, tribes, chiefdoms,** and **states**. This typology was intended both to describe different kinds of society as well as to explain how more complex political forms had developed from simpler ones.

Bands and tribes in this scheme were examples of **non-centralized political systems**, in which power and control over resources are dispersed between members of the society. Chiefdoms and states were examples of **centralized political systems**, in which certain individuals and institutions hold power and control over resources. Although Sahlins and Service (1960) acknowledged that different societies followed different individual evolutionary paths, the tendency was that with increasing population density came more intensive and centralized forms of political organization. Table 10.1 outlines how this classification incorporates politics, economy, size, and population density.

Challenges to Traditional Political Anthropology

Political anthropology's early focus on social structures and political systems was valuable for describing the diverse ways humans create and maintain social order, with or without formal governments. These studies provided holistic insights into

- **State.** The most complex form of political organization, associated with societies that have intensive agriculture, high levels of social stratification, and centralized authority.

- **Non-centralized political system.** A political system, such as a band or a tribe, in which power and control over resources are dispersed between members of the society.

- **Centralized political system.** A political system, such as a chiefdom or a state, in which certain individuals and institutions hold power and control over resources.

TABLE 10.1	A NEO-EVOLUTIONARY TYPOLOGY OF POLITICAL ORGANIZATION			
	NON-CENTRALIZED		CENTRALIZED	
	Band	Tribe	Chiefdom	State
Type of Subsistence	Foraging	Horticulture and pastoralism	Extensive agriculture, intensive fishing	Intensive agriculture
Population Density	Low	Low to medium	Medium	High
Type of Economic Exchange	Reciprocity	Reciprocity and trade	Redistribution through chief, reciprocity at lower levels	Markets and trade; redistribution through state based on taxation
Social Stratification	Egalitarian	Egalitarian	Ranked	Social classes
Ownership of Property	Little or no sense of personal ownership	Lineage or clan ownership of land and livestock	Lineage or clan ownership of land, but with strong sense of personal ownership	Private and state ownership of land
Type of Leadership	Informal and situational; headman	Charismatic headman with some authority in group decision-making	Charismatic chief with limited power, usually based on giving benefits to followers	Sovereign leader supported by aristocratic bureaucracy
Law and Legitimate Control of Force	No formal laws or punishments; right to use force is communal	No formal laws or punishments; right to use force is held by lineage, clan, or association	May have informal laws and specified punishments; chief has limited access to coercion	Formal laws and punishments; state holds all access to use of physical force
Some Examples	!Kung San (Southern Africa); Inuit (Canada, Alaska); Batek (Malaysia)	Yanomamo (South America); Nuer (Sudan); Cheyenne (United States)	Kwakiutl (Canada, Alaska); Precolonial Hawai'i	Aztec (Mexico); Inca (Peru); Euro-American monarchies and representative democracies

Source: Adapted from Ted C. Lewellen, *Political Anthropology: An Introduction* (South Hadley, MA: Bergin & Garvey Publishers, 1983), pp. 20–21.

how political systems worked and how they were related to economic activities, religious beliefs, population density, and the environment.

But reality hardly ever corresponds to these simple theoretical models. For example, a major problem with the bands-tribes-chiefdoms-states typology is that many cases blur the boundaries between types. Take "tribe," for instance. Societies might have tribe-like qualities, such as the Nuer, who have no central political leadership, but because they have a population of 1.8 million people, do not have the same kinds of social relations as a "tribe" of 500 people. Some African chiefdoms have relatively small populations, the size of a typical tribe, but nevertheless have a political organization and pattern of social stratification that seems to prohibit their being classed as a tribe.

Another problem of these typologies is their ignorance of history. Many early political anthropologists originally assumed African or Pacific societies were essentially untouched by contact with the West. But many of these "traditional" political systems were not "traditional" at all, as they had been put in place by the British colonial policy of "Indirect Rule." Indirect Rule allowed local rulers to exercise administrative control over their people through whatever existing power structure was in place when the British arrived. Therefore, the local rulers themselves took instructions from the British colonial supervisors.

The emphasis on static political systems and order came at the expense of understanding the dynamic nature of political processes, characterized by conflict, intrigue, manipulation, and other techniques. As the British anthropologist Lucy Mair (1969) pointed out, political structures only provide individuals with roles. Within a role, individuals make choices and decisions, manipulate others, and strategize, all in the pursuit of power. From this point of view, the proper focus of political anthropology is political power, an issue we turn to next.

THINKING CRITICALLY ABOUT POLITICS

A complex institution like your college or university has many ways of governing the faculty, staff, and student body. These include formal institutions of governance, such as a faculty senate or president's office, as well as less formal associations and belief structures that help maintain order. What are some of these less formal forms of governance, and how do they contribute to the maintenance of order?

What Is Political Power?

The shift from viewing politics as a problem of order to the problem of how people gain and wield power began to flourish in the 1960s and continues to the present. Power is typically considered to be the ability to make people think or act in certain ways, through physical coercion or through more symbolic means, such as persuasion (Kingsolver 1996). Beyond this very general definition, however, there are many nuances to political power.

Defining Political Power

Whether it is an exchange of goods, a religious ceremony, or a conversation between a man and a woman, practically all aspects of human existence are imbued with power. But not all power is *political*. For anthropologists, **political power** refers to how power is created and enacted to attain goals that are presumed to be for the good of a community, the common good (Kurtz 2001:21). Of course, leaders often use political power to serve their own personal or family interests. But what distinguishes political power is the appearance, whether real or not, that it serves the common good.

The exercise of political power requires legitimacy. For power to be legitimate, power must be drawn from a culturally acceptable source. It can come from an independent source—a source outside the individuals that make up a community—such as gods or ancestors, inheritance, some high office, the ability to cure an illness, or the outcome of some legal process, such as an election. Or it can come from a dependent source, that is, power given by other social actors. Power can be *granted* from one leader to another, *delegated* from a leader to a follower for a specific purpose, or *allocated* by the community to a leader (Kurtz 2001:26).

In addition, control over material resources (territory, money, or other culturally defined goods) and human resources (willing followers and supporters) is an essential source of political power. But these two resources are typically not enough for effective political power. Leaders must also control symbolic resources, such as flags, uniforms, badges of rank, or other objects that give meaning to political action (Figure 10.3). Ideological resources justify the exercise of power and allow leaders to manipulate symbolic meaning (Kurtz 2001). There are other important dimensions to political power.

Figure 10.3   Lapel Pin Symbolism. American politicians, such as President Barack Obama and former Senator Arlen Specter pictured here, demonstrate their patriotism—and the fact that they are representatives of American power—by wearing an American flag lapel pin.

- **Political power.** The processes by which people create, compete, and use power to attain goals that are presumed to be for the good of a community.

Political Power Is Action-Oriented

People everywhere gain and manage political power through a combination of decision-making, cooperation, opportunism, compromise, collusion, charm, gamesmanship, strategic alliance, factionalism, resistance, conflict, and other processes. A focus on these processes was central to **action theory**, an approach in the anthropological study of politics that emerged in the 1960s. Action theorists closely followed the daily activities and decision-making processes of individual political leaders like chiefs in African villages or headmen in Amazonian settlements. They argue that politics is a dynamic and competitive field of social relations in which people are constantly managing their ability to exercise power over others (Vincent 1978). In other words, it is not enough to *be* president of the United States. One has to *act* as the president.

To follow political action, one must be familiar with a society's specific rules and codes about who gets to exercise power and under what conditions. Anthropologist F. G. Bailey (1969) compared these codes to those of playing a game. In politics, as in a game, there are *normative rules,* fairly stable and explicit ethical norms by which players must abide, such as honesty, fairness, and so on. There are also *pragmatic rules,* which are the creative manipulations necessary to win the game itself. For example,

- **Action theory.** An approach in the anthropological study of politics that closely follows the daily activities and decision-making processes of individual political leaders emphasizing that politics is a dynamic and competitive field of social relations in which people are constantly managing their ability to exercise power over others.

in U.S. politics, normative rules require political actors to be open, fair, and honest. But we know based on reading the political news in the newspaper that there are also the pragmatic rules of gaining and holding onto power, which often involve favoritism and even outright lying (Lewellen 2003).

Political Power Is Structural

Even as action theorists brought useful attention to the dynamic ways individuals manage political power, it became clear by the 1980s and 1990s that certain power relationships transcend any individual. Political anthropologists began to refer to such power as **structural power**, which is power that not only operates within settings but that also organizes and orchestrates the settings in which social and individual action take place (Wolf 2001:384). "Structure" here means something very different from how the early structural-functionalists understood it. They were interested in social institutions ("structures," as a noun), while this newer perspective focuses on the processes and relationships that shape or "structure" (as a verb) social action and relationships.

In this view, power does not lie in a group or individual's exercise of will over others through domination or manipulation, but is dispersed in many shapes and forms, produced and reproduced through the combined actions of important social institutions, science and other knowledge producers, and people living their everyday lives (Foucault 1978). Anthropologist David Horn (1994) used this approach to study how and why Italians of today accept state intervention in their lives. He traces their acceptance to the rise of social thought, planning, and research around the reproductive health of Italian families after World War I. During this period, the Italian government instituted a census and other scientific and medical programs to measure statistically the population's size, growth rate, and health conditions. Using this information, they instituted new policies of hygiene and family management, including (among others) a 1927 tax on bachelorhood and efforts to eliminate contraception and abortion. Although many of these policies failed, Horn observes that these changes had an important effect on Italians, in that they came to accept the idea that the body is not simply the domain of a private individual, but a social problem that requires scientific and state intervention. As a result they began to willingly accept the idea that they should share intimate details about their reproductive lives with the state and that it has the right to issue directives intended to manage citizens' lives—all of which are ideas that Italians take for granted today.

Another perspective on structural power emphasizes that under capitalism, relations involved in production have drawn people around the globe into a World System (see Chapter 6). These capitalist relations are the primary source of structural power in the world today, making possible the accumulation of capital based on the sale of labor. They are powerful because they constrain, inhibit, and promote what people can and cannot do in their economic and political lives (Wolf 2001:385). For example, a laborer on a banana plantation in Costa Rica has limited prospects for owning or accumulating wealth because all the arable land where he lives has been turned into plantations by foreign companies (Vandermeer and Perfecto 1995). When global demand for bananas drops, plantations lay off laborers, whose livelihood options are limited because they are landless and often undereducated. One of the few options available to them is to stake out a plot of land in the rainforest to grow crops, contributing to the problem of deforestation.

• **Structural power.** Power that not only operates within settings, but that also organizes those and orchestrates the settings in which social and individual actions take place.

Political Power Is Gendered

During the past thirty years, feminist anthropologists have observed that while men tend to dominate formal political processes in most societies, relationships between men and women intersect with political power in complex ways. In a number of societies, women exercise formal leadership and political power. In other settings, women may have very little formal power, but they can mobilize to assert power in response to events.

In many societies, women may be so disempowered politically and socially that their ability to take direct action lies only in the most dramatic action of all, taking one's own life. For example, on the island of New Britain in Papua New Guinea, cases of "revenge suicide" erupt when a woman takes her own life in response to abuse or shame (Figure 10.4). Here young women are powerless figures. But a woman's act of suicide shifts the burden of shame to her tormentor (often a husband), and can even mobilize her own male relatives and other community members to acknowledge the injustice, forcing them to seek accountability from the offending party (Counts 1980). Although taking such actions may be difficult for many Westerners to comprehend, this situation suggests we must consider forms of political power that are available to those we do not conventionally understand to be "powerful."

This point holds true for an issue that has recently gained widespread public attention in Western Europe and North America: the restrictive rules imposed on Islamic women, such as the practice of wearing headscarves restrictions on women mixing with men in public settings, and prohibitions on women driving cars. In many Islamic communities, male clerics justify these with *shari'a,* or customary Islamic law.

🌱 **Figure 10.4   Revenge Suicide in New Guinea.** This painting by contemporary Papua New Guinea artist Apa Hugo from 2003 illustrates how suicide can be used as a weapon of the weak. The caption in Pidgin English written on the painting means: "A man fights with his wife and the wife commits suicide. Her parents are distraught and cry in mourning" (*Man krosim meri na – meri i wari na I go sua sait. Na papa mama I wari na karai I stap*).

Figure 10.5   The Politics of Dress. In Iran, there is a rule that women must conceal their hair from the gaze of unrelated men by wearing a headscarf. Some women subvert the rule by draping a big scarf loosely over their heads and slinging the end over their shoulders, making the hair covering an ornament.

Anthropologist Erika Friedl (1994) observed that Iranian women found ways to subvert these restrictive rules by using these very rules against repressive male religious leaders. Their acts of protest can be something as simple as wearing a headscarf in a modern stylish way (Figure 10.5). Or they can subvert restrictions on attending social gatherings outside the home by making women's pilgrimages to the shrines of local saints. Because these are religious activities, male clerics cannot criticize the women. During these pilgrimages women can gather to exchange gossip and they can even discuss political issues free of the watchful eyes of men.

Political Power in Non-State Societies

To some extent, the exercise of political power differs between state and non-state societies. For example, in non-state societies such as tribal societies of South America and Melanesia, power tends to be temporary and episodic, emerging from personal charisma, not from elections or inheritance from a powerful father. The Amazon headman, for example, is "a first among equals." He assumes his status as leader by being able to persuade followers, not because he controls power or resources on his own. Such leaders, who are sometimes called Big Men, cannot transfer their status and power through inheritance when they die.

A Big Man cannot force others to do anything, but gains influence and authority by giving away wealth and shrewdly persuading others, through a combination of smooth talk and peer pressure, to produce goods they will provide him that he can then redistribute. In their 1970 documentary film *The Feast,* filmmaker Timothy Asch and anthropologist Napoleon Chagnon (1997) show how a Yanomamo headman in southern Venezuela sponsors a feast aimed at building an alliance with another community with which his own community had recently been at war. As headman he could not force anyone to help clear the plaza or cook the plantain soup that would be the centerpiece of the feast. His loud haranguing did little to motivate his fellow clan members, but he leads by example and his clansmen started helping and made it a successful feast, forming a new alliance. Persuasion was his most valuable tool.

In contrast to the status leadership of such a Big Man, the kind of political power your hometown mayor has is a quintessential expression of how political power works in a state society. Your mayor is an office holder, a person who gets power from his or her elected or appointed office. In state societies and chiefdoms, power and authority reside in offices and institutions. Formal rules dictate who can gain an office and the conditions under which it can be gained.

Your mayor holds a mid-level office in a large-scale and highly stratified state. Unlike a Big Man, who knows practically everyone in his social world, your mayor (especially if you live in a large urban area) personally knows few of the people he or she governs, much less the people who created the laws he or she enforces. Mayors use some of the same political skills as a Big Man—persuasion, giving away things, and so forth—but have greater ability to control others and get things done because of greater access to material resources, such as money from taxes, control over a bureaucracy, and an ability to enforce laws. But mayors and other American officials often draw on their personal connections to achieve things, as we suggest in "Thinking Like an Anthropologist: The Power of Personal Connections."

Thinking Like an Anthropologist

The Power of Personal Connections

ANTHROPOLOGISTS BEGIN THEIR research by asking questions. In this box, we want you to learn how to ask questions as an anthropological researcher. Part One describes a situation and follows up with questions we would ask. Part Two asks you to do the same thing with a different situation.

PART ONE: PERSONAL CONNECTIONS IN THE PERSIAN-SPEAKING WORLD

While working for the U.S. State Department in Iran during the 1970s, diplomat Whitney Azoy first encountered the concept *waaseta*, which in Persian refers to "the power of personal connections." *Waaseta* is based on the cultivation of personal relationships by giving and receiving favors. Individuals at all levels of the government use it, from the local village level up all the way to the president's office. The more extensive one's network of personal connections, the greater one's ability to ask for, offer, and call in favors, all of which translate directly to political power. As a diplomat, Azoy found that cultivating *waaseta* helped him pursue the interests of the United States.

When he later became an anthropologist conducting research among Persian speakers in Afghanistan, Azoy once again encountered *waaseta*. He observed that among Afghans, "Your family core group was a given; what really mattered were your personal connections beyond home and hearth. You were defined by it: enabled by knowing some people, limited by not knowing others. 'Name' or reputation—the currency of old-time, hinterland politics among both [traditional rulers] and small peasants was ultimately reckoned by

whom you knew ... and whom you could get to do favors for you" (Azoy 2002:A9). Afghans assumed that Azoy, as an American and a former official in the State Department, had extraordinary personal connections, and they asked him for many favors even long after he left Afghanistan. For instance, after the United States invaded Afghanistan to overthrow the Taliban in 2001 and began developing reconstruction projects, Azoy received a phone call from an Afghan acquaintance with whom he had not spoken in over twenty years. After they caught up on each other's lives, the Afghan asked if Azoy could draw on his *waaseta* in the U.S. government to get money for a reconstruction project. What questions does this situation raise for anthropological researchers?

1. If *waaseta* encompasses all political relationships in Afghanistan, do Afgans view *waaseta* as corruption, as many Americans are likely to do?
2. What limitations does *waaseta* place on developing a modern-style democracy?
3. Is a Western-style democracy, with its ideological commitment to transparency and avoidance of corruption, the only way to have a democracy?

PART TWO: PERSONAL CONNECTIONS IN U.S. POLITICS.

Azoy notes that *waaseta*'s "you-rub-my-back-and-I'll-rub-yours" quality has all the trappings of what we call "corruption." He contrasts it with the rule of law, balance of powers, transparency, and accountability that people in the United States expect of their politicians. But when Azoy made this point to an Afghan acquaintance, the Afghan insisted that American politics is also suffused with *waaseta*. He pointed to the fact that election campaigns are based on the give-and-take of favors between large donors and politicians.

Personal connections are critical to the American government's operations, a fact that very few politicians and bureaucrats hide. In fact, the symbol of a successful, well-connected politician is a smartphone full of phone numbers of other powerful people inside and outside the government with whom he or she has personal connections. If you wanted to understand the role of personal connections in American politics, what questions would you ask as an anthropological researcher?

Afghan Elders Engaging in Waaseta With a British Politician.

The Political Power of the Contemporary Nation-State

- **Nation-states.** Independent states recognized by other states, composed of people who share a single national identity.

Modern states are typically called **nation-states**, independent states recognized by other states and composed of people who share a single national identity. A nation is a population who thinks of itself as "a people" based on sharing—or imagining that they share—a common culture, language, heritage, identity, or commitment to particular political institutions (Robbins 2001:82). The political form of the nation-state originated in Europe several hundred years ago, but has become so common that now all the world's territory falls under the control of one or another nation-state. Even where people are not inclined to think of themselves as a singular "people" because of internal ethnic, religious, and linguistic diversity, they are still members of a nation-state.

Contrary to Locke's idealizations of the "social contract," membership in a nation-state is not necessarily voluntary. For many of the world's peoples, conquest and colonialism forced them into nation-states. Leaders of nation-states exercise various forms of political power to assert control over non-state societies and to ensure the conformity of all their citizens.

Leaders create a sense of unity by drawing symbolic lines between those who are included—often it is some version of the "chosen people"—and those who are excluded. Excluded groups may be defined as enemies (citizens of competing nation-states, or non-state actors such as "terrorists") or as inferior because of racial or ethnic differences. Practically every society makes similar ethnocentric distinctions. But in nation-states, these distinctions often lead to the marginalization of minority societies within the country's boundaries as ethnic or racial "Others." This has been true for American Indians, Australian Aborigines, and indigenous societies in Latin America, among other societies in nation-states.

Modern nation-states exercise power over their citizens by creating and managing information about them using institutionalized surveillance. Techniques of surveillance range from the mundane—national identity cards and censuses, for example—to the more secretive and sinister—such as monitoring social media, wiretapping, and hacking computers. Leaders and citizens alike may justify surveillance as ensuring that citizens receive protection. But surveillance secures and expands leaders' power and authority, by identifying potential opposition or non-conformism threatening their authority.

Many nation-states also use prisons, torture, and violence against citizens who do not conform to dominant values or identities. According to Amnesty International (2008), at least 81 of the 192 nation-states currently conduct torture on their citizens. As many nation-states kill their own citizens for political misdeeds, including criticism of the state, membership in banned political parties, deeds perceived as immoral, economic offenses (burglary, corruption), or for violent crimes (rape, assault, and murder) (Nagengast 1994:120).

Another form of state power is genocide. Although the Nazis during the Holocaust (six million dead, among them Jews, Romani [Gypsies], and homosexuals), typically come to mind, even countries that otherwise claim to respect human equality, such as the United States and Australia, once conducted campaigns of destruction against indigenous peoples (Figure 10.6).

Although nation-states introduce new political dynamics—formalized political parties and bureaucratized elections—it is important to stress that the political mechanisms that we have

Figure 10.6   Trail of Tears. The 1830 Indian Removal Act in the United States forcibly moved Indians from Georgia to Indian Territory (now Oklahoma). This state-sponsored policy cleared Indians from lands desired by whites, leading to the deaths of thousands of Indians.

Anthropologist as Problem Solver

Maxwell Owusu and Democracy in Ghana

SINCE ITS INDEPENDENCE from Britain in 1957, the West African country of Ghana has alternated between civilian- and military-controlled national governments. When the most recent military government (1981–1992) allowed elections in 1992, the Fourth Republic of Ghana emerged, based on a new constitution with a foundation in democratic principles.

An influential actor in that process was Ghanaian-born political anthropologist Maxwell Owusu of the University of Michigan. Owusu served as a consulting member of the Constitutional Experts Committee, which drafted the 1992 constitution proposals. Owusu has been a staunch critic of autocratic and repressive leadership in post-independence Ghana and other African nation-states. He is an advocate of popular participatory democracy. But as an anthropologist he understood the problems of imposing foreign political models—such as Western-style democracy with competing political parties—on African societies with different histories and indigenous political traditions. As he has written (Owusu 1992:384), "African democracy may require the integration of indigenous methods of village co-operation with innovative forms of government, combining the power of universal rights with the uniqueness of each district's or nation's own customs and respected traditions."

A viable solution, Owusu insisted, is to create a decentralized state in which local authorities, primarily chiefs, headmen, and lineage heads, participate directly in state processes and decision-making. The advantage is that local leaders can better identify the needs and priorities of villagers, while being more accountable to their members and communities than are bureaucrats in a state apparatus. The 1992 constitution put this insight to work, creating "District Assemblies" as the basic unit of national government, two-thirds of which are elected and one-third appointed, the latter being mostly traditional leaders or their representatives (Owusu 1992). Owusu observed that far from making chiefs and other non-state political leaders obsolete, these changes have put traditional leaders at the forefront of political change in the nation-state as a whole (Owusu 1996).

Questions for Reflection

1. How does Owusu's notion of participatory democracy, which relies upon decentralization of power toward local traditional leaders, differ from the way local governments at the city, town, or county level work in the United States?

2. Is it likely to be true that local traditional leaders are better able to identify local priorities than national leaders?

Maxwell Owusu.

explored in non-state societies can also operate in state settings. There is no absolute separation between state and non-state political organization. For example, in Benin, national politicians incorporate the same Big Man logic of material redistribution that we considered among the Yanomamo in Venezuela. Political candidates utilize favors from politicians already established in the government—much like *waseeta* in Iran—to build schools and medical clinics in the communities where they seek election. They also hold political rallies in which they ceremonially offer food, drink, and often money to the local community, again to elicit votes. Local people then pick from different candidates based on which candidate seems likely to offer the most largesse in the future. While the Beninese state enjoys an international reputation for a stable and thriving multi-party democracy, this reputation is due more to calculated public relations than to the realities on the ground (Hedges 2014).

Leaders of nation-states also often co-opt local political actors and their power to serve their own or nation-state ends. In post-independence Ghana, for example, where chiefs, headmen, and extended family lineages control village-level resources and political processes, centralized governments have co-opted traditional non-state leaders by rewarding some with high-level positions in the state bureaucracy. Such an appointment to a governmental position makes the leader responsible at the local level for enforcing national laws and mobilizing support for state-led development programs (Owusu 1996). For several decades, anthropologist Maxwell Owusu has researched how this kind of political power works in post-independence Ghana. He has advocated formally incorporating non-state political leaders into nation-state functions. In "Anthropologist as Problem Solver: Maxwell Owusu and Democracy in Ghana," we examine how his ideas have been put to work.

Except for a brief reference to lethal violence and genocide mentioned earlier in the chapter, we have so far discussed the exercise of political power in terms of the cultivation of relationships, persuasion, the collection of information, or the strategic manipulation of others. But violence is also a strategic means of gaining and holding onto political power, which in some societies seems more common and accepted than in others. In the next section, we explore this issue in more detail.

● ●

THINKING CRITICALLY ABOUT POLITICS

As this section shows, different anthropologists have approached political power in different ways. Do you think each of these approaches creates a fundamentally different picture of how political power works? Why or why not?

● ●

Why Do Some Societies Seem More Violent Than Others?

By the 1960s, a number of the societies anthropologists studied were experiencing intense post-independence violence, disruption, and conflict related to the end of European colonialism. This situation prompted an urgent concern to understand the relationship between political power and violence, and why political conflicts in some societies seemed to break out in violence more than conflicts did in other societies. What might be done to end and prevent future violence?

In pursuing answers to these questions, anthropologists have learned that violence is a form of power relations rooted in cultural processes and meanings, just as other strategies of political power, such as persuasion and manipulation, are.

What Is Violence?

Violence is typically defined as the use of force to harm someone or something. It is a highly visible and concrete assertion of power, and a very efficient way to transform a social environment and communicate an ideological message (Riches 1986).

Yet specifying what violence consists of is not always so straightforward, because violence is different things to different people (Eller 2006). Different people will draw the line differently between who or what can experience violence. The same person might acknowledge that shoving a person into a vat of boiling water is violent yet not view placing a lobster, much less a handful of spinach, in that boiling water as violent. Another factor in assessing what is violent is intention. Did the perpetrator mean to do it (violent), or was it an accident (probably not violent)? And rationality: did the perpetrator have control over his or her actions (violent), or was it a case of "losing one's mind" (probably not violent, or at least justified)? And legitimacy: was it a legitimate act, such as a boxer beating on another boxer (sports, not violence), or deviant, such as a man beating his wife (violent)? Even the nature of force: was the force personal, as in one person punching another (violent), or structural, as in economic conditions depriving a child of food (open to debate)? And whether you were a victim, perpetrator, or witness, you are likely to have a different perspective on whether or not an act is violent.

As you read the previous paragraph, you may have found yourself disagreeing with our suggestions of what might be violent and what might not be. This should not be surprising. Even though we might all agree that violence involves some element of harm and an assertion of power over others, people have differing opinions on what constitutes violence. Some of these opinions are individually held, but some are related to differences in how we as members of a particular culture define violence and give meaning to it. Culture shapes not only how people think about violence but also how, why, and when they use it as a form of power over others.

Violence and Culture

Since Hobbes, Europeans and Americans have seen violence as a natural condition of humans. But anthropologists offer two major challenges to this view: (1) neither violence nor its opposite, non-violence, is an inevitable condition of humanity; both are learned behaviors that express themselves in particular social and historic circumstances; and (2) violence is generally not chaotic and arbitrary, but tends to follow explicit cultural patterns, rules, and ethical codes. We consider both of these points here.

Neither Violence Nor Non-Violence Is Inevitable in Human Societies

In recent years, it has become fashionable to think of aggression and violence as genetically determined. But no animal or human carries genes for dominance, aggression, or passivity. These complex social and psychological conditions and states involve biological processes, such as the production of certain hormones, but they are not fixed properties or traits carried by genes.

So how should we deal with claims—some even made by anthropologists—that some societies are fierce and warlike and others peaceful? The answer, of course, is by demonstrating that neither violence nor non-violence is universal (Fry 2006). Two famous examples—the Yanomamo and the Semai—illustrate our point.

- **Violence.** The use of force to harm someone or something.

Figure 10.7   The "Fierce People." In the ethnographic film *The Ax Fight*, from which this image is drawn, the filmmakers represent Yanomamo lives as filled with aggression and near-constant violence. But is it really so?

The Yanomamo

Anthropologist Napoleon Chagnon (1968) described the Yanomamo Indians of southern Venezuela with whom he has worked since the early 1960s as the "fierce people." According to Chagnon, the Yanomamo have an aggressive style about nearly everything they do. They stage brutal raids against enemy settlements, and they routinely have violent responses to their fellow clansmen. Some of the films he produced with filmmaker Timothy Asch (e.g., Asch and Chagnon 1989) vividly depict this fierce approach to life, presenting chest-pounding competitions, ax fights, and raids on enemy groups (Figure 10.7).

But other anthropologists, including Brian Ferguson (1995) and Jacques Lizot (1985), have seen the Yanomamo in a different light, as warm and caring people, who from time to time had to defend themselves against enemies. Filmmaker Asch, who had worked with Chagnon in the field, also produced several films that show a peaceable side of Yanomamo life, including images of a father bathing his children and a husband and wife working on projects together (Asch and Chagnon 1968, 1990a, 1990b). Ferguson's research suggests that Yanomamo fierceness was not the traditional behavior of these Amazonian Indians, but the result of contact with foreigners: missionaries, prospectors, government officials, and anthropologists such as Chagnon, who has come under fire by Yanomami themselves for disrupting their society (Tierney 2002).

The Semai

A similar point can be made about a very different case, the Semai, egalitarian swidden farmers who live in the Malaysian rainforest. Anthropologist Robert Dentan (1968) characterized the Semai as peaceful and non-violent because they committed little or no interpersonal violence during his field research.

The Semai view themselves as peaceful and reject the idea that violence is a natural condition of human life. At the heart of Semai commitment to non-violence is a valued concept of *persusah,* referring to the value of not causing trouble for others. Causing *punan,* a condition that makes someone unhappy or frustrated, is unacceptable to Semai. Semai strive to avoid causing *punan,* and emphasize *persusah.* Acts of power or inequality, such as being stingy, refusing a request, or forcing somebody to obey an order, are especially prone to cause *punan.* Arguments do break out from time to time, but people have found other ways of diffusing tensions besides fighting. Anthropologist Clayton Robarchek (1979), who lived with the Semai in the 1970s, argued that almost all aspects of social life emphasize non-violence and that Semai children are emotionally conditioned to be non-violent and peaceful.

But the Semai are not completely non-violent either. During the Communist insurrection in Malaysia from 1948 to 1960, some Semai became soldiers and a few were renowned fighters. Anthropologist John Leary (1995) worked with these Semai soldiers during the insurrection and argued that the non-violent interpretations of Dentan and Robarchek fundamentally misrepresent these men, who were good soldiers. Although Dentan had consistently described the ethos of the Semai as non-violent and peaceful, he did quote one former soldier who described himself and his comrades in the counterinsurgency as "drunk with blood" (1968:58–59). Robarchek and Dentan (1987) argue that the Semai are indeed socialized to be non-violent, but when they were brought into the counterinsurgency they were socialized as soldiers and trained to kill.

The point of this example is that, as with the Yanomamo, violence and non-violence are not absolute or static conditions. They are the result of cultural attitudes and particular social and historical conditions (Fry 2006).

Explaining the Rise of Violence in Our Contemporary World

Anthropologists have long observed that violence and the threat of violence, far from implying chaos, can actually encourage social order. Contrary to stereotypes of violence as chaotic and anti-social, violent acts are ordered because they reflect culturally specific patterns, rules, and ethical codes. These patterns define when and why violence is acceptable, what forms of violence are appropriate, and who can engage in violent acts.

In news reports pundits routinely explain the rise of violence around the globe as a chaotic outburst of meaningless "tribal" and "ethnic" tensions (Whitehead 2004). The power of such accounts is that they offer a tidy narrative that seems to explain so much of what is going on in our contemporary world. But they are based on a fundamental misunderstanding of the relationship between violence and culture. They also miss the point about how and why people use violence in a conflict at a particular time.

Anthropologists have demonstrated that: (1) it is not inevitable that people from different ethnic groups will fight, and (2) violence and terror are never meaningless, but highly meaningful and even calculated political strategies.

It Is Not Inevitable That Different Ethnic Groups Will Fight

The countries that made up the former Yugoslavia in Southeast Europe, in a region known as the Balkans, share the stereotype of ethnic and religious tribalism. We even have a word for it—"balkanization"—which refers to the fragmentation of society into hostile factions. During the Bosnian civil war in the 1990s, foreign journalists tended to describe acts of violence by Serbs, Croats, and Muslims as "ethnic violence" based on centuries-old hatreds between these ethnic groups.

But this explanation ignores long histories of coexistence, cultural interchange, and peaceful relations that anthropologists had observed in the region (Lockwood 1975; Bringa 2005). In fact, Serbs, Croats, and Muslims interacted regularly and peacefully for decades before the civil war (Figure 10.8).

A more complex understanding of the conflict sees violence as a by-product of a struggle over political power among nationalist leaders after the fall of communism. Seeking to consolidate their hold over political power and state institutions, nationalists on all sides used the media to broadcast daily doses of fear, hatred, and dehumanizing images of people from the other "ethnic" group (Bringa 2005). They used targeted violence on people of other ethnic backgrounds. All of these factors created fear and a sense of powerlessness among ordinary people. So when nationalist leaders eventually called on people to attack their neighbors of different backgrounds, some did just that, leading to now well-known incidents of incredible brutality and horror in places such as Srebenica, site of a mass killing of Bosnian Muslims by Bosnian Serbs (Oberschall 2000).

At the same time, many people found ways to protect their neighbors of different ethnic backgrounds from being attacked. In other words, even in a period of intense, artificially created ethnic conflict, not everybody participated in the violence, and many did not give in to the ethnic hatred that others promoted. Both points undermine any

Figure 10.8   A Peaceful Balkans. At the time of the 1984 Olympic Games in the Bosnian capital city of Sarajevo, commentators celebrated long-standing peaceful relations between Serbs, Croats, and Muslims in this modern city, challenging any notion of "ancient seething hatreds" portrayed in later years.

simplistic story of seething tribalism. Ethnic conflict is not an inevitable condition, and in this case it was manufactured to serve the political and ideological interests of certain leaders.

Violence Is a Meaningful Political Strategy

In the United States we sometimes hear in the media about events like suicide bombings in Israeli and Iraqi markets and cafés, machete attacks on innocent people in Liberia, Rwanda, and Sierra Leone in Africa, or plane hijackings by some militant group, which of course happened in this country on September 11, 2001. Commentators often call these shocking acts "meaningless" and "barbaric." But such acts are never meaningless. They are meaningful—to both victims and perpetrators—although the different sides interpret the violence very differently (Whitehead 2004). For example, families of suicide bombing victims and the families of the suicide bombers themselves comprehend these acts differently. For one side the message is threat and hostility, and for the other it is a message of martyrdom and devotion to a cause.

When people refer to such acts as meaningless and barbaric, they interpret violence as emotional, beyond reason. In fact, violence and the threat of violence are often used as strategic tools for pursuing particular political ends. Consider, for example, the civil war in Sierra Leone (1991–2001), in which at least 50,000 people died. This conflict, waged between the government and a "people's army" called the Revolutionary United Front (RUF), gained widespread notoriety as a barbaric and brutal conflict; images of child soldiers, machete attacks on innocent people, rape, and beheadings circulated globally in the media.

According to British anthropologist Paul Richards (1996), this violence was anything but wanton and mindless. Richards challenged this stereotype, explaining that hand cutting, throat slitting, and other acts of terror were "rational ways of achieving intended strategic outcomes" (Richards 1996:58).

For example, during 1995 the RUF frequently cut off the hands of village women. This practice was strategically calculated to communicate a political message to the RUF's own soldiers and to prevent defections. How could this be so? Richards explains that the RUF expanded by capturing young men and turning them into soldiers. Many defected, returning to their villages at harvest time to help their families. RUF leaders reasoned that they could stop defections by stopping the harvest. To stop the harvest, they ordered the hand amputation of women who participated in harvesting grain. As news spread, the harvests stopped, and defections ended because soldiers did not want the same thing to happen to their own mothers and sisters. Richards does not justify these repulsive acts. Rather, his point is that violence is not "meaningless" but is highly organized in a systematic if brutal fashion.

Not every conflict leads inevitably to violence. We explore this theme in more detail in our final section.

THINKING CRITICALLY ABOUT POLITICS

Since the early years of structural-functionalism, anthropologists have recognized that violence or the threat of violence, far from implying chaos, can encourage social integration and social order. How? Why?

How Do People Avoid Cycles of Aggression, Brutality, and War?

Whenever we watch the news, unsettling images of aggression, brutality, and war flood our consciousness. Yet millions of people around the world rarely if ever have direct experiences of such things in their daily lives. This does not mean that disputes and conflicts do not arise, because they do everywhere, all the time.

But, as we discussed previously, violence is not an inevitable human response to conflict. People always have creative and peaceful ways to manage or settle their disputes. In every society there are people with the ability to intervene in, negotiate, or settle a dispute, actions that are as much an exercise in political power as the ability to wage war (Rasmussen 1991). Working out the problems that arise from those conflicting accounts inevitably touches on who has access to power and what allows them to hold it.

What Disputes Are "About"

Some disputes are explicitly about who can hold political power. But most disputes are also about other matters that are central to the political life of any community (Caplan 1995). Disputes are about material goods, such as who has the right to land and other forms of property. Disputes are about decision-making, such as who gets to decide important matters. Disputes are about social relations, or who gets to do what to whom. Disputes are about the rules, because disputes tend to arise whenever rules are broken, or when the rules themselves are unclear. And disputes are about dividing people or joining them together in new ways, because when arguments happen people take sides.

Most North Americans assume that disputes are about winning and losing. We approach a lawsuit pretty much the same way we approach a sporting event, the point being to vanquish the other side. But for many peoples around the world, disputes are not "about" winning and losing. Neither are sporting events. In both cases, the object of a lawsuit or game is to repair a strained relationship.

When Trobriand Islanders play the game cricket, for example, the goal of the game is to end with a tie, not to win or lose (Kildea and Leach 1975). Sure, the players play hard and even get hurt in the process, but the game is really "about" reaffirming the social relationships that exist among the players and with their communities. Both sides will later claim to have played better and more bravely, but they will have lessened tensions between the two villages. When we look at how people manage disputes around the world, keep in mind that when presented with a dispute, most people prefer to restore harmony by settling the matter to the satisfaction of all parties.

How People Manage Disputes

Legal anthropology, the branch of political anthropology interested in such matters, has identified a number of ways people manage disputes (Nader and Todd 1978). Some strategies are informal, including avoidance, competition, ritual, and play. Others are formal, involving specialized institutions or specialists. The most common of these strategies include adjudication (going to court), negotiation (talking through problems), and mediation (a third party helps resolve the problem).

One of the easiest and most informal ways people handle their disputes is to avoid the matter altogether, which allows tensions to subside. In small-scale communities, people have to get along, and avoiding certain subjects is often the best way of keeping the peace. Even in our society, there are contexts—the workplace, Greek societies, dormitories, families—where some issues are better left untouched, because of the discord they can cause. But people often turn to other informal strategies to handle tensions, such as telling jokes, laughter, gossip, song, duels, sporting contests and other forms of competitive play, ridicule, public humiliation, and even witchcraft accusations (Gulliver 1979; Watson-Gegeo and White 1990; Caplan 1995) (Figure 10.9).

When informal strategies do not work, people usually have more formal means of settling disputes. **Adjudication**, which is the legal process by which an individual or council with socially recognized authority intervenes in a dispute and unilaterally makes a decision, is one possibility. The image of a courtroom with a judge in a robe, a jury, and lawyers comes to mind.

Anthropologist James Gibbs (1963), who conducted fieldwork among the Kpelle [keh-**pay**-lay], rice cultivators of central Liberia, found a different approach to adjudication. Gibbs reported that while Kpelle could take their disputes to government courts, they avoided them because they viewed them as arbitrary and coercive (Gibbs 1963). Kpelle often turned to their own "moot courts," which are hearings presided over by respected kin, elders, and neighbors. Unlike the government courts, which were slow-moving, allowed only limited testimony, and imposed settlements with harsh penalties for the loser, Kpelle moot courts provided a thorough airing of grievances and a quick treatment of the problem before attitudes hardened. Instead of winner-take-all, their goal was to restore harmony. They often found fault with both parties, avoided harsh penalties when there was a clear loser, and negotiated consensual solutions acceptable to all. Moot courts did not have the same enforcement authority as government courts, but because of their emphasis on reconciliation they were especially effective for resolving domestic problems, such as quarrels over inheritance or alleged mistreatment of a spouse, where relationships had to continue after the dispute passed.

In a **negotiation**, the parties themselves reach a decision jointly. As with all other strategies for settling disputes, negotiations never take place in isolation. Broader social relationships and circumstances influence the outcome. For example, British legal anthropologist Phillip Gulliver (1979)—whose research on negotiation in Tanzania has been influential for explaining the cultural importance of negotiation—observed that in a dispute between two close neighbors over land and water rights that took place in a small district in northern Tanzania in 1957, many factors influenced the ability and willingness of each side to negotiate a settlement. For example, one disputant was more popular and better connected in the community, and thus had more allies to push his own agenda. But he was willing to negotiate because, like his rival, he was equally worried that the colonial court could intervene and impose a decision. He also worried that if the dispute was not settled, the other side might use witchcraft and further intensify the dispute.

Mediation entails a third party who intervenes in a dispute to aid the parties in reaching an agreement. Native Hawaiians commonly practice a kind of mediation called *ho'oponopono* (**hoh**-oh-poh-no-poh-no], or "setting to right" (Boggs and Chun 1990). This practice is intended to resolve interpersonal and family problems or to prevent them from worsening. It is based on the belief that disputes involve negative entanglements and setting things right spiritually will lead directly to physical and interpersonal healing (Boggs and Chun 1990). *Ho'oponopono* usually begins

- **Adjudication.** The legal process by which an individual or council with socially recognized authority intervenes in a dispute and unilaterally makes a decision.

- **Negotiation.** A form of dispute management in which the parties themselves reach a decision jointly.

- **Mediation.** The use of a third party who intervenes in a dispute to help the parties reach an agreement and restore harmony.

Figure 10.9   Breakdancing as Dispute Settlement? Breakdancing got its start in New York City in the 1970s. In its early days, street gangs in the South Bronx would battle each other—over turf, because of an affront, or simply to gain respect—through dance. (Photo © Martha Cooper)

when a leader of high status—a family elder, a leader of a community church, or a professional family therapist—intervenes in a dispute, calling the adversaries and all immediate family members to engage in the process. Group participation is especially important because negative entanglements spread beyond those directly involved in the dispute. After opening with prayers, the leader instructs participants in the process and guides a discussion in which all participants are expected to air their grievances and feelings openly and honestly. They direct them to the leader, not to one another, to avoid possible confrontation. At the end, the leader asks all sides to offer forgiveness and release themselves and each other from the negative entanglements.

Is Restoring Harmony Always the Best Way?

It is easy to romanticize dispute settlement traditions whose goal is to restore harmony. Legal anthropologist Laura Nader (1990) observed that harmony and reconciliation are cultural ideologies, and like other ideologies they uphold a particular social order and way of doing things, usually protecting the already powerful.

Nader observed that Zapotec Indians in the southern Mexican village of Talea [tah-**lay**-ah] she studied have a "harmony ideology." Taleans believe "a bad compromise is better than a good fight." They emphasize that people need to work hard to maintain balance and evenhandedness in their relationships with others. They go to local courts frequently, even for very minor disputes, to avoid escalation.

But peace and reconciliation have their price. Nader has seen how these ideologies can prevent a full airing of problems, delay justice, or be used as a form of social control. Harmony ideology sustains a particular power structure, serving the interests of some but not necessarily all.

Since the 1970s, restoring harmony has been a popular strategy in Western countries for conflict resolution studies and practice. Mediation and negotiated settlements deal with disputes from family and work-related problems to complex international clashes, including civil wars and wars between countries (Davidheiser 2007). These techniques are often called Alternative Dispute Management.

While some anthropologists welcome the rise of Alternative Dispute Management (Avruch 1998), Nader (1995, 2001) questions its implicit harmony ideology. She observes that many people involved in civil wars and other large-scale conflicts do not necessarily want harmony. They want justice, fairness, and the rule of law. This is a sentiment expressed by many Mozambicans, for example, whose civil war ended in a mediated settlement in 1992. Many Mozambicans believe the settlement, which brought with it the introduction of foreign aid institutions and International Monetary Fund stabilization policies, actually deepened their woes by generating more poverty and inequality than before the war (Hanlon 1996).

Sometimes confrontation and conflict, not harmony, may be a more appropriate way to bring change for the greater good. For example, in the 1970s Nader (1979) conducted research in collaboration with her brother, the consumer advocate Ralph Nader, on how consumers in industrialized societies deal with faulty products and unscrupulous sellers. What do people do when their washing machine breaks and the manufacturer or retail store they bought it from gives them the run-around? Nader found consumers dissatisfied, even despondent, over fruitless struggles for justice and accountability from corporate giants. Initially Nader recommended consumer advocates and corporations arrange mediation and negotiated settlements, aiming for a harmonious end to conflicts. Many corporations did just that. But consumer satisfaction is now lower than it was in the 1970s, because these processes have not forced real change in the way corporations make their products. Revising her recommendation, Nader (2007) now believes that conflict, confrontation, a more adversarial relationship in court, and aggressively pushing for stronger laws would have been more effective in bringing beneficial change for consumers.

There is not necessarily a "best way" to solve a dispute. If there were, there would be no more disputes! In addition, dispute settlement is never a neutral act. In handling their disputes, people make ideological assumptions and enact social relationships that uphold particular power structures or, as Laura Nader suggests, even challenge those power structures.

● ●

THINKING CRITICALLY ABOUT POLITICS

Think about the last time you had a non-violent dispute in your life. How did you handle it? Was one or more of the strategies we discussed— avoidance, adjudication, negotiation, or mediation—involved? How might the outcome have been different if you had pursued a different strategy than the one you did?

● ●

Conclusion

If you pay much attention to political news on television or the Internet, you may have the impression that politics is mainly about politicians and their political parties, laws, and bureaucratic institutions. This impression offers only part of the story. Politics always involves some element of state power and bureaucratic processes. Every society has individuals who act a lot like North American politicians. From status leaders such as Big Men and councils of elders who settle disputes, to leaders of armed movements organizing violent acts, leaders everywhere use strategy, manipulation, persuasion, control over resources, and sometimes violence to obtain and maintain power over others.

Yet this view of politics is too narrow to appreciate the diverse forms that political power takes around the world. Not all societies train their young to deal with their problems through violence, and even those that accept violence place limits on its use, encouraging more peaceful ways of handling disputes. People not considered conventionally powerful have ways of challenging the power structure in their societies. And while the nation-state is a common political form worldwide, some post-colonial countries, such as Ghana, have explored ways of integrating traditional political structures based on family lineages and chiefly power into the ways the nation-state functions.

Politics is about relationships of cooperation, conflict, and power that exist in any community and at all levels of social life, from the interpersonal and community levels to the national and transnational. The reason that people around the world have so many ways of managing and thinking about those relationships is the same reason cultural diversity persists in the world today: social processes like those involved in politics are always rooted in and emerge from people's everyday social interactions, belief systems, and cultural practices.

KEY TERMS

Reviewing the Chapter

Chapter Section	What We Know	To Be Resolved
Does Every Society Have a Government?	Not every society has a government as we know it, or even makes a distinction between those who govern and those who are governed. Such societies organize their political lives on the basis of principles such as egalitarian social relations, reciprocity, and kinship.	Although classical anthropological studies identified many political processes in non-state societies, anthropologists continue to study and debate how successful these processes have been in confronting the transnational forces that affect almost every society today.
What Is Political Power?	Political power operates in multidimensional ways: it is action-oriented, it is structural, and it is gendered. It also tends to operate in particular ways in non-state contexts as well as in modern nation-states.	Anthropologists debate the relative importance of political power wielded by individuals and structural power shaping fields of social action.
Why Do Some Societies Seem More Violent Than Others?	Neither violence nor non-violence is an inevitable condition. Both are learned behaviors expressed in particular social and historic circumstances.	Most peoples who have been characterized either as peaceful or violent are not uniformly peaceful or violent, yet it is not always clear what conditions might have transformed an otherwise peaceful people into a violent one or vice versa.
How Do People Avoid Cycles of Aggression, Brutality, and War?	Disputes arise in all societies, but they do not necessarily result in aggression, brutality, and war because people everywhere have many peaceful strategies for settling disputes.	Anthropologists continue to debate the effectiveness of the new field of Alternative Dispute Management, especially in cross-cultural and international settings.

Readings

Early twentieth-century anthropologists tended to understand politics in tribal societies as fundamentally an expression of their kinship systems. A classic example is E. E. Evans-Pritchard's 1940 ethnography, *The Nuer: A Description of the Modes of Livelihood and Political Institutions of a Nilotic People* (Oxford: Clarendon Press, 1967). For a comprehensive overview of the field of political anthropology that is as attentive to classic concerns as it is new research directions, see John Gledhill's book *Power and Its Disguises: Anthropological Perspectives on Politics* (Sterling, VA: Pluto Press, 2000).

● ● ● ● ● ● ● ● ● ● ● ● ● ● ● ● ● ● ●

Two books offer a useful overview of how to think anthropologically about violence, including David Riches's edited book *The Anthropology of Violence* (Oxford: Basil Blackwell, 1986), which contains a number of classic articles, and Douglas P. Fry's book *The Human Potential for Peace: An Anthropological Challenge to Assumptions About War and Violence* (New York: Oxford University Press, 2006).

● ● ● ● ● ● ● ● ● ● ● ● ● ● ● ● ● ● ●

Understanding Disputes: The Politics of Argument (Oxford: Berg Publishers, 1995), edited by Pat Caplan, offers a useful introduction to legal anthropology and includes essays by some of the leading figures in the field.

● ● ● ● ● ● ● ● ● ● ● ● ● ● ● ● ● ● ●

Laura Nader's book *Harmony Ideology: Justice and Control in a Zapotec Mountain Village* (Stanford, CA: Stanford University Press, 1990) offers rich ethnographic description of how one community manages disputes to maintain social harmony, but not always to everyone's liking. It pairs well with the film *Little Injustices: Laura Nader Looks at the Law* (Washington, DC: PBS Video, 1981). Though it is now a dated film it offers highly relevant comparative insights into how two societies—Zapotec and U.S.—handle everyday disputes.

● ● ● ● ● ● ● ● ● ● ● ● ● ● ● ● ● ● ●

HARPER'S WEEKLY.

A JOURNAL OF CIVILIZATION.

Vol. XX.—No. 1041.] NEW YORK, SATURDAY, DECEMBER 9, 1876. [WITH A SUPPLEMENT. PRICE TEN CENTS.

Entered according to Act of Congress, in the Year 1876, by Harper & Brothers, in the Office of the Librarian of Congress, at Washington.

Race, Ethnicity, and Class

11

Understanding Identity
and Social Inequality

DURING THE LATE nineteenth century, Irish-Americans became "white." Before then, other Americans considered them a separate racial group that was not white. Even with their light-colored skin, they were believed to be inferior to other Northern Europeans (English, German, French, and Scandinavians) in almost all other respects. The story of their transformation illustrates the fluidity with which racial identities, including whiteness, are culturally constructed.

During the eighteenth century most Irish spoke Gaelic, a Celtic language, and most were Catholic. The English, who had conquered and colonized Ireland during Henry VIII's reign, regarded Irish Catholics as beneath them—a separate and inferior **race** of people, race being a concept that organizes people into groups based on specific physical traits that are thought to reflect fundamental and innate differences. The English system of colonial authority institutionalized this concept of racial inferiority by creating discriminatory laws known as the Penal Codes that denied Irish Catholics the right to vote, to live in incorporated towns, to attend university, and to buy, inherit, or receive gifts of land from Protestants (Ignatiev 1995). This discrimination was based on more than just religious, linguistic, or national differences. It was based on a racial worldview that emphasized Irish inferiority as part of the "natural order of things."

"Equal Burdens." This 1874 image from the cover of *Harper's Magazine* represents caricatures of a black man from the South and an Irishman from the North. Although the Irishman here is identified as "white," Irish immigrants to the United States were not really accepted as "white"—and shared the equal burden of racial discrimination with blacks—until the end of the nineteenth century.

● **Race.** A concept that organizes people into groups based on specific physical traits that are thought to reflect fundamental and innate differences.

During the 1840s and 1850s, the Irish Potato Famine forced large numbers of Irish to emigrate to the United States, where descendants of English settlers also regarded them as an inferior and separate race. They saw Irish and African Americans, or blacks, as closely related, deriding the Irish as "Negroes turned inside out and Negroes as smoked Irish" (Ignatiev 1995). In the early years of mass emigration, Irish often lived side by side with freed slaves in segregated neighborhoods in Northeastern cities like New York and Boston. They worked the same low-prestige jobs and even intermarried.

Within a decade, however, Irish began distancing themselves from blacks and increasingly identifying with whites. Irish workers began monopolizing certain trades and pushing blacks out, sometimes violently. Seeing an opportunity to build its power base in northern cities, the Democratic Party courted Irish voters. Although some Irish leaders rejected the Democratic Party because it supported slavery, a condition they compared to Irish life under English rule, many welcomed the political recognition. In neighborhoods with no black voters, campaigners referred to "the white vote," symbolically redefining the Irish as white. Irish participation and leadership in labor organizations, many of which denied black people membership, also supported the Irish identification with whiteness. By the end of the century, the Irish had achieved a level of social acceptance as white that would have been unimaginable several decades earlier.

The Irish are not alone in "becoming white" in North America. Jews, Italians, Finns, Greeks, Armenians, and certain Latin Americans—all of which at one point were considered inferior non-white racial groups—have become white as well.

No amount of research into the biological features of these groups will explain how and why that transformation took place. The whiteness of all of these groups emerged as a result of the dynamic ways racial identities are constructed, symbolized, and institutionalized in the socially stratified society that is the United States.

Yet most Americans have a worldview that assumes as fact that racial identities are the result of unchanging biological differences. A similar logic, in which *social* differences are misconstrued as inevitable and *natural*, underlies other common social identities, including class, ethnicity, and caste. Although these other concepts differ from race in their particular details, they are similarly justified by people as inevitable, as upholding the natural superiority of some and the inevitable inferiority of others. But as much as people may be invested in the notion that these social identities are rooted in the natural order of things, they are not. They are the product of human culture and social action.

At the heart of an understanding of notions of race, ethnicity, class, and caste is the question around which this chapter is organized: *If differences of identity are not rooted in biology, why do they feel so real, powerful, and unchangeable?* Embedded in this broader question are the following problems, around which this chapter is organized.

Are differences of race also differences of biology?

How is race culturally constructed?

How are other social classifications like ethnicity, class, and caste naturalized?

Are prejudice and discrimination inevitable?

The "natural" order represented in the social hierarchy of any society is supported by social institutions and a rich symbolism that is embedded in most aspects of daily life, much as they were in the changing circumstances of groups like Irish Americans. The categories may feel inevitable, even morally necessary, but like all other cultural phenomena they are constructed and dynamic. In order to show this, we have to begin by dispelling one of the most powerful ideas many Americans hold, that differences of race are rooted in differences of biology.

Are Differences of Race Also Differences of Biology?

In 2005, the U.S. Food and Drug Administration (FDA) approved a new drug called BiDil for treatment of heart failure among African Americans. It is the first drug ever intended and approved for a particular racial group. It works well, too: rigorous studies demonstrate its positive benefits for African American patients. For some scientists and policymakers, the fact that African Americans respond well to this treatment confirms that racial groups have specific biological and genetic characteristics that can be treated with specific drugs.

But these claims do not hold up to critical scrutiny, and there is nothing about this situation which proves that African Americans are biologically different from other racial groups. How can this be? The answer lies in the political, economic, and social reasons this drug was developed in the first place, and the processes of its approval. In recent years, the medical profession and the FDA have been under pressure from Congress and the public to reduce disparities in medical treatment among racial groups. Responding to this pressure and seeing an economic opportunity, the drug manufacturer targeted its efforts in developing BiDil exclusively on African Americans. After demonstrating the success of the drug, the company was able to gain a favorable patent from the FDA, which gives it special commercial protection and enables it to raise capital for the expensive trials among investors who saw the opportunities of marketing to a particular group of people (Brody and Hunt 2006).

But here's the rub: the drug was only tested on African Americans. The drug's manufacturer and various experts have admitted that BiDil will likely work just as well on non–African Americans, but they have not tested it (Brody and Hunt 2006). At no point did the manufacturer or the government identify any unique biological or genetic features of African Americans that explain why BiDil works on them in particular. Nor could they if they tried. It is because it is meaningless to divide humans into distinct biological races.

The Biological Meanings (and Meaninglessness) of "Human Races"

- **Naturalization.** The social processes through which something, such as race, becomes part of the natural order of things.

Since the eighteenth century, European and American scientists have played a key role in the **naturalization** of race—that is, the social processes that make race part of the natural order of things—by producing theories, schemes, and typologies about human differences. Many of these typologies, such as those of nineteenth-century evolutionists, rank races hierarchically (in strata from lower to higher), implying that racial superiority and inferiority are biologically rooted. Other typologies are less ethnocentric and hierarchical. But they all share the same basic flaw. There is no single biological trait or gene unique to any group of people, much less to any group that has been designated "a race." This point is such an important one for anthropologists that we need to examine it in greater detail.

The Problem of Categorizing Humans Into "Races"

Historically, scientists have developed four approaches to categorizing humans into racial groups. The first is trait-based, which isolates certain physical features, such as head size and shape, bodily structure, facial features, lip shape, eye folds, or skin color, to divide people into races according to what seems physically most typical of the group (Johnston 2004). This approach is closely associated with German taxonomist and anthropologist Johann Friedrich Blumenbach (1752–1840), who identified five racial groups—Mongoloid, Caucasoid, Negroid, Malayan, and American Indian—by isolating physical traits like skin color and facial features like eye folds. American folk classifications do something similar with skin color, for example, making distinctions between white, black, red, and yellow skin to denote certain racial groups. Of course, nobody's skin is really any of these colors; they are just convenient markers.

A second approach to categorizing races is based on geographic origins. The Swedish taxonomist Carolus Linnaeus developed such a scheme, dividing humans into four races: African, Asian, American, and European. North American racial models also reflect some elements of this approach, with our division into African-Americans, Asians, Native Americans, Hawaiians/Pacific Islanders, and so forth. In recent years the U.S. Bureau of the Census has used the racial category "Asian and Pacific Islander." The obvious weakness of this model is that political designations, such as Hawaiian and Pacific Islander, and vast continents with tremendous ethnic diversity like Asia, are made into racial groups.

Some anthropologists have refined this geographic approach into a third way of categorizing race called the adaptational approach to racial classification, which refers to the notion that people adapt to the environments in which they live and pass on those adaptations through inheritance (Coon, Garn, and Birdsell 1950). For example, if you look at skin color, people who have lived in lower latitudes of the globe for many generations tend to have darker skin than groups dwelling at higher latitudes. People living in these southern portions of the globe produce more melanin to reflect the ultraviolet rays of the sun, which are stronger near the equator, and this usually dark-brown pigment makes the skin appear darker. Instead of being seen as an indication of inferiority, this adaptation in fact indicates fitness and adaptability. Nevertheless, while people whose ancestors have lived near the equator for a long time tend to be darker-skinned than Northern Europeans, this point suggests only a very general correlation between biology and race, and furthermore, does not translate neatly to the four or five commonly defined races.

A fourth approach builds on advances in population dynamics since the 1950s, and defines races as reproductively isolated breeding populations. This approach moved beyond trait-based and geography-based approaches by focusing on who mates with whom, which allows for the influence of cultural factors, such as religious affiliation or economic status, on the formation of racial groups (Garn 1961). With this approach, the number of races exploded from four to dozens, mainly because there are so many breeding populations in the human species. Taken to the extreme, however, it would also mean that every population qualifies as a race, which muddies the waters between the two concepts (Long 2003).

Each of these four approaches has specific limitations. But there is a common problem shared by all of them, and for that matter, any attempt to categorize humans into races: these typologies rarely describe an actual individual, and they do not characterize whole groups of people. What looks like patently obvious "racial" differences comes from a special way of sampling people. This sampling process isolates one or more visible traits, very often skin color or some other arbitrary phenotypic marker, and marks that trait as representative of a whole group of people. More troubling, that one trait can come to be representative of other characteristics, most notoriously, intelligence, aptitude, and personal character.

Biological Variability in Human Populations

Biological traits and genetic features never vary in neat and easily defined ways, much less in ways that correspond to the "racial" categories Americans are used to recognizing. Because of historical movement, intermingling, and genetic drift (see Chapter 3), human biological variations occur in a continuous fashion. Anthropologists call such variations "clinal" variations, which means that change is gradual across groups and that traits shade and blend into each other (Marks 1995). As a result, something like skin tone—a trait that has often been used as a marker of a racial identity—can be highly variable within any human population, and there are no clear definable lines between actual skin tones.

Biological traits also tend to vary independently of each other. For example, there is no biological connection between the trait of skin tone and any other supposed "racial" trait, such as certain facial features or bodily shapes. In a similar way there is absolutely no physiological parallel or relationship between the superficial trait of skin tone and the biological and social phenomena we call character and intelligence, although this claim tends to be at the heart of many discussions about racial groups.

Finally, visible traits such as skin tone and facial features simply do not reflect important variations in human biological function. Of the many thousands of human biological variations, many are much more consequential than skin tone, nose shape, and hair texture. For example, variations in blood factors, enzymes, and organ function all affect the character of key bodily functions. If there were any valid reason to divide humans into biologically defined groups, any one of the many thousands of traits could provide as valid a basis for classification as could skin color (Cohen 1998). In fact, we do classify people into biologically defined groups all the time, such as by blood type, but we never assign these traits with racial significance. For example, having blood type A suggests only the presence of a certain antigen (the A antigen) on the red blood cells and indicates that someone with this blood type can only donate blood to another person who also has a blood type with that same antigen. But we do not isolate this one characteristic as a necessary and important one upon which to make social divisions, even if it is of biological importance. The traits we *do* isolate as defining racial differences are socially determined and not biologically significant.

Thanks to recent research in genetics, we know several important facts about the human genome, which is the sum of all human genetic material. The first is that there is no single gene that codes race or is unique to any group of people conventionally thought of as a race (Long 2003). The second is that, genetically speaking, humans are a remarkably homogeneous species: there is far greater variation *within* human groups than there is *between* them (Long 2003). In other words, the aggregate sum of variations between the people whose origins lie in Africa is greater than the differences between that group as a whole and all Europeans, Asians, or any other commonly designated "racial" group. But these facts do not imply that race does *not* have biological consequences on people, because it does.

Race *Does* Have Biological Consequences

Even if the origins of racial groups are not genetically or biologically determined, race can *become* biology, by shaping people's biological outcomes due to disparities in access to certain kinds of health care and diets, exposure to certain kinds of diseases, and other factors that can make people either sick or healthy (Gravlee 2009). For example, in the United States there are well-defined differences between racial groups in terms of morbidity and mortality, which refer to incidence of disease and life expectancy. One illustration of this fact is that African Americans have higher rates of many diseases, such as hypertension, diabetes, cancer, stroke, renal failure, cardiovascular disease, and so on, as well as lower life expectancies than white people (Gravlee 2009).

- **Racism.** The repressive practices, structures, beliefs, and representations that uphold racial categories and social inequality.

Race *per se* is not the *cause* of these health inequalities, however. Rather, these health inequalities are the *result* of race, or more specifically **racism**, which anthropologists define as the repressive practices, structures, beliefs, and representations that uphold racial categories and social inequality. One expression of racism is residential segregation by racial group, which has been shown to produce inequalities in health because it constrains opportunities such as access to education, certain occupations, and quality health care. It can also create social environments that influence the spread and distribution of disease (Gravlee 2009). **Discrimination**, which is negative or unfair treatment of a person because of his or her group membership or identity, has also been shown to have embodied consequences on individuals, producing a range of effects from hypertension to lower birth weights (Gravlee 2009). The point here is not that different racial groups do not have differences in biology, but that these differences in biology are the product of social processes and processes of cultural construction. In the next section, we show how race is culturally constructed.

- **Discrimination.** The negative or unfair treatment of an individual because of his or her membership in a particular social group or category.

● ●

THINKING CRITICALLY ABOUT RACE, ETHNICITY, AND CLASS

The idea that racial differences are genetically and biologically determined is widely accepted by the U.S. public, and the contrary and more complicated view just presented has failed to gain widespread traction even as it offers a more empirically valid understanding of the relationship between race and biology. How do you think anthropologists could communicate these ideas and findings to the broader public?

● ●

How Is Race Culturally Constructed?

Like all cultural "realities," the notions that Americans have about race are based on processes that make the artificial seem natural. The development of a particular social order nearly always reflects and upholds this confounding of artificial and natural.

In this case, that social order is one based on systematic patterns of inequality, discrimination, and racism. The key point is that "races" are not self-evident; they are created (Gregory and Sanjek 1994). Scholars refer to the social, economic, and political processes of transforming populations into races and creating racial meanings as **racialization** (Omi and Winant 1996). Racialization always occurs under a particular set of cultural and historical circumstances, which means that different societies racialize groups differently.

Here we examine two examples of racialization, one a familiar example—"blacks" and "whites"—in the United States, and one less familiar to most North Americans, that of Latin America.

- **Racialization.** The social, economic, and political processes of transforming populations into races and creating racial meanings.

The Absence of Race in Colonial Virginia

After the English settled Jamestown in 1607, settlers began to raise tobacco as a cash crop. But labor shortages were a problem, so they brought indentured servants from England. These laborers worked under contract for a certain period of years in exchange for passage to America and necessities like food, clothing, and shelter. The first indentured servants were English, but in 1619, English-speaking Africans living in England came over on similar labor contracts (Parent 2003; Smedley 2007a, 2007b). Some worked off their debts and became freedmen. A number of these African men became prosperous traders and plantation owners and gained rights to vote and serve in the Virginia Assembly, just as any other man with property. Marriages between Africans and non-Africans were not uncommon and carried no stigma. Unlike the Irish, who the English considered racially inferior, the English considered Africans to be equals because of their success at growing food in tropical conditions, their discipline, and their ability to work cooperatively in groups (Smedley 2007a). In sum, in the early 1600s, Africans and their descendants were considered like any other settler as members of the community, interacting with other settlers on an equal footing (E. Morgan 1975).

How Africans Became "Black" and Europeans Became "White" in Seventeenth-Century Virginia

By the mid-1600s the Virginia colony was in crisis (Smedley 2007a). A few men had taken most of the fertile land and poor freedmen had difficulty finding land of their own. Unhappy with their lot, in 1676 thousands of poor freedmen and indentured servants rebelled (Figure 11.1). Most were Europeans, but among them were several hundred of African origin. To prevent future unrest, the leaders began passing laws aimed at controlling laborers. A number of these laws separated out Africans and their descendants, restricting African rights and mobility including, among others, the ability to vote, own property, and marry Europeans (Parent 2003; Smedley 2007a). These laws took away basic rights that African settlers had previously held, and they opened the door to outright slavery, which followed several years later when the English began bringing slaves directly from Africa.

English colonial leaders also promoted a shift in thinking about Africans and their descendants. As slaves from Africa arrived, these Englishmen began drawing distinctions between Africans and Europeans, portraying Africans as uncivilized heathens, intellectually incapable of civilization. Such arguments justified African enslavement. They also began to homogenize all Europeans, regardless of ethnicity, class, or social status. In early public records, the word "Christian" commonly appeared next to the

Figure 11.1   Bacon's Rebellion, Virginia Colony, 1676.

names of Europeans, but was later replaced by "white." Poor whites received land as a way to encourage their identification with the colony's elites, preventing them from siding with Africans. By the end of the seventeenth century, the terms "black" and "white" came to symbolize the differences between the two groups, and the use of this racialized language helped to uphold the artificial lines of difference. Skin color became the chief way of marking status and difference, or as Governor William Gooch of Virginia described, skin color was a "perpetual Brand upon Free Negroes and Mulattos" (Allen 1997:242).

The One-Drop Rule

The biologizing of race as a social category became extreme, particularly after the Civil War. In the south people were defined as "black" if they were believed to have just "one drop" of African blood, meaning a single African ancestor. This notion, called "the one-drop rule," derives from a long-discredited belief that each race had its own blood type, which was believed to correlate with physical appearance and social behavior (Wright 1994:49). Widely promoted in the antebellum South, the rule was a way of enlarging the slave population with the mixed-race children of slaveholders (Figure 11.2).

As in the 1870s, the vast majority of African Americans are of mixed ancestry. Thus, these biological traits were used to justify oppression and inequality as the "natural" order of things. These sharp "racial" lines upheld a particular social and political order and, more importantly, served certain economic interests, especially of those who benefited from cheap African labor.

American racial categories have never been static. Far from it. In "Thinking Like an Anthropologist: Counting and Classifying Race in the American Census," we examine some of this dynamic history in more detail by considering how the U.S. government has classified people in the decennial census, held every ten years since 1790.

Racialization in Latin America

Another powerful demonstration of racialization comes from cross-cultural research in Latin America. In Latin America, the concept of "race" does not exist in many indigenous societies, but exists mainly in societies affected by European colonial expansion. Where racialization has occurred in other societies colonized by Europeans, its results have usually been quite different from the United States because of different histories of European conquest and state-building.

Different societies isolate different markers of racial difference. When dark-skinned middle-class Latin Americans such as Brazilians, Dominicans, Colombians, Cubans, and Puerto Ricans come to the United States, many are shocked to find themselves referred to and treated as "black." In their home countries, they think of themselves and are treated as "white," rarely if ever experiencing the kind of discrimination that is directed toward blacks in America or even in their own countries.

Their home countries have racial inequality and discrimination. Like the English in North America, the Spanish and Portuguese who colonized Latin America controlled African and Indian slaves by defining them as racially inferior and passing laws to control their rights and mobility (P. Wade 1997). But, unlike the English, they did not place such restrictions on sexual contact between Europeans and these other groups, leading to populations with many shades of skin color. As in the United States, "blackness" symbolizes an inferior and savage condition, while "whiteness" is considered civilized and superior. But these conditions are not firmly attached to skin color or other biological traits. They are linked to social behavior, attitude, and social class. "Blacks" may be people of many different shades of skin color, but they are poor and behave in "unrefined" ways, while "whites" act in a refined and courteous manner

Figure 11.2 The One-Drop Rule. Mark Twain's classic 1894 novel *The Tragedy of Pudd'nhead Wilson* depicts the one-drop rule as a farcical tragedy. In it Roxy (pictured here), a slave who is 1/16 black, switches her baby son, who is 1/32 black, with a white baby, knowing her son will grow up with privileges he would never enjoy if people knew he had even had "one drop" of black blood.

Thinking Like an Anthropologist

Counting and Classifying Race in the American Census

ANTHROPOLOGISTS BEGIN THEIR research by asking questions. In this box, we want you to learn how to ask questions as an anthropological researcher. Part One describes a situation and follows up with questions we would ask. Part Two asks you to do the same thing with a different situation.

PART ONE: RACE AND THE 1850 CENSUS

Censuses interest anthropologists because they reveal the role of governments in classifying and categorizing groups of people. In addition, over time census categories change, indicating broader shifts in social categories. The U.S. census has noted the "color" of American residents from the very first census in 1790, but these categories have changed over the next two centuries.

The U.S. Constitution requires a census every ten years to determine how many members each state should have in the House of Representatives. The constitution mentions three kinds of people relevant to the population counted in the allocation of seats in Congress: free persons (each counted as one person), slaves (each counted as two-thirds of a person), and Indians (who were not taxed and not counted until 1860).

The first American census (1790) recorded the head of each household and the number of individuals in each household in basic categories: Whites (by age group and gender), Other Free Persons, and Slaves. From 1800 to 1840 the census expanded the age groupings but used the same basic categories in each household.

In 1850, for the first time the census recorded the name of every person in the United States and its territories. It also recorded the age, gender, color, occupation, and place of birth of every individual. Color is the most interesting classification because the census form mentions three possible categories: White, Black, or Mulatto. The figure shows a form that was filled out in New Orleans's 4th Ward.

Few Americans use the word "mulatto" anymore. It refers to mixed-race people, typically those who are part white and part black. Although the 1850 census doesn't show them, in some parts of the South people informally used even finer grained terms, such as "Quadroon," referring to a person who is one-fourth black and three-fourths white, and "Octoroon," a person who is one-eighth black.

All of these terms are obsolete and now considered offensive. But their use in that era suggests some important

points. One is that Americans acknowledged the existence of people who are racially mixed and sought to classify them. Their use also reflects the same ideology that produced the "one-drop rule," in which mixed-race people are categorized as non-white.

After taking the census, the government produced an official summary of what it learned about the population to share with the public (something it still does). Interestingly, the summary never uses the terms "Black" or "Mulatto." Instead, it distinguishes people in terms of "White," "Free Colored," and "Slave," despite the fact that the terms "Colored" or "Free Colored" never appear on the enumeration forms, as we see in the image.

What questions does this situation raise for anthropological researchers?

1. What does the fact that the census forms used one set of categories but the public summary made use of a different classification tell us about American racial categories in the 1850s?
2. Why is it that it wasn't until the 1850s that the government wanted to record "Mulatto" and "Black"?
3. Although the terms "Mulatto" and "Black" might seem more precise than "Colored," do these competing terminologies suggest an (aborted) effort to change public understandings of race?

PART TWO: THE 2000 AND 2010 CENSUSES

Following categorizations first established in the 2000 census, the 2010 census asked "What is this person's race? Mark one or more Races to indicate what this person considers himself/herself to be." Its list of races includes "White," "Black, African Am., or Negro," and "American Indian or Alaska Native," and uses a wide variety of other "races," including Asian Indian, Chinese, Filipino, Japanese, Korean, Vietnamese, Other Asian, Native Hawaiian, Guamanian or Chamorro, Samoan, Other Pacific Islander, or Some Other Race. In contemporary censuses race is no longer an "either/or" category, and Americans can now check off any number of boxes to reflect the complicated interethnic blending now recognized by Americans. If you wanted to understand the dynamism of racial categories in the contemporary American census, what questions would you ask as an anthropological researcher?

1850 U.S. Census Enumeration Sheet from New Orleans, Louisiana. In southern states like Louisiana, census takers were more sensitive to subtle differences in ethnicity than in most northern states. While northern states distinguished only between black and white as categories, the southern states routinely recognized an intermediary category of mulatto. In this copy of the 1850 enumeration of New Orleans Ward 4, Precinct 3, whites are left blank, blacks are marked "B," and mulattos are indicated with "M." Note that although social status marked by these arbitrary racial categories was clear to everyone, these status differences did not keep whites, blacks, and mulattos from living in the same neighborhoods and even in the same households.

Figure 11.3   *Blanquismo* in the Dominican Republic. Between the 1920s and 1950s, the Dominican dictator Rafael Trujillo (1891–1961), pictured here in the center of the photo, promoted an official policy of *"blanquismo"* [blawn-**keys**-moh], or "whitening" of the population. This policy involved a massacre of black Haitians in 1935, invitations for white Europeans to immigrate to the island, and a celebration of European music, dance, and culture. Under *blanquismo*, dark-skinned individuals could be "white," but their whiteness depended on how closely they identified with European culture and attitudes.

(Figure 11.3). "Black" people are still disadvantaged, but it is more obviously for "cultural" rather than "biological" reasons.

Saying "Race Is Culturally Constructed" Is Not Enough

It is not enough to say that race is culturally constructed, because it might give the impression that race is not "real" (Hartigan 2006). Race is very real, of course, because racial groupings come with discrimination, exploitation, and stigma for some and privilege for others.

Put simply, racism is a potent force in making "race" real, a situation that can have biological consequences on individuals, as we saw previously (Mullings 2005). Racism works through the prejudice that people express against people who are different from them, and through concrete social actions, such as violence or the denial of good wages and access to decent housing, education, and health care. Our point here is to emphasize that the concept of "race" is not a stand-alone concept. It goes hand in hand with prejudicial attitudes and a repressive social order that has real consequences for people's lives.

Of course, race is not the only means by which dominant groups establish and rationalize their social supremacy. In the next section, we consider how categories like ethnicity, class, and caste also operate through processes of naturalization.

● ●

THINKING CRITICALLY ABOUT RACE, ETHNICITY, AND CLASS

Racialization is not something that happened a long time ago; it is an ongoing process even in the United States and Latin America today. Can you think of some examples of how it might still be taking place? Can you identify any conditions today that might shape dynamics of racialization differently from, say, during the period of Virginia Colony?

● ●

How Are Other Social Classifications Like Ethnicity, Class, and Caste Naturalized?

All social hierarchies appeal to and gain support by asserting that social differences are part of the natural order of things rather than arbitrary cultural categories. Yet social hierarchies can be justified and upheld in different ways (Guimarães 1999). While racial ideologies tend to focus on aspects of physical appearance, other systems of classification divide people into groups based on economic status or occupation, behavioral characteristics, common descent, or symbolic purity. What they share in common with racial ideologies is that these divisions are perceived as inevitable and fixed even while in reality they might be quite dynamic. Here we examine three distinct modes of classifying people: ethnicity, which organizes people according to descent; class, which organizes people along lines of poverty and wealth; and caste, which organizes people along lines of symbolic purity.

Ethnicity: Common Descent

Along with race, ethnicity is a salient means of defining group identity and difference in the contemporary world. **Ethnicity** typically refers to membership in a group with a particular history, social status, or ancestry. Instead of the race concept's identification of physical markers as defining people as members of a racial group, members of an ethnic group might be identifiable by any combination of distinctive social characteristics, such as language or dialect, clothing, foodways, etiquette, or bodily modifications such as tattoos or piercings. Americans in particular believe that much can be explained about individuals by knowing their ethnic backgrounds, usually by drawing on common, often negative, stereotypes (Ortner 2006).

The notion of shared "blood" and kinship is generally a central element of ethnicity. Members of ethnic groups often refer to each other as "brothers" and "sisters," might be expected to sacrifice themselves or their interests for the "fatherland" or "motherland," and often believe themselves to be descendants of a common ancestor or ancestral couple (van den Berghe 1999). For these reasons, the ethnicity concept often blends into other terms such as "nation," "nationality," and "tribe." For example, Jews and Muslims, as members of broad "ethnic" communities, not just practitioners of a religion, define themselves—but not each other—as common descendants of Abraham, an important patriarch in both the Old Testament and the Quran. Similarly, the Pathan, pastoralists in Afghanistan and Pakistan, define themselves as an ethnic group, basing their identity on descent through the patrilineage of Qais, a contemporary of the Prophet Mohammed, who converted to Islam (Barth 1969).

By invoking their common descent, ethnic groups establish a distinctive identity and, more important, establish their differences from other groups as natural. A body of scholarship about ethnicity called **primordialism** assumes that ethnicity is largely a natural phenomenon, based on biological, linguistic, and geographical ties to those with whom they have obvious similarities of appearance, geography, language, or socioeconomic context (Tharoor 1999:2).

Despite an appearance of naturalness, however, ethnic groups do not form for genetic reasons. Some members of ethnic groups may eventually come to justify their identities in biological terms, but they are created for political, economic, and cultural reasons. This argument forms the basis of an alternative theory of ethnicity called **instrumentalism**, which asserts that ethnic groups are not naturally occurring or stable, but highly dynamic groups created to serve the interests of one powerful group or another (van den Berghe 1999).

The Rise of Latino/a Ethnic Identity

A powerful illustration of how ethnic groups are established has been playing out in the United States in recent decades through the formation of "Hispanic" or "Latino/a" ethnic identity. With over 53 million people, we often hear that Latinos/as now constitute the largest ethnic minority in the United States. The label refers to immigrants from Latin America and their biological descendants. The "ethnic" label is applied because Latin Americans do not fit neatly into American racial categories based on skin color and other phenotypic characteristics.

- **Ethnicity.** Belonging to a group with a particular history and social status.

- **Primordialism.** A social theory that ethnicity is largely a natural phenomenon, because of biological (i.e., "primordial"), linguistic, and geographical ties among members.

- **Instrumentalism.** A social theory that ethnic groups are not naturally occurring or stable, but highly dynamic groups created to serve the interests of one powerful group or another.

But, as one astute journalist observed, "The theory is that there are no Latinos, only diverse people struggling to remain who they are while becoming something else" (Shorris 2001:9). Most people who would likely identify with the label "Latino" actually do not, preferring to think of themselves primarily in terms of national origin—Mexican, Cuban, Puerto Rican, Colombian, Peruvian, and so forth (Fox 1997). There are a number of reasons for this situation. Different Latin American nations have different customs and identities, and well-developed notions of how they are superior (or inferior) to other Latin American nations. The proximity of Latin America to the United States means that individuals might migrate back and forth between the United States and their Latin American home countries frequently. The ability to remain in close touch with the people and culture of their home countries undermines their sense of common identity with other Latin Americans in the United States. And in cities such as Chicago or New York City, where Mexicans, Dominicans, and Puerto Ricans might live in the same or adjacent neighborhoods, they tend not to think of themselves as members of the same ethnic group—in fact, they may see the others as competitors for the same jobs and resources, even as socially inferior (Fox 1997).

At the same time, however, powerful social forces are driving the construction of a homogeneous ethnic identity out of this diversity. One of these forces is the federal government, which beginning in 1980 included a category for "Hispanic" in the census (it became "Latino" in the 2000 census), as a way of measuring the quantity of immigrants from Latin America. It was also under pressure from Mexican-American and Puerto Rican civil rights groups, who were beginning to demand political recognition in U.S. society and inclusion in the census (Fox 1997). Government funding began flowing to people in the category, new legislation was developed to address them, and newly labeled politicians emerged with ambitions to gain power for themselves and their new constituencies. Market forces have also helped shape the category. For example, new media have emerged targeting that audience, including radio and television stations, such as Univisión, that emphasize a common identity. New consumer products divorced from any single national origin have been created to appeal to a homogeneous group of Latinos (Dávila 2001). A good example of this is the rise of Goya foods as a Latino food distributor serving the entire United States (Figure 11.4).

Class: Economic Hierarchy in Capitalist Societies

Most Americans think of themselves as "middle class," probably because, as the Declaration of Independence states, "all men are created equal." The result of this notion is that class remains largely hidden in American life. The social theorist Karl Marx saw class as the distinction made in capitalist societies between those who control the means of production (factory owners) and those whose labor produces the goods (workers). This definition made sense in the early industrial era but is less relevant to American and European life since the mid-twentieth century. Here we understand **class** to be the hierarchical distinctions between social groups in society usually based on wealth, occupation, and social standing.

The hiddenness of class in American cultural thought means that class tends to be the last factor introduced as an explanation of social success—wealth, privilege, and power—and failure, or poverty and social impotence (Ortner 2006:78). As much as they avoid talking about it directly, however, most Americans recognize that people are born into a particular social position due to the economic situations of their families. Indeed, this fact of birth has profound lifelong consequences, since one's class position typically shapes access to educational and occupational opportunities, possibilities for gaining wealth, even the towns and neighborhoods in which one lives.

- **Class.** The hierarchical distinctions between social groups in society usually based on wealth, occupation, and social standing.

Figure 11.4 Feeding "Latinos." The ethnic group "Latino," referring to a pan-Latin American identity in the United States, is only several decades old. Its emergence is aided by companies like Goya foods, whose commercial success is based on downplaying national tastes and culinary traditions, and emphasizing ingredients found across a wide spectrum of Latin American cuisines.

Being rich or poor is not just a matter of who has or does not have money. There are privileges and exclusions that accompany class hierarchies. Even those rare individuals born into poverty who later strike it rich can find it difficult, if not impossible, to be accepted by other rich people, who exclude those individuals as *nouveau riche* (the "new rich"), a term that implies lack of civilization and refinement.

Several generations ago, Americans regarded class differences as a biological phenomenon. For example, to be wealthy was to be inherently superior, especially in terms of innate intelligence, and to be poor was to be born with inferior intelligence. These ideas have shifted with the growth of the middle class as an intermediary space between the richest and poorest. Americans now naturalize class in other ways, primarily through the languages of race and ethnicity (Ortner 2006). For example, to be a WASP (White Anglo Saxon Protestant) implies upper- or upper-middle-class status; to be Jewish implies middle-class status; and to be African American or Latino implies lower- or lower-middle-class status. We all know that these distinctions are little more than crude stereotypes. Nevertheless, these intersections between class and race explain how Americans naturalize apparently neutral categories like middle, upper, or lower class (Ortner 2006).

The concept of class has had much less relevance in anthropology than in other social sciences (R. Smith 1984). A major reason is that many anthropologists have studied non-capitalist societies where native categories do not correspond with Western economic categories like class (Liechty 2002).

Nevertheless, the spread of capitalism around the world does create owner and worker classes, as well as middle classes with certain characteristic cultural tendencies that transcend national borders. For example, in his study of urban Kathmandu, Nepal (on the northeastern border of India), Mark Liechty (2002) found that the expansion of capitalist markets in recent decades had created a new middle class sandwiched between historically polarized Nepalese elites and commoners. Liechty observed that members of this new middle stratum explicitly distinguish themselves from those above and below them through their consumption of widely circulating consumer goods and mass media, not unlike that of the American middle class. In one passage, he describes a Hindu wedding in the suburbs to which he was invited. Expecting a traditional expression of Nepalese culture, he was surprised at how often a camera crew hired for the occasion interrupted and held up proceedings, even traditional dances. He was especially surprised when an elderly grandmother insisted that the wedding party and camera crew redo a particular bit of the ceremony.

Liechty's broader point is one that many other anthropologists would agree with: the middle class, or any class group for that matter, is not an objective thing "out there," shaped by biological imperatives. Rather, people create and re-create social classes in the context of broader historical and economic processes, often by defining themselves against other groups.

Caste: Moral Purity and Pollution

Caste primarily refers to the system of **social stratification** (the classification of people into unequal groupings) found in Indian society that divides people into categories of moral purity and pollution (U. Sharma 1999). The term derives from the Portuguese word for "pure breed" (*casta*), recognizing that one is born into a caste and should only marry someone of the same caste. Many millions of Indians consider the social divisions associated with their caste system as a "natural" and morally necessary aspect of the human condition.

Just as North Americans "see" race in the most subtle features of somebody's face, hair texture, or skin color, Indians "see" caste in people's occupations, the clothes they

- **Caste.** The system of social stratification found in Indian society that divides people into categories according to moral purity and pollution.

- **Social stratification.** The classification of people into unequal groupings.

wear, how they talk, even their mannerisms. Caste has been described as India's "fundamental institution" (Béteille 1992) because the relationships of inequality upon which it is based are so self-evident and so intertwined with how Indian society works.

Indians actually use two terms for what Westerners have named caste, *varna* [**vahr**-nah] and *jati* [**jah**-tee]. As outlined in classic Hindu religious texts, *varna* refers to the hierarchical division of society into four major groups: Brahmans (priests), Kshatriyas (warriors and rulers), Vaishyas (traders), and Shudras (artisans and servants). Another group outside these four are known as "untouchables." Many occupations and activities are inherently polluting in a ritual sense, such as metal work, leather working, street sweeping, or trash collection. The small minority at the top of this system, the Brahmans (ten percent of the Indian population), are considered the most morally and ritually "pure" and carry the highest social status. Relative purity declines and pollution increases as one moves down the hierarchy.

In actual practice, Indians make many finer social distinctions beyond the four major categories of *varna.* They use the term *jati,* which translates in many Indian languages as "kind" or "species," to designate the actual manifestation of *varna* in practice. *Jati* are the actual social groupings, often based on occupation, that exist in a ranked hierarchy in relation to each other. A single village alone may have more than a dozen *jati.* Each has many internal divisions, so what appears like a single *jati* to outsiders may not actually seem that way to its members (Fuller 2004).

Jati and their many subdivisions are upheld by rigid rules that regulate social conduct, especially social and physical contact between groups and subdivisions. Within multicaste villages, for example, people tend to live in residential clusters separated from other castes. Caste defines the public spaces in which people gather to talk. Higher castes bar lower castes from using certain village wells and other public facilities, such as restaurants. When people of different castes eat together, such as at a wedding feast, they sit in separate caste and subcaste groups and are served in order of rank (Fuller 2004). Many other aspects of life—including whom an individual can marry, do business with, even have bodily contact with—are governed by the same set of strict rules.

The French anthropologist Louis Dumont wrote about Indian caste, arguing that Indian caste is so embedded in how Indians see the world that it is more than just a system of social hierarchy. It is a set of cultural values that understands hierarchy and inequality as natural, that is, as *self-evident* and *morally necessary* conditions of humankind (Dumont 1966:34). Although most anthropologists would agree that caste is ideologically made to seem natural and inevitable, not all agree with Dumont's analysis of Indian society and especially the rigidity he attributes to caste.

Indeed, some Indians have begun to insist that caste no longer exists, because of changing attitudes and the incorporation of ideals like democracy and the creation of formal government affirmative action programs (U. Sharma 1999) (Figure 11.5). This conviction is especially true among some urbanized Indians, where everyday contact between members of different castes—sitting next to each other on a city bus, for instance—has weakened rigid rules governing contact between groups (Krishnamurthy 2004). Nevertheless, while rights of untouchables now exist, discrimination against them and others of low caste persists.

The social inequality upon which caste is constructed tends to be justified as a natural and inevitable aspect of individuals. This naturalization is also true of ethnicity and class, as we have

Figure 11.5   Debating the Indian Census. In recent years, the inclusion of caste categories in the national census has sparked a national debate. Many fear that counting caste in the census grants legitimacy to caste-based politics, while others argue that the data obtained can help plan welfare measures.

seen. However, in each of these cases, just saying a particular form of social inequality is "natural" is never quite enough to fully explain its persistence. Social inequality is also upheld by prejudice and discrimination.

THINKING CRITICALLY ABOUT RACE, ETHNICITY, AND CLASS

The idea that class doesn't exist or is irrelevant in the United States is very powerful, yet social mobility in the United States (the ability to change classes) is restricted. In what ways do you think class mobility is restricted? How is the ideology that Americans have social mobility maintained?

Are Prejudice and Discrimination Inevitable?

In the aftermath of black civil rights leader Martin Luther King Jr.'s assassination in 1968, Jane Elliot, a teacher in the all-white community of Riceville, Iowa, struggled with how to help her third-grade students understand prejudice and discrimination. She developed an exercise in which she divided the students into two groups, one made up of the blue-eyed kids and the other the brown-eyed kids (Figure 11.6). She told the blue-eyed kids that they were better and more intelligent than the brown-eyed kids, and treated them with special favors. She ridiculed the brown-eyed kids as less intelligent and unworthy, and shamed them mercilessly. She encouraged the blue-eyed kids to do the same, and they did (Peters 1970, 2005).

The impact of this experience on each group was remarkable. The blue-eyed kids began to feel superior and treated the brown-eyed kids, even those who were their close friends, with disdain. The brown-eyed kids felt humiliated, powerless, and downtrodden. Then, the next day, Elliot reversed the status of each group. Brown-eyed kids were now on top, and the effects on both groups were the same as before: feelings of pain and powerlessness for some, a sense of superiority for the others. In the course of a single afternoon, Elliot and her class had constructed new social categories that closely resembled racial stereotypes in America. The next day she constructed a different set of social relations between these two classes, with powerful effects on everyone involved.

Elliot's classroom exercise has since become a common technique in anti-discrimination training in schools and organizations. It allows individuals who may never before have experienced **prejudice** (pre-formed, usually unfavorable opinions about people who are different) to experience it firsthand and in a deeply emotional way, to feel what it is like being treated as an inferior minority. It also demonstrates, with tremendous moral force, how the privileged benefit from, and even become complicit with, these attitudes, especially when people in authority (trainers, teachers, officials, or CEOs) authorize and encourage discrimination.

And it raises some questions. Are people naturally disposed to treat humans that are different from them with prejudice? Is discrimination a universal feature of human existence? The answer to both of these questions is no. There is nothing in human nature or biology that makes us treat humans who are different from us as superior or

● **Prejudice.** Pre-formed, usually unfavorable opinions that people hold about people from groups who are different from their own.

▼ **Figure 11.6 Challenging Prejudices.** This image from the 1971 documentary "Eye of the Storm" shows Iowa teacher Jane Elliot discussing her blue-eye/brown-eye exercise with her class.

inferior. Prejudice and discrimination are cultural processes, which is to say, they may feel natural and inevitable, but they are profoundly artificial constructions. Having said that, however, prejudice and discrimination are ubiquitous elements of socially stratified societies, a theme we explore in this section.

Understanding Prejudice

Prejudice takes many forms and has many sides to it. Prejudice too is socially constructed. It is based on taking arbitrary features and assigning qualities of social superiority and inferiority to those qualities. Worldwide, there is a mind-boggling variety of markers upon which prejudices are based. We are most familiar with skin color and hair texture, but other markers include gender behavior that suggests sexual orientation, occupation, family lineage, and religious affiliation. Where they exist, prejudices may feel deep, innate, and natural, but they are not static. As attitudes toward groups change, so do accompanying prejudices.

There is no better illustration of this than the fact that a majority of Americans elected a black president in 2008, which would have been unimaginable only forty years before because of widespread anti-black prejudice. Prejudices tend to express themselves through concrete processes of social rewards and unfair treatment, but they do not always lead to discrimination. In his classic study of prejudice from the 1950s, for example, Gordon Allport (1958) observed that prejudice expresses itself in a continuum from avoidance and non-contact to more aggressive actions, including exclusion, physical attack, and killing.

Most of us learn prejudices at a young age from people whom we regard as authorities, such as parents and other relatives, community leaders, and teachers. This point explains why our prejudices feel so natural. Drawing on insights gained from her studies of race relations in Mississippi during the 1930s, anthropologist Hortense Powdermaker wrote that prejudices are judgments about a whole group of people based on poor reasoning and insufficient evidence. In "Classic Contributions: Hortense Powdermaker on Prejudice," we examine her point in more detail.

The work of Hortense Powdermaker, Jane Elliot, and others involved in anti-racism education has demonstrated that where individuals have learned prejudices they can also *unlearn* them. Unlearning prejudice, however, does not mean that discrimination automatically goes away. The reason is that discriminatory behaviors, where they exist, tend to be structured into people's social relations and institutions.

Discrimination, Explicit and Disguised

Discrimination expresses itself in a range of ways. For example, discriminatory behaviors against so-called racial groups may be a very visible feature of a society, upheld by its laws and openly accepted by social convention, as was true throughout the United States, Europe, and South Africa (among other places) for many decades. Or they may be hidden and subtle, operating in disguised but no less insidious ways. We examine both of these modes of discrimination in turn.

Explicit Discrimination

Most of you could quickly name three or four examples of explicit discrimination on the basis of race, ethnicity, class, or religion. In the South, you could name so-called "Jim Crow laws," which were laws that prevented blacks from voting and exercising other rights between the end of the Civil War and the 1960s. In other parts of the country, such as the West and Southwest, you could point to the forced resettlement

Classic Contributions

Hortense Powdermaker on Prejudice

ANTHROPOLOGIST HORTENSE POWDERMAKER (1896–1970) began study-
ing race relations in Mississippi during the 1930s, making her the first professional anthropologist to conduct ethnographic research in a contemporary American setting. Always
interested in issues of social justice (before her Ph.D. at the London School of Economics in
the 1920s she was a labor organizer), Powdermaker sought to understand how blacks and
whites interacted with each other and the psychological costs of racism.

During the 1940s, she took insights gained from that research to produce the short book
Probing Our Prejudices: A Unit for High School Students, which was required reading in
New York City schools for several decades. In this excerpt from that book, Powdermaker
explains how poor reasoning leads to prejudice.

*Bill plays marbles with a group of boys in his neighbor-
hood, and one of them, John, a Polish boy, cheats. Bill
then concludes that all Poles cheat, and he carries this
idea with him throughout his life. . . .*

*When he is older, Bill reads in the paper that two
Italians who were drunk got into a fight and one
stabbed the other. Bill has never known any Italians
but he swiftly jumps to the conclusion that all Italians
are drunkards and stab each other in the back.*

*Or he hears of a Mexican who stole some money
from his boss, and so, forever after, he thinks of all
Mexicans as thieves.*

*In all three cases Bill concluded that because one
member of a group acted in a certain way, all members of that group will act the same way. This type of
poor reasoning is called false generalization. To gener-
alize is to come to a general conclusion as a result of
learning particular facts or ideas. For example, if you
are a member of a club that functions well at every*
*meeting and lives up to its standards, you may justifi-
ably say, "We have a good club." This is a true generalization based on observation. If, however, you observe
another club during only one of its meetings when
nothing is accomplished, and you say, "That club is no
good," you are making a false generalization, because
you have not based your conclusion on sufficient
evidence.*

*We all suffer from this unfortunate habit of making
false generalizations, especially about racial or religious groups or nationalities other than our own. We
do not make them as frequently about our own group.
If we are white Protestants and a member of our group
cheats, we do not condemn all white Protestants. If
we are Catholics and one of our members lies, we do
not say "All Catholics are liars." In order to be clear-
thinking individuals we must realize this inconsistency
and avoid making false generalizations. (Powdermaker
1944:29–30)*

Questions for Reflection

1. Can you think of other social or political issues beyond race and nationality where
   people make false generalizations?

2. Why do people accept the logical inconsistencies and poor reasoning that lead to
   prejudice?

and control of American Indians, and the exploitation of undocumented Mexican labor. Nazi Germany's programs to place Jews, homosexuals, Roma (Gypsies), and others who did not match "Aryan" ideals into concentration camps where many were killed or died is the classic example of explicit discrimination because it was openly espoused and implemented by political figures and state institutions.

These examples exhibit a broad range of discriminatory action, social exclusion, exploitation of cheap labor, and physical intimidation and violence. What they share in common is that they were practiced openly because they had gained a certain level of social legitimacy and acceptance among members of the higher social strata, and sometimes by the victims themselves. Discriminatory action is often legalized with explicit laws and even bureaucracies to manage and enforce policies of institutionalized coercion and exploitation. Whatever the case, a key feature of discrimination's legitimacy is that authorities who hold political and economic power either encourage or allow widespread discriminatory action because in some way it upholds a social order (blacks as servants to whites, for example) or promotes a new one (a racially homogeneous nation, as in the case of Nazi Germany).

Disguised Discrimination

As plain as these examples of explicit discrimination are, many forms of discrimination can be ambiguous, concealed, and difficult to prove. This fact is especially true where anti-discrimination laws now prohibit the most explicit forms of discrimination, such as in the United States, South Africa, Germany, and other countries once known for past open discrimination against racial or ethnic minorities, the poor, or particular religious groups. Where civil rights struggles have succeeded, there may be a misleading sense that the playing field has become level (Mullings 2005).

So how do we know when discrimination persists? For one, bigotry does not necessarily disappear with changes in formal law. It expresses itself in more subtle ways. For example, throughout the United States, blacks, poor people, and members of certain ethnic minority groups who enter shops and malls may be treated with suspicion and experience "racial profiling," or discrimination based on stereotypes. Shopkeepers and security personnel may keep a close eye on them because of stereotypes of these people as thieves. Real estate agents and landlords may steer potential customers away from areas where they do not "fit in," for racial or socioeconomic reasons, even though laws prevent housing segregation and discrimination. Media reports about crime often mention the accused's race or ethnicity, but only when the suspect is non-white, as if their race or ethnicity is the reason for the crime. Immigrants get tagged with labels like "illegal" and "criminal" and tied to the declining economic fortunes of other working people based on the perception that they take those people's jobs. To many people, especially members of higher status groups, these situations may go unnoticed due to their subtlety or indirectness. All of these issues played into the highly publicized situation in 2012 in Florida in which a young black man, Trayvon Martin, was shot and killed by a neighborhood watch guard, George Zimmerman. The explosion of protests throughout the country when Zimmerman was found innocent often pointed specifically to these issues as preventing justice for Martin.

Another proof of discrimination's existence is in the disadvantage that some groups experience that others do not (Rex 1999). For example, we know that in the United States, the educational outcomes of poor white and poor non-white students tend to be much weaker than white middle- and upper-middle-class students. There are a number of reasons for this situation, but a crucial one has to do with differences in funding levels for elementary and high schools in poor and middle-class areas. This factor directly affects the quality of teachers, the quality of facilities, and the kinds of programs a school can offer, each of which contributes to student success rates and has

Doing Fieldwork

Tamie Tsuchiyama and Fieldwork in a Japanese-American Internment Camp

DURING WORLD WAR II, President Roosevelt ordered the government to move 110,000 Japanese Americans into concentration camps, ostensibly as a way of protecting them from the rage of White Americans after the Japanese bombing of Pearl Harbor. These camps were bleak and uncomfortable places of imprisonment in isolated areas. The program was based on racial stereotyping and the debatable notion that Japanese Americans would try to undermine the war effort against Japan if they remained free to work and live where they wished like other Americans.

The government hired over thirty anthropologists to conduct research in the camps. They carried out empirical research on Japanese American attitudes and social interactions in the camps, as well as applied research to make the camps run more efficiently, trying to make conditions somewhat more acceptable for the internees. Among these anthropologists was Tamie Tsuchiyama (1915–1984), the first Asian American anthropologist trained in the United States. When the war broke out, Tsuchiyama, a second-generation Japanese American, was a graduate student in anthropology at U.C. Berkeley.

In 1942, she began working as a staff researcher on a government-funded Berkeley research project at Poston, a camp in Arizona. Tsuchiyama's situation highlights a number of dilemmas about doing fieldwork, especially the fragility of social relationships upon which fieldwork is based and the complexities of race and identity confronting minority fieldworkers.

Tsuchiyama was herself a camp resident, suffering similar hardships as other internees. But as an anthropologist she also confronted the difficulties surrounding how one conducts research on one's own social group. The vast majority of anthropologists at the time worked in cultures foreign from their own, where as outsiders they could quickly grasp cultural differences. In one's own community, previously formed views of people's behaviors and attitudes can get in the way of a deeper understanding of the culture. Even today, when anthropologists work in their own culture more than ever, this issue is difficult to resolve.

This dilemma was magnified by the complex relationship between who Tsuchiyama was as an anthropologist working for the government, and who she was as a Japanese

🌱 **A Japanese-American Internment Camp During World War II.**

(continued)

Doing Fieldwork (continued)

American. Camp residents mistrusted her as a government spy. Her research was made more difficult because she was a young woman working in the male-dominated domain of politics (the topic she was told to study), and a Hawaiian, whom mainland Japanese Americans saw as different. So she tried to bring little attention to herself and carried out her research semi-clandestinely (Hirabayashi 1999).

Tsuchiyama experienced conflicting emotions about her research subjects. On the one hand, she felt great sympathy for their situation, and complained openly about the discrimination, unfair treatment, and frustration internees experienced. On the other hand, she sometimes experienced feelings of contempt for her informants because they so often treated her with suspicion and resentment (Hirabayashi 1999).

Her advisor at Berkeley claimed all of the credit for her difficult-to-gather research data and findings. By 1944, Tsuchiyama had grown so alienated by what she saw as a colonial situation—the exploitation of her fieldwork and the inequality with her supervisor—that she quit the project. Although she finished her Ph.D. in 1947, she never held an academic position, and Tsuchiyama's status as a pioneer Asian American anthropologist is largely unrecognized.

Some aspects of Tsuchiyama's situation are not exceptional. In fieldwork, there are always questions about who should receive credit for the work when it is published, especially field assistants and other helpers who gather data. These questions get complicated when there are racial inequalities between the anthropologist and field assistants, or when issues of prejudice and discrimination permeate the social environment in which research is being conducted. They highlight how much successful fieldwork relies on a foundation of trust, openness, and fair treatment.

Questions for Reflection

1. How do you think this fieldwork situation might have been different for a white anthropologist?

2. How might this fieldwork situation have been different for Tsuchiyama if she were studying not a Japanese American internment camp but a white American suburb?

3. Most anthropologists at some point feel conflicting emotions about their research subjects. How do you think it is possible to overcome these feelings?

long-term consequences on a student's future educational, employment, and income possibilities (Kozol 1992). The underlying forces driving inequality in educational funding could be traced back to the size of the local tax base or employment levels in a community. Nevertheless, the result over the long term is uneven opportunities for different groups, and previously discriminated-against groups rarely end up on top.

What makes this example so loaded is that it is difficult to identify any single culprit for this situation, or even where the explicit racial or class bias lies. Inequality here is not a matter of personal ignorance (a common explanation for discrimination). On the contrary, it is clear that certain institutional routines and structural forces create and sustain unfair treatment independent of any particular individuals (Mullings 2005).

Since the early years of the discipline, anthropologists have decried both explicit and hidden forms of discrimination, especially racial discrimination, almost as vigorously as they have provided evidence of inequalities. These anti-racist convictions have attracted many minorities to the discipline. But the powerful effects of racism and discrimination can complicate the conduct of ethnographic fieldwork for minority anthropologists, especially when they are researching their own communities. In "Doing Fieldwork: Tamie Tsuchiyama and Fieldwork in a Japanese-American Internment Camp," we consider the difficulties one minority researcher had working in an environment where racial discrimination was a potent social force.

The Other Side of Discrimination: Unearned Privilege

Just as we have shown how discrimination can be disguised, it is possible to show the other side of discrimination, unearned privilege. Structural advantages are often difficult to see. It is easy for most Americans to recognize how skin color puts an individual at a disadvantage, but it is more difficult to identify the advantages and privileges that accrue to lighter skin.

As anthropologist Peggy McIntosh (1997) observes, the privilege that comes with having white skin is "like an invisible weightless knapsack of special provisions, assurances, tools, maps, guides, codebooks, passports, visas, clothes, compass, emergency gear, and blank checks." A small sampling of these privileges includes being able to swear, dress in second-hand clothes, or talk with your mouth full and not have people attribute such things to your race; not being hassled by police or have people cross the street at night simply because of your skin color; and being sure that you can receive medical or legal help without your skin color working against you (Figure 11.7). These privileges exist regardless of whether a white individual does not like colored people or holds racial supremacist ideas. The power of white privilege is that it posits whiteness as the norm and being colored as different, even deviant (Hartigan 2005).

Of course, class differences complicate the picture of white privilege, since many poor whites would justifiably point to severe social disadvantages not experienced by higher class whites (Hartigan 2005). But even these poor white individuals experience privileges not accessible to educated black people. For example, they are rarely pulled over by police because of their "race" in the way many African Americans are for "driving while Black," and other forms of racial profiling.

The broader point here is that social inequality—whether based on racial, class, ethnic, or religious categories—does not rest on discrimination against lower stratum groups alone. It also requires the consent of those who benefit from social inequality, who gain unearned privileges simply by being members of a privileged class (Mullings 2005:684). For anti-discrimination educators such as the ones we mentioned previously, it is not enough simply to demonstrate the existence of prejudice and discrimination. It is also necessary to show how certain people actually receive benefits from that inequality, and to force individuals to face the moral consequences of such situations. It is only when those who benefit accept the immorality of the situation that real social change can happen (McIntosh 1997).

Figure 11.7   Satirizing White Privilege. In a classic 1980s comedy skit, African-American comedian Eddie Murphy satirized white privilege. In the skit, he paints his dark skin color with light-colored make-up to create the impression that he is "white," then walks around New York City. He is shocked by the privileges he enjoys: a shopkeeper gives him a free newspaper, he is served a cocktail on a city bus, and when he asks for a loan at a bank, the bank official gives him the money as a gift.

THINKING CRITICALLY ABOUT RACE, ETHNICITY, AND CLASS

People rarely give up their privileges easily. But, as we have said throughout this chapter, social inequalities and prejudice are cultural processes and thus subject to change. Can you think of any social factors or changes in social relations that might produce a situation in which a group gives up its privileges?

Conclusion

Throughout this chapter we have consistently argued one central point. In spite of the fact that the social categories most of us take for granted feel real, powerful, and unchangeable, there is nothing fixed or inevitable about them. All social hierarchies appeal to a natural order to justify the rankings and categories they assign to different groups. The markers upon which these distinctions are made are arbitrary. If we really want to understand why some people are deemed inferior and others superior, we are better served to explore how belief systems and the dynamics of social power perpetuate prejudice, discrimination, and privilege, rather than searching for any pre-existing biological or moral imperatives.

A final illustration of this point brings us back to where we opened this chapter, with the dynamics of whiteness. Irish Americans today are far less likely to experience discrimination on the basis of their identity than their ancestors did until a century ago. It is now common sense that they are "white." But whiteness has never been a straightforward category. Even today the meanings and markers of whiteness are in flux. For example, Americans have been dropping ethnic identifications that were so common a generation ago—Irish-American, Italian-American, Polish-American, and so on—and adopting a generic "white" label (Gallagher 1997). This process has had the effect of replacing whatever national and ethnic identities groups sought to maintain during the first generations after immigrating to this country, with a homogeneous racial identity that makes no such distinctions.

What is not in flux here—and this is the unfortunate power of racial inequality in American history—is the fact that the idea of race remains a powerful force, even if the individuals and groups assigned to these categories change over time. In hierarchical societies such as ours, inequality is often one of its most enduring features.

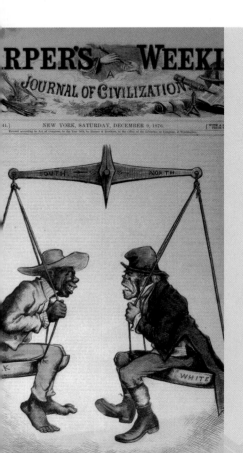

KEY TERMS

Caste p. 279	Instrumentalism p. 277	Race p. 265
Class p. 278	Naturalization, p. 268	Racialization p. 271
Discrimination p. 270	Prejudice p. 281	Racism p. 270
Ethnicity p. 277	Primordialism p. 277	Social stratification p. 279

Reviewing the Chapter

Chapter Section	What We Know	To Be Resolved
Are Differences of Race Also Differences of Biology?	Races are socially, not biologically or genetically, determined. But due to racism and discrimination, race does have consequences on certain people's biological outcomes.	Anthropologists are still working to understand the ways the social dynamics of race and racism express themselves through disparate biological outcomes.
How Is Race Culturally Constructed?	Races are never self-evident; they are culturally constructed through social and historical processes of racialization.	Saying "race is culturally constructed" is not enough because it is also "real." Anthropologists continue to debate the extent to which these realities are purely social or also have biological dimensions.
How Are Other Social Classifications Like Ethnicity, Class, and Caste Naturalized?	All social hierarchies appeal to a natural order to justify themselves. This natural order may feel inevitable, even morally necessary, but like all other cultural phenomena, it is constructed and dynamic.	Race, ethnicity, class, and, in India, caste, interact with each other in complex ways to produce identities. Anthropologists are continuing to work through these complexities.
Are Prejudice and Discrimination Inevitable?	Prejudices are learned attitudes, and as a result they can also be unlearned. Even in the absence of privilege, however, discrimination may persist because it is structured into social relations in sometimes explicit, but more often than not, disguised ways.	Anthropologists continue to debate the main reasons social hierarchies are upheld. Some emphasize that discrimination and oppression against lower stratum groups is the key factor, while others emphasize that it is based on the consent of those who gain unearned privileges simply by being members of a dominant group.

Readings

In recent years, the American Anthropological Association has sought to provoke a national dialogue on race and racism by sharing anthropological perspectives and research on the connections between race, biology, and culture. The website is an excellent resource on the latest thinking in anthropology about race: *Race: Are We So Different?* A Project of the American Anthropological Association: http://www.understandingrace.com/home.html

An analysis of the AAA race website would be usefully paired with the classic text edited by Steven Gregory and Roger Sanjek, *Race* (New Brunswick, NJ: Rutgers University Press, 1994).

For an ethnographically rich study of the construction of Latino identities, especially in popular culture and consumer capitalism, see Arlene Dávila's 2001 book *Latinos, Inc.: The Marketing and Making of a People*. Berkeley: University of California Press.

Whiteness, being such a powerful racial category, has recently drawn the attention of anthropologists seeking to understand how it is constructed. For a useful introduction to the anthropology of whiteness, see John Hartigan Jr.'s book *Odd Tribes: Toward a Cultural Analysis of White People* (Durham, NC: Duke University Press, 2005).

12

Gender, Sex, and Sexuality

The Lives of Women and Men

DURING THE 1990s, the West African country of Liberia was wracked by a civil war. Armed rebels sought to overthrow an oppressive dictatorship. During six years of conflict, at least 200,000 Liberians died and one million fled to neighboring countries as refugees. International news coverage of the conflict included jarring images of mutilated bodies, charred corpses, and child soldiers fighting for the rebels.

Interspersed with these images of brutality was another set of different, yet equally jarring, images. These were images of male rebels dressed in women's clothing, wearing bras and wigs, sometimes striking effeminate poses for the foreign photojournalists. Such a figure is hardly a "soldier" in the Western sense of the term. It contradicts our basic assumptions about the masculinity of war (Moran 1997). Rather than try to explain the meaning of cross-dressing in this society, journalists dismissed it as a bizarre expression of an incomprehensible African mentality.

According to rebels themselves, however, cross-dressing was deliberately taunting, a way to frighten their rivals. It made them feel invincible because they believed it would confuse enemy bullets. Whether cross-dressing actually warded off bullets is beside the point. Set against the backdrop of Liberian attitudes toward the government and its military, and against indigenous notions about the ideal qualities of warriorhood, cross-dressing made particular cultural and political sense.

First and foremost, cross-dressing helped rebels distinguish themselves from the government's uniformed "soldiers," who were despised

Cross-Dressing Warriors? During the Liberian civil war, rebel cross-dressing represented a subtle expression of alternative masculinity and warriorhood.

IN THIS CHAPTER

In What Ways Are Males and Females Different?
- Toward a Biocultural Perspective on Male and Female Differences
- Rethinking the Male-Female Dichotomy
- Hormones and Differences in Male and Female Behavior

In What Ways Are Men and Women Unequal?
- Debating "The Second Sex"
- Taking Stock of the Debate
- Reproducing Gender/Sex Inequalities

What Does It Mean to Be Neither Male Nor Female?
- Navajo *Nádleehé*
- Indian *Hijras*
- "Transgender" in the United States

Is Human Sexuality Just a Matter of Being Straight or Queer?
- Cultural Perspectives on Same-Sex Sexuality
- Controlling Sexuality

because of corruption and their oppression of the populace. Government propaganda had promoted its soldiers as the country's masculine ideal, so cross-dressing was a protest against the soldiers and the state that supported them (Moran 1997). Cross-dressing also helped identify the rebels as "warriors," a social category of subtle complexity, an alternative masculinity commonly recognized in the villages where rebels operated.

The male warriors' use of feminine symbols was meant to be playful. But it also communicated that true warriors are so powerful that they can overcome the biological and social constraints of maleness. In this society, men derive their special powers as warriors from a deliberate mixing of male and female symbols, thus drawing on the power of both.

Cross-dressing was not to last, however. Two years into the war, cross-dressing became less common as rebels adopted a new image of warrior masculinity: the hyper-masculinized image of Rambo, the macho commando, wearing cut-off sleeves and a headband, alienated from society and reporting to no one but himself. The new clothing and bearing continued to differentiate the rebels from government soldiers, this time by tapping into the power and romance of a Hollywood stereotype of strength, an image that brought with it new symbols of power and masculinity.

As wartime Liberia demonstrates, the characteristics people associate with males and females are not set in stone. This point has two important dimensions. First, although all societies distinguish between male and female, the actual boundaries between these categories, and the specific qualities and roles assigned to each, can vary greatly from one society to another. Second, these qualities and roles are not static; they can change quickly, especially in periods of social and political upheaval.

Gender roles always have powerful meanings in any society, leading to the question at the heart of this chapter: *How do relations of gender and sex shape people's lives?* Embedded in this broader question are the following problems, around which this chapter is organized.

In what ways are females and males different?

In what ways are men and women unequal?

What does it mean to be neither male nor female?

Is human sexuality just a matter of being straight or queer?

Gender, sex, and sexuality are at the core of how we define ourselves in contemporary Western culture. But what any society associates with one or another gender is as artificial as any of the other elements of culture we have explored in this book. As we will explain, many other cultures do not even share our basic notion that humans are either male or female, man or woman, and queer or straight. We begin by considering how females and males are different.

In What Ways Are Males and Females Different?

Walk into any kids' clothing store in a North American mall and the message is clear: boys and girls are fundamentally different. The boys' section is stocked with t-shirts in blue and other dark colors emblazoned with images of trucks, guns, or sports equipment, as well as cargo pants in khaki or camouflage. The girls' collection is full of frilly dresses and lace-lined shirts and pants in pastel colors like pink and purple, featuring images of butterflies, flowers, strawberries, and dolls. Judging by these articles, boys are adventuresome, active, and aggressive, while girls are nurturing, domestic, and sentimental (Figure 12.1).

Figure 12.1   Clothing and Sexual Difference. North American ideas about gender differences are powerfully expressed through the colors and characteristics of the clothing they are assigned from the earliest ages.

Although they seem innocent enough in the context of a kid's clothing store, these clothes convey powerful stereotypes about supposed differences in temperament and personality between males and females. In recent decades these stereotypes have become topics of intense debate in the United States, as our culture struggles over issues like why women are excluded from certain kinds of jobs in the military (such as special forces teams) and positions of institutional leadership, and why men dominate certain professions like math and sciences. The issue is not whether our culture distinguishes males and females. The real issue is to explain why our culture constructs these differences in the specific ways it does (Brettell and Sargent 2001). In this section we consider the complex ways that culture and biology intersect to shape male and female differences.

Toward a Biocultural Perspective on Male and Female Differences

The primary explanation our culture gives for differences between males and females is a biological one, suggesting that they are "hardwired" differently. Differences in **sex**, the reproductive forms and functions of the body, are even thought to produce differences in attitudes, temperaments, intelligences, aptitudes, and achievements between males and females. It is not difficult to find evidence that supports this belief. For example, some studies have suggested that in all human societies boys tend to engage in more rough-and-tumble play, while girls tend to be more engaged in infant contact and care, suggesting that such behaviors are determined at a species level (Edwards 1993). Recent studies also indicate that male and female brains function differently: women's left-brained tendencies provide them with superior verbal skills, while men's right-brained tendencies give them superior visual and spatial skills (McIntyre and Edwards 2009).

- **Sex.** The reproductive forms and functions of the body.

But any conclusions about hardwired sex differences are muddied by evidence that culture also shapes male and female preferences and behaviors. Anthropologists refer to the cultural expectations of how males and females should behave as **gender**. For example, the North American association of girls with pink and boys with blue feels natural for American parents. When these children begin choosing their own clothes, it also feels natural to them. But it is thoroughly artificial: relatively few cultures associate a color with a particular gender, and a century ago in the United States, the colors were reversed, boys wearing pink and girls blue (Kidwell and Steele 1989). American attitudes toward boys and girls did not shift; what changed was the gender association of each color, which had consequences for children's clothing preferences. The colors and clothing we associate with boys and girls, and the connotations each

- **Gender.** Cultural expectations of how males and females should behave.

Classic Contributions

Margaret Mead and the Sex/Gender Distinction

Margaret Mead.

SINCE THE BEGINNING of her career in the 1920s, anthropologist Margaret Mead (1901–1978) was interested in the differences between males and females, the cultural roles assigned to each, and how sexual differences shaped an individual's life experiences and personality. Mead was possibly the first social scientist to distinguish between biological sex and culturally distinct gender roles (Viswesaran 1997), which she did in her 1935 book *Sex and Temperament in Three Primitive Societies*. This book, which analyzes sex differences in three Papua New Guinea societies (the Arapesh, the Mundugumor, and the Tchambuli), ends with this influential theoretical reflection on the cultural influences on male and female difference.

The material suggests that we may say that many, if not all, of the personality traits which we have called masculine or feminine are as lightly linked to sex as are the clothing, manners, and the form of head-dress that a society at a given period assigns to either sex. When we consider the behavior of the typical Arapesh man or woman as contrasted with the typical Mundugumor man or woman, the evidence is overwhelmingly in favour of the strength of social conditioning. In no other way can we account for the almost complete uniformity with which Arapesh children develop into contented, passive, secure persons, while Mundugumor children develop as characteristically into violent, aggressive, insecure persons. Only to the impact of the whole of the integrated culture upon the growing child can we lay the formation of the contrasting types. There is no other explanation of race, or diet, or selection that can be adduced to explain them. We are forced to conclude that human nature is almost unbelievably malleable, responding accurately and contrastingly to contrasting cultural conditions. The differences between individuals who are members of different cultures, like the differences between individuals within a culture, are almost entirely to be laid to differences in conditioning, especially in early childhood, and the form of this conditioning is culturally determined. Standardized personality differences between sexes are of this order, cultural creations to which each generation, male and female, is trained to conform. (Mead 1935/1963:280–281)

Questions for Reflection

1. Why would an anthropologist study three different societies in New Guinea to demonstrate that gender roles are culturally constructed rather than innately biological?

2. Some scholars have claimed that Mead's New Guinea examples are cultural stereotypes from within the three cultures she studied. If true, would these indigenous stereotypes undermine or support her claim that gender roles are cultural rather than biological?

carries, are but one example of how culture shapes male and female difference. Anthropologists have long argued for the importance of gender in understanding male and female characteristics, as "Classic Contributions: Margaret Mead and the Sex/Gender Distinction" explores.

The distinction Mead made between sex (biology) and gender (cultural expectations) was influential among anthropologists for decades. But in recent years it has been breaking down because it is difficult to tease apart just how much differences in male and female behavior are caused by "sex," that is, shaped by biology, and how much they are caused by "gender," or cultural expectations (Collier and Yanagisako 1987). We do know that sex-specific biological influences on temperament are strongest during infancy and early childhood. For example, infant boys are more likely to develop their motor skills early, and infant girls are more likely to cry when confronted with unknown people, patterns that are consistent enough to suggest biological differences between the sexes (McIntyre and Edwards 2009). But as children get older, cultural influences on behavior become much stronger. As a result it becomes difficult if not impossible to isolate biological influences on what it means to be male or female.

Another reason the sex-gender dichotomy is breaking down is that "sex" is not simply a product of nature; it is also mediated and produced in the context of a specific culture. In light of this complexity, anthropologists increasingly reject an either-or perspective—that it's *either* biology *or* culture, *either* sex *or* gender—and accept that male-female differences are shaped by a mix of biology, environmental conditions, and sociocultural processes (Worthman 1995).

Reflecting these intellectual shifts, anthropologists are changing their terminology, and commonly refer to the ideas and social patterns a society uses to organize males, females, and those who do not fit either category as **gender/sex systems** (Morris 1995; Nanda 2000). As these older oppositions between culture/gender and biology/sex melt away, more sophisticated biocultural perspectives on male and female differences are emerging (McIntyre and Edwards 2009). Here we examine two illustrations of these new perspectives: rethinking the male-female dichotomy and the role of hormones in human behavior.

- **Gender/sex systems.** The ideas and social patterns a society uses to organize males, females, and those who do not fit either category.

Rethinking the Male-Female Dichotomy

In the idealized world of science textbooks, human beings are a **sexually dimorphic** species, which means that males and females have a different sexual form. Men have X and Y chromosomes, testes, a penis, and various internal structures and hormones that support the delivery of urine and semen. Secondary effects of these hormones include deep voices, facial hair, and in some cases, pattern baldness. Women have two X chromosomes, ovaries, hormones, and an internal structure such as Fallopian tubes that support the movement of ova, pregnancy, and fetal development, and whose secondary effects include breast development and a high voice.

This description is straightforward enough; you already know that nature divides humans into two sexes for the purposes of reproduction. You can probably name some minor exceptions to this rule: some women have facial hair while some men have none, some women have pattern baldness while plenty of men have a full head of hair, and some women speak with deep voices while some men squeak (Fausto-Sterling 2000). And there are plenty of men and women who, for various reasons, cannot reproduce. These variations are not enough to challenge anyone's certainties about the fact of male and female difference.

On more systematic inspection, however, the dichotomy between males and females breaks down significantly. What we actually see is not two distinct categories, but a continuum of sexual possibilities in the human species and the important role culture plays in shaping what biological sex means. Chromosomes, gonads, internal reproductive structures, hormones, and external genitalia vary across our species more than most of you probably realize (Fausto-Sterling 2000). Individuals who diverge from the male-female norm are called **intersex**, meaning they exhibit sexual organs and functions somewhere between male and female or including both male and

- **Sexually dimorphic.** A characteristic of a species, in which males and females have different sexual forms.

- **Intersex.** Individuals who exhibit sexual organs and functions somewhere between male and female elements, often including elements of both.

female elements. For example, some individuals have both ovaries and testes. Other intersexuals may have gonad development with separate but not fully developed male and female organs. Still others may have the ovaries and testes that grow in the same organ. Many intersex individuals are infertile, but not infrequently at least one of the gonads functions well, producing either sperm or eggs.

One reputable estimate puts the frequency of intersex in the United States at 1.7% of all live births (Fausto-Sterling 2000). At 1.7 births per 100, intersex is much more common than an unusual but highly recognizable condition like albinism, which is 1 per 20,000 births. This figure of 1.7% is not universal; some populations have higher rates of intersex, and others lower rates. Yup'ik Eskimos in Alaska, for example, have a higher rate of intersex births: 3.5% of births have Congenital Adrenal Hyperplasia, a condition produced by a genetic mutation that produces masculine genitalia in girls.

Different societies deal with intersex differently. Many cultures do not make anatomical features, such as genitalia, the dominant factors in constructing gender/sex identities, and some cultures recognize that biological sex is a continuum. A number of gender/sex systems do not see intersex individuals as either male or female, but rather place them in an equivalent third social category as we discuss later in the chapter. But European and North American societies—which construct sex as either male or female and tend to focus on genitalia as markers of sex—have considered intersexuality abnormal, sometimes immoral, most recently turning it into a medical problem.

With the development of new medical techniques during the late twentieth century, doctors and parents have gained new powers to "correct" what they view as a medical disorder. These days, for example, pregnant women can often know before birth if they will have an intersex child, at which point they may choose to have an abortion. In the United States, most intersex children are treated shortly after birth with "sex-assignment surgery," in which a doctor eliminates any genital ambiguity through surgery, and doctors counsel the parents to raise the child to correspond with that sexual assignment.

The decisions involved in sex-assignment surgery are rarely medical; they derive from culturally accepted notions about how a boy or girl should look. For example, in the case of a child whom doctors determine will be assigned the sex of "boy," proper penis size and shape is a major concern. For a "girl" it is the size and shape of the clitoris and vagina. Surgeons work hard to create realistic-looking genitalia by removing body parts and using plastic surgery to construct "appropriate" genitalia. But there is no biological norm for penis or clitoris size or shape, and in fact, many boys are born with very small penises which get larger at puberty, and girls born with much larger than average clitorises which present no clinical problems (Fausto-Sterling 2000). The cultural issue surrounding these surgeries is ensuring that the genitals' size and shape will convince others—parents, caretakers, other children, and future spouses—that the person is a male or a female.

Sex-assignment surgery shows that "sex" is not simply a biological phenomenon, but is—*quite literally*—constructed upon cultural assumptions: the assumption that sex is a dichotomy, as well as assumptions about what an ideal male or female should look like. These cultural assumptions stand in contrast to the evidence that human sex is not dichotomous and that natural variations occur in the shape and size of genitalia.

Such surgeries seem well-intentioned—to help intersexuals avoid the emotional burdens of being different in a culture that does not accept sexual ambiguity. However, they have become highly controversial, especially among many intersexuals themselves, who during the past several decades have spoken out against their treatment, sometimes describing it as mutilation (Figure 12.2). They also bring attention to the complex ways that biology and culture intersect to create what we think of as "males" and "females," challenging the injustices they see in our culture's gender/sex system.

Hormones and Differences in Male and Female Behavior

Hormones are chemicals our bodies secrete into the blood stream that regulate many of our bodily functions. These days a lot of people take for granted the power of hormones to shape and improve their lives. Even miniscule amounts of hormones can have transformative effects on our bodies. Athletes take anabolic steroids to build muscle mass and improve their performance, and some older men take testosterone injections to enhance their youthfulness and virility. Women take hormones for birth control and during menopause to moderate hot flashes and mood swings.

Figure 12.2 "Human Rights for Hermaphrodites, Too!" So says this woman's sign from 2009, urging the United Nations Human Rights office in Geneva to declare forced genital operations an abuse of human rights. These days the term "intersex" is generally used instead of hermaphrodite.

Individuals receiving sex-assignment surgeries and sex change operations also take hormones to reduce or enhance certain secondary sex characteristics, such as breasts, body hair, and voice pitch. But the transformative effects of many of these hormones come with a dark side, including liver damage, fluid retention, heart disease, increased rates of cancer, reduced ability to produce sperm in men, and impacts on women's menstrual cycles.

These effects leave us with the impression that hormones play a major role in determining physical and even behavioral differences between males and females. But there is a lot of popular misconception about what hormones do and do not do. One misconception is that certain hormones are linked solely to a specific sex: testosterone to males, and estrogen and progesterone to females. These hormones do play a larger role in one sex than in the other. Estrogen, for example, plays a larger role in women than in men in regulating reproductive cycles. But *both* males and females produce all of these so-called "sex hormones" because they are not connected solely to sexual functions. Hormones are versatile and involved in the growth of several body systems. For example, in addition to producing testosterone, men's testes also produce estrogen, which is involved in bone growth and fertility (Fausto-Sterling 2000).

Popular beliefs in North America hold that sex-specific hormones cause particular behaviors, such as the notion that testosterone causes aggression and the drive to gain social dominance among males. This incorrect belief leads some U.S. states to perform chemical castrations on repeat male sex offenders. The problem is that hormones do not directly cause or trigger any particular behaviors, much less gender-specific behaviors (Worthman 1995). Testosterone by itself does not cause aggression or violence, so efforts to castrate male sex offenders have typically failed to reduce aggressive or violent behaviors (Fausto-Sterling 1992a:126). At best, castration can reduce sexual activity, which is not surprising, since testosterone produced by the testes does regulate sexual potency.

Aggression, dominance, and violence are complex psychological and social states that may involve the production of testosterone, but neither this hormone, nor any other single hormone for that matter, shapes any of these states. Both males and females are capable of aggression and dominance, and societies differ in what they consider to be culturally appropriate levels of aggression expressed by men and women (Brettell and Sargent 2001; Lee 1979). For example, the egalitarian !Kung San (also known as Ju/'hoansi) expect both men and women to be aggressive, although in different ways. !Kung San women engage in verbal abuse while homicides are usually committed by men. To understand when, why, and how !Kung San men or women express aggression, we have to consider not just biological factors influencing behavior, but also the immediate social causes of conflict, the availability of weapons, culturally approved expressions of hostility, and the role of the state and other political-economic factors in driving social conflict (Brettell and Sargent 2001:3).

Related to this whole issue of differences between men and women is yet another enduring question: Are women everywhere subordinate to men because of biological differences between them?

THINKING CRITICALLY ABOUT GENDER, SEX, AND SEXUALITY

In U.S. culture there is a widespread idea that female hormones enable mothers who have given birth to lactate and bond with their babies, providing the basis of effective mothering. While birth and lactation do involve elevated production of certain hormones such as oxytocin, mothering is a complex social relationship as well that must be understood in relation to cultural ideas about effective mothering. What *cultural* ideas do Americans have about effective mothering? Do you think that the production of hormones is necessary to be an effective mother?

Figure 12.3 Batek Headwoman. Batek headwoman Tanyogn in the Malaysian rainforest, plaiting a cord out of black fungus rhizomes to make a bracelet (1976).

In What Ways Are Men and Women Unequal?

Men hold most leadership roles in most societies around the globe. The few exceptions are generally small hunter-gatherer societies like the Batek of the Malay Peninsula in southeast Asia. This small community lives in bands that anthropologists Kirk and Karen Endicott (2008) report are generally egalitarian in their gender roles, to the extent that the band they lived with during their fieldwork had a woman as its headman (Figure 12.3).

But such cases are unusual. In nearly all societies with any degree of social stratification, more men are in leadership roles than women, not only in political roles, but in economic and social roles involving trade, exchange, kinship relations, ritual participation, and dispute resolution (Ortner 1996:176). For example, in the United States today, only 18% of Congressional seats are held by women; in the workplace women earn on average 81% of what their male counterparts earn; and sex discrimination persists in social expectations, such as the notion that women should do housework. Very few of the privileges men have over women are predicated on physical strength. So why is gender/sex inequality such a common feature of many societies?

Rethinking Men

Another influence of focusing on what men and women actually do has involved a rethinking of men. For decades anthropology involved men studying the lives of other men, but until recently very few anthropologists had closely examined men *as men*, that is, how men and women collectively view and shape what "being a man" means, and how men actually perform, or act out, manhood (Gutmann 1997). The anthropological study of **masculinity**, the ideas and practices of manhood, has not just opened new avenues of research for understanding how gender/sex identities are constructed; it has also generated new perspectives on the issue of gender/sex inequality, including the notion that ideals of masculinity are dynamic and do not in themselves necessarily assume male dominance (Figure 12.5).

Anthropologists have observed the existence in many societies of the notion that women are "born" but men are "created" (Gutmann 1997). Some of this could be explained by developmental differences: in females the onset of adult physical characteristics is rapid, once menstruation begins, while among men is it much more gradual. The idea of these differences leads to symbolically assigning women to the category "nature" and men to "culture," a point which, as Sherry Ortner and other feminists have suggested, provides a basis for women's subordinate status. The idea also explains why male initiation rites are such important events in many societies: when boys are ritually transformed into men—fully entered into the realm of culture that they represent—the social order itself is reproduced and affirmed.

Despite the sometimes static pictures of male-female relations that anthropologists depict for a culture, however, the relationship between masculinity and male dominance does change, as anthropologist Matthew Gutmann has pointed out. During the 1990s Gutmann studied how men and women define what "being a man" means in a poor neighborhood of Mexico City (Gutmann 1996). He observed that certain ideals and practices of *machismo*—the Mexican stereotype of the dominant, assertive male—contribute to women's subordination, such as when men expect to eat their meals before women and receive better food, abuse alcohol and hit women, or impose decisions on their families. But many men do not behave in these ways, at least, not all the time. Mexican masculinity has always been more subtle and dynamic than the stereotypes of inflexible, domineering *machos* suggest. One reason is that broader social transformations—greater numbers of women are now working outside the home for money, boys and girls in schools are given equal status, and the feminist movement has influenced Mexican life—contribute to changing perceptions of manhood. Gutmann also observed that women play a key role in shaping ideas of masculinity, one of those ways being to challenge men's domination over them. They argue, cajole, and issue ultimatums to men, forcing them to act contrary to *macho* stereotypes.

By focusing on the dynamic nature of gender/sex inequalities, anthropologists have come to understand that male domination and female subordination are reproduced and performed in complex ways in everyday life. But anthropologists have not only studied "men" and "women." They have also studied people who are not considered, or do not consider themselves, to be either men or women, an issue we deal with in the next section.

Figure 12.5 Maculinity in Transition. Broader social transformations—such as the fact that greater numbers of women are working outside the home for money, boys and girls in schools are given equal status, and the feminist movement—contribute to changing perceptions of manhood, including a new role in parenting.

• **Masculinity.** The ideas and practices of manhood.

● ●

THINKING CRITICALLY ABOUT GENDER, SEX, AND SEXUALITY

Gender/sex inequalities are reproduced and performed in many different ways in daily life. Can you identify examples in the following: Advertising? Sports? Language? Cooking? Shopping at a mall? At the same time, these inequalities are often challenged by both men and women. Can you find examples of such challenges in the same contexts?

● ●

What Does It Mean to Be Neither Male Nor Female?

Although they feel natural, the dichotomies we take for granted—male and female, man and woman—are as artificial and constructed as any society's gender/sex system. Many gender/sex systems around the world are less rigid or constraining than our own, including the one that allowed Liberian rebels to adopt feminine clothing and mannerisms to demonstrate their power as warriors.

In many societies, some people live their lives as neither male nor female. They have a culturally accepted, and in some cases prestigious, symbolic niche and social pathway that is distinct from the cultural life plan of males and females (Herdt 1994). Anthropologists use several terms to refer to this situation. One of these terms is **gender variance**, which refers to expressions of sex and gender that diverge from the male and female norms which dominate in most societies. Another term is **third genders**, recognizing the fact that many societies allow for multiple categories of gender/sex (in actuality ranging anywhere from three to five). Sometimes the terms are used interchangeably, as we do here.

Third gender has often been entangled in debates about **sexuality**, which encompasses sexual preferences, desires, and practices. Third gender has been viewed as a form of homosexuality, since some third gender individuals engage in what appear to be same-sex sexual activities (Herdt 1994). But sexual preferences intersect in complex ways with gender variance. People everywhere establish their gender/sex identities, including normative categories like "man" or "woman," not by sexual practices but through social performance: wearing certain clothes, speaking and moving in certain ways, and performing certain social roles and occupations. Performance is central to establishing one's identity as third gender because other markers of gender/sex, such as anatomy, are not always publicly visible. Indeed, in a number of societies, the performance itself—not any essential features of anatomy or sexual preferences—defines an individual as third gender (Whitehead 1981).

Like other aspects of gender/sex systems, such as the inequalities discussed earlier, gender variance is a dynamic phenomenon. In many societies several different gender/sex systems may even co-exist and interpenetrate, especially in societies whose cultural traditions allowed for gender variance when Western nations colonized these societies. To illustrate these points, we consider three examples of gender variance drawn from different contexts: the Navajo, India, and the contemporary urban United States.

● **Gender variance.** Expressions of sex and gender that diverge from the male and female norms that dominate in most societies.

● **Third genders.** Situation found in many societies that acknowledge three or more categories of gender/sex.

● **Sexuality.** Sexual preferences, desires, and practices.

Navajo *Nádleehé*

Gender variance has been historically documented in over 150 American Indian societies, although it is no longer an important institution except in a few Indian societies. Today, where it exists, American Indian gender variance is often called "two-spirit," meaning an individual has both male and female spirit. The phenomenon has been greatly misunderstood, largely because Western culture lacks the conceptual categories to translate the specific beliefs and customs related to gender variance in these societies (Roscoe 1994). For decades white Americans have used the term *berdache* [burr-**dash**], a derogatory Arabic term that refers to the younger partner in a male homosexual relationship to refer to gender variance among American Indians. This term assumes that gender-variant individuals are homosexual, which is not always the case (Figure 12.6). Western moral thought also categorizes them as deviants when in fact, in a number of Indian societies, third-gender individuals held high social status. Furthermore, Western thinking confuses a wide range of beliefs and customs not shared by all societies into a single phenomenon.

The Navajo, who live in the Four Corners area of the Southwest, present an especially subtle and complex example of how one society has defined multiple genders. In Navajo society, *nádleehé* [nahk-**hlay**] are individuals held in high esteem who combine male and female roles and characteristics. They perform both male roles (such as hauling wood and participating in hunts and warfare) and female roles (such as weaving, cooking, sheepherding, and washing clothes). Some, but not all, *nádleehé* cross-dress. Navajo families have traditionally treated *nádleehé* respectfully, even giving them control over family property. The *nádleehé* participate in important religious ceremonies, and many have become spiritual healers. They also serve as go-betweens in arranging marriages and mediating conflicts.

To understand who becomes a *nádleehé*, it is necessary to understand Navajo ideas about gender (W. Thomas 1997). The Navajo recognize five genders, two of them being male and female. The term *nádleehé* (in English, "one who changes continuously") refers to intersex individuals whom they consider a third gender. The fourth and fifth genders are also called *nádleehé*, but are distinct from intersex individuals. The fourth gender is the Masculine-Female, female-bodied individuals who do not get involved in

🌱 **Figure 12.6   Two Spirit Singers at a Gathering.** Unlike traditional gender variants in American Indian societies, many contemporary Two-Spirit individuals are gay. Due to anti-gay sentiment they often experience hostility and discrimination in their home communities. They also feel alienated from white gay and lesbian society and political activism, which does not acknowledge their unique cultural heritage and the issues of poverty and racism they face as Indians.

reproduction and who work in traditional male occupations (hunting and raiding). Today they often serve as firefighters or auto mechanics. The fifth gender is the Feminine-Male, male-bodied individuals who participate in women's activities of cooking, tending to children, and weaving. Feminine-Males may engage in sexual relations with males, although Navajo do not consider these "homosexual" relationships.

The meanings and status of *nádleehé* have changed. For example, the high social status of *nádleehé* became especially pronounced after the 1890s. The U.S. military forced Navajos onto reservations, undermining men's traditional economic activity of raiding (Roscoe 1994). These changes did not affect women's traditional economic pursuits, especially weaving and sheepherding, in which *nádleehé* also engaged. *Nádleehé* who took advantage of the opportunities presented by these social changes often became wealthy as shepherds and weavers, including the famous weaver Hastíín Klah.

Around the same time, however, Christian missionaries on these reservations tried to eliminate the *nádleehé*. Prominent *nádleehé* began to be more discrete about exposing their identities to the outside world, a situation that continues today (W. Thomas 1997). Although *nádleehé* continue to exist, many young Navajos, especially those raised off reservation, might not identify themselves as *nádleehé* but as "gay" or "lesbian," adopting Western forms of identification that really have nothing to do with traditional Navajo gender notions.

Indian *Hijras*

In India, *hijras* (*hee*-drahs) are a third gender who have special social status by virtue of their devotion to Bahuchara Mata, one of many versions of the Mother Goddess worshipped throughout India (Nanda 1994) (Figure 12.7). *Hijras* are defined as males who are sexually impotent, either because they were born intersex with ambiguous genitalia or because they underwent castration. Because they lack male genitals, *hijras* are viewed as "man minus man." They are also seen as "male plus female" because they dress and talk like women, take on womens' occupations, and act like women

🌱 **Figure 12.7   Hijras in India.**

in other ways—although they act as women in an exaggerated, comic, and burlesque fashion.

Individuals become *hijras* from many religious backgrounds—Hindu, Christian, and Muslim—but their special status emerges from the positive meanings Hinduism attributes to individuals who embody both male and female characteristics and to individuals who renounce normal social conventions. In Hindu thought, males and females exist in complementary opposition. The important Hindu deities—Shiva, Vishnu, and Krishna—have dual gender manifestations. The female principle is active, both life-giving and destructive, while the male principle is inert and latent. When they become *hijras* by undergoing castration (or if they are intersex they can join a *hijra* community), men can become powerful enough to tap into the beneficent and destructive powers of the female principle, as vehicles for the Mother Goddess. *Hijras* are thus viewed as both carrying the ability to bless and inauspicious and stigmatized, and many Indians fear the ability *hijras* have to issue curses.

Hijras live in communes of up to twenty people, led by a *guru* (teacher). They live outside the normal bounds of social convention, having renounced their caste position and kinship obligations. Living marginally like this both stigmatizes them and provides them with social freedom. The primary social role of *hijras* is to provide blessings when a boy is born (a major cause of celebration in India), or at a wedding, to bless the couple's fertility. *Hijras* are typically a raucous presence at these events, making crude and inappropriate jokes, performing burlesque dances, and demanding payment for their services. Although it is stigmatized within *hijra* communities, *hijras* also work as prostitutes, engaging in sex acts with men for pay. *Hijra* prostitutes are not necessarily considered "homosexuals"; Indian society does not consider human sexuality as a dichotomy between homosexuality and heterosexuality as ours does, and *hijras* are not considered males anyway.

Although British colonialism tried to outlaw *hijras*, they continued to exist largely by conducting their initiation rites (including castration of willing males) in secret. In recent decades they have had to adapt to a changing Indian society. Government family planning programs have reduced birth rates, and urban families increasingly live in apartment blocks with security guards who prevent the entrance of *hijras* when they arrive to bless a baby. In response, *hijras* have exploited new economic opportunities, asking for alms of shop owners and expanding prostitution (Nanda 1994:415). They continue to exist mainly because the Indian gender/sex system still considers the combination of male and female as valid and meaningful.

"Transgender" in the United States

Even in the United States, where the culture views gender/sex as either male or female, gender variance exists. Our culture has long recognized the existence of cross-dressers (also known as transvestites), people who wear clothing of another sex/gender. For several decades, it has also been possible for people to undergo sex-reassignment surgery. Individuals do all of these things for various reasons, including erotic pleasure or because they do not accept the social categories that their culture imposes on them. But many in the mainstream have stigmatized these people as deviant, immoral, even mentally ill, and made them the target of violence and hate crimes.

Beginning in the early-1990s, political activists began challenging the stigma and putting pressure on government and society to recognize formally the existence and rights of gender variants in this country. The term these activists use, **transgender**, refers to someone to whom society assigns one gender who does not perform as that gender but has taken either permanent or temporary steps to identify as another

- **Transgender.** Refers to someone to whom society assigns one gender who does not perform as that gender but has taken either permanent or temporary steps to identify as another gender.

Figure 12.8   Transgender Activism in New York City.

gender (Valentine 2003). *Transgender* has become a catch-all term to describe a wide variety of people who had once been seen as separate: transsexuals (people who have had sexual reassignment surgery or strongly desire it), transvestites, drag queens (gay men who wear exaggerated women's clothing, usually for performances), drag kings (women who dress in exaggerated men's clothing), and intersex. It rapidly became a common term in academia, psychiatry, and politics, where transgender activists have been effective in promoting legislation on the issue of hate crimes (Figure 12.8).

And yet many of the people who occupy this category do not necessarily identify themselves as "transgender," suggesting that there is no single community or accepted form of "being transgender" in America. American anthropologist David Valentine has explored this issue in ethnographic research among mostly male-to-female transgender-identified people at drag balls, support groups, cross-dresser organizations, clinics, bars, and clubs in New York City. Valentine observed that many individuals resist the label "transgender" because they see it as including them with so many different groups, thus diluting their own issues (Valentine 2007:101). For example, the psychological and social issues confronting people who cross-dress for erotic pleasure are different from the issues of someone who has undergone sexual reassignment surgery and is struggling with the bodily and personal changes involved in that process. Political activists tend to be white and middle class, while many individuals who reject the transgender label are racial minorities and poor. This difference suggests that philosophical disagreement is not the only problem confronting the use of the transgender label in the United States: class and racial differences play a role too.

This research also raises important issues about the ethics of studying socially vulnerable groups like transgender-identified people. We explore these issues in "Thinking Like an Anthropologist: The Ethics of Research and Advocacy With Transgender People."

The meanings of "transgender" are still in formation, though it is clear our culture still resists accepting people who identify as neither male nor female, because it still does not provide them a legitimate symbolic niche and social pathway. One reason is perhaps that many Americans view transgender through a moralistic lens, as an expression of a perverse sexuality, a notion anthropologists reject. As we show in the next section, sexuality is also a distinctive issue with its own complexities and cultural variability.

THINKING CRITICALLY ABOUT GENDER, SEX, AND SEXUALITY

Societies in which gender variance is common tend to also be societies that are tolerant toward ambiguity and complexity in other areas of life, such as religious beliefs. How and why might a society develop an acceptance of ambiguity and complexity, and beyond gender and religious beliefs, in what other aspects of social life might one expect to see a tolerance for ambiguity?

Thinking Like an Anthropologist

The Ethics of Research and Advocacy With Transgender People

ANTHROPOLOGISTS BEGIN THEIR research by asking questions. In this box, we want you to learn how to ask questions as an anthropological researcher. Part One describes a situation and follows up with questions we would ask. Part Two asks you to do the same thing with a different situation.

PART ONE: NAVIGATING SUFFERING AND SOCIAL EXCLUSIONS IN THE CONSTRUCTION OF A "TRANSGENDER" IDENTITY

In his research among transgender-identified people, anthropologist David Valentine has used ethnographic methods to study how the term "transgender" has been conceived and put to use by activists, academics, politicians, and others. He has also advocated on behalf of transgender people by, for example, joining activist lobbying efforts on Capitol Hill and helping raise public awareness about discrimination against transgender people (Valentine 2003). He was inspired by another anthropologist, Nancy Scheper-Hughes, who argues that anthropologists should not just study social problems but also have an ethical imperative to help alleviate the suffering and preclude the violence they witness during the course of their research. Valentine has seen the violence and suffering that some transgender-identified people experience because of their identity; many of his informants have been attacked and several even murdered.

But the desire to act ethically as an advocate and concerned researcher among one's informants is a complicated matter. Violence, pain, and suffering are inherently complex because different people experience and interpret them differently. For example, Valentine sometimes confronted hostility from transgender-identified individuals who were suspicious of him as a researcher and advocate in their midst. Their mistrust stemmed mainly from his status as a social scientist. Social scientific representations of transgender people have tended to objectify them as pathological and exotic. These representations, some argue, have themselves caused suffering and pain because they influence how powerful social institutions, such as government social service agencies, treat and control transgender people. Although Valentine considers his research important for helping transgender people gain social and political recognition,

he is nevertheless wary that his data and conclusions might themselves cause suffering, or even be construed as violent because of the sensitive stories they recount of transgendered people's lives.

His research findings also put him in a difficult position in relation to his advocacy work. For example, Valentine found that people of color and the poor often had a different experience and notion of being transgender than did white, middle-class activists and academics. Many of the former did not even know what the term "transgender" meant, and others rejected the term as too wide a label, lumping people with different issues. Valentine realized that in their efforts to build a community and identity based on gender variance, transgender activists were ignoring how other powerful social differences—especially race, ethnicity, class, and age—intersected with gender and created suffering of their own among individuals in poor and minority communities. As he argues, "'Transgender' is formed on an implicitly white, implicitly middle-class model of identity-based claims that conceptually—and therefore effectively—excludes the people most at risk for violence" (2003:44). The dilemma for Valentine is what role his research and advocacy plays in creating these exclusions.

Valentine does not have any easy answers for the ethical dilemmas he raises, concluding that effective advocacy is based on careful research that does not simplify the messy, ambiguous, and contradictory meanings of violence, pain, and suffering.

This situation raises a number of questions about anthropological research and advocacy on socially vulnerable and marginalized people, including:

1. How do social differences such as class, race, ethnicity, and age intersect with transgender identity?

2. How do people's meanings and experiences of violence, suffering, and pain affect their attitudes toward the legitimacy of social scientists, and what can social scientists do to gain the trust of vulnerable people?

3. What role should ethnographic research take in support of activists and advocacy for social change? What ethical principles should guide anthropologists who address complex matters like pain, violence, and suffering?

(continued)

Thinking Like an Anthropologist (continued)

PART TWO: THE INSTITUTIONALIZATION OF LGBTQ IDENTITIES

On many college campuses, offices and student groups have been set up to support gay, lesbian, bisexual, transgender, and questioning students and staff, typically combining them all under one roof. If you were invited to conduct an ethnographic study in support of the efforts these offices and student groups are making to change the institutional culture surrounding gender and sexuality in your university, what are some of the questions you might ask as an anthropological researcher?

Is Human Sexuality Just a Matter of Being Straight or Queer?

Most of us assume that sexuality (sexual preferences, desires, and practices) is an either/or issue, that people are *either* heterosexual *or* homosexual. We also assume that most humans are heterosexual. The term we use to indicate heterosexuality—"straight"—implies that it is normal and morally correct, while anything else is deviant, bent, or "queer," a term that once had derogatory connotations but in recent years has been appropriated by gay and lesbian communities and given a more positive connotation.

But human sexuality is far more complex and subtle, something that social scientists began to realize after Indiana University biologist Dr. Alfred Kinsey conducted a series of sexuality studies during the 1940s. Kinsey and his colleagues surveyed the sexual lives and desires of American men and women, discovering that sexuality exists along a continuum. They found, for example, that 37% of the male population surveyed had had some homosexual experience, most of which occurred during adolescence, and at least 25% of adult males had had more than incidental homosexual experiences for at least three years of their lives (Kinsey 1948; Fausto-Sterling 1992b). Many of these men did not think of themselves or lead their lives as "homosexuals"; this suggests quite clearly that in practice people's sexuality does not fall into absolute categories. More importantly, Kinsey's research challenged views of homosexuality that consider it a pathological and deviant condition, indicating that psychologically "normal" people may express their sexuality in many ways (Figure 12.9).

Anthropologists today emphasize that human sexuality is a highly flexible phenomenon ranging along a continuum from asexual (non-sexuality) to polyamorous (love of many). They reject the notion that sexuality is an essence buried deep in a person's psychological self or genetic make-up (Lancaster 2004), or the notion that sexuality is just a matter of personal preference or individual orientation. Instead they argue that like other forms of social conduct, sexuality is learned, patterned, and shaped by culture and the political-economic system in which one lives (Weston 1993). The central role of culture in shaping sexuality can be seen in two issues we explore here: cross-cultural research on same-sex sexuality and how governments seek to shape and control the sexualities of their citizens.

Cultural Perspectives on Same-Sex Sexuality

Anthropological attention to same-sex sexuality goes back to the discipline's early years when in the 1920s a handful of anthropologists wrote about sexual desires and practices in certain non-industrialized societies (Lyons and Lyons 2004). Much of

Figure 12.9   Controversial Knowledge. Kinsey's work was highly controversial during a period in American history when homosexuality and heterosexual promiscuity were considered unacceptable.

that work focused on whether same-sex sexuality was culturally acceptable in non-Western societies. But it was not until the 1960s and 1970s—when the emergence of a gay movement in the United States spurred even greater scholarly attention to issues of sexuality—that anthropologists began paying more consistent attention to issues of sexuality more generally, and the cultural dynamics of same-sex sexuality more specifically (Weston 1993). More recently the global HIV/AIDS pandemic, the visibility of openly gay celebrities in media and television, and the push for legal rights for gays have focused even more anthropological attention on issues of same-sex sexuality (Parker 2001; Lewin and Leap 2009).

Motivated by intellectual and personal concerns to gain comparative perspectives on same-sex sexuality, lesbian, gay, and bisexual-identified ethnographers have played a central role in developing cross-cultural studies of same-sex sexuality (Weston 1993). A number of these ethnographers have written about how their own experience as gay affects their work as anthropologists (Lewin and Leap 1996), a theme we explore in "Doing Fieldwork: Don Kulick and 'Coming Out' in the Field."

One of the difficulties anthropologists studying homosexuality in other societies have faced is the problem of adequately naming what they are studying (Weston 1993). Most North Americans hold the view that people are born straight or gay, implying a fixed and stable condition and identity. This notion originated in the late nineteenth century, when medical science and psychology turned what people had previously considered "perverse" *behaviors* into bio-psychological *conditions* requiring medical intervention. In many other cultures, this idea of same-sex sexuality as a fixed and exclusive condition does not exist. Anthropologists have found in other cultures that same-sex behaviors can exist side by side with heterosexual behaviors, suggesting

Doing Fieldwork
Don Kulick and "Coming Out" in the Field

IN BRAZIL'S THIRD-LARGEST city of Salvador live nearly two hundred *travestis* [trah-**vest**-tees], men who cross-dress and work as prostitutes. *Travestis* adopt female names, clothing styles, hairstyles, make-up, and linguistic pronouns (like "her"). They also ingest hormones and use silicone to acquire feminine bodily features, such as breasts, wide hips, large thighs, and expansive buttocks (Kulick 1998). Such practices might give the impression that these men want to be women or consider themselves "transgender." But in fact they do not self-identify as women, nor do they desire to remove their penises surgically. They consider themselves men—gay men—who desire to have sex with other men—non-gay men—and fashion themselves as an object of desire for those men.

Brazilians are fascinated by *travestis*, several of whom have become national celebrities. But the reality for most *travestis* is that they are discriminated against and poor, living a hand-to-mouth existence, and often dying young from violence, drug abuse, and health problems, particularly AIDS. During the late 1990s, Swedish anthropologist Don Kulick spent a year living among Salvador's *travestis* to understand the day-to-day realities of their lives.

Kulick believes that several factors helped him gain acceptance in the insular *travesti* community. One of these was that *travestis* were open to his involvement in their lives because they viewed Europeans as more liberal and cultivated than Brazilians, and he would not have the same prejudices against their lives that Brazilians would. Another is that when Kulick started his fieldwork he spoke very little Portuguese, and so could not communicate very well. *Travestis* came to see him as a non-threatening presence, someone who would not condemn them.

Kulick believes a third factor played an especially crucial role in his gaining acceptance: he is himself a gay man.

The *travestis* asked about his sexual orientation right away, if he was a *viado* (a "fag"). Kulick observes, "Upon receiving an affirmative answer, *travestis* often nodded and relaxed considerably. My status as a self-acknowledged *viado* implied to the *travestis* that I was, in effect, one of the girls, and that I probably was not interested in them as sexual partners. My behavior quickly confirmed that I was not, and after such preliminaries were out of the way, *travestis* realized that they could continue conversing about the topics—boyfriends, clients, big penises, hormone, and silicone—that occupy their time, without having to worry that I might find such topics uninteresting or offensive" (1998:15).

Previous research on *travestis* had been conducted by heterosexual women and a Brazilian male researcher who had presented himself as a potential client. These studies focused on their work as prostitutes, but these researchers had not gained access to the *travestis'* private worlds. Kulick believes that "coming out" to the *travestis* as an openly gay man facilitated access to confidences and discussions that may not have been granted as easily to other researchers.

Questions for Reflection

1. Kulick argues that an anthropologist's access to this community was benefited by being gay and seen as "one of them." Would this extend to other identities? For example, should women study women's lives and men study men's lives?

2. Although Kulick reports his coming out as positive, it was also risky. What kinds of risks might his coming out have had?

that the assumptions we make about the term "homosexuality"—especially that it is an either/or condition—do not necessarily apply in other cultures.

One example comes from the work of anthropologist Gilbert Herdt, who studied the male initiation rituals of the Sambia people of Papua New Guinea. Boys undergo six elaborate stages of initiation that involve behavior he calls "insemination." To be a strong, powerful warrior requires *jerungdu* (the essence of masculine strength), a substance a boy can only acquire from ingesting the semen of a man. Before insemination the boys must purge harmful feminine essences with a rite that mimics female menstruation: sharp grasses are shoved up the noses of the boys to make them bleed off the lingering essences of their mother's milk. Finally, they receive *jerungdu* in the form of semen directly from young married men on whom they perform fellatio. During the early stages of the initiation the boys are inseminated orally by the young married men at the height of their sexual and physical powers. When the initiates reach later stages of initiation—after marriage but before they become fathers—younger initiates will perform oral sex on them. The final stage of initiation occurs after the birth of their first child. Now in their twenties or thirties, the men have sex only with women, usually their wives, but they can have adulterous trysts in the bush should the opportunity present itself.

Herdt (1981) referred to these initiation activities as "ritualized homosexuality," a term that highlights the homoerotic nature of these rites, since they are sexually arousing for the older men who are fellated. The problem with this terminology is that Western notions of "homosexuality" imply an inborn condition or identity, yet after marriage Sambia men shift their erotic focus to their wives with whom they have intercourse or fellatio. Furthermore, the term implies that these acts are intended for erotic pleasure, while for the Sambia these ritual acts are really intended to develop masculine strength. Herdt and others who study similar rites now refer to them as "semen transactions" or "boy-inseminating rites."

Other contexts raise similar questions about the appropriateness of Western terminology, and also indicate the situational nature of same-sex behaviors. For example, some married Filipina women who migrate to Hong Kong to work as domestic maids consider sexual relationships with other women a "safe" and "moral" alternative to extramarital affairs with men. Affairs with men could end in pregnancy or shame for themselves and their families. So these normally heterosexual women enter into "Hong Kong only" affairs with "tomboys," lesbian women who they view as sensitive and protective, with whom they can share intimacy while away from their families (Pei-Chia 2008). At no point do these women consider themselves "lesbian," and in fact they work hard to keep such relationships concealed from their families.

Anthropologists have also learned that concepts of same-sex sexuality differ across cultures. In Latin American countries like Mexico (Carrier 1976), Nicaragua (Lancaster 1992; 1997), and Brazil (Parker 1989), a man who engages in same-sex practices is not necessarily identified as nor would he consider himself a "homosexual." This notion comes from ideas about passivity and activity in sexual intercourse. For example, Brazilian sexual culture distinguishes being active and being passive participants in sexual intercourse, typically considering the active agent masculine, and the passive agent feminine. The metaphorical language people use to describe sex acts reflects these distinctions: *dar* (darr; "to give") is the passive role of being penetrated during intercourse, while *comer* (koh-**mehr**; "to eat") is the action of penetration (Parker 1989). "Women" and *viados* (a colloquial term meaning "fags" or gay men) are those who "give" (receive penetration), while "men" are the active ones who "eat" (penetrate). The result is that a man who penetrates another man would not consider himself—nor be considered by others—as homosexual, yet the man being penetrated would be considered homosexual.

As Richard Parker (1992), an anthropologist who has studied Brazilian sexual culture, points out, these implicit sexual meanings can have major consequences for designing public health programs. Parker observes that in the early years of the HIV/AIDS crisis, Brazilians uncritically accepted the notion derived from the United States and Europe that HIV/AIDS was a "gay disease" transmitted through homosexual sex and only affecting the homosexual population. To create effective public health interventions, Parker advised, it was necessary to build programs around the specific Brazilian cultural meanings of sexuality, and not ignore the risky behaviors of men who did not consider themselves susceptible to HIV because they were "not gay."

The Sambia and many other examples around the globe contrast with mainstream views of gays and lesbians in the United States, which emphasize homosexuality as a stable identity, around which cohesive social communities are formed. But as anthropologist Ellen Lewin (1993), who has studied lesbian parents in the United States, has found, even in the United States there is more subtlety to this issue than meets the eye. She writes that lesbian parents focus little energy on policing the boundaries of lesbian sexual identity. Instead of claiming an essential identity which they enforce on others, they negotiate their identities constantly in the face of constant demands from children, lovers, fathers and, sometimes, custody disputes over the children. For example, in custody disputes they emphasize themselves not in terms of sexuality but as women who have achieved motherhood and will make "good mothers." As Lewin (1996:107) explains, "Like other people, lesbians and gay men identify themselves along a number of axes, and while sexual orientation is often a salient dimension of their identification, other personal and social characteristics also feed into how they view themselves."

Controlling Sexuality

Long ago, anthropologists observed that every society places limits on people's sexuality by constructing rules about who can sleep with whom. But in the modern world, governments have asserted unprecedented levels of control over sexuality, routinely implementing and enforcing laws that limit the kinds of sexual relations their citizens can have. For example, in dozens of countries around the world, and even in twenty-six U.S. states, adultery is considered "injurious to public morals and a mistreatment of the marriage relationship" (Adultery 2009) and is treated by authorities as a civil offense (subject to fines) or even a crime (subject to jail time). Until the U.S. Supreme Court overturned such laws in 2003, fifteen states still outlawed "sodomy," or same-sex intercourse. In our country, the most contentious public issues—including the abortion debate, gays in the military, and the right of gays to marry—involve questions over whether and how the government should control the sexuality of its citizens.

Family planning programs can also be viewed as another manifestation of government control over sexuality—especially women's sexuality, since such programs tend to focus on women's bodies (Dwyer 2000). China's well-known "One Child Policy," which limits families to one child, has reduced fertility rates and unemployment significantly. But it has also involved unprecedented government control over sexuality, including (until 2002, when it was outlawed) forced abortions and sterilizations of women who exceeded their quota or were deemed unfit to reproduce.

THINKING CRITICALLY ABOUT GENDER, SEX, AND SEXUALITY

Many queer activists in the United States and Europe have accepted and promote the idea that they were "born" homosexual and that they have no choice in the matter. How do you think anthropologists, who view sexuality as culturally patterned, socially conditioned, and not in-born, should respond to this idea?

Conclusion

The concept of sexuality—who can sleep with whom, sexual preferences, and the sexual practices in which people engage—connects back to concepts we considered earlier in this chapter, namely gender and sex. Although they traditionally have distinct definitions, each of these concepts touches on an issue of central importance to human existence, which is our capacity for sexual reproduction. Yet, these concepts are intertwined in complex ways, shaping the ideas and social patterns a society uses to organize males, females, and others who do not fit these neat categories, such as intersexuals.

It is important to remember that how we think of sex, gender, and sexuality, as natural as they feel to us, is not as universal as we may assume. Returning to the Liberian situation of cross-dressing warriors where this chapter opened, it would be quite easy—but deeply mistaken—to explain warrior cross-dressing as some kind of perverted erotic fantasy, just because that is how we tend to think of cross-dressing in our own culture. But cross-dressing Liberian warriors—both the male rebels who wore women's clothing and the women close to the rebel leadership who donned camouflaged uniforms and matching high-heels—were self-consciously engaging with their own traditional notions of sex and gender, specifically mixing male and female symbols to draw on the mystical power of both.

It is also good to remember that matters of sex, gender, and sexuality are not necessarily as stable as they feel to us. Just as Liberian rebels were rather quick to drop cross-dressing in favor of Rambo clothing, our own notions of sex, gender, and sexuality are dynamic as well. Not only does our own society have more diversity and flexibility in sexual practices than our cultural categories tend to acknowledge, the very notion of sexuality as an inborn condition is a relatively new one in Western history. The reason these things feel so stable to us in our everyday experience is that culture—those processes through which the artificial comes to feel natural—is so central to defining sex, gender, and sexuality.

KEY TERMS

Gender p. 293	Masculinity p. 301	Third genders p. 302
Gender variance p. 302	Sex p. 293	Transgender p. 305
Gender/sex systems p. 295	Sexuality p. 302	
Intersex p. 295	Sexually dimorphic p. 295	

Reviewing the Chapter

Chapter Section	What We Know	To Be Resolved
In What Ways Are Males and Females Different?	Every society makes a distinction between "male" and "female." But not all societies attach the same meanings to apparent biological differences, or even think they are important for explaining differences between males and females.	Anthropologists continue to work out the relative influences of biological, environmental, and cultural factors on shaping gender/sex.
In What Ways Are Men and Women Unequal?	Biological differences are not the source of women's subordination. Rather, cultural ideologies and social relations impose on women lower status, prestige, and power than men.	The debate over the universality of women's subordinate status was never resolved, and in recent years new debates have emerged about the extent to which gender inequalities are performed by women and men.
What Does it Mean to Be Neither Male Nor Female?	Many gender/sex systems around the world allow for gender variance and third genders. Gender variants generally establish their unique identities through social performance: wearing certain clothes, speaking and moving in certain ways, and performing certain social roles and occupations.	Western terminology and concepts are not always able to capture the complexity of how other cultures conceive of matters of sex, gender, and sexuality, which raises questions about how to best represent such phenomena.
Is Human Sexuality Just a Matter of Being Straight or Queer?	Human sexuality is variable and patterned by cultural ideologies and social relations. It is also not a fixed or exclusive condition.	Anthropologists continue to work through the complex and subtle ways sexuality interacts with gender and sex, as well as other identities like class, race, and ethnicity.

Readings

The work of biologist Anne Fausto-Sterling, including her book *Sexing the Body: Gender Politics and the Construction of Sexuality* (New York: Basic Books, 2000), offers useful and compelling perspectives on the construction of sex, gender, sexuality, and especially the ways societies have dealt with intersex individuals. Caroline Brettell and Carolyn Fishel Sargent's edited reader, *Gender in Cross-Cultural Perspective* (Third Edition, Englewood Cliffs, NJ: Prentice Hall, 2001) offers a range of anthropological arguments and case studies about these issues.

● ● ● ● ● ● ● ● ● ● ● ● ● ● ● ● ● ● ● ●

For an overview of feminist anthropology and debates over male/female inequality, see Sherry Ortner's book *Making Gender: The Politics and Erotics of Culture* (Boston: Beacon Press, 1996). Amitra Basu's 2010 edited volume *Women's Movements in the Global Era: The Power of Local Feminisms* (Boulder, CO: Westview Press, 2010) offers a recent assessment of the diversity of feminisms that exist in the world.

● ● ● ● ● ● ● ● ● ● ● ● ● ● ● ● ● ● ● ●

Gilbert Herdt's edited book *Third Sex, Third Gender: Beyond Sexual Dimorphism in Culture and History* (New York: Zone Books, 1994) offers a comprehensive overview of gender variance across many cultures. Serena Nanda's book *Neither Man nor Woman: The Hijras of India* (Second edition, Boston:

Cengage, 1999) is a classic ethnographic study of gender variance in India.

• • • • • • • • • • • • • • • • • • • •

Andrew P. and Harriet D. Lyons's book *Irregular Connections: A History of Anthropology and Sexuality* (Lincoln: University of Nebraska Press, 2004) examines anthropology's long fascination with the study of sexuality, as well as the dilemmas it has raised. It pairs well with Don Kulick's recent ethnography of sexuality among transgender prostitutes in Brazil, *Travesti: Sex, Gender, and Culture Among Brazilian Transgendered Prostitutes* (Chicago: University of Chicago Press, 1998).

• • • • • • • • • • • • • • • • • • • •

Kinship, Marriage, and the Family

Love, Sex, and Power

SOAP OPERAS LIKE *General Hospital, The Bold and the Beautiful, Days of Our Lives,* and *The Young and the Restless* are one of the world's most popular and enduring television genres. Every day, hundreds of millions of women and men around the globe tune into one or more of them. Although some of these American soaps have enjoyed international popularity, it is Latin American shows—produced and exported by Mexicans, Venezuelans, Argentines, and Brazilians in particular—that have ruled screens worldwide during the past two decades.

One of the most popular Latin American exports of all time is the Mexican *telenovela* [tay-**lay**-noh-**vell**-ah] (as such shows are called in Spanish) *También los Ricos Lloran* ("The Rich Also Cry"). Produced in 1979, it has enjoyed tremendous popularity and re-broadcasts in dozens of countries throughout the Americas, Europe, Asia, and Africa to the present day. *Telenovelas* usually run for only a few months and have a clear ending, unlike U.S. soaps which are long-running and open-ended—*As the World Turns,* for example, the second longest continuously running TV program in the United States, ran from April 1956 to September 2010 with more than 13,000 episodes.

The basic plot, which many subsequent *telenovelas* have imitated, is as follows. A beautiful and poor young woman named Mariana becomes a maid for a rich and powerful family. She and the youngest son in the family, Luis Alberto, have a scandalous love affair and

Kinship and the Latin American Telenovela. Latin American soap operas called *telenovelas* such as the Mexican show pictured here, "Ni Contigo Ni Sin Ti" ("Neither With You Nor Without You"), have captivated global audiences for decades because of the complicated, if perhaps unlikely, kin relations they present.

317

eventually get married. She has a baby son, Beto, but in a fit of temporary madness she gives him away to an old woman on the street.

During the next eighteen years, Mariana searches desperately for Beto and miraculously finds him when he begins dating Marisabel, who is Mariana and Luis Alberto's adopted daughter (though she doesn't know she's adopted). Mariana tells Marisabel who Beto really is. Marisabel becomes hysterical at the thought of incest with her brother. Mariana does not, however, tell Luis Alberto, fearing he will get angry with her. He gets angry anyway because she spends so much time with Beto that Luis Alberto suspects the two are having an affair. In the final episode Luis Alberto confronts Beto and Mariana with a gun. In the program's final moments, Mariana screams "Son!" Luis Alberto goes ballistic. Beto screams, "Father, let me embrace you!" and the family is, against all odds, reunited at long last.

Dark family secrets, suspicious spouses, unruly children, irresponsible parents, and possible incest make for gripping television, to say the least! But to an anthropologist—if not also for many viewers around the world—the fascination this show holds is not due simply to its unlikely storyline but to its presentation of the complexities of love, sex, and power that are part and parcel of being in any family, anywhere in the world.

Also noteworthy is the show's assumption that blood relations are the central defining relationships in people's lives—after all, Luis Alberto's anger disappears when he realizes Beto is his son, and Marisabel would probably not be so hysterical if she knew Beto wasn't her biological brother. For anthropologists, it is a noteworthy assumption mainly because it reflects one particular culture's way of defining family relationships. Around the world not all cultures give the same weight to biological relatedness for defining a family.

The biological facts of procreation are only one aspect of what it means to have a family. What is more important is how these biological facts are interpreted and the special rights and obligations that these facts confer on individuals. At the heart of anthropology's interest in families is the question: *How are families more than just groups of biologically related people?* Embedded within this larger question are the following questions, around which this chapter is organized.

What are families, and how are they structured in different societies?

How do families control power and wealth?

Why do people get married?

How are technological changes reshaping how people think about family?

The kinds of influence and control people can exert on their relatives varies widely from one society to another. Yet, anthropologists have long recognized that we cannot understand a society until we understand the core relationships of kinship, marriage, and family around which people's social lives are lived. So let us begin by considering what makes a group of relatives a family.

What Are Families, and How Are They Structured in Different Societies?

Families are important in nearly every society. They give members a sense of comfort and belonging and provide them part of their identity, values, and ideals. They control wealth and the material necessities of life. And, importantly, they assign individuals with basic roles, rights, and responsibilities in relation to other relatives.

It probably feels natural to you that your own family does all (or most) of these things. What is *not* natural is how and why your family is organized and achieves these things in the ways it does. Like other aspects of culture we've explored throughout this book, **kinship**—the social system that organizes people in families based on descent and marriage—is patterned in culturally specific and dynamic ways. We begin by exploring its dynamism, and then we examine the different ways families can be organized cross-culturally.

- **Kinship.** The social system that organizes people in families based on descent and marriage.

Families, Ideal and Real

In every society a gap exists between that society's ideal family and the real families that exist, the reason being that all families are dynamic. For example, as individuals grow older they move out of their **natal family**—the family into which they were born and raised—to marry and start their own families. In addition, broader social and economic conditions change the composition, size, and character of the ties between family members, as the example of the American family illustrates.

- **Natal family.** The family into which a person is born and (usually) raised.

"Traditional" American Families

American politicians and religious leaders frequently extol the virtues of the "traditional" family. But just what family do these people have in mind as their model? Most likely, it is some version of the family in the television show *The Adventures of Ozzie and Harriet* (which aired 1952–1966), with a working husband/father who is the head of the household, a loving stay-at-home wife/mother, and two or three children living in a spic-and-span suburban home.

The problem is that the Ozzie and Harriet ideal is not a "traditional" family, but a new pattern—the independent American suburban family—that emerged in the 1950s and lasted for less than twenty years. Only twenty years before then, during the Great Depression of the 1930s, American birth rates had fallen sharply; with limited income most families refrained from having children. The birth rate remained low from 1942 to 1946 because so many men were serving in the military during World War II. But once these millions of men returned they began to marry and start families. The 1950s were a time of unprecedented economic growth, and the baby boom—77 million babies in 15 years—encouraged expansion of new subdivisions filled with these young families. By the late 1950s around 60% of all Americans lived in such families (Figure 13.1).

During the late 1960s and 1970s these young post-war families had grown up, children moved out, and some couples divorced. These changes paralleled changes in

Figure 13.1 Which Is the "Traditional American Family"? Is it the TV sitcom family in *Leave It to Beaver* (left), or the American farm family in the late nineteenth century (the extended family of Harold Harding Cunningham of Wilson County, Tennessee)?

the economy as women began to join the workforce in larger numbers, lowering wages for entry-level jobs. By the 1980s it was hard for young American families to get by on one salary. Two-income households brought in more wages but put stress on couples, who still needed someone to cook their meals, clean their houses or apartments, and look after their children. Nowadays, families tend to have one or two children rather than three or four. Divorce became much more common than ever before in American life, and today only half of American households are headed by a married couple. When divorced couples with kids get remarried, the composition of a family (with multiple sets of step-parents and step-siblings)—and especially the obligations individuals in it have to each other—can get quite complicated. Such families are sometimes referred to as blended families that include full siblings, half-siblings, and step-siblings.

Nuclear and Extended Families

- **Nuclear family.** The family formed by a married couple and their children.

- **Kinship chart.** A visual representation of family relationships.

Still, the **nuclear family**—the family formed by a married couple and their children—is the most important family structure in the United States. Ours is not the only society with nuclear families—nuclear family units occur in and are important to nearly every society around the world. Indeed, for many decades anthropologists wrote of the nuclear family as the most basic unit of kinship (Radcliffe-Brown 1941:2).

Using a basic **kinship chart** (a visual representation of family relationships), we can graph a man's nuclear family easily enough, and we can add another nuclear family for his wife's natal family, and add children (Figure 13.2). Such charts describe the biological connections, such as mother-daughter or father-daughter—without being easily able to express the content of these different relationships. For example, when the child is young the relationship between parent and child may involve teaching and training. But when the widowed mother moves into her son's family, the content of the relationship is entirely different, even though the biological relationship has not changed. The son or daughter may now look after the finances of the aging parent, but they remain her biological child.

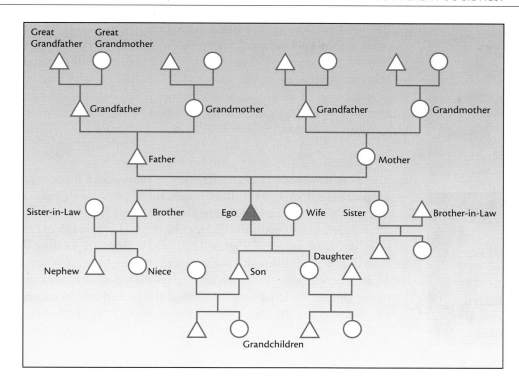

Figure 13.2   A Kinship Chart Plots out All Sorts of Kin Relations. Here the chart shows members of the extended family from a husband/father's perspective. Of course, the chart could be drawn from the wife/mother's perspective as well.

One important feature of nuclear and natal families is that they usually function as **corporate groups,** which are groups of real people who work together toward common ends much like a corporation does. The family's goals are not just the goals of one family member, but of the group as a whole. In every society around the world, families are supposed to look after the needs of all members of the family—parents, children, and any other family members who happen to be in residence.

Family groups may also consist of larger groups of relatives beyond the nuclear family, which anthropologists call **extended families**. Extended families may live together and function as a corporate group or they may merely acknowledge ties with one another. In nineteenth-century America, for example, it was common for households to include a nuclear family at its core, as well as some mix of elderly parents, a single brother or sister, the orphaned children of the wife's sister, and perhaps another niece or nephew. Nowadays, for many Americans only special events like funerals, weddings, and family reunions can bring large extended families together (Figure 13.3).

- **Corporate groups.** Groups of real people who work together toward common ends, much like a corporation does.

- **Extended families.** Larger groups of relatives beyond the nuclear family, often living in the same household.

Clans and Lineages

Sometimes Americans will jokingly refer to their extended family as their "clan." But for anthropologists the term **clan** refers to something different: a special group of relatives who are all descended from a single ancestor. In many societies, links to these ancestors can be quite vague, and in a number of societies these ancestors are animals or humans with distinctive non-human characteristics. Clans are often as important as nuclear families in the small-scale societies anthropologists have studied in Oceania, Africa, and the Americas. So much so that in the 1940s French anthropologist Claude Lévi-Strauss (1969a) challenged the importance of the nuclear family as the basic unit of kinship, arguing instead for the importance of clans as basic units of kinship. Clans typically control land and other resources, as well as any individual member's access to those resources. They are also usually **exogamous**, which means that members of

- **Clan.** A group of relatives who claim to be descended from a single ancestor.

- **Exogamous.** A social pattern in which members of a clan must marry someone from another clan, which has the effect of building political, economic, and social ties with other clans.

Figure 13.3   Extended Families in North America. (Top) An Indian family from the Kainai tribe in the Canadian plains about 1900. (Bottom) An American extended family gathers for a reunion in Mt. Carmel, Illinois, 1904. Everyone in the photo is descended from one deceased couple, parents of seven of the senior women pictured.

the clan must marry someone from another clan, which has the effect of building political, economic, and social ties with other clans. Clans come in three types: patrilineal, matrilineal, and cognatic. **Lineages** are very similar to clans, but lineages tend to be composed of people who are directly descended from known ancestors, while clan membership is often more vague and assumed rather than empirically known.

Patrilineal Clans and Lineages

The most common clans and lineages in nonindustrial societies are **patrilineal**, such as Omaha Indians, the Nuer of South Sudan, and most groups in the Central Highlands of Papua New Guinea. In these societies, clan members claim to be descended through males from the same ancestor (Figure 13.4). These clans are **unilineal** (based on descent through a single descent line, in this case males). Most Americans will easily understand patrilineal descent because in the United States we have traditionally inherited our surnames patrilineally, that is, taking on the family name from the father.

Matrilineal Clans and Lineages

Anthropologists have also observed **matrilineal** clans and lineages that reckon descent through women, and are descended from an ancestral woman (Figure 13.5). In these societies, such as the Trobriand Islanders discussed in other chapters, every man and woman is a member of their mother's clan, which is also the clan of their mother's mother. The other members of this clan include the mother's brother and the mother's mother's brother. A person's strongest identity is with his or her relatives in a mother's clan and lineage.

- **Lineage.** A group composed of relatives who are directly descended from known ancestors.

- **Patrilineal.** Reckoning descent through males from the same ancestors.

- **Unilineal.** Based on descent through a single descent line, either males or females.

- **Matrilineal.** Reckoning descent through women, who are descended from an ancestral woman.

Figure 13.4   Members of a Patrilineage (shaded). Descent is through males.

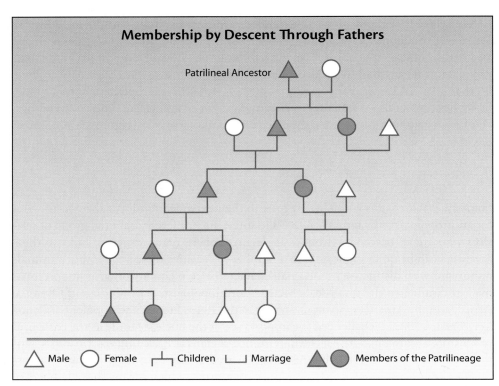

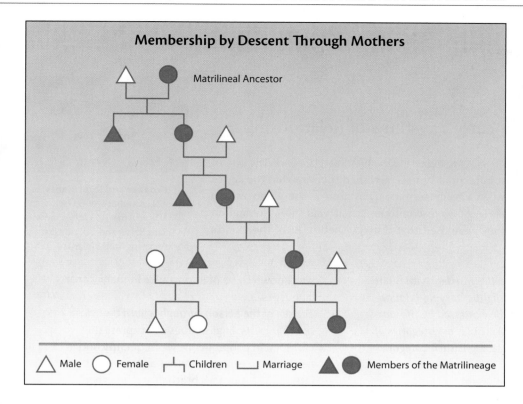

Figure 13.5 **Members of a Matrilineage (shaded).** Descent is through females.

Matrilineality is not the same as matriarchy, in which women hold political power. Matrilineality is only about identity and group membership. In matrilineal societies, land is usually owned by the clan or by a lineage within a larger clan. While women may have some say in who uses clan land for gardens or for gathering material for building houses, it is usually the men in the clan who have control over these resources. As such, a young man will look to his mother's brother for guidance and assistance, just as this uncle had looked to his mother's brother for direction when he was young.

Cognatic Clans

A third kind of clan is the **cognatic** clan (or bilateral clan), such as is found among the Samoans of Central Polynesia. Samoans reckon descent through both the mother and the father, allowing people to be members of both their mother's and their father's clan. The main difference between a cognatic clan and a unilineal clan is that in cognatic clans one can be a member of any of several clans, and in some societies multiple membership is possible or even typical. Matrilineal and patrilineal clans, in contrast, are naturally bounded by who a person's mother or father is, respectively.

- **Cognatic.** Reckoning descent through either men or women from some ancestor.

Kinship Terminologies

Another way to think about the structure of families is to explore terms that people in different societies use to refer to their relatives. Since the 1860s, when American anthropologist Lewis Henry Morgan (1871) collected kinship terminologies from many different languages around the world, anthropologists have collected thousands of different kinship terminologies, but it happens that all of them can be grouped into six basic patterns Morgan had identified. Morgan and several other anthropologists

Classic Contributions

A. L. Kroeber on Classificatory Systems of Relationship

Kroeber and Informants.
A. L. Kroeber (center) with
Native American informants
Sam Batwi and Ishi (the last
surviving Yahi Indian).

IN 1909 ANTHROPOLOGIST A. L. Kroeber (1876–1960) at U.C. Berkeley, one of early American anthropology's most influential figures, published the view that the key to understanding the differences between kinship terminologies around the world was to understand eight general principles. Most were common, but it was the combination of principles and how completely they were used that distinguished most of the world's different kin terminologies.

It is apparent that what we should try to deal with is not the hundreds or thousands of slightly varying relationships that are expressed or can be expressed by the various languages of man, but the principles or categories of relationship which underlie these. Eight such categories are discernible.

1. *The difference between persons of the same and of separate generations.* The distinctions between father and grandfather, between uncle and cousin, and between a person and his father involve the recognition of this category.

2. *The difference between lineal and collateral relationship.* When the father and the father's brother are distinguished, this category is operative. When only one term is employed for brother and cousin, it is inoperative.

3. *Difference of age within one generation.* The frequent distinction between the older and younger brother is an instance. In English this category is not operative.

4. *The sex of the relative.* This distinction is carried out so consistently by English, the one exception being the foreign word cousin. . . .

5. *The sex of the speaker.* Unrepresented in English and most European languages, this category is

well known to be of importance in many other languages. . . .

6. *The sex of the person through whom the relationship exists.* English does not express this category. In consequence we frequently find it necessary to explain whether an uncle is a father's or a mother's brother, and whether a grandmother is paternal or maternal.

7. *The distinction of blood relatives from connections by marriage.* While this distinction is commonly expressed by most languages, there are occasional lapses; just as in familiar English speech the father-in-law is often spoken of as father. . . .

8. *The condition of life of the person through whom the relationship exists.* The relationship may be either of blood or by marriage; the person serving as the bond of relationship may be alive or dead, married or no longer married. Many North American Indians refrain from using such terms as father-in-law and mother-in-law after the wife's death or separation. Some go so far as to possess terms restricted to such severed relationship. . . . Distinct terms are therefore sometimes found for relatives of the uncle and aunt group after the death of a parent. (Kroeber 1909:78–79)

Questions for Reflection

1. Which of these eight classificatory principles are important principles in American kin terms, and which are either less important or not used at all?

2. Give an example of a pair of kin terms used by Americans that illustrates these core principles.

from the cultural evolution school tried to identify some kinship terminologies as more evolved and sophisticated than others. Anthropologist A. L. Kroeber (1909) identified and summarized the basic principles of kinship terminologies by arguing that kinship terminologies are shaped by the kind of clan organization found in a society, not by a group's position on some evolutionary scale. We explore how all kinship systems classify various kin into basic social categories in "Classic Contributions: A. L. Kroeber on Classificatory Systems of Relationship."

This early research on kinship terminologies has been highly influential for two reasons. One of these is the realization that underlying the diversity of terminologies are a few basic systems of organizing people, which we present in Figure 13.6. The second is that anthropologists have come to realize that kinship terminologies do not just provide descriptive names that indicate relationships between individuals, but can also indicate the specific nature of the relationship, rights, and responsibilities that exist between related people. In other words, the term you use to identify a person shapes how you should interact with them. For example, in many American Indian societies, an individual will use the term "father" to refer not just to his biological father, but to his father's brothers or even other men of his father's generation with no direct biological ties. The "father" is expected to interact with his "son" in certain culturally accepted ways, such as providing food or other assistance.

The Problem of Genealogical Amnesia

Another thing kinship terminologies do is help people keep track of their many relatives by assigning categorical terms. But nobody can keep track of everybody. Each society has kinsmen vital to keep track of, while others, usually more distant relatives, are forgotten. Anthropologists refer to this structural process of forgetting whole groups of relatives as **genealogical amnesia**. We explore this phenomenon in more detail in "Thinking Like an Anthropologist: Genealogical Amnesia in Bali, Indonesia, and the United States."

We have seen in this section that whether societies place emphasis on small nuclear family groups or extended kin groups organized as lineages or clans, families organize corporate activities within the group and relationships with people in other groups. Let us turn now to how families control wealth and power.

- **Genealogical amnesia.** Structural process of forgetting whole groups of relatives, usually because they are not currently significant in social life.

- **Teknonymy.** A system of naming parents by the names of their children.

THINKING CRITICALLY ABOUT KINSHIP, MARRIAGE, AND THE FAMILY

Lewis Henry Morgan thought of American kinship as the most rational way of reckoning kin relationships, and he referred to our system as a descriptive rather than classificatory system because relatives on mother's side were called the same thing as on father's side. But, in fact, terms like "aunt," "uncle," and "cousin" group together very different kinds of relatives under the same label, which makes our system a "classificatory" system. Using your own family as an example, discuss how these terms are classificatory even if "mother," "father," "son," and "daughter" are not.

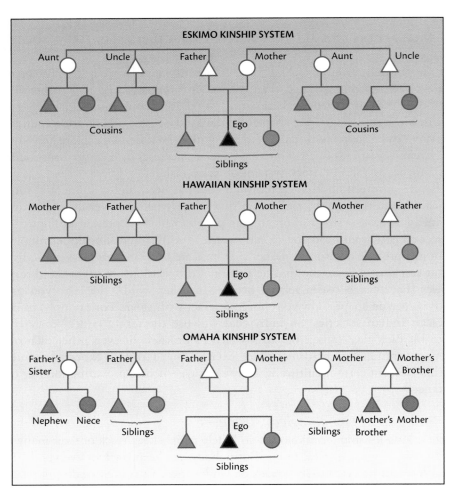

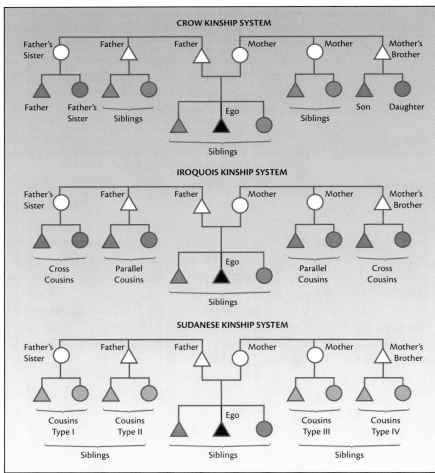

🌱 **Figure 13.6   The Six Basic Systems of Kinship.**
Anthropologists have identified six different basic kinship systems. The differences between them can be understood by how people refer to their different cousins.

Thinking Like an Anthropologist

Genealogical Amnesia in Bali, Indonesia, and the United States

ANTHROPOLOGISTS BEGIN THEIR research by asking questions. In this box, we want you to learn how to ask questions as an anthropological researcher. Part One describes a situation and follows up with questions we would ask. Part Two asks you to do the same thing with a different situation.

PART ONE: GENEALOGICAL AMNESIA AND NAMING PATTERNS ON THE ISLAND OF BALI

In the late 1950s American anthropologists Hildred and Clifford Geertz (1964, 1975) studied Balinese kinship patterns on the lush, tropical island of Bali in Indonesia. The Balinese have a bilateral kinship system, which means that an individual is related equally to relatives in his or her mother's and father's family (much as Americans are). People are more or less "closely" related, at least in theory, to everyone who is descended from any one of their sixteen great-great-grandparents. That is a lot of relatives!

How do the Balinese keep track of them all? The Geertzes found that people don't. While Balinese lived in large extended family groups, the number of relatives they actually interacted with was limited to a few dozen members. Most informants were aware of only a couple hundred kinsmen rather than the thousands that were theoretically possible. The Geertzes referred to this forgetting of relatives as "genealogical amnesia."

Genealogical amnesia was not about how particular individuals literally forgot some of their relatives, but how features of normal social life encourage people to focus on some relatives so that other relatives gradually drift off their radar screen.

The Geertzes learned that genealogical amnesia was not random, but quite systematic. It is the result of a particular naming system. All Balinese have personal names, and as in the United States and other countries, parents often name their children after grandparents, aunts and uncles, and great-grandparents. But after Balinese men and women marry they are no longer called by their personal names; they are referred to as "father of so-and-so" or "mother of so-and-so." As their children get older and marry, they will begin to be referred to as grandfather or grandmother of so-and-so. (Anthropologists call this naming practice **teknonymy**, a system of naming parents by the names of their children.)

In Bali the teknonyms assigned to individuals kept changing over time as people got older. The effect of this was that none of the younger people had ever heard the personal names of their grandparents and great-grandparents. The effect of this rather simple naming system was that everyone knew they were related to everyone who was a descendant of a great-grandparent—who would be known as great-grandparent of so-and-so. But it also obscured relatives, since all the personal names several generations back were no longer used in conversation. Earlier generations were only known by the names of their first-born grandchildren or great-grandchildren, and even these identifications became difficult to pick out of daily conversation after people in those generations had died.

What questions does this situation raise for anthropological researchers?

1. How does being a grandchild of someone with a particular teknonym help you identify other close relatives?
2. What happens to people's knowledge of their common kin ties once their great-grandparents die?
3. How might people be able to identify kin relations more easily if everyone used personal names rather than teknonyms?

🌱 **A Modern Balinese Family Attending a Ceremony.** Most members of this extended family live together in several households inside the same house yard.

(continued)

Thinking Like an Anthropologist (continued)

PART TWO: GENEALOGICAL AMNESIA IN AMERICAN FAMILIES

In the United States, naming practices also produce a systematic pattern of genealogical amnesia. One of the most obvious effects of genealogical amnesia comes from the practice that many women drop their maiden names when they marry. Until the 1970s taking the husband's surname was clearly the most typical pattern. What questions would you ask about genealogical amnesia in the United States as an anthropological researcher?

How Do Families Control Power and Wealth?

Whatever form of family we might find in a society, one of its key functions is controlling and managing its members' wealth. The most obvious way for a family, lineage, or clan group to control its wealth is by defining rights over the productive and reproductive abilities of its women and children, as well as defining the inheritance rights of family members when someone dies. We explore each of these issues in turn next.

Claiming a Bride

In the non-industrial societies anthropologists studied in the early and mid-twentieth century in Africa, South America, and the Pacific, it was clear that women provided much of the labor needed to plant, weed, and harvest food from their fields and gardens. Even though men performed the most active herding and hunting tasks, women often helped with gathering nuts, fruit, greens, and raw materials for houses, and with fishing. Women's labor is critical in these societies, and when a young woman marries, her family loses her efforts in raising or gathering food for the family.

Every person in such societies is valuable, so to compensate another clan for losing a person, the groom's family gives valuables to the bride's family in what has been called bride wealth, bride price payments, or simply **bride price.** Bride price compensates the woman's natal family for the loss of her productive and reproductive activities.

The patrilineal Zulu tribes of southern Africa, for example, traditionally used cattle for their bride price payments. When a young man had identified a young woman that he was interested in as a wife, his male relatives began negotiations about her bride price, which Zulu call *lobola.* These negotiations marked the beginning of the couple's engagement. Typically the man sought the assistance of male relatives in his patrilineage. These gifts from groom to father-in-law consist of a series of gifts, the first gift of several head of cattle occurring at the time of the marriage. Later the man gives gifts of cattle until the entire bride price has been given. Anthropologist Max Gluckman (1940) reported that the South African government viewed these multiple *lobola* payments as a practice that disrupted the flow of

- **Bride price or bride wealth.** Exchange of gifts or money to compensate another clan or family for the loss of one of its women along with her productive and reproductive abilities in marriage.

young men to the mines as laborers. It seems that these men wanted to stay in their villages working to assemble the cattle they needed and were not eager to set off as mine workers. The government plan was to limit *lobola* to eleven head of cattle, all of which should be paid at the time of marriage. This plan, together with a tax levied on each Zulu hut, forced young men to work in the mines but disrupted the normal pattern of marriage, since most wives stayed back in their husband's village and there was no opportunity for the man to build bonds with his father-in-law.

In some tribal societies, other kinds of valuables can be given as bridewealth, including wild game in some Amazon communities or pigs and shell valuables in many New Guinea societies (Figure 13.7). In other societies, a young man has to work for his wife's family for a year or more, performing what can be called bride service.

Recruiting the Kids

As with bride price payments aimed at paying for rights in women, child price payments are another kind of payment to a woman's family intended to buy rights in the woman's children. Such payments compensate the woman's family for a child who belongs to a different clan, and allow the father to recruit the child to his clan. This sort of transaction over children is most typical in societies with patrilineal clans, rather than in those with matrilineal clans, where the children belong to their mother's clan and typically live with her. In some societies, child price payments can be paid all at once, but the power of these transactions can best be understood in societies like the Daribi of the Highland Papua New Guinea, where payments may take place over many years. Anthropologist Roy Wagner (1967, 1969) described these gifts as countering the rights and claims of the child's uncle (mother's brother) over these children. This uncle could claim the child to his clan if the payments were not made. Because so many transactions between clans are about creating alliances, the ongoing series of payments preserve and perpetuate the relationship between child's father and the uncle. In this case, the payments in the form of gifts define and bind the two clans, just as they link the two men in an ongoing alliance. Both men get something from the relationship, including assistance from the other when needed.

🌱 **Figure 13.7 Bride price.** (Top) A Dinka man in east Africa readies his cattle for bride price exchange with his inlaws. (Bottom) Cash has replaced traditional shell valuables in many bride price payments in Papua New Guinea. (Photo © Irene Abdou Photography)

The Dowry in India: Providing a Financial Safety Net for a Bride

Another traditional form of marriage payment occurs in the highly stratified communities of India. Here, high caste families traditionally gave a **dowry** consisting of a large sum of money—or in kind gifts of livestock, furniture, or even electronics—to

● **Dowry.** A large sum of money or in-kind gifts given to a daughter to ensure her well-being in her husband's family.

Figure 13.8   Dowry in Modern India. (Top) A woman from Rajastan shows off part of her dowry. (Bottom) Women protest a woman's death in Jammu caused by problems with her dowry.

a daughter to ensure her well-being in her husband's family. Sometimes the dowry was given, at least in part, to the husband as a way of attracting a prosperous and hard-working husband. The Indian government outlawed the practice of dowry in 1961, but in many parts of the country the practice continues as before.

In recent years abuses of dowry have become common, reaching more than 3,000 incidents a year, attracting the attention of the Indian government, state governments, and international human rights groups. In these cases, members of the husband's family threaten the bride if more dowry is not forthcoming. In the most severe cases, the men's families have even killed the bride because her family would not contribute more dowry (Figure 13.8).

Controlling Family Wealth Through Inheritance

Families also control wealth, property, and power through rules of inheritance. The death of an individual can create a crisis in a family, because members have to decide how to redistribute land and whatever kinds of wealth that person may have held, which can create conflict. Rules of inheritance typically ensure an orderly process, and, more importantly, ensure that wealth and property stay in the family.

In Western countries, such rules have been codified in law for a long time. For example, centuries ago Great Britain acknowledged the right of primogeniture, in which the eldest son inherited a man's entire estate, including all lands and other wealth. Elder brothers might give some allowance to their younger brothers, but these sons had no claim to the estate and they often went into the Church, military, or migrated to distant lands. The goal of primogeniture was to preserve large landed estates together with the money and other wealth needed to maintain them.

Inheritance Rules in Non-industrial Societies

Inheritance rules also exist in small-scale non-industrial societies, in spite of the fact that many lack a formal legal code. In many of these societies the most valuable property is land, but it might also include livestock, locally recognized valuables, vegetables, and rights in people. Not surprisingly, when people die in these societies land and some forms of durable personal property are the most important things to be inherited. In tribal and chiefly societies land is typically controlled by clans or some other form of extended family group.

In any society, inheritance goes to legitimate heirs—typically the children of a socially recognized married couple. But marriage is such a complicated social institution that we should consider what motivates people to get married in the first place as well as the less obvious benefits that come to married people.

THINKING CRITICALLY ABOUT KINSHIP, MARRIAGE, AND THE FAMILY

Although most Americans get engaged thinking the upcoming marriage is about them as a couple, in fact, marriage brings together two sets of families and two sets of friends. Consider the most recent wedding you may have attended, or ask a friend or relative about a wedding they attended as a guest. Discuss who paid for different parts of the celebration (reception, officiant, wedding license, flowers, bridesmaids' dresses, groomsmen's tuxes, gifts to bridesmaids and groomsmen, rehearsal dinner, etc.). Now consider who should give gifts and who these gifts should be given to. How do the dollars and cents of a wedding outline the structure of American families and kin groups?

Why Do People Get Married?

For at least two centuries American pastors, priests, and rabbis have preached that sex is reserved for marriage; it is primarily for procreation. The reality of American life is that sexual behavior is not limited to married couples. The study *Sex in America* (Michael, Gagnon, Lauman, and Kolata 1994) found that, on average, married couples (together with unmarried couples who live together) have sex more often and more regularly than single people. But marriage is about a lot more than sex. In this section we explain why, as well as the diverse forms that marriage can take.

Why People Get Married

For most Americans, marriage should be about love and sex, and we take for granted our individual right to choose a marriage partner. But in most societies around the world marriage is about cultivating political and economic relations between families. In such contexts, a common belief is that marriage is too important to be left to the whims of an individual, and so accepted practice is for family members to choose an individual's marriage partner.

Marriage also provides social recognition of the ties between the couples, if not also their families, as well as social legitimacy to the children. The importance of public recognition partially helps explain why gay and lesbian marriage has become a key issue in the past decade in many societies, including the United States, Canada, Mexico, and Argentina. In places where gay marriage is not legalized, many couples have "commitment ceremonies" whose goal is to bring family members and friends together to publically acknowledge the relationship. In "Doing Fieldwork: Ellen Lewin on Studying Lesbian and Gay Commitment," we explore how so-called commitment ceremonies resemble and differ from mainstream wedding ceremonies in the United States.

Doing Fieldwork

Ellen Lewin on Studying Lesbian and Gay Commitment Ceremonies

CULTURAL ANTHROPOLOGIST ELLEN Lewin is a lesbian who had been in a long-term committed relationship with her partner. Some years into their relationship, the two decided to have a formal commitment ceremony. At the time, no state recognized any form of legal status for same-sex couples. In the mid-1990s Lewin noticed that across the country hundreds of other same-sex couples were holding commitment ceremonies, even though none of these relationships was recognized by any court. These were not legal ceremonies but a public recognition of their relationships.

She began a three-year study of these rituals to understand why these couples were performing ceremonies that had no legal implications whatsoever. Why were gay and lesbian couples, who had been marginalized by mainstream America for so long, adopting the rituals and ceremonies of those who had marginalized them?

Using participant-observation, Lewin observed these ceremonies and conducted open-ended interviews about the ceremonies of twenty-two male and thirty female couples. Her research challenged conventional anthropological methods, because Lewin was in a sense studying her own community. During interviews with couples planning their ceremonies, her informants sometimes relied on her as an "expert" on commitment ceremonies, because she had planned one herself. Throughout three years of research Lewin worked hard to be objective in her interviews, but she feels that having experienced her own commitment ceremony actually gave her insights that might have escaped other researchers.

Some ceremonies were religious services in churches or synagogues, while others were extremely secular. She also observed that some rites were structured to parallel or even mimic wedding ceremonies of the sort that straight couples might have. Yet others were organized almost defiantly in opposition to traditional American wedding ceremonies. Still other gay and lesbian couples objected to the whole idea of a commitment ceremony, arguing that holding such a ritual at all undermined the distinctiveness of being a lesbian or a gay man. She found that "no single lesbian or gay wedding is typical or exemplary." They take on many different forms and styles in ways that straight weddings do not. At the same time she concluded that each expresses many different sorts of symbolic messages simultaneously. All of the ceremonies she observed or studied were acts of accommodation to mainstream culture as much as they were simultaneously acts of resistance and rebellion.

Lewin (1998:44) contends that "same-sex weddings are cultural constructions grounded in a particular social, political, and historical context." A key part of this context at the time was the fact that gay marriage, civil unions, or even domestic partnerships were not recognized anywhere in the United States. These ceremonies drew on meanings from American weddings and common American notions about families, as well as meanings that come directly from the gay and lesbian counterculture. But these rites coopted these meanings, appropriating them for the participants' own personal and political agendas. The ceremonies derived meaning as much in opposition to images of gay promiscuity as they did by challenging straight ideas about family. Her analysis confirms what anthropologists working in exotic communities around the world have long observed: marriages and wedding ceremonies in particular are not just for the bridal couple; they offer powerful statements to the couple's social network.

Questions for Reflection

1. What benefits and disadvantages did Lewin have in being a lesbian anthropologist studying lesbian and gay commitment ceremonies?

2. What different problems might she have encountered if she had been a straight, married woman?

3. Since her commitment ceremony, a number of U.S. states have legalized same-sex marriage. How would this fact change Lewin's research if she conducted her study today?

A Lesbian Commitment Ceremony. Anthropologist Ellen Lewin studied commitment ceremonies for same-sex couples before same-sex marriage was legal in any state in the nation.

Weddings, of course, are important for straight couples as well, which is why so many young brides and their families spend so much time and money staging them. On the one hand, weddings proclaim to the world that the couple is united. But, on the other hand, the wedding ceremony brings the two families together in the same spot, where they acknowledge the couple as a unit.

Forms of Marriage

Just as we have seen the definition of marriage widening in some states and countries to include same-sex marriages, the tendency around the world has increasingly been to limit the number of partners to a couple. In many traditional societies in Africa, Asia, the Americas, and the Pacific, **polygamy** (or plural marriage) was far more common previously than it is today. The most common form of plural marriage was **polygyny**, in which one man is married simultaneously to two or more women. In Africa and Melanesia, having more than one wife indicates an important man with greater wealth, higher social status, or more importance in the community. From a woman's point of view, being in a polygynous marriage can mean that other wives provide support in conducting household duties, such as raising kids, cooking, and so on. But as these indigenous economies have been drawn into the global system, the number of men with two or more wives has declined, as it is increasingly considered too costly and too old fashioned (Figure 13.9).

The other form of plural marriage is **polyandry**, in which one woman has two or more husbands at one time. Few societies around the world are known to have allowed polyandry, and the best known are the Toda, one of the hill tribes in India (Rivers 1906; Dakowski 1990), and the Sherpas of Nepal, who formerly used polyandry to keep large estates from being divided into tiny estates (Ortner 1989). Among both the Todas and the Sherpas, a group of brothers marries the same woman, a practice known as fraternal polyandry that limits the tensions among co-husbands.

Some anthropologists suggest that polyandry is uncommon because of the dominance of men's roles over women's in most societies. Let's consider some of the power that families have over their members.

Sex, Love, and the Power of Families Over Young Couples

All societies around the world have rules about who can have sex with or get married to whom. Parents and other family members may object to certain possible partners, such as if a woman chooses a partner from the wrong socioeconomic, religious, educational, or ethnic background. And there are prohibitions against marriage with people who are too closely related.

The Incest Taboo

Many things can happen within a family, but the one thing that should not happen is marriage. The prohibition on sexual

- **Polygamy.** Any form of plural marriage.

- **Polygyny.** When a man is simultaneously married to more than one woman.

- **Polyandry.** When a woman has two or more husbands at one time.

Figure 13.9 Polygamy Is Largely in Decline Around the World. (Top) An image of a polygamous family in Ramallah in the early 20th century; most Palestinian men have one wife today. The so-called Jack-Mormons of Utah, Colorado, and Texas (bottom), who have broken away from the Mormon Church based in Salt Lake City, are the main exception in the United States and still practice polygyny.

● **Incest taboo.** The prohibition on sexual relations between close family members.

relations between close family members is generally called the **incest taboo**, and this taboo is as close to a universal feature of human societies as anything.

There are two well-known exceptions to the incest taboo, both of which ironically prove this taboo's generality: in ancient Egypt, during the reigns of the pharaohs, and in Hawai'i, before Europeans encountered the islands for the first time in 1778. In both societies ruling monarchs could engage in incest because they were considered living gods, who could only preserve the divine essence of their being by marrying a sibling.

For relationships beyond the nuclear family—such as marriage of cousins—societies vary in what they allow. In Africa, Southeast Asia, South America, Australia, and New Guinea, the incest taboo also includes prohibitions on marriage with some kinds of cousins, particularly in societies with a unilineal clan system. And in most clan-based societies the prohibition on marriage within the clan suggests that this extension of the incest taboo defines the boundaries of the clan, just as the boundaries of incest define the boundaries of the nuclear family.

Why Is There an Incest Taboo?

Social scientists have suggested two general explanations for the incest taboo. The most common is that incest leads to birth defects and the incest taboo prevents these birth defects. The main problem with this explanation is that in small scale societies only incest within the nuclear family, such as brother-sister pairings, leads to higher rates of birth defects. Even then, higher rates of defects does not mean every birth suffers defects. Within a small community of 300 or 500 individuals, the risk of birth defects from marriages between first cousins is not much different from random mating. Everyone in a small community is already interrelated and the odds of deleterious (harmful) gene combinations are effectively the same for marriage with a first cousin and for random pairings.

A second explanation, called the "Westermarck Effect," explains the incest taboo as a natural psychological revulsion toward marriage (or sex) with close relatives. First cousin marriage was common in many places and even in the United States—it is allowed in more than half of the states. For example, during the century or so before the American Revolution, a surprising number of marriages between first or second cousins were recorded, and it was considered an extremely appropriate match. Recently, evolutionary psychologists like Steven Pinker (1997) have adopted this explanation, arguing that natural selection has selected genes that cause us to feel little sexual attraction for people we have grown up with. There are three critiques of this evolutionary model as an explanation for the incest taboo: (1) no gene (or combination of genes) has been identified as linked to the proposed revulsion; (2) the range of relatives prohibited by the incest taboo varies too widely from society to society to be explained by selection; and (3) there is no reason to assume that the revulsion is the cause of the taboo, when it is equally probable that the incest taboo itself generates the psychological revulsion. That is to say, people are repulsed by sibling marriage because it violates the cultural rules of incest.

Both of these explanations assume that the incest taboo emerges from biology. But anthropologists have suggested that the incest taboo emerges from the context of ordinary life rather than from our biology. They point to the research of Melford Spiro (1958), an anthropologist who studied life in an Israeli kibbutz in the 1950s. Spiro found that the adolescents who lived together in large communal settings avoided marrying or even dating members of their communal group. There was no rule against marriage or sex within the group, but there simply was no sexual attraction because they thought of other members as siblings. This situation is not at all unlike what happens in American college co-ed dorms, where there is similar avoidance of sexual liaisons. Sexual relationships within the same dorm produce so many social complications for both parties that some contemporary college newspapers have warned their readers against the "hallway hookup" and "floor incest" (Sivo 2005).

Coed dorms are a concept that would have shocked most Americans fifty years ago, just as people were shocked by the impact that new methods of birth control had on sexual activity in the 1960s and 1970s. But technology is always changing, and reproductive technologies have changed in important ways over the past few decades, producing new situations for families to make sense of and creating new kinds of kin relations.

THINKING CRITICALLY ABOUT KINSHIP, MARRIAGE, AND THE FAMILY

Americans often think that marriage is about "Love." But marriage is also about economics. Being married and having a family cost money. Recent studies have determined that the average age at marriage in the United States has been rising for several decades as middle class incomes have declined. Discuss how the economics of modern American life help shape the decision to get married.

How Are Technological Changes Reshaping How People Think About Family?

In the 1960s, the birth control pill allowed women in Western countries like the United States, France, and Great Britain an unprecedented level of direct control over their sexuality. This technological development contributed to a so-called "sexual revolution" centered around the desire for "casual sex." At first the pill was available only to married women, but by the end of the 1970s it became available to single women in most of the United States as well. For all the entanglements of kinship discussed previously, the prospect of having a child does not facilitate casual sex!

By the 1980s, the technological cutting edge shifted away from efforts to prevent pregnancy to efforts to improve fertility and overcome infertility. In recent decades anthropologists interested in matters of kinship have become attuned to the fact that these new technological developments have begun to complicate people's understandings of kinship relations. We discuss how this might be in two contexts: in-vitro fertilization and surrogacy.

In Vitro Fertilization

People often talk about in vitro fertilization (IVF) as a way to produce "test-tube babies." The technique takes eggs from the mother or some other female donor and sperm from the father or a male donor. Fertilization can occur by incubating an egg and sperm in a Petri dish or, if the donor's sperm count is low, one sperm cell can be injected into the egg. After the embryos have reached the 6- to 8-cell stage they are implanted in the womb of the mother, where some of the embryos can implant in the uterus and lead to a successful pregnancy. Only 25% to 45% of all IVF attempts successfully produce pregnancy. But IVF has become an important procedure, accounting for nearly 1% of all American births annually (Elder and Dale 2000).

The first successful IVF was the birth of Louise Brown in 1978 in England. Since then the procedure has been used in more than 115,000 live births in the United States, creating a variety of new kinship relationships that people never had had to cope with before. For most couples the preferred situation was the mother's egg and father's sperm implanted into the mother, based on the belief that blood relations are the most important. But in situations where a man or woman cannot provide either sperm or an egg, other possibilities present themselves: a mother's egg, donor's sperm; donor's egg, father's sperm; donor's egg and sperm; and any of these in a surrogate uterus. The social relationships between the individuals involved in any of these scenarios do not transfer easily to categories like "mother" and "father," since who provides the biological material may differ from who raises the child or provides the womb to nurture it during pregnancy.

Surrogate Mothers and Sperm Donors

For British anthropologist Marilyn Strathern (1996) the new reproductive technologies offer insights into the ways that ordinary people understand kinship, as these new situations lead to litigation in the courts where families are being defined, constructed, and dismantled in innovative ways because suddenly there are new parties in the family: surrogate mothers, sperm donors, multiple men claiming to be fathers, and the like. As we have seen herein, both biology and social ties are important for creating links between parents and children. Adoption often separates biology and social ties, so that the biological parent has no social ties with the child and the adoptive parents have social ties but no biology. But the new reproductive technologies introduce new ambiguities into the biological facts.

Traditionally, conception always presented some possible ambiguity about biological paternity, since any number of men besides the husband may have had intercourse with a woman. Paternity tests were perceived as conclusive, but most scientists who work in such fields recognize that blood-typing or the more recent DNA tests are never fully reliable. Even when DNA tests indicate the husband as the biological father, his closest kin cannot always be excluded. And, of course, relatives of both the husband and wife are often socially present in the couple's life, making sexual contact between the wife and a brother-in-law possible.

The new reproductive technologies—where sperm donors, egg donors, and IVF are involved—introduce new ambiguities about who was the biological mother or even the biological father. Even eggs and semen from a married couple that are intended to be used for IVF can be inadvertently mixed up with specimens from other individuals before fertilization. And, some gay men wanting a child may request that their semen samples be mixed together intentionally so that one of the men is the biological father, but neither knows whether it is him or his partner. As Strathern suggests, such ambiguities challenge traditional notions that biology and social ties should work together to create kinship bonds between parents and children.

But the most important ambiguity has to do with surrogacy and sperm donors. A surrogate mother is a woman who agrees to have an embryo implanted in her womb. She carries the baby to term, and after the baby is born the child belongs to the couple who provided the embryo. Quite often, couples choose surrogate mothers when the wife is unable to bring a child to term. Surrogate mothers are rarely related genetically to the children they carry to term. But their body has nurtured the child for nine months, which constitutes some ambiguous link between the surrogate mother and the child. When this procedure was beginning to be common in the United States in the 1990s, for example, TV dramas and soap operas often centered their plots on the surrogate who had formed a bond with the fetus and did not want to give up the baby to the couple who had paid all of her expenses over the preceding nine months. Studies by anthropologists of surrogate mothers suggest that very few surrogates have any desire to keep the newborns (Ragoné 1996). Most see their role as quite separate from that of the child's mother; their job is to help unfortunate couples by carrying their babies to term, sometimes (but not always) for a fee.

It is not clear where these new technologies will go in the future, or how the courts will apportion rights to claims on the children of surrogacy, sperm and egg donors, and adoption. Rayna Rapp (1992), for example, has suggested that the next advances "in the study of reproduction will be made from inside a critique of the study of science." After several decades of viewing these new reproductive technologies as simple technological advances, it is becoming clear that parental rights are not about biology but about how people in different cultures choose to interpret and emphasize some biological claims over others. As we saw in some of the most traditional anthropological studies of bride price and child price payments, kinship, marriage, and the family are about claims on people. The courts and the sentiments of the public can easily give some claims more importance than others.

THINKING CRITICALLY ABOUT KINSHIP, MARRIAGE, AND THE FAMILY

Americans have strong feelings that parents have rights over their children, where they can go, what they can participate in, whether they should get vaccines, and so forth. Consider how these parental rights become less clear-cut under the following conditions: (a) the parents have adopted a child, but the birth parents are in the same community, (b) the parents have given up their child for adoption, and they know the family the child lives with, (c) the couple's newborn is the result of the mother's egg and an anonymous sperm donor, who has learned he is the biological father, and (d) the egg was from an anonymous donor, the sperm from the father, and the child was carried to term by a surrogate mother.

Conclusion

Although the tendency in our own culture—if not also the Mexican *telenovela* that opens this chapter—emphasizes that kinship and family are primarily matters of blood relationships, anthropologists view the matter rather differently, having seen the great variety of ways different societies construct families and kinship relations. Not only are families imbued with social and cultural expectations, but the very biological acts of sexual intercourse to conceive children are currently being revised with the rise of new reproductive technologies.

Families are at the heart of most systems of social relationship, although the Israeli kibutzim suggest that communal living situations can in some ways even overwhelm this most basic social unit. In non-industrial societies, families are vitally important to most aspects of social life. But industrialization has put pressure on large families and encouraged individual nuclear families rather than large, unwieldy extended families and clans. And families are important to individuals even when, as in our society, the active family units are pared down to parents and a small number of children.

But no matter how dazzling the diverse kinds of families we might find in different societies, whether matrilineal lineages, patrilineal clans, nuclear families, or some other social form, these ways of understanding and working with relatives seem inherently natural. In nearly every society, they look to their families as one of the most natural and biologically based institutions. Just as we saw in the previous chapter, where ideas of sex and gender seem inherently natural, so too do the families around which we structure our lives.

KEY TERMS

Bride price   p. 328

Clan   p. 321

Cognatic   p. 323

Corporate groups
    p. 321

Dowry   p. 329

Exogamous   p. 321

Extended families   p. 321

Genealogical amnesia
    p. 325

Incest taboo   p. 334

Kinship   p. 319

Kinship chart   p. 320

Lineage   p. 322

Matrilineal   p. 322

Natal family   p. 319

Nuclear family   p. 320

Patrilineal   p. 322

Polyandry   p. 333

Polygamy   p. 333

Polygyny   p. 333

Teknonymy   p. 325

Unilineal   p. 322

Reviewing the Chapter

Chapter Section	What We Know	To Be Resolved
What Are Families, and How Are They Structured in Different Societies?	All societies change their understandings of family, kinship, and social relationship as their societies adapt to new external factors.	It is impossible to predict how any society's system of kinship, marriage, and the family will change without understanding the other social, economic, environmental, and political changes in that society.

How Do Families Control Power and Wealth?	Kin relationships are about social ties between individuals as much as they are about biological ties. All societies have developed ways of ensuring that the family group has some control over collective resources or the labor of its members.	Many anthropologists consider social and cultural factors, such as the desire to control wealth or to exercise power over its members, to be more decisive in explaining how and why people have kinship relations. Yet some insist that there is a biological basis to kin relations, such as those who promote the idea that the incest taboo is biologically based.
Why Do People Get Married?	Marriage can take on many diverse forms, and our own cultural model of basing marriage on love and sex is not important to all societies, especially those in which marriage is about creating social, economic, and political ties with other groups.	Although we know that economics has an impact on who gets married and who does not, it is not clear what the long-term impact of delayed marriage or the growing number of unmarried couples with children will be.
How Are Technological Changes Reshaping How People Think About Family?	Although new reproductive technologies are changing the biological relationships in families, they are not having much impact on the social roles within families, however they become formed.	It is unclear how new reproductive technologies will change how people think of the expectations, relationships, and meanings of kinship.

Readings

The earliest appreciation of the range of variation among the world's societies was published in 1871 by Lewis Henry Morgan, who is otherwise best known for his study of Iroquois. For a view into how kinship studies became a central problem for anthropologists, see Thomas Trautmann's *Lewis Henry Morgan and the Invention of Kinship* (Lincoln: University of Nebraska Press, 2008).

Detailed studies of kinship and social organization did not really begin to appear until the functionalist British school of social anthropology had emerged in the 1920s. Many students from this theoretical school conducted field research in the British colonies in Africa. The classic collection of ethnographic studies is the volume edited by A. R. Radcliffe-Brown and Daryl Forde, *African Systems of Kinship and Marriage* (London: Oxford University Press, 1950). Although the essays remain valid as detailed descriptions of kinship in different tribal groups, the most important essay is Radcliff-Brown's extended discussion, which lays out what was understood of kinship studies at the time.

Two influential texts by American anthropologists on the cultural dynamics of kinship in the United States argue that kinship is never exclusively about biology. These include David Schneider's book *American Kinship: A Cultural Account* (Englewood Cliffs, NJ: Prentice-Hall, 1968), which explores how the study of kinship can reveal fundamental cultural and symbolic meanings Americans hold, and the more recent study by Carol Stack, *All Our Kin* (New York: Basic Books, 1997), which explores the dynamism and fluidity of "family" relations among urban African Americans.

Research on the cultural dimensions of reproductive technologies began exploding during the 1990s. One of the central texts in this vein is Faye Ginsburg and Rayna Rapp's edited volume *Conceiving the New World Order: The Global Politics of Reproduction* (Berkeley: University of California Press, 1995).

Religion
Ritual and Belief

IT WAS THE SOUTH, in the summer of 1965, the darkest days of the civil rights movement in America. The previous year, Ku Klux Klansmen, members of a white supremacist group, had murdered three voting-rights activists in Mississippi. In March the black Baptist civil rights leader Reverend Dr. Martin Luther King, Jr. had called on "clergy of all faiths . . . to join me in Selma for a ministers' march to Montgomery." Hundreds marched, but Alabama State Troopers launched an unprovoked attack on protesters. Two weeks later a white Alabama man slew another civil rights worker. During the summer President Lyndon Johnson signed into law the Voting Rights Act of 1965, but officials in Lowndes County, Alabama, situated between Selma and Montgomery, refused to register any of their non-white citizens to vote, as did those in many other southern counties with large black majorities,

Into this cauldron of politics, fear, and religion came twenty-six-year-old white seminary student Jonathan Daniels of Keene, New Hampshire. Jon had marched through Lowndes County with Rev. King in March 1965, and he spent the summer in Lowndes County protesting racial discrimination and trying to register black voters. In August he participated in a demonstration with Father Richard Morrisroe, a young, white Catholic priest from Chicago, and twenty-seven other activists. All of them were arrested and held for a week in the Lowndes

---

Selma to Montgomery March. The Reverend Dr. Martin Luther King, Jr., drew heavily on religious symbols from the biblical Book of Exodus in his civil rights struggles in 1965. Alabama State Troopers, who attacked protestors during the march, also felt religious conviction in their actions.

County Jail in the quiet little town of Hayneville. After six days, the entire group was released on their own recognizance.

Outside, it was hot and dusty, so Jon and Father Morrisroe set off down the street with two young black women working with the Student Nonviolent Coordinating Committee (SNCC), Ruby Sales and Joyce Bailey, to buy soft drinks at the only store in town that regularly served black customers. As Jon opened the screen door, Special Deputy Sheriff Tom Coleman confronted him, holding a 12-guage shotgun. Coleman shouted, "This store is closed. Get off this goddam property before I blow your goddam brains out, you black bastards." With that he aimed his gun at Ruby Sales. Seeing what was happening, Jon pushed Ruby to the ground and moved between her and the gun. Coleman fired at point-blank range. The blast threw Jon out the door and into the street, killing him instantly. Morrisroe grabbed Joyce's hand and ran down the street with her, as Coleman shot him in the back, wounding him critically. Left behind on the ground, Ruby now caught up with Joyce, grabbed her by the hand, and ran for cover. News accounts reported that a few minutes after the shooting, Coleman called the Alabama Director of Public Safety to say, "I just shot two preachers. Get on down here."

This incident arose because of a set of conflicting beliefs—those that motivated Tom Coleman versus those that motivated Jon Daniels. Today, we may find Coleman's prejudicial belief in the so-called "racial" inferiority of blacks even more difficult to understand than Daniels's religiously inspired altruism. Nevertheless, the bigger issue here is how we make sense of the existence of such different beliefs. It leads us to focus on the phenomenon of beliefs and behaviors, which can vary so radically.

At the heart of anthropology's approach to belief and religion is the question: *Why do people believe things that others consider wrong?* Embedded in this broader question are the following problems, around which this chapter is organized:

How should we understand religion and religious beliefs?

What forms does religion take?

How do rituals work?

How is religion linked to political and social action?

Over the past century anthropologists have come to realize that religious beliefs offer people a roadmap for their behavior: how they should live and how they should understand other people's behaviors, actions, and ideas. At their very heart, religious beliefs create meaning for people through the use of powerful rituals and religious symbols, all of which we discuss in greater depth in this chapter.

How Should We Understand Religion and Religious Beliefs?

Western intellectuals and social scientists have historically found the subject of religion problematic. When scholars in the nineteenth century confronted peoples around the world who held mystical views, most considered these ideas non-scientific mumbo-jumbo. Reinforced by the presence of simple technologies, limited clothing, and simpler ways of life, the existence of what seemed like irrational religious beliefs reinforced the idea that these people were of limited intellectual capacity. But by the 1870s, when anthropology was emerging as an academic discipline, scholars began to look systematically for explanations and theories that would help them understand religious beliefs. Anthropologists came to recognize the cultural importance of religious beliefs early, although theories differed on how to make sense of them.

In this section we consider four different versions or definitions of religion suggested by anthropologists, several of which are still common today. We begin with one of the earliest explanations of religion, offered by British anthropologist Edward Burnett Tylor in 1871. Then we consider two definitions suggested by prominent American anthropologists nearly a century later. Anthony F. C. Wallace suggested that religion concerned "beliefs and rituals concerned with supernatural beings, powers, and forces" (Wallace 1966:5). About the same time, Clifford Geertz (1966) offered a very different definition of religion, suggesting that religion was a system of symbols that made people believe in the reality of these supernatural entities and the moral codes associated with them. Finally, we suggest our own approach to religion that builds on all of the others. In our view, the most effective way to think of religion is that it is a symbolic system that is socially enacted through rituals and other aspects of social life.

Understanding Religion version 1.0: Edward B. Tylor and Belief in Spirits

To make sense of the exotic religious beliefs of non-Western cultures, the British anthropologist Sir Edward B. Tylor (1871) suggested that religion had to do with belief in spiritual beings. For him, primitive religions were based on a fundamental error in thinking. He reasoned that people in all societies had dreams, but the so-called primitive peoples had misinterpreted their dreams as reality, transforming the characters in their dreams into souls or spirits. Tylor called such beliefs in spirits **animism**, which refers to the belief that inanimate objects such as trees, rocks, cliffs, hills, and rivers were animated by spiritual forces or beings. For him the idea that trees and rocks might have souls, or that carved images contained spirits, were just other examples of this same "primitive" misunderstanding. Tylor also reasoned that as societies evolved and became more complex, the supernatural beings they believed in became more complex as well: spirits gave way to demigods and mythical heroes, which gave way to the gods and goddesses of the ancient Greeks and Romans. Finally, these many gods gave way to a single, all-powerful God—which would eventually, in his secular mind, yield to science.

- **Animism.** An early theory that primitive peoples believed which holds that inanimate objects such as trees, rocks, cliffs, hills, and rivers were animated by spiritual forces or beings.

Although many anthropologists later came to reject Tylor's evolutionary theories, his basic approach remained influential in anthropology for many decades. Some influential scholars, like Sir James Fraser, suggested that ideas about magic had predated the idea of souls and spirits, but there was no more evidence for magic as the origin of religious ideas than for dreams. By the Second World War, anthropologists in Great Britain were combining the two theories, writing of "magico-religious" ideas.

Understanding Religion version 2.0: Anthony F. C. Wallace on Supernatural Beings, Powers, and Forces

By the 1950s anthropologists in the United States had long abandoned the idea that American Indians and other non-Western peoples were as primitive as their British counterparts believed. Paul Radin, for example, had published *Primitive Man as Philosopher* (1927) in which he argued that there was nothing simple-minded in the myths, legends, and religious practices of tribal peoples. When American anthropologists began to look at how Indian religions were changing in the context of white expansion and domination, they saw systematic shifts in Indian thinking to make sense of changing times (Figure 14.1).

One of the major figures of this period was Anthony F. C. Wallace, who had studied religious change among the Seneca, one of the Iroquois tribes in upstate New York (1956, 1970). For Wallace, religious change could be observed most easily in the changing religious ceremonies and **rituals** (stylized performances involving symbols that are associated with social, political, and religious activities). But he recognized that rituals only made sense in terms of religious beliefs. His definition of religion became standard in anthropology because it linked beliefs with rituals: "beliefs and rituals concerned with supernatural beings, powers, and forces" (Wallace 1966:5).

- **Rituals.** Stylized performances involving symbols that are associated with social, political, and religious activities.

At the core of Wallace's definition of religion was belief in the supernatural. But in surveying societies around the world, he recognized that some peoples believed in gods or spirits, while others, like the ancient Hawaiians, were concerned with much more amorphous powers and forces that anthropologists had come to call **mana**, which can be understood as raw supernatural power. Just touching things—such as a possession of the chief or even a chief's person—permeated with *mana* could cause sickness or death for any commoner. High-ranking chiefs, whose bodies were believed to possess *mana,* could unintentionally cause harm to any commoner who touched the royal body or who sat at a level higher than that of the chief (Figure 14.2). These ideas concerned the supernatural but were not personalized as spirits, demons, or gods. Ultimately, Wallace grouped all forms of the supernatural together.

- *Mana.* A belief that sacred power inheres in certain high-ranking people, sacred spaces, and objects.

This approach to religious beliefs and behavior bounded the field of religion in ways that fit comfortably with traditional European and American views, which also emphasized the supernatural. But Wallace's definition has several limitations, one of these being that it tended to be static, offering little or no direction for understanding how or why religious ideas and practices are changing. If a society practices some tribal religion but converted to Christianity, Islam, or Buddhism, Wallace's definition could help us document what had changed, but little else. It also could not tell us what difference these changed beliefs make for real people's lives. Moreover, this sense of religion tended to depict deeply religious people and groups as intellectually limited. The biggest failing in Wallace's definition is that it does not explain why people hold onto their religious beliefs and practices with such passion, a limitation that was overcome when anthropologists began understanding religion as based on symbols.

Figure 14.1   The Ghost Dance. The Ghost Dance among the Sioux in 1891 was an innovative religious movement among various tribes in the Great Plains. It was the Sioux's attempt to recover self-respect and control over traditional resources through ritual, but it led to disastrous consequences at Wounded Knee when U.S. Army soldiers misinterpreted the ritual and killed 150 Lakota Sioux.

Figure 14.2 Hawaiian Temple Complex (Heiau) at Kealakekua Bay on Hawai'i's Big Island. This religious center possessed *mana* ("supernatural power"). *Mana* attached to all sacred sites, to persons of noble descent, to ritual carvings of the gods, and to anything the king or nobles touched. For commoners it was dangerous, even deadly, to violate a taboo, touch something with *mana*, or even walk on sacred ground.

Understanding Religion version 3.0: Religion as a System of Symbols

Unsatisfied with Wallace's sense of religion as simply belief in the supernatural, the American cultural anthropologist Clifford Geertz (1966) proposed another kind of definition of religion that could help explain why beliefs are deeply held and motivational, even to the point of negating one's own personal interest as we saw with the example of Jonathan Daniels and Tom Coleman. Geertz argued that religion was a cultural system, or as he put it a "system of symbols." It consisted of five elements:

> Religion is (1) a system of symbols which act to (2) establish powerful, pervasive, and long-lasting moods and motivations in men by (3) formulating conceptions of a general order of existence and (4) clothing these conceptions with such an aura of factuality that (5) the moods and motivations seem uniquely realistic. (1966:4)

This definition has several key features, but most important is that it centers on symbols that seem intensely real and factual. For example, the central symbol in Christianity generally is the most improbable, the notion that after his execution Christ rose from the dead (called the resurrection). Likely or not, hundreds of millions of people around the world accept the resurrection as an historical fact.

Furthermore, the systems of meaning that these symbols generate can create a sense of moral purpose or meaning in people's lives and move them to action. These conceptualizations of the world offer a set of unquestioned assumptions about the world and how it works, called a **worldview**. The notion of culture adopted in this textbook ultimately derives from this understanding of religion as a cultural system. So when we suggest that culture is about symbolic processes that make the artificial and humanly constructed seem natural, we are arguing that culture consists of symbols that are created and given meaning by social life, not just in religious contexts. People's understandings of the world provided by these symbols, like Geertz's religion, seem

● **Worldview.** A general approach to or set of shared unquestioned assumptions about the world and how it works.

uniquely realistic and cloaked in an aura of factuality; the world seems uniquely natural. The symbols describe a "model of" how the world is, as they simultaneously depict a "model for" how the world (morally) should be.

Most anthropologists continue to find Geertz's approach to religion useful. Following Geertz, they have tried to understand the worldview and ethos of a religion, adopting what is often called an **interpretive approach,** a style of analysis that looks at the underlying symbolic and cultural interconnections within a society.

In spite of its strengths, Geertz's explanation does have limitations. Some scholars, for example, have argued that Geertz's definition of religion as a cultural system assumes that people have a basic need for meaning and for making sense of the world, which may or may not be the case (Frankenberry and Penner 1999). Furthermore, anthropologist Talal Asad (1993) has argued that Geertz's definition of religion as a cultural system does not adequately distinguish religion from the domains of science, aesthetics, common sense, or law. Asad has gone further in his criticism, questioning whether we can ever fully understand the emotions people feel during religious experiences, whether rituals, prayers, or social action—all of which are assumed by Geertz's definition (Asad 1993). Still others have charged that it does not pay adequate attention to how institutions and power relations within a society create religious meaning (Eickelman and Piscatori 1996; Foucault 1999).

Perhaps the most significant limitation of Geertz's strategy for understanding religious phenomena is that his definition of religion reads as if he is describing a lone believer sitting quietly surrounded only by his own moods and thoughts as company. But a key feature of religious beliefs and behavior is that they are rooted in social behavior and social action (Figure 14.3). Beliefs get most of their power from being socially enacted repeatedly through rituals and other religious behaviors. By acting together, the community of believers begins to accept the group's symbolic interpretations of the world as if they were tangible, authentic, and real rather than merely interpretation.

- **Interpretive approach.** A kind of analysis that interprets the underlying symbolic and cultural interconnections within a society.

Understanding Religion version 4.0: Religion as a System of Social Action

In July 2013 three million Brazilians turned out to celebrate mass with Pope Francis, the first Roman Catholic Pope from Latin America. In this massive public ritual we can see that religion for these millions is important, but it is also an intensely exciting

Figure 14.3   Expressing Religiosity. Many religious rituals around the world are energetic and boisterous rather than somber, sedate, and pensive as Americans sometimes assume. On the left is a West African ritual performance that brings the Gods into contact with the community, and on the right a modern mega-church in America in which participants take on a vibrant role in the service.

and social experience. It is a very different experience from a single nun on retreat praying quietly by herself for days at a time, periodically eating at a communal meal with other nuns, but with no one speaking. Both experiences are "religious" in that they deal with worshipers' understandings of the world and how important the supernatural power of God is in people's lives. But both religious experiences draw on the social context—being among three million worshipers in Rio and with oneself in the other. Both experiences get their power from being so different from ordinary daily life.

The social experience of religious practice is what makes the beliefs, the organization of religion in daily life, and the religious symbols have meaning for every person present. Most people do not have regular contact with the supernatural. Neither God nor Jesus—to continue with this pair of Catholic ritual experiences—regularly appears in person to most of the congregants in Rio or to the nuns who devote their lives to the church. But the personal meaning they attach to the importance of the intense experiences of the Pope's public mass or the private prayers reinforces for them individually and communally that God and Jesus are real and present in their lives.

Thus, when we speak of religion in this book we feel that **religion** is a symbolic system that is socially enacted through rituals and other aspects of social life. This definition implies several elements that earlier scholars have emphasized:

- **Religion.** A symbolic system that is socially enacted through rituals and other aspects of social life.

1. The existence of things more powerful than human beings. Although in many societies it takes the form of some supernatural force, we prefer to think of it as a worldview or cosmology that situates the place of human beings in the universe.
2. Beliefs and behaviors surround, support, and promote the acceptance that those things more powerful than humans actually exist.
3. Symbols that make these beliefs and behaviors seem both intense and genuine.
4. Social settings, usually involving important rituals, that people share while experiencing the power of these symbols of belief.

The result of these four elements is what we think of as religion. Armed with this sense of religion, let us apply this understanding of religion to one of the great problems of meaning of our time, suicidal bomber attacks: Why do people strap on bombs or board airplanes intending to kill themselves along with many other people?

Understanding Suicide Bomber Attacks

The recent rise of suicide bombings in Iraq, Israel, Afghanistan, and other countries in the Middle East poses a special problem of meaning for many of us: How can people willingly kill themselves, especially in the name of religion? Such ideas are unthinkable to most Americans. Christian and Jewish Americans have long seen suicide as a mortal sin, sometimes even refusing to bury anyone who has committed suicide in consecrated cemeteries. Nowadays, nearly all Americans tend to interpret suicide as evidence that an individual has severe psychological problems. But as anthropologists, we strive to make sense of how a particular cultural context and belief system make such actions meaningful for the persons involved.

Reframing 9/11

A similar problem of meaning was brought home to Americans on September 11, 2001, when nineteen Arab hijackers commandeered four airplanes and crashed them into the World Trade Center, the Pentagon, and a field in Pennsylvania, killing more than 3,000 people as well as themselves (Figure 14.4). President George W. Bush's first official words about the terrorist attack helped define the event for the nation: "Freedom

Figure 14.4   A Problem of Meaning. The terrorist attacks on the United States of September 11, 2001, posed a problem of meaning for Americans: How could anyone kill themselves, just to cause others harm, in the name of religion?

itself was attacked this morning by a faceless coward." Later the same evening, in an address to the nation, the president redefined the event using a different moral language: "Thousands of lives were suddenly ended by evil, despicable acts of terror." In the weeks following the attacks, Bush repeatedly referred to the hijackers as "the evil ones" or "evildoers," using a moral language that pitted good against evil. The president's use of such phrasing was guaranteed to rally public support across the United States, and it worked.

But referring to the 9/11 hijackers as "evildoers" does not help us to understand why they did what they did. One doubts that any of these hijackers thought of themselves as doing evil, and as we have suggested throughout this book, to understand cultural behavior requires a culturally relative approach. "Evil" acts are essentially irrational acts; they make no sense. "Cowardly" acts can only be explained through fear, which is also irrational. The hijackers' actions were carefully planned and deftly coordinated; the attacks do not look like wild and irrational acts. And the fact that the hijackers were willing to die for their beliefs hardly seems cowardly, no matter how wrong the authors of this book and other Americans may feel these acts were. Nevertheless, we have to reframe 9/11 by seeking to understand the specific beliefs and social contexts that produced it.

Situating Al Qaeda in Its Cultural and Religious Context

The key to understanding these acts is that the nineteen terrorists were part of a larger social group, called Al-Qaeda (al-**kay**-dah), whose members shared a certain model for how the world should be, based on religious meanings, values, and actions. They trained under the leadership of Osama bin Laden, a Saudi Arabian who had set up the Al-Qaeda network to wage a **holy struggle** (or *jihad*, in Arabic) against those perceived as oppressing Muslims. Bin Laden's version of Islam is called Wahhabism [wah-**hawb**-ism], an especially conservative reading of Muslim texts and values. Wahhabism is especially critical of the Saudi royal family for its perceived materialism, corruption, and close ties to the West, especially the United States.

Bin Laden's Al-Qaeda developed a strident and radical Islamic ideology, attracting thousands of unemployed Muslim men to training camps in Afghanistan. In these camps Al-Qaeda took on its social character, as individuals from across the Arab world trained, ate, and exercised together (Figure 14.5). Although bin Laden had inherited great wealth from his industrialist father, he lived the simple life of an ascetic, a symbolically loaded image that stood in stark contrast to the luxury of the Saudi royal family.

In Islam *jihad* means "struggle," such as the personal struggles anyone confronts trying to follow Islam's rules for proper, moral living. For example, during the holy

- **Holy struggle.** A conflict—often political or social—that believers see as justified by doing God's work.

Figure 14.5 Creating Meaning Through Social Action. Osama bin Laden with recruits at an Al-Qaeda terrorist camp in Afghanistan. Religious movements get power from the social support, friendship, and comradeship of their members.

month of Ramadan many Muslims "struggle" to fast (not eating or smoking) from before sunrise until sunset. But *jihad* can also mean struggle against non-believers. Images of the Prophet Muhammad's struggle against non-believers trying to kill him in the Quran mimicked bin Laden's own struggle against Saudi royals and provided each with a model of how the world actually was.

Drawing upon such religious imagery in a context where young men spent months in training and talking about little else, bin Laden created a community in which these values and ideas made sense. This community offered a *model of* the world as well as a *model for* how the world should be, and then rooted those beliefs in social action involving guerilla attacks on their enemies. For many hundreds of young Muslim men, participation in the struggle against what they saw as the evil in the West gave meaning to their lives and even led them to willingly sacrifice their own lives to achieve these goals. By creating a social world in which sacrifice strengthened good and righteous acts, bin Laden was able to construct a world where political, religious, and social action were one, a topic we turn to later.

But before considering how religious beliefs and behaviors are linked to social action in the world, it is necessary to turn to another major preoccupation of anthropology of religion, the different forms that religion takes around the world.

● ●

THINKING CRITICALLY ABOUT RELIGION

Consider how each of the four definitions or understandings of religion would explain why a religious cult like the Jim Jones cult in Guyana or the early Mormons in Nauvoo—where they were attacked by non-Mormons—emerged. Alternatively, use these four explanations or definitions to interpret local reaction in your own community toward people with widely different religions.

● ●

What Forms Does Religion Take?

Early anthropologists like Edward B. Tylor largely saw all "primitive" societies as having a "primitive" religion. While anthropologists today reject the notion that some peoples are more "primitive" and others more civilized, it is clear that societies with simple technologies and small populations traditionally had very different religions from those that have formed states with centralized governments and more sophisticated technologies. But there is no evidence that one form inevitably evolves into another as the early anthropologists believed.

The variety of human religions that exists seems to correspond to the kinds of social orders that exist in different scales of society. Societies with small populations, for example, developed few governmental institutions larger than the family, clan, or village, and their religious institutions were typically focused on these same primary institutions. Let us begin by considering clan-based religions and totemism common in small-scale societies, and then turn to religions in larger-scale and socially stratified societies, like polytheism, monotheism, and world religions.

Clan Spirits and Clan Identities in New Guinea

In their social organizations, nearly all New Guinea societies are organized around families and groups of families that belong to the same clan, and these clans are typically associated with particular kinds of spirits. The Ningerum of Papua New Guinea, for example, who have a very low population density of seven to fifteen people per square mile, are concerned with various clan spirits that inhabit their traditional clan lands. These clan spirits have a full range of human emotions, but they become dangerous when they get jealous or angry, whereupon they can cause sickness or even death to people from other clans or even among the children and elders of their own clans. When they are happy and well attended to by the living with gifts of food, especially pork, they bring good harvest in the gardens, success in hunting, and healthy, prosperous families. Conceptually, Ningerum distinguish between various kinds of bush spirits and water spirits associated with particular places on the clan's land, on the one hand, and ghosts of dead members of the clan, on the other. All of their rituals, aside from a few specific healing rites, emphasize dealing with all of these clan-based spirits, and at major feasts pigs are sacrificed to these spirits to honor them with a bit of pork and other gifts made to them.

Among the Elema and Purari tribes of the Papuan Gulf the population densities are much higher, with large villages that traditionally numbered as high as three or four thousand people, larger than all of the Ningerum villages combined. Each village had several large longhouses, where men lived with their brothers and sons in rooms belonging to particular clans or subclans. And on the back wall the men hung a number of carved and painted boards with designs that belonged exclusively to their clan. Traditionally, people believed that their clan spirits lived in the carved boards, so they made offerings in the form of skulls of pigs, crocodiles, and other game from their clan territories to ensure spirits did not cause sickness among clan members. In addition, these clan and subclan groups had various dances at initiation rituals, and the dance costumes depicted various animals that were associated with the particular clan such as crocodiles and the small lizard known as a gecko (Figure 14.6). The systems of totems that are absent among the Ningerum are clearly present in a very simple way among the Elema and Purari tribes.

Figure 14.6   Eharo Mask From Karama Village, Gulf Province, Collected About 1885. The design features the face of a gecko on the body of the mask, and the body and tail extend upward above the face. A pair of "arms" and "legs" are on the left and right of the body, while the tale extends to the top of the mask. Rattan covered with bark cloth, painted with traditional pigments in red, black, and white. The gecko was a totemic emblem for one of the clans in the village, and this mask would have been worn along with ten or more other masks in the same design by men from the gecko clan. (Hood Museum of Art, Dartmouth College, Hanover, New Hampshire)

Totemism in North America

Early anthropologists studying American Indian societies observed that people were identified with particular animals, often claiming to be descended from these animals. These symbols indicated their clans, lineages, tribes, or other social groups with emblems, usually animals, plants, places, and geographic or meteorological features. Anthropologists usually refer to these emblems as totems, and **totemism** as the system of thought that associates particular social groups with specific animal or plant

● **Totemism.** A system of thought that associates particular social groups with specific animal or plant species called "totems" as an emblem.

Figure 14.7   Chiefly Totems. Totemic images identified with the clan and social position of a Kwakiutl chief on Vancouver Island, British Columbia. The main images on the two poles are eagles; other elements associated with the eagle moiety are grizzly bears. The figure at the bottom of the left pole holds a ceremonial copper plaque, suggesting the importance of the chief. These poles capture the social identity, the social position of the chief, and his great accomplishments, all expressed through the carved memorial pole.

species. Totems help create social cohesiveness by stressing group identity, focusing group and private rituals on totems. Some Native American societies simultaneously employed color symbolism, directional symbols, and species as totems. Until the 1920s anthropologists interpreted totemism as evidence of a group's limited intellectual capacity, since people could not possibly be descended from eagles, wolves, or pythons.

Anthropologist Ralph Linton (1924) reported that Americans in the military during the First World War adopted a similar reverential attitude toward emblems like the rainbow (for the 42nd or Rainbow Division) without indicating any psychological problems. Of course, in American culture, this phenomenon is not unique to the military and it is widespread, especially with sports teams named after animals or a particular social group. Fans and players alike typically identify with these totemic emblems, sometimes enacting behaviors that everyone understands as symbolic of the animal or social category of the team emblem, such as the Atlanta Braves tomahawk chop. These are all examples of American totemism, all of which cultivate a sense of belonging to a social order larger than oneself.

Unlike American totemism, however, which is largely secular in orientation, traditional tribal societies usually understood themselves to be related to the totemic animal in some supernatural way. Along the Northwest Coast of North America, for example, the Native society is divided into two halves (anthropologists call these halves "moieties"). One belongs to the Eagle totem, while the other belongs to the Raven totem (Figure 14.7). Within these moieties, each clan is identified with other totems, such as the salmon, the frog, the brown bear, and so on. These animals were also thought to have a special spiritual connection to the members of their social groups and appeared prominently in the origin myths of each clan. Native peoples carved these totems on memorial totem poles, painted them on clan houses, and decorated their blankets with them. In this way, the totems not only marked the sociopolitical order of clans within a village, but through ceremonies and myths they linked people with the supernatural realm.

Shamanism and Ecstatic Religious Experiences

As early as the sixteenth century, European travelers from Russia and central Europe encountered tribes in Siberia whose religious rituals consisted of spiritual leaders called **shamans,** religious leaders who communicate the needs of the living with the spirit world, usually through some form of ritual trance or other altered state of consciousness. These specialists were not political leaders but focused on healing and ensuring the health and prosperity of the community using drum rituals to connect with the spirits. Anthropologists were initially interested in these Siberian shamans because they represented a form of belief in spirits without the particularly special role in a social hierarchy. More recently, anthropologists have focused on the role of **trance** (a semi-conscious state typically brought on by hypnosis, ritual drumming and singing, or hallucinogenic drugs like mescaline or peyote) as an altered psychological state. The shaman's trance can be viewed as an altered state of consciousness that in some societies allows them to do difficult feats that would be impossible in normal circumstances, such as chewing glass or possessing great strength.

- **Shaman.** A religious leader who communicates the needs of the living with the spirit world, usually through some form of ritual trance or other altered state of consciousness.

- **Trance.** A semi-conscious state typically brought on by hypnosis, ritual drumming, and singing, or hallucinogenic drugs like mescaline or peyote.

When viewed in this light, shamanism is an especially widespread phenomenon found in one form or another on all continents, but especially North and South America, Africa, and Asia. The details of these shamanic traditions vary widely around the world, but they are often associated with small-scale societies with more or less egalitarian political structures. Anthropologist Napoleon Chagnon and Timothy Asch's 1973 film *Magical Death* is one of the best known examples of shamanic healing. In this film the Yanomamo shaman heals his family by ingesting hallucinogenic snuff made from a local plant. As in many shamanic traditions, this shaman is assisted by his **spirit familiar** (a spirit that has developed a close bond with the shaman), who helps him see other spirits and heal his children.

The importance of such altered states of consciousness was also explored by anthropologist Barbara G. Myerhoff's (1974) study of the peyote religion of the Huichol [**wee**-choal] Indians of northern Mexico. Myerhoff's key finding is that the rituals of Huichol shamans, including the ritualized hunt for peyote in the Mexican desert, give meaning to the social order of these people. In societies more familiar to Americans, such as some Pentecostal and charismatic Christian traditions, the ecstatic religious experience that has long been associated with shamans is encouraged by members of the congregation through witnessing, singing, and **speaking in tongues** (the phenomenon of speaking in an apparently unknown language, often in an energetic and fast-paced way). Christian churches that practice speaking in tongues typically associate it with the original Pentecost when the followers of Jesus were all gathered together and the Holy Spirit descended on them, causing them to speak in different languages that the others among their group could not understand and had not previously spoken. Anthropologists today have noted that these vocalizations do not correspond to any human language, but symbolically they connect people with God via the Holy Spirit. These individual connections between each participant and the Holy Spirit parallel the egalitarian society they are ritually constructing in their congregations.

Whether it is religions like those of the Ningerum or Elema or totemism among Native American groups, or Shamanism, each of these religious systems draws on a mix of the same sorts of elements. All stress group identities and link these identities to various religious symbols. Symbols are also used in the religions of stratified societies, but the groups they highlight are larger entities or social categories that extend beyond the local, face-to-face community.

- **Spirit familiar.** A spirit that has developed a close bond with a shaman.

- **Speaking in tongues.** The phenomenon of speaking in an apparently unknown language, often in an energetic and fast-paced way.

Ritual Symbols That Reinforce a Hierarchical Social Order

Ritual symbols tend to reinforce the social hierarchy and the political order at the same time they interact with divine beings and powers. In the former kingdom of Benin in what is now Nigeria in West Africa, for example, the Oba (king) was believed to be divine. The fiercest animal in the region, the leopard, became a symbol of royal power, projecting an image of the Oba's power over his people. The Oba's palace was a model for the structure of the cosmos and the social order. People with the higher political and ritual statuses occupied the more central areas, while commoners were only allowed to enter marginal parts of the palace. One feature of Benin religious practice was the Igwe Festival, which was a cleansing ritual expelling evil from the entire kingdom led by the Oba. This ritual sequence served to strengthen and renew the Oba's divine powers. Benin bronze sculptures and reliefs from Benin often depict members of the royal family, offering another way for the Benin to venerate their Oba (Figure 14.8). By strengthening the Oba, the community felt it was

Figure 14.8   Symbols of Royal Authority in the Benin Kingdom. Bronze figures and reliefs represented royal connections to the gods. The focus of all power in the kingdom was in the center of the palace in the person of the Oba. (Hood Museum of Art, Dartmouth College, Hanover, New Hampshire)

- **Polytheism.** A type of religion with many gods.

- **Monotheism.** The belief in a single god.

maintaining the well-being of the kingdom. Among the Benin, the rituals, the palaces, and the royal art together provided a model of the divine nature of the ruler, supporting a social order in which they dominated over all others (Bradbury 1957; Dark 1962, 1982; Eboreime 2003).

Polytheism and Monotheism in Ancient Societies

The kingdoms and dynasties of ancient Egypt provided a similar model of the social order replicated in many of its most important rituals. The Pharaoh was a king ruling over a vast empire of people along the Nile and Mediterranean coast and extending into what is now Israel and the Arabian Peninsula. Everything about Egyptian ritual—as well as the construction of great pyramids and structures like the Sphinx—celebrated a complex hierarchy of officials and priests with the Pharaoh as a divine figure at the head of the state and its religious organizations. But the Pharoah was not the only divine figure; Egyptians held that there were a host of other, more powerful deities, making their religion **polytheistic** (a religion with many gods). All of these gods demanded the attention of humans or, it was thought, they might harm the human world with droughts, plagues, locusts, and floods of the Nile River.

Nearly all of the ancient societies in the Middle East and Mediterranean were polytheistic with complex state rituals, all of which promoted and supported an image of the state and its human leaders as superior to ordinary men. The main exception to polytheism in the Ancient World were the Ancient Hebrews, whose religion focused on a single god called Yaweh. In all likelihood, Yaweh began as a local deity belonging to one of the tribes of Israel, which was worshiped and venerated by one of these groups that became the ancient Hebrews. It seems likely that Yaweh was the deity of Moses's tribe and after the exodus from Egypt under Ramses the Great of the nineteenth dynasty, his clan or tribal deity gradually pushed out Baal and other gods (Armstrong 1994). When the Hebrews established Yaweh as the God of Israel they began a long-term shift to **monotheism**— the belief in a single god. Monotheism set the Hebrews as distinctive in their neighborhood, even though King Tut's father Akhenaten had established his god of the sun (Aten) as the one God during the eighteenth dynasty and promoted monotheism during his reign. But soon after Akhenaten died seventeen years into his reign, monotheism was abandoned and Egypt returned to polytheism. It would not be until two thousand years later with the arrival of Islam that Egyptians would firmly embrace monotheism.

The key feature of monotheism was that it symbolized a single universal faith because the single God was presented as the deity of all, whereas polytheism encouraged different groups to identify with different local gods in much the way totemism works.

World Religions and Universal Understandings of the World

Most of us are more familiar with the universal monotheistic **world religions**—or religions that claim to be universally significant to all people—of Judaism, Christianity, and Islam than the small-scale religions discussed previously. All three of these mono-theistic world religions provided a general message that was applicable to all people, not just the members of a small clan or social group. For the most part, all three provided a positive, uplifting message for adherents, and all three became identified with the ruling governments. All three also became state religions, whose religious message and ritual supported the government of the state.

Christianity and Islam illustrate the ways a local monotheistic religion can become universalized through a set of beliefs and social order. Christianity began in what is now Israel and emerged in communities already practicing Judaism in the first century but only grew and spread when the apostle Paul began evangelizing in the Greek towns of northern Syria, Turkey, and Greece. Expanding membership was possible only after the Jewish requirement of circumcision was abandoned for new converts. Monotheism encouraged a universal, pan-human approach to faith, and there were many people in the Eastern Mediterranean who wanted a religion that made them part of a new, universal, and growing community.

Five centuries later, Islam emerged in the Arabian Peninsula when the Prophet Muhammad received holy scripture in the form of poetry from a single, universal God—called Allah in classical Arabic. Most Americans are startled to learn that the Prophet had one Christian wife and lived peaceably among a mix of Muslims, Jews, and Christians in Medina, until members of one of the Jewish tribes attempted to assassinate him. Jesus, Mary, John the Baptist, Moses, Abraham, and Adam, among others, are discussed at some length in the Quran and all are considered prophets. From a Muslim point of view Muslims, Christians, and Jews are all "people of the book" meaning that each of these has scripture received through prophets from God. But Muslims, being the newest of these three religions, feel that God's message was most accurately received by the Prophet Muhammad. Thus, they feel that Christians and Jews didn't get the entire message from God, in much the same way that many Christian faiths believe that Jews were not given the full faith until Jesus arrived.

Asia has also produced important world religions that reflect particular histories of social stratification and universalistic belief. Hinduism was a polytheistic religion that emerged in India thousands of years ago. Like the polytheistic religions of the Middle East, Hinduism supported the authority of local princes and kings. Most Hindu ritual was focused on achieving good relations between people and various gods. Sometime in the fourth to sixth centuries BCE a man named Siddhartha Gutama emerged as a founder of a new faith called Buddhism in reaction to Hindusim. According to Bhuddist traditions, having been selfishly pursuing his own pleasure through licentious living, he was mysteriously awakened to his misdeeds and pro-moted a life of reflection and active commitment to the Bhuddist path, accepting the Bhudda, the *Dharma* (his teachings), and the *Sangha* (the Buddhist community). Unlike most other religions, Buddhism encourages its members to strive toward greater enlightenment. In this sense Buddhism is neither monotheistic nor polytheis-tic, but as much a moral code of conduct as anything. The rituals often involve medi-tation and devotional rituals aimed at turning people from this-worldly desires (wealth, sex, power, etc.) to concern for other people and all other creatures, and a state of enlightenment called *Nirvana*.

- **World religions.** Religions that claim to be universally significant to all people.

How Does Atheism Fit in the Discussion?

Finally, we must ask if atheists, agnostics, and non-believers have a religion. This question has been a worrisome issue for anthropologists, because traditionally anthropologists have defined religion in terms of a belief in the supernatural, which means that these beliefs have little basis in empirical fact. People believe unusual things because their families and communities believe them, and there are many ritual occasions that require participants to behave as if they believe unverifiable things about God, the afterworld, the life of Jesus or the prophets, and the like.

But taking a step back, if all humans have some sort of worldview, then everyone has some sort of perspective on life analogous to religion. Secular people must also have symbolic systems that give meaning and purpose to their lives. For some, secular rituals that celebrate the state or nation, particular occupations, or other identities may achieve many of the same ends as religious rituals. For others, practicing scientific research may construct a worldview similar to those with more traditional religious beliefs. Geertz's definition of religion was specifically designed to be as useful for secular worldviews with a rich array of secular symbols as it is for more traditional religions.

- - -

THINKING CRITICALLY ABOUT RELIGION

Consider any three different societies we have discussed in this book. Discuss the extent to which scale of society—measured in terms of population or number of people within the same administrative or governing body—is reflected in complexity of technology and complexity of religious concepts. How do these three measures of complexity—population size, technological complexity, and sophistication of religious ideas—match up? What does this kind of comparison tell us about evolutionary models of society?

- - -

How Do Rituals Work?

All rituals have certain key features, including that they are repetitive (happening at set times or before or after certain events) and stylized (following a set order of words or actions). What distinguishes religious ritual from daily habits such as brushing one's teeth (which some of you might think of as a "ritual") is that none of us invests such special significance in tooth brushing. Some rituals, such as rites of passage (discussed later) are especially significant in a person's life. But, before we explain why and how they work, it is important to note that anthropologists have long understood from their studies of non-Western cultures that at the heart of all ritual action exists a particular mode of thought that we call "magical." What do we mean?

Magical Thought in Non-Western Cultures

When Americans think of magic, the image of a party magician pulling rabbits out of top hats or the adventures of Harry Potter may come to mind. But when anthropologists talk of magic only rarely are they speaking about conjuring tricks. Instead, anthropologists discuss **magic** as an explanatory system of causation that does not follow naturalistic explanations—such as being struck by a weapon or infected by some virus—often working at a distance without direct physical contact. Informants nearly always accept these explanations as real, and they often believe deeply that they are frightening or dangerous.

Magic can have many goals, usually goals that are out of reach through an individual taking direct action. The practitioner may want his or her gardens to flourish or his hunt to be successful. She may want the food at her feast to go further than it normally would, or to attract the affections of a handsome young man in a neighboring hamlet. Jealous over another man's abundant successes, a man may want to cause his rival to become ill, or—even more maliciously—he may want his enemy to die. Techniques may involve incantations, spells, unusual behaviors, and the manipulation of any number of special objects, all in an effort to cause some desired event to occur. All of these practices are assumed to occur at a distance with no direct physical contact between the one performing the magic and the object or person upon which he wants to act.

Rarely do anthropologists worry about proving whether magical practices actually bring about their desired ends or not. It is usually enough to understand that members of a community accept that these processes occur. Anthropologists are interested in the particular incantations or the details of the magical rite only because they offer insight into the connections between the magical behaviors or ingredients and their desired ends.

More recently anthropologists have recognized that believing in the existence and efficacy of magic may actually increase a person's anxiety because they may worry about being in danger of some other magic action. But why do these puzzling practices make any sense to the people who practice magic?

Sympathetic Magic: The Law of Similarity and the Law of Contagion

The English anthropologist Sir James G. Frazer coined the term **sympathetic magic** to refer to any magical rite that relied on supernatural powers to produce its outcome without working through a specific supernatural being such as a spirit, demon, or deity (see "Classic Contributions: Sir James G. Frazer on Sympathetic Magic"). Drawing on dozens of examples from around the world, Frazer showed that sympathetic magic works on two principles that he called the law of similarity and the law of contagion. Both involved sympathetic magic because the person or object acted upon did so in sympathy with the magical actions.

The Laws of Magic: Similarities and Contagion

Frazer identified the law of similarities as some point of similarity between an aspect of the magical rite and the desired goal. Informally, this form of magic came to be known as "imitative magic." A good illustration is a so-called "voodoo doll," in which people make a doll or image of their enemy. By poking or stabbing the image they hoped to produce pain in the same part of the victim's body. This principle also works on charms or fishhooks representing a seal that allows fishermen or hunters to catch fish as easily as a seal does. Today, anthropologists often speak of these similarities as metaphors, since the fishhook carved as a seal is not really a seal but merely a hook that resembles a seal (Figure 14.9). Nevertheless, seals are good at catching fish, and this charm on the hook will attract fish.

- **Magic.** An explanatory system of causation that does not follow naturalistic explanations, often working at a distance without direct physical contact.

- **Sympathetic magic.** Any magical rite that relied on the supernatural to produce its outcome without working through some supernatural being such as a spirit, demon, or deity.

Classic Contributions

Sir James G. Frazer on Sympathetic Magic

THE SCOTSMAN JAMES G. Frazer (1854–1941) was one of the earliest anthropologists in Great Britain. He spent his career studying religion in so-called primitive and archaic societies as an armchair anthropologist. He is best known for his multivolume work *The Golden Bough: A Study in Comparative Religion*, first published in two volumes in 1890 and later expanded. Although anthropologists draw on very little of Frazer's work today, they still appreciate his insights about magic. Frazer was the first to offer an explanation of the logic that all magic was based upon—the principle of Sympathetic Magic—which he discusses here.

Sir James G. Frazer, the Classic Armchair Anthropologist.

One of the principles of sympathetic magic is that any effect may be produced by imitating it. To take a few instances. If it is wished to kill a person an image of him is made and then destroyed; and it is believed that through a certain physical sympathy between the person and his image, the man feels the injuries done to the image as if they were done to his own body, and that when it is destroyed he must simultaneously perish. . . .

Magic sympathy is supposed to exist between a man and any severed portion of his body, as his hair or nails;

so that whoever gets possession of hair or nails may work his will, at any distance, upon the person from whom they were cut. This [belief] is world-wide. . . .

Thus we see that in sympathetic magic one event is supposed to be followed necessarily and invariably by another, without the intervention of any spiritual or personal agency. This is, in fact, the modern conception of physical causation; the conception, indeed, is misapplied, but it is there none the less. (Frazer 1890:9–10)

Questions for Reflection

1. Which aspect of sympathetic magic is involved when an athlete wears his or her lucky socks to play a game?

2. Which aspect of sympathetic magic is involved when a boyfriend or girlfriend gives his partner something to keep with him or her during a trip?

Alternatively, a magical rite could follow the law of contagion, in which things that had once been in physical contact with one another could have an effect even when they were no longer in contact. According to the law of contact, mundane objects we've touched or produced as individuals, such as a cigarette butt, a scrap of partly eaten food, hair, nail clippings, sweat, urine, and feces, carry part of our essence, and harmful things done to them by an ill-intentioned magician can by extension hurt us (Figure 14.10).

Applying These Principles to Religious Activities

Although Frazer depicted imitative and contagious magic as occurring in separate situations, it is clear that these two principles often occur together, drawing simultaneously on the similarities and the previous contact. And while Frazer saw magic as

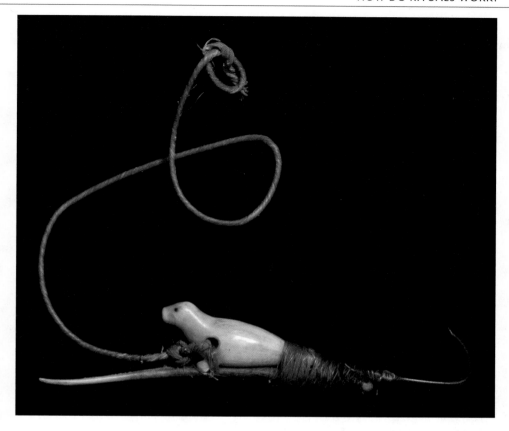

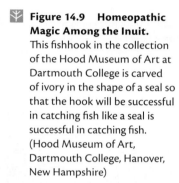

Figure 14.9 Homeopathic Magic Among the Inuit. This fishhook in the collection of the Hood Museum of Art at Dartmouth College is carved of ivory in the shape of a seal so that the hook will be successful in catching fish like a seal is successful in catching fish. (Hood Museum of Art, Dartmouth College, Hanover, New Hampshire)

Figure 14.10 Contagious Magic in Papua New Guinea. A Ningerum man in Papua New Guinea prepares for a pig feast by anointing a pig lengthwise with sago flour in the belief that this rite would make the food go farther. When their guests eat just a little of the pork they will quickly feel full. Anointing the pig uses contagious magic.

distinct and separate from religion, most anthropologists now recognize that magical principles are often invoked in religious rituals.

For example, the Christian ritual of communion embodies both principles of magic. The elements used in the rite—the bread and the wine—are consecrated by the priest or pastor and intended to be consumed by the congregation. This

Figure 14.11   The Christian Eucharist or Communion. The similarity of red wine to blood and wafers to flesh establishes the similarities between the ritual objects and their meaning. Consuming them during the ritual invokes the law of contagion to spread the blessings of God among all the people.

ritual replicates and imitates the Last Supper when Jesus shared bread and wine with his most devoted followers. The Last Supper was held at the start of the Jewish feast of Passover, which reenacts the story of the Jewish exodus from Egypt. Because the meal was part of the Passover, the bread was unleavened and flat like the unleavened matzoh bread that is produced as large flat wafers rather than loaves. Jesus himself is using a metaphor when he holds up the bread announcing that "this is my body" and that the wine "is my blood." The wine is an appropriate element because it resembles blood in color—law of similarity. The wafer resembles the unleavened bread of the Passover meal, which in turn is a symbol for Jesus's flesh. When congregants each eat a consecrated wafer and drink a sip of wine they are linked together as a congregation because they have shared the same wafers and wine—law of contact (Figure 14.11).

Magic in Western Societies

Americans tend to believe that modernization has eliminated magical thought in our culture. Yet many of the elements observed in non-Western societies also occur in contemporary America. In his study of baseball players, for example, anthropologist George Gmelch (1978) found that unlike fielders, who have considerable control in the game, pitchers and batters have much less control. He found that pitchers and batters are much more likely to employ sympathetic magic as a way of asserting some control over their performance. Gmelch noted that players often have lucky jerseys, good luck fetishes, or other objects that become charms. For these players, ordinary objects acquire power by being connected to exceptionally hot batting or pitching streaks. These charms follow the law of similarity. For three months during a winning season, one pitcher Gmelch interviewed followed the exact same routine: at lunch he went to the same restaurant, had two glasses of iced tea and a tuna fish sandwich, and for an hour before the game wore the same sweatshirt and jock strap he had worn the first day of the streak. He was afraid that changing anything he had done before the first winning game might produce a bad result.

Rites of Passage and the Ritual Process

• **Rite of passage.** Any life cycle rite that marks a person's or group's transition from one social state to another.

Now that we understand the importance and persistence of magical thought in ritual, we can explore the most important type of ritual. The **rite of passage** is a life cycle ritual that marks a person's or group of persons' transition from one social state to another. In 1909 the French sociologist Arnold van Gennep (1960) outlined the structure of rituals that marked that passage of individuals from one status to another. Rites of passage include marriage rituals, in which individuals change status from being single to married, or mark the transition from childhood to adulthood. Initiations are common around the world, even in industrial societies such as ours that carries out such rituals in "sweet sixteen parties" for young women, when we graduate from school, and the like. Funerals represent another rite of passage that focuses on the deceased, but is largely about the transition survivors will experience. In "Thinking Like an Anthropologist: Examining Rites of Passage," we explore the link between symbols and the construction of meaning in two American rituals: funerals and graduations.

Thinking Like an Anthropologist

Examining Rites of Passage

ANTHROPOLOGISTS BEGIN THEIR research by asking questions. In this box, we want you to learn how to ask questions as an anthropological researcher. Part One describes a situation and follows up with questions we would ask. Part Two asks you to do the same thing with a different situation.

PART ONE: STATE FUNERAL FOR PRESIDENT RONALD REAGAN

When former President Ronald Reagan died on June 5, 2004, America began a week of national mourning and state ritual that dominated television and radio. State funerals, like inaugurations, are rites of passage that create a model of the state and become a model for how the state should be. Such secular rituals support and help create a sense of nationalism, American pride, a feeling of belonging to the nation, and a way of linking all Americans to state institutions. All funerals, of course, also have an important personal function: disposing of a dead body, and helping the deceased's friends and relatives adjust to the loss. It was no different when President Reagan passed away. Distant relatives and close friends had paid their respects to the president's widow and children. But because of his former role as President of the United States, his death became a rite of passage and transition for all Americans.

The president died in southern California, and the family decided that he would be buried at the Ronald Reagan Presidential Library in Simi Valley, California. The most efficient way to conduct a funeral would be to hold it in California.

⚜ **A Public Funerary Ritual.** Mourners file in to view President Ronald Reagan's flag-draped casket as he lies in state in the rotunda of the United States Capitol building in Washington, D.C., on June 10, 2004.

But most of the ritual occurred in Washington, DC, the center of the government that he led.

Flown to Andrews Air Force base, the flag-draped coffin was brought to the Washington Monument, where it was transferred to a horse-drawn caisson, on which it would proceed slowly up Constitution Avenue to the Capitol. The procession was led by a riderless horse with boots pointed backwards, symbolic of the dead (former) commander in chief. Three pairs of horses pulled the caisson, with riders only on the three left horses. When the procession reached 4th street, twenty-one F15 planes made a flyover, and the coffin was carried the rest of the way up to the Capitol by eight-man teams representing each branch of the military. At this point, there was a 21-gun salute, and the band played "Hail to the Chief" and "The Battle Hymn of the Republic." Mrs. Reagan was waiting inside the Capitol to meet the coffin.

After a short ceremony the president's body was to lie in state in the Rotunda, at the center of the Capitol building. The flag-draped casket rested on the simple pine frame covered with black cloth which had first held the coffin of Abraham Lincoln in 1865. Present were important politicians who had served in the Reagan administration or in the Bush administration. Only the Reagan family was given seats for the ceremony. After the ceremony, Mrs. Reagan and the dignitaries left, but the public was allowed to file in and around the casket throughout the night. Thousands filed past the casket to pay their respects in solemnity and silence until 7:00 the next morning.

The next morning a motorcade took the body to the National Cathedral for the national funeral service, with eulogies from President George W. Bush, former President George H. W. Bush, former British Prime Minister Margaret Thatcher, and former Canadian Prime Minister Brian Mulroney. After the funeral, a motorcade brought the body back to Andrews, whereupon it was flown to California for a private interment ceremony attended only by the Reagan family and close family friends.

What questions does this situation raise for anthropological researchers?

1. How do the ritual symbols, such as the use of a caisson, riderless horse, 21-plane flyover, 21-gun salute, and so on add meaning to the ritual?

(continued)

Thinking Like an Anthropologist (continued)

2. What added meaning was given to the event by holding it in Washington, DC, that could not have been accomplished in the Reagan Library in California?

3. What meaning was created by the particular dignitaries who attended the Rotunda ceremony?

4. What model of social order was conveyed by the particular order in which people viewed the flag-draped casket? What difference did it make that viewing went on for thirty-six hours that would not have been accomplished if it had only lasted for three hours?

PART TWO: YOUR OWN HIGH SCHOOL GRADUATION

Reflect back on your own high school graduation, which was likely marked by special costumes, processions, music, speeches, and some special action (such as shifting the tassel to one side of the hat) that acknowledged your shift from one status to another. Viewing this graduation as a rite of passage, what questions would you ask about this situation as an anthropological researcher?

For anthropologist Victor Turner (1967, 1969), all rituals invoke symbols that can convey the underlying meanings of the ritual. Ritual symbols can consist of objects, colors, actions, events, or words. Often symbols point to, suggest, or take meaning from myths or sacred texts known to participants. Objects, such as the cross or the wine and wafers in Christian church services, refer to key events memorialized in the ritual. The procession of performers or dancers in a tribal ritual may similarly enact key parts of a myth. If an Aboriginal performer in Australia represents an Emu (an ostrich-like bird) totem, his actions may resemble the behavior of the living bird. When American brides wear white they are symbolically expressing their purity, whereas when Chinese wear white at a funeral they are expressing their grief. What is common throughout these examples is that rituals create solidarity and meaning for participants. Part of their power is that they represent tradition for a group of people, and they also create meaning that gets passed from one generation to another.

THINKING CRITICALLY ABOUT RELIGION

Compare the ritual symbols in the Sunday morning television or cable broadcast of a Protestant televangelist with the televised Sunday morning Roman Catholic mass. Although both services are religious rituals for Christian sects, they look very different. How do the different structures in the two services suggest different meanings derived from the same scripture?

How Is Religion Linked to Political and Social Action?

Time magazine's cover for April 8, 1966, asked the provocative question, "Is God Dead?" Playing off of the nineteenth-century German philosopher Friedrich Nietzsche's famous claim that "God is dead"—suggesting that the **secular worldview,** or a worldview that does not accept the supernatural as influencing current people's lives, had finally overtaken the religious one in Europe—*Time* was asking whether the same secularizing trend was at work in America (Figure 14.12). Formal church membership in Europe had declined sharply, to fewer than 10% of the population in some countries, and *Time* was suggesting that perhaps religion would no longer play a role in political action, as it had in the abolition movement and was playing out in the civil rights movement. *Time* was so wrong. More than forty years later, we can see the persistent power of religion in the United States, in politics, in social discourse, in civil rights, and on TV. American church membership has risen gradually since the late 1940s to about 75% of American adults today. So, why was *Time* magazine so wrong?

The main reason is the magazine's false assumption that as a society "modernizes" it begins to value scientific knowledge and reason over religious values and practices. The *Time* authors assumed that secularization would continue to grow, but American churches responded to social change not by ignoring it but by challenging it. Mainline churches like the Episcopalians, Presbyterians, and Methodists began to support the civil rights movement for racial equality. Evangelical churches have tended to resist changes, such as in marriage laws that allowed same-sex marriage and Supreme Court decisions that allowed abortions during the first two trimesters. Churches and other religious organizations became increasingly political, often supporting one political party or the other. In nearly every society, political and religious institutions are not only engaged with one another, they are frequently the same institutions.

The broader point here is that religious values, symbols, and beliefs typically either challenge or uphold a particular social order. We illustrate this point by considering the forceful rise of religious fundamentalisms around the world.

- **Secular worldview.** A worldview that does not accept the supernatural as influencing current people's lives.

🌱 **Figure 14.12   Presenting the Secularization Hypothesis.** *Time* magazine's cover for April 8, 1966, wrongly assumed that the power of religion both in America and around the world was on the decline.

The Rise of Fundamentalism

Since the 1960s, the most significant change in U.S. religion has been how much more active religious organizations have become in public life, particularly among the conservative churches that call themselves **fundamentalist,** people belonging to conservative religious movements that advocate a return to fundamental or traditional principles. Fundamentalist TV preachers have expanded their broadcasting since the early 1980s, and conservative religious groups and religious organizations have been as deeply involved in elections and politics as ever.

As Christians were growing in political clout in America, both Muslim and Jewish communities throughout the Middle East and Asia were experiencing a similar rise in the numbers of religious conservatives. In all three religions, conservative groups have turned to fundamentalism to make sense of and to confront changes that were

- **Fundamentalist.** A person belonging to a religious movement that advocates a return to fundamental or traditional principles.

happening all around them. As in most other societies, fundamentalist religion and politics are deeply engaged with one another.

Understanding Fundamentalism

● **Fundamentalism.** Conservative religious movements that advocate a return to fundamental or traditional principles.

Scholars have had difficulty agreeing to the definition of *fundamentalism.* Traditionally, **fundamentalism** in America has been associated with extremely literal interpretation of scripture, particularly prophetic books in the Bible. Recently the American media has often associated fundamentalism with Islam, violence, extremism, and terrorism, but both views are far too narrow and biased, because most of the world's religions have their own conservative, "back to fundamentals" branches, and most are not so outwardly violent.

To correct these biases, in the 1990s a team of researchers working on the Fundamentalism Project at the University of Chicago studied conservative religious movements within Christianity, Islam, Zionist Judaism, Buddhism, Hinduism, Confucianism, and Sikhism (Marty and Appleby 1991; Almond, Appleby, and Sivan 2003). Not all of these diverse movements rely on literal readings of scripture, and for some groups sacred writings are of little consequence. Nor do fundamentalist groups necessarily reject everything modern. Most have embraced television, computers, the Internet, and other digital technologies to get the word out. And conservative Arab Muslims celebrate the medieval Islamic origins of modern science and technology.

The Fundamentalism Project (Marty and Appleby 1991:viii–x) found several key themes common to all of these conservative religious movements. These include:

- They all see themselves as fighting back against the corrosive effects of secular life on what they envision as a purer way of life. They fight for a worldview that prescribes "proper" gender roles, sexualities, and educational patterns. Their interpretation of the purer past becomes the model for building a purer, Godlier future.
- They are willing to engage in political, even military, battles to defend their ideas about life and death, including issues that emerge in hospitals and clinics dealing with pregnancy, abortion, and the terminally ill.
- They work against others, whether infidels, modernizers, or moderate insiders, reinforcing in the process their identity and building solidarity within their community.
- Most important, fundamentalists have passion, and the most passionate are those who "are convinced that they are called to carry out God's or Allah's purposes against challengers" (Marty and Appleby 1991:x).

Political action among fundamentalists has sometimes taken a more violent course, as the suicide bombings and 9/11 suggest, but in India another minority group with a distinctive religion, the Sikhs, have pushed for fundamentalist values through armed combat and insurrection against the Indian government. We explore this case further in "Doing Fieldwork: Studying the Sikh Militants."

The broader point here is that fundamentalists are not isolated from the world of politics, but are actively engaged in it. What is so striking about fundamentalism for anthropologists is that unlike religion in most small-scale societies, fundamentalism does not typically support the existing political order but fights

Doing Fieldwork

Studying the Sikh Militants

ANTHROPOLOGIST CYNTHIA KEPPLEY MAHMOOD, now at the University of Notre Dame, had been studying religion and conflict in the Indian subcontinent for more than a decade, making frequent visits to India, when she became interested in a fundamentalist movement among members of the Sikh religion. From 1980, a militant group of ethnic Sikhs in the northwestern Indian state of Punjab had been engaged in an armed insurgency aimed at forming a sovereign nation called Khalistan ("Land of the Pure"). This insurgency was built on a fundamentalist religious ideology. Khalistanis identify themselves through both their religious and their ethnic identities. This movement, however, does not represent all or even the majority of Sikh people living in Punjab. Other Sikhs support the idea of independence but reject the violence entailed in winning it.

Wanting to study religion and violence, Mahmood turned her attention to the separatist tensions in Punjab, which were as religious as they were political. Studying a violent religious group presented special problems for the anthropologist, because it was impossible for her to live in a community with the militants, targeted as they were by the Indian government they wanted to overthrow. So Mahmood adopted an innovative strategy by conducting research about militant Sikhs and their movement overseas rather than in India.

Over a period of three years in the early 1990s, Mahmood met intermittently with militant Sikhs in various parts of the United States and Canada to understand the motives, rationale, and ideology of this fundamentalist group. Mahmood's interactions with the Sikhs occurred in restaurants, homes, Sikh temples, and even in prisons. Many of her informants had come to North America as a way of reinvigorating their movement, which was being suppressed by the Indian government in Punjab. Many informants felt that violent acts were reasonable and acceptable responses to the violence that the Indian government had perpetrated against their people. Even though these Sikhs lived overseas, they remained deeply involved in their homeland's affairs. From interviews, Mahmood was able to construct a compelling image of the complex political and religious movement and how participation in it gave meaning to activists based in North America.

Mahmood's interviews posed a variety of ethical issues not present in most kinds of ethnographic research. To protect her informants she had to conceal their identities at every stage in the research, including any identifiers in her field notes. Even though she conducted her study before the terrorist attacks of 9/11, the tapes of her interviews would have posed a danger for her informants if they had fallen into the hands of various law enforcement agencies, because unlike journalists anthropologists have no first amendment rights to protect their sources. Of course, she changed the names of her informants and concealed their identities when she published her book, *Fighting for Faith and Nation: Dialogs with Sikh Militants* (1997).

Questions for Reflection:

1. What is lost by conducting research almost entirely through interviews rather than through participant observation?

2. What ethical complications are involved in studying a militant anti-government religious group?

3. How would these complications be different if one conducted research in the Methodist Church?

A Sikh Temple in India. The vast majority of Sikhs are not militant or violent, just as most Christians, Jews, Muslims, Hindus, and Buddhists are non-violent.

against it. We have seen this in the United States, when the evangelical pastor Jerry Falwell founded a political organization called the Moral Majority in 1979. Members of the Moral Majority were fundamentalists, but they became active in the presidential elections throughout the 1980s, supporting conservative candidates. In recent decades, evangelical Christians with conservative, fundamentalist ideologies have stood in vocal opposition to non-conservative candidates. Despite the organization's name, these fundamentalists did not make up the majority of the American population, although they were a majority in some congressional districts.

What we do see in fundamentalism is that membership and a sense of belonging to a congregation or denomination is an important feature of religious organizations in industrial societies where it is easy for individuals to feel anonymous. Indeed, part of the power of any religious organizations (churches, synagogues, mosques, and other religious centers) is that they bring people together, provide them social support, and give them an identity within a broader secular world. Anthropologists have long understood that this process of belonging and the social action associated with group membership is bolstered by important symbols.

THINKING CRITICALLY ABOUT RELIGION

Consider a secular ritual, like the 4th of July with its parades and fireworks displays in your home town. How do the parades and the speeches and fireworks build symbolic support for the state and federal governments and for the U.S. military? Compare these ritual actions to those in state-centered religions like those in Ancient Egypt, the Roman Empire, or Great Britain in the past century. How do the symbols support the existing government?

Conclusion

A month after Tom Coleman shot Jonathan Daniels in Hayneville, Alabama, an all-white jury found Coleman not guilty of manslaughter. This was a cause of disbelief for many who sympathized with Jon Daniel's worldview. For example, Jon Daniels's hometown newspaper, the *Keene Sentinel,* editorialized that "White Southerners and Northerners who hold [similar] views . . . do not, and apparently cannot, understand why a white man would risk his life to help a Negro register to vote or teach Negro children to read. They simply do not understand that, to men like

Jonathan Daniels, all men are brothers, and skin color means nothing. . . . In dying, not only was Jonathan Daniels minding his own business, but he was attending to His business."

When Jon first went to Alabama, he did so with a moral and religious commitment to what he understood as social justice. His actions were driven by a worldview that called him to help create a world suggested by his reading of scripture and his understanding of God. But at the same time, Tom Coleman acted out of his own worldview, one clearly shared by the jury. At that time in America, many people were proud of their prejudices and found many justifications for them, even in their religions. As much as people today may disapprove of Coleman's actions and of those on the jury, these actions were motivated by a shared set of assumptions about what the world should be like. Coleman acted in defense of that ideal world. Just as Jon's actions made sense in terms of his belief system, Coleman's beliefs and understandings about the world made sense to the large part of his community. Forty years later, racial attitudes in America have changed from where they were in Hayneville in 1965.

No matter whether we agree with such a perspective or not, we can never understand the actions of others without understanding a community's worldview and the powerful moods and motivations it creates. These are the benefits of approaching conflicting beliefs from the "native's point of view."

KEY TERMS

Animism   p. 343

Fundamentalism   p. 364

Fundamentalists   p. 363

Holy struggle   p. 349

Interpretive approach
   p. 346

Magic   p. 357

Mana   p. 344

Monotheism   p. 354

Polytheism   p. 354

Religion   p. 347

Rite of passage
   p. 360

Rituals   p. 344

Shaman   p. 352

Secular worldview   p. 363

Speaking in tongues
   p. 353

Spirit familiar   p. 353

Sympathetic magic   p. 357

Totemism   p. 351

Trance   p. 352

World religions   p. 355

Worldview   p. 345

Reviewing the Chapter

Chapter Section	What We Know	To Be Resolved
How Should We Understand Religion and Religious Beliefs?	Anthropologists have long considered the reasons people have religion and how religions work. While some of the classic approaches have emphasized that religion is about the supernatural, more recent approaches emphasize the symbolic and action-oriented character of religious beliefs.	Many anthropologists accept that we can learn a great deal about the worldviews of the peoples we study, but not all anthropologists believe that we can fully understand how any individual sees and feels about his or her world.
What Forms Does Religion Take?	Traditional societies with limited social stratification tend to have simpler religions than the religions of complex societies, but this correlation is not inevitable.	We don't really know what environmental, political, or social conditions produce more complex forms of religious ideas.
How Do Rituals Work?	Rituals use symbols that convey deep meanings about the world and how it should be. All rituals rely on some version of magical thinking. Ritual symbols themselves rely heavily on metaphor and other kinds of resemblances for conveying meaning.	It is not entirely clear why humans in all societies so readily accept ideas and beliefs that can be so easily shown to be incomplete, if not wrong.
How Is Religion Linked to Political and Social Action?	Religions have always been linked to political organizations and the social order. Anthropologists reject the idea that as the world modernized it would become more secular, drawing on the widespread rise of fundamentalism to demonstrate the continuing social and political importance of religion.	There is no real consensus among anthropologists as to how much political institutions can shape religious symbols, rituals, and worldviews, even though it is obvious that groups in power often try to.

Readings

Nineteenth-century anthropologists were interested in ancient Semitic religions that gave rise to Judaism, Christianity, and Islam (all of which were understood as monotheistic faiths) and how these differed from the religions of Egypt, Mesopotamia, the Hittites, the Persians, and the ancient Greeks and Romans. What interested them was how these pre-Christian religions differed from the religions of Native Americans,

Africans, and Aboriginal Australians, but until the 1920s and 1930s there were few field studies of traditional religions that had not been dramatically transformed by European or American cultures. One of the most important early studies of a traditional religion is E. E. Evans-Pritchard's 1937 classic ethnography, *Witchcraft, Oracles, and Magic Among the Azande* (abridged edition, 1976, Oxford: Clarendon Press), in which

ideas about witchcraft, diviners called oracles, and magic are described and discussed in their natural context in what is now South Sudan.

••••••••••••••••••••

Two more subsequent studies provide examples of more symbolic studies of religion. Clifford Geertz's 1966 article "Religion as a Cultural System" (in Michael Banton, ed., *Anthropological Approaches to the Study of*

Religion, pp. 1–46. ASA Monograph 3. London: Tavistock) explores a symbolic definition of religion that sees religion as a "system of symbols." Victor Turner's book *The Forest of Symbols: Aspects of Ndembu Ritual* (Ithaca, NY: Cornell University Press, 1967) offers a series of explorations of just how such a system of symbols might work in a functioning society in southern Africa.

● ●

For an anthropological perspective on the interactions between Islam and politics, see Dale F. Eickelman and James P. Piscatori's book *Muslim Politics* (Princeton, NJ: Princeton University Press, 1996). Even though it was written before the post-9/11 world, it offers useful analytical tools to understand the complex intersections of religion and political action in the Muslim world.

● ●

If you want to understand the rise of religious fundamentalisms in recent decades, see Martin Marty and R. Scott Appleby's edited volume *Fundamentalisms Observed* (The Fundamentalism Project, Volume 1, Chicago: University of Chicago Press, 1991).

● ●

Medical Anthropology

Health, Illness, and Culture

IN APRIL 2009, breaking news headlines flashed across Americans' TV screens and newspapers announcing that a deadly new strain of influenza identified as swine flu had killed more than 100 people in Mexico City. Influenza is caused by a virus that spreads rapidly through direct contact between individuals, especially hand to hand. But the response to this outbreak demonstrates that disease, even when the biological agent is clear, is about more than viruses and human biology. People in Mexico, the United States, China, and Egypt responded differently to the same outbreak.

In Mexico the epidemic produced a rapid and vigorous response. The government closed schools and universities. The busy streets of Mexico City were practically empty as Mexicans hunkered down in their homes. People wore surgical masks if they went out into the streets.

Soon a few cases were confirmed in several American cities among people who had recently visited Mexico. Although this was a minor news story in the United States, intense TV and radio coverage prompted the Centers for Disease Control (CDC) to issue daily reports. Growing anxiety across the country brought briefings from White House spokespersons, who wanted to show that the government was on the case. But they seemed to heighten rather than calm public anxiety. Several prominent anti-immigrant politicians called for sealing the border with Mexico. Even after six months there had been many fewer deaths in the United States than the more than 20,000 deaths each winter from ordinary seasonal flu.

IN THIS CHAPTER

What Do We Mean by Health and Illness?
- The Individual Subjectivity of Illness
- The "Sick Role": The Social Expectations of Illness

How and Why Do Doctors and Other Health Practitioners Gain Social Authority?
- The Disease–Illness Distinction: Professional and Popular Views of Sickness
- The Medicalization of the Non-Medical

How Does Healing Happen?
- Clinical Therapeutic Processes
- Symbolic Therapeutic Processes
- Social Support
- Persuasion: The Placebo Effect

What Can Anthropology Contribute to Addressing Global Health Problems?
- Understanding Global Health Problems
- Anthropological Contributions to Tackling the International HIV/AIDS Crisis

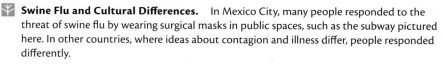

Swine Flu and Cultural Differences. In Mexico City, many people responded to the threat of swine flu by wearing surgical masks in public spaces, such as the subway pictured here. In other countries, where ideas about contagion and illness differ, people responded differently.

In China, the government reacted to the apparent—but false—association between the disease and pigs suggested by the name "swine flu." The Chinese government called for bans on imports of American and Mexican pork. Although this outbreak had nothing to do with pigs, banning American imports of pork made sense as a way of protecting China when they already blamed Americans for the worldwide recession that was barely six months old.

An unexpected response came from Egypt, a country with a large poor population that is routinely critical of the government. Egyptian politicians decided to kill all of their country's pigs as a way of preventing the epidemic from infecting its population. Egypt is a largely Muslim country where, because of Muslims' restriction on its consumption, few people eat pork. Only the Coptic Christians, a small minority group in Egypt, tend pigs and eat pork. Most of the pigs belong to poor Copts, who live around the enormous city dump that serves Cairo, where the pigs consume garbage and waste. Killing the country's pigs would affect only one of Egypt's poorest minority groups, not the larger Muslim population. Stigmatized groups, whether responsible or not, are most likely to be blamed for problems in many cultures.

And then, as suddenly as it had started, swine flu dropped off our TV screens and newspapers during the late spring and early summer as if it had never happened. When the epidemic did return in the late summer and fall it caused few deaths and went largely unnoticed. The initial worldwide response now seems exaggerated, because the epidemic never developed into the deadly worldwide pandemic so many had feared.

In each country officials and ordinary people reacted according to their society's cultural expectations of diseases and their regional experiences of other epidemics. Like all illness episodes, this outbreak was about how people in different cultures respond to disease in distinctive ways they consider reasonable.

As we have argued throughout this book, culture consists of social processes that make the artificial seem natural. In each country, officials and ordinary citizens had seen and heard what seemed "natural" and biological in the news accounts and official reports. Wearing surgical masks seems a "natural" way to protect oneself, but the virus more often spreads through handshakes. Culture shapes not only people's responses to epidemics but even how the human body responds to diseases.

These incidents and reactions lead us to ask a general question about medical anthropology that is central to this chapter: *How does culture influence our experience of health and illness?* We can help answer this question by considering a number of more focused questions around which this chapter is organized.

What do we mean by health and illness?

How and why do doctors and other health practitioners gain social authority?

How does healing happen?

What can anthropology contribute to addressing global health
    problems?

The swine flu epidemic shows how anthropology has a great deal to say about
health and illness. Anthropologists have developed useful tools for understanding the links between culture, reactions to disease, and how our bodies respond
to it. This chapter explores how anthropologists put that knowledge to work in
addressing real-world health crises. Let us first consider how people in different
cultures distinguish between being healthy and being ill.

What Do We Mean by Health and Illness?

At first thought, health and illness seem to be straightforward concepts. Dictionaries
often define the word *health* as the "soundness of body and mind" or as "freedom
from disease" and *illness* as being "unhealthy," or having a "disease," "malady," or
"sickness." The problem is that ideas like "soundness of body" and "malady" do not
suggest any objective measure of when we have health and when it has left us. For
example, most people get sore after a hard workout at the gym, and many people have
mild seasonal allergies and sinus conditions that rarely impair their daily lives, but
which can be annoying. Are these people healthy?

The borderland between health and illness is more ambiguous than we might have
originally assumed. This ambiguity results from two interlaced dynamics: the "subjectivity of illness," which is how people perceive and experience their condition on a
personal level, and the "**sick role**," the culturally defined agreement between patients
and family members to acknowledge that a patient is legitimately sick. We consider
each in turn.

These issues are at the heart of medical anthropology, which is the subfield of anthropology that tries to understand how social, cultural, biological, and linguistic
factors shape the health of human beings (Society for Medical Anthropology 2013).
Doctors tend to focus on treating sickness and disease, while public health officials
have traditionally focused on preventing outbreaks of disease. In many ways medical
anthropologists try to look at the diverse human factors that shape both. Although
more anthropology students are getting jobs in medical anthropology careers than
ever before, there is no single topic that they study or address; they consider many
diverse aspects of illness, its prevention, and its treatment. At its core, medical anthropology begins with the fact that, as much as we might like health and illness to be
objective categories, health and illness are subjective states.

- **Sick role.** The culturally
  defined agreement between
  patients and family members
  to acknowledge that a
  patient is legitimately sick.

The Individual Subjectivity of Illness

Illness is a subjective experience, but it is also shaped by cultural and social expectations. This insight is credited to sociologist Earl L. Koos, who in the 1940s conducted
a classic study of attitudes toward health and illness in a mainstream American community he called Regionville. In his study, he interviewed thousands of ordinary

Americans about being sick. For example, he asked one working-class woman about being sick, to which she replied:

> I wish I really knew what you mean about being sick. Sometimes I've felt so bad I could curl up and die, but had to go on because the kids had to be taken care of, and besides, we didn't have the money to spend for the doctor—how could I be sick? . . . How do you know when you're sick, anyway? Some people can go to bed most any time with anything, but most of us can't be sick—even when we need to be. (Koos 1954:30)

This statement demonstrates both the subjectivity of illness and how health and illness are inherently linked to social behavior and expectations, especially when our symptoms impair us so much that we cannot perform the normal social and economic duties expected of us—jobs, school, and, in this case, caring for her family.

To understand when a particular symptom is considered significant enough to provoke someone to seek medical care, we have to understand the ordinary expectations of the people involved. In the United States, these expectations are linked to issues like social class, gender, age, the kind of work people ordinarily perform, and their routine lifestyles. The poor and working class routinely work more physically, eat less healthy food, and pay less attention to their health concerns than do wealthier people. It is not that lower class people do not care about health, of course. They simply have less time for doctors' visits, work in jobs they could lose if they miss a day, and eat the least expensive foods, which as we discussed in Chapter 7 ("Foodways"), are the processed foods made available by the industrial food system. And they often have less adequate health insurance, or no health insurance at all.

A number of cross-cultural anthropological studies confirm that cultural background also shapes the subjectivity of illness. For example, anthropologist Katherine Dettwyler (2013) conducted research in Mali, a West African nation at the southern edge of the Sahara. There she observed high infection rates of schistosomiasis, a liver and bladder infection caused by a parasitic worm that lives in water. This worm enters the human body through the feet and legs, causing sores on the skin and releasing blood into the urine. Dettwyler found this condition so common in Mali, where she conducted her research, that by puberty nearly all rural men have blood in their urine. Instead of viewing red urine as a shocking symptom, as Americans would, Malians understood it as a normal condition typical of the transition to adulthood. For these adolescents it meant they were becoming men, not that they had an infection (Figure 15.1).

Americans might interpret Malian understandings as ignorance, and perhaps there is some lack of medical knowledge among youth in Mali. But the important point to this example is that people rarely worry about conditions that are very common. Just as manual laborers rarely worry about lower back pain, Malian youth never worry about dark urine but see it as normal and even desirable.

The "Sick Role": The Social Expectations of Illness

Figure 15.1   Undernourished Adolescent in Mali. This condition is caused by a heavy disease load as much as poor nutrition in the diet.

In all societies around the world, when a person is ill there are expectations of how that person, as well as friends and family, should behave. For Americans this typically means the sick person should not go to school or work, should stay in bed and rest, should be given chicken soup, and so on. But these patterns vary cross-culturally. One of this book's authors, Robert Welsch, experienced this kind of cultural difference while conducting field research in Papua New Guinea among the Ningerum people.

One day Welsch noticed that his body ached all over and his forehead burned with a high fever. It was malaria. At first he retired to his bed to rest, but the fever turned into chills, followed by sweats and an even worse body ache. He took anti-malarial pills and aspirin, but the headache became so bad it was unbearable to lay his head on a pillow. Like most Americans he wanted to be by himself and endure this agony alone.

But Ningerum villagers did not sit idly by. As Welsch's condition worsened, more and more of his friends in the village came by the house to sit and chat and smoke. He later realized that most people in the village attributed his sudden symptoms to sorcery: someone in the area had used magic to hurt him, and people expected him to die. If it was sorcery there was nothing anyone in the village could really do for him, but nobody wanted to be accused of having caused his death. The only sure way to avoid suspicion of being a sorcerer was to demonstrate concern. Fortunately for everybody, by the eighth day, the fever broke, the headache and body ache subsided. The villagers who had been keeping vigil for several days went back to their normal activities.

In this instance the anthropologist and the villagers had very different ideas of how they expect patients and caregivers to behave. Anthropologists refer to these unwritten rules as the sick role, or the responsibilities and expected behaviors of sick people by their caregivers (Parsons 1951). To be considered legitimately sick—rather than as malingering, or faking sickness—one must accept specific responsibilities and a new social role, which exempts one from his or her ordinary daily roles and responsibilities such as school or work. Two key aspects of the sick role are to want to get well, and to cooperate with medical experts.

A great example of this phenomenon comes from our own childhoods. During cold and flu season in the winter, many schoolchildren feel under the weather and want to stay home. When a parent agrees to let his or her child stay home, many kids may decide later in the day that it would be fun to go out and play in the snow. But "Dr. Mom" steps in with her authoritative zeal to explain that if you are sick enough to stay home, you are too sick to go outside to play. Playing outside does not demonstrate that you want to get well—which is a key aspect of American ideas of the sick role—and slipping out of the house in defiance of Dr. Mom's explicit orders to stay in bed is not compliance with her medical expertise (Figure 15.2).

Both of these responsibilities, wanting to get well and cooperating to do so, may simultaneously come into play in your own college classes. For example, when absent from a class or especially an exam, the legitimately sick student may need a note from a doctor or clinic, demonstrating that the student wants to get better and has sought medical care.

Welsch found that Ningerum people had a different sick role model, believing that if patients still enjoy a minimum of physical strength, they should themselves deal with the illness. For the Ningerum patient to get help with his or her care and treatment, the patient is obliged to display to family and friends precisely how sick and disabled he or she is. Patients convey this information through their actions or visible physical signs of illness rather than through their words. Startling symptoms such as fainting, bleeding, vomiting, shrieking, and sudden weight loss call family members to action. Patients can also display the severity of their condition by using props like a walking stick to limp cautiously across the village plaza, shedding clothing, refusing to eat, or smearing their chests and legs with mud and dirt. All these actions communicate to family and friends that the patient is sick, and (silently) demand that family

Figure 15.2 Dr. Mom. "Dr. Mom" expects her patient to stay in bed when staying home from school because her child is sick.

members show their sincere concern for the patient. Not to do so would suggest one was not sensitive to a relative's needs—indifference that, to the Ningerum, whose culture prescribes very close kinship ties, would suggest not being fully human.

While culture shapes a community's expectations of the sick role, our medical schools and hospitals have created a culture of medicine that often leads to tensions between the views of professionals and those of lay people. These tensions often have to do with the social authority given to doctors that makes the relationship asymmetric, a topic we consider next.

THINKING CRITICALLY ABOUT MEDICAL ANTHROPOLOGY

The "sick role" as identified and described by Talcott Parsons works well for acute diseases like measles, bad colds, and chicken pox, when patients are expected to (1) want to get better, (2) help in their own care by following medical advice, and for this they are (3) exempt from participating in ordinary social activities and (4) exempt from blame in causing their own sickness.

Compare the sick role from an acute infection with a chronic condition like diabetes, chronic shortness of breath, or severe arthritis.

How and Why Do Doctors and Other Health Practitioners Gain Social Authority?

Medical doctors in the United States have one of the most prestigious, respected, and well paid occupations. The prestige and social authority doctors enjoy, however, is relatively new. Throughout most of the eighteenth and nineteenth centuries, American doctors had low social status. Medicine was not sophisticated, and doctors often doubled as barbers. During the Civil War surgeons were little more than butchers who amputated with large, dirty saws, using no antibiotics, few pain killers, and no antiseptics (Starr 1982).

Many people assume that doctors gained prestige and authority because new medical discoveries and technologies improved their ability to heal people. Antibiotics like penicillin, for example, have made a huge difference in treating disease. But the major advances in health we take for granted today were mostly improvements in preventing diseases rather than curing them. Clean water, sanitation, and other public hygiene programs saved more lives than doctors' treatments have. So how do we explain the social authority of doctors? Medical anthropologists have studied the social authority of healers in many societies. They identify several processes at work, the most important being: the social processes that privilege the healers' perspectives over their patients and the designation of otherwise normal conditions as health problems (Figure 15.3).

The sociologist Eliot Freidson (1970) was among the first to identify the professionalization of the field of medicine as responsible for giving the doctor's perspective privilege over the understandings of ordinary people. It is not that doctors necessarily

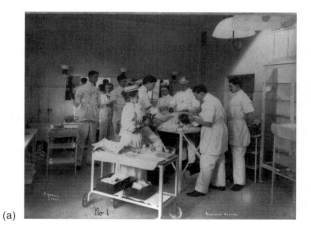

(a)

(c)

(b)

Figure 15.3   Improvements in Public Health. Although use of antiseptics made surgery much safer in the late nineteenth and early twentieth centuries, improvement in life expectancy came from better sanitation and hygiene across the United States, including (a) using antiseptics in the operating room, as this photo from 1900 shows; (b) the use of soaps to promote personal hygiene, as this Lifebouy soap ad from 1900 promises; and (c) street cleaning and the development of improved sewers, such as those implemented in the 1890s in New York which kept the public away from waste of all kinds (note that the street cleaners wore white uniforms in an effort to instill the sense of cleanliness in the public).

knew more about what the patient experiences during an illness, but doctors had been trained how to treat a wide variety of diseases. Subsequently, the medical sociologist Paul Starr (1982) argued that during the twentieth century medical doctors in the United States had used their professional status to increase their incomes, the level of respect they received from the public, and the exclusive right to determine the course of treatment for particular patients. American physicians formed professional associations like the American Medical Association, which allowed them to control how many new doctors were being trained. But while American physicians had achieved professional privileges, great respect, and high salaries, few of these perks were enjoyed by doctors in most other countries. The professional privileges of American doctors had been constructed in a distinctively American way.

The Disease–Illness Distinction: Professional and Popular Views of Sickness

Around the world, patients often view their illnesses differently from the doctors or healers who treat them. In the Western world, patients often feel their doctors do not understand the intensity of their pain and other symptoms. What frequently emerges

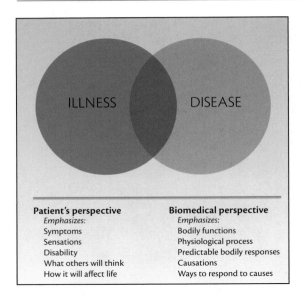

Patient's perspective
Emphasizes:
Symptoms
Sensations
Disability
What others will think
How it will affect life

Biomedical perspective
Emphasizes:
Bodily functions
Physiological process
Predictable bodily responses
Causations
Ways to respond to causes

Figure 15.4   The Disease–Illness Distinction. Patients are concerned with the illness: symptoms, how they feel, and how their activities are affected by these symptoms. Doctors tend to focus on underlying causes of symptoms that they speak of as disease.

- **Disease.** The purely physiological condition of being sick, usually determined by a physician.

- **Illness.** The psychological and social experience a patient has of a disease.

- **Explanatory model of illness.** An explanation of what is happening to a patient's body, by the patient, by his family, or by a health care practitioner, each of which may have a different model of what is happening.

is a clash of professional and popular (or layperson's) understandings that we call the disease–illness distinction, in which doctors focus on **disease**, the purely physiological condition, and patients focus on **illness**, their actual experience of the disease (Eisenberg 1977); see Figure 15.4.

In our culture the doctor, not the patient, has the greater authority in identifying and defining health and illness. Sociologist Eliot Freidson (1970) explained this authority as the result of a social process: "In the sense that medicine has the authority to label one person's complaint an illness and another's complaint not, medicine may be said to be engaged in the creation of illness as a social state which a human being may assume."

American social structure also upholds the doctor's view as the officially sanctioned one. Because of the doctor's professional training, the hospital, governments, insurance providers, and, in extreme cases, even the courts recognize the diagnosis of the physician as legitimate. At the same time, the patient who has to live with the symptoms generally lacks any ability to authorize a prescription or treatment, or even offer an official diagnosis.

Understanding the distinction between doctor and patient perspectives is a key approach in contemporary medical anthropology. In the 1950s and 1960s anthropologists typically accepted Western medicine as superior and authoritative in much the same ways that Freidson suggests. Anthropologists generally assumed that health problems in developing countries were due to ignorance of medical knowledge and technology. A breakthrough came when Arthur Kleinman, a medical anthropologist who conducted research in Taiwan, argued that the key to understanding such differences in perspective is that healers and patients often have different **explanatory models of illness**, which are explanations of what is happening to the patient's body. Kleinman asserted that the goal of medical anthropology research was not to decide who was right in their explanation, but to accept that different people would come to the illness with different concerns and different kinds of knowledge. In "Classic Contributions: Arthur Kleinman and the New Medical Anthropological Methodology," we show an example of this approach.

Kleinman's approach also helped medical anthropologists realize the limitations of scientific knowledge, and they began to challenge whether the doctors always had such special and privileged knowledge. Perhaps the patient understood some aspects of his or her body that the physician did not, and perhaps could not, understand. We have already discussed the subjectivity of pain and other symptoms. But in addition, medical knowledge is constantly changing, so how could doctors always have all the answers for how to treat their patients?

For example, consider what the medical profession has advised about breastfeeding for infants. Breastfeeding was universal until the 1950s, when baby formula was developed, and most American pediatricians promoted formula as a technologically superior way to ensure the health of the baby. By the 1970s new scientific analyses of the contents of breast milk indicated that breast milk contained antibodies that helped the child ward off infections. Rather than viewing breast milk as unsophisticated, the medical world began to see it as nature's way of protecting the child. About the same time in many developing countries, international aid workers were promoting baby formula as a way of producing strong, healthy babies. But by the 1990s, it became clear that this practice was not ideal: babies became malnourished because their poor mothers could not afford enough formula, and where clean drinking water was scarce, mothers often unintentionally used unsanitary water for their baby formula, resulting in much higher rates of fatal diarrhea (Figure 15.5).

Classic Contributions

Arthur Kleinman and the New Medical Anthropological Methodology

Arthur Kleinman.

IN THE MID-1970s physician, psychiatrist, and medical anthropologist Arthur Kleinman (b. 1941) published an essay on the history of medical anthropology. In it he added a short appendix where he introduced a new methodology around the concept of explanatory models, highlighting several cases he had come across in his work at the Massachusetts General Hospital in Boston. One case, excerpted here, offers an especially compelling illustration of his point.

For medical anthropologists, identifying the patients' Explanatory Model (EM) offered a new way of looking at how culture influenced a community's response to symptoms and illness. Rather than seeing an entire community responding uniformly to a set of symptoms, anthropologists now recognized that different individuals in varying relationships to the patient or with different positions in the society held quite varied views, or EMs. Kleinman's approach allowed medical anthropologists to shift the focus of their studies from the society to individuals within the society. And this methodology allowed anthropologists to make sense of how patients in non-Western settings use Western medicine. This new approach allows us to see health care decisions as a tension among different explanatory models.

Mrs. F. is a 60-year-old white Protestant grandmother who is recovering from pulmonary edema secondary to atherosclerotic cardiovascular disease and chronic congestive heart failure on one of the medical wards at the Massachusetts General Hospital. Her behavior in the recovery phase of her illness is described as strange and annoying by the house staff and nurses. While her cardiac status has greatly improved and she has become virtually asymptomatic, she induces vomiting and urinates frequently in her bed. She becomes angry when told to stop these behaviors. As a result of this, psychiatric consultation is requested.

Review of the lengthy medical record reveals nothing as to the personal significance of the patient's behavior. When queried about this behavior, and asked to explain why she is engaging in it and what meaning it has for her, the patient's response is most revealing. Describing herself as the wife and daughter of plumbers, the patient notes that she was informed by the medical team responsible for her care that she has "water in the lungs." She further reports that to her mind the physiology of the human body has the chest hooked up to two pipes, the mouth and the urethra. The patient explains that she has been trying to be

helpful by helping to remove as much water from her chest as possible through self-induced and frequent urination. She analogized the latter to the work of the "water pills" she is taking, which she has been told are getting rid of the water on her chest. She concludes, "I can't understand why people are angry at me." After appropriate explanations, along with diagrams, she acknowledges that the "plumbing" of the body is remarkable and quite different from what she had believed. Her unusual behavior ended at that time.

This amusing but true case study is but a very striking example of the important role played by alternative explanatory models in health care. I use it because it derives from the still poorly understood and inadequately studied popular culture health-care domain, rather than from the far better appreciated and researched folk medical domain (i.e., that section of the health-care system composed of non-orthodox profession and paraprofessional healers—religious healers, quacks, practitioners of chiropractic and osteopathy, and other specialists). Yet it is the former, family- and community-centered beliefs and practices, which has the greatest impact on all forms of health-care-related behavior. (Kleinman 1975:652–653)

Questions for Reflection

1. How might Kleinman's Explanatory Models methodology help anthropologists understand health-care choices in non-Western communities?

2. How does Kleinman's Explanatory Models methodology build on the disease–illness distinction?

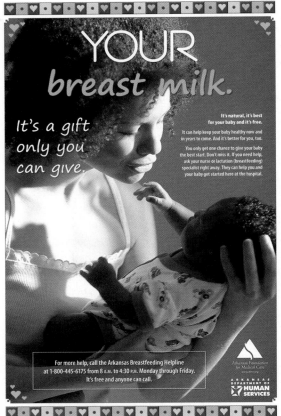

With the spread of AIDS in the developing world, we now know that mothers infected with HIV can give the infection to their infants through breast milk. So, as a result, aid workers are once again, at least, in communities where incidences of HIV infection are high, recommending baby formula. Who knows where the science of breast milk will settle in another generation? But as with nearly every other aspect of medicine, few scientific facts have remained, or will remain, static.

Since medical knowledge is constantly changing, it is no wonder that new diseases and drugs to treat them are constantly emerging. One way these changes emerge is when the professional medical system casts its net of authority out farther, to cover conditions that were not previously understood as medical problems.

The Medicalization of the Non-Medical

Over the past fifty years the health care industry has expanded dramatically, taking over more and more of our individual personal concerns. It has done so by redefining social, psychological, or moral problems as medical concerns. This process of viewing or treating as a medical concern conditions that were not previously understood as medical problems is called **medicalization**.

Alcoholism is a good example of this phenomenon. Excessive use of alcohol has been a problem throughout the history of the United States, producing opposition to it in the form of the temperance movement in the nineteenth and early twentieth centuries, and prohibition in the 1920s. For a long time, alcoholism was seen as a moral failing that caused (usually) men to abandon their jobs and families (Figure 15.6). By the 1980s, psychiatrists, HMOs, and health insurance companies began to view alcoholism as a disease defined as "recurrent substance use resulting in failure to fulfill major role obligations at work, school, home" (American Psychological Association 1994). Defining alcohol abuse as a disease, rather than as a crime, a socially inappropriate behavior, sinful behavior, or moral failing, reclassifies it as a medical concern.

Three major reasons have been suggested for medicalizing the non-medical. The first is financial: pharmaceutical companies, hospitals, and insurance companies stand to make larger profits when they can define a new disease for which they can provide treatment, care, and coverage. A second explanation is that the medicalization enhances the social authority of physicians. A third explanation concerns Americans' current preference for viewing social problems in scientific rather than moral or social terms. In "Thinking Like an Anthropologist: The Emergence of New Disease Categories," we explore how patients and social institutions together created a new disease out of the so-called Gulf War Syndrome.

Figure 15.5   Changing Views on Infant Formula and Breastfeeding. Dr. Benjamin Spock published a series of books beginning in the late 1940s (top) that promoted giving baby formula to infants rather than breast milk. Since the 1970s breastfeeding has had a resurgence in the United States after it became known that a mother's breast milk gave antibodies and partial immunity to infections to her baby (bottom).

• **Medicalization.** The process of viewing or treating as a medical concern conditions that were not previously understood as medical problems.

Up to now we have largely considered how people and their professional healers make sense of and diagnose illness. But a key aspect of the illness experience has to do with how the treatments we get for our illnesses actually help us heal. As with the distinction between health and illness, how the medicines and other treatments we receive help us heal is much more problematic than we might at first assume. It is to the matter of healing that we turn next.

Thinking Like an Anthropologist

The Emergence of New Disease Categories

ANTHROPOLOGISTS BEGIN THEIR research by asking questions. In this box, we want you to learn how to ask questions as an anthropological researcher. Part One describes a situation and follows up with questions we would ask. Part Two asks you to do the same thing with a different situation.

PART ONE: MAKING SENSE OF THE SYMPTOMS OF GULF WAR SYNDROME

In 1990 Iraqi president Saddam Hussein sent his army to invade the independent country of Kuwait. In response, President George H. W. Bush sent some 700,000 American soldiers to the Persian Gulf. During the war the Iraqi army set fire to hundreds of oil wells that spewed dark smoke into the atmosphere. Adding to the perception of environmental devastation, many troops worried that American bombing of Iraqi troop positions had released toxic chemicals into the already putrid atmosphere. Although as it turned out, American bombing did not do this, anxieties over what the air was doing to soldiers' health ran high.

After returning home, more than 10,000 veterans became ill with medically unexplained symptoms, such as chronic fatigue, loss of muscle control, headaches, dizziness, loss of balance, problems with memory, pain in muscles and joints, shortness of breath, and skin problems of various kinds. Most veterans who reported these symptoms attributed their poor health to their service in the Persian Gulf. Most military doctors who examined them found that their conditions resembled what came to be known during the Vietnam War era as post-traumatic stress disorder (PTSD) (called "battle fatigue" during World War II). These war-related conditions are considered anxiety disorders with psychological or psychosomatic roots.

When doctors diagnosed Gulf War veterans' problems as PTSD, most patients objected, claiming that their medical conditions were real and not "in their heads." Veterans had a variety of explanations for their symptoms: long-term contact with nerve agents or chemicals from the burning oil wells or brief encounters with volatile chemical agents. Others interpreted their symptoms as caused by a vaccine for anthrax which all military personnel were injected with before leaving for the Gulf. Although repeated medical examinations could not confirm the explanatory models these patients had developed, and PTSD seemed the most likely cause, veterans began to refer to all these cases as the Gulf War syndrome.

From a medical perspective, most of the symptoms veterans report are subjective, consisting of diffuse pain, fatigue, malaise, and indigestion. Moreover, the range of symptoms seems so varied that physicians systematically rejected any single diagnosis as adequate. In addition, researchers have found the same mortality rates among veterans and other men who never visited the Gulf, suggesting that while the symptoms may be real they are not causing higher than normal death rates among veterans of the Persian Gulf conflict. Nevertheless, veterans formed advocacy groups to defend their definition of these diverse health issues as Gulf War syndrome.

As we have seen, doctors and patients often have very different ways of understanding and interpreting patients' health concerns. And doctors' more authoritative interpretations are difficult for patients to challenge. But in this case there were so many vets with self-diagnosed Gulf War syndrome that veterans groups were able to get congressional attention. The Department of Veterans Affairs formed a study group to investigate the matter, and a federally mandated Research Advisory Committee on Gulf War Veterans' Illnesses (2008) concluded that these illnesses have real biological causes and serious consequences for affected veterans.

The U.S. government now officially recognizes Gulf War syndrome as a disease, even though it has no single cause and no

Gulf War Syndrome, a New Disease Category. Though its origins are in debate, some have associated the prevalence of Gulf War syndrome with burning oil wells in Iraq and Kuwait.

(continued)

Thinking Like an Anthropologist (continued)

common symptoms. And while the official report of the Advisory Committee acknowledged it as a group of real illnesses with genuine effects on veterans, their classification is not a medical classification in the usual sense. But, of course, from the beginning Gulf War syndrome was no simple health problem.

What questions does this situation raise for anthropological researchers?

1. Why should an environmental explanation—exposure to harmful chemical agents—be more appealing to veterans than PTSD?
2. Why would physicians and researchers initially have rejected Gulf War syndrome as a genuine disorder?
3. What role did political pressure by veterans' advocacy groups play here?

PART TWO: MAKING SENSE OF RESTLESS LEG SYNDROME, ERECTILE DYSFUNCTION, AND OTHER PROBLEMATIC DISEASE CLASSIFICATIONS

Consider any one of the new health conditions that have emerged over the past thirty or forty years, such as restless legs syndrome, erectile dysfunction, pre-menstrual syndrome, acid reflux disease, or any of a number of other conditions for which pharmaceutical companies have developed pills, tablets, or capsules as treatments. The American public considers many of these conditions as standard medical diagnoses, even though physicians have not always recognized them. What questions would you ask about the rise of new health conditions as an anthropological researcher?

Figure 15.6   The Temperance Movement. Alcohol use was condemned by members of this early-twentieth-century movement as a moral failing.

THINKING CRITICALLY ABOUT MEDICAL ANTHROPOLOGY

Fifty years ago alcoholism was considered a moral failing, a behavioral problem found when people have no strong moral code to live by and do bad things to their families and others. Compare this earlier understanding of alcoholism with the most common view that alcoholism is a disease. How do you think this shift happened?

How Does Healing Happen?

When Robert Welsch was studying healing practices among the Ningerum, one of his informants came down with malaria. Welsch offered him some anti-malarial tablets, but his informant could not swallow them because they tasted bad. After several days of lying in bed, the man's nephew performed a traditional ritual, smearing clay on his uncle's painful chest, reciting magic words, and apparently removing a packet consisting of some small object wrapped in a banana leaf from the sick man's chest. Within two hours, the man was up and about with his walking stick heading for the spring where he showered, a visible sign to everyone in the village, including the anthropologist, that he was feeling better (see Welsch 1983), see Figure 15.7.

To the Western mind, such examples of traditional healing strain credibility. But anthropologists around the world have observed similar responses to a wide variety of non-medical treatments. We do know that the human body is remarkably resilient. If we cut ourselves superficially while chopping vegetables, the wound will bleed, scab over, and gradually new skin will cover the cut. We do not fully understand how healing works, but we know that healing is more complex than most Americans recognize. Healing is not just about pills and surgeries, but about the meaning that the sick person and the healers give to treatments in a specific cultural context. Healing is a complex biocultural process. Medical anthropologists generally accept that treatments help our bodies heal in four distinct therapeutic processes: (1) clinical processes, (2) symbolic processes, (3) through social support, and (4) through persuasion (Csordas and Kleinman 1996). We consider each of these processes next.

Figure 15.7   The Power of Non-Medical Healing. A Ningerum healer removes a magical packet from a man's leg with magical words, rubbing magical leaves, and sucking to relieve pain in his leg.

Clinical Therapeutic Processes

Most professionals working with Western medicine assume that effective treatment comes from **clinical therapeutic processes**, which involves a doctor observing a patient's symptoms and prescribing a specific treatment, such as a pill. This is the basis upon which most people take over-the-counter medicines, and this is why doctors prescribe specific medicines for us. The medicines have some active ingredient that is assumed to address either the cause or the symptom of a disorder. Thus, an antibiotic is thought to kill a type of bacterium, while a vaccination inserts a small amount of the virus or bacterium—usually already dead—into the blood, which triggers the body's immune system to react by creating antibodies so the body can fight off the infection in the future.

Sometimes doctors understand how these physiological processes work; at other times they may not understand the healing process but assume that it works by some plausible but unproven process. Whatever the case, for medical anthropologists and medical researchers there is still more to understand because these clinical processes do not account for healing such as in the Ningerum case presented earlier.

- **Clinical therapeutic process.** The healing process in which medicines have some active ingredient that is assumed to address either the cause or the symptom of a disorder.

Symbolic Therapeutic Processes

In most tribal societies that medical anthropologists studied in the twentieth century, there were some treatments that used herbs, teas, and potions. The explanatory models used in these societies sometimes drew on clinical models, but often the herbs and potions were important not so much for their chemical properties but for their symbolic ones. Although the chemical composition of the herb or leaf might help the patient heal, people were largely unaware of these properties and used them in rituals for other reasons.

- **Symbolic therapeutic process.** A healing process that restructures the meanings of the symbols surrounding the illness, particularly during a ritual.

In such cases, healing rituals act as a **symbolic therapeutic process** by virtue of their role in structuring the meanings of the symbols used. The symbolism of healing rituals comes from a number of sources, including natural materials. This symbolism often involves fragrant leaves, oils, or potions with rich smells that invoke our olfactory senses and our senses of taste and touch. It can also involve chanting, drumming, singing, and other sounds that set particular moods. Typically, the rituals provide a symbolic temporal progression, as in the form of a mythological story, that the affliction is supposed to follow for the patient to recover and heal.

For example, the French anthropologist Claude Lévi-Strauss (1961) documented a healing ritual among the Kuna [**koo**-nah] Indians of Panama that shows how over a period of many hours the shaman sings, produces smells, and touches a woman in the midst of a difficult birth. Anthropologists usually use the term "shaman" to refer to anyone who performs various kinds of ritual healing practices. The ritual chanting recounts a mythological story in which a child overcomes diverse obstacles to reach its goal. The sounds, the smells, the story, and the touching combine to relax the mother and her baby so the child can emerge from the womb just as the hero of the story reaches his final goal. Csordas and Kleinman suggest that this kind of ritual is very common around the world because so many societies have found it efficacious.

Social Support

- **Social support therapeutic process.** A healing process that involves a patient's social networks, especially close family members and friends, who typically surround the patient during an illness.

The **social support therapeutic process** involves a patient's social networks, who typically surround the patient, much as Welsch found when he became ill while living among the Ningerum. Although relatives and friends may perform some (usually) minor treatments on the patient, the major thrust of this therapeutic process comes from the presence of family members who provide comfort and aid to the sick person. Feeling aided and supported by his or her relatives may affect the patient's bodily functions. For example, diabetics often have better control of their blood sugars when they are with supportive family members, but poorer control when feeling isolated.

Persuasion: The Placebo Effect

- **Placebo effect.** A healing process that works on persuading a patient he or she has been given a powerful medicine, even though the "medicine" has no active medical ingredient.

Persuasion is another powerful therapeutic process. Consider the **placebo effect**, in which a patient is given a non-medicine as if it were a medicine. The classic example of a placebo is a sugar pill given instead of some prescription drug with an active pharmaceutical ingredient. What makes it a placebo is that the sugar pill has a beneficial effect even though it has no pharmacological or clinically active component. Usually, patients are told that they will receive a powerful medication or procedure, even though they will actually receive the placebo. This strategy, however, worries many people, including doctors, because it amounts to lying to a patient; dispensing placebos challenges professional ethical codes of behavior and even some federal laws in the United States.

Up to now it has been hard to explain the placebo's effect clinically, since the placebo seems to work through persuading the patient that the drug is effective. Something must be happening within the patient's body, but it seems to lie outside the bounds of ordinary medicine.

A dramatic illustration of the power of the placebo effect comes from a French study conducted in the 1990s. In this study, researchers divided a group of hospitalized cancer patients with mild to moderate cancer pain into four groups to test the effectiveness of naproxen, at the time a new pain killer that many of you know by the brand name Aleve. None of the patients experienced so much pain that they required opiates, and the study put none of the patients in significant distress. At first these patients were randomly assigned to one of two groups as they came out of cancer surgery. One group was told they would be in a random trial of a powerful new pain reliever and would receive either the test drug or an inert placebo. Members of the second group were told nothing. This second group was unaware they were in a test and would assume that they were receiving standard hospital care. Half of the patients in each group were randomly given either an inert placebo or naproxen, thus creating four groups in all. Nurses, who were unaware of the details of the study, asked patients to evaluate their pain reduction hourly using a pain scale from 1 to 100 that represents the pain experienced (Bergmann et al. 1994; Kaptchuk 2001).

All the patients given naproxen showed a reduction in pain, confirming that naproxen is an effective pain killer. But patients who were given the placebo, and were told they were in the study, had greater pain relief than those patients who were given naproxen but were told nothing about their pain treatment regimen. Figure 15.8 illustrates this study's findings. Even more remarkable: this study suggests something that most researchers were not anticipating and had not appreciated. Figure 15.8 shows the large gap in experiences of pain relief between the two groups who were given naproxen. Theoretically, if we assume that naproxen works physiologically, both groups should have experienced similar levels of pain relief. But they did not; the placebo effect enhanced the pain relief in the test group who received naproxen and were told they were in the trial. In other words, those patients in the test group knew they were in the study and expected to get good results from their pain killer. What this tells us is that the placebo effect probably enhances all clinical interventions whether they are pharmaceuticals, surgeries, or other procedures. When patients *believe* that a pharmaceutical or medical procedure is effective, they regularly see improvements.

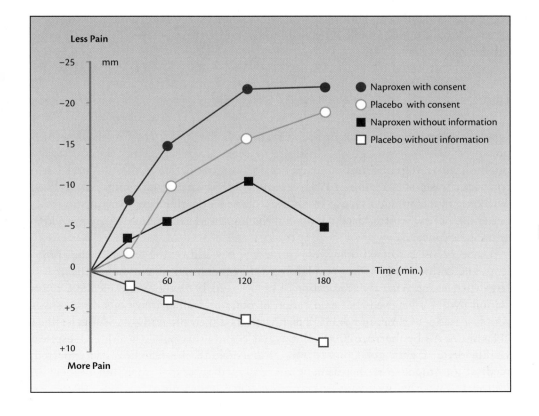

Figure 15.8   Evidence of the Placebo Effect on Pain After Surgery. Everyone in the study who received naproxen experienced pain reduction, but people told about the study who received only the placebo experienced more relief from pain than patients who received naproxen but were not told about the study. (After Bergmann et al. 1994)

The insight that culture and social processes influence the healing process is a powerful insight of medical anthropology. So how do anthropologists put such insights to work? We consider how in our last section.

THINKING CRITICALLY ABOUT MEDICAL ANTHROPOLOGY

We don't understand why or how the placebo effect works, but there is some strong clinical evidence that it does, as the naproxen study shows. Discuss what this study might mean for a doctor prescribing a "powerful" antibiotic or some brand new treatment for a condition in a patient he or she sees in his or her clinic.

What Can Anthropology Contribute to Addressing Global Health Problems?

Anthropologists have long recognized that they can contribute to alleviating global health problems by understanding the health care systems available to different peoples around the world, how diseases are transmitted within and between communities, and how people use the resources available to them. In recent years anthropologists have also become more engaged and proactive in trying to improve health conditions in the communities, countries, and regions in which they work. We explore both of these themes—understanding and actively addressing global problems—in the following subsections.

Understanding Global Health Problems

One of the first attempts at this problem came in the 1950s when medical anthropologists, working through the Institute of Inter-American Affairs, helped design public health programs and rural clinics to promote better health in rural Latin America (Erasmus 1952; Foster 1952; Simmons 1955). Their goal, which they reached with only moderate success, was to find ways for encouraging rural peasants to make better use of newly introduced clinics and the improved vaccinations as a way of lowering infant mortality.

By the 1970s, it seemed that Western medicine would fix the world's health problems, and anthropology's role in explaining different cultural systems of healthcare was largely irrelevant. After the eradication of smallpox in 1979, the World Health Organization (WHO) believed that eradication of polio and other infectious diseases was simply a matter of time, and WHO's planners called their program—unrealistically— "Health for All by the Year 2000." But as AIDS and other public health crises spread worldwide, and even polio proved more intractable than researchers had expected, medical anthropologists increasingly saw the need to double their involvement in understanding what were rapidly becoming global health problems. We explore two issues here: the issue of medical pluralism and patterns of disease transmission.

Understanding Medical Pluralism: Comparing Different Health Care Systems

Medical anthropologists have long recognized that there are many sophisticated non-Western systems of medicine—in places like India, China, and the Arab world—that had been effective for centuries before the medical systems of the United States and Western Europe had developed antiseptics, antibiotics, and vaccines. As India, China, and the Arab world began to establish modern industrial societies, Indian and Chinese health care facilities were integrating Western medicine with their traditional practices. Medicine was not replacing these ancient traditions, but supplementing them. Nearly all other societies draw on more than one medical tradition simultaneously, a concept called **medical pluralism**, which refers to the co-existence and interpenetration of distinct medical traditions with different cultural roots.

An example of medical pluralism comes from anthropologist Carolyn Nordstrom (1988), who studied Ayurveda, a traditional medical system developed in India and Sri Lanka. She found that Ayurveda, while having its own medical schools, was not a single medical tradition. Ayurvedic practitioners diagnose health problems using the classical Ayurvedic practice of reading the pulse, and they mix herbs in specified ways. But practitioners also draw upon traditional Sinhalese (referring to the people of Sri Lanka) medical ideas and practices in what Nordstrom refers to as a mediation of Ayureveda and local Sinhala medicine. She learned that they often mix traditional Sinhalese herbal preparations along with those they have learned at an Ayurvedic college, and that many Ayurvedic healers frequently use stethoscopes and thermometers and dispense standard Western medicines along with their herbal preparations. She also observed that some Sinhalese Buddhist monks incorporated Ayurvedic and Buddhist principles in their therapeutic work, sometimes adding Sinhalese preparations as well (Figure 15.9).

The broader point here is that in an increasingly globalized world, medical anthropologists are learning that all medical systems are now plural systems. Successfully addressing global health problems must take this fact into account.

- **Medical pluralism.** The co-existence and interpenetration of distinct medical traditions with different cultural roots in the same cultural community.

Understanding Patterns of Disease Transmission

Medical anthropologists have also played a key role in making sense of how infectious diseases spread within a population, which is as much an anthropological or sociological task as it is a medical one. For example, anthropologists have played a key role in helping researchers understand the transmission of HIV, which causes AIDS. In the United States and Europe, public health officials have promoted the use of condoms to interrupt the spread of HIV. But promoting condoms has not proved so effective in Africa, Haiti, and certain Southeast Asian countries, each of which had very different cultures of sexuality and patterns of transmission from that in the United States (see also Chapter 12). It was with studying these patterns of transmission that anthropologists played a central role in helping medical researchers understand how culture was shaping HIV transmission.

In Africa, for example, HIV was first noticed along major highway routes where long-haul truckers became infected through heterosexual contacts with infected prostitutes, taking the infection to women in the next truck stop town (Nyamwaya, 1993). Truckers, prostitutes, and truck stops produced ideal conditions for transmission of HIV through these wide-ranging and international social networks. Anthropologist and geographer Ezekiel Kalipeni (2004) suggests that epidemiologists and medical researchers had completely missed seeing these patterns. He argues

Figure 15.9 Medical Pluralism. Modern Ayurveda often adopts elements from biomedicine.

that medical researchers explained the observed distribution of cases in terms of traditional patterns of African sexuality, which the medical community assumed was radically different from those of Western Europe. Traditional culture was demonized; the appearance of modern lifestyles, population growth, social inequality, and mounting poverty that was sending African villagers to urban centers and new forms of employment all went ignored. Anthropologists provided detailed observations of people's ideas about the disease, their explanatory models, and specific information about the sexual practices and behaviors of women as well as men, helping illuminate the patterns of HIV transmission (McGrath et al. 1992; Nyamwaya 1993).

Anthropological Contributions to Tackling the International HIV/AIDS Crisis

As their understanding of global health problems has become more sophisticated, anthropologists have become more assertive in putting their ideas to work. One way they do this is by working with communities to design aspects of the public health system to meet the needs, understandings, and cultural expectations of people in the community. To continue with the example of the HIV/AIDS crisis, we examine the work of Paul Farmer.

Using anthropology's holistic perspective to understand communities and their social problems, anthropologist and physician Paul Farmer (1992) began research for his dissertation in Haiti. As an undergraduate Farmer had majored in anthropology at Duke University. In 1983, before beginning medical school at Harvard, he spent some time in Cange, a community in the mountainous central plateau of Haiti. In this extremely poor area, he could see firsthand that the social, economic, political, and health problems were interconnected. Farmer saw these connections before HIV/AIDS had been identified and before large numbers of AIDS cases had been diagnosed in Haiti. When the AIDS epidemic broke out, the connections between the health of Haitians and socioeconomic and political conditions became even more obvious.

Working with another M.D.-Ph.D. student, Jim Yong Kim, Farmer helped found an organization in the highland district of Cange in 1987. (Kim went on to head the World Bank.) They called this organization Partners in Health (2010) and developed a small health center. The international health community was initially focused on treating AIDS patients and on other public health concerns to slow the spread of AIDS. But Farmer and Kim had larger goals that they saw as related to health in the Haitian community. They began encouraging local people to plant trees in the once lush forested region that had been devastated from poverty and rapid population growth, which led to deforestation as poor Haitians turned to their last resource (trees) to make into charcoal. Farmer and Kim put together an integrated program that attacked the causes of poverty and environmental degradation as a way of improving health. After twenty years of execution of this program, Farmer and Kim saw the district returned to something like its lush original environment and solid improvements in local health (Kidder 2003).

In "Anthropologist as Problem Solver: Nancy Scheper-Hughes on an Engaged Anthropology of Health," we consider another way that anthropologists are becoming increasingly proactive in health problems around the world. These anthropologists and a whole new generation of younger anthropologists are not just observing how health care systems work and don't work, they are also active participants trying to make conditions better.

Anthropologist as Problem Solver
Nancy Scheper-Hughes on an Engaged Anthropology of Health

MEDICAL ANTHROPOLOGIST NANCY Scheper-Hughes has conducted research in a variety of contexts around the world: in the parched lands and shantytowns of northeast Brazil, in the squatter camps of South Africa, and in the AIDS sanatoria of Cuba. In each of these contexts she saw structural poverty and blatant examples of what she called "useless suffering." For years anthropologists have adopted a position of cultural relativism that she feels often puts us in a position of trying to be morally neutral when confronting issues of institutional or state violence against "vulnerable bodies and fragile lives." In her view, to be ethical, anthropologists need to focus critically on the institutions and embedded power relations that shape the health of poor, underserved, and disadvantaged people.

Recently, Scheper-Hughes has been studying the illegal sale of body parts (Scheper-Hughes 2004; Sheper-Hughes and Wacquant 2003). She has interviewed a Brazilian organ trafficker in his prison cell, people whose kidneys had been sold, and other people involved in this trafficking. In July 2009 Scheper-Hughes assisted authorities in arresting a Brooklyn man accused of selling black market kidneys. The *New York Daily News* heralded Scheper-Hughes as having an anthropological "'Dick Tracy' moment" when she turned over information to the FBI that allowed them to bring this suspected organ-trafficker to justice (*Daily News* 2009).

This led to exposing an extensive network that involved people in several countries. She told NPR's Brian Lehrer (National Public Radio 2009), "I had begun to unravel a huge network—a criminal network that really looks like, smells like, a kind of a mafia. The head office of the pyramid scheme originated in Israel; with brokers placed in Turkey; in New York City; in Philadelphia; in Durban; in Johannesburg; in Recife, Brazil; Moldova—all over the place." She went on to say, "And I used my ethnographic investigative skills to just go country-hopping and try to connect the dots. Eventually, it brought me to Isaac Rosenbaum being the head broker for Ilan Peri in Israel, who is the don, basically, of the operation, and who is a slippery guy."

Questions for Reflection

1. To what extent is understanding the perspective of people without a voice a contribution to addressing and resolving those issues?

2. Anthropology has become a much more "hands-on" discipline in the past two decades. But does such involvement in shaping policy get in the way of our being able to understand all perspectives holistically?

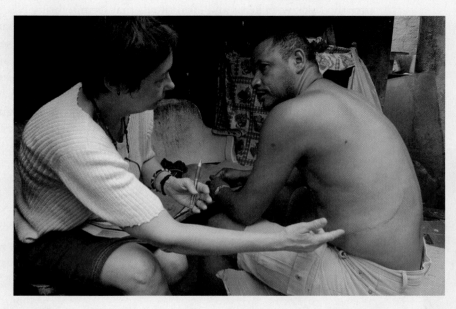

Nancy Scheper-Hughes. Here the anthropologist interviews a man who was trafficked from his home in Recife, Brazil, to Durban, South Africa, so his kidney could be illegally sold. For his kidney he received $6,000, a large sum of money in the slums of Brazil.

THINKING CRITICALLY ABOUT MEDICAL ANTHROPOLOGY

Medical anthropologists have traditionally been involved in public health efforts to vaccinate children, to provide clean drinking water, and more recently to assist with combatting HIV/AIDS. Why would such public health efforts be a natural role for anthropologists rather than involvement in clinical settings that involve physicians and their patients in modern urban settings?

Conclusion

This chapter's focus on issues of our bodies and their impairments reflects what most of us feel, implicitly, is the most natural part of our beings. But how we understand our bodies, and perhaps more important, how we make sense of our bodies' impairments, is inevitably shaped by the culture we have grown up in and by the concerns and preoccupations people around us have.

As we saw with the Spring 2009 outbreak of H1N1 influenza ("swine flu"), discussed in the chapter opener, people living in different cultures, with varying views and cultural expectations, react differently to essentially the same set of facts. In an effort to protect their citizens, each country's leaders approach problems of health and epidemics somewhat differently, because in each case it is not the virus or the epidemiology but the local cultural assumptions that shape these leaders' actions. When individuals become ill in different cultures, they and their families also respond in locally appropriate ways, interpreting the signs, symptoms, and implications in locally meaningful ways.

Recent research even suggests that our bodies respond according to our expectations about the effectiveness of a treatment. Western physicians have nonchalantly dismissed such responses as merely the "placebo effect," but for millennia societies have looked after their sick with herbs and local rituals that seem to bring relief to the sick.

The research medical anthropologists are conducting today comprises some of the most important applied projects in the discipline. But these research projects have demonstrated that global health concerns and modern epidemics are much more than medical problems. Like everything else in life, health and illness are linked to the kinds of society we live in, our biology, the historic traditions that have motivated and shaped our communities, and the meaning and significance we give to these biological and social facts. These linkages taken together are what make us human.

KEY TERMS

Clinical therapeutic process   p. 383

Disease   p. 378

Explanatory model of illness   p. 378

Illness   p. 378

Medical pluralism   p. 387

Medicalization   p. 380

Placebo effect   p. 384

Sick role   p. 373

Social support therapeutic process   p. 384

Symbolic therapeutic process   p. 384

Reviewing the Chapter

Chapter Section	What We Know	To Be Resolved
What Do We Mean by Health and Illness?	A person's culture shapes his or her interpretation of symptoms and understanding of the illness condition.	How people in any particular society will interpret the symptoms of illness can be determined only by detailed evidence from illness episodes in a particular society.
How and Why Do Doctors and Other Health Practitioners Gain Social Authority?	By dealing with human concerns as medical or biomedical problems our society implicitly gives power to health practitioners who can prescribe drugs and other therapies.	It is not entirely clear why some peoples around the world are so ready and willing to give authority to healers, while people in other societies are not willing.
How Does Healing Happen?	Not all healing can be explained by the clinical processes familiar to physicians and medical students. Healing has important social and cultural dimensions.	While the power of the placebo effect is demonstrated, we still don't understand why it can work on our bodies.
What Can Anthropology Contribute to Addressing Global Health Problems?	Clinical solutions to global health problems cannot work effectively without understanding the local culture of the people whose health-related behavior we want to improve, as well as the fact that due to medical pluralism most societies combine distinct healing systems.	Up to now there is no single solution to a health problem that will work in all societies; it is not clear if there are general strategies applicable to most societies.

Readings

One of the most accessible ways that students can enter the world of medical anthropology is through Katherine Dettwyler's *Dancing Skeletons: Life and Death in West Africa* (2nd edition. Long Grove, IL: Waveland Press, 2013). Dettwyler's narrative gives students a sense of what it is like to be a medical anthropologist in a developing country. Anne Fadiman's *The Spirit Catches You and You Fall Down: A Hmong Child, Her American Doctors, and the Collision of Two Cultures* (New York: Farrar, Strauss and Giroux, 1997) offers a glimpse into the tensions between American biomedical culture and an Asian immigrant medical culture, which is as religious as it is medical.

Arthur Kleinman's classic *Patients and Healers in the Context of Culture: An Exploration of the Borderland Between Anthropology, Medicine, and Psychology* (Berkeley: University of California Press, 1980) provided the first modern formulation of medical anthropology as a systematic branch of anthropology, complete with a methodology that could help us understand interactions between patients and health care providers, whether the latter are doctors, traditional healers, new-age consultants, or neighbors. Mary-Jo Delvecchio Good, Paul E. Brodwin, Byron J. Good, and Arthur Kleinman's volume *Pain as Human Experience: An Anthropological Perspective* (Berkeley: University of California Press,

1992) explores how medical anthropologists can study the problem of chronic pain using approaches previously suggested by Kleinman.

Paul Farmer's book, *Pathologies of Power: Health, Human Rights, and the New War on the Poor* (Berkeley: University of California Press, 2004) offers an approach to issues of access to health care resources in a variety of contexts around the world, showing how access to health care is as important as the way patients and healers understand illness.

16 CHAPTER

The Arts

Objects, Images, and Commodities

IN 1935 THE Museum of Modern Art (MoMA) in New York opened the first major exhibition of African art in North America. This exhibition included more than 600 objects from all of the major regions of Sub-Saharan Africa. When museum visitors saw those objects, similar to those in depicted in Figure 16.1, they were presented with carved figures, fetishes, masks and the like, most of which had obvious anthropomorphic (or human-like) features of faces and bodies. Museum-goers could discern faces, eyes, mouths, torsos, legs, and sometimes genitalia that identified the figures as either male or female. But nearly all of these figures were stylized in ways that were unfamiliar to Americans, presenting a problem for most museum-goers: How should they make sense of these oddly shaped bodies and faces?

Some help in answering this question came from *New York Times* art critic Edward Alden Jewell, whose newspaper review of what he referred to as "this strange tribal art" suggested that the public would "probably encounter its principal difficulty" on the aesthetic side (Jewell 1935). Jewell explained that Americans were likely to see these carvings as expressions of poor workmanship and an inability to carve in a realistic or naturalistic fashion, triggering an ethnocentric reaction based on the idea that Africans are primitive people with no artistic ability. Jewell urged museum-goers to look for something deeper than

Rethinking African Art. When Western audiences were first introduced to objects like the Nkisi figure from the Democratic Republic of Congo pictured here, they often responded dismissively and ethnocentrically. They misunderstood African notions of aesthetics. In this Nkisi figure at the Hood Museum of Art at Dartmouth College, each additional element adds meaning and power to the object—the most important here are nails. Each nail pounded into the carving requested some favor from the spirit in this figure, but it also strengthened the spirit. (Hood Museum of Art, Dartmouth College, Hanover, New Hampshire)

Figure 16.1   African Carvings in a Gallery of the Hood Museum of Art at Dartmouth College. (Hood Museum of Art, Dartmouth College, Hanover, New Hampshire)

the sense of cultural superiority many were likely to feel, advising them to check "their preconceived ideas, their prejudices and all narrow standards at the door."

James Sweeney, the curator of the exhibition, went further, arguing that these artworks did not represent the pitiful efforts of "untutored savages" but were the products of skilled carvers who were not trying to carve realistic human-like figures at all, but something else. For Sweeney, these African artists sought to achieve a symbolic, not naturalistic, representation of their subjects. The carvers had intentionally carved in stylized and non-realistic ways to emphasize the symbolic aspects that were most important to the spirits, demons, or gods depicted.

Nowadays, nearly eighty years after the MoMA show, most Americans would recognize this point. They would see these carvings are highly stylized, a feature that we see in our own art, including most of our most popular animated films and cartoons. Many undergraduates who study design and fine art are trained to use highly stylized forms that vaguely represent the naturalistic form of the original. But a century ago, most Americans—many anthropologists among them—assumed that these odd shapes and peculiar bodily forms were evidence that Africans were not physically able to carve realistic forms.

To the contrary, the African carvings intentionally emphasized the symbolic, rather than naturalistic aspects of their subjects. If a carving or mask was made of hardwood, it suggested the strength of the spiritual being that was represented. If it incorporated elements of a large wild creature, such as a lion, it communicated the sense that the figure shared certain traits with a lion, such as strength, domination, speed, and prowess.

The 1935 MoMA show suggests that Africans and Americans approach art very differently and that these objects mean something distinctive in each cultural context. Thinking about these objects and the different ways that different people might understand or appreciate art suggests the question that is central to this chapter: *How do objects and images reflect and shape the world in which we live?* Embedded within this question are several more focused questions, around which this chapter is organized:

How should we look at art objects anthropologically?

Why and how do the meanings of things change over time?

How do certain objects come to represent people's goals and aspirations?

How do images shape the worlds in which people live?

Understanding **aesthetic criteria**—the underlying principles that make something appealing or beautiful—has long been a key aspect of making sense of **art**, which has conventionally been understood to be an expression of human creative skill, usually in the form of painting, sculpture, music, or literature. But for the anthropologist, works of art are not just pretty pictures that hang on the walls of art galleries and museums. Art objects are fundamentally objects that have significance—and multiple dimensions—beyond their aesthetic qualities. Whether it is an African mask, a Picasso painting—or, for that matter, even an everyday object like a bicycle, a bowler hat, or a pair of shoes—the key to what makes any object interesting for anthropological study and reflection is that every object emerges from and exists within a set of human social relationships. Simultaneously, each object tells us something about the social world in which the object was made, used, or displayed. We begin by explaining how anthropologists approach the study of objects.

- **Aesthetic criteria.** The underlying principles that make something appealing or beautiful.

- **Art.** Conventionally understood as an expression of human creative skill, usually in the form of painting, sculpture, music, or literature.

How Should We Look at Art Objects Anthropologically?

Until the 1980s anthropologists tended to look at the study of art in much the same way as art historians did, or, for that matter, how you might before reading this chapter. Although the origins of the objects each field studied were different—anthropologists studied mainly non-Western art, whereas art historians focused mostly on European and American art—they both approached art as a special domain of human experience. Art objects were by definition separate from the objects people use in their daily lives, something hung on a wall or displayed in art museums, galleries, or in places of honor in people's homes. The artist too is someone with a very special, even separate, place in life. Viewed in this way, art was considered an expression of a particular tradition, time, or place, but even more so, an expression of the individual creativity of the artist.

Like art historians, anthropologists recognized that artists, through their creativity, could challenge and affect people's thinking, such as the Spanish surrealist painter Pablo Picasso or the British rock group the Beatles did for the West. But for anthropologists, it was also clear that individual artists used styles and techniques that reflected and reinforced certain consistent cultural patterns, aesthetics, and traditions specific to their own societies.

By the 1980s it had become clear that there were important limitations with this approach to art, however. One of these problems was that many societies do not have a category of "art" that coincides with how we might define art in the United States. Instead, the arts—whether the visual arts, music, or the literary arts—tend to be much more integrated into the daily lives and routines of non-Western people. Moreover, the lives of artists are usually not easily distinguished from the lives of ordinary people. In fact, only in societies with considerable social stratification and occupational specialization is the artist much different from any other member of society. It became increasingly clear that the category of "art" was, in fact, an ethnocentric projection of a Western category onto the cultures of non-Western peoples.

The second problem had to with the kinds of objects anthropologists were considering as art, such as intricately decorated wooden, bamboo, earthenware, or metal objects.

These objects were typically chosen over plain and unornamented tools because of their aesthetic and decorative qualities. But these objects were not made primarily for decorative purposes, and almost anything anthropologists considered art had a social purpose or function, either as a tool or as part of people's ritual lives.

As a result of these insights most anthropologists who have studied the arts since the 1980s have been focusing more generally on *objects* rather than on the category of *art,* which has proved so hard to define in ways that will fit non-Western societies as well as Western cultures. Reflecting this new paradigm, when Robert Layton first published his book *The Anthropology of Art* in 1981, he began his chapter on art and social life with an African example, but not of one of the impressive carvings with which we opened this chapter. He started with an initiation basket of magical charms from the Lega people of Central Africa. The stones, monkey skulls, and other items in this basket would not be considered "art" by most art historians, even though the basket included at least two small crude wooden figures (Layton 1991:54–56). His implicit point was that the proper attention of anthropologists was on objects, rather than the more specialized category of "art objects," because it is objects of all sorts that people everywhere use to construct meanings about the world around them.

The Many Dimensions of Objects

Cultural anthropologists actually have a long history working with objects—from works of art to everyday technologies—in various ways, but it was not until 1985 that anyone attempted to understand that history and systematize it in a meaningful way. In that year historian of anthropology George W. Stocking, Jr. (1985) sought to do just that in a collection of essays about the role objects have played in the history of anthropology. Stocking's book, *Objects and Others: Essays on Museums and Material Culture,* explained that anthropology's history began with the study of objects in museums decades before anthropologists even began conducting their own field research.

Using these collections, the earliest anthropologists classified how civilized, barbaric, or primitive a society was from the kinds of objects they had or did not have, using crude and naïve measures of technologies like pottery and bows and arrows to make conclusions about the cultural progress and sophistication of a society. Later, when anthropologists started conducting fieldwork, they observed ritual life first-hand, noticing the importance of objects in rituals, social exchanges, and political activities. Anthropologists began to look at objects to understand the meaning of rituals, the interconnections between people who exchanged particular objects, or the social stratification within a society that could be seen in the presence or absence of objects in a particular household or community. In a basic sense, this latter approach has endured until the present.

But the importance of Stocking's work is that he felt that when looking at objects it is still too easy to focus only on their obvious physical characteristics. Objects, he said, are multidimensional, and if we really want to understand them, we have to recognize and try to understand not just their three basic physical dimensions—height, width, depth—but four others as well, among them time (history), power, wealth, and aesthetics, making a total of seven dimensions.

The dimension of *time* or *history* refers to the fact that objects in museums came from somewhere and have individual histories. In part this asks when, by whom, and how were they produced, and how did they get here, and also how have interpretations of the object changed over time? The dimension of *power* reveals the relations of inequality reflected in objects, especially why the objects of non-Western people sit in ethnographic museums, while very few non-Western people have museums or repositories where local people can view Western objects. During the heyday of colonialism, European and American anthropologists collected thousands of objects from the peoples they studied, at times without the community giving its consent based on a full knowledge of what was intended to happen to these objects. *Wealth* reflects the fact that people use objects to establish and demonstrate who has wealth and social status. The dimension of *aesthetics* is reflected in the fact that each culture brings with it its own system or patterns of recognizing what is pleasing or attractive, and which configurations of colors and textures are appealing and which are not.

What intrigued Stocking most about objects, especially those now found in museums, was that these things were a historical archive in multiple dimensions that can tell us a great deal about the cultures that made and used these objects as well as the relationships between the societies of the collectors and the communities who originally used them. And because most objects were embedded within local symbolic systems of meaning, the objects themselves could offer a window for understanding the local symbolism that enlivened many other aspects of social life in non-Western communities.

But Stocking's point was more expansive than just being focused on the objects found in art and ethnographic museums. His insights can actually be applied to any everyday object. Consider, for example, a shiny new bicycle.

A Shiny New Bicycle, in Multiple Dimensions

Picture a shiny new bicycle chained to a bicycle rack on your campus (Figure 16.2). Made of a strong yet lightweight alloy, it is fast, sleek, and an exquisite example of modern technology applied to an object that has been around for more than a century. It might even be considered an example of modern artistry, where modern industrial processes combine with aesthetic sensibilities to allow humans and machines swift and elegant movement through city streets. Like all objects, this bicycle has the physical properties of height, length, and width, dimensions that are quite important for any individual mounting one: think of how difficult it is to ride a bicycle that is too big or small.

Objects are defined by more than their physical traits, however. Objects also embody a temporal dimension of having a past, present, and future. The shape and form of this particular object has emerged from improvements on the functions of generations of bicycles, used by generations of cyclists as a childhood toy, as an inexpensive mode of transport, for racing, or for casual weekend riding. If we think of a bicycle in the abstract, we can choose from among all of these meanings and uses of a bicycle. The particular owner of this bicycle has certain associations that come to mind when he or she thinks of a bicycle, and these associations may be quite different from cyclists who race, from mothers who pedal around the neighborhood with their children, or from the bike messenger in a city who spends the day cycling through busy urban traffic. The owner's view of his or her bicycle may be shaped by previous bicycles he or she may have owned; it may be influenced by feelings that the owner is being ecologically "green" and better for the environment than other modes of getting around campus or the city. And such images shape how the owner views himself or herself today or how he or she imagines the future (Vivanco 2013).

This bicycle—like practically every other object North American consumers purchase—is also a commodity that as parts and as a finished product has circulated through a complex economic system, supported by an equally complex set of regulatory rules. As deeply personal as the selection and purchase of an object like a bicycle may be for us as individuals, it was made on an assembly line by dozens of workers, each contributing a small part to the finished effort. We may think of a bicycle like a balloon-tired Schwinn as a quintessentially American invention, but since most bicycle parts are now made and assembled overseas, any particular bike reflects a worldwide network of economic linkages, not to mention the complex set of domestic warehouses and shippers though whose hands this particular bicycle has traveled.

Figure 16.2   The Bicycle, Like Anything, Is a Multidimensional Object.

And in the process of getting this bicycle into the hands of its owner, the manufacturer and the mainstream culture generally have carefully cultivated the current owner's desire to own and use this object. The owner has purchased this particular bicycle and not a more expensive one, and not a beaten-up second-hand one. The owner may even have replaced an older bike with this newer and more efficient one, imagining himself as more of a racer than he really is, or thinking of herself as more environmentally conscious than she might actually be. And our impressions of particular bicycles may be shaped by the images we have seen of them in films, TV programs, ads, and shiny brochures advertising one brand of bicycle (Vivanco 2013).

Finally, this bicycle, like every other object we own, is a useful object, not only for where or how far it can take us, not just in how much it can help keep us healthy from the exercise it provides, not simply from the fuel it saves us, but from the impressions of us that it creates in others as they see us ride.

The point of our bicycle example is that *any* mundane object can help us imagine ourselves, our past, and where we are headed. We may use objects to attract the attention and admiration of others. And our objects may be used by others to classify and stereotype us. Although Stocking's seven dimensions do not cover all the aspects or dimensions suggested about the shiny bicycle, they do offer a simple first glance at how we feel we should look at objects anthropologically.

An Anthropological Perspective on Aesthetics

Now that we have you thinking about objects and not simply pretty things in galleries and museums, we can productively shift back to aesthetics, which you will remember was one of Stocking's seven dimensions of an object. Returning to the African art objects with which we opened this chapter, it is clear that one of the barriers for most Americans to understanding the objects of other cultures is that other people's arts are constructed with very different goals from most American or European art. Those different goals are rooted in different understandings and uses of symbolism across cultures.

The Power of Symbols

By studying the art traditions and objects of non-Western peoples, anthropologists have learned that the complex ideas and understandings about the gods, ghosts, spirits, and other supernatural beings who inhabit their cosmologies are embodied in the physical representations we see in carvings. As we saw, the simple answer to the question "What were African carvers aiming for?" is that these African carvers were not trying to depict the human form, but were displaying the distinctive characteristics of supernatural beings by symbolically representing them as anatomical features. There is every reason to believe that carvers and other people alike imagined that their spirits and demons looked like the carvings. But when one grows up and the only depiction of a particular spirit is the mask or carving that represents the spirit, one will likely understand the spirit to look just like the carvings. In a similar way, although nobody knows what the ancient Hebrew prophet Moses may have looked like, when we hear a discussion of Moses most of us will immediately imagine Charlton Heston, who starred as Moses in the classic 1956 film *The Ten Commandments* (de Mille 1956), because this is the way Moses appears in nearly all popular images of this ancient figure.

Few of us, for example, have seen angels in the flesh, so to speak, yet most Americans have images in our minds of what an angel might look like. These images are derived from the images we have seen of angels around the Christmas holidays in stores, in front of churches, surrounding manger scenes, on postage stamps, and the like. All of these images are an American symbolic construction both for those who believe in angels and those who do not. Whether they exist or not, angels are a cultural construction in American society that we can see in movies, hear about on certain televangelists' broadcasts and radio programs, and buy as amulets or medallions in shops that sell Christian religious paraphernalia such as the amulet pictured in Figure 16.3. In order to make sense of that amulet, we need to understand the history of angel symbolism in American society and culture in addition to the fact that some Americans believe that possessing these angel amulets will in some supernatural way protect them. As the following "Classic Contributions" box shows, anthropologists have long considered the relationship between aesthetics, symbolism, and the meaning of objects.

The Symbols of Power

Just as the aesthetic dimensions of objects shape an object's meaning, powerful people use aesthetics in ways to demonstrate and legitimate their social, political, or religious power. In many traditional African kingdoms, such as those whose artworks now get displayed in museums in places like New York, the kings and chiefs who ruled these communities distinguished themselves from ordinary people with symbols of rank and authority—staffs, chairs, thrones, clothing, and so forth—artfully carved or woven in a particular local style or aesthetic. Similarly, in many religions authorities employ aesthetics to indicate that the holder of an item possesses divine power as well as power here on earth. For example, in the Eastern Orthodox, Roman Catholic, and Episcopal churches, authorities wear certain headgear, sashes around the neck called stoles, and certain robes and hats with distinctive symbolic designs that only popes or bishops can wear (Figure 16.4).

Figure 16.3   Amulets of Angels. For some Americans, owning amulets of angels help them cope with difficulties in their lives.

Figure 16.4   Stoles Change Color With the Church Calendar to Indicate the Following Church Seasons. (1) Advent (purple), the five weeks leading up to Christmas; (2) Christmas (white), worn from Christmas day until Epiphany (the day of Christ's baptism and also the twelfth day of Christmas; (3) Epiphany (green), from Epiphany until the beginning of Lent; (4) Lent (purple, but some Episcopal churches use blue), the forty days of penitence and reflection before Easter, except for Palm Sunday and Good Friday; (5) Palm Sunday and Good Friday (red), symbolizing the martyrdom of Christ; (6) Easter (white), the fifty days from Easter Sunday until Pentecost; (7) Pentecost (green), ordinary time from Pentecost until the beginning of Advent.

Classic Contributions

Nancy Munn on Graphic Signs Among the Walbiri of the Australian Desert

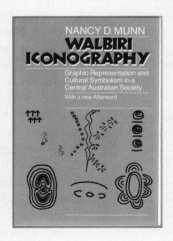

ABORIGINAL PEOPLES OF central and northern Australia use a great deal of symbolism in their religious ceremonies. The rituals employ songs and storytelling about the rituals, nearly all of which refer to ancestral or mythic times—known as the "**dreaming**" or "dream time"—when the ancestors created the natural features of their world as well as the plants and animals that inhabit it. The purpose of their rituals is to insure and maintain for the present generation what the ancestors had set in motion during the dreaming.

While she was a graduate student in the 1950s, American anthropologist Nancy Munn spent a year conducting fieldwork among an Aboriginal group in central Australia called the Walbiri. Her study focused on how men and women use and understand the meanings of symbols and graphic imagery. She was especially interested in how ritual performances used art objects, such as sand paintings, to depict dream time stories of ancestors making their way across the countryside. For example, a line in the sand simultaneously represented a kangaroo's tail as well as a spear, because both are long and straight. But the image also metaphorically represents a boy's penis and becomes part of a larger pattern of culturally standardized metaphoric usages (Munn 1962:978). After identifying from her informants many of these symbolic images, she showed how the meaning-rich dreaming stories were represented visually during the telling.

The innovation in her analysis was to ask how these images came to be associated with the particular meanings given to them by the Walbiri. She concluded that it was the repetitive use of graphic signs in many rituals that created their meaning for participants. The following brief quotation comes from her classic 1962 essay in the *American Anthropologist*, which gives us a brief glimpse into her more complete analysis in her book *Walbiri Iconography: Graphic Representation and Cultural Symbolism in a Central Australian Society* (Munn 1973).

I have suggested that Walbiri Dreaming designs are not isolated or unique forms, but specializations of a more general system or "language" of graphic signs. In the narrative contexts of sand drawing, the use of graphic signs is interlocked with verbal communication, and regular associations between standard graphic forms and certain meaning situations can readily be observed.

An important feature of this usage is that it is part of the repetitive, informal patterns of daily behavior. While particular designs and meanings are secret, the basic core of the graphic system is common knowledge.

We may phrase this in terms of a more general theoretical issue. Complex religious symbols such as Walbiri guruwari designs are the end products of social processes through which meaning is "built into" the signs. In this respect, Malinowski's concept of "context of situation" is as relevant for non-verbal as for verbal sign systems. One important anthropological question is not simply what these end products signify, but how in terms of ongoing sociocultural processes they come to acquire the signification at all. In the Walbiri case a consideration of this problem leads ultimately to an examination of storytelling behavior and the use of graphs in general communication.

Although the Walbiri graphic system is obviously not a code for language morphemes (i.e., a form of writing), it does operate as a visual code for verbally conveyed narrative sequences. That the Dreaming designs have a mnemonic function is apparent. (Munn 1962:981)

Questions for Reflection

1. Can you think of an example of a symbol from a religious tradition you're more familiar with, maybe one that you practice, that is "part of repetitive, informal patterns of daily behavior"? What does that symbol communicate?

2. Munn's theoretical insights are applicable beyond religious contexts and arts. If you wanted to study the social processes through which meaning is "built into" the signs of modern fast food advertising, such as the McDonald's sign, how would you do it?

What sets these objects of power apart is in part their aesthetic style that establishes the objects, and by extension their owners, as important and special. But it is also true that the aesthetic settings and ways in which such objects are used and displayed can also symbolically communicate the power of their owners. An interesting illustration comes from the island of Walis along the north coast of Papua New Guinea, as witnessed by Rob Welsch, one of the authors of this textbook, in 1993. A century earlier, a religious cult leader name Barjani had foretold the coming of Europeans and was believed to be a prophet. After his death, his family's clansmen had erected a shrine for him, where it was believed that people in need of supernatural assistance could leave a small amount of money or tobacco to ensure Barjani's assistance. When Welsch and his colleague, anthropologist John Terrell, went to see the shrine, they were mostly interested in the building's historically important architectural style.

But the real surprise came when they climbed the small ladder to peer into Barjani's shrine. The interior of the small shrine held a single object in a place of honor on a simple but small platform of palm leaves: an old and well-worn bowler hat, much like the one Charlie Chaplin wore in some of his movies. This was Barjani's hat, an object that possessed its power from Barjani's having worn it, but also from being the only object in the shrine. The meaning of this hat, standing out starkly in such an unexpected place, came partly from its association with Barjani and partly from his association with the foreigners he had predicted would come. In addition, the fact that it was a foreign object that few if any other Walis Islanders could have owned must have made it both exotic and valuable as a relic of this local prophet (Figure 16.5).

Although Barjani's hat is for Walis islanders a statement about relations between themselves and powerful outsiders, it is also a window into the historical context of both their society and the changing meaning that this bowler hat has had over its century of existence. To pursue this issue further, let us consider the next question around which this chapter is organized, which is why objects change meaning over time, since Barjani's bowler hat has certainly changed meaning over the past century.

• **Dreaming or the dreamtime.** The mythological period when the ancestors created the natural features of their world as well as the plants and animals that inhabit it.

Figure 16.5 Barjani's Shrine on Walis Island in Papua New Guinea. Inside, the room was empty except for Barjani's bowler hat and offerings or gifts that had been left in exchange for Barjani's help.

THINKING CRITICALLY ABOUT THE ARTS

Most people take the objects around them at face value, but anthropologists think about things in more multidimensional ways. Consider some object, statue, artwork, building, or other physical feature on your campus and outline its different dimensions as an anthropologist might. What new insights about your campus, your school's history, or the school's distinctive local culture do you get from this analysis?

Why and How Do the Meanings of Things Change Over Time?

Anthropologists today study some of the very same museum collections that anthropologists studied over a century ago. But we often come to very different conclusions about the people who made and used the objects in those collections. For example, while early anthropologists might have concluded that a certain bow and arrow in the collections of the Smithsonian Institution in Washington, D.C., represents the cultural and technological inferiority of the society that produced it vis-à-vis Euro-American societies, a contemporary anthropologist working there would reject that view and instead focus on what that bow and arrow might indicate about how that society interacted with its neighbors. What has changed? Maybe one change is that the bow and arrow has deteriorated over time, but that doesn't really explain the difference. More important is the change in interpretation we give to the object. This is a key aspect of what Stocking was getting at when he indicated that objects have a temporal dimension: all objects change over time, *if not in their physical characteristics then in the significance we give to them.*

Around the same time that Stocking was laying out his framework for understanding objects in seven dimensions, another group of anthropologists was developing a set of complementary theories and techniques for analyzing in depth this issue of how objects change over time. Declaring that "things have social lives," they published a book called *The Social Life of Things: Commodities in Cultural Perspective* (Appadurai 1986) in which they laid out some useful concepts and approaches for thinking anthropologically about objects. So how can an *inanimate* object have a *social* life?

The Social Life of Things

The idea that inanimate things have social lives is based on the assumption that things have forms, uses, and trajectories that are intertwined in complex ways with people's lives. Just as people pass through different socially recognized phases of life, objects have "careers" (in the sense of course or progression) with recognizable phases, from their creation, exchange, and uses, to their eventual discard. Along the way, it is possible to identify social relationships and cultural ideologies that influence each period in this career. Across cultures, these relationships and ideologies can vary drastically.

Consider a pair of shoes sold at a mall, for example (Figure 16.6). This pair of shoes may start as cotton fabric and rubber in a Chinese factory. But the shoes mean something quite different there from what they mean to the mall salesperson who rings up your purchase, or from what they mean to you when you wear them to some social event. The shoes may have aged only a few weeks from the time they were made until you wear them; the change in significance comes not from aging, but from moving from one person to another, some of whom see it as a way to make a living, while others see it as a way to look cool at the party next Friday. Economists often talk about each party in this complex chain of economic transactions as "a set of hands." So the shoes pass through the hands of the factory worker who sews the seams and passes it on to the hands of another worker who molds the soles and attaches them to the tops, and another who packs them in a large carton with other shoes. The pair of shoes passes through other hands at the distributor's warehouses and trucks before reaching the store, where it passes through the hands of a sales associate who puts it on a shelf and perhaps rings up the sale. Finally, it reaches your hands when you buy it, and will probably pass through a whole series of other hands when you discard that pair a few years later. That pair of shoes has a complicated life, taking on meanings from the contexts it passes through and, to the sensitive observer, revealing a whole range of complex social relations in the process. And throughout it all the same pair of shoes has changed.

Figure 16.6   The Changes a Humble Shoe Makes. This shoe is not what it seems when you encounter it in a store. It has already had a complex life, and will continue to have a complex life long after you are finished with it.

Three Ways Objects Change Over Time

All objects change over time, but they can do so in different ways. Most objects age and weather with time, of course, usually becoming less significant because they get old and worn out. But for the purposes of understanding the social life of things there are three major ways that objects change over time:

1. The form, shape, color, material, and use may change from generation to generation.
2. An object changes significance and meaning as its social and physical contexts change.
3. A single object changes significance and meaning as it changes hands.

Let us consider a few examples of each of these kinds of changes to illustrate how the social meanings of an object can change over time.

Changing Form From Generation to Generation

Nearly every manufactured product has changed over time as styles and social preferences have changed. While we usually understand these changes as gradual improvements in form or technology, they are just as often due to introducing innovations or differences in style, simply to be different. One of the best examples came from an anthropological study of ladies' fashion.

Just before World War II, anthropologists Alfred Kroeber and Jane Richardson (Richardson and Kroeber 1940) published an analysis of skirt length in women's dresses over the previous 300 years. Studying all sorts of pattern books, sketches, and photographs of women's dresses, they documented how styles of dresses had changed over this period. They found that skirt length had risen and fallen in ways that most women were unaware of. In a more or less predictable way, hem length fluctuated from extremes of long to short over a fifty-year period or cycle (Figure 16.7). Subsequent studies since 1940 have suggested that this cycle has now shortened to about twenty or twenty-five years (Bernard 2011:355).

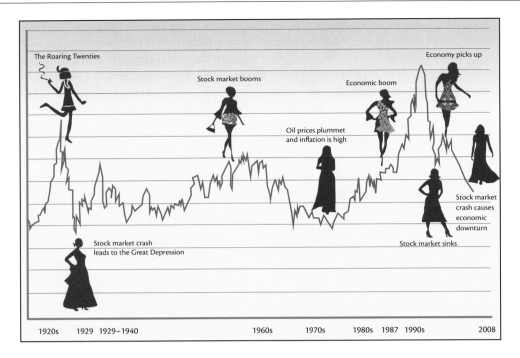

Figure 16.7   Shifting Dress Styles. Although dress styles in Europe and America have changed in many ways from period to period, they reflect cyclical trends and stylistic and aesthetic innovation.

What is the cause of these cyclical changes? There are actually at least two causes. First, fashionable women want to wear the latest fashion, and this desire encourages many others to follow their lead. Second, the factories and seamstresses that have been making women's dresses for 300 years have a vested interest in these objects changing, even if hems will eventually return to their original length. They want to sell new dresses, and the best way to sell new dresses is if the styles change so much that everyone's closet is filled with "old fashioned" dresses.

But there is more to it than simply encouraging new sales, because the symbolism of being fashionable relies on constantly changing preferences. And all aspects of the fashion industry are involved in creating long-term changes that involve thousands and thousands of people in the fashion industry as a whole, from the high-end designers to the most inexpensive stores and even the consignment shops. Nowhere was this vast integration of style and industry captured so succinctly as in Meryl Streep's comments on Anne Hathaway's "lumpy blue sweater" in the 2006 feature film *The Devil Wears Prada* (Frankel 2006).

Miranda (played by Streep) tells her young assistant Andrea (played by Hathaway) that when she goes to her closet to select "that lumpy blue sweater, for instance," Andrea is telling the world that she takes herself too seriously to care about what she wears. But Miranda points out that what Andrea doesn't know is that the sweater is not just blue, turquoise, or even lapis. "It's actually cerulean." She adds that Andrea is "blithely unaware" that some years earlier Oscar de la Renta exhibited cerulean gowns. Then Yves Saint Laurent exhibited cerulean jackets in a military style. Cerulean eventually turned up in collections from no less than eight different designers. The popularity of the work of all these designers meant that cerulean filtered down to department stores, eventually making its way "into some tragic Casual Corner" where Andrea likely found her sweater in some discount bin. Miranda finds it amusing that Andrea thinks that she shows her independence of mind and fashion sense by wearing her lumpy blue sweater, supposedly free from the influence of the fashion industry, when in reality Andrea is wearing a sweater selected for her by the people in her office from stuff Andrea is too good to bother with. As Streep's character suggests, commodities in the modern world are inherently aimed at shaping consumers' preferences by creating fashionable styles, often through print ads and TV commercials, product placements in film, and links between media and commercial outlets.

For over a century, archaeologists have understood the fact that styles and fashions change over time, for example, using pottery styles that were found to have changed over broad regions over decades and centuries to date excavation sites that would otherwise be undateable. As a cooking tool, earthenware pots in the American Southwest became largely obsolete as soon as metal cooking pots became readily available. But, as anthropologist Edwin Wade (1985) shows, the preservation of this traditional style of pottery emerged with the arrival of the Atchison, Topeka, and Santa Fe Railroad to New Mexico after 1880. Pueblo communities that had previously been essentially isolated from the world became directly exposed to outsiders for the first time. Rather than abandoning pottery for metal cooking pots, they began selling their traditional pots to white tourists along the side of the tracks. As time went on, the Pueblo potters adjusted their pottery designs and styles to fit the desires of their tourists. And after the beginning of the Santa Fe Art Market in the 1930s the changes in pottery styles have been shaped by the changing preferences of fine art collectors rather than tourists.

Changing Meaning with Changing Contexts

The last example of shifting pottery styles in response to the shift from local use, to tourist trinket, to sale as fine art also embodies the changing meaning of an object in different contexts: from a useful cooking utensil, to a souvenir of a trip to the Southwest, to examples of fine art ceramics. Here we can see how changing context generates changes in meanings.

Contexts often change as environments and technologies change as well. Tahitians, like other Polynesians, had no knowledge of iron until Europeans first visited their islands (Figure 16.8). On June 18, 1867, the British Captain Samuel Wallis was the first Westerner to reach Tahiti, and that day Tahitians learned about the powerful abilities of iron tools for cutting, chopping, and carving. But after learning about iron tools, Tahitian men started plotting ways they could get access to Wallis's steel. The traditionally stodgy and sexually restrained Tahitian society became transformed almost overnight as men sent their wives, daughters, and sisters out to Wallis's ship,

Figure 16.8 Queen Oberea Welcomes Capt. Samuel Wallis at Tahiti. The queen and the captain exchanged gifts that included some small iron cutting tools that transformed Tahitian society almost immediately.

the HMS Dauphin, to engage in sex in exchange for any sort of iron tools: knives, axes, or even nails that could be fashioned into cutting tools. A year after that the French Captain Bougainville arrived at Tahiti, and a year later Captain Cook first reached Tahitian shores, both of whom found Tahitian women to be so sexually promiscuous that the crew nearly dismantled their small life boats in a quest for much desired nails. On his second voyage Cook brought along quantities of nails and hoop iron to satisfy the local desire for iron. Of course, these interactions with Tahitian women created the stereotype that Polynesians were traditionally very promiscuous, when in fact it was the horny sailors combined with the Tahitian desire for iron that transformed Tahitian society and introduced sexual license to these islands (Howe 1984). Something as simple as a new technology can have profound impacts on local communities.

The introduction of iron and steel tools in New Guinea at the other side of the Pacific usually had a very different impact on local societies. As steel tools became more readily accessible beginning in the 1880s, New Guineans abandoned stone axes and adzes because steel axes and adzes worked so much better. The shift to steel tools made them more dependent on foreigners than before, but most communities abandoned stone tools almost immediately. At first, the reduced demand for stone axes meant that exchange partners who traditionally provided stone axes were much less important than before, leading these villages to find new or different commodities to exchange with their traditional partners. But it also meant that wherever steel was readily accessible, dozens or even hundreds of previously valuable stone axes were suddenly worthless. When anthropologists and other collectors arrived to buy traditional objects, they could purchase piles of stones axes for next to nothing because these objects had no real use in a world with steel axes. When later anthropologists or collectors arrived, there were fewer and fewer axes to be found. After a generation or two, the few stone tools left in the village had become heirlooms, highly desired links to a traditional past.

We can think of this process of change as similar to what happened to the eight-track tape, a magnetic tape that was popular for recording and playing music in the United States between the 1960s and 1980s. When the cassette tape emerged it was more expensive and valuable, and the older eight-track technology lost value and started showing up in yard sales. Today eight track tapes are so rare that they have almost become a museum curiosity. Cassettes themselves were eclipsed by CDs, which are now themselves nearing extinction in favor of downloaded music and video. All of these are changes in our material worlds that have emerged from changing social, economic, and political contexts.

Changing Meaning From Changing Hands

The most powerful examples of objects that change meaning when they pass into different hands come from the situation where an anthropologist or collector buys objects from exotic villagers for a museum. Until steel axes replace stone axes, the collector is buying objects that people feel are useful. But for the collector, the objects are not going to be used except as examples of a traditional society's technology and way of life. Once the object reaches a museum its meaning changes profoundly; it no longer has a useful function but becomes a rare example of something from an exotic culture far away in time and space.

Being in a museum is, of course, not the only force that can change the meaning of an object with the changing of hands. The story of the discovery and exploration of the Americas, which began as a way of reaching the spices in the Spice Islands in what is now Indonesia, is an interesting illustration of another kind of force driving changes in meaning. In Indonesia nutmeg, mace, cloves, and pepper were commonplace and inexpensive crops, readily grown, and traditionally exported to people in other regions. None of these spices was essential for European cooking, and it is a silly

Thinking Like an Anthropologist

Looking at Objects From Multiple Perspectives

PART ONE: NICHOLAS THOMAS
ON ENTANGLED OBJECTS IN FIJI

Anthropologist Nicholas Thomas (1989) was studying British museum collections from Fiji that were acquired in the 1870s around the time that the British government was annexing the Fijian Islands as a colony. He noticed that there was an extraordinarily large number of weapons brought back by sailors, traders, and people with business interests in the islands. The large number of clubs and the so-called cannibal forks were quite appealing to and sought after by wealthy collectors—nearly all of whom were male—probably because such weapons fed their image of tribal societies as vicious and bloodthirsty savages.

Thomas himself did not see these objects as evidence of savagery, as early collectors had. He knew that these wooden forks were used by high-ranking chiefs who were prohibited by taboos from touching food with their fingers as their personal power would in effect poison the food for others. Rarely would these have been used for human flesh. Fijian men could be violent, but they also carried clubs mostly in ceremonial situations as a symbol of their strength and masculine power. But for early collectors in England, who had never visited these tropical islands, clubs presented tangible evidence of an aggressive primitive society they imagined living halfway around the world from Victorian England.

In his research, however, Thomas also found that not everybody interested in these objects bought into the idea

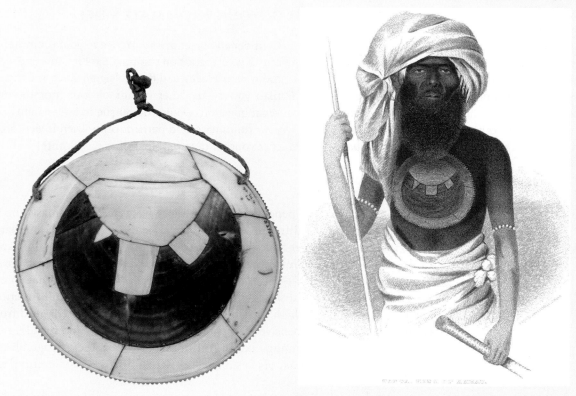

🌱 **Breastplate, Civavonovono, of Whale Ivory, Pearl Shell, and Vegetable Fiber.** This breastplate was collected by Sir Arthur Gordon, first Governor of Fiji between 1875 and 1880. It previously belonged to Ratu Seru Cakobau, Vunivalu (war chief) of Bau, who inherited it from his father, Ratu Tanoa Visawaqa. This breastplate is at the Museum of Archaeology and Anthropology at the University of Cambridge.

(continued)

Thinking Like an Anthropologist (continued)

that Fijians were bloodthirsty savages. For example, he studied how when the Austrian-Scottish traveler and later collector Anatole von Hügel arrived in Fiji in 1874, von Hügel was surprised to find that nobody had attempted to assemble a systematic collection of objects from the islands. Von Hügel was dismissive of the hodge-podge of personal collections he found among the traders and planters in Fiji. For each of them every object had a personal story, "every dish was a cannibal dish, every club had been the instrument of some atrocious murder, and every stain on either was caused by blood" (quoted in Thomas 1989:45). Von Hügel went on to assemble a large personal collection representative of all aspects of Fijian culture. For him these objects as a collection suggested a complex, socially stratified society with a rich culture. He understood his collection not in personal terms but as scientific data.

Thomas also learned that there was yet another set of perspectives on these objects. It happens that von Hügel arrived in Fiji about the same time as the newly appointed colonial governor Arthur H. Gordon. As the first British governor of what became the Crown Colony of Fiji, he viewed Fijian objects very differently from either the traders and planters on the one hand and von Hügel on the other. As representative of Queen Victoria and as head of the Fijian government, Fijian chiefs gave him gifts in nearly every village he visited. He reciprocated with gifts, usually of British manufacture. As a "chief" himself, Gordon negotiated the political relations with other chiefs using Fijian objects, especially the whale tooth ornaments called *tabua*. *Tabua*

were much admired by Fijians, and their possession marked high social status, which was always on the minds of Fijians. For Gordon, Fijian objects were not scientific specimens, as von Hügel viewed them, or evidence of Fijian savagery, as traders and planters viewed them, but tools for promoting government control of the islands and its people.

Thomas concluded that these Fijian objects were "entangled," that is, taken up in complex ways across cultural boundaries based on differing views about the objects. To understand how different parties viewed Fijian objects differently, Thomas began with a set of anthropological questions:

1. How did Fijians view different kinds of objects differently from white people in Fiji?
2. Why did white planters and traders emphasize the bloodthirsty images of Fijians?
3. Why did von Hügel emphasize these objects as scientific specimens rather than as souvenirs?
4. How would the exchange of *tabua* with Governor Gordon enhance his position in the islands?

PART TWO: ENTANGLED OBJECTS IN YOUR ROOMMATE'S LIFE

Consider an object of importance to your roommate (or to one of your friends on campus). Explore how and why your roommate places a different significance on this object than you do or other friends of your roommate might. What questions would you pursue to understand how you, your roommate, and perhaps other friends view an object that your roommate thinks of as significant?

modern-day myth that pepper and other spices were needed to mask the pungent smell of half-rotten meat (rotten meat will never be tasty and edible, no matter what spices are added). Pepper and spices were so hard to get they were only used by the wealthy and noble families, but wealthy Europeans were willing to pay large sums for exotic—and fashionable—spices for their exotic appeal and the fact that an expensive peppercorn in a special dish would show off the owner's wealth and superior nature among their social set. With their importation to Europe, spices changed from being commonplace and inexpensive objects to being highly valued and socially exclusive.

As we see in this "Thinking Like an Anthropologist" box, these geographical movements of objects mean that objects also move across differences in cultural and individual perspective.

Commodities, as we have suggested previously, are examples of the changing significance of objects as these objects change hands. But rather than focus too directly on how commodities create meaning, let us consider how objects represent and even help us create who we are.

● ●

THINKING CRITICALLY ABOUT THE ARTS

Consider some object, photograph, public art installation, memorial, or other feature of your campus. Identify when and why it was installed and the context that led to it becoming a feature of your campus. How has its meaning changed since it was installed or erected? Why is it more or perhaps less meaningful today than when first installed?

● ●

How Do Certain Objects Come to Represent People's Goals and Aspirations?

When we ask how objects can represent our aspirations we are really addressing three interconnected issues: (1) objects express our personal and collective pasts, (2) objects help us express and even formulate our goals and aspirations, and (3) objects can be used in ways that manipulate what our goals and aspirations should be. We consider each of these issues in turn.

The Cultural Biography of Things

To understand how objects help us express our individual pasts it is helpful to consider an idea first proposed by the anthropologist Igor Kopytoff (1986) in an essay included in the book we mentioned before, *The Social Life of Things.* In his essay Kopytoff began by observing the problematic fact that in some societies, including pre–Civil War America, some people were seen as property. By starting with people as property he was forced to recognize that *all* tangible property has a biography that is profoundly shaped by culture. What Kopytoff meant to communicate to anthropologists is that paying attention to the biography of a thing—its life course from its origins through its distribution, uses, and eventual discard—can uncover important social relationships and cultural dynamics.

As an illustration of this concept, think about this: the objects we choose to keep and display in our rooms, houses, and offices remind us of important things in our lives. But they also communicate important things about us to others. Consider, for example, the posters and other objects you or one of your friends has hung up in a dorm room. A poster featuring a basketball or football player, for instance, highlights an interest in certain sports, teams, or players. Some of these objects suggest events or circumstances that are important in shaping who we are. We knew one first-year student from Texas who proudly displayed the lone star flag in his dorm room in a New England college, partly as a reminder of home and partly as a way of expressing his sense of superiority over other students from—in his view—less important states. Flags are often powerful symbols, and his flag was powerful in shaping this student's identity too. Fellow students from other states often saw his flag but had less flattering images of him because in their home communities and social circles bragging about being from Texas, as the flag's presence implies, was a sign of his not understanding how important large East Coast and West Coast states were. These different perceptions of the same symbol are rooted in the differing cultural biographies of the same symbolic object.

Many objects that remind us of our past, who we are, and how we want others to perceive us are ordinary objects that we have bought in a store or online. When iPads were first released by Apple, some students whose families could afford them rushed to buy them, partly for the new functions that the tablets provided but often to show off the fact that they could afford such an expensive item. Now that a majority of students have some sort of tablet or portable device, to distinguish themselves and their devices from those of others, students are selecting colorful covers or decorating their cases with images they find pleasing and personally meaningful. By personalizing these objects, as earlier generations of students did to their laptops and three-ring binders, they are making a mass-produced object into an individualized object like no other. People do these things because these objects can express their personal past.

Individuals are not the only social unit that seeks to imprint a biography onto an object, however. Communities and nations do this too, and as we will see in the following "Doing Fieldwork" box, these processes can become quite complicated in the particular setting of a museum, where preserving objects to remember a collective past is the primary goal.

The Culture of Mass Consumption

People do not simply imprint themselves and their pasts *onto* objects. They also formulate who they are and express themselves *through* objects, especially their goals and aspirations about their lives. A useful vantage point from which to observe this dynamic is in the contemporary **culture of mass consumption**—a term that refers to the cultural perspectives and social processes that shape and are shaped by how goods and services are bought, sold, and used in contemporary capitalism—because this culture is so ubiquitous in so many people's lives.

Karl Marx and the Commodity Fetish

An influential figure in understanding the culture of mass consumption was the German political-economist Karl Marx. In his masterpiece *Capital,* first published in 1867, Marx (1990) observed that with the rise of industrial capitalism in England there was a shift in people's relationships with everyday objects, and mass-produced commodities in particular gained a peculiar new status in people's lives. Before the creation of industrial factories, people made the things they needed or wanted, or got them from individual craftspeople or small-scale cottage industries. A common craftsman, such as a shoemaker, put a great deal of care into his work, and his workmanship was embodied in the shoes that he made. The shoemaker also developed an important social relationship with the buyer of his shoes, who could come to him to be fitted or to have the shoes repaired if something went wrong after he bought them.

But in an industrial factory, a worker makes only part of an object and he or she has no such relationship with either the fruits of his or her labor or with the buyer. The result, Marx asserted, was the creation of a widespread feeling of **alienation**, or antagonistic detachment, between workers and the commodities they produce, as well as between these workers and the buyers of the goods. As this sense of alienation between people and goods expanded, objects were no longer valued as much for how useful they were, or for the human sweat, ingenuity, and social cooperation that went into them. What held people's attention now were issues like wages, working conditions, and the trading values of the commodities. Divorced from the social relationships in which they were once rooted, Marx argued that commodities began to exercise a strange kind of mystical power over people, controlling their attention and becoming

- **Culture of mass consumption.** A term that refers to the cultural perspectives and social processes that shape and are shaped by how goods and services are bought, sold, and used in contemporary capitalism.

- **Alienation.** The antagonistic detachment between workers and the commodities they produce, as well as between these workers and the buyers of the goods.

Doing Fieldwork

Christina Kreps Studies Indigenous Indonesian Perceptions of Museums

LIKE MOST DEVELOPING countries, Indonesia has a large number of regional, provincial, and local museums that illustrate local cultures by putting cultural objects on display. Most of these provincial and regional museums consist of small buildings that house relatively small collections of local ethnographic objects. The number of staff members is usually modest and, despite decades of efforts to professionalize their staff with further training in international museum standards, many smaller museums appear to model themselves on larger national museums or colonial museums in countries like The Netherlands (the former colonial power) or the United States, a country assumed to have the most sophisticated understanding of what a museum should be.

Anthropologist Christina Kreps conducted fieldwork in Central Kalimantan, a rural province in Indonesian Borneo, attempting to study what made these museums distinctively Indonesian. How did Indonesian cultural patterns make the international institution we call the "museum" an Indonesian institution? What she was confronted with was not an Indonesian institution but a transplanted Dutch institution known as a "tropical museum" that resembled the Tropen Museum (literally the 'tropical' museum) in Amsterdam or any of a dozen other anthropological museums in The Netherlands.

🌿 **Float Created for Indonesian Independence Day Parade by Museum Staff in Kalimantan.** The banner on the side of the truck reads: "The Museum and the Preservation of Regional Cultural Arts. Supporting the Development of the People." The float features structures and objects used in a Ngaju-Dayak *tiwah* ceremony.

From interviews with museum directors in Jakarta, the capital, and at the Provincial Museum of Central Kalimantan, it was clear that museum professionals wanted to make both museum staff and the Indonesian public more "museum minded," which means more appreciative of the purpose and functions of a museum. So while Kreps was settling in at the Provincial Museum to observe and study the indigenous aspects of local museums, local staff expected her to become more proficient in using international museum standards. She couldn't just sit back and observe local museum practices, but was expected to help museum staff become "better" at running their museum, even though Kreps herself had limited first-hand understanding of the province and its cultures. For Kreps, a critical dimension of conducting fieldwork meant having to become adept at navigating the gaps between local ideas about how to display objects and international standards.

As Kreps was in the field longer, it gradually became clear that despite the superficial appearance of this museum as a smaller version of any internationally recognized museum, there were distinctive Indonesian and even Kalimantan aspects of museum practice. One example appeared shortly after she arrived during preparations for the Independence Day celebrations held across Indonesia on August 17 every year. Museum staff were preparing a float for the parade through town, and she observed staff loading objects from the collection onto the back of a truck as a kind of moving exhibition. The float included a variety of objects from the permanent collection that were distinctive to the peoples of the province, including structures and objects that were used in a Dayak ceremony. In the West, no museum staff member would display any part of a permanent collection on the back of an open pickup truck. In most American museums staff would only hold an object if they had on a pair of cotton or latex gloves in order to prevent leaving oils from one's skin on an object. Ironically, the banner on the truck announced the theme of the float to the public: "The Museum and the Preservation of Regional Cultural Arts." When Kreps suggested to these staff members that the objects might get damaged during their bumpy ride through town in the truck, one of the staff turned to her with a perplexed look, saying "Oh, it doesn't matter. There are lots of them in the villages" (Kreps 2003:30). Obviously, all of these objects were still commonplace examples of a living culture.

(continued)

Doing Fieldwork (continued)

Kreps found a very different attitude from museum staff when dealing with other kinds of objects of the sort that Indonesians call *pusaka* (literally "heirlooms"). The objects considered *pusaka* in Java, Sumatra, or Sulawesi often include different kinds of old bronze, wooden, or silk objects. But in Central Kalimantan one of the most important object types is a class of *pusaka* known as a dragon jar that consists of an imported ceramic jar that bears the image of a dragon. Imported into Kalimantan and other parts of Southeast Asia from China for centuries, these jars continue to be used in social exchanges locally. For centuries a family's social position and wealth could be estimated by the number of dragon jars that lined the walls of their houses. There were even local "jar experts" in Central Kalimantan, who could determine whether a jar was authentic or "a fake" that was recently made by Chinese craftsmen who make the vessel seem centuries older than it really is. Fine old examples in the homes of important families are often associated with deeply held sacred and religious meanings (Kreps 2003:41–42).

Kreps's research showed that curators and other museum staff had great appreciation for old dragon jars, none of which would ever be loaded onto a parade float. But they had a very different understanding and sense of value for the commonplace cultural objects that were even more indigenous than the ancient but imported Chinese jars. Her insights into the indigenous aspects of museums in Kalimantan have led Kreps to study and encourage people from non-Western cultures to use modern practices with respect to handling and protecting collections while appreciating what local people view as important about these objects beyond their cash value. There is more than one way to preserve culture, while protecting the objects in a museum collection.

Questions for Reflection

Visit your campus museum or gallery, or one in your town, and reflect on the following questions:

1. Can you distinguish "permanent" exhibits from "temporary" or traveling ones? How?

2. What do the "permanent" exhibits tell you about the core interests of the museum?

3. What does the presence of certain objects and images tell you about the museum or the organization that owns or sponsors it?

- **Commodity fetish.** View of Karl Marx that commodities exercise a strange kind of power over people, controlling their attention and becoming objects of obsessive desire and worship.

objects of obsessive desire and worship. He called this obsession "the **commodity fetish**" (Figure 16.9).

It is likely that if he were alive today, Marx would see the commodity fetish as alive and well, for example in the obsessive hype, fascination, even worship given to the latest iPod, smartphone, or Nike athletic shoe. For Marx, consumer culture generates a set of goals and aspirations that are fundamentally anti-social, displacing our ordinary social relationships with the aspiration to accumulate fetish-like commodities.

The Anthropology of Consumption

Marx's understanding of the culture of mass consumption has been influential in anthropology and other social sciences because it explains the changes in human relations that came with the rise of commodity production. But with his focus on commodity *production*, Marx paid little attention to the process of *consumption* and how people actually acquire, use, and make sense of what they consume. Rather than look at consumption as an anti-social act, many anthropologists who study it have concluded that it is a deeply social, not *anti*-social, act. Seeking out and possessing consumer goods is a key means through which people define and express who they are: their social status, economic means, gender identities, aesthetic sensibilities, individual qualities of taste and

Figure 16.9   Keeping in Touch. Modern devices promote the ease they offer for keeping in touch with friends.

discernment, and identification with a certain social class or interest group (Bourdieu 1984; Miller 1987, 1998).

Consider, for example, one key element in a process of consumption: the act of going shopping for the shiny new bicycle discussed previously. We tend to think of shopping as a matter of individual choice or the result of some internal cost-benefit logic where we weigh how much we have to spend with the benefits we expect to get out of buying the object. But shopping is more complicated than that. Many other issues—which are inherently social concerns—go into the decision about where to shop and what to buy, among them: What store do I want to be identified with (versus the one I might be embarrassed to be at)? How will the bicycle I choose allow me to be seen by others? How will the decision to buy a specific bicycle—expensive or inexpensive, handsome or ugly, the latest fashion or technology or last year's model, and so on—affect those who are close to me, such as my family and friends? What bicycle best expresses my goals and aspirations to be someone I want to be or who impresses others: an environmentalist, an athlete, a frugal college student who pinches pennies, etc.? Each of these images suggests a different bicycle and a different kind of decision with distinct social consequences for us as individuals. Shopping, in other words, is only partially a matter of what you like, can afford, or can get access to, as it also involves matters of relationship, identity, social positioning, and the creation of cultural meaning (Miller 1998; Vivanco 2013).

Building off of these sorts of key concepts in studies of consumers and consumer behavior, anthropologists have considered how big businesses advertise their products by playing to the subtle cultural backdrop of modern life that makes one particular product more desirable than another for becoming the kind of person we want to be. Because objects in a consumer society have become a key component in expressing who we are and who we want to be, or at least how we want to be thought of by others, anthropologists have over the past decade studied various classes of consumer goods, ordinary objects through which we explore our individual stories.

How Can Some People Use Objects to Manipulate Us?

If large corporations want to survive and expand they have to convince consumers to buy their products and not those of one of their competitors. To convince you to buy their product they bombard you with advertising that will encourage you to think their product is both necessary for a fulfilling life and that this particular brand is more likely to help you reach your goals than any other brand. Advertisers proudly announce that they are simply passing on useful information to consumers, but we know that they are really trying to convince us that we need *their* product. We think of this ad-making as part of the process of manipulating our world through a symbolic framing or reframing of their products.

Presenting Products to Consumers

Many TV commercials speak to existing needs that people already have—from the basics such as food and clothing to needs that might be considered less basic such as cars or being attractive to other people. The challenge for these ads is to get individuals to realize that their product is the better one for them. So makers of consumer goods segment their audiences, targeting their products toward particular audience demographics, such as gender, socioeconomic class, sexual orientation, and so on.

Most of these ads, like ads for acne creams, are fairly obvious about who they are for and what they do, but there are others that many—perhaps most—Americans do not consciously understand. One set of interesting ads is produced by Budweiser. Any Bud ad is aimed at selling their beer. But how are they trying to convince you that their beer is better than other beer, since they provide no comparisons with other brands and never speak about price? The ad is not really about the beer, but about young men's aspirations to be liked by other guys and having a good time. What they actually present in the commercial is a lot of guys, and usually a bunch of attractive young women, at some sort of party having a good time. If we step back from the ad, we all know that nearly any beer in the same setting would create the same party atmosphere, but here Bud products are framed as being your link to a great party. The ad constructs what its makers feel are what twenty-something men desire and symbolically associates their product with this desired goal to sell their product. Furthermore, by tapping into pre-existing goals and aspirations—the desire to have a good time—the beer company presents their product as able to fulfill these desires.

THINKING CRITICALLY ABOUT THE ARTS

Consider a store near your campus. What are the characteristics of the audience this store hopes to sell to? How does this store market specifically to this demographic group? Give specific details about how the store forms or positions certain products to catch the attention of this target demographic? What aspirations is this store emphasizing to get its target audience's attention? Why might some other marketing display imagery, or array of commodities in the store or in advertising, be less effective in selling this product?

How Do Images Shape the Worlds in Which People Live?

The world we live in is increasingly one in which we are bombarded by visual imagery, more completely than any previous generation. If it is true that the typical American is now exposed to more than 3,000 visual advertisements a day, we have to ask: How do images shape the worlds in which we live? Anthropologists continue to analyze and debate just how culture shapes the ways people process visual images, but there is no doubt in our media-saturated world that images can circulate more quickly, widely, and powerfully across cultural boundaries than ever, making the work of understanding these processes more pressing.

The Power of Visual Media

It may be hard to imagine what life was like for people with few visual outlets. The anthropologist Edmund Carpenter (Bishop and Prinz 2003) visited Papua New Guinea in the 1960s and early 1970s to study reactions of native villagers who had never seen photographs. Carpenter took instant Polaroid pictures and motion picture films of villagers and then documented on film their reactions when he showed them those images. Today, many of these villagers have cell phones and have seen films and TV, but at the time of Carpenter's visit few people had been out of the village, and none of them had ever seen a photograph or moving image of themselves. Carpenter's film shows their stunned reactions and expressions of startled amazement, such as one individual's declaration about his own photographic image, "Oh, what a blow that phantom gave me!" Years later Carpenter reflected on the transformation his experiments in New Guinea had meant for the villagers he encountered, concluding that once people had experienced these photographs their worlds and their senses of self were changed forever.

Carpenter wanted to show that contemporary visual media are powerful forces in shaping people's lives, how they understand their world and imagine their place in it. And it can even have important consequences for cultural diversity. One illustration of this fact is that in one of the villages in which Carpenter did his research, men decided to stop conducting one of the village's most important rituals, a very difficult and trying coming-of-age initiation rite for young men. They explained that now that they had photographs of the rite they didn't need to perform it anymore (Figure 16.10).

One of the criticisms of Carpenter's research is that in introducing people to photographs they had never seen before, he manipulated and forever affected them without their foreknowledge. But Carpenter showed how quickly these individuals grew sophisticated in handling cameras and taking and using pictures themselves, insisting that they were as sophisticated as modern North Americans and Europeans who supposedly had much more experience with visual media. He seemed to be indicating, too, that we are not as special and sophisticated as we like to think we are when we confront visual media, because visual media are always transforming people's worlds.

So Carpenter might say that the ever-present stream of video, ads, commercials, and programing that surrounds most of us as soon as we rise in the morning has presented a great transformation for us too. What is most striking to the anthropologists and other social scientists who have studied this visual world that now surrounds us is that many Americans are not entirely aware of how visual imagery can manipulate us.

Figure 16.10 Seeing in New Ways. Anthropologist Ted Carpenter found that when villagers such as the one pictured here from the Highlands of Papua New Guinea saw themselves, their activities, and their material culture through a camera lens or as a printed image on paper, it changed their worlds forever.

Manipulating Images

One of the most obvious efforts to shape our purchasing behavior is the before-and-after photos for diet, exercise, and body-building programs. Weight-loss regimens, whether selling exercise equipment or diet meals, often show a client before and after use of the product, always with obvious, striking results. A recent blog by a personal trainer entitled "Seduced by the Illusion: The Truth About Transformation Photos" (Dixon 2013) showed how a personal trainer with only 16% body fat could produce dramatic transformation photos that made him look like he had gotten muscular through exercise (Figure 16.11). As he said, "I decided to take my own transformation photos to see what was possible." He asked his girlfriend to take a "before" shot as he let his belly hang out as much as possible. Then he shaved his head, positioned a light to rake across his abs and sucked in his gut and tightened his abs to get the maximum effect "and BOOM! We got our after shot." Both shots were authentic, but each had a different goal, to manipulate the image we would take away from the two images.

Nearly all TV commercials consciously stage their still shots and video footage for effect. Food commercials for hamburgers and ice cream with all the toppings are actually very difficult to photograph, and ad producers routinely avoid the real thing to get the most appetizing shot rather than a soggy bun on a hamburger or a melted ice cream sundae. All of these images are playing to our expectations that emerge from the cultural biography ordinary people apply to the world.

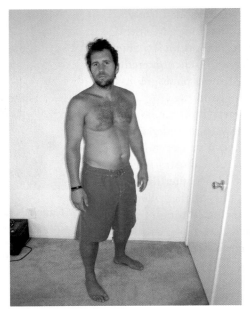

Figure 16.11   Seduced by the Illusion. Personal trainer Andrew Dixon's "before" and "after" shots. These images were actually taken a few hours apart on the same day to illustrate how easily Americans can be seduced into believing something that is not true. Here lighting, shaving, and choice of shorts, along with how he holds and tenses his abs make all the difference.

Manipulation of our impressions is not limited to the crass and commercial side of life but can even be seen in the most scholarly of museum exhibitions. In 1984 Curator William Rubin developed an exhibition for the Museum of Modern Art that attempted to show the links between "primitive" art from Africa and the Pacific, on the one hand, and the works of modern twentieth-century art by Pablo Picasso, Paul Klee, Constantine Brancusi, and many other artists, pairing their "modern" works with pieces from tribal societies in the exhibition. Museum visitors were not viewing random pairings of a tribal artist with a modern one, but carefully chosen tribal pieces like those African objects that had been shown at MoMA in 1935. Picasso, for example, had actually used African tribal sculptures as models for his paintings. Although Rubin presented wonderful examples of both tribal and modern art in the primitive style, the entire exhibition was aimed at constructing an image of continuity between tribal and modern art, even if a specific continuity never actually existed.

Cinema and films are another context in which visual images can be constructed to communicate a persuasive message. One of the most famous Nazi propaganda films was *Triumph of the Will*, directed by Leni Riefenstahl in 1935. Riefenstahl used dramatic footage from Nazi rallies and conventions to glorify the Nazi regime and its promise of future glory for Germans (Figure 16.12). Since World War II and the fall of Nazi Germany, the film has been attacked by many film critics for its blatant propaganda and its attempt to manipulate its viewers. Nevertheless it was quite successful in convincing ordinary Germans to support the Nazi vision of their country and its destiny. Filmmaker Riefenstahl responded in the 1960s that her film was history—not propaganda—because no scene was staged or re-created for the film. Everything in the film was authentic and real. But, of course, each authentic scene in the film was edited to present Nazis in the best light possible, deceiving through omission by ignoring all of the Nazi brutality that had already begun in 1934 when most of the footage was shot.

Figure 16.12   The Power of Visual Persuasion. Hitler and the Nazi leadership in Germany understood very well the power of symbolism and pageantry to persuade Germans to align themselves with the Nazi state.

Web pages and blogs also tend to use lots of video, often heavily edited, to support one particular point or another. We need only think of the many blogs dealing with one conspiracy theory or another, most of which are richly laden with short video clips that present supposed evidence. UFO theorists have for years used photos, most of which in the 1970s and 1980s were doctored in various ways. Now photos can be Photoshopped quite easily to make any point one wants to make, and the technology for video editing is becoming so easy that ordinary people can edit their videos. Like commercials, all films and video clips occur in a world where manipulation of our cultural expectations and personal aspirations is everywhere.

Films Have Social Lives, Too

Of course, one of the critical arguments of the social-life-of-things perspective is that people do not consume objects—in this case manipulated images and messages—in a cultural vacuum. Anthropology, more than any other discipline, has studied what happens when visual imagery circulates globally and crosses cultures, studying up close the processes through which people make sense of the foreign objects like the images and stories in a Hollywood movie or television show. The results can be unexpected, even turning the intended messages on their heads.

One interesting example is the story of how people in a small village in northern Papua New Guinea called Gapun made sense of the series of *Rambo* action films, which star Sylvester Stallone as an estranged and troubled, but heroic, Vietnam veteran who gets himself into fights with the U.S. and Vietnamese governments long after the war is over (Figure 16.13). Western audiences are likely to view the main character, John Rambo, as a strong and self-reliant individual. But as anthropologists Don Kulick and Margaret Willson (2002) discovered when they discussed the films with Gapuners, locals made no such assumptions. Indeed, villagers described Rambo as a "limp and ineffectual" man because he had to be rescued by a tough old woman, his wife, after he was captured by Vietnamese soldiers!

For the anthropologists, this unexpected reading of the films was not based on a misunderstanding of the films, and indeed to call Gapuners' interpretation mistaken would simply perpetuate the racist stereotype of non-Western peoples as backwards and unsophisticated. Rather, Kulick and Willson argued that the villager's interpretation had to be understood in terms of local practices of storytelling, in which villagers freely alter, expand, substitute, transform, and add characters, plots, and moral implications depending on who is listening to the story. Storytelling in Gapun is not simply about describing events, but an active and dynamic process of authoring in its own right, and when Gapuners recount film narratives, they always embed them in local concerns and everyday understandings (Kulick and Willson 2002:276).

This kind of situation, in which people process and interpret foreign products through a local, culturally embedded lens, is common throughout the anthropological literature, and complicates any simplistic notion of a unilateral transmission of any visual message across cultures. More important, it shows that instead of a movie coming in and homogenizing or undermining a local culture, movies too have social lives, and locals—in this case Gapuners, but it could be any number of social groups in the world—can just as powerfully use films to reiterate and confirm who they are in a wider world.

Figure 16.13   Rambo Around the World.
The Rambo films have been wildly popular around the world. But each audience constructs this image according to its own cultural terms.

●●●

THINKING CRITICALLY ABOUT THE ARTS

Middle-aged and older Americans often feel the films and videos that college students enjoy are too fast-paced and violent. Part of their discomfort no doubt comes at least in part from the fact that images seem to them to jump from scene to scene in ways that older Americans rarely saw when they were young. Compare a recent film you have seen with one your parents might have seen when they were young. How do these two films use different patterns of movement from scene to scene? How might these different expectations make some of your favorite films less significant for and less comfortable to watch for older people?

●●●

Conclusion

This chapter began with an art show that took place in a building that is recognizable as an art museum. Although the things on display were not yet considered "art" or the individuals who made them "artists" by Western audiences, nowadays we can all accept that the African masks, figures, and fetishes displayed at the MoMA represent a sophisticated illustration of human artistic expression. But for much of the rest of the chapter, we appear to have strayed from the arts to discussion of things that at first glance might be connected only very weakly to "art," such as bicycles, bowler hats, ethnographic museums, mass consumption, shopping, advertisements, and the Rambo movies.

This route was not accidental. Our goal here has been to show that in order to understand "art" we cannot consider the arts through the lenses of aesthetics and creativity alone, which are commonly accepted as defining features of the arts. To the anthropologist, the symbolic dimensions are of course important to consider in establishing the cultural meaning of any artwork. The fact that in a community specific symbols and visual styles are conventionally recognized and often repeated across different social settings suggests something important about the social and collective dimensions of any form of artistic or stylistic expression. Furthermore, the fact that ideas about aesthetics and what is visually pleasing can differ so markedly across cultures is of great interest for any cultural analysis of the arts.

But just as important to the anthropologist is that these art objects are inherently multidimensional, which shifts attention to the objects themselves and not just what they might communicate. From this vantage point, a whole new set of possibilities opens up for analyzing the human condition and for doing cultural anthropology, focusing on the complex relationships people have with all the things that they create and consume. In this sense, anthropological interest presumes that interest in "art" is about *artifice* and *artifact,* the objects people make, share, visualize, display, and construct meanings about. When we take seriously all the ways people project themselves onto objects, define themselves through objects, and manipulate others using objects and visual images, anthropology is no longer "simply" about people but about the intertwining of people and material things. This intertwining shows that our interpretations of things and visual images are constructed, and in that sense artificial. But because they appear in certain cultural settings and contexts they seem to us natural.

KEY TERMS

Aesthetic criteria   p. 395

Alienation   p. 410

Art   p. 395

Commodity fetish   p. 412

Culture of mass
    consumption   p. 410

Dreaming or the
    dreamtime   p. 401

Reviewing the Chapter

Chapter Section	What We Know	To Be Resolved
How Should We Look at Objects Anthropologically?	All objects, from those considered special because they are art objects to those intended for everyday use, have multiple dimensions.	Stocking's original notion of seven dimensions to objects is a useful starting point for analyzing objects. But there is debate over whether these are always the most useful dimensions for analyzing all objects, as well as which dimensions he may have missed.
Why and How Do Meanings of Things Change Over Time?	All objects change over time, if not in their physical characteristics then in the significance people give to them. Meanings change because of generational change, changes in social and technological context, and as objects change hands.	Anthropologists have not yet systematically explored whether the importance of objects changes and has always changed in the same ways, or if different kinds of societies (literate vs. pre-literate; stratified vs. egalitarian, etc.) change the meanings of things in precisely the same ways.
How Do Certain Objects Come to Represent People's Goals and Aspirations?	In order to address this question, three interrelated issues need to be considered: objects express people's personal and collective pasts; objects help people express and even formulate their goals and aspirations; and objects can be used in ways that manipulate what people's goals and aspirations should be.	Although many anthropologists assume that establishing mass-produced commodities has transformed societies' approach to objects and thus their goals and aspirations, it seems likely that the process of commodification is more complex than recent studies have suggested.

How Do Images Shape the Worlds in Which People Live?

The proliferation of visual imagery has provided new means of imagining oneself and one's community, while at the same time opened up new opportunities for manipulation. It also opens up new opportunities to reiterate basic cultural values and processes.

Anthropologists continue to debate how the spread of communication technologies and visual images shapes people's social lives and cultural meanings.

Readings

From the beginnings of the discipline, anthropologists and archaeologists have been interested in material culture. For a review of traditional approaches to art and materiality in anthropology, see Charlotte M. Otten's edited volume *Anthropology and Art: Readings in Cross-Cultural Aesthetics* (Texas Press Sourcebooks in Anthropology. Austin: University of Texas Press, 1990). Sally Price's *Primitive Art in Civilized Places* (Chicago: University of Chicago Press, 1989) was one of the earliest anthropological efforts to look at the superior knowledge of aesthetics held by art curators, art historians, and anthropologists of art as "constructed." More recently, George E. Marcus and Fred R. Myers strive for a new synthesis for understanding the connections between art and anthropology in *The Traffic in Culture: Refiguring Art and Anthropology* (Berkeley: University

of California Press, 1995). Ruth B. Phillips and Christopher B. Steiner's volume *Unpacking Culture: Art and Commodity in Colonial and Postcolonial Worlds* (Berkeley: University of California Press, 1999) considers the kinds of art objects that anthropologists collected in Third-World countries, drawing on these new approaches about how meaning is constructed.

●●●●●●●●●●●●●●●●●●●●●

Since Arjun Appadurai's collection of essays, *The Social Life of Things: Commodities in Cultural Perspective* (New York: Cambridge University Press, 1986), anthropologists have increasingly looked at how the meanings of objects, including aesthetics, are constructed. One of the most productive areas of research is Daniel Miller's approach in several of his books. Of these, *Material Cultures:*

Why Some Things Matter (Chicago: University of Chicago Press, 1998) offers one of the best approaches to studies of material culture and commodities. Luis Vivanco, a co-author of this book, has applied the social-life-of-things approach to the bicycle in his 2013 book *Reconsidering the Bicycle: An Anthropological Perspective on a New (Old) Thing* (New York: Routledge).

●●●●●●●●●●●●●●●●●●●●●

An excellent overview of the anthropology of media is Kelly Askew and Richard Wilk's 2002 edited volume *The Anthropology of Media: A Reader* (Malden, MA: Blackwell). It has many examples of cross-cultural consumption of cinema, television, radio, and other media.

●●●●●●●●●●●●●●●●●●●●●

Glossary

Note: The number at the end of each definition denotes the chapter in which the term first appears.

Acephalous society. A society without a governing head, generally with no hierarchical leadership. (10)

Action anthropology. Research in which the goal of a researcher's involvement in a community is to help make social change. (5)

Action theory. An approach in the anthropological study of politics that closely follows the daily activities and decision-making processes of individual political leaders emphasizing that politics is a dynamic and competitive field of social relations in which people are constantly managing their ability to exercise power over others. (10)

Adjudication. The legal process by which an individual or council with socially recognized authority intervenes in a dispute and unilaterally makes a decision. (10)

Aesthetic criteria. The underlying principles that make something appealing or beautiful. (16)

Age-grades. Groupings of age-mates, who are initiated into adulthood together. (10)

Agroecology. Integrating the principles of ecology into agricultural production.

Alienation. The antagonistic detachment between workers and the commodities they produce, as well as between these workers and the buyers of the goods. (16)

Animal husbandry. The breeding, care, and use of domesticated herding animals such as cattle, camels, goats, horses, llamas, reindeer, and yaks. (7)

Animism. An early theory that primitive peoples believed which holds that inanimate objects such as trees, rocks, cliffs, hills, and rivers were animated by spiritual forces or beings. (14)

Anthropology. The study of human beings, their biology, their pre-prehistory and histories, and their changing languages, cultures, and social institutions. (1)

Anthropology of development. The field of study within anthropology concerned with understanding the cultural conditions for proper development, or, alternatively, the negative impacts of development projects. (6)

Applied anthropology. Anthropological research commissioned to serve an organization's needs. (1)

Appropriation. The process of taking possession of an object, idea, or relationship. (9)

Archaeology. The study of past cultures, by excavating sites where people lived, worked, farmed, or conducted some other activity. (1)

Armchair anthropologist. An anthropologist who relies on the reports and accounts of others rather than original field research. (5)

Art. Conventionally understood as an expression of human creative skill, usually in the form of painting, sculpture, music, or literature. (16)

Artifactual landscapes. The idea that landscapes are the product of human shaping. (8)

Balanced reciprocity. A form of reciprocity in which the giver expects a fair return at some later time. (9)

Band. A small, nomadic, and self-sufficient group of anywhere from 25 to 150 individuals with face-to-face social relationships, usually egalitarian. (10)

Biocultural. The complex intersections of biological, psychological, and cultural processes. (3)

Biological anthropology. The study of the biological aspects of the human species, past and present, along with those of our closest relatives, the non-human primates. (1)

Biological determinism. The belief that human behaviors and beliefs are primarily, if not solely, the result of biological characteristics and processes. (3)

Bride price or **bride wealth.** Exchange of gifts or money to compensate another clan or family for the loss of one of its women along with her productive and reproductive abilities in marriage. (13)

Call systems. Patterned sounds or utterances that express meaning. (4)

Capitalism. An economic system based on private ownership of the means of production, in which prices are set and goods distributed through a market. (9)

Carrying capacity. The population an area can support. (8)

Caste. The system of social stratification found in Indian society that divides people into categories according to moral purity and pollution. (11)

Centralized political system. A political system, such as a chiefdom or a state, in which certain individuals and institutions hold power and control over resources. (10)

Chiefdom. A political system with a hereditary leader who holds central authority, typically supported by a class of high-ranking elites, informal laws, and a simple judicial system, often numbering in the tens of thousands with the beginnings of intensive agriculture and some specialization. (10)

Clan. A group of relatives who claim to be descended from a single ancestor. (13)

Class. The hierarchical distinctions between social groups in society usually based on wealth, occupation, and social standing. (11)

Clinical therapeutic process. The healing process in which medicines have some active ingredient that is assumed to address either the cause or the symptom of a disorder. (15)

Cognate words. Words in two languages that show the same systematic sound shifts as other words in the two languages, usually interpreted by linguists as evidence for a common linguistic ancestry. (4)

Cognatic. Reckoning descent through either men or women from some ancestor. (13)

Colonialism. The historical practice of more powerful countries claiming possession of less powerful ones. (1)

Commodities. Mass-produced and impersonal goods with no meaning or history apart from themselves. (9)

Commodity fetish. View of Karl Marx that commodities exercise a strange kind of power over people, controlling their attention and becoming objects of obsessive desire and worship. (16)

Comparative method. A research method that derives insights from careful comparisons of aspects of two or more cultures or societies. (1)

Consumers. People who rely on goods and services not produced by their own labor. (9)

Consumption. The act of using and assigning meaning to a good, service, or relationship. (9)

Corporate groups. Groups of real people who work together toward common ends, much like a corporation does. (13)

Creole language. A language of mixed origin that has developed from a complex blending of two parent languages that exists as a mother tongue for some part of the population. (4)

Cross-cultural perspective. Analyzing a human social phenomenon by comparing that phenomenon in different cultures. (2)

Cultural anthropology. The study of the social lives of living communities. (1)

Cultural appropriation. The unilateral decision of one social group to take control over the symbols, practices, or objects of another. (3)

Cultural construction. The meanings, concepts, and practices that people build out of their shared and collective experiences. (2)

Cultural determinism. The idea that all human actions are the product of culture, which denies the influence of other factors like physical environment and human biology on human behavior. (2)

Cultural economics. An anthropological approach to economics that focuses on how symbols and morals help shape a community's economy. (9)

Cultural imperialism. The promotion of one culture over others, through formal policy or less formal means, like the spread of technology and material culture. (6)

Cultural landscape. The culturally specific images, knowledge, and concepts of the physical landscape that help shape human relations with that landscape. (8)

Cultural model. Implicit and typically non-conscious cognitive models shared by a group of people of what is real or natural. (3)

Cultural relativism. The moral and intellectual principle that one should withhold judgment about seemingly strange or exotic beliefs and practices. (1)

Culture. The taken-for-granted notions, rules, moralities, and behaviors within a social group. (1)

Culture and personality school. A school of thought in early and mid-twentieth-century American anthropology that studied how patterns of child-rearing, social institutions, and cultural ideologies shaped individual experience, personality characteristics, and thought patterns. (3)

Culture of mass consumption. A term that refers to the cultural perspectives and social processes that shape and are shaped by how goods and services are bought, sold, and used in contemporary capitalism. (16)

Culture-bound syndrome. A mental illness unique to a culture. (3)

Currency. An object used as a medium of exchange. (9)

Customs. Long-established norms that have a codified and lawlike aspect. (2)

Delayed reciprocity. A form of reciprocity that features a long lag time between giving and receiving. (9)

Descriptive linguistics. The systematic analysis and description of a language's sound system and grammar. (4)

Development anthropology. The application of anthropological knowledge and research methods to the practical aspects of shaping and implementing development projects. (6)

Diffusionists. Early twentieth-century Boasian anthropologists who held that cultural characteristics result from either internal historical dynamism or a spread (diffusion) of cultural attributes from other societies. (6)

Discrimination. The negative or unfair treatment of an individual because of his or her membership in a particular social group or category. (11)

Disease. The purely physiological condition of being sick, usually determined by a physician. (15)

Diversity. The sheer variety of ways of being human around the world. (1)

Division of labor. The cooperative organization of work into specialized tasks and roles. (9)

Dowry. A large sum of money or in-kind gifts given to a daughter to ensure her well-being in her husband's family. (13)

Dreaming or **the dreamtime.** The mythological period when the ancestors created the natural features of their world as well as the plants and animals that inhabit it. (16)

Ecological anthropology. The specific vein with environmental anthropology that studies directly the relationship between humans and natural ecosystems. (8)

Ecological footprint. A quantitative tool that measures what people consume and the waste they produce. It also calculates the area of biologically productive land and water needed to support those people. (8)

Economic anthropology. The subdiscipline concerned with how people make, share, and buy things and services. (9)

Economic system. The structured patterns and relationships through which people exchange goods and services. (9)

Ecosystem. Natural systems based on the interaction of non-living factors and living species. (8)

Enculturation. The process of learning the social rules and cultural logic of a society. (2)

Environmental anthropology. The field that studies how different societies understand, interact with, and make changes to the natural world. (8)

Environmental determinism. A theory that attempts to explain cultural characteristics of a group of people as a consequence of specific ecological conditions or limitations. (8)

Environmental justice. A social movement addressing the linkages between racial discrimination and injustice, social equity, and environmental quality. (8)

Ethics. Moral questions about right and wrong and standards of appropriate behavior. (1)

Ethnicity. Belonging to a group with a particular history and social status. (11)

Ethnobiology. The subfield of ethnoscience that studies how people in non-Western societies name and codify living things. (8)

Ethnocentrism. The assumption that one's own way of doing things is correct, while dismissing other people's practices or views as wrong or ignorant. (1)

Ethnographic method. A prolonged and intensive observation of and participation in the life of a community. (1)

Ethnohistory. The study of cultural change in societies and periods for which the community had no written histories or historical documents, usually relying heavily on oral history for data. Ethnohistory may also refer to a view of history from the native's point of view, which often differs from an outsider's view. (5)

Ethnopsychology. The study of culturally specific ideas of personhood, self, emotion, and other psychological states. (3)

Ethnoscience. The study of how people classify things in the world, usually by considering some range or set of meanings. (4)

Evolution. The adaptive changes organisms make across generations. (1)

Exchange. The transfer of objects and services between social actors. (9)

Exiles. People who are expelled by the authorities of their home countries. (6)

Exogamous. A social pattern in which members of a clan must marry someone from another clan, which has the effect of building political, economic, and social ties with other clans. (13)

Explanatory model of illness. An explanation of what is happening to a patient's body, by the patient, by his family, or by a health care practitioner, each of which may have a different model of what is happening. (15)

Extended families. Larger groups of relatives beyond the nuclear family, often living in the same household. (13)

Fieldnotes. Any information that an anthropologist writes down or transcribes during fieldwork. (5)

Fieldwork. Long-term immersion in a community, normally involving first-hand research in a specific study community or research setting where people's behavior can be observed and the researcher can have conversations or interviews with members of the community. (1)

Food security. Access to sufficient nutritious food to sustain an active and healthy life. (7)

Foodways. Structured beliefs and behaviors surrounding the production, distribution, and consumption of food. (7)

Foraging. Obtaining food by searching for it, as opposed to growing or raising it. (7)

Formal economics. The branch of economics that studies the underlying logic of economic thought and action. (9)

Functionalism. A perspective that assumes that cultural practices and beliefs serve purposes for society. (2)

Fundamentalism. Conservative religious movements that advocate a return to fundamental or traditional principles. (14)

Fundamentalist. A person belonging to a religious movement that advocates a return to fundamental or traditional principles. (14)

Gender. Cultural expectations of how males and females should behave. (12)

Gender variance. Expressions of sex and gender that diverge from the male and female norms that dominate in most societies. (12)

Gender/sex systems. The ideas and social patterns a society uses to organize males, females, and those who do not fit either category. (12)

Gene flow. The movement of genes though interbreeding or intermarriage in humans between distinct populations so the two populations become more similar or maintain shared traits. (3)

Genealogical amnesia. Structural process of forgetting whole groups of relatives, usually because they are not currently significant in social life. (13)

Genealogical method. A systematic methodology for recording kinship relations and how kin terms are used in different societies. (5)

General purpose money. Money that is used to buy nearly any good or service. (9)

Generalized reciprocity. A form of reciprocity in which gifts are given freely without the expectation of return. (9)

Genetic drift. Random sampling effects—not natural selection—that bring changes to the distribution of traits within a population. (3)

Geneticization. The use of genetics to explain health and social problems over other possible causes. (3)

Globalization. The widening scale of cross-cultural interactions caused by the rapid movement of money, people, goods, images, and ideas within nations and across national boundaries. (6)

Government. A separate legal and constitutional domain that is the source of law, order, and legitimate force. (10)

Green Revolution. The transformation of agriculture in the Third World that began in the 1940s, through agricultural research, technology transfer, and infrastructure development. (7)

Headnotes. The mental notes an anthropologist makes while in the field, which may or may not end up in formal fieldnotes or journals. (5)

Holism. Efforts to synthesize distinct approaches and findings into a single comprehensive interpretation. (1)

Holistic perspective. A perspective that aims to identify and understand the whole—that is, the systematic connections between individual cultural beliefs and practices—rather than the individual parts. (3)

Holy struggle. A conflict—often political or social—that believers see as justified by doing God's work. (14)

Horizontal migration. Movement of a herding community across a large area in search of whatever grazing lands may be available. (7)

Horticulture. The cultivation of gardens or small fields to meet the basic needs of a household. (7)

Human Relations Area Files (HRAF). A comparative anthropological database that allows easy reference to coded information about several hundred cultural traits for more than 150 societies. The HRAF allows statistical analysis of the relationship between the presence of one trait and the occurrence of other traits. (5)

Hybridization. Persistent cultural mixing that has no predetermined direction or end-point. (6)

Illness. The psychological and social experience a patient has of a disease. (15)

Immigrants. People who enter a foreign country with no expectation of ever returning to their home country. (6)

Incest taboo. The prohibition on sexual relations between close family members. (13)

Industrial agriculture. The application of industrial principles to farming. (7)

Industrialization. The economic process of shifting from an agricultural economy to a factory-based one. (1)

Informant. Any person an anthropologist gets data from in the study community, especially people interviewed or who provide information about what they have observed or heard. (5)

Instrumentalism. A social theory that ethnic groups are not naturally occurring or stable, but highly dynamic groups created to serve the interests of one powerful group or another. (11)

Intensification. Processes that increase agricultural yields. (7)

Interpretive approach. A kind of analysis that interprets the underlying symbolic and cultural interconnections within a society. (14)

Interpretive theory of culture. A theory that culture is embodied and transmitted through symbols. (2)

Intersex. Individuals who exhibit sexual organs and functions somewhere between male and female elements, often including elements of both. (12)

Intersubjectivity. The realization that knowledge about other people emerges out of relationships and perceptions individuals have with each other. (5)

Interview. Any systematic conversation with an informant to collect field research data, ranging from a highly structured set of questions to the most open-ended ones. (5)

Kinship. The social system that organizes people in families based on descent and marriage. (13)

Kinship chart. A visual representation of family relationships. (13)

Lactase persistence. Continuation of lactase production beyond early childhood that allows a person to digest milk and dairy products. (7)

Language. A system of communication consisting of sounds, words, and grammar. (4)

Language ideology. Widespread assumptions that people make about the relative sophistication and status of particular dialects and languages. (4)

Laws. Sets of rules established by some formal authority. (10)

Life history. Any survey of an informant's life, including such topics as residence, occupation, marriage, family, and difficulties, usually collected to reveal patterns that cannot be observed today. (5)

Limited purpose money. Objects that can be exchanged only for certain things. (9)

Lineage. A group composed of relatives who are directly descended from known ancestors. (13)

Linguistic anthropology. The study of how people communicate with one other another through language and how language use shapes group membership and identity. (1)

Linguistic relativity. The idea that people speaking different languages perceive or interpret the world differently because of differences in their languages. (4)

Localization. The creation and assertion of highly particular, often place-based, identities and communities. (6)

Magic. An explanatory system of causation that does not follow naturalistic explanations, often working at a distance without direct physical contact. (14)

Mana. A belief that sacred power inheres in certain high-ranking people, sacred spaces, and objects. (14)

Market. A social institution in which people come together to exchange goods and services. (9)

Masculinity. The ideas and practices of manhood. (12)

Matrilineal. Reckoning descent through women, who are descended from an ancestral woman. (13)

Means of production. The machines and infrastructure required to produce goods. (9)

Mediation. The use of a third party who intervenes in a dispute to help the parties reach an agreement and restore harmony. (10)

Medical pluralism. The co-existence and interpenetration of distinct medical traditions with different cultural roots in the same cultural community. (15)

Medicalization. The process of viewing or treating as a medical concern conditions that were not previously understood as medical problems. (15)

Migrants. People who leave their homes to work for a time in other regions or countries. (6)

Mind. Emergent qualities of consciousness and intellect that manifest themselves through thought, emotion, perception, will, and imagination. (3)

Modes of subsistence. The social relationships and practices necessary for procuring, producing, and distributing food. (7)

Money. An object or substance that serves as a payment for a good or service. (9)

Monotheism. The belief in a single god. (14)

Morphology. The structure of words and word formation in a language. (4)

Multi-sited ethnography. An ethnographic research strategy of following connections, associations, and putative relationships from place to place. (6)

Mutation. Seemingly random changes in an organism's genetic code. (3)

Natal family. The family into which a person is born and (usually) raised. (13)

Nation-states. Independent states recognized by other states, composed of people who share a single national identity. (10)

Natural selection. The process through which the natural environment selects those individuals with the most suitable characteristics for that environment to have more successful offspring than other, less well adapted individuals. (3)

Naturalization. The social processes through which something, such as race, becomes part of the natural order of things. (11)

Nature and nurture. A kind of shorthand for biological (nature) and cultural or environmental (nurture) influences. (3)

Negative reciprocity. A form of reciprocity in which the giver attempts to get something for nothing, to haggle one's way into a favorable personal outcome. (9)

Negotiation. A form of dispute management in which the parties themselves reach a decision jointly. (10)

Neoclassical economics. Economic theories and approaches that study how people make decisions to allocate resources like time, labor, and money in order to maximize their personal benefit. (9)

Neural plasticity. The moldability and flexibility of brain structure. (3)

Non-centralized political system. A political system, such as a band or a tribe, in which power and control over resources are dispersed between members of the society. (10)

Norms. Typical patterns of actual behavior as well as the rules about how things should be done. (2)

Nuclear family. The family formed by a married couple and their children. (13)

Nutrition transition. The combination of changes in diet toward energy-dense foods (high in calories, fat, and sugar) and declines in physical activity. (7)

Obesity. The creation of excess body fat to the point of impairing bodily health and function. (7)

Open-ended interview. Any conversation with an informant in which the researcher allows the informant to take the conversation to related topics that the informant, rather than the researcher, feels are important. (5)

Overweight. Having abnormally high fat accumulation. (7)

Participant observation. The standard research method used by sociocultural anthropologists that requires the researcher to live in the community he or she is studying to observe and participate in day-to-day activities. (5)

Participatory action research. A research method in which the research questions, data collection, and data analysis are defined through collaboration between the researcher and the subjects of research. A major goal is for the research subjects to develop the capacity to investigate and take action on their primary political, economic, or social problems. (5)

Pastoralist societies. Groups of people who live by animal husbandry, which is the breeding, care, and use of domesticated herding animals such as cattle, camels, goats, horses, llamas, reindeer, and yaks. (7)

Patrilineal. Reckoning descent through males from the same ancestors. (13)

Person. The socially recognized individual. (3)

Phenotype. The visible characteristics of an organism. (3)

Philology. Comparative study of ancient texts and documents. (4)

Phonology. The systematic pattern of sounds in a language, also known as the language's sound system. (4)

Pidgin language. A mixed language with a simplified grammar, typically borrowing its vocabulary from one language but its grammar from another. (4)

Placebo effect. A healing process that works on persuading a patient he or she has been given a powerful medicine, even though the "medicine" has no active medical ingredient. (15)

Political ecology. The field of study that focuses on the linkages between political-economic power, social inequality, and ecological destruction. (8)

Political power. The processes by which people create, compete, and use power to attain goals that are presumed to be for the good of a community. (10)

Politics. Those relationships and processes of cooperation, conflict, and power that are fundamental aspects of human life. (10)

Polyandry. When a woman has two or more husbands at one time. (13)

Polygamy. Any form of plural marriage. (13)

Polygyny. When a man is simultaneously married to more than one woman. (13)

Polytheism. A type of religion with many gods. (14)

Postcolonialism. The field that studies the cultural legacies of colonialism and imperialism. (6)

Prejudice. Pre-formed, usually unfavorable opinions that people hold about people from groups who are different from their own. (11)

Prestige economies. Economies in which people seek high social rank, prestige, and power instead of money and material wealth. (9)

Primordialism. A social theory that ethnicity is largely a natural phenomenon, because of biological (i.e., "primordial"), linguistic, and geographical ties among members. (11)

Proto-language. A hypothetical common ancestral language of two or more living languages. (4)

Psychological anthropology. The subfield of anthropology that studies psychological states and conditions. (3)

Qualitative methods. A research strategy producing an in-depth and detailed description of social activities and beliefs. (1)

Quantitative methods. A methodology that classifies features of a phenomenon, counting or measuring them, and constructing mathematical and statistical models to explain what is observed. (1)

Race. A concept that organizes people into groups based on specific physical traits that are thought to reflect fundamental and innate differences. (11)

Racialization. The social, economic, and political processes of transforming populations into races and creating racial meanings. (11)

Racism. The repressive practices, structures, beliefs, and representations that uphold racial categories and social inequality. (11)

Rapid appraisal. Short-term, focused ethnographic research, typically lasting no more than a few weeks, about narrow research questions or problems. (5)

Reciprocity. The give-and-take that builds and confirms relationships. (9)

Redistribution. The collection of goods in a community and then the further dispersal of those goods among members. (9)

Refugees. People who migrate because of political oppression or war, usually with legal permission to stay in a different country. (6)

Religion. A symbolic system that is socially enacted through rituals and other aspects of social life. (14)

Rite of passage. Any life cycle rite that marks a person's or group's transition from one social state to another. (14)

Rituals. Stylized performances involving symbols that are associated with social, political, and religious activities.

Salvage paradigm. The paradigm which held that it was important to observe indigenous ways of life, interview elders, and assemble collections of objects made and used by indigenous peoples. (1)

Scientific method. The standard methodology of science that begins from observable facts, generates hypotheses from these facts, and then tests these hypotheses. (1)

Secondary materials. Any data that come from secondary sources such as a census, regional survey, historical report, other researchers, and the like that are not compiled by the field researcher. (5)

Secular worldview. A worldview that does not accept the supernatural as influencing current people's lives. (14)

Self. An individual's conception of his or her fundamental qualities and consciousness. (3)

Sex. The reproductive forms and functions of the body. (12)

Sexuality. Sexual preferences, desires, and practices. (12)

Sexually dimorphic. A characteristic of a species, in which males and females have different sexual forms. (12)

Shaman. A religious leader who communicates the needs of the living with the spirit world, usually through some form of ritual trance or other altered state of consciousness. (14)

Sick role. The culturally defined agreement between patients and family members to acknowledge that a patient is legitimately sick. (15)

Social institutions. Organized sets of social relationships that link individuals to each other in a structured way in a particular society. (2)

Social sanction. A reaction or measure intended to enforce norms and punish their violation. (2)

Social stratification. The classification of people into unequal groupings. (11)

Social support therapeutic process. A healing process that involves a patient's social networks, especially close family members and friends, who typically surround the patient during an illness. (15)

Sociolinguistics. The study of how sociocultural context and norms shape language use and the effects of language use on society. (4)

Speaking in tongues. The phenomenon of speaking in an apparently unknown language, often in an energetic and fast-paced way. (14)

Spheres of exchange. Bounded orders of value in which certain goods can be exchanged only for others. (9)

Spirit familiar. A spirit that has developed a close bond with a shaman. (14)

State. The most complex form of political organization, associated with societies that have intensive agriculture, high levels of social stratification, and centralized authority. (10)

Stops. Sounds that are formed by closing off and reopening the oral cavity so that it stops the flow of air through the mouth, such as the consonants p, b, t, d, k, and g. (4)

Structural power. Power that not only operates within settings, but that also organizes those and orchestrates the settings in which social and individual actions take place. (10)

Structural-functionalism. An anthropological theory that the different structures or institutions of a society (religion, politics, kinship, etc.) functioned to maintain social order and equilibrium. (10)

Structuralism. An anthropological theory that people make sense of their worlds through binary oppositions like hot-cold, culture-nature, male-female, and raw-cooked. These binary oppositions are expressed in social institutions and cultural practices. (7)

Substantive economics. A branch of economics, inspired by the work of Karl Polanyi, that studies the daily transactions people engage in to get what they need or desire. (9)

Surplus value. The difference between what people produce and what they need to survive. (9)

Sustainable agriculture. Farming based on integrating goals of environmental health, economic productivity, and economic equity (7)

Sustainable development. Development that meets the needs of the present without compromising the ability of future generations to meet their own needs (WCED 1987). (8)

Swidden agriculture. A farming method in tropical regions in which the farmer slashes and burns small area of forest to release plant nutrients into the soil. As soil fertility declines, the farmer allows the plot to regenerate to forest. (7)

Symbol. An object, idea, image, figure, or character that represents something else. (2)

Symbolic therapeutic process. A healing process that restructures the meanings of the symbols surrounding the illness, particularly during a ritual. (15)

Sympathetic magic. Any magical rite that relied on the supernatural to produce its outcome without working through some supernatural being such as a spirit, demon, or deity. (14)

Syntax. Pattern of word order used to form sentences and longer utterances in a language. (4)

Taste. A concept that refers to the sense that gives humans the ability to detect flavors, as well as the social distinction associated with certain foodstuffs. (7)

Teknonymy. A system of naming parents by the names of their children. (13)

Theory. A collection of tested and repeatedly supported hypotheses. (1)

Third genders. Situation found in many societies that acknowledge three or more categories of gender/sex. (12)

Totemism. A system of thought that associates particular social groups with specific animal or plant species called "totems" as an emblem. (14)

Tradition. Practices and customs that have become most ritualized and enduring. (2)

Traditional ecological knowledge. Indigenous ecological knowledge and its relationship with resource management strategies. (8)

Trance. A semi-conscious state typically brought on by hypnosis, ritual drumming, and singing, or hallucinogenic drugs like mescaline or peyote. (14)

Transactional orders. Realms of transactions a community uses, each with its own set of symbolic meanings and moral assumptions. (9)

Transgender. Refers to someone to whom society assigns one gender who does not perform as that gender but has taken either permanent or temporary steps to identify as another gender. (12)

Transhumance. Regular seasonal movement of herding communities from one ecological niche to another. (7)

Transnational. Relationships that extend beyond nation-state boundaries without assuming they cover the whole world. (6)

Tribe. A type of pastoralist or horticulturist society with populations usually numbering in the hundreds or thousands in which leadership is more stable than that of a band, but usually egalitarian, with social relations based on reciprocal exchange. (10)

Unilineal. Based on descent through a single descent line, either males or females. (13)

Value. The relative worth of an object or service that makes it desirable. (9)

Values. Symbolic expressions of intrinsically desirable principles or qualities. (2)

Violence. The use of force to harm someone or something. (10)

World culture. Norms and values that extend across national boundaries. (6)

World religions. Religions that claim to be universally significant to all people. (14)

World systems theory. The theory that capitalism has expanded on the basis of unequal exchange throughout the world, creating a global market and global division of labor, dividing the world between a dominant "core" and a dependent "periphery." (6)

Worldview. A general approach to or set of shared unquestioned assumptions about the world and how it works. (14)

References

Adultery. 2009. "Adultery: Criminal Laws, Enforcement of Statutes, as a Defense, Divorce, Cross-Reference." Accessed on 8/18/09: http://law.jrank.org/pages/4112/Adultery.html.

Alatas, Syed Hussein. 1977. *The Myth of the Lazy Native: A Study of the Image of the Malays, Filipinos, and Javanese from the Sixteenth to the Twentieth Century and Its Function in the Ideology of Colonial Capitalism.* London: Routledge.

Allen, Theodore W. 1997. *The Invention of the White Race.* Vol. 2. London: Verso.

Allport, Gordon. 1958. *The Nature of Prejudice.* Abridged edition. New York: Doubleday Anchor Books.

Almond, Gabriel, A., R. Scott Appleby, and Emmanuel Sivan. 2003. *Strong Religion: The Rise of Fundamentalisms Around the World.* Chicago: University of Chicago Press.

American Psychological Association. 1994. *Diagnostic and Statistical Manual of Mental Disorders: DSM-IV.* Washington, DC: American Psychological Association.

Ames, Michael. 1999. How to Decorate a House: The Re-negotiation of Cultural Representations at the University of British Columbia Museum of Anthropology. *Museum Anthropology,* 22(3):41–51.

Amnesty International. 2008. "Amnesty International Report 2008: State of the World's Human Rights." Accessed on 7/25/08: http://report2008.amnesty.org/eng/report-08-at-a-glance.html

Amuyunzu-Nyamongo, Mary. 2006. "Challenges and Prospects for Applied Anthropology in Kenya." In Mwenda Ntarangwi, David Mills, and Mustafa Babiker, eds., *African Anthropologies: History, Critique and Practice,* pp. 237–49. Dakar: CODESRIA.

Anderson, Eugene N. 2005. *Everyone Eats: Understanding Food and Culture.* New York: NewYork University Press.

Appadurai, Arjun, ed. 1986. *The Social Life of Things: Commodities in Cultural Perspective.* Cambridge: Cambridge University Press.

Appadurai, Arjun. 1996. *Modernity At Large: Cultural Dimensions of Globalization.* Minneapolis: University of Minnesota Press.

Armelagos, George, and Alan Goodman. 1998. "Race, Racism, and Anthropology." In Alan Goodman and Thomas Leatherman, eds., *Building a New Biocultural Synthesis: Political-Economic Perspectives on Human Biology,* pp. 359–78. Ann Arbor: University of Michigan Press.

Armstrong, Karen. 1994. *A History of God: The 4,000-Year Quest of Judaism, Christianity and Islam.* New York: Ballantine Books.

Asad, Talal. 1993. *Genealogies of Religion: Discipline and Reasons of Power in Christianity and Islam.* Baltimore: John Hopkins University Press.

Asch, Timothy, and Napoleon Chagnon. 1968. *Children Play in the Rain.* Film. Somerville, MA: Documentary Educational Resources.

Asch, Timothy, and Napoleon Chagnon. 1989. *The Ax Fight.* Video-cassette. Watertown, MA: Documentary Educational Resources.

Asch, Timothy, and Napoleon Chagnon. 1990a. *A Father Washes His Children.* Videocassette. Watertown, MA: Documentary Educational Resources.

Asch, Timothy, and Napoleon Chagnon. 1990b. *A Man and His Wife Make a Hammock.* Videocassette. Watertown, MA: Documentary Educational Resources.

Asch, Timothy, and Napoleon Chagnon. 1997. *The Feast.* Videocassette. Watertown, MA: Documentary Educational Resources. [Released as 16 mm film, 1970.]

Atran, Scott. 2001. "The Vanishing Landscape of the Petén Maya Lowlands: People, Plants, Animals, Places, Words, and Spirits." In Lisa Maffi, ed., *On Biocultural Diversity: Linking Language, Knowledge, and the Environment,* pp. 157–76. Washington, DC: Smithsonian Institution Press.

Avruch, Kevin. 1998. *Culture and Conflict Resolution.* Washington, DC: United States Institute of Peace.

Azoy, Whitney. 2002. "Waaseta (Personal Connections)." *Bangor Daily News,* Feb. 9–10, 2002, A9–10.

Bailey, F. G. 1969. *Stratagems and Spoils: A Social Anthropology of Politics.* London: Basil Blackwell.

Banerjee, Abhijit V., and Esther Duflo. 2006. *The Economic Lives of the Poor.* MIT Department of Economics Working Paper No. 06–29. Cambridge, MA.

Barth, Frederick. 1969. *Ethnic Groups and Boundaries: The Social Organization of Culture Difference.* New York: Little Brown & Co.

Bartlett, Robert. 1982. *Gerald of Wales, 1146–1223.* Oxford: Oxford University Press.

BasisonLine.Org. 2003. The Curse of the Bambino—Don't Bet on It. *The Wager* 8(43): 1–7. Accessed Feb 28, 2005: http://www.basisonline.org/2003/10/the-wager-vol-3.html

Basu, Amitra, ed. 2010. *Women's Movements in the Global Era: The Power of Local Feminisms.* Boulder, CO: Westview Press.

Bates, Daniel G. 1998. *Human Adaptive Strategies: Ecology, Culture, and Politics.* Boston: Allyn and Bacon.

Benedict, Ruth. 1934. *Patterns of Culture.* Boston: Houghton Mifflin.

Benedict, Ruth. 1946. *The Chrysanthemum and the Sword: Patterns of Japanese Culture.* Boston: Houghton Mifflin.

Berger, Peter L., ed. 1999. *The Desecularization of the World: Resurgent Religion and World Politics.* Washington, DC: Ethics and Public Policy Center.

Bergmann, J. F., O. Chassany, J. Gandiol, P. Deblois, J. A. Kanis, J. M. Segresta, C. Caulin, R. Dahan. 1994. A Randomized Clinical Trial of the Effect of Informed Consent on the Analgesic Activity of Placebo and Naproxen in Cancer Pain. *Clinical Trials Meta-Analysis* 29:41–47.

Beriss, David. 2005. Review of Reckoning with Homelessness. *American Anthropologist* 107(4): 729–30.

Berlin, Brent, and Paul Kay. 1969. *Basic Color Terms: Their Universality and Evolution.* Berkeley: University of California Press.

Berlin, Brent. 1973. Folk Systematics in Relation to Biological Classification and Nomenclature. *Annual Review of Systematics and Ecology* 4:259–71.

Bernard, Russell H. 2011.*Research Methods in Anthropology: Qualitative and Quantitative Approaches.* Lanham, MD: AltaMira Press.

Béteille, André. 1992. Caste and Family in Representations of Indian Society. *Anthropology Today* 8(1):13–18.

Bird-David, Nurit. 1992. Beyond the "Original Affluent Society": A Culturalist Reformulation. *Current Anthropology* 33(1): 25–47.

Bird-David, Nurit. 1993. "Tribal Metaphorization of Human-Nature Relatedness: A Comparative Analysis." In K. Milton, ed., *Environmentalism: The View from Anthropology,* pp. 112–25. London: Routledge.

Bishop, John Melville, and Harold E. L. Prinz, 2003. *Oh! What a Blow that Phantom Gave Me!: Edmund Carpenter.* DVD Video. West Hills, CA: Media Generation.

Blim, Michael. 2000. Capitalisms in Late Modernity. *Annual Reviews of Anthropology* 29:25–38.

Boas, Franz. 1889. Die Ziele der Ethnologie. *Gemeinverständliche Vorträge gehalten im Deutsche Gesellig-Wissenschaftlichen Verein* 16:3–30. New York: Herman Bartsch.

Boas, Franz. 1912. Changes in the Bodily Form of Descendants of Immigrants. *American Anthropologist* 14(3):530–562.

Boas, Franz. 1940. *Race, Language, and Culture.* New York: Macmillan.

Bodley, John. 1999. *Victims of Progress.* 4th Edition. New York: McGraw-Hill.

Boggs, Stephen T., and Malcolm Naea Chun. 1990. "Ho'oponopono: A Hawaiian Method of Solving Interpersonal Problems." In Karen Ann Watson-Gegeo and Geoffrey White, eds., *Disentangling: Conflict Discourse in Pacific Societies,* pp. 123–53. Stanford, CA: Stanford University Press.

Bohannon, Paul, and Laura Bohannon. 1968. *Tiv Economy.* Evanston, IL: Northwestern University Press.

Boserup, Ester. 1965. *The Conditions of Agricultural Growth: The Economics of Agrarian Change Under Population Pressure.* London: G. Allen & Unwin.

Bourdieu, Pierre. 1984. *Distinction: A Social Critique of the Judgement of Taste.* Cambridge, MA: Harvard University Press.

Bourgois, Philippe. 1995. *In Search of Respect: Selling Crack in El Barrio.* New York: Cambridge University Press.

Bradbury, R. E. 1957. *The Benin Kingdom and the Edo-speaking Peoples of South-Western Nigeria.* London: International African Institute.

Brettell, Caroline B., and Carolyn F. Sargent, eds. 2001. *Gender in Cross-Cultural Perspective.* 3rd Edition. Upper Saddle River, NJ: Prentice Hall.

Bringa, Tone. 2005. "Haunted by Imaginations of the Past: Robert Kaplan's Balkan Ghosts." In Katherine Besteman and Hugh Gusterson, eds., *Why America's Top Pundits Are Wrong: Anthropologists Talk Back,* pp. 60–82. Berkeley: University of California Press.

British Association for the Advancement of Science. 1899. *Notes and Queries on Anthropology.* 3rd Edition. London: The Anthropological Institute.

Brockington, Dan. 2002. *Fortress Conservation: The Preservation of the Mkomazi Game Reserve.* Bloomington: Indiana University Press.

Brody, Howard, and Linda Hunt. 2006. BiDil: Assessing and Race-Based Pharmaceutical. *Annals of Family Medicine* 4(6): 556–560.

Brown, Michael. 2003. *Who Owns Native Culture?* Cambridge: Harvard University Press.

Brownell, K. D. 2002. "The Environment and Obesity." In C. G. Fairburn and K. D. Brownell, eds., *Eating Disorders and Obesity: A Comprehensive Handbook.* 2nd Edition, pp. 433–8. New York: Guilford Press.

Bullard, Robert. 1994. *Dumping in Dixie: Race, Class, and Environmental Quality.* 2nd Edition. Boulder, CO: Westview Press.

Bulmer, Ralph. 1967. Why Is the Cassowary Not a Bird? *Man* 2:5–25.

Burling, Robbins. 1971. *Man's Many Voices: Language in Its Cultural Context.* New York: Holt, Rinehart and Winston.

Caplan, Pat, ed. 1995. *Understanding Disputes: The Politics of Argument.* Oxford: Berg Publishers.

Caputo, John, and Mark Yount, eds. 1993. *Foucault and the Critique of Institutions.* University Park: Pennsylvania State University Press.

Carey, Benedict. 2007. Brainy Parrot Dies, Emotive to the End. *New York Times* Sept. 11, 2007. Accessed July 20, 2010: http://www.nytimes.com/2007/09/11/science/11parrot.html?_r=1

Carrier, James. 1995. *Gifts and Commodities: Exchange and Western Capitalism Since 1700.* London: Routledge.

Carrier, James. 1996a. "Exchange." In Alan Barnard and Jonathan Spencer, eds., *Encyclopedia of Social and Cultural Anthropology,* pp. 218–21. London: Routledge.

Carrier, James. 1996b. "Consumption." In Alan Barnard and Jonathan Spencer, eds., *Encyclopedia of Social and Cultural Anthropology,* pp. 128–9. London: Routledge.

Carrier, Joseph M. 1976. Family Attitudes and Mexican Male Homosexuality. *Urban Life* 5(3):359–75.

Carrithers, Michael. 1996. "Person." In Alan Barnard and Jonathan Spencer, eds., *Encyclopedia of Social and Cultural Anthropology,* pp. 419–23. London: Routledge.

Carroll, John B., ed. 1956. *Language, Thought, and Reality: Selected Writings of Benjamin Lee Whorf.* Cambridge: Technology Press of Massachusetts Institute of Technology.

Carsten, Janet. 1989. "Cooking Money: Gender and the Symbolic Transformation of Means of Exchange in a Malay Fishing Community." In J. Parry and M. Bloch, eds., *Money and the Morality of Exchange,* pp. 117–41. Cambridge: Cambridge University Press.

Chagnon, Napoleon, and Timothy Asch. 1973. *Magical Death.* Watertown, MA: Documentary Educational Resources.

Chagnon, Napoleon. 1968. *Yanomamö: The Fierce People.* New York: Holt, Rinehart and Winston.

Chakrabarty, Ankita. 2012. India in Race with China to Become Global Diabetic Capital. *ZeeNews,* 14 November 2012. Accessed on 8/12/13: http://zeenews.india.com/exclusive/india-in-race-with-china-to-become-global-diabetic-capital_5848.html

Chambers, Robert. 1997. *Whose Reality Counts? Putting the Last First.* 2nd Edition. London: Intermediate Technology Publications.

Chossudovsky, Michel. 1997. *The Globalization of Poverty: Impacts of IMF and World Bank Reforms.* Atlantic Highlands, NJ: Zed Books.

Cohen, Mark Nathan. 1998. *Culture of Intolerance: Chauvinism, Class, and Racism in the United States.* New Haven: Yale University Press.

Colchester, Marcus. 2003. "The Vth World Parks Congress: Parks for People or Parks for Business?" *World Rainforest Movement Bulletin No. 75,* October 2003. Accessed on February 15, 2005: http://www.wrm.org.uy/bulletin/75/parks.html.

Collier, Jane, and Sylvia Yanagisako, eds. 1987. *Gender and Kinship: Essays Toward a Unified Analysis.* Stanford, CA: Stanford University Press.

Connor, Linda. 1982. Ships of Fools and Vessels of the Divine: Mental Hospitals and Madness, A Case Study. *Social Science and Medicine* 16:783–94.

Coon, C. S., S. M. Garn, and J. B. Birdsell. 1950. *Races.* Springfield, IL: Thomas.

Counihan, Carole. 1999. *The Anthropology of Food and Body: Gender, Meaning, and Power.* New York: Routledge.

Counts, Dorothy A. 1980. Fighting Back Is Not the Way: Suicide and the Women of Kaliai. *American Ethnologist* 7:332–51.

Cronon, William. 1983. *Changes in the Land: Indians, Colonists, and the Ecology of New England.* New York: Hill and Wang.

Csordas, Thomas, and Arthur Kleinman 1996. "The Therapeutic Process." In Carolyn F. Sargent and Thomas M. Johnson, eds., *Medical Anthropology: Contemporary Theory and Method,* pp. 3–20. Revised Edition. Westport, CT: Praeger.

D'Andrade, Roy. 1990. "Cultural Cognition." In Michael Posner, ed., *Foundations of Cognitive Science,* pp. 795–830. Cambridge, MA: MIT Press.

Dakowski, Bruce. 1990. "Everything Is Relatives: W. H. R. Rivers." In *Pioneers of Social Anthropology: Strangers Abroad* (Documentary Film Series). Videorecording. Princeton: Films for the Humanities and Sciences.

Daltabuit, Magalí, and Thomas Leatherman. 1998. "The Biocultural Impact of Tourism on Mayan Communities." In Alan Goodman and Thomas Leatherman, eds., *Building a New Biocultural Synthesis: Political-Economic Perspectives on Human Biology,* pp. 317–38. Ann Arbor: University of Michigan Press.

Dark, Philip J. C. 1962. *The Art of Benin: A Catalogue of an Exhibition of the A. W. F. Fuller and Chicago Natural History Museum Collections of Antiquities from Benin, Nigeria.* Chicago: Chicago Natural History Museum.

Dark, Philip J. C. 1982. *An Illustrated Catalogue of Benin Art.* Boston: G. K. Hall.

Darwin, Charles. 1859. *On the Origin of Species by Means of Natural Selection: Or, The Preservation of Favoured Races in the Struggle for Life.* London: J. Murray.

Davidheiser, Mark. 2007. Overview of Peace and Conflict Resolution Study and Practice. *Anthropology News* Oct:11–12.

Dávila, Arlene. 2001. *Latinos, Inc.: The Marketing and Making of a People.* Berkeley: University of California Press.

de Castro, Fabio, and David McGrath. 2003. Moving toward Sustainability in the Local Management of Floodplain Lake Fisheries in the Brazilian Amazon. *Human Organization* 62(2): 123–33.

Delaney, Carol. 1988. Participant Observation: The Razor's Edge. *Dialectical Anthropology* 13(3): 291–300.

de Mille, Cecil B., director. 1956. *The Ten Commandments.* Hollywood, CA: Paramount Pictures.

Dentan, Robert Knox. 1968. *The Semai: A Non-Violent People of Malaya*. New York: Holt, Rinehart, and Winston.

Dentan, Robert Knox, K. Endicott, A. G. Gomes, and M. B. Hooker. 1997. *Malaysia and the "Original People": A Case Study of the Impact of Development on Indigenous Peoples*. Boston: Allyn and Bacon.

Dettwyler, Katherine A. 2013. *Dancing Skeletons: Life and Death in West Africa*. 2nd Edition. Prospect Heights, IL: Waveland.

Dixon, Andrew. 2013. "Seduced by the Illusion: The Truth About Transformation Photos." *Huffington Post,* 24 July 2013. Accessed 24 July 2013: http://www.huffingtonpost.com/andrew-dixon/weight-loss-secrets_b_3643898.html

Douglas, Mary. 1966. *Purity and Danger: An Analysis of the Concepts of Pollution and Taboo*. New York: Praeger.

Douglas, Mary, and Baron Isherwood. 1978. *The World of Goods*. Harmondsworth: Penguin.

Dressler, William. 2005. What's Cultural About Biocultural Research? *Ethos* 31(1): 20–45.

Dreyer, Edward L. 2007. *Zheng He: China and the Oceans in the Early Ming Dynasty, 1405–1433*. New York: Pearson Longman.

Dumont, Louis. 1966. *Homo Hierarchicus: The Caste System and Its Implications*. Chicago: University of Chicago Press.

Dwyer, Leslie. 2000. "Spectacular Sexualities: Nationalism, Development, and the Politics of Family Planning in Indonesia." In Tamar Mayer, ed., *Gender Ironies of Nationalism: Sexing the Nation,* pp. 25–62. New York: Routledge.

Eboreime, Joseph. 2003. *The Installation of a Benin Monarch: Rite de Passage in the Expression of Ethnic Identity in Nigeria*. Paper from the ICOMOS 14th General Assembly. Accessed March 3, 2005. http://www.international.icomos.org/victoriafalls2003/papers/B3–1%20-%20Eboreime.pdf

Edwards, Carolyn P. 1993. "Behavioral Sex Differences in Children of Diverse Cultures: The Case of Nurturance to Infants." In Michael E. Pereira and Lynn A. Fairbanks, eds., *Juvenile Primates: Life History, Development, and Behavior,* pp. 327–38. New York: Oxford University Press.

Eickelman, Dale F., and James Piscatori. 1996. *Muslim Politics*. Princeton: Princeton University Press.

Eisenberg, Leon. 1977. Disease and Illness: Distinctions Between Professional and Popular Ideas of Sickness. *Culture, Medicine and Psychiatry* 1(1): 9–23.

Elder, Kay, and Brian Dale. 2000. *In Vitro Fertilization*. 2nd Edition. Cambridge: Cambridge University Press.

Eller, Jack David. 2006. *Violence and Culture: A Cross-Cultural and Interdisciplinary Approach*. Belmont, CA: Thomson Wadsworth.

Endicott, Kirk, and Karen Endicott. 2008. *The Headman Was a Woman: The Gender Egalitarian Batek of Malaysia*. Long Grove, IL: Waveland Press.

Erasmus, Charles John. 1952. Changing Folk Beliefs and the Relativity of Empirical Knowledge. *Southwestern Journal of Anthropology* 8(4): 411–28.

Erlich, Paul R. 1968. *The Population Bomb*. New York: Ballantine Books.

Escobar, Arturo. 1991. Anthropology and the Development Encounter: The Making and Marketing of Development Anthropology. *American Ethnologist* 18:658–82.

Escobar, Arturo. 1995. *Encountering Development: The Making and Unmaking of the Third World*. Princeton: Princeton University Press.

Escobar, Arturo, Sonia Alvarez, Adusta E. Dagnino. 1998. "Introduction: The Cultural and the Political in Latin American Social Movements." In Arturo Escobar, Sonia Alvarez, and E. Dagnino, eds., *Cultures of Politics/Politics of Culture: Revisioning Latin American Social Movements,* pp. 1–32. Boulder, CO: Westview Press.

Esteva, Gustavo. 1992. Development. In Wolfgang Sachs, ed., *The Development Dictionary,* pp. 6–25. London: Zed Books.

Evans-Pritchard, E. E. 1940. *The Nuer: A Description of the Modes of Livelihood and Political Institutions of a Nilotic People*. Oxford: Oxford University Press.

Evans-Pritchard, E. E. 1961. *Anthropology and History: A Lecture Delivered at the University of Manchester with Support of the Simon Fund for the Social Sciences*. Manchester: Manchester University Press.

Eyer, Diane. 1993. *Mother-Infant Bonding: A Scientific Fiction*. New Haven, CT: Yale University Press.

Fabian, Johannes. 1971. On Professional Ethics and Epistemological Foundations. *Current Anthropology* 12(2): 230–2.

Fabian, Johannes. 2001. *Anthropology with an Attitude: Critical Essays*. Palo Alto: Stanford University Press.

Fairhead, James, and Melissa Leach. 1996. *Misreading the African Landscape: Society and Ecology in a Forest-Savanna Mosaic*. Cambridge: Cambridge University Press

Farmer, Paul. 1992. *AIDS and Accusation: Haiti and the Geography of Blame*. Berkeley: University of California Press.

Fausto-Sterling, Anne. 1992a. *Myths of Gender: Biological Theories About Women and Men*. 2nd Edition. New York: Basic Books.

Fausto-Sterling, Anne. 1992b. Why Do We Know So Little About Human Sex? *Discover Magazine*. June 1992. Accessed on 8/19/09: http://discovermagazine.com/1992/jun/whydoweknowsolit64

Fausto-Sterling, Anne. 2000. *Sexing the Body: Gender Politics and the Construction of Sexuality*. New York: Basic Books.

Fazioli, K. Patrick. 2014. The Erasure of the Middle Ages from Anthropology's Intellectual Genealogy. *History and Anthropology* 25(3):336–355.

Ferguson, James. 1994. *The Anti-Politics Machine: "Development," Depoliticization, and Bureaucratic Power in Lesotho*. Minneapolis: University of Minnesota Press.

Ferguson, R. Brian. 1995. *Yanomami Warfare: A Political History*. Santa Fe: School of American Research Press.

Field, Les, and Richard G. Fox. 2007. "Introduction: How Does Anthropology Work Today?" In Les Field and Richard G. Fox, eds., *Anthropology Put to Work,* pp. 1–19. Oxford: Berg Publishers.

Finney, Ben R. 1973. *Big Men and Business: Entrepreneurship and Economic Growth in the New Guinea Highlands*. Honolulu: University of Hawaii Press.

Fluehr-Lobban, Carolyn. 2003. *Ethics and the Profession of Anthropology: Dialogue for Ethically Conscious Practice*. Walnut Creek, CA: AltaMira Press.

Food and Agriculture Organization of the United Nations (FAO). 2012. *Undernourishment Around the World*. Accessed on 9/11/13: www.fao.org/docrep/016/i3027e/i3027e02.pdf

Foster, George M. 1952. Relationships between Theoretical and Applied Anthropology: A Public Health Program Analysis. *Human Organization* 11(3): 5–16.

Foucault, Michel. 1978. *The History of Sexuality:* Vol. 1. *An Introduction*. Trans. Robert Hurley. New York: Vintage Books.

Foucault, Michel. 1999. *Religion and Culture*. Selected and edited by Jeremy R. Carrette. New York: Routledge.

Fox, Geoffrey. 1997. *Hispanic Nation: Culture, Politics, and the Constructing of Identity*. Tucson: University of Arizona Press.

Frankel, David, director. 2006. *The Devil Wears Prada*. DVD. Beverly Hills, CA: 20th Century Fox Home Entertainment.

Frankenberry, Nancy, and Hans H. Penner. 1999. Clifford Geertz's Long-Lasting Moods, Motivations, and Metaphysical Conceptions. *Journal of Religion* 79(4): 617–40.

Fratkin, Elliot. 2003. *Ariaal Pastoralists of Kenya: Surviving Drought and Development in Africa's Arid Lands*. 2nd Edition. Boston: Allyn and Bacon.

Frazer, James G. 1890. *The Golden Bough: A Study in Comparative Religion*. 1st Edition. 2 Vols. London: Macmillan.

Frazer, James G. 1900. *The Golden Bough: A Study in Magic and Religion*. 2nd Edition. 3 Vols. London: Macmillan.

Frazer, James G. 1911–1915. *The Golden Bough: A Study in Magic and Religion*. 3rd Edition. 12 Vols. London: Macmillan.

Freidson, Eliot. 1970. *Profession of Medicine: A Study of the Sociology of Applied Knowledge*. New York: Dodd, Mead.

Friedl, Erika. 1994. "Sources of Female Power in Iran." In Mahnaz Afkhami and Erika Friedl, eds., *In the Eye of the Storm: Women in Post-Revolutionary Iran*, pp. 151–68. Syracuse, NY: Syracuse University Press.

Friedman, Jonathan. 1994. *Cultural Identity and Global Process.* London: Sage Publications.

Friedman, Jonathan. 1999. "The Hybridization of Roots and the Abhorrence of the Bush." In Michael Featherstone and Scott Lash, eds., *Spaces of Culture: City-Nation-World,* pp. 230–55. London: Sage.

Fry, Douglas. 2006. *The Human Potential for Peace: An Anthropological Challenge to Assumptions About War and Violence.* New York: Oxford University Press.

Fuller, C. J. 2004. *The Camphor Flame: Popular Hinduism and Society in India.* Princeton, NJ: Princeton University Press.

Gallagher, Charles. 1997. "White Racial Formation: Into the Twenty-First Century." In Richard Delgado and Jean Stefancic, eds., *Critical White Studies: Looking Behind the Mirror,* pp. 6–11. Philadelphia, PA: Temple University Press.

García-Canclini, Nestor. 1995. *Hybrid Cultures: Strategies for Entering and Leaving Modernity.* Minneapolis: University of Minnesota Press.

Gardner, R. Allen, Beatrix T. Gardner, and Thomas E. van Cantfort, eds. 1989. *Teaching Sign Language to Chimpanzees.* Albany: State University of New York Press.

Garn, Stanley. 1961. *Human Races.* Springfield, IL: C. C. Thomas.

Geertz, Clifford. 1963. *Agricultural Involution: The Processes of Ecological Change in Indonesia.* Berkeley: University of California Press.

Geertz, Clifford. 1966. "Religion as a Cultural System." In Michael Banton, ed., *Anthropological Approaches to the Study of Religion,* pp. 1–46. ASA Monograph 3. London: Tavistock.

Geertz, Clifford. 1973. *The Interpretation of Cultures: Selected Essays.* New York: Basic Books.

Geertz, Clifford. 1988. *Works and Lives: The Anthropologist as Author.* Stanford, CA: Stanford University Press.

Geertz, Hildred, and Clifford Geertz. 1964. Teknonymy in Bali: Parenthood, Age-Grading, and Genealogical Amnesia. *Journal of the Royal Anthropological Institute of Great Britain and Ireland* 94(2): 94–108.

Geertz, Hildred, and Clifford Geertz. 1975. *Kinship in Bali.* Chicago: University of Chicago Press.

Gellner, Ernest. 1983. *Nations and Nationalism.* Ithaca, NY: Cornell University Press.

Gennep, Arnold van. 1960. *The Rites of Passage.* Trans. by Monica B. Vizedom and Gabrielle L. Caffee. Chicago: University of Chicago Press. [Orig. published 1909 in French]

Ghani, Ashraf, and Clare Lockhart, eds. 2009. *Fixing Failed States: A Framework for Rebuilding a Fractured World.* New York: Oxford University Press.

Gibbs, James L., Jr. 1963. The Kpelle Moot. *Africa* 33(1): 1–11.

Gibson, Kathleen. 2005. "Epigenesis, Brain Plasticity, and Behavioral Versatility: Alternatives to Standard Evolutionary Psychology Models." In Susan McKinnon and Sydel Silverman, eds., *Complexities: Beyond Nature and Nurture,* pp. 23–42. Chicago: University of Chicago Press.

Gledhill, John. 2000. *Power and Its Disguises: Anthropological Perspectives on Politics.* London: Pluto Press.

Gluckman, Max. 1940. Analysis of a Social System in Modern Zululand. *Bantu Studies* 14:1–30, 147–74.

Gmelch, George. 1978. Baseball Magic. *Human Nature* 1(8): 32–39.

Goldschmidt, Walter. 2000. A Perspective on Anthropology. *American Anthropologist,* 102(4): 789–807.

Gonzalez, Roberto. 2001. *Zapotec Science: Farming and Food in the Northern Sierra of Oaxaca.* Austin: University of Texas Press.

Gordon, Robert J. 2005. *The Bushman Myth: The Making of a Namibian Underclass.* 2nd Edition. Boulder, CO: Westview Press.

Gould, Stephen Jay. 1981. *The Mismeasure of Man.* New York: W. W. Norton.

Gow, David. 1993. Doubly Damned: Dealing with Power and Praxis in Development Anthropology. *Human Organization* 52(4): 380–97.

Gravlee, Clarence. 2009. How Race Becomes Biology: Embodiment of Social Inequality. *American Journal of Physical Anthropology* 139:47–57.

Green Belt Movement. 2005. "Achievements." Accessed on March 20, 2005: http://www.greenbeltmovement.org/achievements.php.

Gregory, Steven, and Roger Sanjek, eds. 1994. *Race.* New Brunswick: Rutgers University Press.

Grimm, Jakob. 1822. *Deutsche Grammatik.* Göttingen: Dieterichsche Buchhandlung.

Grove, Richard. 1995. *Green Imperialism: Colonial Expansion, Tropical Island Edens and the Origins of Environmentalism, 1600–1860.* Cambridge: Cambridge University Press.

Gudeman, Stephen. 1986. *Economics as Culture: Models and Metaphors of Livelihood.* London: Routledge & Kegan Paul.

Gudeman, Stephen. 2001. *The Anthropology of Economy: Community, Market, and Culture.* Oxford: Blackwell.

Guha, Ramachandra. 2000. *Environmentalism: A Global History.* New York: Longman.

Guimarães, Antonio Sérgio Alfredo. 1999. "Racism and Anti-Racism in Brazil." In Roger S. Gottlieb (series ed.) and Leonard Harris (volume ed.), *Key Concepts in Critical Theory: Racism,* pp. 314–30. Amherst, NY: Humanity Books.

Gulliver, Phillip H. 1979. *Disputes and Negotiations: A Cross-Cultural Perspective.* New York: Academic Press.

Gutmann, Matthew C. 1996. *The Meanings of Macho: Being a Man in Mexico City.* Berkeley: University of California Press.

Gutmann, Matthew C. 1997. Trafficking in Men: The Anthropology of Masculinity. *Annual Review of Anthropology* 26:385–409.

Haeri, Niloofar. 1997. The Reproduction of Symbolic Capital: Language, State, and Class in Egypt. *Current Anthropology* 38(5): 795–805, 811–16.

Haeri, Niloofar. 2003. *Sacred Language, Ordinary People: Dilemmas of Culture and Politics in Egypt.* New York: Palgrave Macmillan.

Hale, Kenneth L. 1992. On Endangered Languages and the Safeguarding of Diversity. *Language* 68(1): 1–3.

Hanlon, Joseph. 1996. Strangling Mozambique: International Monetary Fund "Stabilization" in the World's Poorest Country. *Multinational Monitor* 17(7–8) July/August: 17–21.

Hannerz, Ulf. 1992. "The Global Ecumene." In *Cultural Complexity: Studies in the Social Organization of Meaning,* pp. 217–67. New York: Columbia University Press.

Hansen, Karen Tranberg. 2000. *Salaula: The World of Secondhand Clothing and Zambia.* Chicago: University of Chicago Press.

Harding, Sandra. 1994. "Is Science Multicultural? Challenges, Resources, Opportunities, Uncertainties." In D. Goldberg, ed., *Multiculturalism: A Critical Reader,* pp. 344–70. Oxford: Blackwell.

Harris, Marvin. 1979. *Cultural Materialism.* New York: Random House.

Harris, Olivia. 1980. "The Power of Signs: Gender, Culture, and the Wild in the Bolivian Andes." In C. P. MacCormack and Marylin Strathern, eds., *Nature, Culture, and Gender,* pp. 70–94. Cambridge: Cambridge University Press.

Hartigan, John, Jr. 2005. *Odd Tribes: Towards a Cultural Analysis of White People.* Durham, NC: Duke University Press.

Hartigan, John, Jr. 2006. Saying "Socially Constructed" Is Not Enough. *Anthropology News,* February 2006, p. 8.

Harvey, L. P. 2007. *Ibn Batuta.* London: I. B. Tauris & Oxford Centre for Islamic Studies.

Hastrup, Kirsten, and Peter Elass. 1990. Anthropological Advocacy: A Contradiction in Terms. *Current Anthropology* 31(3): 301–11.

Haviland, William A., Robert J. Gordon, and Luis A. Vivanco, eds. 2006. *Talking About People: Readings in Cultural Anthropology.* New York: McGraw-Hill.

Hawkins, Dana. 2001. The Dark Side of Genetic Testing. *U.S. News and World Report* 2/19/01. Accessed on 9/1/06: http://www.usnews.com/usnews/news/articles/010219/archive_005280.htm

Hedges, Nathan T. 2014. Patron-Client Relations in Modern Benin: Exploring Political Process in the Nation-State. Unpublished paper in the authors' possession.

Herdt, Gilbert H. 1981. *Guardians of the Flutes: Idioms of Masculinity.* New York: Mcgraw-Hill.

Herdt, Gilbert H. 1994. Introduction: Third Sexes and Third Genders. In Gilbert Herdt, ed., *Third Sex, Third Gender: Beyond Sexual Dimorphism in Culture and History,* pp. 21–81. New York: Zone Books.

Hill, Jane H. 1978. Apes and Language. *Annual Review of Anthropology* 7:89–112.

Hill, Jane H. 1993. Hasta la vista, baby: Anglo Spanish in the American Southwest. *Critique of Anthropology* 13(2): 145–76.

Hill, Jane H. 1998. Language, Race, and White Public Space. *American Anthropologist* 100:680–9.

Hirabayashi, Lane Ryo. 1999. *The Politics of Fieldwork: Research in an American Concentration Camp.* Tucson: University of Arizona Press.

Ho, Karen. 2009. *Liquidated: An Ethnography of Wall Street.* Duke University Press.

Hobbes, Thomas. 1651. *Leviathan, or, the matter, forme, & power of a common-wealth ecclesitical and civill.* London: Andrew Crooke.

Hobbes, Thomas. 1909. *Leviathan.* Oxford: Clarendon Press.

Hoben, Alan. 1995. Paradigms and Politics: The Cultural Construction of Environmental Policy in Ethiopia. *World Development* 23(6):1007–1021.

Hobsbawn, Eric, & Ranger, Terence (eds.). (1983) *The Invention of Tradition.* Cambridge: Cambridge University Press.

Hopper, Kim. 1988. More Than Passing Strange: Homelessness and Mental Illness in New York City. *American Ethnologist* 15(1): 155–67.

Hopper, Kim. 2002. When (Working) in Rome: Applying Anthropology in Caesar's Realm. *Human Organization* 61(3): 196–209.

Horn, David. 1994. *Social Bodies: Science, Reproduction, and Italian Modernity.* Princeton, NJ: Princeton University Press.

Howe, K. R. 1984. *Where the Waves Fall: A New South Sea Islands History from Its First Settlement to Colonial Rule.* Honolulu: University of Hawaii Press.

Hruschka, Daniel, Daniel Lende, and Carol Worthman. 2005. Biocultural Dialogues: Biology and Culture in Psychological Anthropology. *Ethos* 33(1): 1–19.

Hsu, F. L. K. 1972. "Psychological Anthropology in the Behavioral Sciences." In F. L. K. Hsu, ed., *Psychological Anthropology,* pp. 1–19. Cambridge, MA: Schenkman Publishing Co.

Hubert, Annie. 1997. "Choices of Food and Cuisine in the Concept of Social Space among the Yao of Thailand." In Helen MacBeth, ed., *Food Preferences and Taste: Continuity and Change,* pp. 157–166. Providence: Berghahn Books.

Human Terrain Systems (HTS). 2010. Overview. Accessed on 7/31/10: http://humanterrainsystem.army.mil/overview.html

Humphrey, Caroline. 2002. *The Unmaking of Soviet Life: Everyday Economies After Socialism.* Ithaca: Cornell University Press.

Huntington, Samuel. 1996. *The Clash of Civilizations and the Remaking of World Order.* New York: Simon and Schuster.

Ignatiev, Noel. 1995. *How the Irish Became White.* New York: Routledge.

Igoe, James. 2004. *Conservation and Globalization: A Study of National Parks and Indigenous Communities from East Africa to South Dakota.* Belmont, CA: Wadsworth.

Inda, Jonathan, and Renato Rosaldo, eds. 2002. *The Anthropology of Globalization: A Reader.* Malden, MA: Blackwell.

International Obesity Task Force (IOTF). 2013. "The Global Epidemic." World Health Organization Fact Sheet. Accessed on 9/10/13: http://www.iaso.org/iotf/obesity/obesitytheglobalepidemic/

Irving, Judith. 2006. Edward Sapir. MITECS. Accessed on 7/3/14: http://ai.ato.ms/MITECS/Entry/irvine.html

Jewell, Edward Alden. 1935. African Negro Art on Exhibition Here: An Unusual Show Opens with Reception at Museum of Modern Art. *New York Times,* 19 Mar 1935.

Johnston, Francis E. 2004. "Race and Biology: Changing Currents in Muddy Waters." Paper presented at the conference "Race and Human Variation: Setting an Agenda for Future Research and Education," held September 12–14, 2004 in Alexandria, Virginia. Available at: http://www.understandingrace.com/resources/papers_activity.html

Kalipeni, Ezekiel. 2004. *HIV and AIDS in Africa: Beyond Epidemiology.* Malden, MA: Blackwell.

Kaplan, David, and Robert A. Manners. 1972. *Culture Theory.* Prospect Heights, IL: Waveland Press.

Kaptchuk, Ted J. 2001. The Double-blind, Randomized, Placebo-controlled Trial: Gold Standard or Golden Calf? *Journal of Clinical Epidemiology* 54:541–9.

Kearney, Michael. 1995. The Local and the Global: The Anthropology of Globalization and Transnationalism. *Annual Review of Anthropology* 24:547–65.

Keller, Ellen Fox. 2000. *The Century of the Gene.* Cambridge: Harvard University Press.

Khanmohamadi, S. 2008. The Look of Medieval Ethnography: William of Rubruck's Mission to Mongolia. *New Medieval Literatures* 10(1):87–114.

Kidder, Tracy. 2003. *Mountains Beyond Mountains.* New York: Random House.

Kidwell, Claudia Brush, and Valerie Steele, eds. 1989. *Men and Women: Dressing the Part.* Washington, DC: Smithsonian Institution Press.

Kildea, Gary, and Jerry Leach. 1975. *Trobriand Cricket: An Ingenious Response to Colonialism.* DVD. Berkeley, CA: Berkeley Media.

Kingsolver, Ann. 1996. "Power." In Alan Barnard and Jonathan Spencer, eds., *Encyclopedia of Social and Cultural Anthropology,* pp. 445–8. London: Routledge.

Kinsey, Alfred. 1948. *Sexual Behavior in the Human Male.* Philadelphia: W. B. Saunders.

Kirkpatrick, John, and Geoff White. 1985. "Exploring Ethnopsychologies." In Geoff White and John Kirkpatrick, eds., *Person, Self, and Experience: Exploring Pacific Ethnopsychologies,* pp. 3–32. Berkeley: University of California Press.

Kleinfield, N. R. 2006. Modern Ways Open India's Doors to Diabetes. *The New York Times,* September 13, 2006. Accessed on 9/13/06: http://www.nytimes.com/2006/09/13/world/asia/13diabetes.html?ex=1166936400&en=8322bd1c8904e016&ei=5070

Kleinman, Arthur. 1975. "Social, Cultural and Historical Themes in the Study of Medicine in Chinese Societies: Problems and Prospects for the Comparative Study of Medicine and Psychiatry." In A. Kleinman et al., eds. *Medicine in Chinese Cultures: Comparative Studies of Health Care in Chinese and Other Societies. Papers and Discussions from a Conference Held in Seattle, Washington, U.S.A., February 1974,* pp. 589–657. Washington, DC: U.S. Department of Health, Education, and Welfare.

Koos, Earl Lomon. 1954. *The Health of Regionville.* New York: Columbia University Press.

Kopytoff, Igor. 1986. "The Cultural Biography of Things: Commoditization as Process." In Arjun Appadurai, ed., *The Social Life of Things: Commodities in Cultural Perspective,* pp. 64–91. New York: Cambridge University Press.

Korten, David. 1995. *When Corporations Rule the World.* West Hartford, CT: Kumarian Press.

Kozol, Jonathan. 1992. *Savage Inequalities: Children in America's Schools.* New York: Harper Perennial.

Krech, Shepard. 1999. *The Ecological Indian: Myth and History.* New York: W. W. Norton.

Kreps, Christina F. 2003. *Liberating Culture: Cross-Cultural Perspectives on Museums, Curation, and Heritage Preservation.* London: Routledge.

Krishnamurthy, Mathangi. 2004. Resources and Rebels: A Study of Identity Management in Indian Call Centers. *Anthropology of Work Review* 25(3–4): 9–18.

Kroeber, Alfred L. 1909. Classificatory Systems of Relationship. *Journal of the Royal Anthropological Institute of Great Britain and Ireland* 39:77–84.

Kulick, Don. 1998. *Travesti: Sex, Gender, and Culture Among Brazilian Transgendered Prostitutes.* Chicago: University of Chicago Press.

Kulick, Don, and Margaret Willson. 2002. "Rambo's Wife Saves the Day: Subjugating the Gaze and Subverting the Narrative in a

Papua New Guinean Swamp." In Kelly Askew and Richard Wilk, eds., *The Anthropology of Media: A Reader*, pp. 270–85. Malden, MA: Blackwell.

Kurtz, Donald V. 2001. *Political Anthropology: Paradigms and Power.* Boulder, CO: Westview Press.

Labov, William. 1990. "Intersection of Sex and Social Class in the Course of Linguistic Change." *Language Variation and Change* 2(2): 205–54.

Labov, William, Sharon Ash, and Charles Boberg. 2006. *The Atlas of North American English: Phonetics, Phonology, and Sound Change: A Multimedia Reference Tool.* Berlin: Mouton de Gruyter.

Lakoff, Robin. 1975. *Language and Woman's Place.* New York: Harper and Row.

Lancaster, Roger. 1992. *Life Is Hard: Machismo, Danger, and the Intimacy of Power in Nicaragua.* Berkeley: University of California Press.

Lancaster, Roger. 1997. On Homosexualities in Latin America (and Other Places). *American Ethnologist* 24(1): 193–202.

Lancaster, Roger. 2004. The Place of Anthropology in a Public Culture Shaped by Bioreductivism. *Anthropology News* 45(3): 4–5.

Larner, John. 1999. *Marco Polo and the Discovery of the World.* New Haven, CT: Yale University Press.

Layton, Robert. 1981. *The Anthropology of Art.* New York: Columbia University Press.

Layton, Robert. 1991. *The Anthropology of Art.* 2nd Edition. Cambridge: Cambridge University Press.

Leacock, Eleanor. 1981. *Myths of Male Dominance.* New York: Monthly Review.

Leary, John. 1995. *Violence and the Dream People: The Orang Asli and the Malaysian Emergency, 1948–1960.* Athens, OH: University Center for International Studies.

Lechner, Frank, and Boli, John. 2005. *World Culture: Origins and Consequences.* Malden, MA: Blackwell.

Ledeneva, Alena V. 1998. *Russia's Economy of Favors: Blat, Networking and Informal Exchange.* Cambridge: Cambridge University Press.

Lederman, Rena. 1990. "Pretexts for Ethnography: On Reading Field Notes." In Roger Sanjek, ed., *Field Notes: The Making of Anthropology*, pp. 71–91. Ithaca, NY: Cornell University Press.

Lee, Richard. 1969. "!Kung Bushmen Subsistence: An Input-Output Analysis." In Andrew P. Vayda, ed., *Environment and Cultural Behavior*, pp. 47–79. Garden City, NY: Natural History Press.

Lee, Richard. 1979. *The !Kung San: Men, Women, and Work in a Foraging Society.* Cambridge: Cambridge University Press.

Lentz, Carola. 1999. "Changing Food Habits: An Introduction." In Carola Lentz, ed., *Changing Food Habits: Case Studies from Africa, South America, and Europe*, pp. 1–25. Newark, NJ: Harwood Academic Publishers.

Lester, Toby. 2002. Oh, Gods. *Atlantic Monthly* 289(2): 37–45.

Lévi-Strauss, Claude. 1961. "The Effectiveness of Symbols." In *Structural Anthropology*, pp. 186–205. New York: Basic Books.

Lévi-Strauss, Claude. 1969a. *The Elementary Structures of Kinship.* Boston: Beacon Press.

Lévi-Strauss, Claude. 1969b. *The Raw and the Cooked.* New York: Harper & Row.

Lewellen, Ted C. 2003. *Political Anthropology: An Introduction.* 3rd Edition. Westport, CT: Praeger.

Lewin, Ellen. 1993. *Lesbian Mothers: Accounts of Gender in American Culture.* Ithaca, NY: Cornell University Press.

Lewin, Ellen. 1996. "Why in the World Would You Want to Do That?": Claiming Community in Lesbian Commitment Ceremonies. In Ellen Lewin, ed., *Inventing Lesbian Cultures in America*. pp. 105–30. Boston: Beacon Press.

Lewin, Ellen. 1998. *Recognizing Ourselves: Ceremonies of Lesbian and Gay Commitment.* New York: Columbia University Press.

Lewin, Ellen, and William L. Leap, eds. 1996. *Out in the Field: Reflections of Lesbian and Gay Anthropologists.* Urbana: University of Illinois Press.

Lewin, Ellen, and William L. Leap, eds. 2009. *Out in Public: Reinventing Lesbian/Gay Anthropology in a Globalizing World.* Malden, MA: Wiley-Blackwell.

Lewontin, Richard. 1991. *Biology as Ideology: The Doctrine of DNA.* New York: Harper Perennial.

Lewontin, Richard C., Steven Rose, and Leon J. Kamin. 1984. *Not in Our Genes: Biology, Ideology, and Human Nature.* New York: Pantheon Books.

Lieberman, Leslie Sue. 1987. "Biocultural Consequences of Animals Versus Plants as Sources of Fats, Proteins, and Other Nutrients." In Marvin Harris and Eric B. Ross, eds., *Food and Evolution: Toward a Theory of Human Food Habits*, pp. 225–60. Philadelphia: Temple University Press.

Liechty, Mark. 2002. *Suitably Modern: Making Middle Class Culture in Kathmandu.* Princeton, NJ: Princeton University Press.

Lienhardt, Godfrey. 1961. *Divinity and Experience: The Religion of the Dinka.* Oxford: Clarendon Press.

Lindholm, Charles. 2005. "An Anthropology of Emotion." In Conerly Casey and Robert B. Edgerton, eds., *A Companion to Psychological Anthropology: Modernity and Psychocultural Change*, pp. 30–47. Malden, MA: Blackwell Publishing.

Linton, Ralph. 1924. Totemism and the A. E. F. *American Anthropologist* 26:296–300.

Lippman, Abby. 2001. The Power of Naming Things Genetic. Review of "Sociological Perspectives on the New Genetics." *Second Opinion* 7:99–100.

Little, Peter, and Michael Painter. 1995. Discourse, Politics, and the Development Process: Reflections on Escobar's "Anthropology and the Development Encounter." *American Ethnologist* 22(3): 602–609.

Lizot, Jacques. 1985. *Tales of the Yanomami: Daily Life in the Venezuelan Forest.* Trans. by Ernest Simon. Cambridge: Cambridge University Press.

Locke, John. 1690. *Two Treatises on Goverement: In the former, the false principles, and foundation of Sir Robert Filmer, and his followers, are detected and overthrown. The latter is an essay concerning the true original, extent, and end of civil government.* London: Awnsham Churchill.

Locke, John. 2003. *Two Treatises on Government: And a Letter Concerning Toleration.* New Haven, CT: Yale University Press.

Lockwood, William G. 1975. *European Moslems: Economy and Ethnicity in Western Bosnia.* New York: Academic Publishers.

Long, Jeffrey. 2003. *Human Genetic Variation: The Mechanisms and Results of Microevolution.* Paper presented at the American Anthropological Association 2003 annual meeting on November 21, 2003 in Chicago, Illinois. Accessed on 5/24/07 at: http://www.understandingrace.com/resources/papers_author.html

Lovgren, Sven. 2003. "Map Links Healthier Ecosystems, Indigenous Peoples." *National Geographic News*, February 27, 2003. Accessed on February 15, 2005: http://news.nationalgeographic.com/news/2003/02/0227_030227_indigenousmap.html

Lyons, Andrew P., and Harriet D. Lyons. 2004. *Irregular Connections: A History of Anthropology and Sexuality.* Lincoln: University of Nebraska Press.

MacBeth, Helen. 1997. *Food Preferences and Taste: Continuity and Change.* New York: Berghahn Books.

MacKinnon, Katherine, and Agustín Fuentes. 2005. "Reassessing Male Aggression and Dominance: The Evidence from Primatology." In Susan McKinnon and Sydel Silverman, eds., *Complexities: Beyond Nature and Nurture*, pp. 83–105. Chicago: University of Chicago Press.

Mahmood, Cynthia Keppley. 1997. *Fighting for Faith and Nation: Dialogues with Sikh Militants.* Philadelphia: University of Pennsylvania Press.

Mair, Lucy. 1969. *Anthropology and Social Change.* New York: Humanities Press.

Malinowski, Bronislaw. 1922. *Argonauts of the Western Pacific: An Account of Native Enterprise and Adventure in the Archipelagoes of Melanesian New Guinea.* London: Routledge & Kegan Paul.

Malinowski, Bronislaw. 1935. *Coral Gardens and Their Magic: A Study of the Methods of Tilling the Soil and of Agricultural Rites in the Trobriand Islands.* London: G. Allen & Unwin.

Malinowski, Bronislaw. 1948. *Magic, Science and Religion and Other Essays.* Boston: Beacon Press.

Malotki, Ekkehardt. 1983. *Hopi Time: A Linguistic Analysis of the Temporal Concepts of the Hopi Language.* Berlin: Mouton.

Mamdani, Mahmood. 1972. *The Myth of Population Control: Family, Caste, and Class in an Indian Village.* New York: Monthly Review Press.

Marcus, George. 1995. Ethnography in/of the World System: The Emergence of Multi-Sited Ethnography. *Annual Review of Anthropology* 24:95–117.

Mark, Jason 2006. "Will the End of Oil be the End of Food?" *Alternet.org.* Accessed on 4/14/07: http://www.alternet.org/envirohealth/41023/.

Marks, Jonathan. 1995. *Human Biodiversity: Genes, Race, and History.* New York: Aldine de Gruyter.

Marty, Martin E., and R. Scott Appleby, eds. 1991. *Fundamentalisms Observed.* The Fundamentalism Project, Volume 1. Chicago: University of Chicago Press.

Marwick, M. G. 1952. Social Context of Cewa Witch Beliefs. *Africa* 22:120–35, 215–33.

Marx, Karl. 1990. *Capital: A Critique of Political Economy.* New York: Penguin.

Mauss, Marcel. 1954. *The Gift: The Form and Reason for Exchange in Archaic Societies.* Trans. W. D. Halls. New York: W. W. Norton & Company.

McCabe, Terrence. 1990. Turkana Pastoralism: A Case Against the Tragedy of the Commons. *Human Ecology* 18(1): 81–103.

McDonald, James H. 1993. Corporate Capitalism and the Family Farm in the U.S. and Mexico. *Culture & Agriculture* 45/46:25–28.

McGrath, J. W., C. B. Rwabukwali, D. A. Schumann, J. Pearson-Marks, R. Mukasa, B. Namande, S. Nakayiwa, and L. Nakyobe. 1992. Cultural Determinants of Sexual Risk Behavior among Baganda Women. *Medical Anthropology Quarterly* 6(2):153–61.

McIntosh, Peggy. 1997. "White Privilege and Male Privilege: A Personal Account of Coming to See Correspondences through Work in Women's Studies." In Richard Delgado and Jean Stefancic, eds., *Critical White Studies: Looking Behind the Mirror,* pp. 291–9. Philadelphia: Temple University Press.

McIntyre, Matthew H., and Carolyn Pope Edwards. 2009. The Early Development of Gender Differences. *Annual Review of Anthropology* 38:83–97.

McKenna, James J. 1996. Sudden Infant Death Syndrome in Cross-Cultural Perspective: Is Infant-Parent Cosleeping Protective? *Annual Review of Anthropology* 25:201–16.

McKinnon, Susan, and Silverman, Sydel. 2005. "Introduction." In Susan McKinnon and Sydel Silverman, eds., *Complexities: Beyond Nature and Nurture,* pp. 1–22. Chicago: University of Chicago Press.

Mead, Margaret. 1928. *Coming of Age in Samoa: A Psychological Study of Primitive Youth for Western Civilization.* New York: William Morrow.

Mead, Margaret. 1935/1963. *Sex and Temperament in Three Primitive Societies.* New York: William Morrow.

Meigs, Anna. 1997. "Food as a Cultural Construction." In Carole Counihan and Penny Van Esterik, eds., *Food and Culture: A Reader,* pp. 95–106. New York: Routledge.

Menzies, Gavin. 2002. *1421: The Year China Discovered America.* London: Transworld Publishers.

Merry, Sally Engle. 2003. Human Rights Law and the Demonization of Culture. *Anthropology News* 44(2) February:4–5.

Michael, Robert T., John H. Gagnon, Edward O. Lauman, and Gina Kolata. 1994. *Sex in America: A Definitive Survey.* Boston: Little Brown.

Michaels, Eric. 1994. *Bad Anthropological Art: Tradition, Media, and Technological Horizons.* Sydney: Allen and Unwin.

Miller, Daniel. 1987. *Material Culture and Mass Consumption.* Oxford: Basil Blackwell.

Miller, Daniel, ed. 1995. *Acknowledging Consumption: A Review of New Studies.* London: Routledge.

Miller, Daniel. 1998. *A Theory of Shopping.* Ithaca, NY: Cornell University Press.

Mintz, Sidney. 1992. A Taste of History. *The Higher Perspective,* May 8, pp. 15, 18.

Mohanty, Chandra Talpade. 1991. "Under Western Eyes: Feminist Scholarship and Colonial Discourses." In Chandra Talpade Mohanty, Ann Russo, and Lourdes Torres, eds., *Third World Women and the Politics of Feminism,* pp. 333–58. Indianapolis: Indiana University Press.

Money, John. 1985. *Destroying Angel: Sex, Fitness, and Food in the Legacy of Degeneracy Theory, Graham Crackers, Kellogg's Corn Flakes, and American Health History.* Buffalo: Prometheus Books.

Moran, Mary. 1997. "Warriors or Soldiers? Masculinity and Ritual Tranvestism in the Liberian Civil War." In Louise Lamphere, Helena Ragone, and Patricia Zavella, eds., *Situated Lives: Gender and Culture in Everyday Life,* pp. 440–50. Chicago: University of Chicago Press.

Morgan, Edmund. 1975. *American Slavery, American Freedom.* New York: W. W. Norton.

Morgan, Lewis Henry. 1871. *Systems of Consanguinity and Affinity of the Human Family.* Washington: Smithsonian Institution.

Morris, Rosalind C. 1995. All Made Up: Performance Theory and the New Anthropology of Sex and Gender. *Annual Review of Anthropology* 24:567–92.

Mullings, Leith. 2005. Interrogating Racism: Toward an Antiracist Anthropology. *Annual Review of Anthropology* 34:667–93.

Munn, Nancy D. 1962. Walbiri Graphic Signs: An Analysis. *American Anthropologist* 64(5, pt. 1): 972–84.

Munn, Nancy D. 1973. *Walbiri Iconography: Graphic Representation and Cultural Symbolism in a Central Australian Society.* Ithaca, NY: Cornell University Press.

Munson, Barbara. 1999. Not for Sport. *Teaching Tolerance Magazine.* Accessed on 7/31/10: http://www.tolerance.org/magazine/number-15-spring-1999/not-sport.

Murray, Gerald. 1987. "The Domestication of Wood in Haiti: A Case Study in Applied Evolution." In R. M. Wulff and S. J. Fiske, eds., *Anthropological Praxis: Translating Knowledge into Action,* pp. 223–40. Boulder, CO: Westview Press.

Myerhoff, Barbara G. 1974. *Peyote Hunt: The Sacred Journey of the Huichol Indians.* Ithaca, NY: Cornell University Press.

Nabhan, Gary Paul. 1997. *Cultures of Habitat: On Nature, Culture, and Story.* Washington, DC: Counterpoint.

Nabhan, Gary Paul. 2001. "Cultural Perceptions of Ecological Interactions: An 'Endangered People's' Contribution to the Conservation of Biological and Linguistic Diversity." In Lisa Maffi, ed., *On Biocultural Diversity: Linking Language, Knowledge, and the Environment,* pp. 145–56. Washington, DC: Smithsonian Institution Press.

Nadasdy, Paul. 2005. The Anti-Politics of TEK: The Institutionalizaton of Co-Management Discourse and Practice. *Anthropologica* 47(2): 215–32.

Nader, Laura. 1979. Disputing without the Force of Law. *Yale Law Journal* 88(5): 998–1021.

Nader, Laura. 1990. *Harmony Ideology: Justice and Control in a Zapotec Mountain Village.* Stanford, CA: Stanford University Press.

Nader, Laura. 1995. Civilization and Its Negotiators. In Pat Caplan, ed., *Understanding Disputes: The Politics of Argument,* pp. 39–63. Oxford: Berg Publishers.

Nader, Laura, ed. 1996. *Naked Science: Anthropological Inquiry into Boundaries, Power, and Knowledge.* New York: Routledge.

Nader, Laura. 2001. "The Underside of Conflict Management—in Africa and Elsewhere." *IDS Bulletin* Vol. 32, no. 1:19–27.

Nader, Laura. 2007. "What's Good About Conflict?" *Anthropology News* 48(6): 14–15.

Nader, Laura, and Harry F. Todd, eds. 1978. *The Disputing Process—Law in Ten Societies.* New York: Columbia University Press.

Nagengast, Carole. 1994. Violence, Terror, and the Crisis of the State. *Annual Review of Anthropology* 23:109–36.

Nanda, Serena. 1994. "Hijras: An Alternative Sex and Gender Role in India." In Gilbert Herdt, ed., *Third Sex, Third Gender: Beyond Sexual Dimorphism in Culture and History*, pp. 373–417. New York: Zone Books.

Nanda, Serena. 2000. *Gender Diversity: Crosscultural Variations*. Prospect Heights, IL: Waveland Press.

Nash, June. 1981. Ethnographic Aspects of the World Capitalist System. *Annual Review of Anthropology* 10:393–423.

Nash, June. 2007. Consuming Interests: Water, Rum, and Coca-Cola from Ritual Propitiation to Corporate Expropriation in Highland Chiapas. *Cultural Anthropology* 22(4): 621–39.

Nash, Manning. 1958. *Machine Age Maya*. Glencoe, IL: Free Press.

Natcher, David C., Susan Hickey, and Clifford G. Hickey. 2005. Co-Management: Managing Relationships, Not Resources. *Human Organization* 64(3): 240–50.

National Public Radio. 2009. Brian Lehrer interviews Nancy Scheper-Hughes, 24 July 2009. http://www.wnyc.org/shows/bl/episodes/2009/07/24/segments/137306

National Solidarity Programme. 2014. "NSP Basic Introduction." Accessed on 6/1/2014: http://www.nspafghanistan.org/default.aspx?sel=109.

Nederveen Pieterse, J. 2004. *Globalization and Culture: Global Mélange*. Lanham, MD: Rowman & Littlefield.

New York Daily News. 2009. Anthropologist's 'Dick Tracy Moment' Plays Role in Arrest of Suspected Kidney Trafficker. *New York Daily News* (24 July 2009). Accessed 18 August 2009. http://www.nydailynews.com/news/ny_crime/2009/07/24/2009-07-24_seven_year_quest_to_end_rosenbaum_evil_work_pays_off.html

Nietschmann, Bernard. 1992. *The Interdependence of Biological and Cultural Diversity*. Occasional Paper No. 21. Center for World Indigenous Studies, December 1992.

Norberg, Johan. 2006. "How Globalization Conquers Poverty." Accessed on 11/19/06: http://www.cato.org/special/symposium/essays/norberg.html.

Nordstrum, Carolyn R. 1988. Exploring Pluralism: The Many Faces of Ayurveda. *Social Science and Medicine* 27(5): 479–89.

Nyamwaya, D. O., 1993. Anthropology and HIV/AIDS Prevention in Kenya: New Ways of Cooperation. *AIDS and Society* 4(4): 4, 8.

O'Connor, James. 1998. *Natural Causes: Essays in Ecological Marxism*. New York: Guilford.

Oberschall, Anthony. 2000. The Manipulation of Ethnicity: From Ethnic Cooperation to Violence and War in Yugoslavia. *Ethnic and Racial Studies* 23(6): 982–1001.

Omi, Michael, and Howard Winant, eds. 1996. Racial Formation in the United States. 2nd Edition. New York: Routledge.

Ong, Aihwa. 1988. The Production of Possession: Spirits and the Multinational Corporation in Malaysia. *American Ethnologist* 15(1): 28–42.

Ortner, Sherry B. 1971. On Key Symbols. *American Anthropologist* 75:1338–46.

Ortner, Sherry B. 1974. "Is Female to Male as Nature is to Culture?" In Michelle Rosaldo and Louise Lamphere, eds., *Woman, Culture, and Society*, pp. 67–88. Stanford, CA: Stanford University Press.

Ortner, Sherry B. 1989. *High Religion: A Cultural and Political History of Sherpa Buddhism*. Princeton, NJ: Princeton University Press.

Ortner, Sherry B. 1996. *Making Gender: The Politics and Erotics of Culture*. Boston: Beacon Press.

Ortner, Sherry B. 2006. *Anthropology and Social Theory: Culture, Power, and the Acting Subject*. Durham, NC: Duke University Press.

Owusu, Maxwell. 1992. "Democracy and Africa: A View from the Village. *Journal of Modern African Studies* 30(3): 369–96.

Owusu, Maxwell. 1996. Tradition and Transformation: Democracy and the Politics of Popular Power in Ghana. *Journal of Modern African Studies* 34(2): 307–43.

Parent, Anthony S., Jr. 2003. *Foul Means: The Formation of Slave Society in Virginia, 1660–1740*. Chapel Hill: University of North Carolina Press.

Parker, Richard. 1989. Acquired Immunodeficiency Syndrome in Urban Brazil. *Medical Anthropology Quarterly* 1(2): 155–75.

Parker, Richard. 2001. Sexuality, Culture, and Power in HIV/AIDS Research. *Annual Review of Anthropology* 2001, 30:163–79.

Parkin, David, and Stanley Ulijaszek, eds. 2007. *Holistic Anthropology: Emergence and Convergence*. New York: Berghahn Books.

Parry, Jonathan, and Maurice Bloch, eds. 1989. *Money and the Morality of Exchange*. Cambridge: Cambridge University Press.

Parsons, Talcott. 1951. *The Social System*. Glencoe, IL: The Free Press.

Partners in Health. 2010. Partners in Health web page. http://www.pih.org/

Patel, Raj. 2007. *Stuffed and Starved: The Hidden Battle for the World Food System*. London: Melville House.

Patterson, Penny, Director. 2003. *Koko and Friends*. Videorecording, produced by the Gorilla Foundation, distributed by Dave West, Utah Film and Video.

Peet, Richard and Michael Watts, eds. 2004. *Liberation Ecologies: Environment, Development, Social Movements*. 2nd Edition. London: Routledge.

Pei-Chia, Lan. 2008. "Global Cinderellas: Sexuality, Power, and Situational Practices Across Borders." In Stevi Jackson, Lui Jieyu, and Woo Juhyun, eds., *East Asian Sexualities: Modernity, Gender, and New Sexual Cultures*, pp. 33–51. London: Zed Books.

Peters, William, producer. 1970. *Eye of the Storm*. Human Relations Film Series. Videocassette. New York: Insight Media.

Peters, William, producer. 2005. *A Class Divided*. PBS Video. (Originally broadcast Mar. 26, 1985 on *Frontline*.)

Petryna, Adriana. 2002. *Life Exposed: Biological Citizenship After Chernobyl*. Princeton, NJ: Princeton University Press.

Pinker, Steven. 1994. *The Language Instinct*. New York: W. Morrow and Co.

Pinker, Steven. 1997. *How the Mind Works*. New York: Norton.

Piot, Charles. 1999. *Remotely Global: Village Modernity in West Africa*. Chicago: University of Chicago Press.

Polanyi, Karl. 1944/1975. *The Great Transformation*. New York: Octagon Books.

Pottier, Johan. 1999. *The Anthropology of Food: The Social Dynamics of Food Security*. Cambridge: Polity Press.

Powdermaker, Hortense. 1944. *Probing Our Prejudices: A Unit for High School Students*. New York: Harper and Brothers Publishers.

Pretty, Jules. 2002. *Agri-Culture: Reconnecting People, Land, and Nature*. London: Earthscan.

Price, David. 2002. Past Wars, Present Dangers, Future Anthropologies. *Anthropology Today* 18(1): 3–5.

Radcliffe-Brown, Alfred R. 1941. The Study of Kinship Systems. *Journal of the Royal Anthropological Institute of Great Britain and Ireland* 71(1/2): 1–18.

Radcliffe-Brown, Alfred R. 1952. *Structure and Function in Primitive Society: Essays and Addresses*. Glencoe, IL: Free Press.

Radin, Paul. 1927. *Primitive Man as Philosopher*. New York: D. Appleton and Co.

Ragoné, Helena. 1996. Chasing the Blood Tie: Surrogate Mothers, Adoptive Mothers and Fathers. *American Ethnologist* 23(2): 352–65.

Rahnema, Majid, and Victoria Bawtree. 1997. *The Post-Development Reader*. London: Zed Press.

Ramos, Alcida Rita. 1990. Ethnology Brazilian Style. *Cultural Anthropology* 5(4): 452–72.

Ramos, Alcida Rita. 2000. Anthropologist as Political Actor: Between Activism and Suspicion. *Journal of Latin American Anthropology* 4(2)/5(1): 172–89.

Rapp, Rayna. 1992. "Anthropology: Feminist Methodologies for the Science of Man." In S. R. Zalk and J. Gordon-Kelter, eds., *Revolutions in Knowledge: Feminism in the Social Sciences*, pp. 79–92. Boulder, CO: Westview Press.

Rapp, Rayna. 1999. *Testing Women, Testing the Fetus: The Social Impact of Amniocentesis in America*. New York: Routledge.

Rappaport, Roy. 1984. *Pigs for the Ancestors: Ritual in the Ecology of a New Guinea People*. 2nd Edition. Prospect Heights, IL: Waveland Press.

Rasmussen, Susan. 1991. Modes of Persuasion: Gossip, Song, and Divination in Tuareg Conflict Resolution. *Anthropological Quarterly* 64(1): 30–46.

Research Advisory Committee on Gulf War Veterans' Illnesses. 2008. Research Advisory Council on Gulf War Veterans' Illnesses web page. http://www1.va.gov/rac-gwvi/

Rex, John. 1999. "Racism, Institutionalized and Otherwise." In Roger S. Gottlieb (series ed.) and Leonard Harris (volume ed.), *Key Concepts in Critical Theory: Racism,* pp. 141–160. Amherst, NY: Humanity Books.

Richards, Audrey. 1939. *Land, Labor, and Diet in Northern Rhodesia: An Economic Study of the Bemba.* Oxford: Oxford University Press.

Richards, Paul. 1996. *Fighting for the Rainforest.* London: James Currey.

Richardson, Jane, and Alfred L. Kroeber. 1940. Three Centuries of Women's Dress Fashions: A Quantitative Analysis. *University of California Anthropological Records* 5(2): i–iv, 100–53.

Riches, David. 1986. "The Phenomenon of Violence." In David Riches, ed., *The Anthropology of Violence,* pp. 1–27. Oxford: Basil Blackwell.

Riefenstahl, Leni, director. 1935. *Triumph of the Will.* Film.

Ritzer, George. 1996. *The McDonaldization of Society: An Investigation into the Changing Character of Contemporary Social Life.* Thousand Oaks, CA: Pine Forge Press.

Rivers, William H. R. 1906. *The Todas.* London: Macmillan.

Rivoli, Pietra. 2005. *The Travels of a T-Shirt in the Global Economy: An Economist Examines the Markets, Power, and Politics of World Trade.* Hoboken: John Wiley & Sons.

Robarchek, Clayton A. 1979. Learning to Fear: A Case Study of Emotional Conditioning. *American Ethnologist* 6(3): 555–67.

Robarchek, Clayton A., and Robert Knox Dentan. 1987. Blood Drunkenness and the Bloodthirsty Semai: Unmaking Another Anthropological Myth. *American Anthropologist* 89(2): 356–65.

Robben, Antonius. 1989. *Sons of the Sea Goddess: Economic Practice and Discursive Conflict in Brazil.* New York: Columbia University Press.

Robbins, Richard. 2001. *Cultural Anthropology: A Problem-Based Approach.* 3rd Edition. Itasca, IL: F. E. Peacock Publishers, Inc.

Robbins, Richard. 2005. *Global Problems and the Culture of Capitalism.* 3rd Edition. Boston: Pearson/Allyn and Bacon.

Rosaldo, Michelle Zimbalist. 1974. "Woman, Culture, and Society: A Theoretical Overview." In Michelle Rosaldo and Louise Lamphere, eds., *Woman, Culture, and Society,* pp. 17–42. Stanford, CA: Stanford University Press.

Rosaldo, Michelle Zimbalist. 1984. *Knowledge and Passion: Ilongot Notions of Self and Social Life.* Cambridge: Harvard University Press.

Rosaldo, Renato. 1989. *Culture and Truth: The Remaking of Social Analysis.* Boston: Beacon Press.

Roscoe, Will. 1994. "How to Become a Berdache: Toward a Unified Analysis of Gender Diversity." In Gilbert Herdt, ed., *Third Sex, Third Gender: Beyond Sexual Dimorphism in Culture and History,* pp. 329–72. New York: Zone Books.

Rubin, William, ed. 1984. *Primitivism in 20th Century Art: Affinity of the Tribal and the Modern.* New York: Museum of Modern Art.

Sahlins, Marshall. 1965. "On the Sociology of Primitive Exchange." In M. Banton, ed., *The Relevance of Models for Social Anthropology,* pp. 123–236. ASA Monographs, 1. London: Tavistock.

Sahlins, Marshall. 1972. *Stone Age Economics.* Chicago: Aldine-Atherton.

Sahlins, Marshall. 1976. *Culture and Practical Reason.* Chicago: University of Chicago Press.

Sahlins, Marshall. 1999. Two or Three Things That I Know About Culture. *Journal of the Royal Anthropological Institute* 5(3): 399–421.

Sahlins, Marshall, and Elman Service, eds. 1960. *Evolution and Culture.* Ann Arbor: University of Michigan Press.

Sandweiss, Stephen. 1998. "The Social Construction of Environmental Justice." In David E. Camacho, ed. *Environmental Injustices, Political Struggles: Race, Class, and the Environment,* pp. 31–57. Durham, NC: Duke University Press.

Sanjek, Roger. 1990. "Vocabulary for Fieldnotes." In Roger Sanjek, ed., *Fieldnotes: The Making of Anthropology,* pp. 71–91. Ithaca, NY: Cornell University Press.

Sapir, Edward. 1929. The Status of Linguistics as a Science. *Language* 5(4): 207–14.

Saussure, F. de. 1916. *Cours de linguistique générale.* Paris: Payot.

Saussure, F. de. 1986. *Course in General Linguistics.* LaSalle, IL: Open Court.

Sayer, Andrew. 2000. Moral Economy and Political Economy. *Studies in Political Economy* Spring 2000: 79–103.

Scheper-Hughes, Nancy. 1995. The Primacy of the Ethical: Propositions for a Militant Anthropology. *Current Anthropology* 15:227–83.

Scheper-Hughes, Nancy. 2004. Parts Unknown: Undercover Ethnography of the Organs-trafficking Underworld. *Ethnography* 5:29–73.

Scheper-Hughes, Nancy, and Loïc Wacquant, eds. 2003. *Commodifying Bodies.* Thousand Oaks, CA: Sage Publications.

Schlosser, Eric. 2001. *Fast Food Nation: The Dark Side of the All-American Meal.* Boston: Houghton Mifflin Company.

Segal, Daniel A., and Sylvia J. Yanagisako, eds. 2005. *Unwrapping the Sacred Bundle: Reflections on the Disciplining of Anthropology.* Durham, NC: Duke University Press.

Seligman, Rebecca. 2005. Distress, Dissociation, and Embodied Experience: Reconsidering the Pathways to Mediumship and Mental Health. *Ethos* 33(1): 71–99.

Sharma, Devinder. 2004. *Farmer's Suicides.* ZeeNet. Accessed on 12/20/06: http://zcomm.org/znetarticle/farmers-suicides-by-devinder-sharma/

Sharma, Ursula. 1999. *Caste.* In Frank Parkin (series ed.), *Concepts in the Social Sciences.* Buckingham: Open University Press.

Sheridan, Michael. 2006. "Linguistic Models in Anthropology 101: Give Me the Cup." In P. Rice and D. McCurdy, eds. *Strategies in Teaching Anthropology,* pp. 54–56. 4th Edition. Upper Saddle River, NJ: Prentice Hall Professional.

Shore, Bradd. 1996. *Culture in Mind: Cognition, Culture, and the Problem of Meaning.* New York: Oxford University Press.

Shorris, Earl. 1992. *Latinos: A Biography of the People.* New York: W. W. Norton.

Shorris, Earl. 2001. *Latinos: Biography of a People.* New York: W. W. Norton & Company.

Shweder, Richard. 2003. *Why Do Men Barbeque? Recipes for Cultural Psychology.* Cambridge: Harvard University Press.

Sillitoe, Paul. 2002. Contested Knowledge, Contingent Classification: Animals in the Highlands of Papua New Guinea. *American Anthropologist* 104(4): 1162–71.

Silverblatt, Irene. 1988. "Political Memories and Colonizing Symbols: Santiago and the Mountain Gods of Colonial Peru." In Jonathan Hill (Ed.), *Rethinking History and Myth: Indigenous South American Perspectives on the Past,* pp. 174–94. Urbana: University of Illinois Press.

Simmons, Ozzie G. 1955. Popular and Modern Medicine in Mestizo Communities of Coastal Peru and Chile. *Journal of American Folklore* 68(1): 57–71.

Singer, Merill. 1996. Farewell to Adaptationism: Unnatural Selection and the Politics of Biology. *Medical Anthropology Quarterly* 10(4): 496–515.

Sivo, Ellen. 2005. The DOs and DON'Ts of College Romance. *The Vermont Cynic* Nov. 29, 2005. http://media.www.vermontcynic.com/media/storage/paper308/news/2005/11/29/LifeAndStyle/The-Dos.And.Donts.Of.College.Romance-1115738.shtml

Sloane, Patricia. 1999. *Islam, Modernity, and Entrepreneurship Among the Malays.* New York: St. Martin's Press.

Small, Meredith. 1998. *Our Babies, Ourselves: How Biology and Culture Shape How We Parent.* New York: Anchor Books.

Smedley, Audrey. 2007a. *The History of the Idea of Race . . . And Why It Matters.* Paper presented at the conference "Race, Human Variation and Disease: Consensus and Frontiers," Warrenton, Virginia, March 14–17, 2007. Available at: http://www.understandingrace.com/resources/papers_author.html

Smedley, Audrey. 2007b. *Race in North America: Origin and Evolution of a Worldview.* 3rd Edition. Boulder, CO: Westview Press.

Smith, Adam. 1776/1976. *An Inquiry into the Nature and Causes of The Wealth of Nations.* Chicago: University of Chicago Press.

Smith, M. Estellie. 2000. *Trade and Tradeoffs: Using Resources, Making Choices, and Taking Risks.* Long Grove, IL: Waveland Press.

Smith, Raymond T. 1984. Anthropology and the Concept of Social Class. *Annual Review of Anthropology* 13:467–94.

Society for Medical Anthropology. 2014. What Is Medical Anthropology? Accessed 6/1/14: http://www.medanthro.net/9/comment-page-1/#comment-36

Spielman, Katharine A., and James F. Eder. 1994. Hunters and Farmers: Then and Now. *Annual Review of Anthropology* 23:303–23.

Spiro, Melford E. 1958. *Children of the Kibbutz.* Cambridge: Harvard University Press.

Spittler, Gerd. 1999. "In Praise of the Simple Meal: African and European Food Culture Compared." In Carola Lentz, ed., *Changing Food Habits: Case Studies from Africa, South America, and Europe,* pp. 27–42. Newark, NJ: Harwood Academic Publishers.

Spitulnik, Debra. 1998. "Mediating Unity and Diversity: The Production of Language Ideologies in Zambian Broadcasting." In Bambi B. Shieffelin, Katharyn A. Woolard, and Paul V. Kroskrity, eds., *Language Ideologies: Practice and Theory,* pp. 163–88. New York: Oxford University Press.

Starr, Paul. 1982. *The Social Transformation of American Medicine.* New York: Basic Books.

Stiles, Daniel. 1993. Nomads on Notice. *Natural History* 102(9): 51–56.

Stocking, George W., Jr., ed. 1985. *History of Anthropology:* Vol. 3. *Objects and Others: Essays on Museums and Material Culture.* Madison: University of Wisconsin Press.

Stoffle, Richard, Rebecca Toupal, and Nieves Zedeño. 2003. "Landscape, Nature, and Culture: A Diachronic Model of Human-Nature Adaptations." In H. Selin, ed., *Nature Across Cultures: Views of Nature and the Environment in Non-Western Cultures,* pp. 97–114. London: Kluwer Academic Publishers.

Stonich, Susan. 1995. "Development, Rural Impoverishment, and Environmental Destruction in Honduras." In M. Painter and W. Durham, eds., *The Social Causes of Environmental Destruction in Latin America,* pp. 63–99. Ann Arbor: University of Michigan Press.

Strathern, Marylin. 1988. *The Gender of the Gift: Problems with Women and Problems with Society in Melanesia.* Berkeley: University of California Press.

Strathern, Marylin. 1990. *The Gender of the Gift: Problems with Women and Problems with Society in Melanesia.* Reprint. Berkeley: University of California Press.

Strathern, Marilyn. 1996. "Enabling Identity? Biology, Choice and the New Reproductive Technologies." In S. Hall and P. du Gay, eds., *Questions of Cultural Identity,* pp. 37–52. London: Sage.

Strong, Pauline. 1996. Animated Indians: Critique and Contradiction in Commodified Children's Culture. *Cultural Anthropology* 11(3): 405–24.

Sturtevant, William. 1964. "Studies in Ethnoscience." In A. Kimball Romney and Roy G. D'Andrade, eds., *Transcultural Studies of Cognition,* pp. 99–131. Menasha, WI: AAA.

Tainter, Joseph. 2006. Archaeology of Overshoot and Collapse. *Annual Review of Anthropology* 35:59–74.

Tannen, Deborah. 1990. *You Just Don't Understand: Men and Women in Conversation.* New York: Morrow.

Taussig, Karen-Sue. 2005. "The Molecular Revolution in Medicine: Promise, Reality, and Social Organization." In Susan McKinnon and Sydel Silverman, eds., *Complexities: Beyond Nature and Nurture,* pp. 223–47. Chicago: University of Chicago Press.

Tharoor, Shashi. 1999. The Future of Civil Conflict. *World Policy Journal* 16(1): 1–11.

Thomas, K. 1983. *Man and the Natural World: Changing Attitudes in England, 1500–1800.* New York: Oxford University Press.

Thomas, Mark. 2008. *Belching Out the Devil: Global Adventures with Coca-Cola.* London: Ebury Publishing.

Thomas, Nicholas. 1989. Material Culture and Colonial Power: Ethnological Collecting and the Establishment of Colonial Rule in Fiji. *Man* 24(1):41–56.

Thomas, Wesley. 1997. "Navajo Cultural Constructions of Gender and Sexuality." In Sue-Ellen Jacobs, Wesley Thomas, and Sabine Lang, eds., *Two-Spirit People: Native American Gender Identity, Sexuality, and Spirituality,* pp. 156–73. Urbana: University of Illinois Press.

Thomson, Rob, Tamar Murachver, and James Green. 2001. Where Is the Gender in Gendered Language? *Psychological Science* 12:171–5.

Tierney, Patrick. 2002. *Darkness in El Dorado: How Scientists and Journalists Devastated the Amazon.* New York: W. W. Norton.

Toren, Christina. 1996. "Psychological Anthropology." In Alan Barnard and Jonathan Spencer, eds., *Encyclopedia of Social and Cultural Anthropology,* pp. 456–61. London: Routledge.

Trevor-Roper, Hugh R. 1983. "The Invention of Tradition: The Highland Tradition of Scotland." In Eric Hobsbawn and Terence Ranger (Eds.), *The Invention of Tradition,* pp. 15–41. Cambridge: Cambridge University Press.

Trubek, Amy. 2008. *The Taste of Place: A Cultural Journey Into Terroir.* Berkeley: University of California Press.

Truman, Harry S. 1949. Inaugural Address, January 20, 1949. Accessed on 6/3/14: http://www.bartleby.com/124/pres53.html

Tsing, Anna Lowehaupt. 2000. The Global Situation. *Cultural Anthropology* 15(3): 327–60.

Tsing, Anna Lowehaupt. 2005. *Friction: An Ethnography of Global Connection.* Princeton, NJ: Princeton University Press.

Turner, Victor. 1967. *The Forest of Symbols: Aspects of Ndembu Ritual.* Ithaca, NY: Cornell University Press.

Turner, Victor. 1969. *The Ritual Process: Structure and Anti-Structure.* Chicago: Aldine.

Two Bears, Davina R. 2006. Navajo Archaeologist Is Not an Oxymoron: A Tribal Archaeologist's Experience. *American Indian Quarterly* 30 (3–4): 381–7.

Tylor, E. B. 1871. *Primitive Culture: Researches into the Development of Mythology, Philosophy, Religion, Art, and Custom.* London: John Murray.

U.S. Census Office, J. D. B. DeBow, Superintendent. 1853. *The Seventh Census of the United States: 1850.* Washington, DC: Robert Armstrong, Public Printer.

Ulijaszek, Stanley. 2007. "Bioculturalism." In David Parkin and Stanley Ulijaszek, eds., *Holistic Anthropology: Emergence and Convergence,* pp. 21–51. New York: Berghahn Books.

Ulijaszek, Stanley J., and Hayley Lofink. 2006. Obesity in Biocultural Perspective. *Annual Reviews of Anthropology* 35:337–60.

Underhill, Paco. 2005. *Call of the Mall: A Walking Tour Through the Crossroads of Our Shopping Culture.* New York: Simon and Schuster.

Urry, James. 1972. "*Notes and Queries on Anthropology* and the Development of Field Methods in British Anthropology, 1870–1920." In *Proceedings of the Royal Anthropological Institute of Great Britain and Ireland* for *1972,* pp. 45–57. London: The Royal Anthropological Institute.

Valentine, David. 2003. "The Calculus of Pain": Violence, Anthropological Ethics, and the Category Transgender. *Ethnos* 68(1): 27–48.

Valentine, David. 2007. *Imagining Transgender: An Ethnography of a Category.* Durham, NC: Duke University Press.

van den Berghe, Pierre. 1999. "Ethnicity as Kin Selection: The Biology of Nepotism." In Roger S. Gottlieb (series ed.) and Leonard Harris (volume ed.), *Key Concepts in Critical Theory: Racism,* pp. 50–73. Amherst, NY: Humanity Books.

Vandermeer, John, and Ivette Perfecto. 1995. *Breakfast of Biodiversity: The Truth About Rainforest Destruction.* Oakland, CA: Food First.

Veseth, Michael. 2005. *Globaloney: Unraveling the Myths of Globalization.* Lanham, MD: Rowman & Littlefield.

Vincent, Joan. 1978. Political Anthropology: Manipulative Strategies. *Annual Review of Anthropology* 7:175–94.

Viswesaran, Kamala. 1997. Histories of Feminist Ethnography. *Annual Review Anthropology* 26:591–621.

Vivanco, Luis. 2013. *Reconsidering the Bicycle: An Anthropological Perspective on a New (Old) Thing.* New York: Routledge.

Wackernagel, Mathis, Larry Onisto, Alejandro Callejas Linares, Ina Susana López Falfán, Jesús Méndez García, Ana Isabel Suárez Guerrero, et. al. 1997. *The Ecological Footprints of Nations: How Much Nature Do They Use? How Much Nature Do They Have?* Report manuscript. Toronto: International Council for Local Environmental Initiatives.

Wade, Edwin L. 1985. "The Ethnic Art Market in the American Southwest, 1880–1980." In Richard Handler (series ed.) and George W. Stocking, Jr. (volume ed.), *History of Anthropology: Vol. 3. Objects and Others: Essays on Museums and Material Culture,* pp.167–91. Madison: University of Wisconsin Press.

Wade, Peter. 1997. *Race and Ethnicity in Latin America.* London: Pluto Books.

Wagner, Roy. 1967. *The Curse of Souw: Principles of Daribi Clan Definition and Alliance.* Chicago: University of Chicago Press.

Wagner, Roy. 1969. "Marriage Among the Daribi." In R. M. Glasse and M. J. Meggitt, eds. *Pigs, Pearlshells, and Women: Marriage in the New Guinea Highlands,* pp. 56–76. Englewood Cliffs, NJ: Prentice Hall.

Wallace, Anthony F. C. 1956. Revitalization Movements: Some Theoretical Considerations for Their Comparative Study. *American Anthropologist* 58: 264–81.

Wallace, Anthony F. C. 1966. *Religion: An Anthropological View.* New York: Random House.

Wallace, Anthony F. C. 1970. *The Death and Rebirth of the Seneca.* New York: Knopf.

Wallman, Joel. 1992. *Aping Language.* Cambridge: Cambridge University Press.

Wapner, Paul. 1996. *Environmental Activism and World Civic Politics.* Albany: State University of New York Press.

Warren, Kay. 1998. *Indigenous Movements and Their Critics: Pan-Maya Activism in Guatemala.* Princeton: Princeton University Press.

Warren, Kay. 1998. *Indigenous Movements and Their Critics: Pan-Maya Activism in Guatemala.* Princeton, NJ: Princeton University Press.

Watahomigie, Lucille, and Akira Yamamoto. 1992. Local Reactions to Perceived Language Decline. *Language* 68(1): 10–17.

Watson, James L., and Melissa L. Caldwell, eds. 2005. *The Cultural Politics of Food and Eating: A Reader.* Malden, MA: Blackwell Publishing.

Watson-Gegeo, Karen Ann, and Geoffrey White, eds. 1990. *Disentangling: Conflict Discourse in Pacific Societies.* Stanford, CA: Stanford University Press.

Watters, Ethan. 2011. *Crazy Like Us: The Globalization of the American Psyche.* New York: Free Press.

Wax, Murray, and Felix Moos. 2004. Anthropology: Vital or Irrelevant. *Human Organization* 63(2): 246–7.

Weiner, Annette B. 1976. *Women of Value, Men of Renown: New Perspectives in Trobriand Exchange.* Austin: University of Texas Press.

Weiner, Annette B. 1988. *The Trobrianders of Papua New Guinea.* Fort Worth, TX: Harcourt Brace Jovanovich College Publishers.

Welsch, Robert L. 1983. "Traditional Medicine and Western Medical Options Among the Ningerum of Papua New Guinea." In Lola Romanucci-Ross, Daniel E. Moerman, and Laurence R. Tancredi, eds., *The Anthropology of Medicine: From Culture Toward Medicine,* pp. 32–53. New York: Praeger.

Werner, Cynthia, and Duran Bell, eds. 2004. *Values and Valuables: From the Sacred to the Symbolic.* Lanham, MD: Rowman Altamira.

Westermark, George D. 1998. History, Opposition, and Salvation in Agarabi Adventism. *Pacific Studies* 21(3): 51–71.

Weston, Kath. 1993. Lesbian/Gay Studies in the House of Anthropology. *Annual Review of Anthropology* 22:339–67.

White, D. Steven. 2010. "The Top 175 Global Economic Entities, 2010." World Wide Website accessed on 1/24/14: http://dstevenwhite.com/2011/08/14/the-top-175-global-economic-entities-2010/

White, Geoff. 1992. "Ethnopsychology." In Theodore Schwartz, Geoff White, and Catherine Lutz, eds., *New Directions in Psychological Anthropology,* pp. 21–46. Cambridge: Cambridge University Press.

White, Geoff, and Catherine Lutz. 1992. "Introduction." In Theodore Schwartz, Geoff White, and Catherine Lutz, eds., *New Directions in Psychological Anthropology,* pp. 1–20. Cambridge: Cambridge University Press.

White, Leslie. 1949. *The Science of Culture: A Study of Man and Culture.* New York: Farrar, Strauss.

Whitehead, Harriet. 1981. "The Bow and the Burden Strap: A New Look at Institutionalized Homosexuality in Native North America." In Sherry Ortner and Harriet Whitehead, eds. *Sexual Meanings: The Cultural Construction of Gender and Sexuality,* pp. 80–115. Cambridge: Cambridge University Press.

Whitehead, Neil L. 2004. "Cultures, Conflicts, and the Poetics of Violent Practice." In Neil Whitehead, ed., *Violence,* pp. 3–24. Santa Fe: School of American Research.

Wiley, Andrea. 2004. "Drink Milk for Fitness": The Cultural Politics of Human Biological Variation and Milk Consumption in the United States. *American Anthropologist* 106(3): 506–17.

Wiley, Andrea. 2011. *Reimagining Milk.* New York: Routledge.

Wilk, Richard, and Lisa Cliggett. 2007. *Economies and Cultures: Foundations of Economic Anthropology.* 2nd Edition. Boulder, CO: Westview Press.

Wise, Timothy A. 2007. *Policy Space for Mexican Maize: Protecting Agro-Biodiversity and Promoting Rural Livelihoods.* Global Development and Environment Institute Working Paper No. 07–01, Tufts University, Medford, MA.

Wolf, Eric. 1984. *Europe and the People without History.* Berkeley: University of California Press.

Wolf, Eric. 2001. *Pathways of Power: Building an Anthropology of the Modern World.* Berkeley: University of California Press.

Woolard, Kathryn A. 1998. "Introduction: Language Ideology as a Field of Inquiry." In Bambi B. Shieffelin, Kathryn A. Woolard, and Paul V. Kroskrity, eds., *Language Ideologies: Practice and Theory,* pp. 3–47. New York: Oxford University Press.

World Commission on Environment and Development (WCED). 1987. *Our Common Future.* Report. Oxford: Oxford University Press.

Worthman, Carol M. 1995. "Hormones, Sex, and Gender." *Annual Review of Anthropology* 24:593–616.

Wright, Lawrence. 1994. One Drop of Blood. *New Yorker,* July 25, pp. 46–55.

Wuerthner, George. 2003. Welfare Ranching: Assessing the Real Cost of a Hamburger. *Vegetarian Voice.* Accessed on March 15, 2005: http://www.navs-online.org/environment/cattle_ranching/welfare_ranching.php

Yardley, Jim. 2012. Malnutrition Widespread in Indian Children, Report Finds. *New York Times,* January 10, 2012. Accessed on 8/12/13: http://www.nytimes.com/2012/01/11/world/asia/malnutrition-in-india-is-widespread-report-finds.html.

Young, Michael W. 1998. *Malinowski's Kiriwina: Fieldwork Photography 1915–1918.* Chicago: University of Chicago Press.

Photo Credits

CHAPTER 1

Opening image (p. 2): Captain Samuel Wallis (1728–1830) being received by Queen Oberea on the Island of Tahiti (colour litho), Gallina, Gallo (1796–1874)/Private Collection/The Stapleton Collection/ The Bridgeman Art Library; **Figure 1.1 (p. 7):** Photo courtesy of Cowan's Auctions Inc., Cincinnati, OH; **Figure 1.2 (p. 9):** OUP; **Classic Contributions (p. 11):** PRM 1998.271.35. Copyright Pitt Rivers Museum, University of Oxford; **Figure 1.3 (p. 13):** OUP; **Figure 1.4 (p. 13):** Photo: Ed Ewing; **Doing Fieldwork (p. 16):** Courtesy of Robert L. Welsch; **Figure 1.5 (p. 18):** OUP; **Figure 1.6 (p. 19):** Photo by Luis A. Vivanco; **Figure 1.7 (p. 20):** Photo by Joshua A. Bell and Robert L. Welsch; **Figure 1.8 (p. 22):** © FAO/Alessandra Benedetti; **Figure 1.9 (p. 22):** Andrew Curry; **Figure 1.10 (p. 23):** Courtesy of James McKenna; Figure 1.11 (p. 23): Courtesy of Akira Yamamoto; **Figure 1.12 (p. 25):** Image courtesy of National Archives and Records Administration; **Thinking Like an Anthropologist (p. 26):** Photo by Marco Di Lauro/Getty Images

CHAPTER 2

Opening image (p. 30): AP Photo/Scott Boehm; **Figure 2.1 (p. 34):** Peters, JM. 1977. Pictorial Communication. Capetown, South Africa: David Philip. p. 90; **Figure 2.2 (p. 35):** Photo by KMazur/ WireImage; **Figure 2.3 (p. 37)** PATRICK KOVARIK/AFP/Getty Images; **Classic Contributions (p. 39):** Image courtesy of the National Anthropological Archives, Smithsonian Institution, MNH 8301; **Figure 2.4 (p. 41):** Wikimedia Commons; **Figure 2.5 (p. 43):** JIJI PRESS/AFP/Getty Images; **Figure 2.6 (p. 45):** from *The Silent Friend* by R. and L. Perry & Co. (1847), via Archive.org; **Figure 2.7 (p. 46, top):** Image courtesy of the Library of Congress Prints and Photographs Division Washington, DC; **(bottom):** www.healthexhibits.com. Used with permission; **Thinking Like an Anthropologist (p. 48):** OUP; **Anthropologist as Problem Solver (p. 50):** University of British Columbia Archives, Photo by Frank Nowell [UBC 1.1/1643]; **Figure 2.8 (p. 51):** Broddi Sigurðarson/UN/Flickr

CHAPTER 3

Opening image (p. 54): © Horizon International Images Limited/Alamy; **Figure 3.1 (p. 57, top):** © cusoncom/iStockphoto; **(bottom):** © PA; **Figure 3.2 (p. 59):** © Heritage Image Partnership Ltd/ Alamy; **Classic Contributions (p. 62):** Courtesy of the Library of Congress (LC-USZ62-114649); **Figure 3.3 (p. 64):** © Charles Martin/National Geographic Society/Corbis; **Anthropologist as Problem Solver (p. 65):** Photo by Nancy Travers, 2009, courtesy of Kim Hopper; **Figure 3.4 (p. 66):** Documentary Educational Resources; **Figure 3.5 (p. 66):** YASUYOSHI CHIBA/AFP/Getty Images; **Figure 3.6 (p. 70):** from *Types of Mankind* by J. C. Nott and Geo. R. Gliddon (1854), via Archive.org; **Figure 3.7 (p. 71):** Darrell Gulin/Getty; **Figure 3.8 (p. 73):** OUP; **Thinking Like an Anthropologist (p. 76):** via Google Books

CHAPTER 4

Opening image (p. 80): © Image Source/Alamy; **Figure 4.1 (p. 84):** Ron Cohn/Gorilla Foundation/ koko.org; **Figure 4.2 (p. 85):** OUP; **Figure 4.3 (p. 86):** OUP; **Figure 4.4 (p. 89):** Sawayasu Tsuji/ Getty; **Figure 4.5 (p. 90):** © Jake Warga/Corbis; **Figure 4.6 (p. 91):** © PABLO MARTINEZ MONSIVAIS/AP/Corbis; **Figure 4.7 (p. 91):** Image courtesy of Zoe Cormack; **Classic Contributions (p. 93):** Ruth Benedict Papers, Archives & Special Collections Library, Vassar College; **Figure 4.8 (p. 94):** © Stapleton Collection/Corbis; **Figure 4.9 (p. 95):** color chart courtesy of WCS Data Archives, http:// www.icsi.berkeley.edu/wcs/data.html; **Figure 4.10 (p. 97):** Courtesy of Robert L. Welsch; **Figure 4.11 (p. 97):** JOHN MAHONEY/THE GAZETTE; **Thinking Like an Anthropologist (p. 100, left):** © Ellen Jo Roberts; **(right):** © NoDerog/iStockphoto; **Doing Fieldwork (p. 102):** © gulfimages/Alamy

CHAPTER 5

Opening image (p. 106): Lara Jo Regan/Gallerystock; **Thinking Like an Anthropologist (p. 110):** AP Photo/Brian Kersey; **Figure 5.1 (p. 112):** Manuscript Division, Library of Congress (50a); **Figure 5.2**

(p. 112): Courtesy of Robert L. Welsch; **Figure 5.3 (p. 113):** Courtesy of Luis A. Vivanco; **Figure 5.4 (p. 115):** Cambridge Museum of Archaeology and Anthropology; **Figure 5.5 (p. 117):** Courtesy of Library of the London School of Economics and Political Science, MALINOWSKI/3/ARG/1; **Classic Contributions (p. 118):** Courtesy of Library of the London School of Economics and Political Science, MALINOWSKI/3/B/18/1; **Figure 5.6 (p. 120):** Human Relations Area Files: hraf.yale.edu; **Figure 5.7 (p. 120):** Image courtesy of Cambridge Museum of Archaeology and Anthropology N.22900.ACH; **Figure 5.8 (p. 121):** (AP Photo) Jim Bourdier; **Figure 5.9 (p. 123):** Smithsonian Institution, National Anthropological Archives; **Figure 5.10 (p. 123):** Courtesy of the Bateson Idea Group; **Anthropologist as Problem Solver (p. 125, top):** © Fiona Watson/Survival; **(bottom):** © Survival International; **Figure 5.11 (p. 127):** Courtesy of Philippe Bourgois

CHAPTER 6

Opening image (p. 133): Image courtesy of PAW Media/Warlpiri Media Association— pictured are Bruno Jupurrurla Wilson (L) and Jason Japaljarri Woods (R); **Figure 6.1 (p. 136):** Wikimedia Commons; **Figure 6.2 (p. 137):** RAJESH JANTILAL/AFP/Getty Images; **Figure 6.3 (p. 138):** Redrawn from Segal, A. (1993) *An Atlas of International Migration.* London: Hans Zell Publishers. Copyright remains with the estate of Aaron Segal; **Thinking Like an Anthropologist (p. 139):** Image courtesy of Lynsey Addario; **Classic Contributions (p. 141):** Image courtesy of Sydel Silverman; **Figure 6.4 (p. 143):** © Per-Anders Pettersson/Corbis; **Figure 6.5 (p. 145):** Paul Jeffrey/kairosphotos.com; **Figure 6.6 (p. 148):** KIRILL KUDRYAVTSEV/AFP/Getty Images; **Figure 6.7 (p. 149):** Image courtesy of the Krannert Center for the Performing Arts; **Doing Fieldwork (p. 151):** AP Photo/Igor Kostin

CHAPTER 7

Opening image (p. 156): © Tom Pietrasik/Corbis; **Figure 7.1 (p. 160, top):** Christer Fredriksson/Lonely Planet Images/Getty; **(bottom):** Tim E White/Photolibrary/Getty; **Figure 7.2 (p. 161):** © Found Image Press/Corbis; **Figure 7.3 (p. 165):** The Game Must End Soon, a Peasant Carrying a Clergyman and a Nobleman, 1789 (coloured engraving) (see also 158273), French School, (18th century)/Musee de la Ville de Paris, Musee Carnavalet, Paris, France/The Bridgeman Art Library; **Thinking Like an Anthropologist (p. 167, top):** © Jamie Grill/Tetra Images/Corbis; **(bottom):** © Visual Ideas/Camillo Morales/Blend Images/Corbis; **Figure 7.4 (p. 168):** © Marcos Delgado/epa/Corbis; **Figure 7.5 (p. 170):** © Anthony Bannister/Gallo Images/Corbis; **Figure 7.6 (p. 172):** Courtesy Robert L. Welsch; **Figure 7.7 (p. 173):** © Alex Treadway/National Geographic Society/Corbis; **Figure 7.8 (p. 174):** © Ocean/Corbis; **Anthropologist as Problem Solver (p. 176, top):** Teresa Mares. Used with permission; **(bottom):** © Lynn Stone/AgStock Images/Corbis

CHAPTER 8

Opening image (p. 184): AP Photo/Eraldo Peres; **Figure 8.1 (p. 188):** Drawn after "Pueblos Indígenas y Ecosistemas Naturales en Centroamérica y el Sur de México," National Geographic/Center for the Support of Native Lands; **Figure 8.2 (p. 189):** Jason Beaubien/NPR; **Figure 8.3 (p. 195):** not in copyright; **Figure 8.4 (p. 198):** Col. Roosevelt standing beside a water buffalo which he has shot (sepia photo), Roosevelt, Kermit (1889–1943)/Gilder Lehrman Collection, New York, USA/The Bridgeman Art Library; **Doing Fieldwork (p. 201, top):** Courtesy of James Fairhead; **(bottom):** Courtesy of Melissa Leach; **Figure 8.5 (p. 203):** OUP; **Thinking Like an Anthropologist (p. 204):** © Image Source/Alamy; **Figure 8.6 (p. 206):** © Bettmann/CORBIS

CHAPTER 9

Opening image (p. 210): © Peter Turnley/Corbis; **Figure 9.1 (p. 213):** AP Photo/PBS; **Figure 9.2 (p. 216):** David Klein; **Classic Contributions (p. 217):** Photo by Ulf Andersen/Getty Images; **Figure 9.3 (p. 219):** RichardMcGuire.ca; **Figure 9.4 (p. 223):** from *Argonauts of the Western Pacific* by Bronislaw Malinowski (1922); **Thinking Like an Anthropologist (p. 224):** Malinowski/3/5/19, LSE Library collections; **Figure 9.5 (p. 225):** Photo By Getty Images; **Figure 9.6 (p. 227):** Imaginechina via AP Images; **Figure 9.7 (p. 228, top):** Staatlichen Museums für Völkerkunde München via Wikimedia Commons; **(bottom):** © James Leynse/Corbis; **Figure 9.8 (p. 230):** AP Photo/Richard Drew; **Anthropologist as Problem Solver (p. 232):** AP PHOTO/KEYSTONE, Martial Trezzini

CHAPTER 10

Opening image (p. 236): by Apa Hugo, courtesy of Robert L. Welsch; **Figure 10.1 (p. 239):** © Anthony Bannister/Gallo Images/Corbis; **Classic Contributions (p. 241):** Courtesy of Pitt Rivers Museum University of Oxford; **Figure 10.2 (p. 242):** REUTERS/Alessia Pierdomenico; **Figure 10.3 (p. 245):** © Ron Sachs/Pool/CNP/Corbis; **Figure 10.4 (p. 247):** by Apa Hugo, courtesy of Robert L. Welsch; **Figure 10.5 (p. 248):** © Michel Setboun/Corbis; **Thinking Like an Anthropologist (p. 249):** AP Photo/Murad Sezer; **Figure 10.6 (p. 250):** Woolaroc Museum, Bartlesville, Oklahoma; **Anthropologist as Problem Solver (p. 251):** Courtesy of Maxwell Owusu and Shafica Ahmed; **Figure 10.7 (p. 254):** Image Still from *The Ax Fight* by Timothy Asch and Napoleon Chagnon, 1975, courtesy of Documentary Educational Resources; **Figure 10.8 (p. 255):** AP Photo; **Figure 10.9 (p. 259):** © Martha Cooper

CHAPTER 11

Opening image (p. 264): Illustration courtesy of harpersweekly.com; **Figure 11.1 (p. 272):** *The Burning of Jamestown* by Howard Pyle (1901), via Wikimedia Commons; **Figure 11.2 (p. 273):** from *Pudd'nhead Wilson and Those Extraordinary Twins* by Mark Twain (1894), via HathiTrust; **Thinking Like an Anthropologist (p. 275):** Courtesy of Robert L. Welsch; **Figure 11.3 (p. 276):** © Bettmann/CORBIS; **Figure 11.4 (p. 278):** © Patti McConville/Alamy; **Figure 11.5 (p. 280):** AFP/Getty Images; **Figure 11.6 (p. 281):** ABC News; **Doing Fieldwork (p. 285):** National Archives; **Figure 11.7 (p. 287):** Saturday Night Live

CHAPTER 12

Opening image (p. 290): PASCAL GUYOT/AFP/Getty Images; **Figure 12.1 (p. 293):** © Iris Images/Corbis; **Classic Contributions (p. 294):** Photo by George Rose/Getty Images; **Figure 12.2 (p. 297):** FABRICE COFFRINI/AFP/Getty Images; **Figure 12.3 (p. 298):** Courtesy of Kirk and Karen Endicott; **Figure 12.4 (p. 299, top):** Photo by Keystone/Getty Images; **(bottom):** Photo by David Fenton/Getty Images; **Figure 12.5 (p. 301):** Jonatan Fernstrom/The Image Bank/Getty Images; **Figure 12.6 (p. 303):** Photo by David Victor. Used with permission by the Pride Foundation; **Figure 12.7 (p. 304):** INDRANIL MUKHERJEE/AFP/Getty Images; **Figure 12.8 (p. 306):** HECTOR MATA/AFP/Getty Images; **Figure 12.9 (p. 309):** Time & Life Pictures/Getty Images

CHAPTER 13

Opening image (p. 316): LatinContent/Getty Images; **Figure 13.1 (p. 320, left):** Michael Ochs Archives/Getty Images; **(right):** Courtesy of the Library of Congress (LC-DIG-ppmsca-08768); **Figure 13.2 (p. 321):** OUP; **Figure 13.3 (p. 322, top):** James Willard Schultz, Photographer. Merrill G. Burlingame Special Collections at Montana State University Libraries; **(bottom):** Courtesy of Robert L. Welsch; **Figure 13.4 (p. 322):** OUP; **Figure 13.5 (p. 323):** OUP; **Classic Contributions (p. 324):** UC Berkeley, Hearst (Phoebe A.) Museum of Anthropology; **Figure 13.6 (p. 326):** OUP; **Thinking Like an Anthropologist (p. 327):** © Trevor Thompson/Alamy; **Figure 13.7 (p. 329, top):** © Irene Abdou Photography; **(bottom):** Courtesy of Robert L. Welsch; **Figure 13.8 (p. 330, top):** Courtesy of Rolf Lunheim; **(bottom):** REUTERS/Adnan Abidi; **Doing Fieldwork (p. 332):** JENNIFER LAW/AFP/Getty Images; **Figure 13.9 (p. 333, top):** Courtesy of the Library of Congress (LC-DIG-ppmsca-13196); **(bottom):** AFP/Getty Images

CHAPTER 14

Opening image (p. 340): © BH/AP/Corbis; **Figure 14.1 (p. 344):** from The ghost-dance religion and the Sioux outbreak of 1890 by James Mooney (1896), via Archive.org; **Figure 14.2 (p. 345):** SSPL/Getty Images; **Figure 14.3 (p. 347, left):** Dan Kitwood/Getty Images; **(right):** AP Photo/Jessica Kourkounis; **Figure 14.4 (p. 348):** Jennifer S. Altman/WireImage; **Figure 14.5 (p. 349):** press hand-out; **Figure 14.6 (p. 351):** 53.65.13194/probably Elema People/Eastern Papuan Gulf; Papua New Guinea; Melanesia; Oceania/*Barkcloth Mask (Eharo)*, collected 1885/Bark cloth, rattan, plant fiber and pith, natural pigment (black, white, and red)/Overall: 29 1/2 × 14 1/2 × 4 15/16 in. (75 × 36.8 × 12.5 cm)/Hood Museum of Art, Dartmouth College, Hanover, New Hampshire; **Figure 14.7 (p. 352):** Courtesy of the Library of Congress (LC-USZ62-47016); **Figure 14.8 (p. 354):** 2001.51.34345/Yoruba people/Nigeria/Guinea Coast/Africa/Scepter, 19th century/Bronze with leather bound handle/

Overall: 14 3/8 × 4 3/16 × 2 3/16 in. (36.5 × 10.7 × 5.5 cm)/Hood Museum of Art, Dartmouth College, Hanover, New Hampshire; gift of Peter H. Voulkos; photography by Jeffrey Nintzel; **Classic Contributions (p. 358):** NPG x37001 Sir James George Frazer © National Portrait Gallery, London; **Figure 14.9 (p. 359):** 29.58.7934/Inuit/Canada/Arctic/North America/*Fishhook Decorated with an Ivory Seal*, late 19th or early 20th century/Brass, copper, ivory, and sinew/Hood Museum of Art, Dartmouth College; photography by Jeffrey Nintzel; **Figure 14.10 (p. 359):** Courtesy of Robert L. Welsch; **Figure 14.11 (p. 360):** AP Photo/Chris Clark; **Thinking Like an Anthropologist (p. 361):** Mario Tama/Getty Images; **Figure 14.12 (p. 363):** "Is God Dead?" from TIME; 4/8/1966; **Doing Fieldwork (p. 365):** Frank Bienewald/LightRocket via Getty Images

CHAPTER 15

Opening image (p. 370): Joe Raedle/Getty Images; **Figure 15.1 (p. 374):** AP Photo/Jerome Delay; **Figure 15.2 (p. 375):** IS_ImageSource/iStock; **Figure 15.3 (p. 377, top left):** Courtesy of the Library of Congress (LC-USZ62-19404); **(right)** not in copyright; **(bottom left)** Source: Courtesy of the Library of Congress (LC-USZ62-19404); **Figure 15.4 (p. 378):** OUP; **Classic Contributions (p. 379):** Photo by Mr. Hong, Haohan, by permission of Pan Tianshu; **Figure 15.5 (p. 380, top):** Photo by Jay Colton/The LIFE Images Collection/Getty Images; **(bottom):** Arkansas Foundation for Medical Care. Used with permission; **Thinking Like an Anthropologist (p. 381):** AP Photo/Matt Dunham; **Figure 15.6 (p. 382):** © Minnesota Historical Society/CORBIS; **Figure 15.7 (p. 383):** Courtesy of Robert L. Welsch; **Figure 15.8 (p. 385):** drawn after Bergmann et al. 1994; **Figure 15.9 (p. 387):** Luis Davilla/age fotostock/SuperStock; **Anthropologist as Problem Solver (p. 389):** © Organs Watch

CHAPTER 16

Opening image (p. 392): 996.22.30233/Solongo style/Kongo people/Angola/Democratic Republic of Congo/Central Africa/Africa/Nkisi Nkondi, Power Figure, 19th century/Wood and mixed medium/Overall: 23 in. (58.42 cm)/Overall: 23 1/16 in. (58.5 cm)/Hood Museum of Art, Dartmouth College: purchased through the Mrs. Harvey P. Hood W'18 Fund, the William B. Jaffe and Evelyn A. Jaffe Hall Fund, the William B. Jaffe Memorial Fund, the William S. Rubin Fund, the Julia L. Whittier Fund and through gifts, by exchange; photography by Jeffrey Nintzel; **Figure 16.1 (p. 394):** Installation view(s) of Evolving Perspectives: Highlights from the African Art Collection at the Hood Museum of Art, Dartmouth College, Hanover, New Hampshire, January 26, 2013–April 6, 2014; photography by Jeffrey Nintzel; **Figure 16.2 (p. 397):** Courtesy of Luis A. Vivanco; **Figure 16.3 (p. 399):** © Penalope/iStockphoto; **Figure 16.4 (p. 399, left):** © Bob Daemmrich/Alamy; **(right):** © ZUMA Press, Inc./Alamy; **Classic Contributions (p. 400):** by permission of the University of Chicago Press; **Figure 16.5 (p. 401):** Courtesy of Robert L. Welsch; **Figure 16.6 (p. 403):** craftvision/iStock; **Figure 16.7 (p. 404):** Courtesy of Paradigm PR; **Figure 16.8 (p. 405):** Captain Samuel Wallis (1728–1830) being received by Queen Oberea on the Island of Tahiti (colour litho), Gallina, Gallo (1796–1874)/Private Collection/The Stapleton Collection/The Bridgeman Art Library; **Thinking Like an Anthropologist (p. 407 left):** Museum of Archaeology and Anthropology, University of Cambridge, MAA Z 2730; **(right):** via Wikimedia Commons; **Doing Fieldwork (p. 411):** Christina Kreps; **Figure 16.9 (p. 412):** CREATISTA/Shutterstock; **Figure 16.10 (p. 415):** Image Still from *Oh What A Blow That Phantom Gave Me* by John Bishop and Harald Prins, 2003, courtesy of Documentary Educational Resources; **Figure 16.11 (p. 416):** Courtesy of Andrew Dixon; **Figure 16.12 (p. 416):** Roger Viollet/Getty Images; **Figure 16.13 (p. 417):** Photo by Donna Callejon, 2007

WORLD MAP (INSIDE BACK COVER)

Copyright © Philip's

List of Boxes

Index

Page numbers in bold indicate pictures or illustrations. Those in italic indicate tables or maps.